Financial Analysis and Modeling Using Excel and VBA

Founded in 1807, John Wiley & Sons is the oldest independent publishing company in the United States. With offices in North America, Europe, Australia, and Asia, Wiley is globally committed to developing and marketing print and electronic products and services for our customers' professional and personal knowledge and understanding.

The Wiley Trading series features books by traders who have survived the market's ever changing temperament and have prospered—some by reinventing systems, others by getting back to basics. Whether a novice trader, professional, or somewhere in-between, these books will provide the advice and strategies needed to prosper today and well into the future.

For a list of available titles, visit our web site at www.WileyFinance.com.

Financial Analysis and Modeling Using Excel and VBA

SECOND EDITION

CHANDAN SENGUPTA

John Wiley & Sons, Inc.

First edition published by John Wiley & Sons, Inc., in 2004.

Published by John Wiley & Sons, Inc., Hoboken, New Jersey.
Published simultaneously in Canada.

For general information on our other products and services or for technical support, please contact our Customer Care Department within the United States at (800) 762-2974, outside the United States at (317) 572-3993 or fax (317) 572-4002.

Wiley also publishes its books in a variety of electronic formats. Some content that appears in print may not be available in electronic books. For more information about Wiley products, visit our web site at www.wiley.com.

Library of Congress Cataloging-in-Publication Data:

Sengupta, Chandan.
Financial analysis and modeling using Excel and VBA / Chandan Sengupta. — 2nd ed.
p. cm. — (The Wiley finance series)
Includes index.
Rev. ed. of: Financial modeling. c2004.
ISBN 978-0-470-27560-3 (paper/CD-ROM)
1. Finance—Mathematical models. 2. Investments—Mathematical models. 3. Microsoft Excel (Computer file) 4. Microsoft Visual Basic for applications. I. Sengupta, Chandan. Financial modeling. II. Title.
HG106.S46 2010
332.0285′554—dc22

2009035135

Printed in the United States of America.

10 9 8 7 6 5 4 3 2 1

For Preety

Contents

Part Four Financial Modeling Using VBA

About This Book

This second edition of *Financial Analysis and Modeling Using Excel and VBA* is designed for use with Excel 2007 as well as earlier versions of Excel going back to Excel 1997. It has been thoroughly updated and expanded to cover all the new features of Excel 2007 including its new efficient user interface—the Ribbon. Excel 2007 introduced many new powerful features, and depending on your needs you may benefit significantly from upgrading to Excel 2007. I have included a chapter discussing the important additions and improvements in Excel 2007 to help you decide if you would benefit from upgrading or you want to continue with the Excel version you are already familiar with.

Users of the first edition of this book will notice that its name has been expanded to include "Financial Analysis" because the book should be equally useful to both those who are interested in financial analysis and those who are interested in financial modeling. In reality, there is little difference between financial analysis and financial modeling. Most Excel spreadsheets that finance people create for financial analysis are actually financial models; they just do not look at them that way. Most people think of financial modeling as something esoteric and complex that is reserved for specialists. But that is not true. You will be able to develop more powerful and useful spreadsheets to do financial analysis if you start viewing them as financial models and applying to them the basic principles of financial modeling. I discuss this in more detail in the first chapter.

I have added several new chapters to cover in more detail topics and Excel features that you can use to develop more powerful models and spreadsheets faster than before. For example, you can use the significantly improved Pivot Table in Excel 2007 to create, in minutes, spreadsheets and models to analyze data that may otherwise take you hours. I have covered Pivot Tables in detail. Similarly, there are now new comprehensive chapters on writing formulas that can make decisions, doing statistical analysis, answering what if questions, finding iterative solutions to problems and so on that show you how to best use Excel's built-in functions and tools in these areas.

Excel and its built-in programming language Visual Basic for Applications (VBA) remain the premier tools for most financial analysis and modeling. This book will help you learn and improve your financial analysis and modeling skills, making the best use of Excel and VBA.

From the First Edition

How do you get to Carnegie Hall? You practice, practice, practice.

The same is true of financial modeling. The only way you can learn to develop good financial models is by practicing a lot. Fortunately if you learn and practice modeling the right way, you will not have to practice even one-tenth as hard as a performer does to get to Carnegie Hall.

The primary objectives of this book are to show you how to learn and practice financial modeling the right way and to provide you with a wide range of real-world financial models—over 75 of them—to imitate and use for practice so that you can be on your way to financial modeling's Carnegie Hall. Financial modeling is an essential skill for finance professionals and students, and Excel and its built-in programming language, Visual Basic for Applications (VBA), are the preferred tools for the job. However, modeling using Excel and VBA is rarely presented as an integrated subject in books or classrooms. The result is that both practitioners and students follow time-consuming trial and error approaches to modeling and end up with models that are not sufficiently flexible and powerful.

This book, designed for self-study, classroom use, and reference, presents a comprehensive approach for developing simple to sophisticated financial models in all major areas of finance using both Excel and VBA. The approach is based on my long experience in the business world developing a wide variety of financial models and in the classroom teaching an MBA course in financial modeling that students find very useful not just in their other course work but in their subsequent professional careers as well.

Developing good financial models requires combining knowledge of finance, mathematics, and Excel and VBA using modeling skill. In each of these areas, the following is what I assume you already know and what you will learn from this book.

In finance and mathematics, I assume that you have the necessary basic knowledge. Nonetheless, in each chapter I have included a review of the theory and concepts you will find useful for working on the models within that chapter. Because I cover a wide range of topics in the book, I think some of this material will be new to you. By immediately applying the newly acquired knowledge to "real world" problems, you will expand your knowledge of finance in some areas in which you may have been interested for some time.

In Excel, I assume you know the basics, and I cover the advanced features of Excel that you need for modeling in detail. You may be amazed to find out how much those whiz kids from Redmond have squeezed into Excel that many of us do not even know about.

VBA will be one of the most important things you learn from this book. I assume that you know nothing about it. VBA is a powerful and very useful tool that people who have Excel already have sitting inside their computers. Unfortunately, very few people use it because they are afraid of learning "programming." I will teach you VBA and modeling with VBA using a simple class-tested approach. The key is to learn VBA as a language the same way you learned your mother tongue—by imitating how to say things you want to say, without worrying about learning all the rules of grammar or trying to acquire a large vocabulary that you do not need. You will be surprised to find out how little you have to learn to be able to develop models with VBA that are often more useful, powerful, and flexible than Excel models.

Finally, I assume that you are new to modeling. Even if you have some experience, you will quickly find yourself challenged as you build on your skills. You will learn by imitating and practicing on numerous models from all areas of finance, and you will be able to challenge yourself further by developing extensions to these models.

I have not tried to cover every type of financial model that you may need to develop over the years, nor have I tried to cover modeling in depth for one or two particular areas of finance (such as derivatives). The reality—and my assumption—is that once you develop your financial modeling skill and learn to use Excel and VBA well, you will be able to develop models for any problem as long as you know the financial theory and mathematics needed to solve it conceptually. I have therefore focused on helping you develop the skill of financial modeling, and the best way to develop that skill is to work on a broad range of models instead of narrowly focusing on any one area of finance.

The CD that accompanies this book includes complete working versions of all the models in the book. In the text I provide the modeling strategy for each problem, detailed instructions on how to build each model, and thorough analysis of all the VBA codes for the models. I also explain how you can cover the material following different learning tracks depending on your background, how much time you have, and how good you want to become in financial modeling.

The book and the CD also include several special tools (for example, a VBA Quick Reference and a selected list of the most useful Excel and VBA built-in functions) that you can personalize, add to over time, and keep easily accessible on your computer's hard disk.

Financial modeling is finance in action. It is challenging and it is a lot of fun. I hope this book will show you how to have fun with it and benefit from it at the same time.

CHAPTER 1

Introduction to Financial Analysis and Modeling

Although many people think that financial analysis and financial modeling are very different, they are actually two sides of the same coin. If you have been developing Excel worksheets to solve financial problems, chances are you have been developing financial models without knowing it. Your financial analysis worksheets would be more useful if you viewed them as financial models and incorporated in them some of the basic principles and characteristics of financial models.

Let me explain what I mean by first addressing the question, What is a financial model? A simple, practical answer is that a financial model is designed to represent or capture in mathematical terms the relationships among the variables of a financial problem so that it can be used to answer "what if" questions or make projections.

This may sound a little abstract. So let us look at a simple, concrete example. Suppose you are using a spreadsheet to calculate, based on your taxable income, what your after-tax income was last year. Income tax rates vary in steps (brackets) for different income levels. So you cannot simply calculate your taxes by multiplying your taxable income by one tax rate (30%, for example) and subtracting it from your taxable income to get the after-tax income.

Consider two approaches to setting up a spreadsheet to calculate the after-tax income. In the first approach, you enter your taxable income in a cell, in a second cell you write the formula to calculate the taxes by manually looking up and incorporating the different tax rates for the different applicable tax brackets, and then write a formula in another cell to calculate your after-tax income by subtracting the total taxes from the taxable income in the first cell.

This type of spreadsheet solution is generally considered financial analysis; it is not a useful financial model. Why? Because it does not capture the key mathematical relationship between taxable income and taxes. The result is that if you now try to answer the "what if" question, *What would my after-tax income* *have been if my taxable income were $10,000 higher?* you will have to modify your spreadsheet.

However, taking a different approach, you can set up your spreadsheet to calculate the taxes on any taxable income (using Excel's lookup functions to automatically look up the necessary tax brackets and tax rates from a tax table) and use the computed tax number to calculate your after-tax income. You will then have a financial model, because it will capture the relationship between taxable income and taxes. You will also be able to use this model to answer the "what if" question I posed before.

As you can see, with a little extra effort and change in the way you think, you can develop most financial analysis spreadsheets in the form of a financial model, which will be more useful. Most of the time you want to solve the same financial problems as a financial analyst and a financial modeler. Since by thinking and acting like a financial modeler you can develop more useful spreadsheets, I suggest that you start viewing financial modeling and financial analysis as one and the same. As you go through this book you will find that most of the solutions to financial problems that I call models are just slightly more sophisticated versions of financial analysis spreadsheets.

So from here on, I will use the two terms interchangeably and you should think of them the same way. Do not be intimidated by the term *modeling*. There is nothing complex about it.

Before going on, let me mention that on Wall Street, financial modeling is often used to exclusively refer to derivatives modeling. But that is only one special albeit vast and important area of financial modeling. As you will see in this book, in finance we develop many other types of models as well. So even if you do not have any interest in developing derivatives models, it is almost certain that as a finance professional you will be involved in developing many other types of models.

In creating financial models, you always have to keep in mind that you want to capture as many of the interdependencies among the variables of the model as possible. In addition, you want to structure your models in such a way that it is easy to ask "what if" questions, that is, change the values of the independent variables and observe how they affect the values of the key dependent variables. You also should recognize that some of the relationships, as in the case of taxes, are easy to establish and exact; but many others will be approximate or even unknown. You will have to come up with them based on financial theory, analysis of data, and so on, and coming up with these relationships is one of the major challenges of financial modeling. Generally, the more of these relationships you can come up with and incorporate into your model, the more useful your model will be.

My Assumptions about You and the Users of Your Models

In this book I assume that you know the basics of finance and can solve by hand most of the problems for which you will be creating models. I also assume that you are familiar with the basics of Excel and have experience creating spreadsheet solutions to at least simple problems. You do not need to have knowledge of Excel's advanced features or of modeling; I will cover both in detail. You also do not need to have any knowledge of VBA. A key objective of the book is to teach you VBA and modeling using VBA from scratch by way of an easy and effective method.

Another important assumption I am making is that you will be developing the models primarily for your own use or for use by people who have some experience with Excel, but not necessarily with VBA. When you create models for use by people who have little or no familiarity with Excel, it requires adding special user interfaces to make the models easy to use. One must build into them special features to make them "bulletproof"—that is, to make sure that the models will not crash or produce wrong results if someone enters inappropriate inputs. I will discuss some design methods and Excel features that make models easier to use and more "bullet-resistant." Most everyday modelers do not need to go beyond this.

Excel and VBA as Modeling Tools

Even in the mid- to late 1990s, Excel was not considered a powerful enough tool for serious financial modeling, in part because the PCs available at the time had speed and memory limitations. With advances in PCs and improvements in Excel itself, the table has now turned completely: Excel has become the preferred tool for creating all but the largest and most computationally intensive financial models. The advantages of Excel for financial modeling are so obvious that it is not necessary to go into them. However, for those who have not worked with other programs or programming languages for modeling, it is worthwhile to point out that one of the important advantages of Excel is that with Excel you can create excellent output with very little work. You should learn to take full advantage of Excel's power in this respect.

If Excel is so good, then, why bother with VBA? VBA is a programming language, and if you do not know anything about programming languages, it will be difficult for you to appreciate the advantages of VBA at this point. Let me touch on only a few key reasons here, and I will answer the question in greater detail when we discuss modeling with VBA.

Despite its power, Excel has many limitations, and there are many financial models—some even relatively simple ones—that either cannot be created in Excel or will be overly complex or cumbersome to create in Excel. What's more, when you create a highly complex model in Excel, it can be difficult to understand, debug, and maintain. VBA generally offers a significant edge in all these respects.

The problem that most people have with VBA is that it is one more thing to learn, and they are somehow afraid of trying to learn a programming language. The reality is that if you follow the right method, learning a programming language is not particularly difficult—especially if you selectively learn what you will really use (as we will do in this book) and not let yourself get lost in all the other things you can do with VBA but probably never will. The truth is that you do not need to learn all that much to be able to create very useful and powerful financial models with VBA. What you will need is a lot of practice, which you will get as you go through this book. VBA offers you the best of both worlds: you can take advantage of all the powers of Excel including its ability to easily create excellent outputs, and supplement them with VBA's additional tools and flexibility.

Independent and Dependent Variables

We can say that the purpose of a model is to calculate the values of certain dependent variables for the values provided for its independent variables. It is therefore important to understand the difference between independent and dependent variables.

Independent variables are also called the input or external variables. The model's user or creator inputs the values of these variables—they are not calculated by the model. These are the variables you change to ask "what if" questions. For example, in our simple model the taxable income is an independent variable.

A model may also include a special type of input variable called a parameter. Parameters are independent variables in that their values are also provided by the creator or user of the model. The difference is that their values are expected to remain constant or change infrequently within the context of the model. For example, the tax rates and the tax brackets in our simple model can be considered parameters of the model because their values have to be provided for the model to work, but these values are not expected to change frequently. As you create a model, it is useful to keep the parameters together but separate from the other independent variables. They should still be easy to see and change, however.

The variables whose values are calculated by the model are called the calculated or dependent variables. Some of them may be intermediate variables, calculated for use in other calculations. Others are of primary interest to the user and are the output variables of the models. Models are almost always created to observe how the values of the output variables will change with changes in the values of one or more independent variables. Dependent variables are the ones whose values we want to project or determine when we ask "what if" questions.

It is possible to distinguish between intermediate dependent variables and output dependent variables; intermediate dependent variables are used in further calculations, whereas output dependent variables are not. This is generally not a useful distinction, however. It is better to look at the dependent variables of primary interest as the output variables of the model irrespective of whether they are used in further calculations. One must also recognize that, from time to time, some dependent variables that were previously not considered output variables of a model can become so and vice versa.

STEPS IN CREATING A MODEL

Whether you are creating a financial model using Excel or VBA, you must take a systematic approach. A systematic approach always involves planning ahead and this takes some time. Most people do not like to plan and think they can save time by starting to build a model right away without spending time on planning. However, for all but the simplest models, not taking the time upfront to do some planning and not taking a systematic approach ends up being both frustrating and a waste of time.

Here are the key steps you should follow in creating both Excel and VBA models. The details vary somewhat depending on whether you are working with Excel or VBA, and I will discuss them in later chapters. You should keep two other things in mind. First, in practice, you do not have to follow the steps strictly in this order, nor do you have to finish one completely before going onto the next one. Most of the time you will have to go back and forth to some extent. It will depend on the circumstances. Second, over time, you should try to create your own variation on this basic approach and learn to adapt it to different situations.

Excel and VBA are flexible tools and you can usually make changes almost at any stage without a great deal of difficulty. But this still will take more time than if you do it right the first time, and making changes later increases the chances of missing some of the other changes that have to go with them.

Step 1: Define and Structure the Problem

In real life, problems rarely come neatly defined and structured. Unless you take the time upfront to define and structure the problem and agree on them with the user (your boss, for example), you may end up having to extensively change the model you first create. When your boss asks you a question whose answer requires developing a model, she often has only a vague idea of what she is really seeking. As a finance person and a modeler, you are responsible for putting it all in more concrete terms before proceeding.

Start by discussing and defining why the model is needed and what decisions, if any, will be made based on its output—that is, what questions the model is supposed to answer. Then establish how accurate or realistic the outputs need to be. As we discussed, all models have to capture the relationships among their variables, and discovering and quantifying these can take a lot of time. How much effort you put into doing this should depend on how important the project is and how accurate or realistic the outputs need to be.

Step 2: Define the Input and Output Variables of the Model

Make a list of all the inputs the model will need and decide who will provide them or where they will come from. This is crucial. For example, if you are creating a model to do the business plan for your company, the inputs must come from the business managers. You cannot just guess what sales growth rates they will be able to achieve, how much they will have to spend on plants and equipment to support those sales growths, and so forth. You may not need the actual numbers upfront, but the list of inputs should be established based on your discussions with the business managers so that you can make them independent variables in your model. Otherwise you may have go back later on and change a lot of things in the model.

Make a list of the tabular, graphical, and other outputs the model needs to create. To some extent, these should be driven by the decisions that will be made based on them. One advantage of Excel is that a lot of the output can be just printouts of your spreadsheets, provided the spreadsheets have been laid out properly. If you plan ahead and lay out your spreadsheets with the outputs in mind, you will save yourself a lot of time later on.

Step 3: Decide Who Will Use the Model and How Often

Who will use the model and how often it will be used make a lot of difference. In this book, I am assuming that you are developing the models either for your own use or for use by others who are familiar with Excel and understand the model, at least to some extent. When you create models for others' use, it involves much more work. You have to make sure that these people cannot enter data that do not make sense, they cannot accidentally damage parts of the model, and they can get the necessary outputs automatically and so forth. These are collectively called the user interface, and the more elegant, more easy to use, and more robust you want to make a model, the more work it is. You also have to plan for many of these features ahead of time.

How frequently a model will be used is another important issue. If a model is going to be used only once in a while, then it does not matter if it takes a long time to run or if it takes some extra work every time to create the outputs. A model that will be used frequently, however, should be designed differently.

Step 4: Understand the Financial and Mathematical Aspects of the Model

It is important to remember that the computer cannot do any thinking; you have to tell it exactly how all the calculations in the model will have to be done. In most situations, if you do not know how you would do the calculations by hand, you are not going to be able to write the necessary formulas or instructions for the computer to do it. It does not pay to start building the model until you are sure you could solve the problem by hand.

It usually takes beginners a lot of time to create a model and they often think that it is their Excel or VBA skills that are slowing things down. This may be partly true, but at least as often the problem is in their understanding of the finance and mathematics of the model they are trying to create. You will save lot of time if you do not even sit down in front of the computer to create a model until you are sure that you know how to solve the problem.

Step 5: Design the Model

There are two aspects to designing a model. One is to sketch the steps that Excel or VBA will have to follow to solve the problem. For simple models, you may want to write down only the broad steps or perhaps even do it in your head. For more complex problems, however, you should work on paper and use a degree of detail that suits your level of experience and the complexity of the problem. The less experience you have, the more detailed the sketch should be. Once again, remember that this may seem like a waste of time, but ultimately it will save you time compared to plunging into your spreadsheet or VBA program without such a sketch of the model.

The other aspect of design is planning how the model will be laid out in Excel or VBA. Are you going to do the entire model in one spreadsheet (or VBA module) or split it into several spreadsheets (or VBA modules or procedures)? Editing an Excel or VBA model is easy. So you do not have to decide every detail ahead of time, but you need to have an overall design in mind or on paper depending on the complexity of the problem and your level of experience.

As I discussed before, you also need to think about the kind of user interface you want to create and the reports you want the model to produce.

Step 6: Create the Spreadsheets or Write the VBA Codes

For most models, this is the big step. Most of this book covers the details of this step, so there is no need to get into them here.

Step 7: Test the Model

Almost no model works correctly the first time it is used; you have to find the problems (bugs) and fix them. The bugs that prevent the model from working at all or produce obviously wrong answers are generally easier to find and fix. However, models often include hidden bugs that create problems only for certain values or certain combinations of values for the input variables. To find them, you have to test a model extensively with a wide range of input variables.

You have to take somewhat different approaches to testing and debugging a model depending on whether you are working with Excel or VBA. Both Excel and VBA provide some special tools for this purpose; I will discuss these tools and provide suggestions on how to debug models in Excel and VBA in later chapters. Here are a few helpful hints that apply to both:

- There is no standard approach to testing and debugging a model. You almost always have to use your ingenuity to figure out what will be the best way to test and debug a particular model. Your ability to do so will improve with experience.

- The better you understand a problem and a model, the easier it will be to debug it. If you understand how changes in certain independent variables affect the values of certain dependent variables, then you can change the values of the independent variables to see if the dependent variables are changing in the right direction and by the right orders of magnitude. This is one of the best tools, especially for debugging large models, and you should do a lot of testing using this approach. You can also use this approach to hunt down the sources of the problems: Starting from a value that looks wrong, backtrack through the values of the intermediate dependent variables to see where the problem may be originating. This approach may sound somewhat vague and abstract, but with experience you will find that you can locate and fix most bugs rapidly using this approach.
- Checking a model's output against hand-calculated answers is a common and effective approach to debugging. In some situations, doing hand calculations may not be practical, but you may be able to use Excel itself to do some side calculations to test individual parts of the model.

Step 8: Protect the Model

Once you have completed a model, and especially if you are going to give it to others to use, you should consider protecting it against accidental or unauthorized changes. In addition, you may also want to hide parts of the model so that others cannot see certain formulas, data, and so on. Excel provides several flexible tools that you can use to hide and protect parts or all of your model. A good strategy is to cluster and color code all the input cells of a model and protect and hide everything else in the workbook.

There is less need to protect VBA modules because most users do not even know how to open them. Nonetheless, if you think it is necessary, you can protect parts of your VBA models as well.

Step 9: Document the Model

Documenting a model means putting in writing, diagrams, flowcharts, and so on, the information that someone else (or you yourself in the future) will need to figure out what it does, how it is structured, and what assumptions are built into it. One can then efficiently and effectively make changes to (update) the model if necessary.

For large systems (for example, the reservation systems for airlines), the amount of necessary documentation can be enormous; it is often put on CDs for easy access and use. Professional system development organizations have elaborate standards for documentation, because different pieces of large systems are developed by different people—many of whom may not be around for very long. Also, it is almost certain that the systems will have to be constantly updated.

Over time, anyone who creates models develops his own system of documentation. As long as you keep in mind the objectives I mentioned before, you have a lot of leeway to come up with your own system as well. Both Excel and VBA offer a number of features that let you easily do a lot of the documentation as you work on your model. You should take full advantage of them and do as much of your documentation as possible while creating the model.

This is important for two reasons. First, if you write your documentation when things are fresh in your mind, it will save you time later and you will be less likely to forget to document important things. Second, everyone hates (or learns to hate) documentation. It is no fun at all, especially if you try to do it all at once at the end of the project. If you do not work on the documentation until the end, chances are you will never do it. Then, if you have to use the model again a few months later or have to update it, you will end up spending hours or even days trying to figure out what you did. Do your documentation as you go along and finish it immediately after your model is done.

You have to take somewhat different approaches to when you document Excel and VBA models. I will discuss how in the appropriate later chapters.

Step 10: Update the Model as Necessary

This is not a part of the initial model development, but almost all models require updating at some point, either because some things have changed or because you want to adapt it to do something else. This is where the documentation becomes useful. Depending on how much updating is involved, you may want to go through all of the above steps again. You should also thoroughly update the documentation and include in it the information on who updated it, when and why, and what changes were made.

HOW THIS BOOK IS ORGANIZED

To use this book effectively, it will be helpful to understand some of my thinking behind its organization. Modeling is a skill that you can develop only by creating a variety of models. Once you have developed the basic skill, you should be able to create increasingly complex models—as long as you understand the finance and mathematics of the underlying problems. In some ways, it is like learning a language, especially when you are working with VBA. Once you learn the language, you can say new things in that language—you can make up sentences that you have never heard before. I therefore emphasize learning the language by exposing you to a variety of models in different areas of finance instead of concentrating on one particular area like derivatives or trying to anticipate and include every model you may need to develop.

For both Excel and VBA, I have provided one part that covers the "grammar" of the language (Parts One and Three) and then a second part that provides examples of its use (Parts Two and Four) to create models.

I suggest that you start with Part One to become familiar with all the powerful Excel features that are indispensible for creating good financial models and saving time. In this new edition Part One includes several new chapters covering these features in groups in detail so that you can learn them well and take full advantage of them in your models.

Let me give you two examples. In your models you would often want Excel to take different actions depending on whether one or a combination of conditions are satisfied. If you do not automate this process then the user will have to look at intermediate results and manually direct computations and actions to proceed in one direction or another. This will be inefficient and only some knowledgeable users will be able to use your model. Excel has tools that you can use to automate the process and Chapter 5: Making Decisions and Looking Up Values covers the relevant Excel tools in detail. If you study this chapter well before getting into creating models, you will save a lot of time. Similarly, Chapter 6: Analyzing Databases covers the special Excel tools for analyzing and viewing data from large databases efficiently and in various ways. One of these, PivotTable, is a powerful and useful tool that can save you hours of writing your own models to do the same analysis.

In most chapters in Part Two, I have included a section called "Review of Theory and Concepts." These are the theories and concepts of finance that you will need to work on the models in that chapter. If you are familiar with them, you can skip them and go on to the models. If you want to refresh your memory and understanding, the material is there.

You will notice that many of the modeling chapters in Parts Two and Four have the same titles. There is a reason for including such parallel chapters. It has been my experience that the easiest way to learn modeling with VBA is to start with problems that you can already model in Excel, because then you already know a lot about the problem and you can focus on the VBA aspects of it. In many cases, the parallel VBA models also demonstrate that even if you can model a problem using Excel, using VBA can provide additional flexibility, power, and so on. Most of the VBA chapters include additional models that are cumbersome or impossible to create using Excel.

What this means is that you may be better off covering Parts One and Two before you go on to the VBA parts. However, if you are already good at modeling with Excel and are primarily interested in learning VBA and modeling using VBA, you can start with Part Three. Then, as you cover the chapters of Part Four, you can review the corresponding chapters in Part Two as necessary.

Because there are certain differences between Excel-based models and VBA-based models, I have provided in the first chapters of both Parts Two and Four additional information on how to develop good models using them. I have also included suggestions on how best to use the material in both parts to improve your modeling skills rapidly. You will progress faster if you read and follow these suggestions instead of taking a haphazard approach.

PART One

Excel for Financial Analysis and Modeling

CHAPTER 2

Excel 2007 and the Previous Versions

This book is specifically written for working with Excel 2007. However, you will be able to use it equally easily and well with Excel 97 and any later version of Excel. Excel 2007 looks and feels very different from the previous versions of Excel and has a few powerful new features. But unless you think you would need those features, you do not have to update to Excel 2007 right away to be able to create good financial models.

In this chapter I will briefly discuss what is new in Excel 2007 and which new features you may find particularly useful for certain types of work. With that information you should be able to decide if you want to upgrade to Excel 2007 now or wait until the next version of Excel comes out. (Although no one knows for sure, from the point of view of financial modeling, the next version of Excel is not likely to add many great new features. If you upgrade to Excel 2007 now, chances are it will be fine for your financial modeling work for at least the next five years.)

For those of you who choose to continue working with an earlier version of Excel, whenever I use a feature exclusive to Excel 2007 I will point that out, and also suggest workarounds if available.

The New Features in Excel 2007

If you have been working with an earlier version of Excel or are familiar with more than one previous version, what will strike you immediately when you open Excel 2007 is that it looks and feels very different from all of them; the change from even Excel 2003, the immediate previous version, is much bigger than that between any two earlier versions.

The changes in Excel 2007 are not just skin deep. Excel 2007 is a complete rewrite of the program, although as a user you will primarily notice the new user interface and a number of new features. Most of the rest works the same way as before.

In this section I will briefly cover the new user interface and the major new or significantly improved features. I do not cover the user interface in great detail because once you have a general idea of how it works, you will find it much easier to learn it by experimenting on your own as you need to learn new aspects. Reading about it in a book is neither very interesting nor very productive. And then there is always the Help. As to the new features, I will cover the ones that are particularly useful for financial modeling in sufficient detail in later chapters.

The New User Interface

Before I get into the new user interface let me also remind you that when we get used to doing something in a certain way for years, it is very difficult to change to a new way. It is natural to resist the new way and try to fall back to the old way as much as possible. Most people have this reaction to the new user interface and some even start hating it. While the jury is still out on whether the new user interface will catch on or will be another fiasco like the new Coke or some of the "improvements" Microsoft tried in the past, after spending some time with it I have concluded that the new interface is much easier and more efficient to work with than the old ones, once you get used to it. So no matter how unhappy you feel about it in the beginning, just keep going for a while and chances are pretty soon you won't even miss the old interface.

The interface in the old Excel and other Office applications could be called a menu and toolbar interface. To do most things you clicked on a menu item and then clicked on additional menu items from a dropdown list. You could also select commands from one or more toolbars, many of which you could customize for the way you work. The problem Microsoft faced is that as it added features to Excel over the years, the menus became longer, the toolbars became more numerous, and it became increasingly difficult to find the commands you need. Many heavy users of Excel learned and fell back on keyboard shortcuts instead of hunting for commands in menus or toolbars. But that does not work for all commands, plus unless you use Excel all the time, it is difficult to remember all those keyboard shortcuts. And keeping too many toolbars open cluttered up the worksheet too much. (Incidentally, if over the years you have learned and gotten used to relying heavily on keyboard shortcuts, you will be happy to know that most of them will work with Excel 2007 as well.)

In all 2007 Office applications Microsoft has moved to a Ribbon and tab interface, which makes it possible to access most commands more easily.

THE OFFICE ICON

All Office 2007 applications now have what Microsoft calls the Office icon at the top left corner of the screen. This is essentially equivalent to the old File menu. Clicking on it drops down a menu containing familiar file commands such as Save and Print. Some menu items have an arrow on their right, and clicking on it opens up a fly-out menu with additional choices.

An important item on this menu is the Excel Options button in the bottom bar. Clicking on it opens a dialog box with many tabs. Microsoft has consolidated and organized all options that you need to customize your Excel work environment in this dialog box. These were spread out in many different menus in the previous versions of Excel, and as the number of available options grew, it became increasingly difficult to find them. Unfortunately, even now it is not always easy to locate an option you are looking for, primarily because there are so many of them. But chances are that any option you are looking for is somewhere in this dialog box, and if you take a few minutes to look through and familiarize yourself with how the options are organized under the different tabs, finding the right Excel option should be much easier now.

THE RIBBON

The all-new Ribbon that stretches across the top of the Excel screen contains all the features of Excel organized under a series of named tabs. The Ribbon consists of many underlying ribbons that come to the front when you click the tab of that ribbon (e.g., Home, Insert). Within the ribbon for each tab, related commands are organized in groups with the group name at the bottom. Note that while you have to click on a tab to open its ribbon, you do not have to click on a group name to access the items inside it; you can directly click on an icon or work with other items within a group. The grouping and group names are there to help you find a command faster.

There are nine tabs on the Ribbon that will always be visible (except as noted below). A few additional contextual tabs become visible and available only when you work with certain features of Excel 2007 (e.g., Table Tools). I will discuss these tabs when I introduce these features.

The nine permanent tabs are:

Home: The Excel features that you are likely to use most often are on this ribbon. Most of these features should be familiar to you. You may want to pay special attention to the features in the Styles group in case you are not familiar with them.

Insert: You will use features in this group to insert charts, shapes, and so on, in your worksheet. The PivotTable and Table features in the Tables group may be new to you. We will discuss them in detail in a later chapter.

Page Layout: All the commands you need to control the appearance of your worksheet and set up your pages for printing are located in this ribbon. In addition, it gives you access to the Themes features of Excel 2007.

Formulas: This ribbon gives you direct access to the various groups of functions in the Function Library. You will also use this ribbon to manage names you assign to cells and ranges, and to access the Formula Auditing features.

Data: This tab consolidates all of Excel's features for working with internal or external data. For example, you will use features in this ribbon to set up data validation, to sort or filter data, and so on.

Review: This ribbon consolidates the features for checking spelling, working with cell comments, and protecting and sharing your work.

View: The features that let you view your work in various ways (e.g., by freezing panes, zooming in and out, viewing worksheets side by side) are conveniently consolidated in this tab.

Developer: You will use the features in this tab when you write or record VBA macros. If this tab is not visible, you can turn it on by going to the Popular tab of the Excel Options dialog box and choosing Show Developer Tab in the Ribbon in the Top options for working with Excel section.

Add-Ins: This tab becomes visible only after you install any add-ins to Excel.

Minimizing the Ribbon

If you want to minimize the Ribbon for some reason (primarily to be able to see more of your worksheet on the screen), press Ctrl+F1 or right-click the Ribbon anywhere in its active area and select Minimize the Ribbon. This will leave the Office icon and the Ribbon tabs visible and hide the rest of the Ribbon. To use any of the commands in a tab, click the tab name and the ribbon for that tab will open up temporarily. After you select a command, the Ribbon will automatically go back to the minimized state.

To permanently switch the Ribbon back to the open state, press Ctrl+F1 again or right-click anywhere in the visible part of the Ribbon and choose Minimize the Ribbon (to deselect it).

THE QUICK ACCESS TOOLBAR (QAT) AND CUSTOMIZING IT

The new user interface offers a customizable Quick Access Toolbar (QAT) which always remains visible. You can add to it icons (from any ribbon) for the commands that you use frequently so that every time you need one of them you do not have to first open the ribbon in which it is located.

Initially the QAT is located above the Ribbon next to the Office icon and offers the following command icons: Save, Undo, Redo, and Quick Print. You can move the QAT below the Ribbon by clicking the dropdown arrow at the right edge of the QAT and selecting Show Below the Ribbon. You can move the QAT back next to the Office icon by opening the same dropdown menu and selecting Show Above the Ribbon.

To add any command icon to the QAT (from any ribbon), right-click that icon and select Add to Quick Access Toolbar. You can add up to 90 commands to the QAT, but getting anywhere close to that number will be overkill. If you limit yourself to only those commands that you really want to have handy at all times, using the QAT can significantly increase your efficiency.

To customize the QAT further, right-click on it and choose Customize Quick Access Toolbar, which will give you access to all the different tabs in the Excel Options dialog box. From there customizing the QAT is a matter of only a few clicks.

THE SHORTCUT MENUS AND THE MINI TOOLBAR

As in the earlier versions of Excel, in Excel 2007 you can access context-sensitive shortcut menus by selecting or putting the mouse-pointer on almost anything in your worksheet. Most often the command you need will be on this menu, and being able to choose a command right near your mouse-pointer instead of having to go back to the Ribbon to look for it will save you a lot of time.

Also, when you open a shortcut menu, very often (depending on the context) a Mini toolbar containing some of the most commonly used tools from the Home tab appears above the shortcut menu box. Using this Mini toolbar when you need any of these tools can be another efficiency booster.

FINDING SOME OF THE OLD TOOLS AND DIALOG BOXES

To force you to give Excel 2007 a good try, Microsoft, probably consciously, has not provided any way of switching back to the old menu and toolbar system in Excel 2007. But all is not lost. At the right end of the bars containing many of the group names in the ribbons you will notice a small arrow. Clicking on any of these arrows generally brings up one of the familiar old dialog boxes related to the commands in that group. Most of the time you can do everything you need to do using the commands on the ribbon in that group, but sometimes you may find it easier or necessary to open and use one of those old dialog boxes.

Other New Features

In this section I discuss the other new features of Excel 2007 in the approximate order of their importance for financial modeling and analysis work. I have provided enough description here for you to judge if a new feature will be useful for the type of work you do most with Excel. If you do not fully understand the capabilities and uses of a new feature from the brief description here, consult the chapter that includes more on it.

PIVOTTABLE

PivotTable is one of the most sophisticated features of Excel. It existed in earlier versions of Excel also; but the PivotTable in Excel 2007 is much more powerful and easier to use.

You use pivot tables to work with flat databases. A flat database is essentially data organized in a rectangular range—literally in an Excel worksheet or figuratively in an external database—where the data consist of the same characteristics or properties for a number of similar entities. For example, it can be a database of employees of a company, where each row of data in the database represents one employee and holds her name, address, telephone number, social security number, date of birth, and so on. If you work with flat databases, especially large ones, then it may be worthwhile for you to upgrade to Excel 2007 just to have access to the new, improved PivotTable.

Using a pivot table you can view and summarize the data in a flat database almost in any way you want to look at it to understand the data and make decisions. Once you get somewhat used to working with pivot table, it takes only a few clicks to organize the data the way you want to view it, and only a few more clicks to look at it from a very different perspective. You can also summarize the data in many ways, create pivot charts from the data, and so on.

In a way you can look at PivotTable as a modeling tool because with it you can quickly get answers that would otherwise take a lot of time to get if you had to build the model yourself. Also, most of the time to shift to a different perspective you may need to build a new model, whereas with pivot table it is a matter of a few more clicks. The flexibility and time-saving features of pivot table are amazing.

TABLE

Excel 2007 introduces a new feature called Table that can make working with flat databases very convenient and efficient. (Excel 2007 calls it just table, which I find confusing because in Excel we use the word *table* in many different contexts. So in this book I call this new feature Table with the *T* capitalized to avoid any confusion.)

Using tools incorporated in the Table, you can easily sort and filter the data in the Table, insert summary formulas (to calculate totals, averages, etc.) in the bottom row of the Table, and so on. You can also apply attractive formatting to the Table with a single click and take other actions quickly.

One powerful feature of Table is that you can easily remove duplicate data from the database. If you have not worked with large databases, you may not appreciate the usefulness of this feature. This can be a great time saver.

If you need to work with flat databases, especially large ones, just being able to access the Table feature may make it worthwhile to upgrade to Excel 2007. Of course, you can do most of the things Table can do for you by writing your own Excel formulas. Also, previous versions of Excel have a feature called list that has some of the functionalities of Table. But for the right job, Table is a far superior tool.

PROFESSIONAL QUALITY CHARTS

Excel 2007 has an all-new charting engine that can create much more attractive, professional quality charts. But Excel 2007 does not include any new chart types. If you create many charts, especially for upper-management or important presentations, then the superior chart quality capability can easily justify upgrading to Excel 2007.

CONDITIONAL FORMATTING

As in the previous versions of Excel, Excel 2007 allows you to use conditional formatting (that is, specify that the formatting in a cell be determined by the content of the cell). But conditional formatting in Excel 2007 is a lot more powerful and much easier to use. For example, now you can easily add gradients, heat maps, and in-cell data bars as part of conditional formatting, to make your data or model outputs much easier to visualize. You can also use more complex conditions than you could in the earlier versions of Excel.

AUTOCOMPLETE FOR ENTERING FORMULAS

Excel 2007 introduces a new AutoComplete feature that makes entering functions and formulas more efficient and error-free. When you are entering a formula, Excel 2007 tries to anticipate functions, cell or range names, etc., that you may want to use and presents them in a dropdown list. If you want to use any of those, you can just select them from the list, thus eliminating the need for looking for them or the chance of making spelling errors. The list also shows the arguments of the functions. The list presented is context sensitive and keeps changing as you progress with writing your formula.

ONE INTEGRATED FUNCTION LIBRARY

In the earlier versions, many useful Excel functions were included in the Analysis ToolPak and you could not reach them from the function library. In Excel 2007 all Excel functions have been integrated into one function library so that you can more easily work with all available functions. Excel 2007 offers only a few new functions, none of much significance for financial modeling work.

STYLES AND THEMES

It is always important to make the outputs of your models attractive and easy to understand. Otherwise your audience, especially senior executives, may not pay attention to your results no matter how great the underlying model may be. Unfortunately, most people do not appreciate the importance of presentations or are not good at creating attractive ones.

Excel 2007 introduces a large gallery of predefined styles and themes that you can apply with just a few clicks to make your outputs look attractive and professionally coordinated in colors, font styles, effects, and so on. What is more, themes can be coordinated with other Microsoft Office applications (e.g., Word and Power Point) to produce great looking reports or presentations.

I do not cover styles and themes in this book. But if you upgrade to Excel 2007 you should definitely learn about them simply by experimenting on your own or from the Help or general Excel books, and start applying them to your work.

A MUCH LARGER GRID

The grid, that is, the worksheet, in the earlier versions of Excel is limited to 65,536 rows and 256 columns. It is unlikely that you ever ran into that limitation in developing financial models (unless you were working with very large databases or for some reason needed to put daily data or several years of weekly data across the columns instead of down the rows). The grid in Excel 2007 has been expanded to 1,048,576 rows by 16,384 columns. You will never need that big a grid, and at least for now you will not be able to use all of it in any PC. But I hope this will remove any worries you may have had about running out of room in your worksheet.

Many other limits have been extended as well. For example, you can now use up to 64 levels of nesting instead of just 7 as in previous versions. But unless you are a professional programmer developing a large system, you probably would never want to use more than 3 or 4 levels of nesting. For similar reasons, most of the other limit increases will not matter to you for financial modeling.

One increase in limit that may matter to you is that the number of levels of undo (that is, backtracking) has been increased in Excel 2007 to 100 from 16 in previous versions. I strongly advise against relying on undo to go back to a much earlier point of your work. As I discuss in a later chapter, you will be much better off saving your work frequently under different version numbers for your workbooks, that is, in systematically named different files, and keeping track of major changes you make from one version to another. Nonetheless, in an emergency when you have not been following that advice, the maximum undo level of 100 can be a lifesaver. (Remember that once you save a workbook without changing its name, you overwrite the previous version under the same name and cannot undo anything in that workbook even in Excel 2007.)

PAGE LAYOUT VIEW

In Excel 2007 you can set up and preview how your outputs will look in print using the commands in the Page Layout ribbon. This is similar to what you did in the earlier versions of Excel using the Page Setup dialog box. But the new feature is better in many ways. For example, you can edit and fine-tune your outputs while you are in the Page Layout ribbon, which you cannot do in the older Page Setup dialog box.

CONSOLIDATED OPTIONS

In all versions of Excel you can set numerous options to customize your work environment and control how Excel works in many situations. For example, you can set the recalculation option to control if you want Excel to automatically recalculate everything in your workbook every time you make a change or you want it to wait until you manually force a recalculation. Over the different versions of Excel the number of such options has grown significantly and been spread all over the place even though a large number of them are consolidated in one dialog box.

Excel 2007 has consolidated all such options in just one, easily accessible dialog box where all the options are grouped into a number of tabs. (To open this options dialog box click the Office icon at the top left corner of your Excel window and then click the Excel Options button in the bottom bar.)

New File Formats in Excel 2007

Over the years the format for Excel files has undergone some internal changes that we users (as opposed to techies) have been able to ignore. In the previous versions of Excel, when we save an Excel file, it is saved with a .xls extension and the same file format works with all versions of Excel from 97 to 2003. Also, the .xls files can include both worksheets and macro sheets. (Incidentally, .xls files are binary files.)

In Excel 2007 Microsoft has introduced two new eXtensible Markup Language (XML) file formats for Excel files to make Excel files more compatible with many applications other than Excel. Another advantage of the new XML file format is that the new files are actually zip-compressed text files. The two new file formats that you will use most are:

- XLSX: This is the default file format for Excel 2007. It does not allow macros. Files with this extension are called Excel Workbook.
- XLSM: This format allows for the inclusion of VBA macros. Files with this extension are called Excel Macro-Enabled Workbook.

Excel 2007 also offers an Excel Binary Workbook option. Files in this format can be loaded and saved faster. But you are not likely to need this extra speed and should generally avoid using this format. There are also four other new file formats that you are not likely to need.

Excel 2007 can still open the old .xls files and save files in that format. If you want to share Excel files with others who may not have Excel 2007 you should save your Excel files in this format. But keep in mind that the .xls file format may not work with some of the new features of Excel 2007. (When you try to save an Excel 2007 file with such incompatible features in the .xls format, Excel will give you a warning and help you decide what you want to do.)

If you know at the beginning that you will want to share a workbook you are creating with Excel 2007 with others using earlier versions of Excel and would prefer to lose as little as possible in transfers back and forth, then start with a workbook in the .xls format, that is, immediately after you create a new workbook in Excel 2007 save it as a .xls file and then do your work using that file.

You can also open and save files in Excel 2007 formats in Excel XP and Excel 2003 using the Office 2007 Compatibility Pack. You can download it from the Microsoft web site (http://office.microsoft.com) and install it in the computer running those earlier versions of Excel. But if your operating system and Excel do not have the required service packs installed, then downloading and installing the Compatibility Pack can be a little cumbersome because you would have to first install the required service packs. Often as a simple alternative you can ask whoever sent you the Excel 2007 file to resend it in .xls format. Either way there may be some loss of functionality in translation, however.

CHAPTER 3

Excel Basics

In this book, I assume that you already know the basics of Excel—that is, you have been using Excel for some time and can create spreadsheet solutions for simple financial and other problems, plot charts to present your results, and print out your results. So rather than cover all the basics of Excel in detail, I will first offer some general suggestions here on how to improve your Excel skills. I will then list all the basic features of Excel that you are likely to use extensively. In the process I will also point out things to which you should pay special attention and provide other guidance on the safe and efficient use of Excel.

If you are not familiar with any of these basic features of Excel, you should learn it now using Excel's online Help or other general Excel books. Knowing these basic features well is essential for learning the advanced features covered in the next chapters as well as for developing your financial modeling skills.

Incidentally, throughout the book I refer to all the things you can do with Excel (or VBA) as *features*. Features include everything from the various ways that you can move around a worksheet to the many sophisticated tools, built-in functions, and so on, that Excel offers. Although Excel has literally thousands of features, in most of your modeling you will use only a selected group of them; however, you will need to know this group of features well. This is the group of features that I will cover in this part of the book.

I should also point out that the distinction I am drawing between basic and advanced features is somewhat arbitrary. For example, you will find that in the next chapter I cover in detail how to write formulas with relative and absolute references, enabling you to create formulas in other cells to do similar calculations simply by copying and pasting the original formula into them. Many people consider this to be one of the basic features of Excel because a lot of Excel's power derives from this feature. I cover some such features in detail in the next chapter instead of just listing them as basic features here because they are so important that you must know them very well. The distinction between basic and advanced is not important. What is important is that after you cover these chapters on Excel in this part of the book, you will be able to use Excel more effectively and more efficiently as you develop financial models.

Improving Your Excel Skills

SAVING YOUR WORKBOOKS

Although you probably have heard hundreds of times by now that you should save your workbooks frequently, the importance of the message generally does not sink in until you have suffered a major disaster of your own. If your luck has held up so far, do not push it. Develop the habit to save your workbooks—which are files in Windows parlance—frequently. You should also learn to do it the right way as described here. Remember that you can never be too protective of your files. You should also establish and follow a plan to periodically back up your files from the hard disk on your computer to some removable storage medium like external hard disks or CDs.

To guard against the loss of any of your current work, save your workbook by clicking the floppy disk icon on the Quick Access Toolbar, by pressing Ctrl+S, or by selecting Office ⇨ Save every time you have made substantial changes or additions to your workbook. Depending on your pace of work, at times this may mean saving every few minutes—at other times, much less frequently. (You cannot save any individual worksheet of a workbook; Excel always saves entire workbooks.)

Here is something very important about saving workbooks that you should keep in mind. Whenever you save a workbook, Excel overwrites the copy you had saved previously under the same name with the current workbook, and the old copy is permanently lost. Also, once you save a workbook, you will not be able to use Excel's Undo to backtrack to any earlier step. So, as I will discuss shortly, you should periodically save your workbooks under a different version name following a system you design to suit your own circumstances.

Using Excel's AutoRecover

In Excel 2002, AutoRecover has replaced the AutoSave of the older versions. It is a useful improvement, and it keeps working in the background once you turn it on.

If you have the AutoRecover turned on and your computer or Excel encounters a problem or stops responding, you will be able to recover most, if not all, of the work that you have not saved yet. To turn on AutoRecover, select the Office icon and then the Excel Options button in the bottom row. In the Excel

Options dialog box that opens, select the Save tab. Select Save AutoRecover Info Every and enter a time interval in the text box next to it. You can also specify an AutoRecover save location. At the specified intervals, Excel will save the necessary information to update your workbook(s) from the last manual save so that if you set the interval at 5 minutes, at worst you will lose only the last 5 minutes of work. There is a good chance, however, that you will not lose any work at all. (The AutoRecover feature is available in Excel 2002 onwards. In these earlier versions you have to select Tools ⇨ Options and then the Save tab in the Options dialog box.)

I do not think this is a substitute for the procedure I recommend below for saving your workbook frequently and at times under a different version name. However, if you are using Excel 2002 or a later version, you should definitely have AutoRecover turned on at all times with an appropriate time interval setting.

To learn more about AutoRecover and to find out how you recover a file if necessary, look in Help.

Using Excel's AutoSave (in Excel 97 and 2000)

AutoRecover is not available in Excel 97 and Excel 2000. Instead you have a feature called AutoSave. It is not as good, but it is still a useful feature.

If in those versions you want Excel to remind you to save your workbooks at a set time interval, turn on Excel's AutoSave. Select Tools ⇨ AutoSave to open the AutoSave dialog box. Select the check box labeled Automatic Save Every and then enter an appropriate interval in the Minutes box. (You may want to change the interval from time to time to suit your pace of work.) Decide if you want to save only the active workbook or all open workbooks, and then select the check box labeled Prompt Before Saving. It is important to select this option because otherwise Excel will automatically save your workbook(s) at the specified interval without asking you and overwrite the previously saved copy of the workbook. You may not always want this to happen.

If you select the Prompt Before Saving option, a dialog box will pop up at the specified intervals to remind you to save, and will offer you several options. If you are not working with Excel at that time, the name of the workbook will start blinking in the Windows Task Bar at the bottom of your screen to draw your attention. Do not click Save mechanically in the dialog box. You may not want to save the workbook(s) right at that moment, and you may not want to save all the open workbooks (in case you had selected that option when you had set up the AutoSave). I generally click Skip or Cancel and then save the workbook(s) promptly once I am ready to do so.

(If you cannot find AutoSave in the Tools menu, you have to install it. Select Tools ⇨ Add-Ins to go to the Add-Ins dialog box, select Autosave Add-in, and click OK.)

Saving Workbooks under Different Version Names

Whenever you save a workbook using any of the three methods I mentioned before, Excel overwrites the copy you had saved previously under the same name, and the old copy is permanently lost. At times, this may not be what you want. For example, you may later discover some mistakes you made along the way and want to go back to an earlier point to start over. Or you may want to go back to an earlier point and take a different direction with your model. Remember that you can backtrack using Excel's Undo only through the changes you have made since you saved the workbook the last time. Once you save a workbook you cannot backtrack to any earlier stage.

I find it safer and more convenient to save my workbooks under different version numbers as I go along so that I can easily backtrack as much as I want. I include in the name of my first workbook of a model the version number V1 (for example, "Retirement Planning V1"). As I work, I keep saving the normal way. After I have made some progress or get to a point that I may want to revisit later, I select Office ⇨ Save As and in the file name increase the version number by 1 (for example, from V1 to V2) before saving the workbook. If I think it will be helpful later on, I also add a few words to the new workbook name to identify where I was at that point. (Note that Excel considers a workbook with even a slightly different name to be a totally different workbook. Excel does not recognize them as different versions of the same workbook. This is why when you use this method, a file with a V2 in its name will not overwrite a file with an otherwise identical name but V1 in it.)

Another advantage of this approach is that if somehow the version of the workbook you saved last gets corrupted—it does happen mysteriously from time to time—you will lose a relatively small amount of work and will not have to restart from scratch.

As you gain experience, you may want to modify this approach to suit your own circumstances and know how often you need to create a new version. To avoid clutter, delete earlier versions at the end of each session that you do not think you will need anymore. If you do not clean up promptly, it may take more time later to decide which versions you want to delete and which ones you want to keep.

Keep in mind that if you use the workbook's name anywhere within the workbook (for example, in a formula) or in any other workbook, then you will have to update those references with the new name using Find & Select ⇨ Replace; Excel will not do it automatically.

USING EXCEL'S ONLINE HELP

Excel has extensive built-in (called online) Help that is particularly useful because it is always right there for you to access. Most people, however, do not take the time to learn how to use it properly to take full advantage of it. Invest a few minutes to learn how the system works and then keep using it. You will quickly become familiar with it, and it will save you a lot of time and frustration over the years.

The system offers explanations of varying quality and clarity, but most of it is pretty good. Sometimes you may have difficulty finding what you are looking for and you may have to look for it in a few different ways. Finally, keep in mind that it is often much easier to follow complex explanations or instructions if you read them on paper instead of on the screen. So learn to print out the Help screens.

Using Help in Excel 2007

Finding Help has been considerably simplified in Excel 2007. You can at anytime click the Help icon (a question mark, near the right end of the row with the tabs) to open the Excel Help dialog box, enter what you are looking for in the box to the left of Search and click Search. With a little practice you will quickly learn how to search using the words and phrases that Excel recognizes most easily.

Finding Help in Previous Versions of Excel

In the previous versions Excel has gone through several different approaches to finding Help. If you are using an earlier version of Excel, you will benefit from the rest of the discussions on finding Help. If you are using Excel 2007 you can skip the rest of the discussion on finding Help, however.

In the previous versions there are two primary ways to access the online Help—through the Office Assistant and directly through the full Help window. (In Excel 2002, there is a small window at the right end of the menu bar labeled Ask a Question, which works like the Office Assistant, except that it is always open and never gets in your way.) In addition, there are a few shortcuts for getting Help for certain items, which I will discuss first.

Getting Help with Menu Commands and Toolbar Buttons

To see the name of any toolbar button, place the mouse pointer on it and wait a few seconds. The name will appear in a small box.

For context-sensitive help on a menu command, a toolbar button, or any other component of the Excel window, select Help ⇨ What's This? (or, press Shift+F1). This will turn the mouse pointer into an arrow with a question mark next to it. Now point at any menu command, toolbar button, or other component and click on it to see a description of the item in a pop-up box. (Press Esc to close the pop-up box or to switch back to the regular mouse pointer.)

Getting Help with the Options in Dialog Boxes

To get Help with any option when you are in a dialog box, click on the "?" button near the right end of the dialog box's title bar. This will turn your mouse pointer into an arrow with a question mark next to it. You can then click on an option to get a description of it. You can also right-click on an option and then click on the What's This? box that pops up to get a description of the option.

Using the Office Assistant to Get Help

Using the Office Assistant is normally the fastest way to get help on things other than the ones I mentioned in the previous two sections. Office Assistant is the character (generally a paper clip) that may be already sitting on your worksheet. If it is not, you can bring it up by selecting Help ⇨ Show the Office Assistant. (Most of the time, pressing F1 will also do the same. See more on this later.)

To get help on any topic, click on the Office Assistant, which will open a pop-up window. In the box near the bottom of the window, type a description of what you want help on, and click Search. You do not have to type in a full sentence or question; you can just type in one or more keywords that you think Excel will recognize. After searching, the Assistant will show you a list of topics. Click the one that sounds closest to what you are looking for and the Microsoft Excel Help window will open up with the help information. Working with this Help window and finding additional information by clicking on various items it presents is fairly straightforward. Remember that once you start exploring the related topics by clicking on them, you can move back and forth among them by using the left and right arrows in the top pane of the Help window.

If the help information is not what you are looking for, click on the Office Assistant again to go back to the pop-up window with your original inquiry and list of topics. Now you can click on another topic or make another inquiry.

The only problem with finding help on something with the Office Assistant is that you often have to know the keywords Excel uses for it. Otherwise, Excel may not be able to find it. If a search is not coming up with the kind of topics you are looking for, search for what you need using alternate guesses for keywords that Excel may be using. If this does not work, then click on the Show icon in the Microsoft Excel Help window to search for help in the three other ways described in the next section. (The Show icon is the one at the left end of the series of icons in the top pane. It looks like a page with a left arrow attached to it.)

In Excel 2002, you can also use the Ask a Question window at the right end of the menu bar as an alternative to Office Assistant's question window.

Customizing the Office Assistant: You can customize the Office Assistant in many different ways. To see what options are available, right-click the Office Assistant and then select Options, which will bring up the Office Assistant dialog box. To see the description of any of the options, follow the method I described in the previous section.

Hiding versus Turning Off the Office Assistant: You can both Hide the Office Assistant and turn it off. The key difference is that if you Hide it, pressing F1 (or selecting Help ⇨ Microsoft Excel Help) will bring up the Office Assistant; if you turn it off, pressing F1 will open up the full Help window with three tabs in a left panel where you can look for help in three different ways. You can hide the Office Assistant by right-clicking on it and then selecting Hide. To turn off the Office Assistant, clear the check box next to Use the Office Assistant in the Options tab of the Office Assistant dialog box. In either case, you can activate the Office Assistant again by selecting Help ⇨ Show the Office Assistant.

Using the Full Help Window to Get Help

You can get to the full Help window (which has two panes, one with three tabs) in two ways. If the Office Assistant is turned off (not just hidden), then pressing F1 will take you directly there. Otherwise, F1 will bring up the Office Assistant. Type in any question, click Search, and select one of the suggested topics to bring up the Help window. Now click on the Show icon to bring up the second pane of the Help window with three tabs. In the full Help window, you can search for help in three different ways using the three different tabs.

Contents Tab: In this tab, the help topics are arranged like chapters in a book with each chapter marked with a book icon. To open the list of topics included in a chapter, you can either double-click the book icon for the chapter or click on the plus sign on its left. A chapter may also include sections marked by book icons, which work the same way. (You can collapse the list of sections and topics in a chapter by clicking on the minus sign on the left of the book icon.)

This tab is particularly helpful if you want to learn about some aspect of Excel instead of looking for help on something specific. Also, if you have not been able to find help on something through the Office Assistant because you did not use the right keyword, you may be able to find it through this tab by guessing which chapter and section includes the information you need.

Answer Wizard Tab: This tab works like the Office Assistant. You type your question or keyword in the top window and click Search. A list of topics appears in the window below and you can get help by clicking on one of them.

Index Tab: This tab works like the index at the back of a book and you have to search by keywords. You can type in a keyword in the first window or you can scroll through the second window to get to the right keyword. The list is quite long, however. So you may save time if you type in a keyword or the first one or two letters of it to go to the correct area in the keyword list fast. At this point, you can scroll to get to the right keyword and double-click on it to see a list of topics in the window below. Click on a topic to get help.

LEARNING EXCEL FEATURES

You can save a lot of time by learning Excel features the right way and thoroughly. The best way to learn any Excel feature is to use the "try and check" method, which means you try it out in a few simple made-up examples (generally on a new worksheet) and check to make sure that it is working the way you think it should work and that it gives you the right answers. (You can check the answers using a hand calculator.)

If you try to learn a feature by using it immediately in a large model, it may be difficult for you to know if the feature is working properly or not. If it does not work, it may take a long time to figure out if you are using the feature incorrectly or if there is a problem in some other part of your model. Once you have learned a feature by working through some simple examples, use it in bigger models soon. Without some practice early on you will forget what you learned; however, if you have to go back and learn it again it will take much less time.

Remember that most Excel features are designed to be intuitive: if you understand what a feature is supposed to do, you may be able to figure out how it works just by trial and error. This is a good approach to take because the more features you figure out on your own, the better you will get at doing so and the more confidence you will develop with Excel. But do not become too stubborn to look for help if you cannot get a feature to work in two or three trials. Sometimes you can easily waste hours trying to make a feature work by trial and error. Also, it is good to look up a feature in Excel's Help or a book just to make sure that you do not miss something else the feature can do or some shortcuts you could take.

The Basic Excel Features

As I mentioned earlier, I will list in this section the features that you probably already know well and will use all the time. Check your knowledge against the list, close any gaps you may have in your knowledge in these areas, and pay special attention to the pointers I have provided on some of the features.

KEEPING YOUR WORKBOOKS AND RELATED FILES ORGANIZED

Learn to keep your workbooks and other files organized using the Windows system for organizing files and folders (also called directories). It is generally helpful to keep all your files—Excel files, Word files, Power Point files, and so on—related to a project in one folder. If a project has a large number of files or several different kinds of files, you may want to save them in a few different folders within the project folder. If your files and folders have descriptive names and are well organized, it will be much easier for you or someone else to find them at a later date. (Learn to use Windows Explorer or some other utility program to organize your folders and files.)

NAMING WORKBOOKS AND WORKSHEETS

Learn the rules and restrictions for naming workbooks and worksheets. Always use short but descriptive names for them.

FINDING THE COMMANDS YOU NEED

As I discussed in an earlier chapter, in Excel 2007 all commands have been organized in the Ribbon. Take a few minutes to familiarize yourself with the general organization of the Ribbon for the Excel features you will need most often. You will learn how to access the commands for more features as you learn them in the following chapters.

If you are using one of the earlier versions of Excel, learn to use the menus in the menu bar and the submenus available under each menu. Many of the submenus lead to additional features and options. Learn them as you need them. Also learn to call up and use the context-sensitive shortcut menus by selecting whatever you want to work on (for example, a cell or a chart) and then right-clicking.

Note that when you open a menu from the menu bar, the dropdown list may initially show only a few of the submenu items (including those you used recently) instead of all the submenu items available under the menu. You can see the rest by clicking on the downward-pointing double arrows at the bottom, or, if the right option is active in your Excel, the rest of the submenu items will appear automatically after you wait a few seconds. If you find the wait irritating, select Tools ⇨ Customize and in the Options tab deselect Menus show recently used commands first. (This will make the same change in all the Office applications on your computer.)

WORKING WITH WORKSHEETS

Learn to insert, delete, rename, and hide worksheets. Also learn to move or copy a worksheet within the same workbook or to a different workbook. After you create a copy of a worksheet, remember to give it an appropriate new name.

WORKING WITH ROWS, COLUMNS, AND CELLS

Learn to do the following:

- Select one or more contiguous or noncontiguous complete rows, complete columns, and cells (ranges).
- Insert, delete, cut, copy, and paste rows, columns, and cells.
- Change column widths and row heights.
- Wrap around text in a cell.
- Hide rows, columns, and formulas or contents of a cell. (These are discussed in a later chapter.)

Excel also lets you select ranges in multiple sheets, and you can make other kinds of special selections using Home ⇨ Editing ⇨ Find & Select ⇨ Go to Special (in earlier versions of Excel use Edit ⇨ Go To command and then choose Special). Most people never need to use these features, however. Learn them if and when you need to use them.

USING THE TOOLBARS

In previous versions of Excel, you should learn how to access the primary toolbars—the Standard Toolbar, the Formatting Toolbar, and the Drawing Toolbar—and use the tools available on each. This will help you develop speed. Note that you can move a toolbar to a different location or make it free-floating to get it out of your way. You can also customize the existing toolbars and create your own custom toolbars, although you may never need to do either.

USING KEYBOARD SHORTCUTS

To work with Excel faster, you may want to learn how to do most things in Excel using just the keyboard and save the time of going back and forth between the keyboard and the mouse and using the mouse. You could use such keyboard shortcuts in earlier versions of Excel also, but in Excel 2007 it is even easier to do so.

Excel 2007

You can easily access and execute any command on the Ribbon from the keyboard. To start, press the Alt key, which will display the pop-up "keytips" for all the tabs on the ribbon as shown in Figure 3.1. (A keytip is the number or letter or multiple letter combination you see next to each command and can type in to execute the

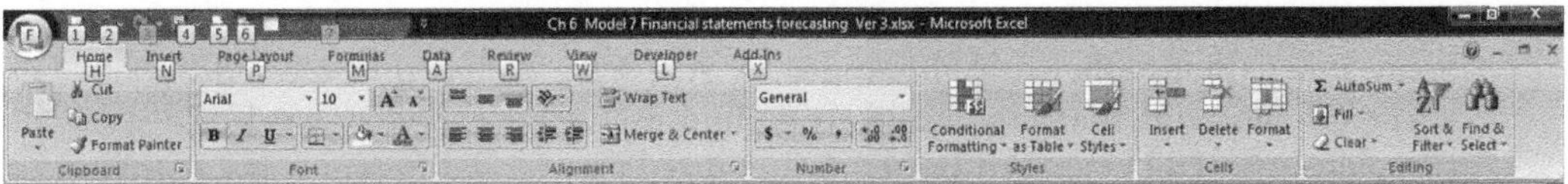

FIGURE 3.1 Keytips displayed when the Alt key is pressed.

command.) You can now type in the keytip to choose a particular tab and display its ribbon with new keytips for all the commands on it. (You do not have to hold down the Alt key or press it again.) Depending on the command, pressing any of the new keytips will either execute the command or open a small menu that you can select from using the arrows on the keyboard or by pressing new keytips.

This essentially represents the best of both worlds. As you start remembering the Alt plus key combinations needed to do the things that you do most often in Excel, you will use those combinations without even looking at the keytips. But if you forget a key combination, you can find it instantly on the screen.

Once you have pressed the Alt key, you can also select and execute commands using the keyboard arrows and Enter. For example, after you press the Alt key, you can scroll through the tabs using the left and right arrows and then enter a tab and its ribbon by pressing the down arrow once you are at the tab you need. In the ribbon you can again scroll through the commands using the arrows and execute a command by pressing Enter.

Of the two options, using the keytips, especially after you have automatically memorized the combinations you use most often, will be faster.

Most of the old keyboard shortcuts (e.g., Ctrl+S to save a workbook) still work in Excel 2007, and some of these shortcuts can be even faster. To learn more about these key combinations search in Help for "accessibility" and then look under Keyboard shortcuts in the 2007 Office system (which offers training and practice) and Shortcut keys in Office 2007 and go from there.

Earlier Versions of Excel

If you are using an earlier version of Excel you should find the following discussion on keyboard shortcuts helpful.

To open the dropdown window for any menu, you can press Alt+ the letter underlined in the menu name (for example, Alt+V to open the View menu). In the pull-down list of a menu command or in any dialog box, if any submenu or option name or label has an underlined letter, you can activate it by pressing that letter on the keyboard. This feature is not case sensitive. You do not have to press Shift+ the letter even if the letter is capitalized in the name or label.

Note that the keyboard shortcuts for many submenu items (for example, Copy in the Edit menu) are shown next to them in the dropdown menus where they appear. There are also shortcuts for navigating the worksheet and doing many other things efficiently. In Appendix A, I have included a selected list of keyboard shortcuts that you are likely to find useful for everyday work. To see complete lists of all keyboard shortcuts organized in several different ways, search in Excel's Help under "keyboard shortcuts." You may want to personalize the list in Appendix A by adding to it other shortcuts you want to learn and use. However, remember that unless you use a shortcut frequently, you will soon forget it. So learn only the ones you think you will use, especially the ones that work across several office applications. For example, Ctrl+S saves the current workbook in Excel and also the current document in Word.

NAVIGATING THE WORKSHEET

Learn to navigate a worksheet efficiently using the arrow keys, the mouse, the scroll bars, and the PgUp and PgDn keys. You can jump to a specific cell by typing in its number or name (if you have given it a name) in the Name Box (located at the left end of the formula bar) and pressing Enter. Alternately, to jump to a named cell, click on the arrow next to the Name Box to see a dropdown list of all the cell names you have defined in the workbook. To jump to a particular cell, click on the cell name.

Also learn to jump to particular cell numbers and named cells using the Go To command by pressing Ctrl+G.

To navigate large models efficiently, give descriptive names to cells that mark the beginnings of various sections of the model (or give each section a range name) and then use one of the above methods to move quickly from one section to another.

FORMATTING

It is important to make your models (worksheets) easy to understand and use and their outputs attractive. Learn to use the myriad Excel formatting options available to do this, but use formatting judiciously and in good taste. If you use too many different fonts, font sizes, colors, borders, and shadings, your worksheet may become unattractive and more difficult to read.

Aligning texts and numbers properly in the cells makes a big difference in the look of your worksheet. For example, the column headings in tables should be aligned the same way (mostly right adjusted) as the numbers below them. Also, it often looks nicer if a table title is centered across the full table width. It is easy to change alignments and you should learn all the options available.

Make sure that the titles and headings of your tables and charts are clear and all labels are descriptive but short. For numbers, use the fewest number of decimal places necessary and be consistent throughout the model, that is, use the same number of decimal places for similar variables throughout.

ENTERING AND WORKING WITH FORMULAS

Learn to enter formulas both by typing in cell references and pointing at the relevant cells, and to create formulas by copying and pasting formulas you have already created. To save time and avoid making typographical errors and other mistakes, create formulas by pointing at cells or by copying and pasting whenever possible. (See the more detailed discussion on creating formulas by copying and pasting in a later chapter.)

Learn the order in which Excel performs the mathematical operations within a formula and how you can use parentheses to change this order to suit your needs. You may also want to use parentheses in a formula even when it is not essential, either to make the formula more readable or to make doubly sure that Excel will do the calculations in the exact order you have in mind.

To make your formulas easier to understand and check, keep them short and use named variables whenever possible. One way to keep your formulas short is to do your calculations in steps. For example, assume that you are calculating the total sales for a company with 15 divisions that are organized under 4 groups. Rather than write a formula with 15 cell addresses in it to calculate the total sales for the entire company in one step, first calculate the total sales for each group (in 4 different cells) and then calculate the total sales for the company by adding the total sales for the 4 groups. Even where there is no natural intermediate step like this, you can create some logical intermediate steps to keep your formulas relatively short and simple.

USING PASTE SPECIAL

Learn to use Paste Special in conjunction with Copy to paste in various special ways (for example, to paste only the format of a number). Learn the uses of Transpose and Paste Link in Paste Special.

Sometimes you may want to freeze the values in certain cells that have been calculated by the formulas in these cells so that even when the values of the underlying variables change, the values in these cells will not change anymore. To do this, select the cells, select Copy to copy the cells, select Paste Special to bring up the Paste Special dialog box, choose the Values option under Paste, and click OK. (Here you are copying the values in the cells and overwriting the formulas in the cells with those values.)

CONTROLLING THE WORKSHEET VIEW

Excel provides a few options to let you view different parts of your worksheet and sometimes multiple sheets in the same window or in multiple windows on the screen. Learn how to do the following:

- Open multiple windows to view and work with different parts of the same worksheet or different worksheets at the same time.
- Split a worksheet into two or four panes in the same window to work with the different parts of it simultaneously.
- Freeze panes to scroll through a worksheet while the column and row headings (or several columns on the left and several rows at the top) remain visible.

USING UNDO AND REDO

Learn how you can backtrack one step at a time by clicking the Undo repeatedly. Once you have backtracked one or more steps, you can move forward through those same steps by repeatedly clicking Redo. These buttons can save you a lot of time and agony if you change your mind about something you have done or discover an error after you have moved ahead several steps in your work. Remember that you can backtrack only through the steps you have taken since you last saved your worksheet. To allow yourself more flexibility, see the earlier discussion on saving your workbook under different version names.

CUSTOMIZING THE EXCEL WORK ENVIRONMENT

In Excel 2007 all options to customize your Excel work environment have been consolidated in the Excel Options dialog box under various tabs. To open this dialog box click the Office icon and then the Excel Options button in the bottom row. Familiarize yourself with the numerous options available under the different tabs.

In the previous versions of Excel the options are somewhat scattered in various places. But the Options submenu under the Tools menu offers a large number of them (organized under several tabs in the Options dialog box) to customize your work environment. Familiarize yourself with the options available in this dialog box.

For example, to have Excel show the formulas instead of the numbers in a worksheet, you have to go to the Options dialog box, click the View tab, select Formulas in the Window options section, and then click OK. (Note that this procedure changes the column widths and you may want to adjust them to fit your screen or a printed page.) There are additional customizing options available in the Customize submenu under the Tools menu.

CONTROLLING WHEN FORMULAS ARE CALCULATED

Learn to use the options in the Formulas tab of Excel Options in Excel 2007 (the Calculation tab in Tools ⇨ Options in earlier versions) to control when the formulas in your workbook will be calculated. Generally the Automatic option should be selected so that whenever you enter or edit data and formulas all formulas that depend on them are recalculated.

However, if you are working with a model that includes a large number of complex formulas or uses large data tables, you may want to select one of the other options to postpone recalculations. Make sure, though, that you manually force recalculations (by pressing F9) before relying on any of the results you see. Keep in mind that with a fast, modern PC you will rarely need to turn off automatic calculation. Often when people turn off automatic calculation, they forget it and end up with wrong or puzzling results. So if your model produces wrong or puzzling results, one of the first things you should check is if the automatic calculation is turned on.

While the automatic calculation is turned off, you can press F9 to force recalculation of formulas in all open workbooks or Shift+F9 to recalculate formulas only in the active worksheet.

PRINTING

You must be able to create attractive, well-formatted printed reports from your models. Learn to do the following by using the options and tools that Excel provides to create such reports efficiently:

- Specify what you want to print.
- Specify orientation, scaling, margins, and center your printout within the page.
- Create headers/footers and have them automatically include filename, date, time, page number, and so on.
- Repeat certain rows and columns on each printed page, include row and column headings (that is, the row and column numbers), print gridlines, and print pages in desired order.
- Preview and make adjustment to the pages before printing.
- Control where pages break in your printouts.

CREATING CHARTS

Charts are essential for making compelling presentations of the outputs of your model. Excel provides very good chart-making capabilities, and learning to use them to create various kinds of properly formatted and labeled charts efficiently is important.

Learn to make the different types of charts you can create with Excel, but pay special attention to XY (Scatter) charts because you will probably use them most often. Choosing the right chart type, using the right colors, and other formatting, (including the proper titles, labels, and so on) are important for getting your message across effectively.

After you have created a chart, you should be able to do the following:

- Move and resize a chart.
- Relocate an embedded chart to a chart sheet and vice versa.
- Change the chart type.
- Modify various chart elements such as the chart area and the plot area.
- Modify the chart titles and legends.
- Change chart gridlines.
- Modify the axes, especially their scales.
- Format a chart's data series.
- Display data labels in a chart.
- Add a trend line.

Remember that experimenting is one of the best ways to improve your charting skills.

WORKING WITH MORE THAN ONE WORKBOOK

You can open and work with several workbooks at a time and a model can extend over several workbooks as well. However, a model will be easier to create and will work more smoothly if you confine it and all the associated data to one workbook. If your model has to extend over several workbooks, then learn how to link data and formulas in different workbooks and which books have to be open to update and run your model.

When several workbooks are open at the same time, you can switch from one to another in two easy ways: (1) Click the icon with the workbook name in the Windows taskbar at the bottom of your screen, or (2) Press Alt+Tab which will open a pop up box with icons for all the open windows. Hold down the Alt key and press Tab repeatedly to cycle through the icons until the right window is selected and then release Alt to open the selected window. (Notice that as you cycle through the icons for the various open windows, their names appear in the box below the row of icons.)

USING THE SCROLL LOCK

If you turn on the Scroll Lock by pressing the ScrLk key (SCRL will be displayed on the Status bar), you can scroll through a worksheet while the active cell remains selected. You can use this feature to check out something at a different part of a large worksheet and then return to the active cell quickly by pressing Ctrl+Backspace.

CHAPTER 4

Advanced Excel Features

In this chapter, I will discuss a series of advanced Excel features that are used often in financial models. Even if you are familiar with some of these features, you may not know them well and may have difficulty learning them thoroughly from other general Excel books or Excel's online Help. You do not need to learn all of them right away. The Overview of each feature tells you what you may use it for and how often you are likely to use it. You should read the Overviews for all of these features to get an idea of what tools you have access to and then learn the ones that you think you will use now. You can come back and learn the others as you need them.

The large number of built-in functions and analysis tools that Excel provides is one of its most important advanced features. They are so important and numerous that I will cover them in several subsequent chapters organized by their category, such as statistical functions and financial functions.

I start with a general discussion of the built-in functions and analysis tools and then present the other features in the approximate order of how frequently you are likely to use them; I have started with the ones you will probably use all the time and ended with the ones you will probably use occasionally in special situations. Be aware, however, that this ordering may not apply to you perfectly. Use your own judgment about the relative importance of these features.

Learning the Features Efficiently

I will explain most features by walking you through one or more examples of its use. To learn a feature efficiently, copy its example(s) from the workbook for this chapter from the CD, clear all the cells other than those with headings, labels, and input data (the cells shaded gray), and then work through the example following the instructions. Once you are sure you have the right solution, you may want to compare it with the completed example from the CD. If necessary, repeat the process and also try out the feature on some other examples you make up for yourself. Do not try to learn a feature by looking through the completed example first. You will learn much faster if you work through the example first on your own. Also, do not try to use the feature in a large model until you are sure you fully understand how to use it. You will get many opportunities to practice these features in the models you will develop in later chapters.

Remember that the fastest way to learn any Excel feature is to experiment with it.

Excel's Built-In Functions and the Analysis ToolPak

Excel provides numerous useful built-in functions in several different categories as well as several useful analysis tools in the Analysis ToolPak. Note that certain functions that used to be included in the Analysis ToolPak in the earlier versions of Excel have now been integrated into the function library in Excel 2007. In Excel 2007 the Analysis ToolPak has only analysis tools. Appendix C provides a list of selected Excel and VBA functions available, with descriptions.

Many people look at functions as "black boxes." You input the arguments, and the functions provide the answers. In a way this view is true, but it is also somewhat dangerous. It is true that you can get answers by providing the arguments, but in many cases, especially for financial and statistical functions, if you do not understand how a function calculates its answer, there is some chance that you will use it incorrectly and get wrong answers. You should therefore make an effort to understand exactly how a function does its calculations before using it. It is also important to understand how Excel treats inputs that are not numbers, and so on, in order to use a function or tool correctly.

Arguments of Functions

Most functions require arguments (inputs) that you enter in a pair of parentheses after the function name. Even for the few functions that do not require arguments, you have to include an empty pair of parentheses.

You can, of course, enter values as arguments. You can also use cell/range references or cell/range names, expressions (that is, formulas that Excel can evaluate), and other functions. As long as Excel can unambiguously evaluate what you provide to come up with a value for the argument, it will accept it. If you are in doubt about whether you can input an argument in a certain way or how Excel will interpret it, check it first in a small, made-up example.

For arguments, it is generally preferable to enter cell/range references or cell/range names instead of values because then you can easily change them if necessary. Also, make sure that you enter the required extra commas if you are not providing values for one or more optional argument. However, you can omit the extra commas for optional arguments that are at the end of the list of arguments, that is, are not followed by any other argument for which you are providing values.

Entering Functions

There are two ways to enter functions in formulas: you can type in the function name and the arguments or you can let Excel help you do it more safely. In Excel 2007 in the Formulas ribbon you can click on any of the function category icons in the Function Library group and then choose the function you want from the dropdown list that opens. In earlier versions choose them from the Paste Function dialog box, followed by the Function Arguments dialog box. (In Excel 2007 you can reach the same Insert Function dialog box using Formulas ⇨ Function Library ⇨ Insert Function.)

I find it easier and safer to use the second approach because the Function Arguments dialog box helps both in entering the arguments and in making sure that you enter all the arguments. If you see a scroll bar on the right side of the boxes for entering arguments, it indicates that there are more arguments than can be shown in the space available, and you have to scroll down to enter values for all of them. (If the Function Argument dialog box gets in your way, left-click on it, hold down the button, and drag the dialog box out of the way.)

Installing and Accessing the Analysis ToolPak

The Analysis ToolPak is part of Excel, that is, it is included in your Excel installation CDs and the necessary files are even copied to your hard disk when you install Excel. But you must install it before you can use the tools (and functions in earlier versions) included in it.

In Excel 2007, if the Analysis ToolPak has already been installed then you will see a Data Analysis icon in the Analysis group of the Data tab. If you don't see the Data Analysis icon, then install the Analysis ToolPak as follows: Select Office ⇨ Excel Options ⇨ Add-Ins. At the bottom of the dialog box in the dropdown list next to Manage select Excel Add-ins and click Go. In the Add-Ins dialog box that comes up, select Analysis ToolPak (and also Analysis ToolPak – VBA if you are going to work with VBA) by clicking the box next to it, and back out by clicking OK.

In earlier versions of Excel Select Tools ⇨ Add-Ins, in the Add-Ins dialog box check the box to the left of Analysis ToolPak, and click OK.

To access the Analysis ToolPak in Excel 2007 select Data ⇨ Analysis ⇨ Data Analysis. In the Data Analysis dialog box that opens, select the tool you want to use and click OK.

A Key Difference between Functions and Tools in the Analysis ToolPak

There are some overlaps among tools in the Analysis ToolPak and available functions, especially in the area of statistical analysis. Generally the tools are meant for doing more comprehensive analysis than you can do with the corresponding functions. Another key difference is that you can include the functions in worksheet formulas and they will get automatically recalculated whenever any changes are made to the workbook (assuming automatic calculation is turned on). The tools in the Analysis ToolPak cannot be automated (unless you use VBA). You use them to get onetime results, and if anything changes you will have to manually run the tool again. So you cannot use these tools in models that will be run by users who will not know enough or remember to rerun the analysis with the tool when the data changes.

COPYING FORMULAS USING ABSOLUTE AND RELATIVE CELL REFERENCES

Overview

The ability to create formulas in many cells by copying them from one cell is one of the most powerful and timesaving features of Excel. It is no exaggeration to say that without this feature, spreadsheet programs like Excel would never have gained the popularity that they have. It is that important.

For your formulas to work properly in the new cells, however, you have to use the right combination of absolute and relative cell references when creating the formula you copy. This can get complex, especially if you are developing a large model. To learn to use this feature effectively, you will need to thoroughly understand how it works and practice a lot.

Let us use the following example to illustrate this feature.

Example: A publisher sells books to stores A and B at a discount of 40% of the list price. Calculate the publisher's revenues at the list prices and its actual revenues for years 2006, 2007, and 2008. The list prices of the books and the sales volumes for each store for the three years are given.

Figure 4.1 shows the results of the example.

Copying Using Relative Cell Reference

Make a copy of the example from the worksheet "Copying formulas" and clear all the cells other than the input and label cells. In B10 enter the formula =B9*B6 to calculate the year 2006 sales at list price for Store A. Now copy and paste the formula into cells C10 and D10 for years 2007 and 2008. Without realizing it you just used the relative cell reference. But what does this mean?

If you look at cell C10, the formula reads =C9*C6, which is different from the formula you had in B10 because when copying the formula, Excel intelligently modified it. Excel recognized that you do not want to copy the formula literally. Instead, what you really want is to multiply the values in the cells 1 row and 4 rows above the cell into which you are pasting the formula, that is, for the copied formula, it used cell addresses relative to the address of the cell into which you are pasting the formula.

	A	B	C	D	E
1	**Calculating Publisher's Revenue**				
2					
3	Discount to book stores	40%			
4					
5		**2006**	**2007**	**2008**	
6	Book price (list)	$20	$30	$25	
7					
8	**Store A**				
9	Sales volume	1,000	2,500	4,000	
10	Revenue at list price	$20,000	$75,000	$100,000	
11	Actual revenue after discount	$12,000	$45,000	$60,000	
12					
13	**Store B**				
14	Sales volume	2,500	5,000	7,000	
15	Revenue at list price	$50,000	$150,000	$175,000	
16	Actual revenue after discount	$30,000	$90,000	$105,000	
17					
18					

FIGURE 4.1 Example of copying formulas using various types of cell references.

Unless you tell Excel to do otherwise—we will see in a moment how you do this—Excel copies formulas using relative cell references. This is what you want most of the time.

Copying Formulas with Absolute Cell References

To calculate the actual year 2006 revenue (after discount) from Store A, in B11 enter the formula =B6*B9*(1-B3) and then copy and paste it into cells C11 and D11. However, when you do this, the values in both of these cells equal the revenues at list prices shown in the cells above, which is obviously wrong. What happened?

As before, Excel copied the formula using relative reference. The formula in C11 therefore reads =C6*C9*(1-C3). But C3 is blank or zero and is not the discount the bookstores get. This is what caused the problem. You really wanted Excel to continue using B3 and not change it to C3 or D3 as you pasted the formula into the different cells. You can specify this by changing the original formula in B11 to =B6*B9*(1-$B$3), where the $ signs in $B$3 tell Excel that in pasting the formula, it should not modify the cell reference relative to the cell where the formula is being pasted. The $B$3 is called an absolute cell reference, which is not modified when formulas are copied and pasted.

If you now copy and paste the new formula into cells C11 and D11, you will get the right answers. If you look into the pasted formulas, you will see that Excel has left the $B$3 part of it as is in both of these cells.

Copying Formulas with Mixed Cell References

To calculate the year 2006 revenue at list price from Store B, now copy the formula from cell B10 and paste it into cell B15. This again gives you an answer that is obviously wrong. What happened here is that in copying the reference to cell B6 (the book's list price) in the formula, Excel used relative reference and changed it to B11, which is not the book's list price.

To avoid this problem you can try to make the reference to the cell B6 absolute. Go back and change the formula in B10 to =B9*$B$6 and then copy and paste it into cells B15:D15. Now the result in the cell B15 is correct but those in C15 and D15 are not correct—the formulas there are using the book price from cell B6 instead of from cells C6 and D6, as they should.

To solve this problem, change the formula in B10 to =B9*B$6, which makes the column name B of B6 relative but the row number 6 absolute. This is called mixed reference and it tells Excel that in copying and pasting the formula for the book price, it should make the column number relative, that is, change it as it is pasted into cells in different columns (because in each year you want the price to come from the column for that year). However, it will make the row number absolute because the price is always in row 6. You can now copy and paste the correct formula from B10 into B15:D15. To keep your formulas consistent, you should paste the corrected formula into cells C10 and D10 as well.

Now if you go back, correct the formula in B11 to =B9*B$6*(1-$B$3), and copy and paste it into the appropriate cells, your model will work.

Choosing the Right Cell Reference When Creating Formulas

Whenever you create a formula to be copied and pasted into other cells, you should think ahead to decide which type of cell reference to use for each cell address in the formula. It is easier to learn to make the right choice through practice and trial and error than by studying some abstract rules. Nonetheless, if you want some rules, here they are:

- If when you copy a formula into other cells in the same row you do not want the column letter of a cell reference in it to change, then that cell address should use mixed references with absolute reference for the column.
- If when you copy a formula into other cells in the same column you do not want the row number of a cell reference in it to change, then that cell address should use mixed references with absolute reference for the row number.
- If when you copy a formula into other cells anywhere in your model you do not want the column letter and the row number of a cell reference in it to change, then that cell address should use absolute reference. To look at it another way, if the value of a variable will come from one particular cell

throughout your model (as with the discount rate in our example), then you should use absolute reference for its cell address.
- For all other cell addresses in formulas, use relative reference.

Remember to always check if a copied formula is working properly using hand calculations or other methods.

Additional Notes

- You can enter an absolute or mixed reference manually by inserting the $ sign in the appropriate places in a formula's cell address or you can do it using the F4 key. To learn how the latter works, place your cursor on a cell address as you are creating or editing a formula, then press the F4 key a few times and observe how the cell address cycles through different types of cell reference.
- When you cut and paste, that is, move (instead of copy and paste) a formula, Excel duplicates the formula exactly as it was in its original position; it does not modify the cell references in it in any way. This is true regardless of whether they are absolute, relative, or mixed.
- You can safely insert rows and columns in a sheet in which you already have formulas with various types of cell references. Excel automatically modifies your formulas to make sure that they will continue to work correctly. To see how Excel makes the adjustments, insert some rows and columns in the example you just worked on and observe how the formulas change.

CREATING NAMES FOR CELLS AND RANGES

Overview

Formulas written using cell or range addresses can get difficult to understand and check because you have to keep referring to the cells used in the formulas to remember what is in a particular cell. You can make your formulas easier to understand and check if you give cells and ranges short descriptive names and use those names instead of cell or range addresses in your formulas. Also, you can jump directly to a named cell or range, which will save a lot of time if you are working with a large worksheet.

Choosing Names

Excel lets you give names to cells and ranges and use those names as variables that represent the cells and ranges as well as their values. You can view the names as alternatives to the cell and range addresses.

Excel requires that all cell and range names start with a letter, but otherwise you can use any combination of letters and numbers in a name. A name cannot have an embedded space and the only symbols you can use in a name are the underscore and the period. For example, January Sales is not a valid name but January_Sales and January.Sales are.

It is important to choose names that are not just valid but also make your formulas easier to read and your model easier to work with. If you are going to develop a large model, it will pay to spend some time upfront to develop a good naming convention that you will use consistently throughout the model. Taking a planned approach from the beginning will save time, although you can create or change names later and substitute them in formulas you have already written.

You should always use descriptive names. Keep your names short, but do not make them so cryptic that three months later you will have difficulty remembering what a particular name means or what naming convention you used. You should try to keep your names between 3 and 10 characters long.

Over time, everyone develops a particular naming style. For example, JanuarySales, January_Sales, and January.Sales are all valid and descriptive names; you may like one more than the others. You may also prefer to shorten it to JanSales or Jan_Sales, for example.

Any name you define in a workbook is available for use in all the worksheets in that workbook. Normally you can use a name only once in a workbook; that is, you cannot define it differently in different worksheets. You can get around this limitation, however, by using a special naming procedure that also gives you additional power. (See the section called "Using workbook and worksheet level names" later in this chapter.)

Creating Names Manually

There are two ways to create names manually. Select the cell or range you want to name and then do one of the following:

- Click the Name Box (at the left end of the Formula Bar), type in the name you want to assign, and press Enter. You must press Enter to create the name. If you just move away by clicking on some other area of the worksheet, Excel will not create the name. Note that whenever you select a cell or a range that already has a name, the name appears in the Name Box. (You cannot change an existing name or assign an additional name to the same cell or range using this method.)
- In Excel 2007 select Formula ⇨ Define Names ⇨ Define Name ⇨ Define Name to go to the New Name dialog box. Type in the name you want to create in the box for name. The cell or range you are naming should already show in the box for Refers to. From the dropdown list for Scope choose if

you want the name to be valid only in a particular worksheet or in the entire workbook. Add any comments in the Comment box and click OK.

- In earlier versions of Excel select Insert ⇨ Name ⇨ Define. In the box labeled Names in workbook, type the name you want to assign and then click OK. Notice that the cell or range address along with the worksheet name is shown in the box at the bottom labeled Refers to.

If you insert rows or columns that move a cell or a range or expand or contract a range that you have named, Excel will automatically make the necessary adjustments.

Creating Names Automatically

You can use existing texts in adjacent cells to automatically create names for one or a series of cells in a worksheet. Suppose you are working with a worksheet like the one in Figure 4.2 and want to name the cells B4 through B8 using the texts in cells A4 through A8. To do so, select the range A4:B8 and then select Formula ⇨ Define Names ⇨ Create from Selection to open the Create Names from Selection dialog box. (In previous versions select Insert ⇨ Name ⇨ Create to open the Create Names dialog box.) Note that Excel has already checked the box labeled Left column because it rightly guessed that you want to use the texts in the column to the left to create the names. Click OK and Excel will create the names for you.

Quite often the existing texts you are using as labels in your worksheet may not be exactly what you want to use for names. For example, in this case you probably wanted to name cell B4 something like MondaySales or MoSales instead of Monday. Rather than create the names manually one at a time, you can put the desired names in the column on the right as I have done and then automatically

	A	B	C	D
1	**Creating Names Automatically**			
2				
3		**Sales**		
4	**Monday**	100	MoSales	
5	**Tuesday**	250	TuSales	
6	**Wednesday**	300	WeSales	
7	**Thursday**	250	ThSales	
8	**Friday**	200	FrSales	
9				
10				

FIGURE 4.2 Example of creating names automatically using text in adjacent cells.

create the names using the texts from column C instead of column A. After that, if you want to, you can clear the names in column C. However, you may want to leave them in for reference.

Note that if a text you are trying to use will result in an invalid name (for example, if it has a space in it), Excel will modify it to create a valid name—Monday Sales will be modified to Monday_Sales. But sometimes the modifications that Excel makes may not be what you want. Make sure that the texts you are using will result in valid names and always double check the names you create using the automatic procedure.

Defining Names with Different Types of Cell and Range References

Names created using any of the above methods use absolute references for cells or ranges. When you use one of these names in a formula and copy and paste that formula, the name will behave like an absolute cell reference.

Excel will allow you to create names with relative or mixed cell references as well. But they are rarely used, and you should avoid them because they can be confusing and work in unexpected ways.

The Name Manager

Excel 2007 has a new feature called Name Manager to make it easy to work with names once they have been created using the Name Manager dialog box. To open this dialog box (shown in Figure 4.3), select Formula ⇨ Define Names ⇨ Name Manager or press Ctrl+F3. You can use this dialog box to edit a name, that is, change the name you assigned to a cell or range, assign a new cell or range to an existing name, delete a name, change the scope of the name from worksheet level to workbook level or vice versa, and change the comment you had saved with a name. You can also create a new name from this dialog box by clicking the New button, which will take you to the New Name dialog box we saw before.

Another important feature of this dialog box is that its filtering capability can be very useful for large models. Clicking the down arrow next to Filter near the top-right of the dialog box drops down a menu offering options to filter the list of names in the workbook in several ways. For example, you can choose to see only workbook-level names.

Assigning Multiple Names to the Same Range

In general, the same cell or range can have multiple names. Unless you have a good reason to do so, however, avoid multiple names; they can create confusion. To assign additional names to a cell or range that already has a name, you cannot use the Name Box; you have to use the New Name (Define Name in older versions of Excel) dialog box as described before.

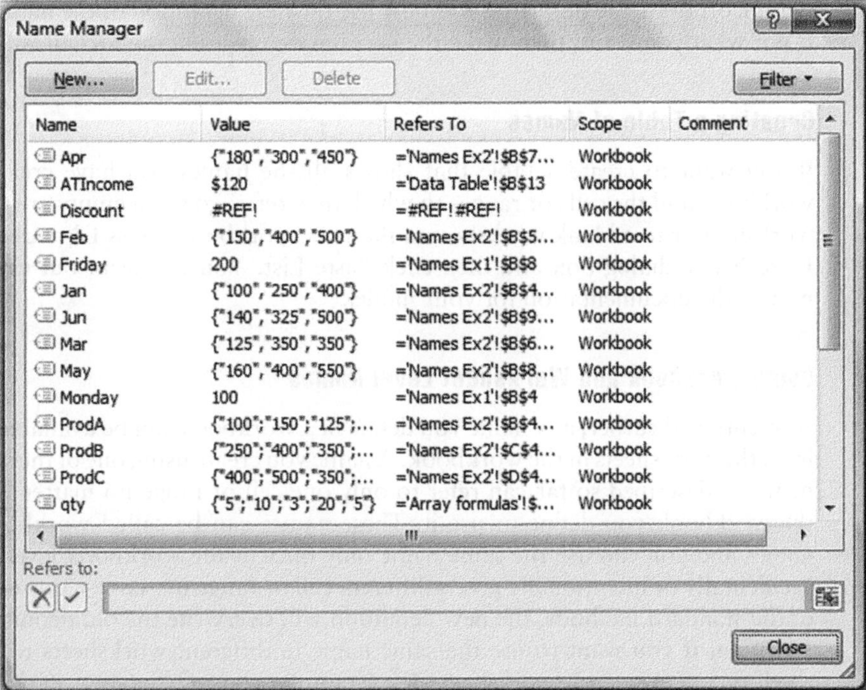

FIGURE 4.3 The Name Manager dialog box.

Deleting Names

To delete an existing name, in Excel 2007 use the Name Manager. In earlier versions of Excel go to the Define Name dialog Box by selecting Insert ⇨ Name ⇨ Define, select the name in the list of names, and click the Delete button.

Changing Names

To change the name of a cell or range, first create the new name using the New Name (Define Name in older versions) dialog box and then delete the old name. Note that the new name will not be automatically substituted in existing formulas that are using the old name. To learn how to substitute the new name in place of the old name in existing formulas, see the section called "Changing names in existing formulas" later in this chapter.

Redefining Names

If you want to change the cell or range to which an existing name refers, it is easiest to delete the old name and then assign it to the new cell or range. Existing formulas that incorporate the old name will now use the new definition of the name. If this is not what you want, then make the necessary changes in the formulas.

Creating a Table of Names

If you want to create a table that shows all the names you have created in a workbook and the cells or ranges to which they refer, go to an empty area of your worksheet or to a blank worksheet in the same workbook, press F3 to display the Paste Name dialog box and then click Paste List. You can print out this list as part of the documentation for your model.

Using Workbook and Worksheet Level Names

As mentioned earlier, any name you define in a workbook can be available for use in all the worksheets in the workbook. A name you create using one of the standard methods described so far can refer to only one cell or range no matter where in the workbook you define or use it. These names can be called workbook-level names and you can use the same name only once at the workbook level. (If you accidentally or intentionally give a different cell or range the same name using one of the standard methods, the new definition will overwrite the old definition.)

What if you want to use the same name in different worksheets to refer to a cell or range in each worksheet? For example, you may have several identical worksheets in a workbook, each with data and a model to analyze the data for a month. You want to use the same name (for example, Sales) in each worksheet to refer to the sales for that month.

You can do so by creating what may be called worksheet-level names. In Excel 2007 you can designate a name as worksheet or workbook level at the time you create it using the New Name dialog box.

In earlier versions of Excel, go to the worksheet where you want to create a worksheet-level name, select the cell or range, click the Name Box, and then enter the name of the worksheet and an exclamation point followed by the name you want to use (for example, January!Sales in the worksheet named January). If the worksheet name has a space in it, you have to enclose it in a pair of single quotation marks (for example, 'January 2002'!Sales). You can also use the Define Name dialog box to do the same.

Notice that this name will show in the dropdown list next to the Name Box or in the lists in the Define Name or Paste Name dialog boxes only when you access them from the worksheet which is associated with that name. If you open the dropdown list or either dialog box from a different worksheet, the name will appear only if you have defined it for that worksheet as well.

When you use a worksheet-level name in its own worksheet, you can use the name by itself without the worksheet name. To use a worksheet-level name from one worksheet in a different worksheet you have to use the full name, that is, include the appropriate worksheet name.

Creating worksheet-level names is extra work. Why would you want to do it? Because at times it can be a powerful tool. Suppose you have created a model on a worksheet to analyze the data for January and your model uses several names. When the February data comes in, ideally you want to be able to do the same analysis for February by creating a copy of the January worksheet and then entering the February data. This simple procedure will work fine if you created and used worksheet-level names in the January worksheet, but it will not work if you used workbook-level names that referred to data specific to a month. (When you copy a worksheet or a part of it that includes formulas that use worksheet-level names to a different worksheet, Excel automatically creates and uses corresponding worksheet-level names in the new worksheet.)

You can also use the same name at the workbook and worksheet levels. This, however, takes additional understanding of which one will take precedence under what circumstances and may cause confusion or errors. To be safe, avoid using the same name at both the workbook and worksheet levels.

Creating Other Types of Names

There are two other types of names you should be aware of, although you may use them only in special situations.

If you are working with the sales data for three products for six months as shown in Figure 4.4, you may want to name the range B4:B9 as ProdA and the range B4:D4 as Jan and so on. You can create the names one at a time using one of the techniques we have discussed before, or, to do it faster, select the entire table A3:D9, select Insert ⇨ Name ⇨ Create, and click OK. You can now use these range names in formulas like =SUM(Jan) to find the total sales for January. What is more interesting is that you can now refer to the sale for January for ProdA (that is, the cell B4) in formulas by Jan ProdA because the cell containing the datum is at the intersection of these two ranges. (You have to put a space

	A	B	C	D	E	F
1	Using Advanced Naming Techniques					
2						
3		ProdA	ProdB	ProdC		
4	Jan	100	250	400		
5	Feb	150	400	500		
6	Mar	125	350	350		
7	Apr	180	300	450		
8	May	160	400	550		
9	Jun	140	325	500		
10						
11						

FIGURE 4.4 Example of using advanced naming techniques.

between the names of the two intersecting ranges.) For example, you can write a formula like =Jan ProdA+Mar ProdB, which is easy to read.

You can also name a range that extends over the same cell or range in several worksheets in a workbook. This can come in handy when you are working with a series of similarly laid out worksheets (for example, each with data for a month). Excel calls it 3-D reference and to learn how to use it, search in Help for "3-D reference."

USING NAMES IN FORMULAS

Overview

You can make your formulas much easier to understand and check if you write them using a judicious mix of short, descriptive names and cell and range addresses. In formulas, names and cell addresses have their own advantages and disadvantages. Once you become familiar with using both, you will find the mix that is right for a specific situation.

Incorporating Names in Formulas

You can enter names in formulas in a few different ways. You can manually type in the names instead of cell addresses as you write a formula or, better yet, use the pointing method to write formulas. With this method, Excel will automatically use names instead of addresses for cells and ranges that you have already named.

You can also have Excel paste a name into a formula. To do so, when you get to the point in a formula where you want to enter a name, press F3, which will bring up the Paste Name dialog box. Now double-click the name you want to insert or select it and click OK.

Changing Names in Existing Formulas

In Excel 2007 when you change the name of a cell or a range, Excel will automatically substitute it in any existing formula that uses the old name.

In the earlier versions of Excel this automatic substitution may not occur. (Check by testing.) To make the necessary substitutions, select Edit ⇨ Replace to bring up the Replace dialog box. In the box titled Find what, enter the old name; in the box titled Replace with, enter the new name and then click the Replace All button.

Applying New Names to Existing Formulas

When you create new names for cells and ranges, Excel will not automatically substitute them for the corresponding cell or range addresses in existing formulas. To do so, select Formula ⇨ Defined Names ⇨ Define Name ⇨ Apply Names to bring up the Apply Names dialog box. (In previous versions of Excel use Insert ⇨ Name ⇨ Apply to bring up the Apply Names dialog box.)

In the list of names in the Apply Names box, select the name(s) you want substituted in the existing formulas and then click OK. (You can leave the two check boxes at the bottom selected, or, to be safer, you may want to deselect the check box labeled Ignore Relative/Absolute.) Note that when you use Apply Names with a newly created name, it replaces references to the cell only in formulas on the same worksheet and not in formulas in the other worksheets that refer to the cell. So if you are creating a multi-sheet model, make sure you create all the names you plan to use before writing your formulas and then use the names as you create the formulas.

Using Names with Different Types of Cell or Range References

Names created using any of the standard methods use absolute references for cells or ranges. When you use one of these names in a formula and copy and paste that formula, the name will behave like an absolute cell reference.

Excel will allow you to create names with relative or mixed cell references as well. But they are rarely used, and you should avoid them because they can be confusing and work in unexpected ways. As we will see later, if you have to develop a large, complex model where the formulas are likely to become long and difficult to understand and check, you may be better off developing it in VBA instead of Excel.

Limitations of Using Names in Formulas

Unfortunately, using names in formulas is not as useful as it appears in the beginning. One of the reasons that spreadsheet programs like Excel have become so popular is that if you create a complex formula in a cell using the a proper mix of relative, mixed, and absolute cell references, you can copy it into hundreds of cells where it will work properly—the program will make the necessary adjustments to the formula as it is pasted into the different cells. Because names can be used primarily in place of absolute references, they cannot help much to make these complex formulas easier to read or check. As you will find out, VBA can be of great help in situations where formulas get unwieldy.

A1 AND R1C1 REFERENCE STYLES

Overview

Most of the time you reference (address) cells in Excel using what is called the A1 style. Excel offers a second style, called the R1C1 style. You may not use it often with Excel, but you will use it a lot when working with VBA.

How the Two Styles Work

Generally, your worksheet names columns by letters across the top and rows by numbers down the side. This is called the A1 reference style. In this style, you refer to a cell by its column letter followed by the row number (D5, for example). A formula in cell D5 may look like =A2+B3. (If your worksheet is currently showing numbers across the top, just keep reading.)

In Excel's other reference style, called the R1C1 reference style, both columns and rows are referred to by numbers going across the top and down the side. In this style, the cell D5 will be referred to as R5C4 because it is in row 5 and column 4. (Note that here you put the row number first, which is the opposite of the convention for the A1 style.) To switch your worksheet to the R1C1 style, select Office ⇨ Excel Options ⇨ Formulas and then, in the Working with formulas section, select R1C1 reference style. (In older versions of Excel select Tools ⇨ Options, then the General tab, and then the check box for R1C1 reference style under Settings.) To go back to the A1 style you have to deselect this check box.

If you switch to the R1C1 style, you will find formulas harder to read because they use what is called the relative reference. For example, the formula =A2+B3 in cell D5 will now read =R[-3]C[-3]+R[-2]C[-2] because the cell A2 is 3 rows above and 3 columns to the left of (that is, relative to) the cell D5 and so on. The easiest way to understand how this works is to write a few simple formulas with your worksheet in the A1 style, switch to R1C1 style, and then look at the formulas again.

Although formulas in the R1C1 style look complex to write, you can create them easily using the pointing method. Simply point to the cells you want to refer to in a formula instead of trying to type the correct relative references of the cells into the formulas. Luckily you almost never need to use the R1C1 style when working in Excel. However, it will be useful when you start working in VBA, and there you will use it in a way that is easy and intuitive.

USING COMMENTS IN CELLS

Overview

You can insert a detailed comment in any cell to document its content. This is a very helpful and easy-to-use feature that you should utilize extensively.

Working with Comments

Cell comments are very useful for adding information to individual cells in your worksheet for future reference. However, it is wise to insert in cells only those comments that will not need to be updated repeatedly as you progress. It is easy to forget to update them when they should be updated, and that can create confusion later on.

Inserting comments: To insert a comment in a cell (also called attaching a comment), select the cell, right-click, and select Insert Comment in the shortcut menu. A small window with your name already inserted will come up. You can resize the window by dragging any of the handles. Type in your comment and then close the window by clicking anywhere outside the window. You can also bring up the window for inserting a comment by selecting Review ⇨ Comments ⇨ New Comment (Insert ⇨ Comment in previous versions of Excel) or by pressing Shift+F2. (Note that you can also include objects other than text in the comment window although you are not likely to have much use for this option.)

Editing comments: To edit an existing comment in a cell, select the cell and press Shift+F2, or right-click to open the shortcut menu and select Edit Comment. Alternately, you can select Review ⇨ Comments ⇨ Edit Comments (Insert ⇨ Edit Comment in previous versions of Excel).

Deleting comments: To delete a comment, select the cell, right-click, and then select Delete Comment in the shortcut menu.

Displaying comments: You have three choices on how to display the comments in your workbook. In Excel 2007 select Office ⇨ Excel Options ⇨ Advanced. In the Display section you will see three options under For cells with comments, show. Choose the one you want. The indicator here means a small red triangle at the upper-right corner. Most of the time you will want the second option, Indicators only, and comments on hover. You can show all comments in a worksheet by selecting Review ⇨ Comments ⇨ Show all comments.

In previous versions of Excel, Select Tools ⇨ Options and then the View tab. Look under Comments. If you select Comment indicator only, a small red triangle will show in the upper-right corner of each cell with a comment attached to it. Whenever you move the mouse pointer over such a cell, the comment will show. If you select Comment and indicator, then all the comments in your workbook will show next to their cells. You can hide both the comments and their indicators by selecting None.

Copying comments: If you copy a cell with a comment and paste it in another cell, the comment will be copied and pasted along with everything else. If you want to copy and paste only a comment, copy the cell that has the comment, select the target cell, right-click, and select Paste Special in the shortcut menu. Then, under Paste in the Paste Special dialog box, select Comments, and click OK.

Printing comments: You can print out one comment or all the comments in a worksheet, either next to the cells they are attached to or at the end of the worksheet. To learn how, search in Help under "Print a worksheet with comments." Note that to print comments, you have to also print the worksheets that contain them.

DATA VALIDATION

Overview

Most models will not work or will produce wrong answers if the user enters inappropriate input data. Data validation is a useful tool to guard against such mistakes. You can use data validation to restrict what data can be entered into an input cell or range of input cells. For example, you can specify that the user will be allowed to enter only numbers and not text, or only whole numbers between 0 and 10, in a particular input cell.

An important use of data validation is to easily create a dropdown list in an input cell so that a user can enter data simply by selecting from the list.

Setting Up Simple Data Validation

Select an empty cell and then select Data ⇨ Data Tools ⇨ Data validation ⇨ Data Validation (or Data ⇨ Validation in earlier versions of Excel) to open the Data Validation dialog box. Click the Settings tab and open the dropdown list in the box below Allow to see the available options. They are mostly self-explanatory. For example, if you want to restrict entries to only whole numbers, select that option, and then open the dropdown list under Data to see what forms of restriction you can specify. Depending on what you select here, you will have to enter a specific value(s) in the box(es) below.

One important choice in the dropdown list under Allow is List. You will use it when you want to restrict cell entries to the data from a list you specify. If the list is short (for example, you want the user to enter only P or C), enter the valid entries, separated by commas, in the box under Source. Note that you do not have to enclose text entries in quotation marks and the data validation test is case sensitive (that is, if your list includes Jan, Excel will not allow a user to enter jan). To create a longer list of valid entries, type them either down a single column or across a single row on the same worksheet, making sure that you do not include any blank cells in the list. Then provide reference to the range by selecting it while your cursor is in the Source box. You can also name the range and enter the name of the range preceded by an equal sign (e.g., =MyList).

If you want Excel to show, in the restricted cell (when it is selected), a drop-down list of the valid entries that the user can choose from instead of typing in an entry, make sure that the check box to the left of In-cell dropdown is selected. Leave the check box to the left of Ignore blank selected.

To have Excel display an appropriate message if a user attempts to enter invalid data into the restricted cell, click the Error Alert tab. In the box under Title, enter a title for the message box if you want, and in the box for Error message, type in the message you want to be displayed. To prevent a user from making an unacceptable entry, choose Stop in the box under Style. If you choose

Warning or Information for Style, the user will be able to enter invalid data, although she will see a warning or information message box.

If you want a message displayed whenever a cell with data validation is selected, you can enter it in the Input Message tab.

To impose the same data restrictions to a range of cells, select the range instead of just one cell before you go through the steps of setting up the data validation.

Using Formulas to Create Data Validation Rules for a Cell

The Allow dropdown list in the Data Validation dialog box includes an option called Custom, which we have not discussed yet. This is a powerful option in that it allows you to create sophisticated data validation rules that you cannot create using the other options. When you choose Custom, you can enter, in the box under Formula, a logical test or condition (of any complexity). When a user enters data in a cell restricted with this option, Excel evaluates the formula, accepts the data if the formula evaluates to TRUE, and rejects the data if the result is FALSE. (You must have Stop selected as Style in the Error Alert tab.)

To take a simple example, if you want to restrict inputs to cell J15 to only text, you would choose Custom and enter in the Formula box = ISTEXT(J15). The formula can be a lot more complex, but it should include reference to the cell J15 because you want Excel to test if with the data being entered in J15 the condition is satisfied.

To create the same data validation, instead of entering the formula =ISTEXT(J15) in the Formula box as before, you could enter the formula in some cell other than J15 (say A1) and then enter =A1 in the Formula box when creating data validation for J15. In this case when a user enters data in J15, the cell A1 evaluates to TRUE or FALSE depending on that input, and Excel uses that value to decide if the input data will be accepted or not. This may seem complex or convoluted, but once you think about it a little, it should make perfect sense.

Using Formulas to Create Data Validation Rules for a Range

You can also use the Custom option to easily create sophisticated data validation for a range of cells. Suppose you want to restrict all cells in the range A1:C20 to text entries only. Select the range A1:C20 and then open the Data Validation dialog box. Choose Custom under Allow, type =ISTEXT(A1) in the formula box, and click OK. Now if you try to enter 123 in cell B11, Excel will stop you.

To understand how this worked, select any cell in the range other than A1 (say B11) and open the Data Validation dialog box. You will see that the Formula box reads =ISTEXT(B11). What happens is that when you are working with a range and enter a formula in the Formula box, you have to write the formula using the address of the top-left cell (here A1) of the range because it is the active cell. After you finish with the Data Validation dialog box, Excel copies the same formula in all the other cells in the range using relative reference. That is how the Custom formula for B11 gets copied as =ISTEXT(B11).

Obviously, when you use the Custom option for a range instead of a single cell, the formula for condition has to be inserted in the Formula box in the Data Validation dialog box. You cannot put it in a cell and refer to it in the Formula box as you could for a single cell.

With a little practice you should now be able to create sophisticated restrictions on a single cell or a range of cells with little work.

An Important Limitation of Data Validation

If you paste data into a restricted cell (copied from somewhere) instead of typing it in, the data validation of the restricted cell will be deleted. Neither the data you paste nor any future data entry into the cell will be checked and restricted any longer. Unfortunately, there is no simple way to guard against this problem.

CONTROLS

Overview

You use Excel's controls all the time, although you probably do not know them by that name. All those check boxes you select, the buttons you click, and so on, are called controls, and you can add some of them to your Excel models. They are useful in creating elegant and convenient user interfaces, particularly for models that will be used by people with little or no knowledge of Excel. For example your model may require a user to run a macro that you have created. You can add a properly labeled command button control to your worksheet and link it to the macro so that the user can run the macro by clicking the button.

Most financial modelers, however, though, do not need to spend the extra time it takes to create bulletproof models with user-friendly interfaces. They mostly create models for themselves or others who are reasonably familiar with Excel, and in such models controls are not particularly useful.

Adding Controls

Most of the discussion in this and the next section apply to Excel 2007 as well as earlier versions of Excel. However, the procedure to add a control to a worksheet is somewhat different in earlier versions. I will discuss that later in a separate section.

Excel 2007 offers two different sets of controls: Form controls and ActiveX controls. The latter are easier to work with. Here I will discuss only one ActiveX control, the SpinButton (also called the spinner), which we will use often. Once you learn how to work with it, it should be easy for you to use any of the other ActiveX controls if you want to do so. From here on I will use the word control to refer exclusively to ActiveX controls; this discussion does not apply to Form controls. (Note that controls are most effectively used in VBA in conjunction with UserForms. But I will not cover controls in VBA because using them in VBA requires learning a number of other things, none of which will be useful to most financial modelers.)

To add a control to your worksheets, select Developer ⇨ Controls ⇨ Insert. The activeX controls available are shown in the bottom of dropdown icon list. To see the name of a control put the cursor on it and wait a few seconds.

To set up or make changes to a control, you have to be in the design mode. At this point you should be automatically in the design mode and the Design Mode (toggle) icon next to the Insert icon should be highlighted. If it is not, click on it. When you are finished, you will have to click it again to get out of the design mode before you can work on anything else.

The Spinner

The Spinner control has two arrows that you can click repeatedly to increase or decrease, in steps, the value in a cell you link to the Spinner. It is a convenient way to change the value of a variable quickly instead of having to type in new values for each step. You can choose the maximum and minimum values as well as the size of the step.

To add a spinner to your worksheet, click on the Spinner icon. This turns your cursor into a cross. Move the cursor to the top left corner of the cell where you want to insert the spinner (say, B3). Click and hold down the left mouse button, drag the cursor to cover the cell, and then release the mouse button. Excel will insert a spinner in B3 with handles around it. (You can control the size of the spinner by dragging your cursor over a smaller or larger area, or you can adjust the size by dragging one of the handles.)

To customize the spinner, click the Properties icon next to the Design Mode icon. This will open the Properties dialog box, where you can set the properties for the spinner to activate and customize it. Familiarize yourself with the properties. Note that the properties are listed in two different tabs. Both show the same properties, one alphabetically and the other categorized. Normally you will need to set just a few of the properties as follows:

- The LinkedCell refers to the cell whose value the spinner will control. For now, enter C3 in the box next to LinkedCell.
- The Max and Min are the maximum and minimum values the LinkedCell will have. For now, leave them at 100 and 0. You can enter any whole numbers for these, including negative numbers.

- The SmallChange determines the step size. You can specify any whole number for it. For now, leave it at 1.
- The Orientation determines if the spinner arrows will be oriented horizontally or vertically. To change it, select Orientation, open the dropdown list in the box next to it, and choose the orientation you want.

You can control the size of the spinner by specifying the Width and Height properties, but it is easier to change the size by dragging the handles that appear when you select the spinner in the design mode.

Once you have finished setting the properties, close the Properties dialog box by clicking the Close button at top right. To see how the spinner works, get out of design mode. Then click on either arrow of the spinner. You will see that the value in C3 will change between 0 and 100 in steps of 1.

What if you want the value to change in steps of 0.1 instead of 1? In D3 enter the formula =0.1*C3. Now as you click the arrows the value in D3 will change in steps of 0.1 and will range between 0 and 10. So even though the Max, Min, and SmallChange are limited to whole numbers, you can use a second cell and a suitable multiplier as we just did to get any range and step size you want in that cell. (You will, of course, have to specify the Max, Min, and SmallChange appropriately as you change the multiplier.)

How do you use a spinner in a model? We will see many applications throughout the book. For a simple example, let us assume that you have created a model in which interest rate is an independent variable and the price of a bond is one of the dependent variables. You can use a cell like D3 here for the interest rate and cycle through different values of interest rate using the up or down spinner buttons to see how the price of the bond changes.

Note that you can still manually enter any value in C3. You are not limited to the spinner's specified range and step to set values for the independent variable the spinner controls.

Adding a Spinner in Earlier Versions of Excel

In the earlier versions, you add controls to your worksheets from the Control Toolbox. To access it, select View ⇨ Toolbars and then click the Control Toolbox. It shows the most commonly used controls. To see the name of each tool in this Toolbox, put the cursor on it and wait a few seconds. The three icons in the top section are for working with the controls. The ones in the middle section are for the various controls. Take a few minutes to check the names of all of them. If you click on the icon at the bottom, you will see a list of many more controls that are available (although I do not think you will ever need to use any of them).

To set up or make changes to a control, you have to be in the design mode. The first tool in the Control Toolbox gets you into and out of the design mode. If it looks pressed (and reads Exit Design Mode when you put the cursor on it), then you are in the design mode. Otherwise you have to click it to get into the design mode, and when you are finished, you will have to click it to get out of the design mode before you can work on anything else. To close the Control Toolbox, click the Close button at the right end of its title bar. To add a spinner to your worksheet, open the Control Toolbox as described before and make sure you are in the design mode. Now click on the Spinner icon; this turns your cursor into a cross. Move the cursor to the top left corner of the cell where you want to insert the spinner (say, B3). After this point proceed as we discussed before.

CUSTOM NUMBER FORMATS

Overview

Although Excel provides a wide range of standard formatting options for numbers, at times you may want to display numbers in a format that is not included in any of the standard categories. For example, none of the standard formatting options lets you add text to a number or create a financial statement in thousands or millions of dollars. However, Excel gives you the option to create custom number formats using a series of codes, and such formats can be both useful and impressive.

Creating Custom Formats

To create or modify a custom number format code, you need to understand the structure of a custom number format and the codes used to create such a format. For an explanation of the structure, search in Help under custom number format (in previous versions of Excel search under Custom format and select Create a custom number format from the list of options). Once you understand the structure you can specify different formats for positive numbers, negative numbers, and zero values, and you can even specify a different color for each.

The Help also explains the codes. Briefly, you create number formats using digit placeholders # or 0 (zero) combined with decimal points and commas (as thousands separators) if you want them. The two placeholders work as follows:

- # displays only significant digits and does not display insignificant zeros.
- 0 (zero) displays insignificant zeros if a number has fewer digits than there are zeros in the format.

The difference between # and 0 as placeholders is that a number will be displayed with at least as many digits as there are zeros in the format (padded with zeros if necessary). If a number has more digits to the right of the decimal point than there are placeholders in the format, the number is rounded to as many decimal points as there are placeholders. However, if the number has more digits to the left of the decimal points than there are placeholders, the extra digits are displayed.

	A	B
1	**Examples of Custom Number Formats**	
2		
3	**To display**	**Use this code**
4		
5	635 as 00635	00000
6	1350.639 as 1350.6	#.# or #.0 or #######.#
7	7.5 as 7.500	#.000
8	.7 as 0.7	0.#
9	14 as 14.0 and 153.758 as 153.76	#.0#
10	12000 as 12,000	#,###
11	12,000,000 as 12000	#,
12	12,000,000 as 12,000	#,###,
13	12,000,000 as 12	#,###,,
14	1 as 1,000	#",000"
15	0.6 as 1,000,000	#",000,000"
16	Funding needed is $2.0 million	"Funding needed is" $#,###.0,, "million"
17		
18		

FIGURE 4.5 Examples of custom number formats.

You can add texts to a format by including them in quotation marks.

You create a custom number format in the Format Cells dialog box. To open this dialog box, select the cell you want to format, right-click to open the shortcut menu and select Format Cells (or select Format ⇨ Cells in previous versions of Excel), and then choose the Number tab. In the Category list, click a category (for example, Currency) and a built-in format that resembles the format you want. Then, in the Category list, click Custom. In the Type box, edit the number format codes to create the format you want. Alternately, you can start with the Custom category, select one of the built-in formats that resembles the format you want, and modify it as needed.

It is easiest to understand how these various options work by looking at the examples in Figure 4.5. A little experimenting will rapidly improve your skill at creating custom number formats.

Two Useful Custom Number Formats

In financial models (such as in models of financial statements), you often want to display a number in thousands or millions—that is, scale it by a multiple of 1,000. To do so, at the end of the format add one comma to display the number in thousands, two commas to display it in millions, and so on. (See the examples in Figure 4.5.)

At times you may want to hide the number in a cell, that is, make the cell appear blank (for aesthetic or other reasons), no matter what the number is. To do so, custom format the cell with just one semicolon (;). If you want the cell to appear blank only when the value in it is zero, custom format it with only #s as placeholders. Then a number with a value of zero will not be displayed because it does not have any significant digit.

HIDING AND PROTECTING

Overview

After you have spent a lot of time developing a model, you may want to protect your workbooks, worksheets, or some cells, objects, and so on, in them from unauthorized or accidental changes. You may also want to hide one or more worksheets or formulas in certain cells so that no one can see them. Excel provides several tools and options for such protecting and hiding.

Hiding a Workbook

To hide the active workbook, select View ⇨ Windows ⇨ Hide. In older versions of Excel select Window ⇨ Hide. To unhide hidden workbooks, select View ⇨ Windows ⇨ Unhide (Window ⇨ Unhide in older versions of Excel.) From the list of hidden workbooks that opens select the workbook you want to unhide and click OK (or double-click the name of the workbook). When you quit Excel, you will see a dialog box with a message asking you if you want to save changes to the hidden workbook. If you click Yes, the workbook window will remain hidden the next time you open the workbook.

Hiding Worksheets

To hide the active worksheet in a workbook, select Home ⇨ Cells ⇨ Format. In the dropdown window select Hide & Unhide under Visibility and then select Hide Sheet. (In older versions of Excel select Format ⇨ Sheet ⇨ Hide.) If you want to hide more than one worksheet at one time, you can select them by holding down Ctrl and clicking on their tabs before going through the previous steps.

To unhide one or more hidden worksheets, go back to the same fly-out menu we used to hide sheets and select Unhide Sheet. From the dialog box showing the list of hidden worksheets, select the worksheet you want to unhide and click OK. You can unhide worksheets only one at a time.

Since all workbooks must have at least one worksheet visible, Excel will not let you hide the last worksheet in a workbook remaining unhidden. If necessary, though, you can switch it with a hidden worksheet by first unhiding one of the hidden worksheets, or you can insert a blank worksheet and hide the other worksheet.

Hiding and Unhiding Rows and Columns

To hide one or more rows (or columns), select the rows, right-click to bring up the shortcut menu, and click Hide. Alternately, after you have selected the rows, select Home ⇨ Cells ⇨ Format ⇨ Hide & Unhide ⇨ Hide Rows. (In older versions of Excel select Format ⇨ Row and then click Hide.) When Excel hides a row, it does not renumber the rows to exclude the hidden rows. To find out if a worksheet has hidden rows, look down the row numbers to see if any of them are missing. Where rows have been hidden you will also notice a slightly thicker line than is found elsewhere between rows. Hidden rows are not printed and data in them are not included in charts. If you create a chart and then hide some rows or columns that included data used in the chart, the chart will look different or incomplete. Other than these effects, hidden rows are used in all calculations as if they were not hidden.

To display hidden rows, select cells in the row above and the row below them, go back to the fly-out menu we used to hide rows and click Unhide Rows. (In older versions of Excel select Format ⇨ Row, and click Unhide.) If you want to use the shortcut menu, select the row above and below the hidden rows, right-click to bring up the shortcut menu, and click Unhide.

If the first row or column of a worksheet is hidden, select Home ⇨ Find & Select ⇨ Go To (or press F5). Type A1 in the reference box and click OK. Then use Unhide Rows or Unhide Columns as before.

Password-Protecting a Workbook

You can protect a workbook from access by unauthorized users by requiring a password to open it. In Excel 2007 there are two ways to password-protect a workbook. Select Office ⇨ Prepare ⇨ Encrypt Document, enter a password (twice as prompted), and click OK. Alternately, select Office ⇨ Save As to open the Save As dialog box. Click the dropdown arrow next to Tool at the bottom and select General Options. In the dialog box, enter a password in the box next to Password to open, click OK, reenter the password as requested and then click OK again. Then save the workbook.

If you protect your workbook using any of the above methods, once a user opens it with the password, he will be able to make changes to any part of the workbook that is not protected as discussed a little later. If you want a user to be able to only open and look through the workbook but not make any changes in the General Options dialog box we used in the second method, enter a password in the box next to Password to modify. With this protection in place the workbook will always open in Read-Only mode. In this case the user will not be able to make changes to the workbook and save it under the same name unless he has this second password. In other words, he will not be able to change your original file, but he can make modifications and save the workbook under a different name.

In the same dialog box you can check the Read-Only recommended option instead of requiring a password for making modifications. In this case at the time a user opens the workbook, Excel will suggest to open the workbook in Read-Only mode, but the user can override the suggestion.

In earlier versions of Excel, use Tools ⇨ Protection ⇨ Protect Workbook.

Remember that passwords are case sensitive, and if you forget or lose the password, you will permanently lose access to the workbook (or the protected elements, as discussed below). Keep in mind that this password protection can protect you against most people, but not professional intruders. They can break the password or use other tricks to get into your workbook and protected elements. So always assume that your information will not be protected if your computer falls into the wrong hands.

Protecting a Workbook's Structure

You may wish to prevent others from changing the structure of a workbook, that is, from moving, deleting, adding, hiding, unhiding, or renaming worksheets in the workbook. To do this, select Review ⇨ Changes ⇨ Protect Workbook to display the Protect Workbook dialog box and check the box on the left of Structure. You can also check the box next to Windows to prevent a user from resizing or moving the workbook window. You can also provide passwords for these protections in the box provided in the dialog box.

To remove the protection, select Review ⇨ Changes ⇨ Unprotect Workbook.

In older versions of Excel use Tools ⇨ Protection ⇨ Protect Workbook to get to the Protect Workbook dialog box.

Protecting an Entire Worksheet

To protect the entire active worksheet in Excel 2007, select Review ⇨ Changes ⇨ Protect Sheet to open the Protect Sheet dialog box as shown in Figure 4.6. Leave the top-left box selected. You can enter a password if you want, keeping in mind my earlier comments about passwords.

In the window under Allow all users of this workbook to you can pick and choose what you want protected. The options are self-explanatory. The first two options, Select locked cells and Select unlocked cells, which are selected by default, allow a user to move around and look through a worksheet but not make any changes to it. You would generally want to leave these options selected and then make additional selections for your situation.

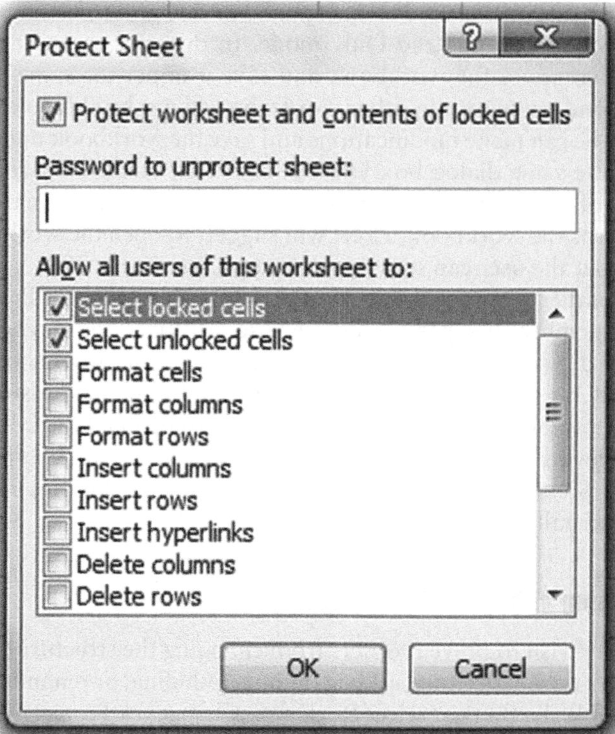

FIGURE 4.6 The Protect Sheet dialog box.

After you have selected the options you want, click OK to complete protection.

To unprotect a protected worksheet, activate the worksheet and then select Review ⇨ Changes ⇨ Unprotect Sheet.

In earlier versions of Excel, you have to select Tools ⇨ Protection ⇨ Protect Sheet and check one or more of the following options as appropriate:

- **Contents:** To prevent changes to cells on worksheets or to data and other items in the charts, and to prevent viewing of hidden rows, columns, and cell formulas. (Hiding cell formulas requires an additional step which is discussed later.)
- **Objects:** To prevent changes to graphic objects on worksheets or charts.
- **Scenarios:** To prevent changes to the definitions of scenarios on a worksheet.

Here again you can assign a password to create additional protection. The previous comments on passwords apply here as well.

To unprotect the active sheet, select Tools ⇨ Protection ⇨ Unprotect Sheet.

To Hide Formulas in Cells

Protecting the contents of a worksheet as above will prevent anyone from changing the formulas in cells, but people will still be able to see them. If you want to hide the formula in a cell, you have to first format the cell as hidden before protecting the worksheet. To do so, select the cells whose formulas you want to hide and then open the Format Cells dialog box by right-clicking and choosing Format Cells from the shortcut menu. In the dialog box, select the Protection tab, check the Hidden box, and click OK. Now if you protect the sheet as before, the formulas in those cells will no longer be visible. Remember that you have to protect the sheet after the above step for the Hidden option to take effect.

Leaving Selected Cells Unprotected

You would often want to leave the input cells or some other cells in a protected worksheet unprotected so that the user can enter data or make changes in them. To do so, select the cells you do not want to protect, go to the Protection tab in the Format Cells dialog box as I discussed earlier, uncheck the Locked box, and click OK. Note that all cells in a sheet have Locked checked by default and all the cells that you do not specifically unlock before protecting a sheet will be protected automatically. So if you want selected cells to remain unprotected, you have to first deselect Locked for them and then protect the worksheet.

CUSTOM VIEWS

Overview

You may sometimes want to view the same workbook or worksheet in different ways. For example, you may want a worksheet to show all the columns and rows, or you may want to see it with certain rows and columns hidden. Once you have set up your workbook in the way you want to see it for a certain type of analysis or for printing a certain type of report, you can save the settings as a named custom view. You can create several named custom views of a workbook for different purposes and switch from one to another as needed. This saves the time and work of having to create the same settings again and again or maintaining several different workbooks with the different settings.

Understanding Custom Views

A custom view effectively lets you look at your workbook through a particular lens that you create. It is important to understand that creating a custom view does not change the underlying workbook in any way. It just creates a lens through which you can view your workbook whenever you want, and you can create and save many such lenses under different names.

Each custom view includes the entire workbook even though two views may differ only in the way that one particular worksheet appears in them. The settings stored for each custom view include: column widths, display options, window size and position on the screen, window splits or frozen panes, the sheet that is active, and the cells that are selected at the time the view is created. You can also save hidden rows and columns, filter settings, and print settings by selecting the appropriate options.

Creating, Displaying, and Deleting a Custom View

Set up the workbook the way you want and then select View ⇨ Workbook Views ⇨ Custom Views (in earlier versions of Excel View ⇨ Custom Views). In the Custom Views dialog box that opens click Add, in the Add View dialog box in the Name box type in a name for the view, under Include in View select the options you want, and click OK.

To display a custom view, open the Custom Views dialog box as before and in the list under Views select the name of the view you want and click Show.

You can delete a view from the same dialog box.

Using a Custom View to Print Reports

If you want to create several different reports (printouts) from the same Excel workbook, you may find that setting up each report can be quite time-consuming. You can avoid having to set up any report again by creating a custom view that includes the workbook and printer setting for the report. (Remember to choose the appropriate options when you create the view.)

To print out the same report in the future, open the view you want and print.

ARRAYS AND ARRAY FORMULAS

Overview

An array is a collection of elements, most often a group of contiguous cells in a row or a column in a worksheet, and sometimes the cells in a square or rectangular range. Arrays are of interest because you can use them to write a special type of formula, called an array formula, which is more compact than a regular formula. Array formulas have certain advantages and disadvantages, and after considering them you may never want to use array formulas. However, you still need to be at least familiar with arrays and array formulas because some of Excel's built-in functions and some of the tools in the Analysis ToolPak use them.

A Note of Caution

If you are familiar with matrix algebra, note that you can use arrays to represent vectors and matrices and use certain Excel functions to do matrix calculations with them. However, calculations on arrays using array formulas do not follow the rules of matrix algebra. Do not confuse the two different ways of using arrays.

Using Arrays in Built-In Function

Many of Excel's built-in functions give you the option to enter single cells or arrays as arguments, and some will take only array arguments.

For example, the arguments for the SUM function can be individual cells or arrays. If you want to sum the values in cells A1, A2, and A3, you can write it as =SUM(A1,A2,A3) or as =SUM(A1:A3) using the array A1:A3. You probably have been writing formulas like the second one all along without realizing that you were using arrays.

Some built-in functions also produce array outputs and say so in their descriptions. You will be able to use them once you become familiar with array formulas.

Creating Array Formulas

You can write array formulas that have to be entered in multiple cells, that is, in an array, and produce multiple results that occupy those cells (that is, the array), or you can write array formulas that occupy only one cell and produce one result. Let us look at an example to see both uses.

Suppose you bought a stock in several lots over time at different prices as shown in columns A and B of Figure 4.7. You want to calculate your total investment and the average price you paid. (As shown in B13, a lot is 100 shares.)

You can calculate the cost for each lot (as in column C) by entering in C5 the formula =A5*B5*$B$13 and then copying it into C6:C9. To calculate the total investment, you then insert in C10 the formula =SUM(C5:C9).

To do the same calculation using an array formula and show the result for each lot separately (as in column C), select D5:D9 and in D5 enter the formula =(A5:A9*B5:B9*$B$13). Then, instead of pressing Enter, press Ctrl+Shift+Enter. This last step is critical because it tells Excel that you want the formula entered as an array formula in all the selected cells. If you select any cell in D5:D9, you will see it has the same formula, and the formula is enclosed in a pair of braces ({}). This is Excel's way of writing array formulas. You cannot type in the braces, however. Excel enters them automatically when you enter an array formula using the special combination of keys I mentioned.

	A	B	C	D	E	F
1	**Example of Using Array Formulas**					
2						
3	Lots purchased	Price paid	Cost for lot	Cost for lot	Cost for lot	
4			(Regular formulas)	(Array formula)	(Using names)	
5	5	$40.00	$20,000.00	$20,000.00	$20,000.00	
6	10	$35.00	$35,000.00	$35,000.00	$35,000.00	
7	3	$43.00	$12,900.00	$12,900.00	$12,900.00	
8	20	$42.00	$84,000.00	$84,000.00	$84,000.00	
9	5	$32.00	$16,000.00	$16,000.00	$16,000.00	
10	Total investment		$167,900.00			
11						
12						
13	Shares/lot	100				
14						
15	Total investment	$167,900.00				
16	Average cost	$39.05				
17						
18						

FIGURE 4.7 Example of using array formulas.

Let us now understand this formula. It is easiest to view an array formula like this one as a set of parallel formulas (in this case, 5 parallel formulas, because each array here has 5 elements). Excel takes the corresponding elements from each array to break down the array formula into a set of 5 ordinary formulas like =A5*B5*$B$13 and then evaluates them separately. Since the 5 component formulas will produce 5 separate results, they have to go into 5 cells. This is why an array formula like this one has to be entered into an array with 5 elements. Note that all the arrays in an array formula must have the same number of elements. However, you can also include single-value elements like $B$13 here, which Excel effectively interprets as an array with the same number of elements as the others with the same value for all of its elements.

As we just saw, to use an array in an array formula you do not have to define the arrays in any special way. You just use them as ranges in the array formulas as we did before. We could also give the arrays names and write the array formula using the names as I have done in E5:E9. To duplicate it, name the array A5:A9 qty and the array B5:B9 stkPrice. Now select E5:E9, enter the formula =qty*stkPrice*$B$13, and press Ctrl+Shift+Enter.

To calculate the total investment using an array formula, select B15, enter the formula =SUM(A5:A9*B5:B9*$B$13), and press Ctrl+Shift+Enter. In this case, Excel will first evaluate the array formula inside the parentheses and produce the 5 results as before. Then, because the results are now arguments of a SUM function, Excel will add them up and enter the result in B15. This is an example of an array formula that occupies only one cell and produces only one result.

To calculate the average price, we can use another array formula. Select B16, enter the formula =SUM(A5:A9*B5:B9)/SUM(A5:A9), and press

Ctrl+Shift+Enter. Combining array formulas with Excel's built-in functions, as we have done here, you can do a large number of calculations in just one cell.

Editing an Array Formula

If you want to edit a multi-cell array formula, you have to edit the entire array (range) at the same time; you cannot edit the cells within it individually because the different cells cannot have different formulas. Select the entire range or any cell within it, press F2, edit the formula, and then press Ctrl+Shift+Enter. This will change the formula in all the cells in the array.

Expanding and Contracting Array Formulas

Suppose you want to add another transaction to the model by inserting a new row. Excel will not let you insert a row within an array that contains an array formula until you remove the array formula or convert it into ordinary formulas. Select D5:D9, press F2, and then press Ctrl+Enter. This will enter individual formulas (which will look a little strange if you look into them) into all the cells in the array. You have to do the same with E5:E9. Now insert the row, select the new range D5:D10, press F2, and then press Ctrl+Shift+Enter. Do the same with the new range in column E as well.

Advantages and Disadvantages of Array Formulas

The most important advantage of array formulas in financial modeling is that you can use them to make some of your formulas very compact, especially when you use single-cell array formulas incorporating Excel's built-in functions (as we did to calculate the average cost). Another advantage is that Excel will not let you or a user accidentally change or overwrite a multi-cell array formula. However, Excel will not protect against overwriting a single-cell array formula.

One disadvantage of array formulas is that they can get cryptic and difficult to read. A second disadvantage is that because most Excel users are not familiar with array formulas, your average colleague may not be able to understand a model that uses array formulas. Finally, as we saw, expanding or contracting an array formula (for example, adding more transactions to our model) is somewhat cumbersome.

You should know about array formulas, but decide for yourself if you want to use them in your models.

OUTLINE

If you are working with hierarchical data (such as financial statements) that use various levels of subtotals, you can use Excel's outline feature to control the level of detail that is displayed. You can switch between the various levels with just one or two clicks of the mouse. It is also useful for creating reports with various levels of details. For example, you may want to switch between full financial statements with all line items showing to summary statements that show only the titles and subtotals for major categories.

You may find this feature useful in simple situations. However, working with outlines in more complex situations can get cumbersome, especially if you want to add line items and categories after you have first set up an outline. You can do similar things using custom views and may not want to learn or use this additional feature. If you want to learn more about the outline feature, look in Help.

CHAPTER 5

Making Decisions and Looking Up Values

One reason Excel is so useful is that it can do an enormous number of complex calculations accurately and fast. But if it could do only straightforward calculations, then it would not be half as useful as it is. A significant part of its usefulness or power comes from the fact that in Excel you can write formulas to make various kinds of decisions equally quickly and accurately.

What do we mean by making decisions? Making decisions means choosing which path or action to take out of several possibilities depending on the results of one or more conditions or tests. If you think about it you will realize that this is very similar to what we mean by making decisions and how we make decisions in real life as well, even though we generally do not explicitly think about what conditions or tests we are considering to decide what action we would take.

In financial models, you will often need to use Excel's decision-making abilities. Although most Excel users know how to set up simple decision making in Excel, they cannot create complex decision structures, and they think that the problem is that they do not know Excel well enough or do not know all the necessary features. But most of the time the real problem is that to set up a decision-making structure you have to first lay out in clear and precise steps exactly how a decision is to be made. Since we do not make decisions in such clear and precise steps, it takes some conscious practice to learn and document the steps of a decision. Once you have thought through and documented exactly how a decision is to be made, translating it into Excel formulas is not that difficult.

In this chapter, I will introduce Excel's decision-making tools. But more important, by using several examples I will show you how can break down a decision into steps and then translate it into Excel's language. Learning to create decision structures is very important for financial modeling. You should devote the necessary time and effort to learn it well and then practice writing decision-making formulas at every opportunity you get.

I will also cover two other groups of Excel's features that act very much like decision making. The first is looking up the value for something from a list or table depending on certain specified conditions or tests. This is a very powerful use of Excel. The second is formatting one or more cells differently depending on their content. This capability, called conditional formatting, is very useful to make your data or model outputs more clear and attractive. The conditional formatting feature has been significantly enhanced in Excel 2007. You will be able to use conditional formatting with its full power only if you are using Excel 2007.

Logical Values

Excel includes two logical values, TRUE and FALSE, which you can use in formulas or which can be the results of certain computations. (How and why you use them will become clear a little later.) For Excel to recognize these as logical values and not confuse them with text, you have to write them in your formulas in all capitals, as shown, and without the quotation marks normally used for texts. Excel also provides two functions, TRUE() and FALSE()—they do not take any arguments—which return the values TRUE and FALSE. These functions are provided only for compatibility with other spreadsheet programs. You will not need to use them because entering TRUE or FALSE anywhere is the same as entering the equivalent function.

Making Decisions

Excel offers several logical functions that you can use to give your formulas simple to fairly complex decision-making abilities. The IF function is the workhorse of this group and you will use it extensively in financial models. You use the IF function to tell Excel to do one thing if the condition or logical test you specify in it is satisfied (that is, evaluates to TRUE) and do a different thing if the condition is not satisfied (that is, evaluates to FALSE). Although the IF function is simple to understand and use, you can use it in various creative and advanced ways to generate results that can look miraculous because they can make it look like your model can think. The only way to learn to write good decision-making formulas is to look at a lot of them and write them whenever you have a need.

There are a few other functions that you will use extensively, often with the IF function, to give your formulas decision-making ability. These are AND and OR, which Excel categorizes as logical functions, and MAX and MIN, which are included in the statistical category. Excel's logical function category also includes the functions IFERROR (a new function in Excel 2007, not available in earlier versions) and NOT. You will use these less often, but you should know about them.

In creating decision-making formulas, sometimes you will also need to use some functions from Excel's lookup and reference functions category. We will mostly discuss them in the later section on looking up values.

The Comparison Operators

Excel offers six comparison operators to create conditions that you want to test either for standalone use or for use inside functions or other formulas. These are: = (means equal to), > (means greater than), < (means less than), >= (means greater than or equal to), <= (means less than or equal to), and <> (means not equal to).

When Excel evaluates an expression with one of these operators, it generates the logical value TRUE or FALSE. To see a standalone use, enter 50 in cell A1 in a worksheet and in cell A2 enter the formula =A1>60. When you press Enter after entering this formula, cell A2 will read FALSE because in this case the value in A1 is not greater than 60. If you write the formula in A2 as =A1>A10 then if the value in cell A1 is greater than the value in A10, you will see TRUE in cell A2, and if the value in A1 is less than or equal to A10, then cell A2 will show FALSE.

Note two important points. First, when you use comparison operators, be careful about choosing the one that exactly reflects what you mean. For example, the formula =A1>60 is not the same as =A1>=60. The first will produce the result FALSE if the value in A1 is 60, whereas the second will produce the result TRUE in the same situation. As we saw above, if you write the formula =A1>A10, then if the value in cell A1 is greater than the value in A10, you will see TRUE in cell A2, and if the value in A1 is less than or equal to A10, then cell A2 will show FALSE. If you do not choose your comparison operator carefully you may get an unexpected answer as we saw in the situation where A1 is equal to A10.

Second, the result of the operation with a comparison operator is always TRUE or FALSE—a logical value—and you can use this result in other formulas in your worksheet. In our example, if any other formula in your worksheet uses the reference A2, Excel will substitute in it the value TRUE or FALSE for A2. So any formula that uses A2 must be written to use these logical values, or else you may get an error or wrong answer. If it becomes necessary to substitute numerical values for TRUE or FALSE (e.g., you use it in a calculation, by mistake or otherwise), Excel substitutes 1 for TRUE and 0 for FALSE. This means that (in our example) if in A3 you enter the formula =A1+A2, you will get the result 50 or 51 depending on whether the logical value in A2 is FALSE or TRUE. Most of the time you would write such a formula by mistake rather than to do a calculation of this type, but in this situation Excel will not flag this as an error. So be careful.

The IF Function

The structure of the IF function is:

IF(logical_test,value_if_true,value_if_false)

The logical_test can be any value or expression that can be evaluated to TRUE or FALSE (for example, F33>100). Value_if_true and value_if_false can be simple or complex expressions (including other functions). Excel evaluates only one of these expressions depending on whether the result of the logical_test is TRUE or FALSE and enters the result in the cell (that is, in the same cell in which the IF function appears). The value_if_true part is often referred to as the true leg of the IF and the value_if_false as the false leg.

Try this simple example. In cell B1 of an empty worksheet, enter the formula =IF(A1<=0,"Negative","Positive"). Now if you enter a negative number or zero in cell A1, cell B1 will read Negative; for numbers greater than zero in A1, it will read Positive.

Nested IF Functions

The second and third arguments of the IF function can include additional IF functions to create more sophisticated decision structures. This is called using nested IF functions.

Suppose the interest rate on a loan will be 6% if the loan amount is less than $1 million, 5% for loan amounts between $1 and $2 million, and 4% for loans above $2 million. You want the appropriate interest rate to be entered in cell B1 depending on the size of the loan in cell A1. To do this, enter the following formula in B1:

=IF(A1<1000000,0.06,IF(A1<2000000,0.05,0.04))

Now if A1 is less than 1000000 the condition of the outer IF function will be satisfied and the interest rate will be 0.06 or 6%. If the condition is not satisfied, however, then Excel will evaluate the condition in the inner (nested) IF function and act on its result. See how this works by entering different values in A1.

Note two things. First, as with all functions, the result of an IF function is entered in its own cell. In this case you can use the interest rate in B1 (that is, use the cell address B1) in other calculations in your model that need to use the interest rate. Second, as I mentioned earlier, you have to make sure that the conditions you set up exactly reflect your intentions. For example, when you look at it closely, this formula says the interest rate will be 5% for a loan size equal to or greater than 1000000 but less than 2000000. The problem says "between $1 and $2 million," which is vague.

You can, of course, include additional IF functions in both the true and false legs of the IF function, and you can nest IF functions in up to 64 layers in Excel 2007 and 7 layers in earlier version. But you should avoid more than three layers of nesting because beyond that point the formulas start to get difficult to read and interpret and your chances of making a mistake go up.

The IFERROR Function

This is a very useful new function introduced in Excel 2007. It returns a value you specify if a formula evaluates to an error (e.g., $N/A, #VALUE!); otherwise, it returns the result of the formula. You can use it to trap and handle errors in a formula.

The syntax is:

IFERROR(value,value_if_error)

Value is the value, cell reference, or formula that is checked for an error. Value_if_error is the value to return if the formula evaluates to an error.

For example if you have the formula =IFERROR(A1/B1, "Error in calculation") in cell F57 and B1 is 0 (zero), then F57 will read "Error in calculation." If B1 is not zero and the result of the division is 5 then F57 will read 5.

The AND and OR Functions

The AND and OR functions are used to create more complex conditions. The AND function has the structure AND(logical1,logical2, ...) where the arguments are conditions. The AND function returns TRUE only if all its arguments are TRUE; otherwise it returns FALSE. For example, the formula =AND(A1>0,B1>0,C1>0) will return TRUE only if A1, B1, and C1 are all greater than 0. If any one of these conditions is not true then the AND function will return FALSE.

The OR function has the same structure, but it returns TRUE as long as at least one of its arguments is TRUE. So the formula =OR(A1>0,B1>0,C1>0) will be TRUE as long as any one (or more) of A1, B1, and C1 is greater than 0.

You can enter formulas like the ones I just showed in a cell, and the cell will say TRUE or FALSE depending on the result of the statement. If one of the formulas using AND or OR is in A2, you can write an IF function (say, in B2) such as =IF(A2=TRUE,0,1). More often, you will use AND or OR functions within IF functions to create more complex conditions.

There is one more logical function: NOT. It reverses the logic of its argument—that is, the result of NOT(TRUE) is FALSE and vice versa.

The MAX and MIN Functions

These functions respectively return the largest and smallest values in a list of arguments. The structure of these functions is MAX(number1,number2 ...) and MIN(number1,number2 ...), where the arguments can be numbers, references (that is, cell addresses for numbers), and ranges. They can also be arrays, text, and logical values, but in those cases you would need to be careful; otherwise you may end up with unexpected results.

Excel lists these functions in the statistical functions category. I am including them here as well because, as we will see, you can often use these in creating formulas that make decisions.

EXAMPLES OF CREATING DECISION-MAKING FORMULAS

Example 1: Calculating Income Tax, Version 1

Let us develop an increasingly more complex and realistic model for calculating income tax to see how logical functions, especially the IF function, can be used to have Excel make decisions. (Income tax in these examples refers to only the Federal income tax.)

Income tax is calculated on a taxpayer's taxable income, which is arrived at after making a series of adjustments to the taxpayer's salaries and wages and income from other sources. (For simplicity in our examples I will use the terms *income* and *taxable income* interchangeably.)

To start with a simple example, let us assume that a taxpayer does not have to pay any taxes on income up to $40,000, and pays taxes at the rate of 20% of any income in excess of $40,000.

The simple model is shown in Figure 5.1. The model has three inputs: taxable income; income not taxed, which is the income level below which the taxpayer does not have to pay any income tax; and tax rate. Even though in this example the income not taxed is a fixed $40,000 and the tax rate is 20%, it is always better to set them up as input variables in separate cells and not hard-code them into formulas.

The formula in B7 for calculating the income tax is:

=IF(B3>B4,B5*(B3-B4),0).

Let us analyze this formula. The first part inside the IF, B3>B4 is the logical test or condition that all IF functions require as the first argument. If the condition evaluates to TRUE, that is, B3 is greater than B4, then Excel does the calculation of the second argument—it calculates the income tax as 20% of the income above $40,000. In this case Excel enters (shows) this value in B7. If the condition

	A	B	C	D	E
1	**Simple Income Tax Calculation**				
2					
3	Taxable income	$60,000			
4	Income not taxed	$40,000			
5	Income tax rate	20%			
6					
7	Income tax	$4,000			
8					
9					
10					

FIGURE 5.1 Example 1: Simple income tax calculation.

	A	B	C	D	E
1	**Tax Calculation with Three Tax Brackets**				
2					
3	Taxable income	$120,000			
4	Lower Income threshold for bracket 2	$40,000			
5	Lower Income threshold for bracket 3	$100,000			
6	Income tax rate for bracket 2	20%			
7	Income tax rate for bracket 3	25%			
8					
9	Income tax	$17,000			
10					
11					
12					

FIGURE 5.2 Example 2: Calculating income tax when there are three tax brackets.

evaluates to FALSE, that is, if B3 is less than or equal to B4, Excel executes the third argument and shows 0 in B7.

Although this is almost the simplest possible example of using logic and the IF function, you can see that your formula is now making decisions about how to calculate the income tax depending on the taxable income, and you could not automate even this simple calculation without using IF.

Whenever you write formulas using logic, you should thoroughly test them to make sure that they will produce correct results for all possible inputs. In this case you should test you formula by entering a wide range of values for the three input variables.

Example 2: Calculating Income Tax, Version 2

Now let us complicate the example a little. Let us assume that you have to calculate income tax as in Example 1 up to an income of $100,000, but for all income above that the tax rate goes up to 25%. Note that you still pay 20% taxes on the portion of the income between $40,000 and $100,000 and pay 25% taxes only on the portion of the income above $100,000. In income tax language, we now have three tax brackets: a 0% bracket for income up to $40,000, a 20% bracket for income between $40,000 and $100,000, and a 25% bracket for income above that. The tax rates are also called the marginal tax rates. (Some people count this as two tax brackets by ignoring the 0% bracket.)

The model for this example is shown in Figure 5.2. We now have five input variables. Because the lower income threshold for the highest tax bracket is the same as the upper income threshold for the tax bracket below it, we do not need to separately include the income threshold for the second bracket, and so on.

We now need to use nested IF functions to write the formula to calculate the tax. The tax calculation formula in B9 is:

```
=IF(B3<=B4,0,(IF(B3<=B5,(B6*(B3-B4)),(B6*(B5-B4)+B7*(B3-B5)))))
```

It is not as complicated as it looks. Let us go through it in steps. The condition for the outer IF function is B3<=B4. If this evaluates to TRUE, that is, income is less than or equal $40,000, which is the upper threshold of the lowest bracket (the same as the lower threshold of the second bracket), then Excel executes the true leg of this IF and enters the tax as 0.

If the condition is not satisfied, that is, income is over $40,000 and the test evaluates to FALSE, then we would need to determine if the income is below or above $100,000. So if the condition B3<=B4 is not satisfied, then Excel goes on to execute the second or false leg of the outer IF, which is the part after the comma following the 0.

This is a second or nested IF function, and it again has to start with a condition. In this case the condition B3<= B5 tests if the income is less than or equal to or greater than $100,000. If the condition is met and income is less than or equal to $100,000, then the first leg of this IF function, (B6*(B3-B4)), is executed to calculate income tax at the 20% rate on income above $40,000.

If the condition is not met, meaning income is over $100,000, then the income tax calculation has two parts. The tax has to be calculated at the 20% rate for the income between $40,000 and $100,000 (that is, on $60,000) and added to tax calculated at 25% on income above $100,000. This is the calculation that is done in the formula (B6*(B5-B4)+B7*(B3-B5), which is the second leg of the inner or nested IF function.

You have to use parentheses appropriately both to satisfy Excel's requirements and to make your formula readable. For example, at the very least, the inner IF function needs to have its three arguments enclosed in a pair of parentheses. The first leg of the inner IF, the formula B6*(B3-B4) does not have to be enclosed in a pair of parentheses, but doing so, as I have done, makes the formula easier to read.

An important point to note is that in this example there are actually three possibilities: income below $40,000, income between $40,000 and $100,000, and income above $100,000, and taxes have to be calculated in three different ways (counting calculating the tax as 0 for income below $40,000). And we needed only two IFs to cover these three possibilities. This will always be the case. You will always need one fewer IF than the possibilities you need to cover because you can write your IFs in such a way that the default will cover one of them.

Also note that we could have written the condition of the outer IF as B3>B4, in which case the current second leg of this outer IF (that is, the nested IF) would have had to be made the first, or true, leg by putting it in the second position and the 0 would have had to be made the second, or false, leg. I wrote the condition the way I did to make the 0 the first leg because I think that makes the formula easier to read. This is a matter of taste.

Needless to say, when you write a longer and more complicated decision-making formula like this one, you have to test it extensively by varying all the input variables and checking the results with hand calculations to makes sure that your formula does the right calculations under all conditions.

	A	B	C	D	E
1	**Tax Calculation with Three Tax Brackets Using Cell Names**				
2					
3	Taxable income	$120,000	<== Income		
4	Lower Income threshold for bracket 2	$40,000	<== Thresh2		
5	Lower Income threshold for bracket 3	$100,000	<== Thresh3		
6	Income tax rate for bracket 2	20%	<== Rate2		
7	Income tax rate for bracket 3	25%	<== Rate3		
8					
9	Income tax	$17,000			
10					
11					
12					

FIGURE 5.3 Example 2: Calculating income tax with three tax brackets and cell names.

Even though this is a relatively simple problem, the formula for calculating income tax looks long and complex. This is why I said earlier that you should avoid writing formulas with more than three layers of nested IF functions.

This formula is also difficult to read because you have to keep referring back to which variable each cell address stands for. You can make a formula like this easier to read (and check) if you give the cells short but descriptive names, as I have done in Figure 5.3. Here I have inserted the cell names shown in column C into the corresponding cells in column B. The formula in B9 now reads:

=IF(Income<=Thresh2,0,(IF(Income<=Thresh3,(Rate2*(Income-Thresh2)),(Rate2*(Thresh3-Thresh2)+Rate3*(Income-Thresh3)))))

You could make the formula more compact by using even shorter names, such as rt3 for Rate3 and so on. Incidentally, after I named the cells, I did not have to rewrite the formula using the names. I chose Formula ⇨ Defined Names ⇨ Define Name ⇨ Apply Names, selected all the names on the list in the dialog box that opened up, and clicked OK. If you give the cells the appropriate names before you write a formula and use the pointing method to create it (that is, instead of entering a cell number in the formula by typing, click the cell when you want to enter its address in the formula), Excel will automatically enter the cell name instead of the cell number.

Using Decision Trees to Represent Logic

As the decision-making needs of your problems grow and you have to use several levels of nested IF functions or other logical functions, you will need to think through your logic in a systematic way and somehow put it down on paper (or a computer screen) before you write your formulas. Otherwise, it will be nearly impossible to write a formula with the correct logic and debug it. Also, such documentation can help others, and even you, at a later date to understand the logic you used.

	A	B	C	D	E	F
1	**Decision Tree for Calculating Income Tax with Three Tax Brackets**					
2						
3						
4						
5						
6						
7		Yes	Tax = 0			
8						
9	income <= thresh2?					
10				Yes	Tax = rate2* income over thresh2	
11		No	income <= thresh3?			
12				No	Tax= (rate2* thresh3 less thresh2) + (rate3*income over thresh3)	
13						
14						
15						

FIGURE 5.4 Example 2: Decision tree for calculating income tax.

When you are using IF functions, it is intuitive to write down your logic using a decision tree structure where each node represents an IF function and the two branches that emanate from a node represent the true and false legs. Most people start by drawing something like that on the back of an envelope, then move on to a bigger sheet of paper, and so on. I prefer to do it on an Excel worksheet as shown in Figure 5.4. The advantages are that the worksheet can stay in the same workbook as the model, I can make changes easily, and I can never run out of space because I can always add more rows and move the tree down and extend it to the right as needed.

Figure 5.4 is my representation of the decision tree for Example 2. The condition of the first IF function I need is in A9. If this condition is TRUE then what has to be done next is entered in C7 next to the Yes in B7, which indicates that this is the true leg of the IF. If the condition in A9 is FALSE then the next step is in C11 next to the No in B11. C11 is the nested IF function and has its own true and false legs, and so on.

You should keep the descriptions in A9 and the similar other cells brief. You should generally put down in words what action is to be taken or calculation to be made, and not write down the actual equations as I have done (for illustration). Nonetheless, one advantage of using a worksheet is that you can put as much information in the cells in your tree as you want by wrapping the text around inside a cell. Also, if you start running out of room for the upper branches of the tree, you can move down the whole tree by inserting rows at the top.

You can also use similar structures to write down logics involving AND and OR. Generally it is best to develop your own style for documenting your logic by experimenting.

Example 3: Calculating Income Tax, Version 3

We are now ready to create a model for more realistic Federal income tax calculation based on the actual Federal tax brackets and rates that applied to the tax year 2008. The tax table that applied to a taxpayer whose filing status is single is shown Figure 5.5. Although there are some technical definitions of the different tax statuses such as single, married, and so on, we will assume they just mean what the names imply. The tax tables vary for filers with different tax status.

The first line of the table says that the tax for someone with a taxable income between $0 and $8,025 is 10% of income. The second line applies to someone with a taxable income between $8,025 and $32,550. The tax for such a person is $802.50 (shown in column F, representing the tax on the first $8,025 of income at the 10% rate) plus tax at the rate of 15% on the income over $8,025 (shown in column I). The subsequent lines are to be read the same way except that the last line applies to all income above $357,700.

The tax calculation is similar to that in Example 2 except that since there are several more tax brackets, if we try to write a tax calculation formula similar to the one there we will have a very long formula with several levels of nested IF functions. Such a formula will be both difficult to write and check.

We can adopt many different simpler approaches. Let us look at one. In cell B9 I entered a formula that would calculate the tax for someone with an income below $8,025. The formula reads:

=IF(AND(B$3>D9,B$3<=E9),(F9+H9*(B$3-I9)),0)

Here I am using the logical function AND to create the condition for the IF function. Within the AND function, the first argument, B$3>D9, checks if the income is greater than the lower income limit for this tax bracket and the second argument, B$3<=E9, tests if the income level is less than or equal to the upper limit. This line of the table applies only to income levels that satisfy both of these conditions. If both conditions are satisfied, they will both evaluate to TRUE and therefore the AND will evaluate to TRUE as well. In that case the condition for the IF function will be TRUE and the tax will be calculated using the formula for the true leg of the IF, that is, (F9+H9*(B$3-I9)). Since F9 is zero (blank), I could have omitted it. But because the amount in the F column will need to be incorporated in the calculation formulas in the subsequent lines and whenever possible we should write formulas that can be copied and pasted in other similar cells, I have included the F9 here.

If either of the tests in the AND function is not satisfied, then this line does not apply. The AND will evaluate to FALSE, and Excel will execute the second leg of the IF function, which in this case is 0. So by itself this line does not calculate the tax correctly for other income levels.

But let us now copy and paste the formula in B9 to cells B10:B14. The result is that for the input income level of $130,000 in cell B3, the tax is calculated in

	A	B	C	D	E	F	G	H	I	J
1	**Calculating Federal Income Tax for Single Filers**									
2										
3	Taxable income	$130,000								
4	Income tax	$30,378.25								
5				**Filing status:**	**Single**					
6				**If your taxable income is:**		**The tax is:**				
7				Over	But not over				of the amount over	
8										
9		$0.00		$0	$8,025			10%	$0	
10		$0.00		$8,025	$32,550	$802.50	+	15%	$8,025	
11		$0.00		$32,550	$78,850	$4,481.25	+	25%	$32,550	
12		$30,378.25		$78,850	$164,550	$16,056.25	+	28%	$78,850	
13		$0.00		$164,550	$357,700	$40,052.25	+	33%	$164,550	
14		$0.00		$357,700		$103,791.75	+	35%	$357,700	
15										

FIGURE 5.5 Example 3: Calculating Federal income tax for single filers.

B12 because row 12 applies to this income level and the tax in all the other rows will show zeros.

To make our model output look good, we want to enter the tax amount from cell B12 in cell B4. But we cannot simply enter =B12 in B4 because for other income levels the tax in B4 will have to be taken from other cells. To take the tax amount from the cell that applies to a particular income level, we use the MAX function and enter the formula =MAX(B9:B14) in B4. This works because there will be only one non-zero tax amount in the range B9:B14 and MAX will enter that value in cell B4. We could also use SUM(B9:B14) to get the same result.

At this point it looks like we are done. But enter an income of $400,000 and you will see that the tax comes out as 0. Why is that? Take a closer look at the formula in B14, which is the same as those in the cells B9:B13 because we created them all using copy and paste. Tax for an income of $400,000 should be calculated in line 14, but with $400,000 as the income the second test of the AND function in this cell evaluates to FALSE, which makes the condition of the IF FALSE, and the tax comes out as 0.

Because this last line of the tax table applies to all income above $357,000, we do not need to impose a test for the upper limit in the condition for IF in this cell and we can eliminate the AND function. Enter the formula =IF(B$3>D14,(F14+H14*(B$3-I14)),0) in cell B14, and now the tax for $400,000 will be $118,596.75, which is the correct result.

Example 4: Calculating Income Tax, Version 4

We can now incorporate one more level of realism in our model. As I mentioned earlier, there are different tax tables for taxpayers with different filing status. Figure 5.6 shows the tax table for single taxpayers, which we used in Example 3, and also the tax table for a married couple filing jointly, labeled here simply as Married. We want to enhance the model so that a user can enter his filing status and get the right tax amount. This model will work for only single and married filers, but you should be able to extend it easily for other filing statuses.

In B10:B15 and B22:B27 I have entered the same tax computation formula we developed in the previous example. In cell B5 we need to enter the tax amount depending on whether the taxpayer is single or married. The tax payer enters this information in cell B4. The formula in cell B5 is:

=IF(B4="Single",MAX(B10:B15),MAX(B22:B27))

If the taxpayer enters Single in B4, the condition of the IF evaluates to TRUE and the tax amount is taken from B10:B15. Otherwise it is taken from B22:B27.

When you want to do a test like this using user input in an IF function, it is safer to restrict what the user can enter for input. Otherwise the user may have the spelling wrong or may enter an unexpected word and get a wrong result.

	A	B	C	D	E	F	G	H	I	J
1	**Calculating Federal Income Tax for Single and Married Filers**									
2										
3	Taxable income	$400,000								
4	Filing status	Single								
5	Federal income tax	$118,596.75								
6				**Filing status:**	**Single**					
7				**If your taxable income is:**		**The tax is:**				
8				Over	But not over				of the amount over	
9										
10		$0.00		$0	$8,025			10%	$0	
11		$0.00		$8,025	$32,550	$802.50	+	15%	$8,025	
12		$0.00		$32,550	$78,850	$4,481.25	+	25%	$32,550	
13		$0.00		$78,850	$164,550	$16,056.25	+	28%	$78,850	
14		$0.00		$164,550	$357,700	$40,052.25	+	33%	$164,550	
15		$118,596.75		$357,700		$103,791.75	+	35%	$357,700	
16										
17										
18				**Filing status:**	**Married**					
19				**If your taxable income is:**		**The tax is:**				
20				Over	But not over				of the amount over	
21										
22		$0.00		$0	$16,050			10%	$0	
23		$0.00		$16,050	$65,100	$1,605.00	+	15%	$16,050	
24		$0.00		$65,100	$131,450	$8,962.50	+	25%	$65,100	
25		$0.00		$131,450	$200,300	$25,550.00	+	28%	$131,450	
26		$0.00		$200,300	$357,700	$44,828.00	+	33%	$200,300	
27		$111,575.00		$357,700		$96,770.00	+	35%	$357,700	
28										
29										

FIGURE 5.6 Example 4: Calculating Federal income tax for single and married filers.

If you select cell B4, a dropdown arrow appears next to it and the user is restricted to choosing from the dropdown list. It is easy to create this constraint using data validation. Make B4 the active cell and then choose Data ⇨ Data Tools ⇨ Data Validation ⇨ Data Validation. In the Settings tab of the Data Validation dialog box that opens, open and choose List from the dropdown list under Allow and in the box under Source, type "Single" and "Married" separated by a comma. Then click OK.

If you want to incorporate a few other filing statuses, you could use nested IF functions to extend the formula in cell B5 or find some other solution.

Example 5: Implementing Dividend Policy

You will often need to create models to create projected financial statements for a corporation and incorporate in the model various financial policies the management wants to follow. For example, in such a model a corporation may want to incorporate the policy that it will pay out 40% of income in dividends (that is, target a payout ratio of 40%), but will never increase per share dividend by more than 10% in any year.

The model is shown in Figure 5.7. The numbers for 2008 are actuals and those for 2009 to 2012 are projections. In real life you cannot change actuals, which are historical numbers for past years, but when you are building a model you may sometimes want to change them to check that your model responds properly. In this case we are not concerned with how the future net income and average number of shares outstanding are projected. The earnings per share are calculated from those two.

In the model I have made both the target payout ratio and the maximum allowed increase in dividend per share from one year to the next input variables and have named C3 payout and C4 maxgr. This will make it easy to change values of these variables in the model.

The last two rows, the Memo rows, are not needed. I have included them (and management often wants to see them) to understand which policy constraint is driving the dividend in a particular year.

The formula in C13 to project the dividend for 2009 is:

```
=IF((C9*payout/C10>(1+maxgr)*B13),B13*(1+maxgr),C9*payout/C10)
```

The same formula is copied over to D14:F14 using relative reference.

The condition of the IF function checks if the per share dividend calculated using the target payout ratio (here 40%) will exceed the previous year's dividend per share by more than the maximum allowable year to year growth rate (here 10%). If this is true then dividend per share is calculated (in the true leg) as 10% more than the previous year's dividend per share. Otherwise (in the false leg) dividend per share for the year is calculated at a payout ratio of 40%.

	A	B	C	D	E	F	G	H
1	**Implementing Dividend Policy**							
2								
3	Target payout ratio	40%	<== payout					
4	Maximum allowed annual per share dividend growth	10%	<== maxgr					
5								
6								
7		**Historical**		**Forecast Period**				
8		2008	2009	2010	2011	2012		
9	Net income	$1,351	$1,400	$1,500	$1,600	$1,700		
10	Average number of shares outstanding	1000	1050	975	1100	900		
11	Earnings per share	$1.35	$1	$2	$1	$2		
12								
13	Dividend per share	$0.60	$0.53	$0.59	$0.58	$0.64		
14	Total dividend	$600	$560	$572	$640	$576		
15								
16	Memo:							
17	Dividend per share at 40% pay out ratio	$0.54	$0.53	$0.62	$0.58	$0.76		
18	Dividend per share at 10% over previous year		$0.66	$0.59	$0.65	$0.64		
19								
20								

FIGURE 5.7 Example 5: Implementing dividend policy.

In addition to providing useful information for management, the two Memo lines are also helpful to check if the model is working properly. The dividend in any year should be the smaller of the dividend rates calculated based on the two approaches. Because here we are already calculating the dividend per share using both constraints, instead of using the IF function in C13, etc., we could have used the formula =MIN(C17,C18).

In our model (using the projected numbers we have used) the dividend per share declines from the previous year in both 2009 and 2011. Companies generally resist reducing dividends unless there is no other alternative. So after looking at the results your manager may ask you to fix the model so that per share dividend is never allowed to go down. (In real life models are often updated based on such discussions.)

A simple formula to implement this additional constraint for 2009 in C13 can be =MAX(B13,MIN(C17,C18)), and the same formula can be copied to the corresponding cells for the other years. Notice that we have now used MIN and MAX to do the work of the logical function IF. Whenever several conditions are involved, it is often easier to write a more understandable formula combining MIN, MAX, OR and AND. This, of course, required the extra step of calculating the values in rows 17 and 18.

For practice, modify the formula in C13 to include the additional constraint using IF and see if you like that one step approach better than the multistep approach to make your formulas clearer.

So far we have entered only positive earnings for the forecast years. If you enter a negative earning, the model will produce unrealistic, negative dividends. How do we fix this problem? We have to ask management, what the company's policy would be in such years. Companies are generally reluctant to cut dividends even in bad times. But sometimes management may have no choice but to cut dividends. If management wants to include an additional financial policy, such as that the company will cut back per share dividend by 50% in unprofitable years, how would you incorporate that in your model? Suppose management decides that if it has losses only for one year, it will not change the dividend per share from the previous year, but it will cut back dividend by 50% if there are two consecutive years of losses. Once again, practice by implementing this dividend policy. Keep in mind that you have to first define a dividend policy before you can implement it in your model.

Example 6: Determining the Rank of a Poker Hand

This example involves ranking a five-card poker hand according to the rules of poker. I have chosen this example because it offers the opportunity to demonstrate and challenge you to write some fairly complex decision-making formulas.

Poker has clearly defined rules for ranking hands. Even people who do not know poker or have never played any card game can easily understand these rules and learn to rank poker hands (by referring to the ranking table) within a few minutes. But as we will see, writing formulas to do the same is much more difficult.

Let us start by understanding the rules of ranking poker hands. A deck (or pack) of cards consists of 52 cards divided into four suits called Spades (s), Hearts (h), Diamonds (d), and Clubs (c) of 13 cards each. Ten of the 13 cards of each suit are numbered 1 to 10, and then there are 3 picture cards called Jack (J), Queen (Q) and King (K). (A deck also includes two jokers, but we will not consider them.)

For our purpose, we will assume that each poker hand consists of five cards drawn at random from one deck of cards.

A few points to note:

- The ranking or value of the cards within each suit in descending order is: A (Ace or the 1 card), K, Q, J, and then 10, 9, 8, . . . 2. This order also determines whether three or more cards are consecutive or in sequence. So A, K, Q, J are consecutive cards, and so on. One exception is that the Ace can also be counted as 1. Therefore, A, 2, 3 are also consecutive or in sequence. In our programs we will assign values of 11, 12, 13, to J, Q, and K, respectively, and the values of both 14, and 1, to A. Which value of A we use will depend on the context.
- In poker all suits have equivalent rank, which means that a 3 of Spades is neither higher nor lower than a 3 of Clubs. However, they are not exactly the same either because in some situations whether two or more cards in a hand are of the same suit matters.
- Because we will assume that all the five-card hands we will work with at any one time are drawn at random from one deck of cards without replacement, no card can appear more than once in the same hand.
- Although in referring to cards the words *rank* and *value* mean the same thing, from here on we will only use the word *value* when referring to individual cards and reserve the word *rank* to refer to the rank of a hand according poker rules.

The top part of Figure 5.8 shows the ranks of various poker hands. For example, if a hand consists of A, K, Q, J, 10 of the same suit (any suit), then it is called a Royal Flush, which is the highest ranking hand in poker. Its rank is 1. A hand where all cards are consecutive and of the same suit, but the highest card is not an Ace (e.g., 10, 9, 8, 7, 6 of Clubs) is called a Straight Flush and is ranked 2. You should look through the description of the hands of all the 10 ranks and make up your own examples of hands of each rank to make sure you fully understand the ranking system. (A pair is two cards with the same value. They obviously cannot be of the same suit because we are using only one deck, as explained earlier.)

	A	B	C	D	E	F	G
4	**Name**	**Description**	**Definition**		**Rank**		
5							
6	**Royal Flush**	All of one suit, all cosecutive from from Ace down	1		FALSE		
7	**Straight Flush**	All of one suit, all consecutive starting below ace	2		FALSE		
8	**Four of a Kind**	Four cards of same value	3		TRUE		
9	**Full House**	Three cards of one value and the other two a pair	4				
10	**Flush**	All of one suit, but all not consecutive	5		FALSE		
11	**Straight**	All cards consecutive but all not of same suit	6				
12	**Three of a Kind**	Three cards of one value, but other two not a pair	7				
13	**Two Pairs**	Two pairs, each of a different value	8				
14	**One Pair**	One pair, other three cards of different values	9				
15	**High Card**	Any hand not in one of the other categories	10				
16							
17							
18							
19	**For analysis first order a hand by card values**						
20							
21		**The hand to be ranked (in descending order by value)**	**Value**	**Suit**			
22							
23		Highest card	10	s			
24		Second highest card	9	s			
25		Third highest card	9	s			
26		Fourth highest card	9	s			
27		Lowest card	9	h			
28							
29		All cards in hand of same suite?		FALSE			
30		Midddle three cards are of same value?		TRUE			
31							
32							

FIGURE 5.8 Example 6: Determining the rank of a poker hand.

The user would enter a test hand of five cards in C23:D27. Each card is represented by its value (2 to 14) in column C and suit (s, h, d, c) in column D. The user has to enter the cards in descending order of value. (As we will see, this makes writing the logic for ranking significantly easier.) I have named the cells C22 to C27 as z1v, z2v . . . z5v and cells D22 to D27 as z1s, z2s . . . z57. This will make our formulas easier to write and read.

Our objective is to write formulas in E6 to E15 so that the value in each cell will read TRUE if the specified hand is of the rank defined in that row and FALSE otherwise.

Let us start by writing a formula in D29 to determine if all the five cards in the hand the user entered are of the same suit. (We will see shortly how this will be helpful.) The formula in D29 reads =AND(z1s=z2s,z2s=z3s,z3s=z4s,z4s=z5s), which is a simple test. If all of the cards are of the same suit, each of these conditions will be TRUE and therefore the result of the AND function will be TRUE. If even one card is of a different suit, one of the equal tests will fail and the result of the AND will be FALSE.

It is tempting to think that if this result is TRUE then E10 should also read TRUE, that is, the rank of the hand would be 5 because the hand has five cards of the same suit. But this is not correct. If the hand has five consecutive cards of the same rank, then the hand will have rank of 1 or 2 and not 5.

Let us now write the formula for C6. This is a simple formula that reads =AND(D29,z1v=14,z5v=10). This first argument checks if all the cards are of the same suit by looking at D29, the second checks if the highest card has a value of 14, and the third argument checks if the lowest card has a value of 10. Why does this work? Because if the cards have been entered in descending order and are of the same suit, and the highest card is an Ace (value 14) and the lowest card is a 10, then the cards in between must be K, Q and J. If we did not require that the cards be entered in descending order, then this test would not have worked.

Next we write the formula for C7, which is:

=OR(AND(D29,z1v<>14,(z1v-z5v)=4),AND(D29,z1v=14,z5v=2,
(z2v-z5v)=3)).

This looks complex, but is not. Let us analyze its two pieces. The first AND tests if all the cards are of the same suit, if the highest card is something other than an Ace, and the difference between the values of the highest and the lowest card is 4. As before, given that all cards are of the same suit, if the last test in this AND is true then the cards are in sequence. The middle test makes sure that the top card is not an Ace, because if it were, and the other two tests were satisfied, then this would be a hand of rank 1 and not rank 2.

But a hand can be of rank 2 in another way also. If all cards are of the same suit, the hand includes an Ace (entered as 14), and the other four cards are 5, 4, 3, 2, then the Ace can be counted as 1 to complete the five card sequence. This is what the second AND tests. (The test should be clear if you think it through.)

Since the hand would be of rank 2 if either of the AND functions produces a TRUE result, I have put them inside an OR to test for that.

We can now write the formula for E10, that is rank 5. If all five cards are of the same suit, but the hand is not of rank 1 or 2, it is of rank 5 by default. So I am using the formula =AND(D29,NOT(E6),NOT(E7)). The NOT function inverts a TRUE to FALSE, that is NOT(TRUE) produces the result FALSE and NOT(FALSE) produces the result TRUE. For a hand to be of rank 5 we want D29 to be TRUE, but E6 and E7 to be FALSE. Think why using the two NOT functions in this formula performs precisely the test we want to be satisfied for a hand of rank 5.

A rank 3 hand requires that it include four cards of the same value. Since the cards have been entered in descending order, the only way this can happen is if the middle three cards have the same value plus the top or bottom card has the same value as well. In D30 I use the formula =AND(z2v=z3v,z3v,z4v) to test if the middle three cards have the same value. Then in E8 I use the formula =AND(D30,OR(z1v=z2v,z4v=z5v)), which performs the test I explained.

I will leave it to you as an exercise to come up with the formulas for the other ranks. Some of them will become complex and long. But working through them will significantly improve your skill of writing formulas that can make decisions.

In writing logical formulas for this and other examples keep in mind that you can often simplify your formulas by doing the tests in steps instead of doing all of them in one formula. This is particularly true if you would need to repeat the same test in several formulas. For example, in this example, we tested if all the cards in the hand are of the same suit in cell D29 and used the result in the formulas in cells E6, E7, and so on.

Looking Up Values

Excel offers several functions to look up values from a table or from the arguments of the function itself. For example, as we saw, you may want to look up tax rates and base tax amounts from a tax table to calculate taxes due. You may want to consult a table of detailed information on inventory for the cost and availability of particular products. These Excel functions will help you do such things easily.

The functions covered in this section are listed in the Excel functions library in the Lookup and Reference group. I will cover only those functions from this group that you are likely to use in financial modeling. There are a few other functions in this group that you may use only in special situations. You should generally familiarize yourself with what else is available by looking in Excel's Help under Lookup and Reference functions.

LOOKUP (Vector Form)

Looks in a one-row or one-column range for a value and returns a value from the same position in a second one-row or one-column range. (This is called the vector form of LOOKUP. There is a second form of the LOOKUP function known as the array form. It is better to use the HLOOKUP or VLOOKUP to do what the array form does.)

The syntax of the vector form of the LOOKUP function is:

LOOKUP(lookup_value,lookup_vector,result_vector)

Lookup_value is the value that LOOKUP searches for in the first vector. Lookup_value can be a number, text, a logical value, or a name or reference that refers to a value.

Lookup_vector is a range that contains only one row or one column. The values in it can be text, numbers, or logical values. The values in lookup_vector must be placed in ascending order: . . . ,−2, −1, 0, 1, 2, . . . , A-Z, FALSE, TRUE; otherwise, LOOKUP may produce a wrong answer. Uppercase text and lowercase text are considered equivalent.

Result_vector is a range that contains only one row or column. It must be the same size as lookup_vector.

If LOOKUP cannot find the lookup_value, it matches the largest value in the lookup_vector that is less than the lookup_value. This makes it possible to look up values where the lookup_value falls in a range instead of matching a specific value.

If the lookup_value is smaller than the smallest value in the lookup_vector, LOOKUP gives the #N/A! error value.

Example: The tax table in Figure 5.5 provides information for calculating taxes for a single filer given her taxable income. In the table, the marginal tax rate is 10% and the base tax amount is $0 for taxable income up to $8,025; for income between $8,025 and $32,550 they are 15% and $802.50, respectively; and so on.

Here is how you will use the LOOKUP function to look up the marginal tax rate and the results you will get for various taxable incomes.

=LOOKUP(29000,D9:D14,H9:H14) will return 15%
=LOOKUP(55000,D9:D14,H9:H14) will return 25%
=LOOKUP(400000,D9:D14,H9:H14) will return 35%

HLOOKUP, VLOOKUP

HLOOKUP and VLOOKUP are parallel functions that work the same way.

HLOOKUP searches for a value in the top row of a table or an array (range) of values and then returns the value from a specified row in the same column of the table or array.

VLOOKUP searches for a value in the leftmost column of table or array (range) and then returns a value from a specified column in the same row of the table or array.

Use HLOOKUP when your comparison values are located in a row across the top of a table of data, and you want to look down a specified number of rows. Use VLOOKUP when your comparison values are located in a column to the left of the data you want to find.

The syntax of the HLOOKUP function is:

HLOOKUP(lookup_value,table_array,row_index_num,range_lookup)

Lookup_value is the value to be found in the first row of the table. Lookup_value can be a value, a reference, or a text string.

Table_array is a table of information in which data is looked up. Use a reference to a range or a range name. The values in the first row of table_array can be text, numbers, or logical values. If range_lookup is TRUE, then the values in the first row of table_array must be placed in ascending order. (See LOOKUP for a definition of ascending order.)

Row_index_num is the row number in table_array from which the matching value will be returned. A row_index_num of 1 returns the first row value in table_array, a row_index_num of 2 returns the second row value in table_array, and so on.

Range_lookup is a logical value that specifies whether you want HLOOKUP to find an exact match or an approximate match. If TRUE or omitted, an approximate match is returned. In other words, if an exact match is not found, the largest value that is less than lookup_value is returned. If FALSE, HLOOKUP will look for an exact match. If one is not found, the error value #N/A! is returned. This argument is optional, and if omitted it is assumed to be TRUE.

Here is how you will use the VLOOKUP function to look up the base tax amounts from the tax table in Figure 5.5.

=VLOOKUP(140000,D9:I14,3) will return $16,056.25
=VLOOKUP(63000,D9:I14,3) will return $4,481.25
=VLOOKUP(140000,D9:I14,3,FALSE) will return #N/A!
(no exact match)

You could also use VLOOKUP to look up the marginal tax rates as follows:

=VLOOKUP(140000,D9:I14,5,TRUE) will return 28%

Example 7: Calculating Income Tax, Version 5

We can now use the VLOOKUP function to rewrite the income tax calculation formulas we developed in Example 6 using the IF function. These are shown in Figure 5.9.

If we want to calculate taxes only for a single filer, the formula in B5 would be:

=VLOOKUP(B3,D10:I15,3)+VLOOKUP(B3,D10:I15,5)*(B3-VLOOKUP(B3,D10:I15,1))

Although it looks complex, it is actually a simple formula that uses the VLOOKUP function three times: first to find the base tax amount from column F, which is column 3 within the tax table, then to look up the marginal tax rate from column H, and finally to look up the base (the lower threshhold) income amount for the selected tax bracket.

To make the model work for both single and married filers, you can use an IF function in B5, and have it look up values from the table in D10:I15 for single filers and from the table in D22:I27 for married filers. The formula will be fairly long, but straightforward.

You can simplify the formula by calculating the tax for single and married filers separately in two different cells—B30 and B31 in this example—and then use an IF function in B5 to pick the right tax amount depending on whether the user specifies a single or married filer.

	A	B	C	D	E	F	G	H	I	K
1	**Calculating Federal Income Tax for Single and Married Filers**									
2										
3	Taxable income	$40,000								
4	Filing status	Single								
5	Federal income tax	$6,343.75								
6				**Filing status:**	**Single**					
7				**If your taxable income is:**		**The tax is:**				
8				Over	But not over				of the amount over	
9										
10				$0	$8,025			10%	$0	
11				$8,025	$32,550	$802.50	+	15%	$8,025	
12				$32,550	$78,850	$4,481.25	+	25%	$32,550	
13				$78,850	$164,550	$16,056.25	+	28%	$78,850	
14				$164,550	$357,700	$40,052.25	+	33%	$164,550	
15				$357,700		$103,791.75	+	35%	$357,700	
16										
17										
18				**Filing status:**	**Married**					
19				**If your taxable income is:**		**The tax is:**				
20				Over	But not over				of the amount over	
21										
22				$0	$16,050			10%	$0	
23				$16,050	$65,100	$1,605.00	+	15%	$16,050	
24				$65,100	$131,450	$8,962.50	+	25%	$65,100	
25				$131,450	$200,300	$25,550.00	+	28%	$131,450	
26				$200,300	$357,700	$44,828.00	+	33%	$200,300	
27				$357,700		$96,770.00	+	35%	$357,700	
28										
29										
30	Tax for single filer	$6,343.75								
31	Tax for married filer	$5,197.50								
32										
33										

FIGURE 5.9 Example 7: Calculating income tax using VLOOKUP.

The formula in B30 is the same as the formula we looked at a little earlier:

=VLOOKUP(B$3,D$10:I$15,3)+VLOOKUP(B$3,D$10:I$15,5)*(B$3-VLOOKUP(B$3,D$10:I$15,1))

And the formula in B31 is similar except that it specifies the range D22:I27. The formula in B5 is =IF(B4="Single",B30,B31).

MATCH

Returns the relative position of an item in a range of contiguous cells in a row or a column that matches a specified value. Even though the function is called MATCH, as with the lookup functions, it does not need to find an exact match (unless you specifically require it). Use MATCH instead of one of the LOOKUP functions when you need the position of an item in a range instead of the item itself.

The syntax of the MATCH function is:

MATCH(lookup_value,lookup_array,match_type)

Lookup_value is the value you use to find the value you want to find in a table.

Lookup_array is a range of contiguous cells containing possible lookup values. It can be an array or an array reference.

Match_type is the number −1, 0, or 1. Match_type specifies how Microsoft Excel matches lookup_value with values in lookup_array.

- If match_type is 1, MATCH finds the largest value that is less than or equal to lookup_value. Lookup_array must be placed in ascending order: . . . −2, −1, 0, 1, 2, . . . , A-Z, FALSE, TRUE.
- If match_type is 0, MATCH finds the first value that is exactly equal to lookup_value. Lookup_array can be in any order.
- If match_type is −1, MATCH finds the smallest value that is greater than or equal to lookup_value. Lookup_array must be placed in descending order: TRUE, FALSE, Z-A, . . . 2, 1, 0, −1, −2, . . . , and so on.
- This argument is optional. If match_type is omitted, it is assumed to be 1.

We can use the MATCH function to find the row number for a certain taxable income in Figure 5.5 to get the following results:

=MATCH(64000,D9:D14,1) will return 3. =MATCH(32550,D9:D14,0) will return 3. =MATCH(64000,D9:D14,0) will return #N/A! (no exact match). =MATCH(64000,D9:D14,−1) will return #N/A! (values not in descending order).

Note that the 3 in the above examples indicates the relative position within the array, that is, it means the third row of the array and not the row number 3 in the Excel worksheet. Of course, if the array started in Excel's row number 1, then the number returned would also refer to Excel's row number.

CHOOSE

Based on a specified index number (1st, 2nd, etc.), this function chooses a value from the list of its arguments. The arguments can be numbers, cell references, defined names, formulas, functions, or text.

Suppose you want to see in a cell the day of the week based on the value of 1 to 7 that the user enters in another cell (with 1 for Monday and so on). In cell A2 of a worksheet enter the formula =CHOOSE(A1,"Mon", "Tue", "Wed", "Thur", "Fri", "Sat", "Sun"), and then in A1 enter 3. A2 will now read Wed because that is the third value in the list.

To make many creative uses of CHOOSE look up more about it in the Help.

INDEX

Returns the value of an element in a table or an array, selected by the row and column number indexes.

The syntax of the INDEX function is:

INDEX(array,row_num,col_num)

Array is a range of cells.

Row_num selects the row in array from which to return a value. If row_num is omitted, column_num is required.

Col_num selects the column in array from which to return a value. If col_num is omitted, row_num is required.

We can use the INDEX function to look up any value in the tax table in Figure 5.5 by specifying its row and column numbers within the table as follows:

=INDEX(D9:I14,2,3) will return $802.50

If the array has more than one row and more than one column, and only row_num or col_num is used, INDEX returns an array of the entire row or column of the array. If you need to use this option, you will have to enter the formula as an array formula in an appropriate size range. For example, if you want the entire second column of the tax table, you can select A9:A14, type in the formula =INDEX(D9:I14,,2) and then press Shift+Ctrl+Enter. This will copy the second column of the tax table to the range A9:A14.

(There is a second form of the INDEX function called the reference form, which you are not likely to use.)

OFFSET

Returns the reference—let us call it the resulting reference for clarity—to a single cell or a range of cells that is a specified number of rows and columns from a cell or range of cells.

The syntax of the OFFSET function is:

=OFFSET(base_reference, rows, columns, height, width)

Base_reference is the reference to the base cell or range from which the resulting reference is to be calculated.

Rows is the number by which the row number of the resulting reference is to be offset from that of the base_reference. If rows is a positive number then the row number of the resulting reference will be higher than that of the base_reference. If rows is a negative number then the row number of resulting reference will be lower than that of the base_reference.

Columns work in a similar way.

Heights and width specifies the number of rows and columns to be included in the resulting reference. (These can be omitted if you want a resulting reference to be just one cell.)

If you enter the function by itself in a cell and the reference created is a single cell, then its value will be displayed. If you want similar results when the reference created is a range of cells, then you will have to enter it as an array formula in an array of appropriate dimensions. Alternately, you can do other things with the created reference when it is a range of cells, for example, sum the values in the reference range by using the OFFSET function as an argument of the SUM function.

Other Related Functions

The Lookup and Reference function group includes a few other functions that you may find useful sometimes. These are: ADDRESS, COLUMN, COLUMNS, INDIRECT, ROW, ROWS, and TRANSPOSE. These are simple to use. Familiarize yourself with them from the Help so that if you think one of them may be useful in a model you are working on, you can look up more details about it.

Conditional Formatting

Conditional formatting involves decision making in a somewhat different sense. You use conditional formatting to ask Excel to format a cell or group of cells differently depending on their own contents or their contents relative to the contents of a specified range of cells; in other words, depending on whether certain conditions are satisfied. That is the decision-making aspect of it.

This is an abstract description and you are probably wondering how useful that can be. It can be very useful in visualizing your data or model output. Let us consider a few examples to understand how.

You are probably already familiar with and have been using conditional formatting without realizing it. Chances are you have used formats where negative numbers are formatted with parentheses around them or are shown in red with parentheses around them. This is conditional formatting except that in this case the conditional formatting is built into the format you picked from the formatting dialog box.

You may think that negative numbers will stand out even better if their cells are shaded in some color as well. Or if you have the total one-year returns for 100 funds and want to highlight those with higher than average returns, returns in the top 10%, and so on, you can use conditional formatting to do that.

Conditional formatting has been around in several previous versions of Excel, but it had limited features and was not used much because it was not very useful. In Excel 2007 conditional formatting is a significantly more powerful feature. You will not have access to most of these powerful features unless you upgrade to Excel 2007. So if after reading this section you feel that the presentation of your data and outputs can significantly benefit from the use of conditional formatting, then consider upgrading to Excel 2007.

Like many other features of Excel, you can learn conditional formatting much more easily by experimenting on your own on the screen instead of reading pages of descriptions. So I will cover conditional formatting briefly, primarily to point out the various things you can do with it. If any of those is of interest to you, just try to apply it to your worksheet and I am certain it will not take more than a few minutes of trying.

To apply conditional formatting to any range of cells, select them and then select Home ⇨ Styles ⇨ Conditional Formatting to see the options available (see Figure 5.10). Let me go through one of these options to explain how you apply conditional formatting.

You use the first option, Highlight Cells Rules, to highlight cells that meet rules you specify. Clicking the arrow on the right will open the fly-out menu shown in Figure 5.11 with the choice of the kinds of rules you can specify. You can specify special formatting for cells with values greater than certain values, less than certain values, and so on.

When you choose one of these options (in this case Greater Than ...), you will see a dialog box similar to the one shown in Figure 5.12 where, in the box on the left, you can enter the value (or reference to a cell) that is to be used for the test and from the dropdown list on the right you can select the formatting that should be applied to the cell if the specified condition is met. In this dropdown list Excel offers you several predesigned formats and also the option to create your own customized format.

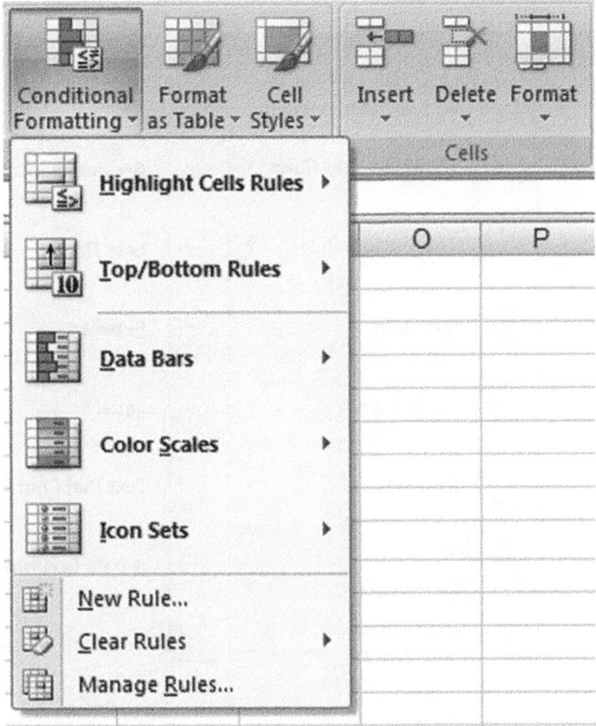

FIGURE 5.10 Conditional formatting menu.

The other choices you can make (shown in Figure 5.11) for setting rules are self-explanatory. If none of these rules meet your need, you can click More Rules at the bottom, which will open the dialog box New Formatting Rule (shown in Figure 5.13). It gives you the flexibility to create your own more specific rule and the format you want to apply when the rule is satisfied for a cell.

One important thing to keep in mind is that even though you can apply conditional formatting to just one cell, more often you would apply the same conditional formatting to a range of cells so that cells that meet the specified condition will stand out from the ones that do not.

The other choices in the conditional formatting menu (Figure 5.12) are:

Top/Bottom Rules: This offers several options to highlight the top 10 items, top 10% items, and so on in a range of cells.

Data Bars: This option allows you to create a bar chart in the cells where the bar lengths are proportional to the values in the cells.

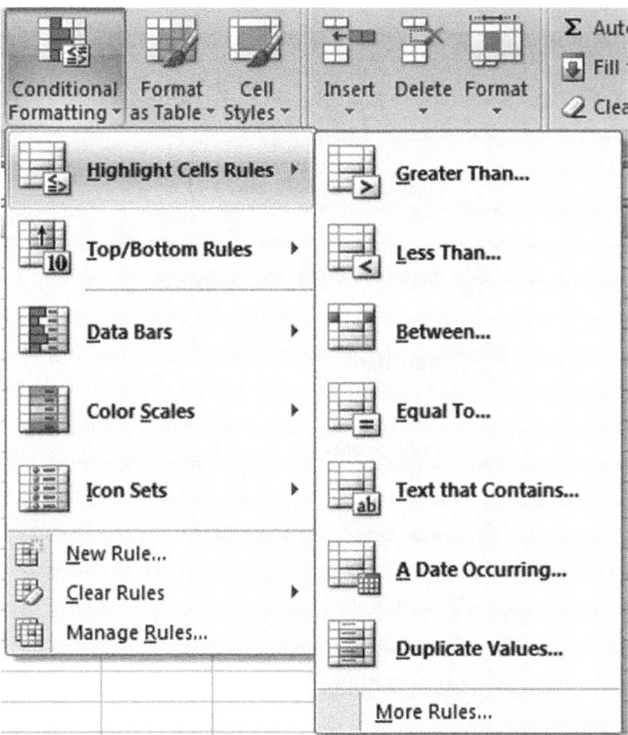

FIGURE 5.11 Options under Highlight Cells Rules.

Color Scales: This option allows you to specify background colors to the cells proportional to the values in the cells. Some people also call them heat maps because you can choose formatting so that the higher value cell in a range will have darker colors (and look hotter).

Icon Sets: You can use this option to include different icons in a cell depending on conditions. For example, you can choose to show an up arrow in a cell where

Greater Than

Format cells that are GREATER THAN:

with Light Red Fill with Dark Red Text

OK Cancel

FIGURE 5.12 Dialog box for setting conditions and formatting.

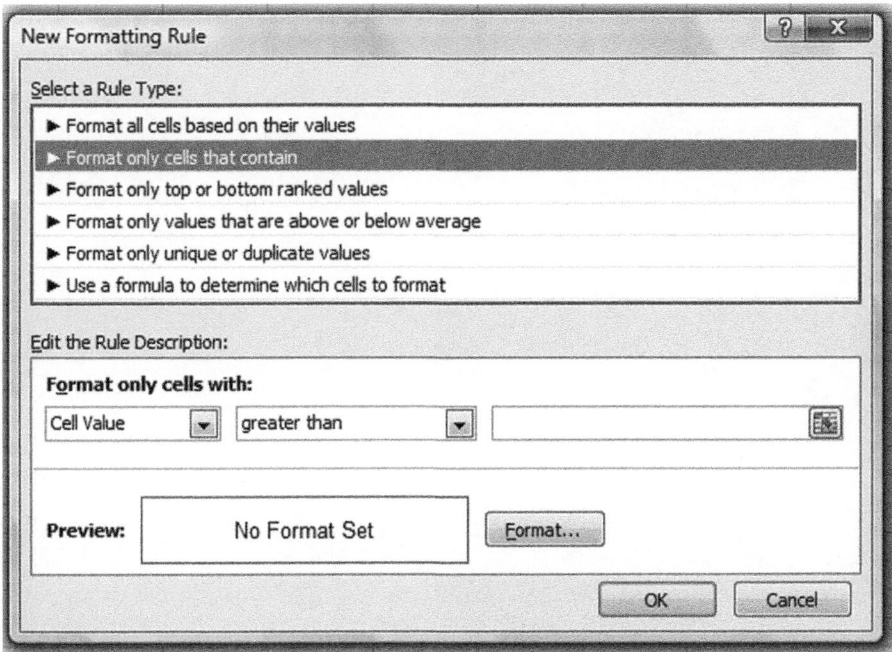

FIGURE 5.13 Dialog box for creating custom rules and formats.

the value in a cell is up from the previous cell, a down arrow in a cell where the value is down, and so on. You can choose to show both the value and the icon in a cell or just the icon.

New Rules: Opens the dialog box we saw in Figure 5.13, which you can use to create your own logical formulas for conditions and specify custom formatting.

Manage Rules: This option presents a dialog box that you can use to create, edit and otherwise manage your rules.

CHAPTER 6

Analyzing Databases

In finance and many other fields we often need to analyze data from flat databases to answer questions, draw conclusions, and make decisions. Excel provides four powerful and highly efficient tools—Sort, Filter, Table, and PivotTable—for such analysis. Analyzing databases with these tools does not constitute modeling in a strict sense. On the other hand, if these tools were not available, we would have to spend a lot of time creating our own models to do the same type of analysis with the data. So it is important to learn these various database analysis tools and use them wherever possible to avoid having to develop your own models.

Let us start by clearly understanding what a database is. A database is information or data about a number of similar entities, such as stocks, customers, employees, or inventory items (which can number in tens to millions), organized to make it easy to access and work with the data efficiently. In a flat database the data is organized—conceptually or actually—in rows and columns similar to an Excel worksheet. Each row (called record in the language of database) represents or holds the data for one entity, and each column (called field) holds the same information for the different entities. For example, in an employee database, each row will hold data for one employee, and the employee name, address, and so on, will go into different columns in the same row. The key is that in a flat database each column holds the same information for each employee. Such a database is called a flat database because conceptually it can be arranged on a flat piece of paper in rows and columns.

Most of the time we work with flat databases or slices of data extracted from more complex databases that can be represented as flat databases. All the Excel tools we will discuss in this chapter are meant to be used with flat databases. So here and throughout the book we will use the term database to exclusively refer to flat databases.

THE MUTUAL FUND PORTFOLIO

Throughout this chapter we will use the stock mutual fund portfolio shown in Figure 6.1 to illustrate the different Excel data analysis features. In many of the figures in the book I have hidden some columns and shown only the first few rows of data to make the figures more readable. The corresponding files on the CD always include the full portfolio.

This is the snapshot at one point in time of the stock mutual fund portfolio of a large investor. The portfolio shows data on 86 mutual funds, although the investment in some of the portfolios at the time of this snapshot is zero. We can view this portfolio as a flat database.

Note that most of the data for this portfolio is made up to highlight the capabilities of the various data analysis features of Excel I want to illustrate. Do not spend any time wondering why a particular fund is shown as more risky than another or compare the data for a fund with its actual historical data. Obviously, you should not use any information from this table to make any investment decision.

The first row is a title or header row. We will use the header for each column as the name of that particular data field. Each subsequent row holds data for one mutual fund, that is, represents a data record.

Here's what the various fields represent:

- The Ticker and Name columns hold the ticker symbol and name of each fund.
- The Investment Value ($000) column shows the market value (in thousands of dollars) of the shares the portfolio holds in a particular fund.
- The Fund Type is Domestic if the fund invests in domestic stocks and Foreign if it invests in foreign (that is, other than U.S.) stocks. (Most mutual funds invest exclusively in domestic or foreign stocks, although there are some funds, called World Stock funds, that invest in a mix of domestic and foreign stocks.)
- The Size Category shows whether a fund holds Small cap, Medium cap, or Large cap stocks. In the investment world, cap refers to the market capitalization, that is, the total market value, of a company. The dividing market values between the categories are somewhat arbitrary and depend on who is doing the categorization.
- The Style Category shows whether a fund mostly holds Value stocks or Growth stocks. As the names imply, value stocks are supposed to be stocks that represents good value because they are cheap relative to their "intrinsic" value, and growth stocks are supposed be stocks of companies that are expected to grow faster than the average company. While the market cap of a company at any point in time is an objective number, whether a stock is a value stock or a growth stock is always a subjective judgment even though investors often use quantitative measures to make the value/growth split. Value and growth investing are considered distinct investment styles, and that is why this field is called the Style Category.

◇	A	B	C	D	E	F	G	H	I	J	K	L	M	N	O	P	Q	R
1	Ticker	Name	Investment Value ($000)	Fund Type	Size Category	Style Category	Risk Rank	Return Rank	Current Price	52-Week High	52-Week Low	Return 2003 (%)	Return 2004 (%)	Return 2005 (%)	Return 2006 (%)	Return 2007 (%)	Avg. Market Cap ($mil)	Fund Total Assets ($mil)
2	BGRFX	Baron Growth	844	Domestic	Small	Growth	1	2	28.81	55	25.3	31.8	26.6	5.7	15.5	6.6	2,105	6,207
3	JALCX	James Equity	1,114	Domestic	Medium	Value	3	1	5.77	12.1	5.47	26.6	22.1	15.1	16.2	3.6	5,665	10
4	DISVX	DFA Intl Small Cap Value I	0	Foreign	Medium	Value	3	2	9.84	22.3	9.25	66.5	34.8	23.2	28.4	3.0	816	4,467
5	HRVIX	Heartland Value Plus	1,064	Domestic	Small	Value	1	3	17.77	28	15.3	53.6	17.0	1.3	13.6	4.7	988	627
6	MEIIX	MFS Value I	924	Domestic	Large	Value	1	3	16.61	29.6	14.5	25.1	15.5	6.6	21.1	8.0	40,512	13,231
7	VASCX	Van Kampen Small Cap Growth A	403	Domestic	Small	Growth	1	1	6.95	12.8	6.14	39.0	21.8	12.9	12.8	21.2	1,609	486
8	AEPGX	American Funds EuroPacific Gr A	1,671	Foreign	Large	Value	3	3	26.86	57.1	24.7	32.9	19.7	21.1	21.9	19.0	30,505	71,157
9	BLUEX	Brandywine Blue	613	Domestic	Large	Growth	1	3	19.21	36.5	17.5	29.4	19.3	8.4	10.9	23.5	21,544	2,846
10	DREQX	Dreyfus Growth Opportunity Z	671	Domestic	Large	Growth	1	3	5.26	10	4.66	27.7	5.7	5.6	8.0	14.2	31,587	126
11	HIMGX	Harbor Mid Cap Growth Inv	1,010	Domestic	Medium	Growth	1	2	4.87	9.81	4.13	45.0	8.5	19.3	12.4	22.6	4,372	426
12	FCNTX	Fidelity Contrafund	326	Domestic	Large	Growth	1	3	43.39	78.8	38.9	28.0	15.1	16.2	11.5	19.8	34,720	47,670
13	NMTAX	Columbia Marsico 21st Century A	1,976	Domestic	Large	Growth	1	3	8.7	17.4	7.57	48.6	21.9	8.0	18.5	19.9	19,157	4,707
14	TMCGX	Turner Emerging Growth Investor	1,142	Domestic	Small	Growth	1	1	29.55	65.6	26.7	49.3	23.2	10.9	14.7	17.3	958	332
15	JATTX	Janus Triton	0	Domestic	Small	Growth	3	1	7.7	16.5	6.38	28.1	18.1	3.5	15.9	20.7	1,327	123
16	FPPFX	FPA Perennial	1,365	Domestic	Medium	Growth	2	2	19.36	38.5	17.2	37.9	16.3	12.8	4.1	7.1	2,193	215
17	VASVX	Vanguard Selected Value	1,753	Domestic	Medium	Value	1	1	11.21	21.8	9.7	35.2	20.4	10.7	19.1	-0.2	5,152	2,423
18	JAOSX	Janus Overseas	1,611	Foreign	Large	Growth	1	3	21.84	61.2	20	36.8	18.6	32.4	47.2	27.8	6,114	4,345
19	SGGAX	DWS Large Company Growth A	141	Domestic	Large	Growth	2	3	19.4	30.6	17.4	24.7	4.2	7.9	6.9	12.4	38,715	189
20	TIVFX	Tocqueville International Value	1,627	Foreign	Small	Value	3	1	7.82	16.1	7.35	53.7	21.7	21.1	17.0	1.4	10,534	114

FIGURE 6.1 The mutual fund portfolio.

- Risk Rank and Return Rank refer to the riskiness and expected return of a fund. Here, for both, 1 is the highest rank and 3 is the lowest rank. A fund with a Risk Rank rating of 1 is low risk and a rating of 3 is high risk, and a fund with a Return Rank rating of 1 is expected to earn high returns and one with a rating of 3 to earn low returns. So a fund with both Risk Rating and Return Rating of 1 will be a low risk, high expected return fund and most desirable.
- Current Price, 52-Week High, and 52-Week Low refer to prices and are self-explanatory. Investors often look at the current price relative to those highs and lows to make investment judgments.
- The calendar year return numbers (e.g., Return 2003 (%)) represent total returns, that is, returns with dividends reinvested.
- Average Market Cap ($mil) shows the average market cap of the stocks a fund holds. (This information is generally used to assign a fund to the Large, Medium, or Small cap category.)
- Fund Total Assets ($mil) shows the total value of the fund's holdings. This is also called the size of the fund. A fund with large total assets is called a large fund and so on, but do not confuse this with the fund's Size Category. The latter depends on the average size of the stocks the fund holds. So you can have a large cap fund that is small in size.

It will be useful for you to get used to the basic database terminology. To that end, in the rest of this chapter I will use the following terms interchangeably:

- Database, data range, and table. (Note that Excel has a feature called table, which is similar to what we generally mean by a table, but it also incorporates special data analysis tools. Excel calls it table, but that confuses it with a generic table. So for clarity I will use Table for this particular Excel feature and table to refer to generic tables of data, although this will be a departure from Excel's terminology.)
- Record and row
- Field and column

For Excel's data analysis features to work properly your database should have only one row of headings. If you need multiple line headings use wrap text within the cell as I have done.

Sorting

Sorting data is probably the most basic operation in data analysis. Sorting is rearranging the rows of a database based on the values of one or more of its columns. We often want to sort a database in a certain order to make the data easier to understand and work with, or to answer questions about or make decisions based on the data. For example, we may want to sort the fund portfolio by the ticker of the funds in alphabetical order to make it easier to find a fund and information about it if we know its ticker.

During the sort, we cannot move just the ticker (that is, just one field) by itself from one row to another because that would separate the rest of the data for the fund from its ticker and scramble the database. During a sort, entire rows of data have to be moved to new positions to maintain the integrity of each data record.

SORTING ON ONE FIELD

To sort the fund portfolio database on any column, select any cell in that column and choose Home ⇨ Editing ⇨ Sort & Filter ⇨ Sort A to Z. Notice that you do not have to define the range of the database on the spreadsheet; Excel can guess it and assumes that the first row of the range contains titles or headers and not data. Figure 6.2 shows how the fund database looks when sorted by the ticker alphabetically. You can sort in reverse alphabetical order by choosing Sort Z to A instead of A to Z. (As mentioned earlier I have hidden some of the columns to make the figure more readable. This does not affect the result of the sort. When a row is moved during a sort, all visible and hidden fields of a record are moved together.)

Here is some additional information about simple sorts:

- You can sort data by fields that contain text, numbers, or date and time. Texts can be alphanumeric, but in that case you have to think through if the sorted data will come out in the order you want when you sort alphabetically.
- You can also sort data by cell color, font color, and icon. If you need to do that, consult Excel's Help.
- You cannot sort by partial contents of a field. For example, if you have full names (including middle initials) of employees in a field, you cannot sort the database just by last name. If you want to sort by last name, you will have to split the name into separate last name, first name, and middle initial columns and then sort by the last name. (As we will see a little later, once you have split the name field, you can then sort by last name and after that by first name and middle initial, as is customary.)
- You cannot sort by values calculated based on one or more fields. For example, you cannot sort the database on the average rate of return for the funds for the years 2003 to 2007. To do so, you will have to first create (that is, add to your database) a new column with a formula to calculate the average returns from the other columns and then sort by that column.

	A	B	C	D	E	F	G	H	I	L	Q	R
1	Ticker	Name	Investment Value ($000)	Fund Type	Size Category	Style Category	Risk Rank	Return Rank	Current Price	Return 2003 (%)	Avg. Market Cap ($mil)	Fund Total Assets ($mil)
2	ACIOX	American Century Intl Opport Instl	1,395	Foreign	Medium	Growth	3	3	3.63	40.3	1,328	67
3	AEPGX	American Funds EuroPacific Gr A	1,671	Foreign	Large	Value	3	3	26.86	32.9	30,505	71,157
4	ARTIX	Artisan International Inv	384	Foreign	Large	Growth	2	3	13.74	29.1	24,859	6,494
5	ARTKX	Artisan International Value	1,866	Foreign	Medium	Value	3	3	16.45	56.6	6,597	835
6	ARTQX	Artisan Mid Cap Value	1,957	Domestic	Medium	Value	1	1	11.74	36.8	3,738	2,501
7	ATHAX	American Century Heritage A	175	Domestic	Medium	Growth	2	3	11.04	21.2	7,177	1,612
8	BARAX	Baron Asset	577	Domestic	Medium	Growth	3	1	35.23	27.3	4,963	3,741
9	BCSIX	Brown Capital Mgmt Small Co Instl	1,493	Domestic	Small	Growth	3	1	22.66	41.7	930	297
10	BEGRX	Mutual Beacon Z	718	Domestic	Large	Value	3	2	8.67	29.4	17,065	4,141
11	BGRFX	Baron Growth	844	Domestic	Small	Growth	1	2	28.81	31.8	2,105	6,207
12	BLUEX	Brandywine Blue	613	Domestic	Large	Growth	1	3	19.21	29.4	21,544	2,846
13	BMCIX	BlackRock U.S. Opportunities Instl	1,072	Domestic	Medium	Growth	1	1	22.45	47.8	3,454	862
14	BREAX	BlackRock International Opp A	1,907	Foreign	Medium	Growth	3	1	19.61	48.6	9,477	858
15	BRWIX	Brandywine	1,015	Domestic	Medium	Growth	3	2	19.45	31.5	5,432	2,442
16	BUFSX	Buffalo Small Cap	257	Domestic	Small	Growth	2	1	14.99	51.2	1,127	1,067
17	CHASX	Chase Growth	0	Domestic	Large	Growth	2	3	13.53	17.9	48,207	453
18	CSCPX	CMG Small Cap Value	1,205	Domestic	Small	Value	1	3	7.65	28.1	671	19
19	CSIEX	Calvert Social Investment Equity A	1,511	Domestic	Large	Growth	2	2	22.15	22.3	25,261	836
20	DISVX	DFA Intl Small Cap Value I	0	Foreign	Medium	Value	3	2	9.84	66.5	816	4,467

FIGURE 6.2 Portfolio alphabetically sorted on ticker.

- Hidden rows are not moved when you sort rows. Most of the time you will want to sort all rows in the database and therefore should make sure before sorting that no row in the database is hidden. But in rare situations when you do not want certain rows moved during a sort, hide them before sorting. As I mentioned earlier, when you do a row sort, data even in hidden columns are moved with their rows.

SORTING USING CUSTOM LISTS

You can also sort data in an order other than a standard order such as alphabetical. For example, you may want to sort the fund portfolio database by the Size Category field and put the small cap stock funds at the top, the medium cap ones next, and the large cap ones at the bottom. To do a sort like this you have to use a Custom List to tell Excel the order in which you want the values of a field sorted. If the Custom List you need does not already exist, you can easily create and save it for future use. (Excel comes with four Custom Lists for sorting by the days of the week and the months of the year.)

To do the sort, choose Home ⇨ Editing ⇨ Sort & Filter ⇨ Custom Sort to display the Sort dialog box shown in Figure 6.3. From the dropdown list under Column choose Size Category, which should show in the box next to Sort by. The box under Sort on should show Values. If it shows something else, choose Values from the dropdown list under Sort On.

Next open the dropdown list under Order and choose Custom List. This will open the Custom Lists dialog box shown in Figure 6.4. In the List entries box enter Small, Medium, Large in that order in three separate lines by pressing Enter

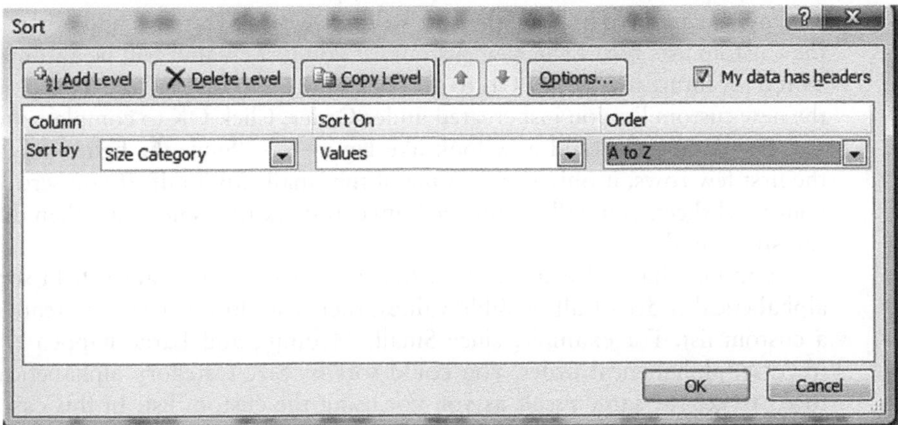

FIGURE 6.3 Sort dialog box to sort by Size Category.

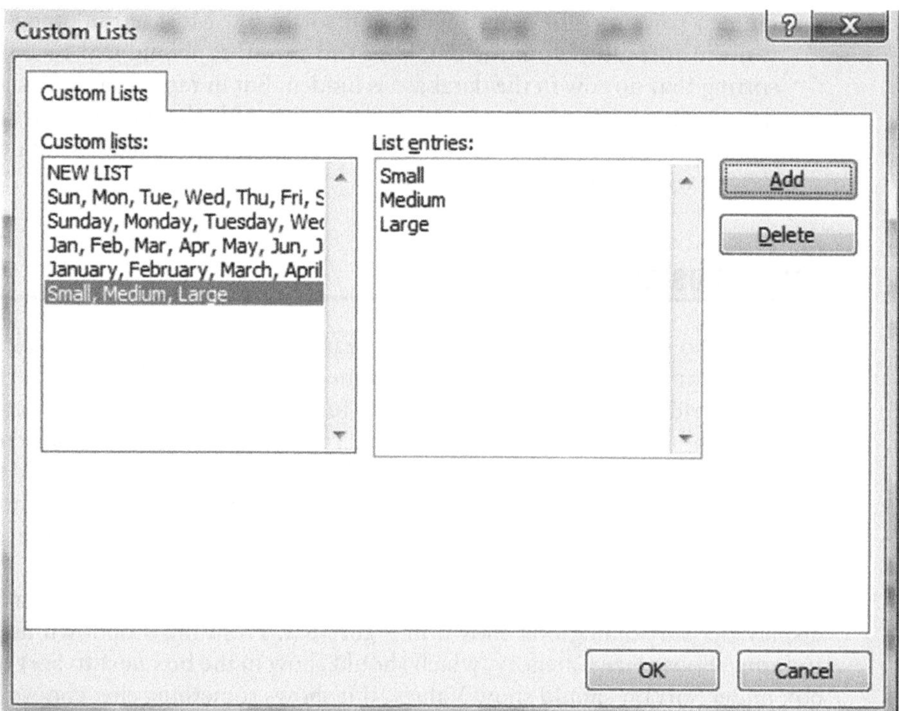

FIGURE 6.4 Custom Lists dialog box to sort by Size Category.

after each, and then click the Add button. (The list should be in the sorting order you want and must include all possible values for the sort field. Also, be careful with the spellings. If you do not spell the possible values for a field exactly as they appear in the database, the sort will not work.) This will add a new line in the Custom lists box. (The new custom list you just created will be automatically stored for future use.) Click OK to get back to the Sort dialog box. You should see the new custom list you just created under Order. Click OK to complete the sort.

The database should now look like Figure 6.5. (Since the figure only shows the first few rows, it only shows some of the small cap funds. If you scroll down your worksheet, you will see the medium cap stock funds next and then the large cap stock funds.)

You may have already realized that if in a sort you want a field sorted in alphabetical order of all possible values, then you do not need to create or use a custom list. For example, since Small, Medium, and Large happen to be in (reverse) alphabetical order, you could sort by Size Category alphabetically (Z to A) to get the same result as you got using the custom list. In this case using the custom list was a matter of taste. However, when the order you want is not alphabetical, you have to use a custom list.

	A	B	C	D	E	F	G	H	I	L	Q	R
1	Ticker	Name	Investment Value ($000)	Fund Type	Size Category	Style Category	Risk Rank	Return Rank	Current Price	Return 2003 (%)	Avg. Market Cap ($mil)	Fund Total Assets ($mil)
2	BGRFX	Baron Growth	844	Domestic	Small	Growth	1	2	28.81	31.8	2,105	6,207
3	VASCX	Van Kampen Small Cap Growth A	403	Domestic	Small	Growth	1	1	6.95	39.0	1,609	486
4	TMCGX	Turner Emerging Growth Investor	1,142	Domestic	Small	Growth	1	1	29.55	49.3	958	332
5	JATTX	Janus Triton	0	Domestic	Small	Growth	3	1	7.7	28.1	1,327	123
6	VSGIX	Vanguard Small Cap Growth Index Instl	1,668	Domestic	Small	Growth	1	3	10.94	43.1	1,285	3,304
7	PRIDX	T. Rowe Price International Discovery	937	Foreign	Small	Growth	1	1	22.15	65.3	1,216	1,373
8	MIDAX	MFS International New Discovery A	694	Foreign	Small	Growth	2	3	12.12	48.6	3,497	1,780
9	LSBAX	Lord Abbett Small-Cap Blend A	138	Domestic	Small	Growth	3	3	10.04	52.4	1,059	1,054
10	NCLEX	Nicholas Limited Edition I	280	Domestic	Small	Growth	2	2	12.67	39.6	1,150	123
11	EPIEX	Epoch International Small Cap Inst	463	Foreign	Small	Growth	2	2	11.16	42.1	2,339	151
12	SSCTX	RidgeWorth Small Cap Growth Stock I	1,500	Domestic	Small	Growth	1	1	8.65	45.6	1,069	330
13	WAAEX	Wasatch Small Cap Growth	765	Domestic	Small	Growth	2	1	18.83	37.4	1,223	523
14	LAUAX	Columbia Acorn USA A	881	Domestic	Small	Growth	1	3	14.91	46.3	1,477	920
15	NBMVX	Neuberger Berman Small Cap Growth Adv	1,166	Domestic	Small	Growth	1	3	8.6	33.4	1,483	228
16	BUFSX	Buffalo Small Cap	257	Domestic	Small	Growth	2	1	14.99	51.2	1,127	1,067
17	VINEX	Vanguard International Explorer	751	Foreign	Small	Growth	1	1	8.57	57.4	1,447	1,079
18	HRSCX	Eagle Small Cap Growth A	399	Domestic	Small	Growth	2	2	19.39	40.4	885	235
19	BCSIX	Brown Capital Mgmt Small Co Instl	1,493	Domestic	Small	Growth	3	1	22.66	41.7	930	297
20	MSSCX	Managers Small Cap	259	Domestic	Small	Growth	2	2	10.14	44.3	806	44

FIGURE 6.5 Portfolio sorted by Size Category.

MULTIPLE SORT

Sometimes you may need to sort a database on more than one field to view the data from a different perspective. For example, you may want to sort or group the funds in the portfolio first into Domestic and Foreign stock funds, then each group into Value and Growth funds, and finally each of those groups into Small, Medium, and Large cap funds. Such multiple sorts are easy to do in Excel.

Start again by choosing Home ⇨ Editing ⇨ Sort & Filter ⇨ Custom Sort to open the Sort dialog box. In the dialog box, from the dropdown list under Column choose Fund Type and under Order choose A to Z. Next click the Add Level button (at top left in the dialog box) to open a new sort level, and there, under Column choose Style Category and under Order choose Z to A. For the third sort open another sort level by clicking the Add Level button again. Under Column choose Size Category and under Order choose Custom List to open the Custom Lists dialog box, and then select the custom list you created in the previous example. Now click OK to close the Custom Lists dialog box. The Sort dialog box should now look like Figure 6.6. Click OK to close the Sort dialog box and complete the sort.

The fund portfolio should now look like Figure 6.7. Often after doing a multiple field sort, it is useful to rearrange a few columns to see the effect of the sort more clearly. In this example, if you move the Style Category column to the position between the Fund Type and Size Category columns, the purpose and effect of the sort will be more apparent. Also, scroll down your spreadsheet to see the full result of the sort.

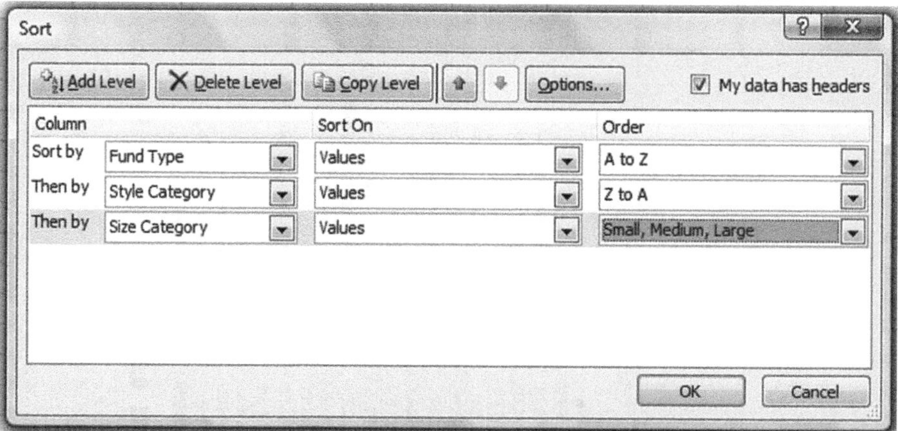

FIGURE 6.6 Sort dialog box set up to sort by three fields.

	A	B	C	D	E	F	G	H	I	J	O	P
1	Ticker	Name	Investment Value ($000)	Fund Type	Size Category	Style Category	Risk Rank	Return Rank	Current Price	Return 2003 (%)	Avg. Market Cap ($mil)	Fund Total Assets ($mil)
2	HRVIX	Heartland Value Plus	1,064	Domestic	Small	Value	1	3	17.77	53.6	988	627
3	RSQCX	Royce Special Equity Consult	765	Domestic	Small	Value	2	2	13.44	35.5	713	456
4	VSMCX	Van Kampen Small Cap Value C	190	Domestic	Small	Value	2	2	9.18	38.1	1,053	364
5	JSCVX	Janus Small Cap Value Inv	424	Domestic	Small	Value	2	2	16.22	36.8	1,330	1,069
6	EAVSX	Eaton Vance Small-Cap Value A	519	Domestic	Small	Value	1	1	9.46	32.7	1,453	17
7	PVFAX	Paradigm Value	516	Domestic	Small	Value	2	1	30.78	60.9	917	86
8	CSCPX	CMG Small Cap Value	1,205	Domestic	Small	Value	1	3	7.65	28.1	671	19
9	TASVX	Target Small Capitalization Value	1,784	Domestic	Small	Value	2	3	12.59	47.1	1,617	369
10	JALCX	James Equity	1,114	Domestic	Medium	Value	3	1	5.77	26.6	5,665	10
11	VASVX	Vanguard Selected Value	1,753	Domestic	Medium	Value	1	1	11.21	35.2	5,152	2,423
12	TRMCX	T. Rowe Price Mid-Cap Value	558	Domestic	Medium	Value	2	1	13.88	39.0	5,259	4,844
13	ARTQX	Artisan Mid Cap Value	1,957	Domestic	Medium	Value	1	1	11.74	36.8	3,738	2,501
14	HRSVX	Heartland Select Value	1,692	Domestic	Medium	Value	2	2	16.72	35.7	5,136	259
15	MEIIX	MFS Value I	924	Domestic	Large	Value	1	3	16.61	25.1	40,512	13,231
16	BEGRX	Mutual Beacon Z	718	Domestic	Large	Value	3	2	8.67	29.4	17,065	4,141
17	VEIPX	Vanguard Equity-Income	1,802	Domestic	Large	Value	3	3	15.9	25.1	46,628	3,736
18	PRFDX	T. Rowe Price Equity Income	1,012	Domestic	Large	Value	3	1	16.58	25.8	30,710	15,324
19	LSGIX	Loomis Sayles Value Y	0	Domestic	Large	Value	2	1	13.58	26.2	44,593	338
20	YACKX	Yacktman	409	Domestic	Large	Value	1	3	9.43	33.0	33,410	297
21	DODGX	Dodge & Cox Stock	527	Domestic	Large	Value	3	1	70.65	32.3	38,890	32,430
22	BGRFX	Baron Growth	844	Domestic	Small	Growth	1	2	28.81	31.8	2,105	6,207
23	VASCX	Van Kampen Small Cap Growth A	403	Domestic	Small	Growth	1	1	6.95	39.0	1,609	486
24	TMCGX	Turner Emerging Growth Investor	1,142	Domestic	Small	Growth	1	1	29.55	49.3	958	332
25	JATTX	Janus Triton	0	Domestic	Small	Growth	3	1	7.7	28.1	1,327	123

FIGURE 6.7 Portfolio sorted by Fund Type, Style Category, and Size Category.

The Importance of the Sorting Order

In a multiple sort the order in which the sorting is done affects the result. For example, in the sort we just looked at, the database is first sorted by Size Category, then the sorted database is re-sorted by Style Category, and finally the resulting database is sorted by Fund Type. To follow the effects of the sorts in steps, manually sort the portfolio one column at a time in this order and check that your sorted portfolio looks the same as the sorted portfolio we got before. Note that this manual sorting order is the reverse of the order in which we specified the sort in the Sort dialog box. (What actually happens is that Excel does the sorting in the reverse order of the order you specify in the Sort dialog box, that is, it starts with the bottom sort in the list and works its way up, which is the same order as you would use to do the sort manually.)

To see more clearly why the sorting order matters, manually sort the database again one column at a time in the reverse order, that is, first by Fund Type, then by Style Category, and finally by Size Category. The sorted portfolio will now look very different and will provide a different perspective on the data.

Another way to choose the right sorting order is to sort starting with the least significant column and work your way up in the order of significance to the most significant column. In our example the most significant column is the Fund Type because we want the other sorts to happen with each fund type. So you should sort on this column last and so on.

Think through why and how the order of the sort matters and experiment with the database to understand clearly how you should choose and specify the right sorting order to get the result you want.

Editing a Multiple Sort

When you specify a multiple sort using the Sort dialog box, Excel saves the sort. You can then edit it as needed. You can add and delete sort levels using the Add Level and Delete Level buttons in the Sort dialog box. You can also move a sort (line) in the dialog box up or down by selecting it and then clicking the up or down arrow next to the Copy Level button. Each click moves a sort line up or down by one level.

Filtering

We often need to find and work with only those records or rows in a database that meet certain criteria. You can use Excel's AutoFilter or Filter feature to do so based on a wide range of criteria you specify. The rows that do not meet the criteria are hidden, and you can copy, find, edit, format, chart, and print the subset of filtered rows (that is, the rows not hidden) without rearranging or moving them. In other words, once you have filtered the database, Excel treats the hidden rows as if they do not exist, which makes it possible to work with the filtered database efficiently.

As we will see, you can easily create sophisticated filtering criteria to meet your needs. You can also filter by more than one column. (Note that if you have manually or conditionally formatted a range of cells by cell color or font color, you can filter by these colors as well. You can also filter by an icon set created through a conditional formatting. I will not cover these criteria here. Refer to Excel's Help if you want to use them to filter.)

FILTERING ON A SINGLE COLUMN

Suppose we want to work with only the domestic stock funds in the fund portfolio. The simplest way to do so is to select any cell in the Fund Type column that has the value Domestic, and right-click on it. In the menu that appears choose Filter, and then in the next menu select Filter by Selected Cell's Value to hide all rows (in this case the Foreign fund rows) that do not meet the criterion.

Note that Excel also inserts a dropdown arrow in the header cell of every column (except the Fund Type column) that you can use to filter further on any of them. The header cell of the Fund Type column has a different icon (the filter icon) to indicate that the database is currently filtered on that column. If you rest the cursor arrow on that icon, it shows the filtering criteria used.

An alternative way to do the same filtering would be to select any cell in the database and choose Home ⇨ Editing ⇨ Sort & Filter ⇨ Filter (or Data ⇨ Sort & Filter ⇨ Filter). This inserts the filter dropdown arrow in all the header cells. You can now click on the down arrow in the Fund Type header cell. This opens a menu that lists all the values in the database in the Fund Type field. To filter on any value (in this case only Domestic), you have to leave only the box to the left of it selected and unselect all the other values. To filter on several values, select all of them and unselect all the others. For short lists you can do so by clicking the appropriate boxes. For a longer list, using a combination of the boxes next to Select All and certain values may be faster. (Find out by experimenting.)

To clear a filter, that is, unhide the rows that were hidden by a filter, click the filter icon in the header cell and click Clear Filter From <Column Name>. To clear all filters and remove the filtering down arrows from the header cells choose Data ⇨ Sort & Filter ⇨ Filter.

Now let us try a more sophisticated filtering on the Ticker field. Suppose we want to see only the funds whose tickers start with the letter T or higher in the alphabet. Open the filter menu by clicking the down arrow in the header cell Ticker. Then choose Text Filters ⇨ Custom Filters to open the Custom AutoFilter dialog box as shown in Figure 6.8. Click the dropdown arrow in the top left box and select is greater than or equal to. In the box next to it enter TAAAA and click OK. The filtered portfolio will now look like Figure 6.9.

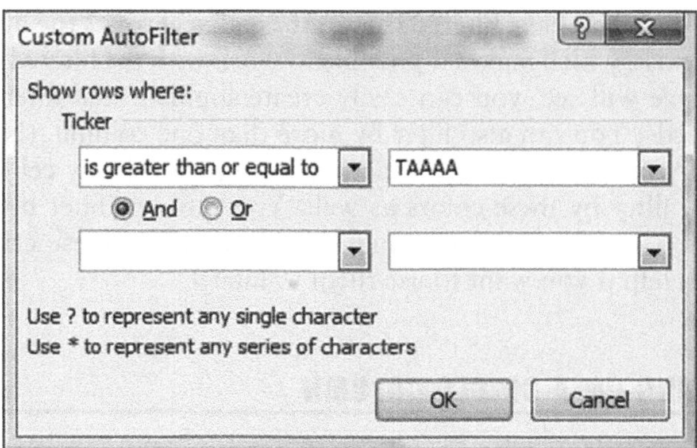

FIGURE 6.8 Custom AutoFilter dialog box.

Take a closer look at the Custom AutoFilter dialog box. You can create sophisticated filtering criteria by combining the various filtering logic provided in the dropdown menus of the left boxes and the values you provide in the boxes to their right. In our example, we used the criteria greater than or equal to and the value TAAAA because the tickers we want to retain would all be greater than or equal to TAAAA.

You can also filter on the same field based on two criteria. For example, if you want to filter tickers that start with the letters D to L, you would create a Custom AutoFilter dialog box that looks like Figure 6.10.

You can combine the two criteria with And or Or by choosing the appropriate button in the Custom AutoFilter dialog box. You can also use the wild characters ? (to represent any single character) and * (to represent any series of characters) to specify values in the right boxes.

To filter on numerical fields, Excel provides many choices. For example, you can filter the portfolio for funds with Fund Total Assets higher than the average Fund Total Asset for all the funds in the portfolio. To do so, click the filter arrow in that field, choose Number Filters and then choose Above Average. Take a look at what other choices are available in this menu.

If you want to filter on more complex criteria, choose Data ⇨ Sort & Filter ⇨ Advanced. Then click the Help button (?) to learn how to use this feature.

FILTERING ON MULTIPLE COLUMNS

You can filter a database on several columns one at a time. The effect of the filtering will be additive, that is, each filter will be applied to only the rows remaining after the previous filters. Unlike with sorting, the order in which you filter does not affect the final result. You can also clear each filter individually to unhide the rows that were hidden because of that particular filtering criterion.

	A	B	C	D	E	F	G	H	I	L	Q	R
1	Ticker	Name	Investment Value ($000)	Fund Type	Size Category	Style Category	Risk Rank	Return Rank	Current Price	Return 2003 (%	Avg. Market Cap ($mil)	Fund Total Assets ($mi
7	VASCX	Van Kampen Small Cap Growth A	403	Domestic	Small	Growth	1	1	6.95	39.0	1,609	486
14	TMCGX	Turner Emerging Growth Investor	1,142	Domestic	Small	Growth	1	1	29.55	49.3	958	332
17	VASVX	Vanguard Selected Value	1,753	Domestic	Medium	Value	1	1	11.21	35.2	5,152	2,423
20	TIVFX	Tocqueville International Value	1,627	Foreign	Small	Value	3	1	7.82	53.7	10,534	114
23	VSGIX	Vanguard Small Cap Growth Index Instl	1,668	Domestic	Small	Growth	1	3	10.94	43.1	1,285	3,304
26	VSMCX	Van Kampen Small Cap Value C	190	Domestic	Small	Value	2	2	9.18	38.1	1,053	364
33	VEIPX	Vanguard Equity-Income	1,802	Domestic	Large	Value	3	3	15.9	25.1	46,628	3,736
34	TRMCX	T. Rowe Price Mid-Cap Value	558	Domestic	Medium	Value	2	1	13.88	39.0	5,259	4,844
49	WAAEX	Wasatch Small Cap Growth	765	Domestic	Small	Growth	2	1	18.83	37.4	1,223	523
67	VINEX	Vanguard International Explorer	751	Foreign	Small	Growth	1	1	8.57	57.4	1,447	1,079
72	YACKX	Yacktman	409	Domestic	Large	Value	1	3	9.43	33.0	33,410	297
73	TAVIX	Third Avenue International Value	275	Foreign	Medium	Value	2	3	10.59	54.7	2,788	1,071
74	TBGVX	Tweedy, Browne Global Value	1,781	Foreign	Small	Value	2	2	17.52	24.9	10,009	3,846
75	VWIGX	Vanguard International Growth	753	Foreign	Large	Value	2	3	11.87	34.5	24,094	11,033
83	TASVX	Target Small Capitalization Value	1,784	Domestic	Small	Value	2	3	12.59	47.1	1,617	369
85	TCMSX	TCM Small Cap Growth	1,209	Domestic	Small	Growth	3	1	17.18	44.7	1,627	330

FIGURE 6.9 Portfolio filtered for Ticker starting with T and higher letters.

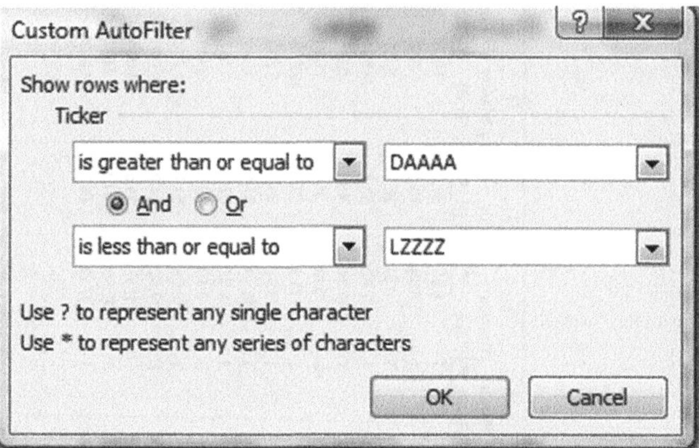

FIGURE 6.10 Custom AutoFilter dialog box with two filtering criteria.

COMBINING FILTERING AND SORTING

You can combine filtering and sorting to produce more sophisticated results. Recall that once you have filtered the database, Excel treats the hidden rows as if they do not exist. Always filter your database first on one or more criteria and then sort the remaining rows. This is safer and easier to understand.

Suppose we want to look at funds with more than $5 billion in assets in the order of their total returns for 2007. First filter the database on the Fund Total Assets column for values greater than 5,000 and then sort it largest to smallest on the Return 2007 column. The database will now look like Figure 6.11.

Tables

To make managing and analyzing databases easier, Excel 2007 has introduced a new powerful feature called Table. Any database can be easily converted to a Table, which makes several new Excel features available to work with and to analyze the data.

(Excel calls this feature *table*, but that confuses it with a generic table. So for clarity I will use *Table* with the *T* capitalized for this Excel feature and *table* to refer to generic tables of data, although this will be a departure from Excel's terminology.)

Table is a new feature introduced in Excel 2007. Excel 2003 has a feature called Lists that has some of the functionalities of Table. But Table is a much more powerful feature with many additional capabilities. If you are using Excel

	A	B	C	D	E	F	G	H	I	J	K	P	Q	R
1	Ticker	Name	Investment Value ($000)	Fund Type	Size Category	Style Category	Risk Rank	Return Rank	Current Price	52-Week High	52-Week Low	Return 2007 (%	Avg. Market Cap ($mil)	Fund Total Assets ($mi
4	NEWFX	American Funds New World A	1,798	Foreign	Large	Growth	3	1	28.83	65.42	26.33	32.9	12,065	10,191
12	HAINX	Harbor International Instl	1,178	Foreign	Large	Value	2	2	35.59	78.85	31.95	21.8	30,865	17,123
18	FCNTX	Fidelity Contrafund	326	Domestic	Large	Growth	1	3	43.39	78.8	38.92	19.8	34,720	47,670
23	ARTIX	Artisan International Inv	384	Foreign	Large	Growth	2	3	13.74	35.84	12.39	19.7	24,859	6,494
25	AEPGX	American Funds EuroPacific Gr A	1,671	Foreign	Large	Value	3	3	26.86	57.1	24.7	19.0	30,505	71,157
31	FDIVX	Fidelity Diversified International	750	Foreign	Large	Growth	2	2	18.99	43.78	17.33	16.0	22,170	29,296
33	VWIGX	Vanguard International Growth	753	Foreign	Large	Value	2	3	11.87	28.77	10.74	16.0	24,094	11,033
37	DODFX	Dodge & Cox International Stock	978	Foreign	Large	Value	2	2	21.56	50.53	19.33	11.7	24,565	24,960
48	SGOVX	First Eagle Overseas A	1,661	Foreign	Small	Value	1	2	16.51	27.81	15.6	8.4	3,879	6,002
54	MEIIX	MFS Value I	924	Domestic	Large	Value	1	3	16.61	29.6	14.45	8.0	40,512	13,231
58	LACAX	Columbia Acorn A	1,382	Domestic	Medium	Growth	2	3	16	31.83	13.59	7.4	1,900	10,666
61	BGRFX	Baron Growth	844	Domestic	Small	Growth	1	2	28.81	54.99	25.3	6.6	2,105	6,207
67	PRFDX	T. Rowe Price Equity Income	1,012	Domestic	Large	Value	3	1	16.58	30.65	14	3.3	30,710	15,324
77	DODGX	Dodge & Cox Stock	527	Domestic	Large	Value	3	1	70.65	157.44	60.19	0.1	38,890	32,430
88														

FIGURE 6.11 Funds with over $5 billion in assets sorted on 2007 return.

2003 and after reading this section you think that Table will be a useful for your work, then instead of learning Lists you will be better off upgrading to Excel 2007. Because Table is far superior to Lists, I will not cover Lists here.

The key advantages of converting a database into a Table are:

- Activating any cell in a Table brings up a new contextual tab in the ribbon called Table Tools. As with the other tabs in the ribbon, clicking on the Table Tools tab brings up all the special tools available for Table.
- One of the new tools in Table Tools makes it possible to apply to a Table one of many standard background and text color formatting styles with just one or two clicks to make the database look attractive and more readable.
- When you convert a database into a Table Excel automatically adds the dropdown arrow next to each header to use for data sorting and filtering.
- You can easily remove duplicate rows (that is, records) of data from a database once you have converted it into a Table. This is a very useful feature because removing such duplicates otherwise is not easy.
- You can add calculated columns to a Table more easily. When you write the calculation formula in one cell of the column, Excel automatically copies it to all the rows.
- You can write formulas that use data from the table with a structured reference, which makes it easier to read and understand the formulas because the formulas use the column names instead of cell numbers.
- You can easily add a Total Row at the bottom of a Table to show, for each column, a summary value (e.g., total, average) calculated from the data in its column.

CREATING A TABLE

You can either convert an existing database (that is, a range already filled with properly organized data) or a blank range that you will fill in with data later into a Table. To convert a rectangular range already populated with data to a Table, activate any cell in the range and choose Insert ⇨ Tables ⇨ Table (or press Ctrl + T). This will bring up the Create Table dialog box. In the window below Where is the data for your table? Excel shows its guess for the range of your database. If Excel's guess is correct, click OK. Otherwise correct the range, make sure that the box to the left of My table has header is selected or unselected as appropriate, and then click OK. If your database does not have any blank rows or columns and is separated from other data by at least one row and column, which generally should be the case, then Excel will most likely make the right guess. In any case, your database or the specified blank range will now be converted into a Table.

To convert a blank range into a Table, in the dialog box you will have to enter the range and indicate if your Table will have a header row. By default a Table has a header row and every Table column has filtering enabled in the header row so that you can filter or sort the data in the Table quickly.

Excel automatically applies the default style, that is, background and font colors, to the Table. You can experiment with and select a different style from selections provided in Table Styles (at the right end of the ribbon) under Table Tools ⇨ Design. (To see all the available styles you will have to scroll down on the scroll bar at the right side of the Table Styles area.)

You can also create and use custom styles. If you convert a range that already had formatting applied to parts of it, then just applying a Table style will not work. You will have to first clear the existing formatting. For these issues look in Excel's Help.

Naming a Table

At the time you create a Table, Excel gives it a default name. To see the name, select Table Tools ⇨ Design and look at the box under Table Name in the Properties area of the ribbon. You can give the Table a different name at any time by typing it in the box. There are a few naming rules (e.g., it cannot contain a space). Excel will prevent you from violating them.

Printing a Table

To print a Table, click the Microsoft Office Button (at the top left corner of the Excel window) or press Ctrl+P, and under Print what click Table.

Converting a Table back to a Range

To convert a table back to a range, select any cell in the Table and then Table Tools ⇨ Design ⇨ Tools ⇨ Convert to Range.

WORKING WITH A TABLE

Keeping the Table Headers Visible

You often have to scroll down or keep scrolling down your worksheet to see all the data rows in a range or Table. For a regular range doing so makes the header row of the range, if there is any, disappear after a point (unless Freeze Panes is used). In a Table scrolling down replaces the worksheet header letters (the A, B, C ...) with the Table headers to keep them visible, which is very convenient. Unfortunately, the dropdown arrows next to the table headers do not remain visible. So to sort or filter using the dropdown arrows you have to scroll up until those arrows became visible again.)

Selecting a Column or Row

To select a column (with or without its header) or row in a Table, select any cell in the column or row of the Table, right-click to open the context menu, click Select and then make the appropriate choice. Note that for a column you have the choice of including or not including the header of the column. The key difference between selecting a column or row in a Table and a regular spreadsheet is that for a Table the selection extends only to the edge of the table; the entire column or row of the worksheet is not selected. This, of course, is very helpful when you want to apply formatting, paste formulas, and so on. You can also select a Table column or row by putting your cursor near the top of a column's header cell or just to the left of a row's first cell, at which point the cursor turns into an arrow, and clicking.

Setting Table Style Options

The Table Tools ⇨ Design ⇨ Table Style Options group provides a number of options that lets you control how a Table displays certain elements in the Table. You activate a Table Style Option by putting a check mark in the box to its left.

You can display the header row by selecting that option and hide it by deselecting it.

Selecting Banded Rows or Banded Columns makes alternate rows or columns of different colors to make it easier to read along a row or column of a Table.

Selecting the First Column or Last Column applies special formatting to them to make them stand out.

Selecting the Total Row adds the very useful special new row to the bottom of the Table. I discuss it a little later.

Inserting a Column or Row

To insert a column to the left or a row above a cell in a Table, select and right-click the cell, choose Insert from the dropdown menu, and then click the appropriate option. In a regular spreadsheet area these steps insert a cell; but in a Table they insert a column or row.

To expand the Table by adding a new column or row next to the current edge of the Table, just start entering data in the new column or row and Excel will automatically expand the Table. You can also add one or more columns and rows to a Table by clicking and dragging the control at the lower-right corner of the bottom-right cell. (When you put your cursor properly on this control, it will turn into a two-headed diagonal arrow.) Note that to add one or more rows to the bottom of your Table using the first method or to expand a Table by dragging the corner, you will need to hide the Total Row first (if it is showing).

Deleting a Column or Row

To delete a column or row in a Table, select any cell in that column or row, right-click to open the shortcut menu, select Delete, and then make the appropriate choice. To delete several contiguous columns or rows, start by selecting the appropriate contiguous cells and then use the same procedure. (Note that in the regular areas of a spreadsheet the same steps would delete one or more cells and not columns or rows.)

ADDING AND USING A TOTAL ROW

As we just discussed, you add a Total Row at the bottom of a Table by selecting the corresponding option in the Table Styles Options group. Total Row is a misnomer in that each cell in this row can be used to show a summary value (e.g., total, average) calculated from the data in its column. It is not limited to showing only the total of the column. Different cells in this row can show different types of summary values.

You add this special row by selecting the Total Row option. Selecting any cell in this row displays a dropdown arrow, and clicking on it opens a dropdown list that shows the different summary value calculations you can choose from. The choices are self-explanatory. You can also use functions not on the list by selecting More Functions from the dropdown list. This opens the Function dialog box to give you access to other functions.

What I have said so far makes the Total Row seem like a convenient feature, but nothing you could not have created yourself by adding formulas to cells at the bottom of a Table. The one thing that makes the Total Row different and powerful is that the calculated summary values shown in this row are based on only the rows in the Table that are visible. So if you filter the table in different ways, the values in the Total Row will be automatically updated to show results based on only the filtered data.

Here is an example to show the power of this feature. In Figure 6.12 I have converted the mutual fund portfolio to a Table and shown the average fund size in the Fund Total Assets column in the Total Row by selecting Average from the dropdown list for that cell. The average is 4,520.

Now suppose I want to find the average fund size for only domestic funds. To see this number I only have to filter the Fund Type column on Domestic. As shown in Figure 6.13, the average is 3,093. This excludes the hidden rows (that is, the Foreign funds).

To realize the power of this feature, think about how you would calculate the average size of only the Domestic funds without the Table feature and how much time it would take you then to calculate the average size of only Domestic Large Cap funds. In a Table you can do this with just a few clicks.

◇	A	B	C	D	E	F	Q	R	S
1	Ticker	Name	Investment Value ($000)	Fund Type	Size Category	Style Category	Avg. Market Cap ($mil)	Fund Total Assets ($mil)	
2	BGRFX	Baron Growth	844	Domestic	Small	Growth	2,105	6,207	
3	JALCX	James Equity	1,114	Domestic	Medium	Value	5,665	10	
4	DISVX	DFA Intl Small Cap Value I	0	Foreign	Medium	Value	816	4,467	
5	HRVIX	Heartland Value Plus	1,064	Domestic	Small	Value	988	627	
6	MEIIX	MFS Value I	924	Domestic	Large	Value	40,512	13,231	
7	VASCX	Van Kampen Small Cap Growth A	403	Domestic	Small	Growth	1,609	486	
8	AEPGX	American Funds EuroPacific Gr A	1,671	Foreign	Large	Value	30,505	71,157	
9	BLUEX	Brandywine Blue	613	Domestic	Large	Growth	21,544	2,846	
10	DREQX	Dreyfus Growth Opportunity Z	671	Domestic	Large	Growth	31,587	126	
11	HIMGX	Harbor Mid Cap Growth Inv	1,010	Domestic	Medium	Growth	4,372	426	
12	FCNTX	Fidelity Contrafund	326	Domestic	Large	Growth	34,720	47,670	
13	NMTAX	Columbia Marsico 21st Century A	1,976	Domestic	Large	Growth	19,157	4,707	
14	TMCGX	Turner Emerging Growth Investor	1,142	Domestic	Small	Growth	958	332	
15	JATTX	Janus Triton	0	Domestic	Small	Growth	1,327	123	
16	FPPFX	FPA Perennial	1,365	Domestic	Medium	Growth	2,193	215	
17	VASVX	Vanguard Selected Value	1,753	Domestic	Medium	Value	5,152	2,423	
18	JAOSX	Janus Overseas	1,611	Foreign	Large	Growth	6,114	4,345	
19	SGGAX	DWS Large Company Growth A	141	Domestic	Large	Growth	38,715	189	
20	TIVFX	Tocqueville International Value	1,627	Foreign	Small	Value	10,534	114	
21	FDSSX	Fidelity Stock Selector	0	Domestic	Large	Growth	31,143	595	
22	CSIEX	Calvert Social Investment Equity A	1,511	Domestic	Large	Growth	25,261	836	
23	VSGIX	Vanguard Small Cap Growth Index Instl	1,668	Domestic	Small	Growth	1,285	3,304	
24	RSQCX	Royce Special Equity Consult	765	Domestic	Small	Value	713	456	
25	FDIVX	Fidelity Diversified International	750	Foreign	Large	Growth	22,170	29,296	
26	VSMCX	Van Kampen Small Cap Value C	190	Domestic	Small	Value	1,053	364	
27	BRWIX	Brandywine	1,015	Domestic	Medium	Growth	5,432	2,442	
28	DODFX	Dodge & Cox International Stock	978	Foreign	Large	Value	24,565	24,960	
29	BREAX	BlackRock International Opp A	1,907	Foreign	Medium	Growth	9,477	858	
30	ARTKX	Artisan International Value	1,866	Foreign	Medium	Value	6,597	835	
31	BEGRX	Mutual Beacon Z	718	Domestic	Large	Value	17,065	4,141	
32	ACIOX	American Century Intl Opport Instl	1,395	Foreign	Medium	Growth	1,328	67	
33	VEIPX	Vanguard Equity-Income	1,802	Domestic	Large	Value	46,628	3,736	
34	TRMCX	T. Rowe Price Mid-Cap Value	558	Domestic	Medium	Value	5,259	4,844	
35	PRIDX	T. Rowe Price International Discovery	937	Foreign	Small	Growth	1,216	1,373	
36	MIDAX	MFS International New Discovery A	694	Foreign	Small	Growth	3,497	1,780	
37	JORNX	Janus Orion	1,374	Domestic	Medium	Growth	13,136	2,687	
38	ATHAX	American Century Heritage A	175	Domestic	Medium	Growth	7,177	1,612	
39	PRFDX	T. Rowe Price Equity Income	1,012	Domestic	Large	Value	30,710	15,324	
40	LSGIX	Loomis Sayles Value Y	0	Domestic	Large	Value	44,593	338	
41	LSBAX	Lord Abbett Small-Cap Blend A	138	Domestic	Small	Growth	1,059	1,054	
42	NCLEX	Nicholas Limited Edition I	280	Domestic	Small	Growth	1,150	123	
43	JSCVX	Janus Small Cap Value Inv	424	Domestic	Small	Value	1,330	1,069	
44	EAVSX	Eaton Vance Small-Cap Value A	519	Domestic	Small	Value	1,453	17	
45	EPIEX	Epoch International Small Cap Inst	463	Foreign	Small	Growth	2,339	151	
46	SSCTX	RidgeWorth Small Cap Growth Stock I	1,500	Domestic	Small	Growth	1,069	330	
47	CHASX	Chase Growth	0	Domestic	Large	Growth	48,207	453	
48	MERDX	Meridian Growth	1,668	Domestic	Medium	Growth	3,317	1,040	
49	WAAEX	Wasatch Small Cap Growth	765	Domestic	Small	Growth	1,223	523	
50	OAKEX	Oakmark International Small Cap I	890	Foreign	Small	Value	823	424	
51	MGRAX	MFS International Growth A	394	Foreign	Large	Growth	19,951	670	
52	LAUAX	Columbia Acorn USA A	881	Domestic	Small	Growth	1,477	920	
53	LOMMX	CGM Mutual	560	Domestic	Large	Growth	64,823	458	
54	ARTQX	Artisan Mid Cap Value	1,957	Domestic	Medium	Value	3,738	2,501	
55	PVFAX	Paradigm Value	516	Domestic	Small	Value	917	86	
56	FBRVX	FBR Focus	502	Domestic	Medium	Growth	2,220	661	
57	PITIX	Principal International Growth Inst	1,807	Foreign	Large	Growth	18,803	1,243	
58	BARAX	Baron Asset	577	Domestic	Medium	Growth	4,963	3,741	
59	NBMVX	Neuberger Berman Small Cap Growth Adv	1,166	Domestic	Small	Growth	1,483	228	
60	EKJAX	Evergreen Large Company Growth A	1,037	Domestic	Large	Growth	38,484	229	
61	HAINX	Harbor International Instl	1,178	Foreign	Large	Value	30,865	17,129	
62	BUFSX	Buffalo Small Cap	257	Domestic	Small	Growth	1,127	1,067	
63	NEWFX	American Funds New World A	1,798	Foreign	Large	Growth	12,065	10,191	
64	CSCPX	CMG Small Cap Value	1,205	Domestic	Small	Value	671	19	
65	OIGYX	Oppenheimer International Growth Y	1,185	Foreign	Large	Growth	11,037	1,926	
66	ARTIX	Artisan International Inv	384	Foreign	Large	Growth	24,859	6,494	
67	VINEX	Vanguard International Explorer	751	Foreign	Small	Growth	1,447	1,079	
68	LAIAX	Columbia Acorn International A	1,744	Foreign	Medium	Growth	1,495	2,724	
69	HRSCX	Eagle Small Cap Growth A	399	Domestic	Small	Growth	885	235	
70	LACAX	Columbia Acorn A	1,382	Domestic	Medium	Growth	1,900	10,666	
71	BCSIX	Brown Capital Mgmt Small Co Instl	1,493	Domestic	Small	Growth	930	297	
72	YACKX	Yacktman	409	Domestic	Large	Value	33,410	297	
73	TAVIX	Third Avenue International Value	275	Foreign	Medium	Value	2,788	1,071	
74	TBGVX	Tweedy, Browne Global Value	1,781	Foreign	Small	Value	10,009	3,846	
75	VWIGX	Vanguard International Growth	753	Foreign	Large	Value	24,094	11,033	
76	EALCX	Eaton Vance Large-Cap Growth A	649	Domestic	Large	Growth	39,910	70	
77	HFMCX	Hartford Midcap A	1,053	Domestic	Medium	Growth	4,123	1,727	
78	IEGAX	AIM International Small Company A	1,803	Foreign	Medium	Growth	934	264	
79	LSAIX	Loomis Sayles Mid Cap Growth Instl	330	Domestic	Medium	Growth	4,448	91	
80	SGOVX	First Eagle Overseas A	1,661	Foreign	Small	Value	3,879	6,002	
81	BMCIX	BlackRock U.S. Opportunities Instl	1,072	Domestic	Medium	Growth	3,454	862	
82	MSSCX	Managers Small Cap	259	Domestic	Small	Growth	806	44	
83	TASVX	Target Small Capitalization Value	1,784	Domestic	Small	Value	1,617	369	
84	HRSVX	Heartland Select Value	1,692	Domestic	Medium	Value	5,136	259	
85	TCMSX	TCM Small Cap Growth	1,209	Domestic	Small	Growth	1,627	330	
86	DODGX	Dodge & Cox Stock	527	Domestic	Large	Value	38,890	32,430	
87	OAKIX	Oakmark International I	1,005	Foreign	Large	Value	14,365	2,772	
88	Total							4,520	
89									

FIGURE 6.12 Portfolio converted to table and showing average size for all funds.

◇	A	B	C	D	E	F	Q	R	S
1	Ticker	Name	Investment Value ($000)	Fund Type	Size Category	Style Category	Avg. Market Cap ($mil)	Fund Total Assets ($mil)	
2	BGRFX	Baron Growth	844	Domestic	Small	Growth	2,105	6,207	
3	JALCX	James Equity	1,114	Domestic	Medium	Value	5,665	10	
5	HRVIX	Heartland Value Plus	1,064	Domestic	Small	Value	988	627	
6	MEIIX	MFS Value I	924	Domestic	Large	Value	40,512	13,231	
7	VASCX	Van Kampen Small Cap Growth A	403	Domestic	Small	Growth	1,609	486	
9	BLUEX	Brandywine Blue	613	Domestic	Large	Growth	21,544	2,846	
10	DREQX	Dreyfus Growth Opportunity Z	671	Domestic	Large	Growth	31,587	126	
11	HIMGX	Harbor Mid Cap Growth Inv	1,010	Domestic	Medium	Growth	4,372	426	
12	FCNTX	Fidelity Contrafund	326	Domestic	Large	Growth	34,720	47,670	
13	NMTAX	Columbia Marsico 21st Century A	1,976	Domestic	Large	Growth	19,157	4,707	
14	TMCGX	Turner Emerging Growth Investor	1,142	Domestic	Small	Growth	958	332	
15	JATTX	Janus Triton	0	Domestic	Small	Growth	1,327	123	
16	FPPFX	FPA Perennial	1,365	Domestic	Medium	Growth	2,193	215	
17	VASVX	Vanguard Selected Value	1,753	Domestic	Medium	Value	5,152	2,423	
19	SGGAX	DWS Large Company Growth A	141	Domestic	Large	Growth	38,715	189	
21	FDSSX	Fidelity Stock Selector	0	Domestic	Large	Growth	31,143	595	
22	CSIEX	Calvert Social Investment Equity A	1,511	Domestic	Large	Growth	25,261	836	
23	VSGIX	Vanguard Small Cap Growth Index Instl	1,668	Domestic	Small	Growth	1,285	3,304	
24	RSQCX	Royce Special Equity Consult	765	Domestic	Small	Value	713	456	
26	VSMCX	Van Kampen Small Cap Value C	190	Domestic	Small	Value	1,053	364	
27	BRWIX	Brandywine	1,015	Domestic	Medium	Growth	5,432	2,442	
31	BEGRX	Mutual Beacon Z	718	Domestic	Large	Value	17,065	4,141	
33	VEIPX	Vanguard Equity-Income	1,802	Domestic	Large	Value	46,628	3,736	
34	TRMCX	T. Rowe Price Mid-Cap Value	558	Domestic	Medium	Value	5,259	4,844	
37	JORNX	Janus Orion	1,374	Domestic	Medium	Growth	13,136	2,687	
38	ATHAX	American Century Heritage A	175	Domestic	Medium	Growth	7,177	1,612	
39	PRFDX	T. Rowe Price Equity Income	1,012	Domestic	Large	Value	30,710	15,324	
40	LSGIX	Loomis Sayles Value Y	0	Domestic	Large	Value	44,593	338	
41	LSBAX	Lord Abbett Small-Cap Blend A	138	Domestic	Small	Growth	1,059	1,054	
42	NCLEX	Nicholas Limited Edition I	280	Domestic	Small	Growth	1,150	123	
43	JSCVX	Janus Small Cap Value Inv	424	Domestic	Small	Value	1,330	1,069	
44	EAVSX	Eaton Vance Small-Cap Value A	519	Domestic	Small	Value	1,453	17	
46	SSCTX	RidgeWorth Small Cap Growth Stock I	1,500	Domestic	Small	Growth	1,069	330	
47	CHASX	Chase Growth	0	Domestic	Large	Growth	48,207	453	
48	MERDX	Meridian Growth	1,668	Domestic	Medium	Growth	3,317	1,040	
49	WAAEX	Wasatch Small Cap Growth	765	Domestic	Small	Growth	1,223	523	
52	LAUAX	Columbia Acorn USA A	881	Domestic	Small	Growth	1,477	920	
53	LOMMX	CGM Mutual	560	Domestic	Large	Growth	64,823	458	
54	ARTQX	Artisan Mid Cap Value	1,957	Domestic	Medium	Value	3,738	2,501	
55	PVFAX	Paradigm Value	516	Domestic	Small	Value	917	86	
56	FBRVX	FBR Focus	502	Domestic	Medium	Growth	2,220	661	
58	BARAX	Baron Asset	577	Domestic	Medium	Growth	4,963	3,741	
59	NBMVX	Neuberger Berman Small Cap Growth Adv	1,166	Domestic	Small	Growth	1,483	228	
60	EKJAX	Evergreen Large Company Growth A	1,037	Domestic	Large	Growth	38,484	229	
62	BUFSX	Buffalo Small Cap	257	Domestic	Small	Growth	1,127	1,067	
64	CSCPX	CMG Small Cap Value	1,205	Domestic	Small	Value	671	19	
69	HRSCX	Eagle Small Cap Growth A	399	Domestic	Small	Growth	885	235	
70	LACAX	Columbia Acorn A	1,382	Domestic	Medium	Growth	1,900	10,666	
71	BCSIX	Brown Capital Mgmt Small Co Instl	1,493	Domestic	Small	Growth	930	297	
72	YACKX	Yacktman	409	Domestic	Large	Value	33,410	297	
76	EALCX	Eaton Vance Large-Cap Growth A	649	Domestic	Large	Growth	39,910	70	
77	HFMCX	Hartford Midcap A	1,053	Domestic	Medium	Growth	4,123	1,727	
79	LSAIX	Loomis Sayles Mid Cap Growth Instl	330	Domestic	Medium	Growth	4,448	91	
81	BMCIX	BlackRock U.S. Opportunities Instl	1,072	Domestic	Medium	Growth	3,454	862	
82	MSSCX	Managers Small Cap	259	Domestic	Small	Growth	806	44	
83	TASVX	Target Small Capitalization Value	1,784	Domestic	Small	Value	1,617	369	
84	HRSVX	Heartland Select Value	1,692	Domestic	Medium	Value	5,136	259	
85	TCMSX	TCM Small Cap Growth	1,209	Domestic	Small	Growth	1,627	330	
86	DODGX	Dodge & Cox Stock	527	Domestic	Large	Value	38,890	32,430	
88	Total							3,093	
89									

FIGURE 6.13 Portfolio filtered to show only domestic funds and their average size.

Note that when you convert a range to a Table, Excel adjusts the width of each column to show the full name of the field and the down arrow next to it (used for filtering and sorting) in one row without using wraparound, as I did until now. So you may want to adjust the column widths after converting a database range to a Table or hide some columns that are not relevant to the analysis you are doing (as I have hidden many columns that are not relevant to this example).

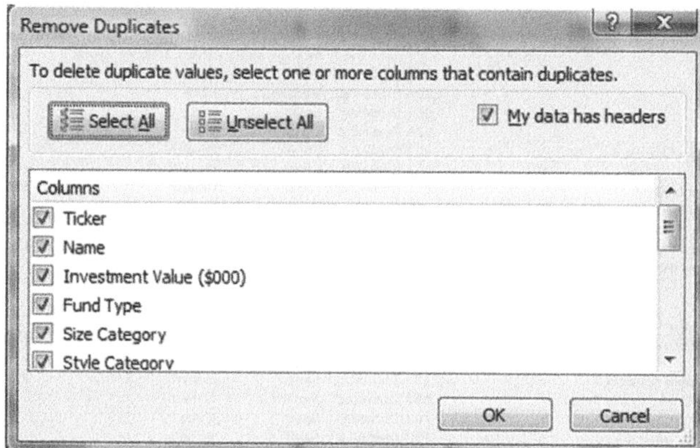

FIGURE 6.14 Remove Duplicates dialog box.

REMOVING DUPLICATE DATA ROWS FROM A TABLE

Databases often include duplicate records that need to be deleted. Without the Table feature you would have to do it manually, which will generally take a lot of time. Moreover, in a large database you are likely to miss some of the duplicates. Table makes it easy to delete duplicate records.

To remove duplicate rows from a Table, select any cell in the Table and then choose Table Tools ⇨ Design ⇨ Tools ⇨ Remove Duplicates, which will open the Remove Duplicates dialog box as shown in Figure 6.14. As the default all the column names will be selected, which means that only rows that have identical values in all columns will be considered duplicates and all but one of them will be deleted. However, once in a while you may want to exclude one or more columns from the comparisons, which means rows with identical values in all the other columns will be considered duplicates even if they have different values in the columns excluded. To exclude a column from the comparison, remove the check mark from the box to its left. When you have the appropriate columns selected, click OK. Excel will remove the duplicate rows and display a message showing how many duplicate rows were found.

Note that Excel compares the values as displayed on the worksheet to determine whether two values are identical or not; it does not compare the underlying values. So make sure that all values in each column are formatted identically before you use Remove Duplicates.

SORTING AND FILTERING A TABLE

Sorting and filtering works the same way in a Table, as we discussed earlier. For convenience, Excel automatically inserts the down arrows in the header row for sorting and filtering when you convert a range to a Table.

USING STRUCTURED REFERENCES WITH TABLES

One important feature of Table is that you can write formulas to do calculations with the data in a Table using the Table name and column names that are easier to create and read than the formulas that you would normally write using cell references. This is called writing formulas using structured references. One additional advantage of using structured references to do your calculations is that your formulas will automatically adjust for many changes you make to a Table.

I will briefly illustrate what it means to write formulas using structured references and some of its advantages, but I will not cover this advanced topic in detail. If after learning the basics you think that it would be helpful for you to use structured references in your application, refer to Excel's Help for additional examples.

Automatically Creating Table Formulas with Structured References

Suppose in our mutual fund database we want to calculate the difference between the 2007 and 2006 total returns. As shown in Figure 6.15, I started with the full database and hid columns C through N to focus on Return 2006 and Return 2007 columns. To add a new column to show the difference, I typed 2007 vs. 2006 Return in cell S1, which automatically expanded the Table by a column. Then I selected any cell in that column and entered the necessary formula to calculate the difference the normal way using the pointing method. In other words, I selected any cell in that row, typed =, selected the cell in the same row in the column Return 2007 (%), typed a – sign, selected the cell in the same row in column Return 2006 (%), and pressed Enter.

Excel entered the following formula in the cell and copied it in all other cells as well to produce the result you can see:

> =Table1[[#This Row],[Return 2007 (%)]]-Table1[[#This Row],[Return 2006 (%)]]

This formula is written with structured reference, that is, it refers to the cells with names that refer to the Table. Although the formula looks long and its format looks unfamiliar, once you look at closely, it is actually easy to understand and read. It starts with Table1 because that is the default name of the Table, which I could have changed, as explained earlier, to a more meaningful name (e.g., FundPortfolio).

The formula uses brackets instead of parentheses. The segment [#This Row],[Return 2007 (%)] refers to the cell in the same row as the formula in the column Return 2007 (%). You should now be able to understand the formula and appreciate that it is much easier to read than if it were written with cell numbers in the normal way. If you select any other cell in this new column you

	A	B	O	P	Q	R	S
1	Ticker	Name	Return 2006 (%)	Return 2007 (%)	Avg. Market Cap ($mil)	Fund Total Assets ($mil)	2007 vs. 2006 Return
2	BGRFX	Baron Growth	15.5	6.6	2,105	6,207	-8.9
3	JALCX	James Equity	16.2	3.6	5,665	10	-12.6
4	DISVX	DFA Intl Small Cap Value I	28.4	3.0	816	4,467	-25.4
5	HRVIX	Heartland Value Plus	13.6	4.7	988	627	-8.9
6	MEIIX	MFS Value I	21.1	8.0	40,512	13,231	-13.1
7	VASCX	Van Kampen Small Cap Growth A	12.8	21.2	1,609	486	8.4
8	AEPGX	American Funds EuroPacific Gr A	21.9	19.0	30,505	71,157	-2.9
9	BLUEX	Brandywine Blue	10.9	23.5	21,544	2,846	12.6
10	DREQX	Dreyfus Growth Opportunity Z	8.0	14.2	31,587	126	6.3
11	HIMGX	Harbor Mid Cap Growth Inv	12.4	22.6	4,372	426	10.2
12	FCNTX	Fidelity Contrafund	11.5	19.8	34,720	47,670	8.2
13	NMTAX	Columbia Marsico 21st Century A	18.5	19.9	19,157	4,707	1.4
14	TMCGX	Turner Emerging Growth Investor	14.7	17.3	958	332	2.7
15	JATTX	Janus Triton	15.9	20.7	1,327	123	4.8
16	FPPFX	FPA Perennial	4.1	7.1	2,193	215	3.0
17	VASVX	Vanguard Selected Value	19.1	-0.2	5,152	2,423	-19.3
18	JAOSX	Janus Overseas	47.2	27.8	6,114	4,345	-19.5
19	SGGAX	DWS Large Company Growth A	6.9	12.4	38,715	189	5.5
20	TIVFX	Tocqueville International Value	17.0	1.4	10,534	114	-15.5

FIGURE 6.15 Inserting formulas in a Table with structured reference.

will find that the formula in it is the same because in this case Excel does not have to copy the formula in the other cells using relative reference.

You can write the formula the normal way using cell numbers as well. For example, in cell S8 you can type in the formula =P8-O8, and Excel will automatically copy it up and down the column, but in this case the copies will use relative reference.

One key advantage of converting the database to a Table is that if you add a row to it, whether at the bottom or somewhere in the middle, Excel will automatically copy the formula in the corresponding cell of the new row. This happens whether you create the formula using structured reference or normal reference.

PivotTable

PivotTable is one of the most powerful and sophisticated features of Excel. (We will use the term PivotTable to refer to this Excel feature or tool and pivot table or pivot table report to refer to the tables created using the PivotTable feature.) It enables us to organize and summarize the data in a database in tables from various points of view to better understand the information contained in the data, draw conclusions, make decisions, and take actions. Even for a relatively small database the raw data can be overwhelming and not very useful until it is properly organized and summarized. For databases that contain thousands or millions of pieces of data, as many do, the raw data is essentially useless until it is organized and summarized.

We can, of course, use other features of Excel to organize and summarize data. What is so useful and powerful about PivotTable is that it makes the task fast, error free, and almost painless. It often takes just a few clicks of the mouse to create a pivot table. Furthermore, most of the time we want to look at data in many different ways. If we create a summary table using the other Excel features, creating many different tables or modifying a table after we have created it can be time-consuming. Modifying a pivot table or creating a new one generally takes only a few additional clicks.

Another way to think about PivotTable is to recognize that we generally want to ask questions about the data in a database. PivotTable makes it possible to quickly create tables to answer such questions. For example, for the mutual fund investment portfolio we have been looking at, the investor may ask the question, "How much money do I have invested in funds in each of the three size categories?" We can quickly create a pivot table to answer that question. After that, the investor may wonder, "Is the distribution similar for domestic and foreign funds?" PivotTable can quickly modify the previous table to answer this question. And so on.

THE BASIC STRUCTURE OF A PIVOT TABLE

Figure 6.16 shows a pivot table created from the mutual fund database. Before discussing how I created it, let us first understand the basic structure of a pivot table. All pivot tables have the same basic structure, which you must clearly understand from the beginning to learn efficiently.

The area A1:D8 is the pivot table, which shows how the fund holdings (Investment Value) in the portfolio are distributed among the three different types of funds by Size Category (Small, Medium, and Large) and within each Size Category the allocations to the two Style Categories—Growth and Value. This pivot table also shows both row and column totals so that it is easy to see that the total Investment Value of the portfolio is $81,652 of which $27,675 is invested in small-cap funds and so on. (Note that the investment values are in thousands of dollars, so that the $81,652 is actually $81,652,000. Also, the amounts are not properly formatted with dollar signs and commas. As we will see, even when you create a pivot table from a Table or worksheet range where the data is formatted the way you want, the formatting will not automatically carry over to a pivot table. You will have to format the data again in the pivot table, although that is very little work. Another point to note is that the total row and column are not essential parts of a pivot table. You can show or omit them, and you can also replace them with other kinds of summary information.)

It is important and helpful to keep in mind, especially when you are first learning about pivot tables that PivotTable is just a tool to create tables to see and show your data in a helpful way. The table should aim to answer a specific question that you or your audience want answered. So it is best to start by clearly thinking through (and even writing down or sketching out on paper) exactly how you want your table laid out—what values you want to see in the body of the table and how you want them broken down along the rows and across the columns of the table.

A pivot table can have up to four distinct areas: the row area, the column area, the value area, and the report filter area. One or more of these can be omitted.

The Row Area

In our example A4:A7 is the row area. Most of the time you will have at least one field in the row area. The row area generally has fields that represent groups or categories. In this example Size Category is the field in the row area, and the three rows of the table represent the three different size categories in the database. (The elements of a field that appear as a row or column header in a pivot table are called items.)

The Column Area

In our example B3:C4 is the column area. The column area is generally used for categories, time periods (months, quarters, etc.), and so on that you want to see

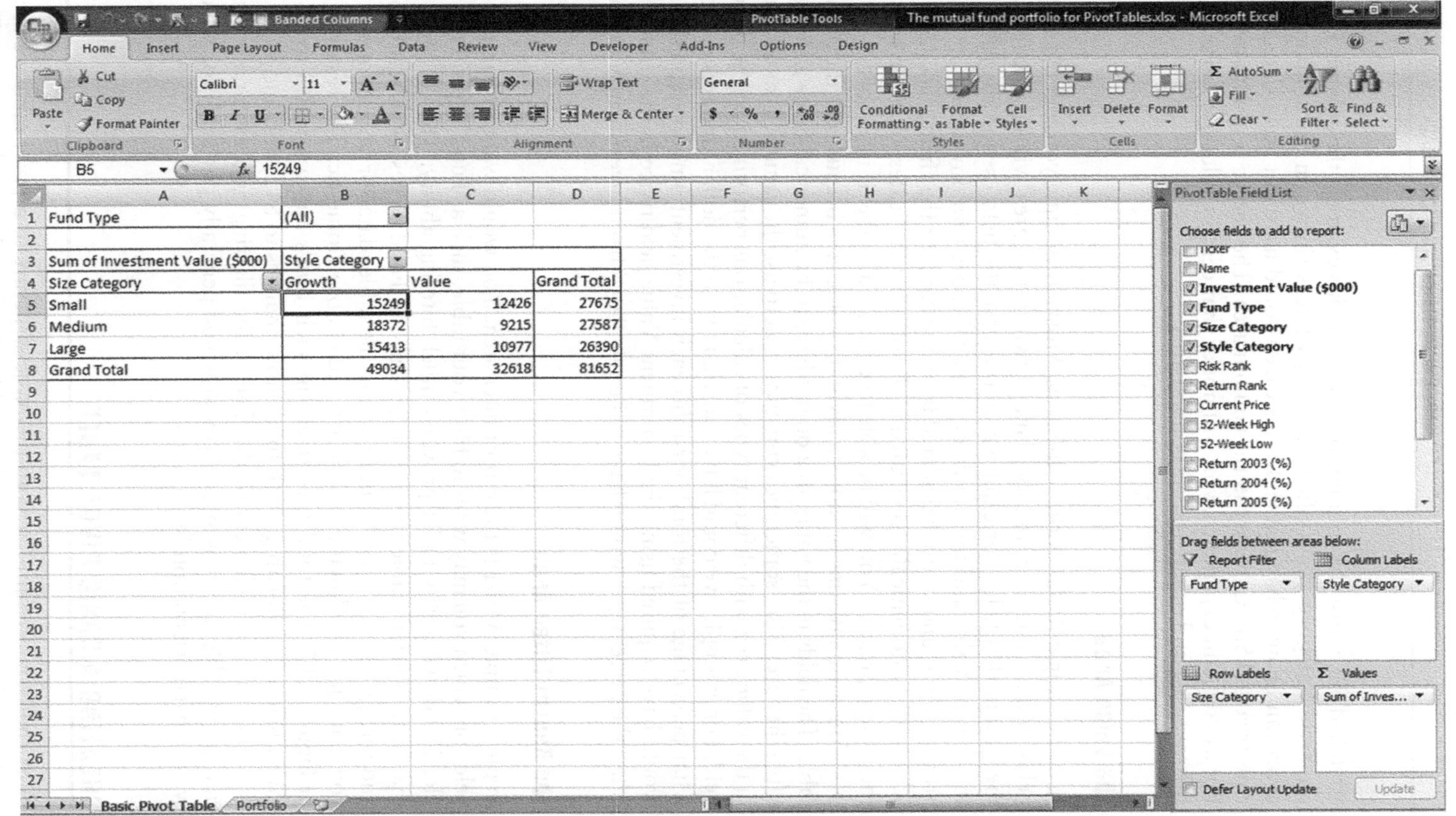

FIGURE 6.16 The basic structure of a pivot table.

stretched out across the columns of a table. In this example the column area shows the Style Category. As is often the case, what is shown in the column and row areas can be interchangeable. In this case I could have put Style Category in the row area and Size Category in the column area. The choice was a matter of taste. But as you gain experience, you will notice that certain fields are more suited for the row area and others for the column area.

The Value Area

In our example B5:C7 is the value area. Most of the time you will put numerical fields in the value area and the data shown in this area will be calculated from the data in that field. For example, in this case the field used in the value area is Investment Value and the numbers in the table are total investment in small-cap growth funds, and so on, calculated from the data for that field. (The label in A3, which was automatically generated by PivotTable, indicates what the numbers in the table represent. You will be able to change this label if necessary.)

You must have one or more fields in the value area because it is the body of the table. The fields in the value area do not have to be numerical fields although very often they are. Also, sometimes you may want to use the same field more than once in the value area with different types of calculations performed on the data in the field. For example, we could have shown, next to the dollar amounts in the table, what percentage of the total portfolio each investment amount represents. This would have required using the Investment Value field twice in the value area because the percentages would have to be calculated from Investment Value as well.

The Report Filter Area

In our example A1:B1 is the report filter area. You would want to put in this area fields on which you may want to filter your table, such as Fund Type in this example. The down arrow in B1 provides quick filtering ability. The All there means that in the current table the data represents all Fund Types, that is, all domestic and foreign funds. If you want to see, in the table, data for only domestic funds, you can click the down arrow in B1 and choose Domestic. The result is shown in Figure 6.17. The total investment in such funds appears in D8 as $50,344, investment in small-cap growth funds now changes to $12,404, and so on.

Choosing each element of the field in the filtering area essentially creates a new pivot table in a new page. So you would generally put fields for which you want a page orientation in this area.

CREATING A BASIC PIVOT TABLE

Now that you are familiar with the basic structure of a pivot table we are ready to discuss how you create a pivot table for a database either from a Table or

	A	B	C	D	E
1	Fund Type	Domestic			
2					
3	Sum of Investment Value ($000)	Style Category			
4	Size Category	Growth	Value	Grand Total	
5	Small	12404	6467	18871	
6	Medium	11523	7074	18597	
7	Large	7484	5392	12876	
8	Grand Total	31411	18933	50344	
9					
10					
11					

FIGURE 6.17 Report filter set to show data for only domestic stock funds.

worksheet range, by going through the steps I took to create the pivot table we have been discussing. Although you can create a pivot table directly from a database that resides on a worksheet as a range, it is generally preferable to convert the range into a Table and then create the pivot table from the Table. The advantage is that if you create a pivot table from a Table and later add new rows to the Table, Excel will automatically update the corresponding pivot table. If your pivot table is created from a range, then after such a change you will have to remember and manually change your pivot table for the change in the underlying data range.

I created this pivot table from the mutual fund portfolio database we have been using except that I have replaced the Risk Rank number 1 by Low, 2 by Medium, and 3 by High, and for Return Rank I have replaced 1 by High and so on. This modified database is included in the CD in the Pivot Tables workbook. You should use this database to follow the discussion in this section.

In working with PivotTable most things can be done in more than one way. I will mostly show you one of them—the one that I think is most intuitive and easiest to use. There are often faster shortcuts to do certain things, but unless you work with PivotTable regularly, you will find it difficult to remember the shortcuts. Start by learning to work with PivotTable the way I show you here, and later if you want to learn the faster ways, look them up in Excel's Help or refer to an advanced Excel book that covers PivotTable in detail or one written exclusively for working with PivotTable.

To start, activate any cell in the Table or data range where the database resides and then select Insert ⇨ Tables ⇨ PivotTable ⇨ PivotTable, which will open the Create PivotTable dialog box shown in Figure 6.18. As a default the Select a table or range will show as selected and Excel will guess and show a Table name or worksheet range in the box next to Table/Range. Also, as a default under Choose, where you want the PivotTable report to be placed, choose New Worksheet and then click OK. (Note the other choices in this dialog box. You may want to use one of them on other occasions.)

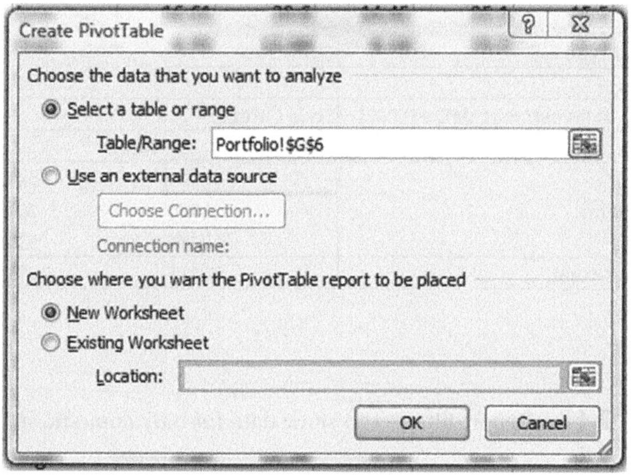

FIGURE 6.18 Create PivotTable dialog box.

Excel will open a new worksheet as shown in Figure 6.19. Notice the new tab, PivotTable Tools in the top line of this window and two new tabs, Options and Design, under it. These two tabs give you access to two new ribbons for working with PivotTable. Initially, as here, Excel will show the Options ribbon.

Look through the different elements in the panel on the right side of the screen, titled PivotTable Field List. The top section lists all the fields in your database, and at the bottom are four boxes where you will tell Excel which fields you want to be placed in the various areas (e.g., the report filter area) of the pivot table you want to create.

A few pointers about this panel: If you click on the down arrow in the icon at the right end of the second row in this panel, you will see options to rearrange this panel in several different ways. You may want to experiment with these, but I find the default layout (as shown here) to be the most convenient to work with. You can also move the whole panel to other locations using its title bar. But I prefer to leave it docked along the right edge, which is its default location. Finally, after you create a pivot table, this panel will be visible only when one of the cells in the pivot table is selected. You can intentionally or accidentally make the panel temporarily disappear by selecting a cell outside the pivot table.

Because we want the Size Category in the row area, click (and hold down your left mouse button) the Size Category in the field list and drag and drop it in the Row Labels box in the bottom section of the panel. (You could also right-click on the name of the field to open a small menu that would let you select the area where you want this field to go.) Drag and drop the Style Category field in the Column Labels box, the Investment Value field in the Values box, and the Fund Type field in the Report Filter box.

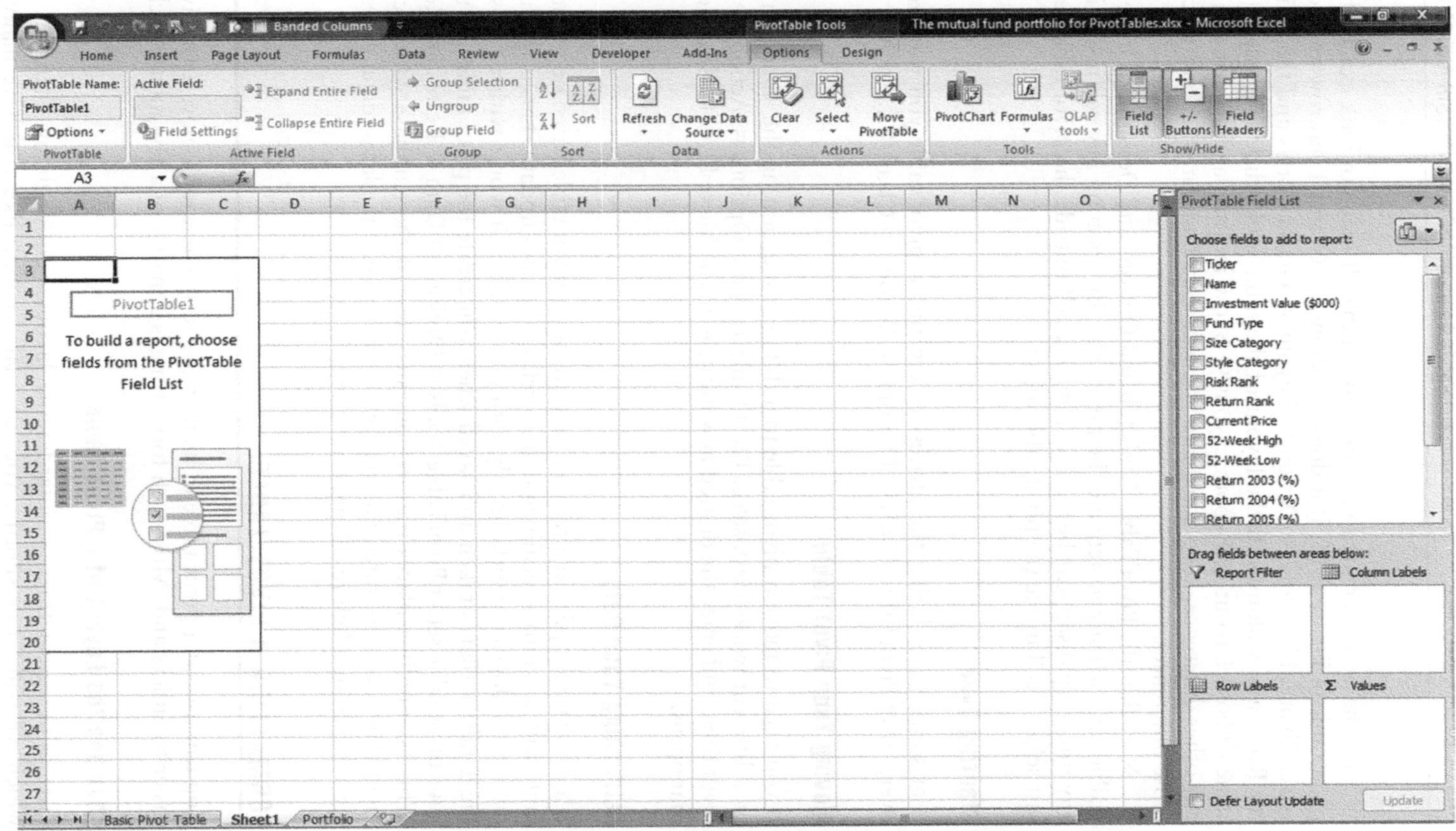

FIGURE 6.19 View of worksheet at the beginning of creating a pivot table.

You have now created your first pivot table. It may not look exactly like the pivot table in Figure 6.16. If it does not show the Grand Total row and column, select PivotTable Tools ⇨ Design ⇨ Layout ⇨ Grand Totals and then click On for Rows and Columns. If the layout of the table looks different, select (on the same ribbon) Layout ⇨ Report Layout ⇨ Show in Tabular Form. If you notice any other difference, keep going and you will soon find out what may be causing those differences.

Note that the PivotTable Tools tab and Options and Design tabs under it are visible only when you activate the pivot table by selecting any cell inside it. If at any time they disappear because you have a cell outside the pivot table selected, just select a cell inside the pivot table again.

Starting Over

If at some point during the process of creating a pivot table you want to start over, select PivotTable Tools ⇨ Options ⇨ Actions ⇨ Clear ⇨ Clear All.

Moving Your Pivot Table

If you need to move a pivot table to a different location (in the same worksheet or a different worksheet), select PivotTable Tools ⇨ Options ⇨ Actions ⇨ Move PivotTable and enter the desired new location in the Move PivotTable dialog box that opens.

Refreshing Your Data

If a database is updated after you have created a pivot table based on it, the pivot table will not automatically update to reflect the data update. This is because the pivot table does not work directly with the database. It works with a snapshot of the database that is taken and saved when you create the pivot table. To update your pivot table select PivotTable Tools ⇨ Options ⇨ Data ⇨ Refresh ⇨ Refresh. (This essentially replaces the previous snapshot of the database with a current one.) Unless you are sure that your pivot table reflects the latest data, you should always refresh it before relying on the data in it.

FORMATTING A PIVOT TABLE

You can format a pivot table in many ways to make it look more attractive and easier to understand. Most such formatting is a matter of a few mouse clicks.

Changing the Layout of a Pivot Table

PivotTable offers three standard table layouts, although by changing styles, which we will cover shortly, you can make it look like you have many more layout choices.

	A	B	C	D
1	Fund Type	(All)		
2				
3	Sum of Investment Value ($000)	Style Category		
4	Size Category	Growth	Grand Total	
5	Small	15249	15249	
6	Medium	18372	18372	
7	Large	15413	15413	
8	Grand Total	49034	49034	
9				

FIGURE 6.20 Pivot table showing only growth funds.

You can change the layout of a pivot table by selecting PivotTable Tools ⇨ Design ⇨ Layout ⇨ Report Layout to open the menu showing the three choices. The layout we have seen so far is the one you get by selecting the Show in Tabular Form choice. This choice creates a table that looks like a regular Excel table (with grid lines and all) except that it offers you the Style Category and Size Category dropdown arrows, which you can use to further customize your table.

For example if you want to show only growth funds in the three size categories, click the dropdown arrow next to Style Category, click the box on the left of Value in the dropdown menu, and then click OK. Your pivot table will now look like Figure 6.20, which shows only growth funds, and the dropdown arrow next to Style Category will change to the filter icon to indicate that the table has been filtered and is not showing all style categories anymore.

If you choose Show in Compact Form in the Report Layout menu, your pivot table will look like Figure 6.21. This is the default layout for pivot tables. As the name implies, this is a more compact format, and it does not show grid lines.

	A	B	C	D	E
1	Fund Type	(All)			
2					
3	Sum of Investment Value ($000)	Column Labels			
4	Row Labels	Growth	Value	Grand Total	
5	Small	15249	12426	27675	
6	Medium	18372	9215	27587	
7	Large	15413	10977	26390	
8	Grand Total	49034	32618	81652	
9					

FIGURE 6.21 Pivot table in compact form.

	A	B	C	D	E
1	Fund Type	(All)			
2					
3	Sum of Investment Value ($000)	Style Category			
4	Size Category	Growth	Value	Grand Total	
5	Small	15249	12426	27675	
6	Medium	18372	9215	27587	
7	Large	15413	10977	26390	
8	Grand Total	49034	32618	81652	
9					

FIGURE 6.22 Pivot table in outline form

Choosing Show in Outline Form in the Report Layout menu will make the pivot table look like Figure 6.22. This is similar to the Tabular Form but does not show the grid lines.

If you look closely, you will see some differences among the three layouts in column widths and other details. The differences will be more noticeable for more complex pivot tables, especially those with layers, as we will see a little later. Because changing layouts is so easy, you can always try out all three layouts with a pivot table you create to see which you like best for a particular situation.

Applying Styles to a Pivot Table

Excel offers a large number of color-coordinated styles that you can apply to your pivot tables to make them look attractive with a few clicks. To see the choices available, click the bottom down arrow in the scroll bar on the right side of PivotTable Styles group in the Design tab of PivotTable Tools. You will have to scroll down in the box that opens to see all the choices.

To preview how your table will look when you apply a particular style, just hover your cursor arrow on the style. You can quickly view many styles, and when you find one that you like, click on it. You can also style a pivot table with banded rows or columns, which makes reading larger tables easier. You can remove a style you have applied by selecting the first (top-left) style in the style window.

As with report layouts, experiment with different styles until you find the one that works best for a particular pivot table.

Formatting the Values in a Pivot Table

Even if you create your pivot table data from a Table or worksheet range where you had formatted the data the way you want to show it, this formatting will not carry over to the pivot table; you will have to format it again. Fortunately this is very little work.

In any of your pivot tables right-click a cell number in the values area and, from the shortcut menu, choose Value Field Settings. In the dialog box that opens, click the Number Format button at bottom-left (in the Summarize by tab). This will open the familiar Format Cells dialog box for numbers. Select the formatting you want and click OK in this box, and OK again in the previous box to finish formatting the data.

MODIFYING PIVOT TABLES

We will now look at how to modify pivot tables using the many powerful features of PivotTable to answer more questions about the data.

Rearranging a Pivot Table

You could have created a table like the simple one we created "manually" using Excel features you already know, although it would have taken you much longer. But now suppose that after you look at the table you think it would be nicer if the style categories were shown down the rows of the table and the size categories across the top. If you had created the table manually, it would have taken a lot of time to make the change. But to make the change in your pivot table, you just drag and drop the Size Category field from the Row Labels box to the Column Labels box and drag and drop the Style Category field from the Column Labels box to the Row Labels box. That's it. Your pivot table should now look like Figure 6.23.

Rearranging your pivot table by swapping fields in the column and row areas, replacing one field by another in those areas, and changing the field you want to show in the value are simple matters. Just add or remove the fields from the appropriate boxes at the bottom of the right panel.

	A	B	C	D	E	F
1	Fund Type	(All)				
2						
3	Sum of Investment Value ($000)	Size Category				
4	Style Category	Small	Medium	Large	Grand Total	
5	Growth	15249	18372	15413	49034	
6	Value	12426	9215	10977	32618	
7	Grand Total	27675	27587	26390	81652	
8						

FIGURE 6.23 The rearranged pivot table.

You can also choose to filter your pivot table by a different field, more than one field, or not filter it at all.

Adding Layers to a Pivot Table

Once you have looked at your pivot table you may decide you want to see how much of the money invested in each size category is invested in high, medium, and low expected return funds. In a manually created table this will be a lot of additional work. In a pivot table, it is literally a matter of one drag and drop move.

In the right panel drag and drop the Return Rank field in the Row Labels box. You will now have a Return Rank line under the previous Size Category line in that box and your pivot table will look like Figure 6.24. (If your table looks different, it is probably because this table is shown in the Tabular Form and you may be using a different report layout. Also, the return ranks in your table may not be sorted in the proper High, Medium, and Low order. You will learn in the section on sorting a little later how to get this order right.)

The table is now a lot more informative. But you can also easily collapse it to show the information in the summarized form as you had before. You can click on the minus signs to the left of Small, Medium, or Large in the Size Category to hide the detailed breakdown by return rank and expand the information again by

	A	B	C	D	E	F
1	Fund Type	(All)				
2						
3	Sum of Investment Value ($000)		Style Category			
4	Size Category	Return Rank	Growth	Value	Grand Total	
5	⊟Small	High	$8,457	$2,662	$11,119	
6		Medium	$2,245	$4,821	$7,066	
7		Low	$4,547	$4,943	$9,490	
8	Small Total		$15,249	$12,426	$27,675	
9	⊟Medium	High	$10,977	$5,382	$16,359	
10		Medium	$4,443	$1,692	$6,135	
11		Low	$2,952	$2,141	$5,093	
12	Medium Total		$18,372	$9,215	$27,587	
13	⊟Large	High	$5,851	$1,539	$7,390	
14		Medium	$3,446	$3,879	$7,325	
15		Low	$6,116	$5,559	$11,675	
16	Large Total		$15,413	$10,977	$26,390	
17	Grand Total		$49,034	$32,618	$81,652	
18						
19						

FIGURE 6.24 Pivot table with a second layer added to the row area.

	A	B	C	D	E
1	Fund Type	(All)			
2					
3	Sum of Investment Value ($000)	Column Labels			
4	Row Labels	Growth	Value	Grand Total	
5	⊟Small	$15,249	$12,426	$27,675	
6	High	$8,457	$2,662	$11,119	
7	Medium	$2,245	$4,821	$7,066	
8	Low	$4,547	$4,943	$9,490	
9	⊟Medium	$18,372	$9,215	$27,587	
10	High	$10,977	$5,382	$16,359	
11	Medium	$4,443	$1,692	$6,135	
12	Low	$2,952	$2,141	$5,093	
13	⊟Large	$15,413	$10,977	$26,390	
14	High	$5,851	$1,539	$7,390	
15	Medium	$3,446	$3,879	$7,325	
16	Low	$6,116	$5,559	$11,675	
17	Grand Total	$49,034	$32,618	$81,652	
18					

FIGURE 6.25 Pivot table with two layers in row area in compact form.

clicking the plus signs that appear in those boxes when the details are collapsed. (You can do so for any or all of the size categories.)

You can also use the dropdown arrow next to the Return Risk header to open a dialog box to show or hide one or more of the return ranks in each Size Category.

Depending on your data and objective, you can add more layers to the row area and also to the column area using the same drag and drop method.

You can make the table look different by changing the Report Layout. For example, if you change the Report Layout to the Compact Form, your table will look like Figure 6.25. Notice that the compact form offers Row Labels and Column Labels filters (indicated by dropdown arrows next to them) instead of filters by field names (e.g., Size Category) in the Tabular Form. But these are equivalent, because if you open the Row Labels dropdown menu you will see further filtering choices for Size Category and Return Rank.

Adding Grand Totals and Subtotals to a Pivot Table

The pivot tables we created so far automatically added grand totals and subtotals. You can control which of these will be shown and where.

	A	B	C	D	E
1	Fund Type	(All)			
2					
3	Sum of Investment Value ($000)	Column Labels			
4	Row Labels	Growth	Value	Grand Total	
5	⊟Small				
6	High	$8,457	$2,662	$11,119	
7	Medium	$2,245	$4,821	$7,066	
8	Low	$4,547	$4,943	$9,490	
9	Small Total	$15,249	$12,426	$27,675	
10					
11	⊟Medium				
12	High	$10,977	$5,382	$16,359	
13	Medium	$4,443	$1,692	$6,135	
14	Low	$2,952	$2,141	$5,093	
15	Medium Total	$18,372	$9,215	$27,587	
16					
17	⊟Large				
18	High	$5,851	$1,539	$7,390	
19	Medium	$3,446	$3,879	$7,325	
20	Low	$6,116	$5,559	$11,675	
21	Large Total	$15,413	$10,977	$26,390	
22					
23	Grand Total	$49,034	$32,618	$81,652	
24					

FIGURE 6.26 Pivot table with subtotals at bottom and blank rows added.

To control grand totals, select PivotTable Tools ⇨ Design ⇨ Layout ⇨ Grand Totals. This will bring up four options that are self-explanatory. Try out all four to see how they affect your table.

Clicking the Subtotals icon next to the Grand Totals icon shows you the options for subtotals, which are also self-explanatory. Again, experiment with them to see how they affect the look of your table.

The Blank Rows icon in the same Layout group offers you the option to add (and remove) a blank row after each item to make your table more readable. Figure 6.26 shows the pivot table (in Compact Form) we have been working with, showing subtotals at bottom of each size category followed by a blank row.

Showing Values in a Pivot Table in Different Ways

When you dragged and dropped the Investment Value field in the Values box, Excel assumed that in each cell of the value area of your PivotTable you want to show the total amount of investment. This is the default assumption if the field is a numerical field. If the field has any data other than numerical data (including blanks) then the PivotTable treats it as a text field and shows counts, that is, the number of data points. But you have the option to show other summary measures in the value area.

Suppose, in the table we have created, we want to show not just the distribution of investment in dollars but also the percentage of the total portfolio each of those investments represents. To do so we will have to use the Investment Value field twice in the Values box because both the values we want to show will have to be calculated from data in this field.

Start by dragging and dropping the Investment Value field again in the Values box. In the pivot table select any of the values in the second column of investment values, right-click to open the shortcut menu, and click on Value Field Settings to open the dialog box of the same name. Click the Show values as tab and open the list of your options by clicking the dropdown arrow in the box under Show values as. Look through all the options available and then select % of total. In the box next to Custom name enter % of Portfolio or some other header you want to see for the new column you are adding. (If you do not enter a name here, Excel will use a default name that you probably will not like.) When you click OK you will see the percent distribution in the pivot table next to each investment amount. If you do not like the formatting of the percent field, select any value in that column, go back to the Value Field Settings dialog box, click the Number Format button at bottom-left and set the format. Your table should now look like Figure 6.27.

This table is a lot more informative and you can answer many additional questions about the portfolio using this table. For example, in the last row you can see that 60.1% of the portfolio is invested in growth stocks and 39.9% in value stocks. You can answer many other questions about the investment distribution in the portfolio by looking at the different rows and columns. What if you want to know what percent of growth stock investment is in small-cap stocks? You can calculate this figure by dividing 18.7% (from C10) by 60.1% (from C21). But you can find it even more easily by clicking the dropdown arrow next to Column Labels in B3 and selecting Growth in the dropdown menu (that is, by filtering the table for the style category Growth). You will see the answer 31.1% in C10 of the filtered table.

You can answer questions about the distribution of investments in Domestic and Foreign funds by using the Report Filter in B2.

You, of course, were not limited to making Investment Value the second field for the value area of table. You could have picked any other field and any of the other Show value as options that you saw earlier when you selected % of total for this analysis. It all depends on what questions you want to answer.

	A	B	C	D	E	F	G	H
1	Fund Type	(All)						
2								
3		Column Labels						
4		Growth		Value		Total Investment	Total % of Portfolio	
5	Row Labels	Investment	% of Portfolio	Investment	% of Portfolio			
6	⊟Small							
7	High	$8,457	10.4%	$2,662	3.3%	$11,119	13.6%	
8	Medium	$2,245	2.7%	$4,821	5.9%	$7,066	8.7%	
9	Low	$4,547	5.6%	$4,943	6.1%	$9,490	11.6%	
10	Small Total	$15,249	18.7%	$12,426	15.2%	$27,675	33.9%	
11	⊟Medium							
12	High	$10,977	13.4%	$5,382	6.6%	$16,359	20.0%	
13	Medium	$4,443	5.4%	$1,692	2.1%	$6,135	7.5%	
14	Low	$2,952	3.6%	$2,141	2.6%	$5,093	6.2%	
15	Medium Total	$18,372	22.5%	$9,215	11.3%	$27,587	33.8%	
16	⊟Large							
17	High	$5,851	7.2%	$1,539	1.9%	$7,390	9.1%	
18	Medium	$3,446	4.2%	$3,879	4.8%	$7,325	9.0%	
19	Low	$6,116	7.5%	$5,559	6.8%	$11,675	14.3%	
20	Large Total	$15,413	18.9%	$10,977	13.4%	$26,390	32.3%	
21	Grand Total	$49,034	60.1%	$32,618	39.9%	$81,652	100.0%	
22								

FIGURE 6.27 Pivot table with percent distribution added.

Summarizing Data in a Pivot Table in Different Ways

You can also summarize the data in the table in different ways. For example, you may want to show how the number of funds break down among size and style categories and return ranking.

To see this, you start with the pivot table we saw in Figure 6.24. Select any cell in the value area of the table and open the Value Field Settings dialog box. Look at the choices under Summarize value field by. The very first choice is Sum, which is the default choice Excel makes for numerical fields. Count, the next choice, is the default option for non-numerical fields and also numerical fields that have any blanks. This option uses the Excel function COUNTA(), which counts all cells other than blank ones. Take a look at the other available options and then select Count. In the box next to Custom Name enter Number of Funds (to overwrite the default name that Excel would otherwise use) and click OK.

Your table would now look like Figure 6.28, which shows the distribution of the 86 funds in the portfolio by size and style categories. You can get the distributions for the Domestic and Foreign funds using filtering as before.

Note that to count the number of funds it was not necessary to use the Investment Value as the field in the value area of the table. Many other fields could be used, and they all would have provided the same results because in this case Excel is only counting the cells with data in them and not looking at the data in the cells.

	A	B	C	D	E	F
1	Fund Type	(All)				
2						
3	Number of Funds		Style Category			
4	Size Category	Return Rank	Growth	Value	Grand Total	
5	⊟Small	High	10	3	13	
6		Medium	5	5	10	
7		Low	5	4	9	
8	Small Total		20	12	32	
9	⊟Medium	High	9	4	13	
10		Medium	4	2	6	
11		Low	3	2	5	
12	Medium Total		16	8	24	
13	⊟Large	High	5	3	8	
14		Medium	3	4	7	
15		Low	10	5	15	
16	Large Total		18	12	30	
17	Grand Total		54	32	86	
18						

FIGURE 6.28 Pivot table showing number of funds.

GROUPING FIELDS

You can use the grouping feature of PivotTable to manually or automatically group fields in a pivot table to summarize your data in ways that you cannot do with the tools we have looked at so far. You would generally want to group data in three types of fields: date fields, numerical fields, and text fields. In financial modeling being able to group date and numerical fields can be very useful. Let us look at a few examples to understand what is meant by grouping and how grouping can be useful in looking at your data.

Grouping Date Fields

Figure 6.29 shows part of a database containing three data fields for a stock: Date, Closing Price, and Volume. You cannot tell much about how the stock price and trading volume varied over this period by looking at this daily data. It would be a lot easier to draw some conclusions if you could group the data by month and show the highs and lows and total trading volume for each month. You can easily create a pivot table to summarize your data by months using grouping. (The database has daily prices going back to the beginning of 2007. The figure shows only a part of the data.)

	A	B	C	D
1	Date	Closing Price	Volume	
2	2/13/2009	57.1	12563900	
3	2/12/2009	57.78	14424600	
4	2/11/2009	57.33	14692600	
5	2/10/2009	56.73	16612000	
6	2/9/2009	58.5	9357000	
7	2/6/2009	58.51	11458700	
8	2/5/2009	58.11	14781300	
9	2/4/2009	57.96	11429500	
10	2/3/2009	58.58	13181700	
11	2/2/2009	57.69	10933900	
12	1/30/2009	57.69	13858500	
13	1/29/2009	58.28	16159300	
14	1/28/2009	58.56	18096400	
15	1/27/2009	57.54	14771500	
16	1/26/2009	56.55	16347800	
17	1/23/2009	55.97	21334000	
18	1/22/2009	56.87	19146100	
19	1/21/2009	56.36	22306100	
20	1/20/2009	56.75	23153700	
21	1/16/2009	57.44	20746500	
22	1/15/2009	57.62	20383600	
23	1/14/2009	57.95	16707900	
24	1/13/2009	58.84	15513400	
25	1/12/2009	58.34	15253100	
26	1/9/2009	59.05	14698300	

FIGURE 6.29 Daily closing price and transaction volume for a stock.

Create a pivot table as before and drag and drop the Date field in the Row Labels box and the Closing Price (twice) and Volume fields in the Values box. To group the date rows in the table into months, select any date in the pivot table, right-click, and open the Grouping dialog box. The dialog box will show the range of dates in the database. Since we want to include all the available dates, we don't need to change the starting and ending dates, but you could change them to do the monthly grouping for only part of the database. In the box under By, select both Months and Years and click OK. (If you select only Months then all Januaries from the different years will be grouped together and so on, which is not what you want.)

	A	B	C	D	E
1					
2					
3		Values			
4	Row Labels	Highest Closing Price	Lowest Closing Price	Total Volume	
5	⊟2007	68.4	59.77	3032240300	
6	Jan	67.76	66.07	175594400	
7	Feb	67.01	62.93	192375400	
8	Mar	62.45	60	318147400	
9	Apr	65.12	60.1	248968100	
10	May	64.56	61.82	280281700	
11	Jun	63.6	60.73	259962000	
12	Jul	63.8	59.77	290358700	
13	Aug	62.49	60.55	331077300	
14	Sep	65.7	61.65	220556400	
15	Oct	66.25	63.95	232885800	
16	Nov	68.4	63.91	284862700	
17	Dec	68.3	66.7	197170400	
18	⊟2008	72.22	55.33	3735191300	
19	Jan	68.31	62.18	339978400	
20	Feb	63.85	61.88	218925600	
21	Mar	65.38	61.33	274621800	
22	Apr	67.37	65.27	221952400	
23	May	68.26	64.88	219962000	
24	Jun	66.96	63.57	228287700	
25	Jul	69.03	64.64	308621600	
26	Aug	71.7	68.1	224063800	
27	Sep	72.22	66.9	367504200	

FIGURE 6.30 Daily stock price and volume data grouped by month and year.

At this point, by default both Volume and Closing Price fields are summed in the value area. Select any data point in the first Closing Price column, right-click, and open the Value Field Settings dialog box. Next to Custom Name enter Highest Closing Price, from the options under Summarize value field by, select Max, and click OK to finish. Set the second Closing Price to show the lowest closing price for each month and change the header for the Volume field to Total Volume (also using the Value Field Setting dialog box). Your pivot table should now look like Figure 6.30. (The figure shows only part of the pivot table.)

Note that you can easily summarize this pivot table by year by clicking on the minus signs in the little boxes on the left of each year.

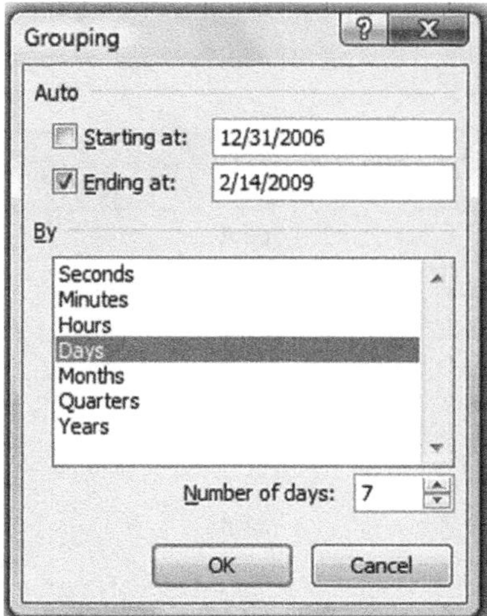

FIGURE 6.31 The Grouping dialog box set to group by weeks.

In the box below By in the Grouping dialog box (Figure 6.31) you used to group by months, Quarters is another option, but weeks is not. What if you want to group daily data by week? It is simple. To group by weeks, in the list under By, select only Days and set Number of days to 7 in the box below using its spinner. You have to do one more thing. Depending on whether you want to count weeks from Sunday or Monday, you have to enter in the box next to Starting at, a date that was a Sunday or a Monday and deselect the box to the left. Then click OK. (In Figure 6.31 I have entered the date 12/31/06, which was a Sunday, to count my weeks as starting on Sundays. Even though the database and pivot table do not include the date 12/31/06, Excel did not complain.)

Obviously, if you need to do so, you can group the dates into any of 1 to 7 day periods using the same method.

Grouping Numeric Fields

An easy and useful application of grouping numeric fields is showing frequency distributions in a pivot table. One of the fields in our mutual fund data base is Return 2007 (%). It may be useful to see how these returns were distributed, that is, how many fell in different ranges.

Create a new pivot table by dragging and dropping this same field in both the Row Labels and Values boxes. Select any return in the row area of the pivot table and open the Grouping dialog box as before. Because this is a numeric field and not a date field, the dialog box looks different, as shown in Figure 6.32. Excel has automatically entered the lowest and highest values in the Return 2007 field in

FIGURE 6.32 The Grouping dialog box for numeric fields.

the Starting at and Ending at boxes. It has also suggested a step increment of 10 in the box next to By. For the moment let us accept those values by clicking OK.

In the Row Labels column you will now see ranges starting with −8.33–1.67. This range starts with the lowest value in the field of −8.33, which Excel suggested and we accepted as the low end of this group, and based on the step increment of 10, the high end for this range is set as (−8.33 + 10 =) 1.67. The next groups are created in similar ways. By default the numbers in the value area are the sums of the returns for all the funds that had returns in the specified range. This is not meaningful.

To create a frequency distribution, that is, show how many funds had returns in each range, in the value area we want to see in the value area the number of funds, that is, counts. Select any cell in the value area and open the Value Fields Setting dialog box using the shortcut menu. In the Custom Name box, type Number of Funds, and from the options under Summarize value field by, select Count. Then click OK.

It will also be nicer to use ranges that are not as large and have limits in round numbers. To make these changes, select any cell in the row area and open the Grouping dialog box again. Deselect the boxes on the left of Starting at and Ending at and enter −10 and 50 in the boxes to their right. (We already know that these values will cover the full range of data in the field.) Change step increment to 5 in the box next to By and click OK. Your pivot table should now look like Figure 6.33.

With this understanding of how grouping works for numeric fields, you should be able to make many imaginative uses of this feature in pivot tables you develop.

Grouping Text Fields

You can also group text fields. For example, you may decide to create a pivot table where you use Size Category as the first field in the row area and the fund names as the second field in that area. Then you may want to group certain funds

	A	B	C
1			
2			
3	Row Labels	Number of Funds	
4	-10--5	1	
5	-5-0	6	
6	0-5	19	
7	5-10	17	
8	10-15	13	
9	15-20	13	
10	20-25	10	
11	25-30	2	
12	30-35	2	
13	35-40	2	
14	45-50	1	
15	Grand Total	86	
16			

FIGURE 6.33 Frequency distribution created by grouping a numeric field.

in each size category as the preferred funds in that category, and so on. At this point you know enough about pivot tables and grouping to be able to learn to use grouping of text fields by experimenting on your own and using Excel's Help. Give it a try and have fun.

SORTING AND FILTERING PIVOT TABLES

The principles and tools for filtering and sorting, which we discussed at length early in this chapter, remain the same when you apply them to pivot tables, but they work a little differently.

Sorting

When we created the first pivot table (Figure 6.16), in your version the rows under Size Category probably came out in the order Medium, Large, and Small, because by default pivot table field values (also called items) are sorted in ascending sequence. On the other hand, in the figure the rows are sorted in the order Small, Medium, and Large, which makes more sense. How did I get it to come out differently? By using a custom list, which we discussed in the section on sorting.

To see how sorting works in pivot tables, re-create the simple pivot table again as shown in Figure 6.34. Notice that now my pivot table also shows the

	A	B	C	D	E
1	Fund Type	(All)			
2					
3	Sum of Investment Value ($000)	Style Category			
4	Size Category	Growth	Value	Grand Total	
5	Large	15413	10977	26390	
6	Medium	18372	9215	27587	
7	Small	15249	12426	27675	
8	Grand Total	49034	32618	81652	
9					

FIGURE 6.34 The simple pivot table with row items sorted in ascending alphabetical order.

Large, Medium, Small order. To sort this field in the more desirable order, select any of those three cells, right-click, select Sort from the menu, and then select More Sort Options to open the Sort dialog box. Click More Options at bottom-left to open the More Sort Options dialog box. Make sure that AutoSort is not selected. Chances are the box under First key sort order reads Normal. Click on the dropdown arrow on the right of that box. You will now see several custom sorting lists as shown in Figure 6.35. Select the last custom list Small, Medium, Large. Click OK. (If you do not see this custom list, you will need to go out from these dialog boxes and create it following either the method we discussed earlier under sorting or the alternative one I will discuss shortly. Excel saves all custom sorting lists you create and shows them to you when you need to do a sort using a custom list.)

You should now be back at the Sort dialog box. Make sure you do not have Manual selected under Sort options. You can select either Ascending or Descending. In this case, which one you select does not matter because you are actually using a custom list. Click OK and your pivot table will now show the three items in the Size Category sorted in the order you want.

You can also sort the pivot table by the values in any column of the value area. For example, if you want the table sorted in the descending order of how much the portfolio has invested in Growth funds, select any value in the Growth column, right-click to open the shortcut menu, click Sort, and then choose Sort Largest to Smallest. As you would expect, Excel will move whole rows as it sorts and not just cells in one column. So in the row area Medium will now be in the first position because the largest investment in growth funds is in medium-cap funds.

So far we have not seen any difference between how sorting works for a pivot table and for a Table or range. Now let us see how it works when you have two layers in the row area, as we had before in Figure 6.25. Here again the second layer items were nicely sorted as High, Medium, and Low, which is not in alphabetical order. I used another custom sorting list to get this right. If your pivot table did

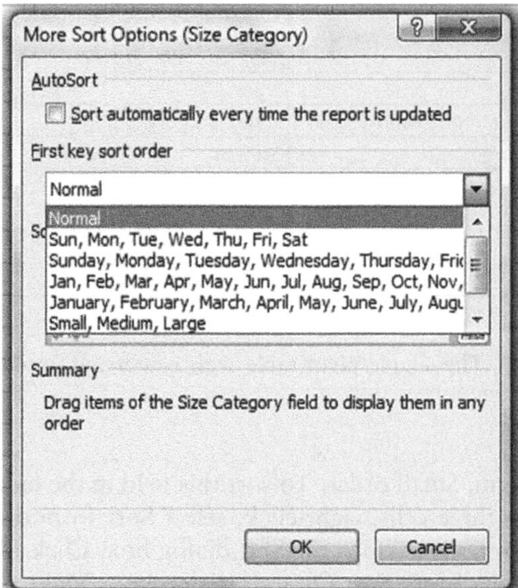

FIGURE 6.35 The More Sort Options dialog box.

not have this order right, first create a custom sorting list of High, Medium, Low. You can create it by going through the steps we discussed in the sort section early in this chapter, or you can access the Custom Lists dialog box directly as follows: Click the Office button at top-left of your Excel screen, select Excel Options at the bottom, and select Popular. In the last line of the first section in this tab click Edit Custom Lists. This will open the Custom Lists dialog box. Create the new custom list and back out.

Once you have the necessary custom list in place, select any of the cells in the second layer in the row area and go through the same steps we did to sort the first layer. What is interesting is that, as you would want, Excel will sort the Return Rank items as High, Medium, and Low under all three size categories. You do not have to do this sort separately for each size category.

Once you go through these examples and understand why they work the way they do, you should be able to figure out how to do any type of sort in pivot tables by experimenting.

Filtering

The simplest way to do filtering in pivot tables is to add the fields you want to filter on to the Report Filter box. Then you can do your filtering using the dropdown arrows next to the field names in the report filter area of your pivot table. (In addition, filtering arrows are already added to the fields in row and column areas.)

OTHER FEATURES OF PIVOTTABLE

I have now covered all the features of PivotTable that you need to know to start using this powerful tool. PivotTable has a few more features that you may find useful at times. One of them is PivotChart, which you can use to create charts from your pivot tables. Creating charts from pivot tables using PivotChart offers certain advantages over creating charts from pivot table data the regular way. You can also create and use Calculated Fields and Calculated Items in your pivot tables. But this feature is somewhat cumbersome.

I suggest that you first learn the features I have covered here well before trying to learn the above two or other PivotTable features.

CHAPTER 7

Answering What-If Questions

We create models primarily to project values of output (dependent) variables in order to make decisions and take actions. Such projections are never perfect, in part because we can never specify the necessary input (independent) variables exactly; those are almost always estimates or assumptions. So we are rarely interested in the values of the dependent variables for just one set of independent variables. More often we want to know how the output values will change if certain input values turn out to be different or we choose to make them different (for example, we decide to make only half as much investment in new plant and equipment). In other words, a key reason we build financial models is to be able to answer what-if questions.

Excel includes two useful tools to answer the two types of what-if questions we generally ask. In the first type, we are interested in looking at the projected values of one or more dependent variables for a series of values of one or two independent variables. Excel's data table feature is designed to answer this type of question. In the second type, we want to see the values of a selected group of dependent variables for a set of values for a selected group of independent variables. A specific set of values for a selected group of independent variables is called a scenario. The Excel tool to answer what-if questions about scenarios is called the Scenario Manager.

Excel includes in its what-if group a third tool called Goal Seek. I believe Goal Seek fits in better in the group of tools for finding iterative solutions, which I cover in a separate chapter.

Independent and Dependent Variables

People often have problems with data tables and some other features of Excel because they do not clearly understand the concepts of independent and dependent variables. Independent variables are the inputs to a model. They are not calculated in the model; the user has to provide them. They are called independent because they can be changed independently, at the user's choice. In the worksheets, the cells for independent variables have only input numbers or text and not any formula.

Any value calculated within the model is a dependent variable because its value depends on the values of other independent and dependent variables. Some dependent variables are the final outputs of a model; others may be intermediate values used to calculate other dependent variables. In the worksheets, any cell that has a formula in it represents a dependent variable.

In a model, the value of any dependent variable always depends—directly or indirectly—on one or more independent variables, but it does not have to depend on the values of all the independent variables of the model. When you use an Excel feature that assumes that a dependent variable, x, depends on a particular independent variable, y (for example, when you are trying to find out how the value of x varies with values of y), make sure that the x depends on y. Not paying attention to this often creates a lot of confusion and wastes hours of time.

If you prefer, you can use the terms input and output variables instead of independent and dependent variables. But remember that dependent variables are not only the ultimate outputs of a model, they include all the intermediate calculated variables as well.

Data Tables

Overview

Excel's Data Table tool is designed to create dynamic tables showing how some of the results (outputs) of the model would look for a series of different values for one or more of the inputs to your model. You can use Data Table to create two types of data tables: A one-input data table (also called one-variable data table) allows you to show the values of several dependent (output) variables for a range of values for one independent (input) variable. A two-input data table allows you to show the values of one dependent (output) variable for ranges of values for two independent (input) variables.

Creating a One-Input Data Table

A one-input data table displays the values of one or more dependent variables of a model for a series of values (that you specify) of one independent or input variable.

Let us look at the simple example shown in Figure 7.1. It is a model for calculating the after-tax income of a business that buys and sells just one product. During the time period in the example, it sold 100 units of the product at $12 each and its only cost was that of buying the product at $10 each. The business's income tax rate is 40%.

	A	B	C	D	E	F	G	H	I	J
1	**Examples of Data Tables**									
2										
3	Number of units sold	50			**One-input Data Table**					
4					Revenue	AT Income				
5	Sales price/unit	$11			550	$30				
6	Revenue	$550		50	$550	$30				
7				100	$1,100	$60				
8	Purchase price/unit	$10		150	$1,650	$90				
9	Cost of goods sold	$500		200	$2,200	$120				
10				250	$2,750	$150				
11	Before-tax income	$50		300	$3,300	$180				
12	Income tax (40%)	$20								
13	After-tax income	$30								
14					**Two-input Data Table**					
15				$30	10	11	12	13	14	
16				50	$0	$30	$60	$90	$120	
17				100	$0	$60	$120	$180	$240	
18				150	$0	$90	$180	$270	$360	
19				200	$0	$120	$240	$360	$480	
20				250	$0	$150	$300	$450	$600	
21				300	$0	$180	$360	$540	$720	
22										
23										
24										

FIGURE 7.1 Example of data tables.

In this model, there are three independent variables: the number of units sold, the sales price, and the purchase price. (There is actually a fourth independent variable, the income tax rate, but we are treating it as a constant and not a variable.) There are five dependent variables: revenue, cost of goods sold, before-tax income, income tax, and after-tax income.

Let us say we want to create a table to show what the revenue and the after-tax income of the business will be for the number of units sold shown in cells D6:D11. If you were to do this manually, you would take each of these values for the independent variable number of units sold, enter it in cell B3 of the model, look up the revenue in cell B6, and enter it in the table. Data Table does it exactly the same way. It has to know where to get the range of independent variables we are interested in, in which cell of the model it should enter the values of the independent variable, in which cell it should look up the values of the dependent variable, and where in the table it should enter the values of the dependent variable. Here is how we have to give Data Table this information.

We want the revenues to go into cells E6:E11. In E5 enter =B6 to tell Data Table that the values of the dependent variable, which it should enter below E5, will come from cell B6. (The safest way to do this is to enter = in E5, click B6, and press Enter.) For convenience, you can enter the label "Revenue" in E4. (It does not mean anything to Excel; the label, just like all other labels, is for your and the user's convenience.) Similarly, the after-tax incomes will go into cells F6:F11. In F5 enter =B13 to indicate where the after-tax income number will come from. Put a label in F4.

Now select D5:F11, and select Data ⇨ Data Tools ⇨ What-If Analysis ⇨ Data Table to open the Data Table dialog box. (In earlier versions of Excel you have to select Data ⇨ Table to open the Table dialog box.) Since the values of the independent variable are in a column (D6:D11) and not in a row, click the box next to Column input cell and then click B3 because that is where the values of the independent variable have to be substituted. Click OK and Excel will fill up the table with the values for revenue and after-tax income.

Note that you have to strictly follow the structure of the table because this is what tells Data Table where to get the independent variable values and so on. This means that you cannot leave a blank column to the right of the column of independent variables, you cannot have a blank row between the row (row 5 here) where you are specifying the dependent variable cells of the model and the row where the column of the independent variable values start (row 4), and so forth. Most problems with data tables arise from not strictly following the table structure.

You could have provided the values for the independent variable across a row instead of down a column and changed the other things accordingly. For a one-input data table, you have to enter a cell number in only one of the two boxes in the Data Table dialog box, depending on whether the values for the independent variable are in a column or a row. In a one-input data table, you can include as many dependent variables as you want. To do so in our example, we would have to create additional columns the same way we created the first two.

People often find the numbers in the cells E5 and F5 confusing because they do not belong to the output table. You can handle this problem in a few different ways. You can separate them by using a border for the table, as I have. You can hide that row (row 5 here) provided it does not hide useful information in some other column in the same row (as it would in this case). Alternately, you can hide the numbers in these cells using a custom formatting. To do so, in the Home ribbon click the small diagonal arrow at bottom-right of the Number group to open the Format Cells dialog box. (In earlier versions of Excel select Format ⇨ Cells.) Then, in the Numbers tab in the Category list, choose Custom. In the Type box, type in a semicolon (;). Finish by clicking OK. The cells will now appear blank, but if you select one of them, the formula in it will appear in the formula bar.

Creating a Two-Input Data Table

A two-input data table displays the values of one dependent variable of a model for ranges of values for two independent or input variables.

In our example, to see how the after-tax income will vary with the number of units sold and sales price/unit, you can create a two-input data table as follows.

Enter the desired values for the number of units sold in D16:D21 and the desired values for sales price/unit in E15:I15, making sure to leave the corner cell, D15, empty. In D15 enter =B13 to indicate from where the values for the dependent variable should be picked up. Now select D15:I21 and open the Data Table dialog box as before. In the box labeled Row input cell, enter B5 (preferably by pointing) to indicate that the values in the top row relate to the independent variable sales price/unit, and in the box labeled Column input cell, enter B3. Click OK to complete the table.

The number in the corner cell, D15, may look confusing to a user. Once again, you can border the table as shown to make it clearer or use the custom formatting I discussed under one-input data table to hide the content of the corner cell.

As you can see, you have to create a separate table for every dependent variable that you want to study with a two-input data table. Remember to always strictly follow the structure of the table.

Two other points are worth making. First, a dependent variable in a model may be only one or two calculations away from an independent variable, as in this simple example, or it may be two hundred calculations away (in large, complex models). Conceptually it makes no difference. You can use all dependent variables in a model in data tables.

Second, sometimes a particular dependent variable may not depend on one or more of the input variables in a model. If you pair them in a data table, you will find that the data table is showing the same value of the dependent variable in all cells in a column or a row. Think through your model to decide if this is correct (in which case there is no point in using them in the same data table) or if there is a bug in your model.

Data Tables Are Dynamic

Data tables are dynamic, which means that if anything is changed in the model that should change the values of a table's dependent variable(s), then the table will be automatically updated. To see this, change the purchase price/unit to $11 and see how the values in the tables change. This automatic process of updating is one of the major advantages of using data tables.

Data tables are also arrays. Click on any cell in the data table and you will see a formula that looks a little strange and is enclosed in a pair of braces ({}). One implication of this is that you cannot edit any of the cells in the data table by themselves. You can only change the entire data table by going through the steps you used to create them. (For more on this, see the section "Arrays and Array Formulas" in Chapter 4: Advanced Excel Features.)

An Important Restriction

The input and output cells that a data table uses must be on the same worksheet in which you are creating the data table. This is something you need to keep in mind before developing any model for which you may want to use data tables. Otherwise you may end up having to redo some of the work.

If you already have a multi-worksheet model in which the relevant input and output cells are on different sheets, you can create a data table by effectively creating new input and output cells on the same worksheet by linking them to the original input and output cells on the different worksheets.

Let us say you want to create a data table on worksheet A when an input cell is in worksheet B and an output cell is in worksheet C. Choose a cell in worksheet A (say, D1) to create a new input cell and link it to the original input cell in worksheet B. To do so, select the original input cell in worksheet B, enter an equal sign (=) in it, select worksheet A, click on D1, and then press Enter. Now whatever you enter in D1 in worksheet A will be mirrored in the original input cell in worksheet B. So you have created a new input cell and any data for this input will now have to be entered here; the original input cell is not an input cell anymore. To create a new output cell in worksheet A, select that cell, enter an equal sign (=) in it, select worksheet C, select the original output cell, and press Enter. The output value from the cell in worksheet C will now be mirrored in this new cell in worksheet A. If you need to create additional input and output cells, repeat the procedure.

Now you can create your data table in worksheet A using the new linked input and output cells in it. Instead of using a new worksheet A, you could have used worksheets B or C, in which case you would have had to create fewer links.

If you are creating a large, multi-sheet model, chances are your inputs will be on one worksheet. It will be easiest to create your data tables on that sheet by creating linked output cells on it as necessary.

Using Data Tables to Create Charts

Data table is an efficient tool to create charts (using the values from the data table) showing the relationship between a dependent variable and an independent variable of a model. Because data tables are dynamic, if you use the data in a data table to create a chart then the chart will be automatically updated whenever you make any changes in the model. Keep this tool in mind for such applications.

Scenario Manager

Overview

Scenario Manager is the other Excel feature that lets you create tables to show how some of the outputs of a model vary with some of its inputs. In each table created using Data Table, you can show how a dependent variable varies with (at most) two independent variables. In a table created with Scenario Manager, you can show the values of any number of dependent variables for several sets of values (each called a scenario) of a group of independent variables.

What Is a Scenario?

In modeling, a scenario is a specific set of values for all the input variables of a model. Suppose you have created a model to forecast the financial statements for a business over the next five years. You may want to see what some important balance sheet ratios will look like if the economy takes a downturn. For this, you have to first define what you mean by the economy taking a downturn by specifying what the value of each independent variable will be when this occurs. That is a scenario. You may call this a pessimistic scenario and decide to create and look at several other scenarios as well.

Using the Scenario Manager

The Scenario Manager lets you create a table showing the values of the set of dependent variables you are interested in for as many scenarios as you want. Although the definition of each scenario must include specific values for all independent variables of the model, you generally change the values of only a few of the independent variables from one scenario to another when you compare several scenarios; the others remain the same. To keep the table focused, you may choose to show in it the values for only those changing independent variables.

As with Data Table, you could create this table by manually changing the input data in their respective cells in the model and then copying the values of the dependent variables to a table. The Scenario Manager automates the process and saves you a lot of time.

Let us look at how it works using the same example we used for Data Table. Let us define a pessimistic scenario in which the company will sell only 50 units at a price of $11 each and an optimistic scenario in which it will sell 125 units at $13 each. In both scenarios, the other independent variables will remain at the same levels as shown in the model. The output variables we are interested in seeing are revenue and after-tax income. Name the independent and dependent variable cells as follow: B3 Sales, B5 SPrice, B6 Revenue, and B13 ATIncome.

To create a scenario table, you have to first create your scenarios. Select Data ⇨ Data Tools ⇨ What-If Analysis ⇨ Scenario Manager (Tools ⇨ Scenarios in earlier versions of Excel) to open the Scenario Manager dialog box as shown in Figure 7.2. To create a new scenario, click the Add button, which will bring up the Add Scenario dialog box. In the Scenario name box, type "Pessimistic." In the Changing cells box, enter the address of the cells for the independent variables whose values you want to change separated by commas. In this case they are B3 and B5. Once your cursor is in the box, the best way to enter them is to select cell B3, put a comma after the cell address in the box, select cell B5, and then click OK.

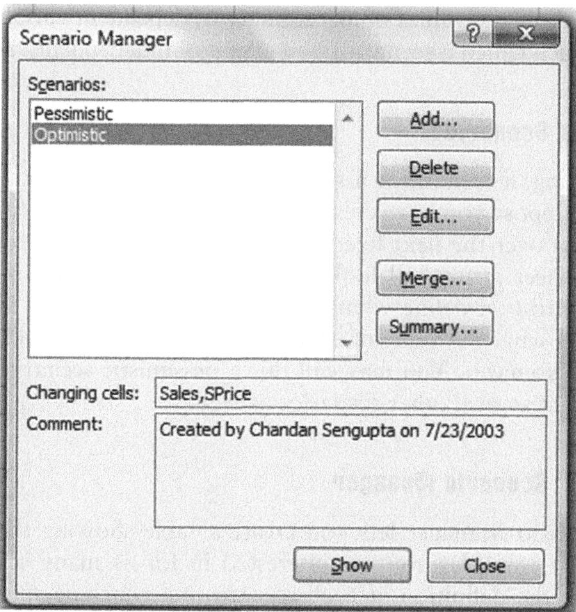

FIGURE 7.2 The Scenario Manager dialog box.

In the Scenario Values dialog box that comes up, enter 50 in the box next to Sales and 11 in the box next to SPrice to define the scenario. (The values that were showing in the boxes when this dialog box first opened are the current values in the model.) Notice that because you named the cells, Excel prompts you with the cell names, which is helpful. Click OK to finish creating this scenario.

To create the optimistic scenario, click the Add button again and repeat the previous steps. However, in this case you do not need to reenter the cell addresses in the Changing cells box; you just need to enter the values for Sales and Price in the Scenario Values dialog box.

Next, to create the scenario table, in the Scenario Manager dialog box, click the Summary button. In the Scenario Summary dialog box in the Results cells box, enter the addresses for the dependent variables you want to show in your table, separated by commas. (As before, do so by selecting the cells.) In Report type, select Scenario summary, then click OK. Scenario Manager will create the scenario table as shown in Figure 7.3 in a new worksheet. Note the following about the table:

- In addition to the two scenarios you defined, it also shows a column with the current values for comparison.
- For independent variables for which you do not specify new values to define your scenarios, the Scenario Manager uses the current values in your model.

	A	B	C	D	E	F	G
1							
2		Scenario Summary					
3				Current Values:	Pessimistic	Optimistic	
4		Changing Cells:					
5			Sales	100	50	125	
6			SPrice	$12	$11	$13	
7		Result Cells:					
8			Revenue	$1,200	$550	$1,625	
9			ATIncome	$120	$30	$225	
10		Notes: Current Values column represents values of changing cells at					
11		time Scenario Summary Report was created. Changing cells for each					
12		scenario are highlighted in gray.					
13							
14							

FIGURE 7.3 Scenario summary report created by Scenario Manager.

Remember that a scenario is defined by the values for all independent variables even though only a few of them may be shown in the table.

- Although the table looks fancy, it is a regular Excel table and you can change and reformat it in any way you want.
- This table is a one-time snapshot; it is not a dynamic table. If you change any of the values in the model, even the values in the Current Values column will not change.
- For cells that are named, the table uses the names instead of the cell addresses, which makes the table easier to read. Otherwise it will use the cell addresses, which look cryptic. If you do not name the cells beforehand, you can manually change the cell addresses that the table uses as labels to whatever labels you want for a particular row in a scenario.
- Both the independent and dependent variables are shown in the order you entered them. The more you think ahead, the less reformatting and rearranging of the table you will have to do.
- In each scenario you can change up to 32 independent variables. The table can show any number of dependent variables and scenarios. Even though we used it here for a simple model, it will work for huge, complex models as well.

In this example, to create the scenario table, in the Scenario Manager dialog box, as Report type, select Scenario summary. This format works well when you have only a few scenarios. When you work with many scenarios, you may want to choose Scenario PivotTable report as the Report type to get more flexibility.

Before leaving this example, go back to the Scenario Manager dialog box and look at the various options there, which are mostly self-explanatory. For additional information, search in Help under "Create a scenario."

An Important Restriction

As with data tables, the input and output cells you use in a Scenario Manager must be on the same worksheet. This is something you need to keep in mind before developing any model for which you may want to use the Scenario Manager. If necessary, for multi-sheet models you can use the approach that I discussed under Data Table, of creating linked input and output cells on the same worksheet.

CHAPTER 8

Finding Iterative Solutions

For many financial problems, it is often convenient or necessary to find a solution by trial and error. What does that mean? For example, we may want to know what sales growth rate will be necessary for a company to earn a certain earnings per share (EPS) in three years. Once we have built a model for the company with sales growth rate as one of its independent variables, we can change it in steps until the target EPS is achieved. (This assumes holding all other independent variables of the model constant.) Instead of looking for just the sales growth rate that will be necessary, we may also want to know what combination of certain independent variables, constrained in certain ways, could achieve the same target. Once again, we can find the answer by systematically varying the independent variables, that is, by trial and error. But this time it may take a lot of work.

The trial and error method is also called the iteration method, and there are many mathematical techniques (actually a whole branch of mathematics) to find iterative solutions to problems efficiently. Excel provides two tools—Goal Seek and Solver—for finding such iterative solutions. In addition, in certain circumstances you can find iterative solutions using a third Excel feature called circular reference.

In this chapter I will cover these three Excel features. Circular reference is the feature you are likely to use most often. Goal Seek is a handy tool, but not very powerful. Solver, on the other hand, is one of Excel's most sophisticated and powerful tools, and it takes a certain amount of mathematical knowledge to use it safely and well. You will not use it much in finance.

CIRCULAR REFERENCE

Overview

Most of the time the formula in a cell (say, H32) in your model will depend on values in other cells whose values do not, directly or indirectly, depend on the value of H32 itself. In other words, when Excel calculates the formula in H32, it expects that the values of all the cells referred to in the formula are already known. However, sometimes a formula in a cell may, directly or indirectly, refer to the cell it is in. This is called circular reference. This can happen because you made a mistake along the line, but there are also times when you may create one or more circular references in your model intentionally because it is a handy tool to solve certain types of problems.

Unintentional Circular Reference

If you accidentally create a circular reference, and if Enable iterative calculation (or, Iteration in previous versions of Excel) is not turned on (see the later discussion of what this means), you will see a long message on circular reference and you will also see the word Circular in the status bar at the bottom of your screen. Click OK and Excel will show a Help screen with information on how to track down and fix the problem.

Using Circular Reference Intentionally

You can use circular reference intentionally as a tool to solve a certain type of problem. It will be easiest to understand how by working through an example. Before we begin, select Office ⇨ Excel Options ⇨ Formulas and under Calculation Options make sure Enable iterative calculation is not selected. If it is selected, deselect it. (In earlier versions of Excel, select Tools ⇨ Options. Then in the Calculation tab of the Options dialog box, make sure that the check box for Iteration is not selected. If it is selected, deselect it.)

For our example, we will look at a company that has a policy of contributing 2% of its operating income to charity. Create a simple income statement for the company as shown in Figure 8.1 in the "No circular reference" column. Here, the formula in B8 is =B7*B14.

Now suppose the company decides that it wants to contribute 2% of its net income (rather than operating income) to charity. In this case, you will have a circular reference when you try to model the company's income statement: The net income will depend on the charitable contribution because it is tax deductible and will affect taxes, but the charitable contribution itself will depend on the net income because of the new policy.

If you were doing the calculations manually, you could solve the problem using algebraic equations. You could also solve it using trial and error or iteration. To use the trial and error method, you would take a guess at the contribution (for example, start with the number from the previous version), calculate the net income, calculate a new contribution as 2% of the net income, calculate a new net income based on that, and so on until the values change very little in successive iterations and the charitable contribution becomes very close to 2% of net income.

	A	B	C	D
1	**Using Circular Reference**			
2				
3		No circular reference	With circular reference	
4				
5	Revenue	$100,000	$100,000	
6	Costs	$70,000	$70,000	
7	Operating income	$30,000	$30,000	
8	Charitable contribution	$600	$356	
9	Income before tax	$29,400	$29,644	
10	Income tax	$11,760	$11,858	
11	Net income	$17,640	$17,787	
12				
13				
14	Contribution rate	2%	2%	
15	Tax rate	40%	40%	
16				
17				

FIGURE 8.1 Solving a problem using circular reference.

To create the model reflecting the new policy, copy B5:B15 into C5:C15 and in C8 enter =C11*C14. You will immediately see a circular reference message. Click Cancel to continue. The message will go away, but you will notice that the answer is wrong because the charitable contribution amount does not equal 2% of net income. To have Excel solve the problem by iteration, go back and select Enable iterative solution (or Iteration in earlier versions) the same way you made sure earlier that it was not selected. Once you click OK to close the dialog box, Excel will do the iterations and come up with the right answers. (Conceptually, Excel does it the same way you would do it when using trial and error.)

How to Set Up a Circular Reference

Some people get confused about how to set up a circular reference intentionally to solve the type of problem we discussed. As you saw, you do not have to do anything special. Just enter the formulas as usual without worrying about circular reference. If iteration is already turned on, you will not see any message. If it is not, turn it on when you see the message. That's it. But check (using hand calculations if necessary) to make sure that the iteration process produced the right answer because sometimes it may not.

Should you keep iteration turned on at all times? I would say, No. Keeping iteration off, unless you are intentionally setting up circular references, will flag any circular reference you may create by accident. If iteration is always on, accidental circular references may go unnoticed and introduce errors into your models. However, if it is not turned on when you are using circular reference intentionally, your model may not update properly when you change inputs or some formulas. So turn it on or off judiciously.

Controlling the Accuracy of Your Answer

You can control the accuracy of the answer and how long you want Excel to try to produce an answer before stopping. To see how, go back to the dialog box where you selected Enable iterative calculation. In the box for Maximum Iterations, specify the number of iterations that Excel should try before stopping (even if it does not reach an answer with the desired accuracy). The value you enter in the Maximum Change box controls the accuracy of your answer. It says iteration should stop when the values of the variables involved change from one trial to the next by an amount smaller than this number. Iteration will stop as soon as one of the two conditions is satisfied. If you leave these boxes blank, Excel uses default values of 100 and 0.001, respectively. (In earlier versions of Excel, select Tools ⇨ Options and then the Calculation tab. You can set the two conditions here in the section for Iteration.)

Unless you have a huge model, each iteration takes almost no time on a modern PC. You can therefore set the Maximum Iterations quite high. Nonetheless, you should set a reasonable number (100 or so to start with) just in case there is a bug in your program or some other problem that keeps the iterations going without getting closer to the answer. In the Maximum Change box you should put a fairly small number to get an accurate answer, again because in most cases the time that it takes to get there will be miniscule. However, if you are working with a computation-intensive model, you will probably want to play around with these specifications to get the level of accuracy you need without wasting too much time.

Circular Reference in Larger Models

In large models you may need to set up several circular references, and the circularity in each may involve many cells. Excel will easily work through them. But before setting up complex or several circularities in a model, think through the circularities you are setting up and make sure exactly why you need them and through what path (that is, series of cells) the formula in a cell depends on the value of the cell itself. Circular reference is a powerful and useful tool as long as you use it by design and full understanding and not by accident.

GOAL SEEK

Overview

Once you have created a model, you may want to find out what the value of a particular independent variable will have to be for a dependent variable to achieve a target value. You can use Goal Seek to answer this question. Goal Seek is a useful tool, but it can deal with only one independent variable and one dependent variable at a time. If your model has several independent and dependent variables and you want to find the best combination of values of a selected group of independent variables to achieve certain targets (for example, the best combination of ingredients A and B that can produce a product at a particular price or at the cheapest price), you will not be able to do it with Goal Seek. For such more complex problems you will have to use Solver, which we will discuss a little later.

Using Goal Seek

To learn Goal Seek quickly, it will help to have a clear understanding of independent (input) and dependent (output) variables.

Let us look again at the example we used for data tables (Figure 8.2). You want to find out how many units you will have to sell to achieve an after-tax income of $300 if other things remain the same. It is crucial to recognize that whenever you use Goal Seek, you assume that the values of all the independent variables other than the one you are going to change will remain at their current values in the model.

To answer the question, you could manually change the value in cell B3 in steps until the value in B13 reaches $300. Goal Seek automates this process for you and does it essentially the same way you would do it manually—by trial and error or iteration.

To find an answer by iteration, Goal Seek has to know in which cell it has to enter the various trial values (B3 here), what target value you are looking to achieve ($300), and which cell has to reach that target value (B13).

	A	B	C
1	**Using Goal Seek**		
2			
3	Number of units sold	50	
4			
5	Sales price/unit	$11	
6	Revenue	$550	
7			
8	Purchase price/unit	$10	
9	Cost of goods sold	$500	
10			
11	Before-tax income	$50	
12	Income tax (40%)	$20	
13	After-tax income	$30	
14			
15			

FIGURE 8.2 Using Goal Seek to find a solution.

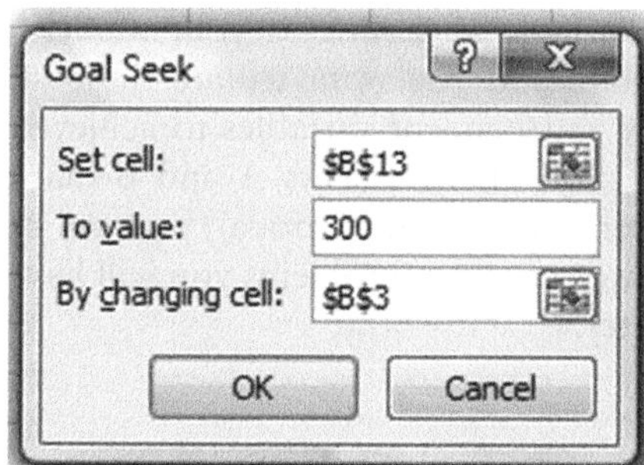

FIGURE 8.3 The Goal Seek dialog box.

To use Goal Seek, select Data ⇨ What-If Analysis ⇨ Goal Seek (or Tools ⇨ Goal Seek in previous versions of Excel) to open the Goal Seek dialog box as shown in Figure 8.3. In the box for Set cell, enter B13 (preferably by pointing)—this is the cell of the dependent (target) variable. In the box for To value, enter 300 because that is your target value. (Note that you have to enter a numerical value here; you cannot enter the address of a cell where you may have specified your target value.) In the box for By changing cell, enter B3—this is the cell of the independent variable. Click OK. The dialog box Goal Seek Status (Figure 8.4) will open with the answer. Read through its contents and also note that the values for the particular independent and dependent variables in your worksheet have been changed to the answer. If you click OK at this point, those changes will become permanent. If you click Cancel, the changed values will go back to the original values.

There are two points to keep in mind:

First, for Goal Seek to work, the value of the dependent variable (the target cell) must depend on the value of the independent variable (the changing cell).

Goal Seek Status

Goal Seeking with Cell B13 found a solution.

Target value: 300
Current value: $300

Step | Pause | OK | Cancel

FIGURE 8.4 The Goal Seek Status dialog box.

If changing the value of the independent variable does not change the value of the target dependent variable, then you will not be able to find a solution either manually or using Goal Seek. Second, you can, of course, use Goal Seek with models of any size.

Some Limitations of Goal Seek

Goal Seek is useful, but it has a few important limitations:

- The most important limitation is that it can deal with only one pair of independent and dependent variables at a time. You can still change other independent variables, but you will have to do it manually and tabulate the results manually. In our example, if you wanted to create a table to show what combinations of sales volume and sales price would achieve the $300 after-tax profit, you would have to run Goal Seek as before several times, each time with a different value for sales price in B5, and then note the answers in a table.
- You cannot automate the use of Goal Seek, so you cannot set up your model for a user who does not know how to use Goal Seek to get the kind of answers you can get using Goal Seek. (However, as we will see, you can automate Goal Seek using VBA.)
- Goal Seek does not retain its settings. Every time you run it, you have to enter all the values in the dialog box again.

The Solver overcomes some of these problems.

SOLVER

Goal Seek is a handy tool to find what value of an independent variable is necessary to achieve a target value for a dependent variable of a model (holding all other independent variables constant). Solver, which is a more sophisticated tool, can do much more.

The Solver is more powerful than Goal Seek in three ways:

1. Solver can look for three different types of solutions. It can maximize or minimize the value of a target cell (the dependent variable) or, like Goal Seek, it can find a solution that makes the value of the target cell equal to a value you specify. (A solution is a set of values for the independent variables or the changing cells of the problem.)
2. Unlike Goal Seek, Solver can find a solution by varying several different independent variables of the model simultaneously, that is, it can work with many changing cells.

3. It can find the solution subject to a number of constraints that you specify for the individual independent variables or linear combinations of them (the changing cells).

As with Goal Seek, for Solver to be able to find a solution, the value of the target cell must change as the values in the changing cells are changed. In other words, if the value of the dependent variable does not depend on the values of the independent variables you specify as changing cells, then no solution can be found.

Let us discuss a classical problem that Solver is often used to solve to understand the capabilities of Solver in concrete terms. Suppose your company produces one product, stores it at a number of warehouses around the country, and delivers it to a number of geographically dispersed retail stores. The cost of shipping depends on the distance between a retail store and the warehouse from which it receives its shipments. At a certain point in time the company has a book of orders from the different retail stores and a list of inventories at the different warehouses. It wants to decide how much product should be shipped from each warehouse to each retail store to minimize the total shipping cost to the company.

Clearly if the company has enough inventory in each warehouse to supply all the orders from the stores nearest to it, then the solution is trivial: You would supply each store from its nearest warehouse. But generally, that would not be the case. So the problem to solve is that the company wants to minimize the total shipping cost (the dependent variable in a target cell) by deciding how much product to supply to a particular store from various warehouses (the independent variables or changing cells), subject to the constraints that each warehouse can supply at most as much product as it has (the constraints). For other reasons you may need to impose additional constraints.

A Few Cautionary Notes

Before we look at an actual example to see how Solver works, let me offer a few cautionary notes. First, Solver is a highly sophisticated tool, and unless you have had at least one course in linear programming or something similar, you may have difficulty correctly specifying a problem for Solver. Second, even when you set up your problem correctly in Solver, you may get a wrong answer. Unless you know enough you may not even recognize that the answer you got is wrong. This, of course, can be dangerous. Third, beginners often try to use Solver for problems that are not suitable for it or do not require its use. Many such problems can be solved with some thinking and simple worksheet formulas. In the example we discussed, if each warehouse has enough inventory to supply its nearest stores, then there will be no need to use Solver. But people who don't see the obvious solution try to solve this trivial problem with Solver.

In finance you will not encounter problems that you must solve using Solver very often. So your primary initial objective should be to get a general understanding of the type of problems you can solve with Solver and work on developing a better understanding of Solver only when you need to use it.

Installing and Accessing Solver

Solver is part of Excel, that is, it is included in your Excel installation CDs and the necessary files are even copied to your hard disk when you install Excel. But you still need to install it before you can use it.

In Excel 2007 if Solver has already been installed, then you will see a Solver icon in the Analysis group of the Data tab. If you don't see the Solver icon, then install Solver as follows: Select Office ⇨ Excel Options ⇨ Add-Ins. At the bottom of the dialog box in the dropdown list next to Manage, select Excel Add-Ins and click Go. In the Add-Ins dialog box that comes up, select Solver by clicking the box next to it, and back out by clicking OK. In earlier versions of Excel Select Tools ⇨ Add-Ins, in the Add-Ins dialog box check the box to the left of Solver and click OK.

To access Solver in Excel 2007 select Data ⇨ Analysis ⇨ Solver.

A Solver Example

We want to maximize the value of:

$$3a + 2b + 5c$$

where a, b, and c are the three independent variables of the problem.

This may seem abstract, but you can think of a, b, and c as the quantities of three products a company sells at profit margins of \$3, \$2, and \$5 per unit of sales, respectively. In that case the formula is the total profit from sales, and the company wants to maximize the total profit.

None of a, b, and c can be negative. This is one set of constraints. There are also the following additional constraints:

$$3a + b <= 10$$
$$b + 2c <= 6$$
$$2a + b + c <= 8$$

Let us see how we set up this problem for Solver.

First, we label B4, B5, B6 (Figure 8.5, but you will have blanks or zeros in the cells until you run Solver) as the cells for the three independent variables. These will be our changing cells.

	A	B	C
1	**Using Solver**		
2			
3	**Independent variables**		
4	a	2.5	
5	b	0	
6	c	3	
7			
8	**Target cell**	22.5	
9			
10	**Constraints**		
11	First constraint <=10	7.5	
12	Second constraint <=6	6	
13	Third constraint <=8	8	
14			
15			

FIGURE 8.5 Setting up a problem to be solved by Solver.

Next, in B8 we enter the formula =3*B4+2*B5+5*B6 to make it the target cell.

Finally, we enter the constraint formulas in cells B11, B12, B13. For example, the formula in B11 is =3*B4+B5.

Now select Data ⇨ Analysis ⇨ Solver to open the Solver Parameters dialog box as shown in Figure 8.6. Enter the target cell address B8 in the Set Target Cell

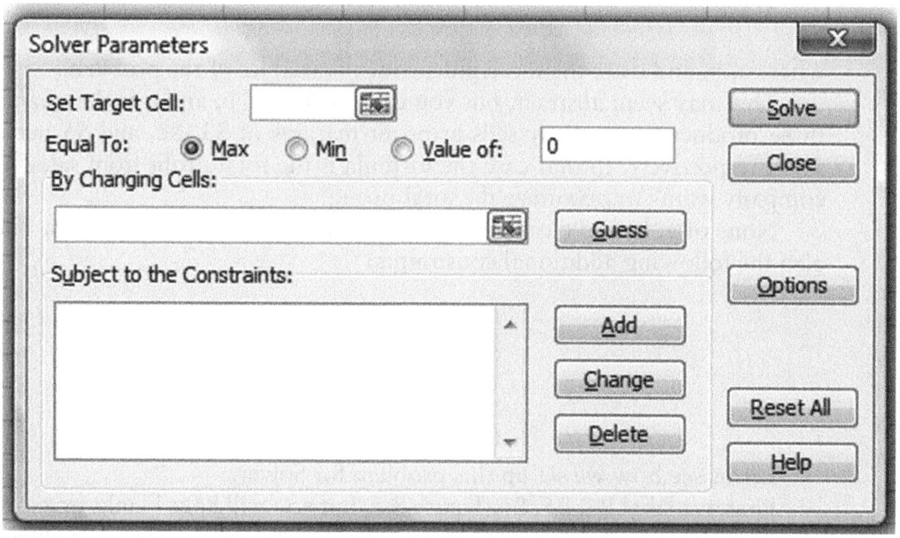

Solver Parameters
Set Target Cell:
Equal To: Max Min Value of: 0
By Changing Cells:
Guess
Subject to the Constraints:
Add
Change
Delete
Solve
Close
Options
Reset All
Help

FIGURE 8.6 Solver Parameters dialog box.

box (preferably by pointing). In the Equal To line choose Max. Under By Changing Cells enter the addresses of the three independent variable cells separated by commas.

Now we have to enter the constraints, one at a time. Click Add to open the Add Constraint dialog box. The first constraint we want to enter is a>=0. Enter the cell address of a, B4, under Cell Reference. From the dropdown list in the next box select >=, and then under Constraint enter 0. Click Add. You will be back at the Solver Parameters dialog box and see the constraint you just created listed in the Subject to the Constraints box.

Add all the other constraints the same way, one at a time. When you are done, your Solver Parameters dialog box should look like Figure 8.7. Now click Solve to let Solver find the solution.

When Solver is done—in this case as soon as you click it—the Solver Results dialog box (Figure 8.8) will open and you will see the solution (that is, the values of the independent variables, the maximum target value, and so on filled out in the worksheet as we saw in Figure 8.5). You can choose to keep the Solver solution or restore the original values in your worksheet by choosing one of the buttons here. You can also ask for one or more of the reports offered on the right (just click on the ones you want). If you choose a report or just want to save the scenario (by clicking the Save Scenario button), Excel will ask for a name of the scenario. Enter a name and click OK.

Larger problems have to be set up the same way. So once you understand the concepts of target cell, changing cells, and constraints, you will have no difficulty in

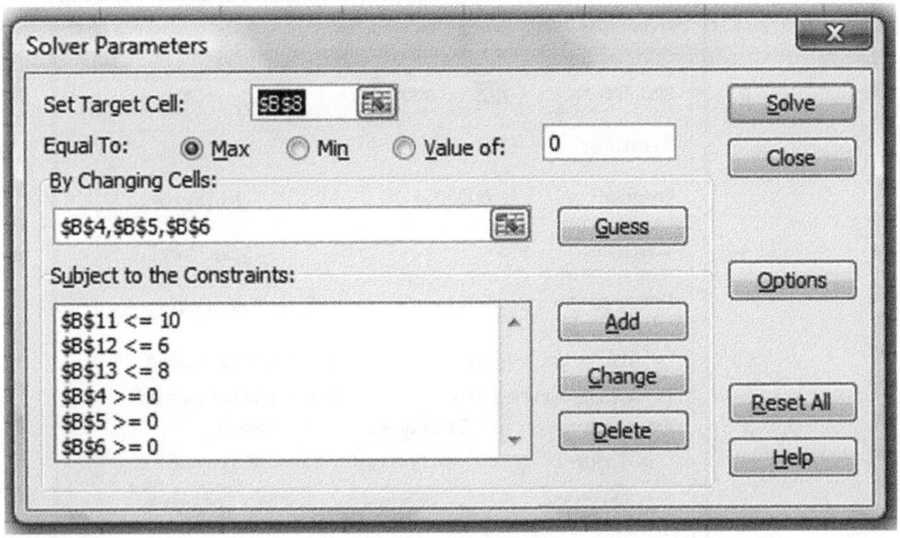

FIGURE 8.7 Solver Parameters dialog box fully set up.

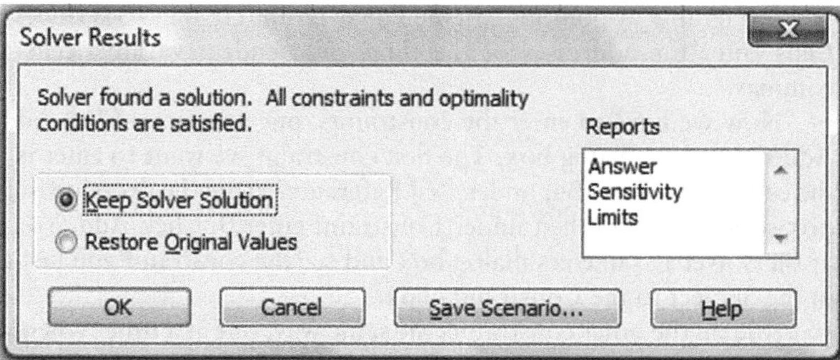

FIGURE 8.8 Solver results dialog box.

filling out the Solver Parameters dialog box and running Solver. The key challenge is to decide what dependent variable you want to maximize and what constraints you have to impose, and then set up your worksheet in an organized way.

The Solver Options Dialog Box

Before solving your problem, you can choose certain options from the Solver Options dialog box (Figure 8.9), which you can reach by clicking the Options button in the Solver Parameters dialog box.

FIGURE 8.9 Solver Options dialog box.

Many of the options are self-explanatory, and unless you are solving a large problem, you would not need to change the default values. Some others (for example, those under Estimates, Derivatives, and Search) are for advanced users.

Selecting Assume Linear Model can speed up Solver, but this will matter only for large models. You should choose it only if the relationships in your problem are linear.

Selecting Use Automatic Scaling can sometimes improve the result when there are large differences in magnitude among the different variables.

CHAPTER 9

Doing Statistical Analysis

In the Statistical group of its function library Excel provides a large number of statistical functions. In addition Excel includes an add-in called Analysis ToolPak, which incorporates a number of tools for doing more comprehensive statistical analysis. Together the statistical functions and the tools in the Analysis ToolPak cover most types of statistical analysis that you would need to do in finance and include in your models. So you should familiarize yourself with what functions and tools are available and then learn them in more detail when the need arises. (Note that in the earlier versions of Excel many functions were included in the Analysis ToolPak, which have now been integrated into the function library in Excel 2007. If you are using an earlier version of Excel and cannot find a function I mention in the function library, you will have to first install the Analysis ToolPak, as explained later.)

In both the function library and Excel's Help, functions are listed alphabetically. This is not very helpful. Here I will group together statistical functions and tools from the Analysis ToolPak by usage to make it easier for you to find the function or tool you need for any situation.

Many people look at functions as "black boxes." You input the arguments, and the functions provide the answers. In a way this view is true, but it is also dangerous. You should be especially careful about using the statistical functions and tools. They make it seem easy to do statistical analysis. The reality, though, is that trying to do any statistical analysis without knowing the underlying theory is dangerous—you may use a function or tool incorrectly or misinterpret the results. So take the time to know the underlying statistical theory before using any of these functions or tools. The explanations and examples I have provided for them are enough to learn to use them, but not enough to fully understand the underlying theory and especially the pitfalls.

For more on general information about how to use the functions and the Analysis ToolPak, see the discussions in the chapter on advanced Excel features. One point to keep in mind is that some statistical functions need range arguments and need to be entered in an appropriate range of cells as array formulas. Pay

	A	B	C	D	E
1	Month	Price	Return (%)	Ln Return (%)	
2	Feb-09	764.90	-7.38	-7.67	
3	Jan-09	825.88	-8.57	-8.95	
4	Dec-08	903.25	0.78	0.78	
5	Nov-08	896.24	-7.48	-7.78	
6	Oct-08	968.75	-16.83	-18.42	
7	Sep-08	1164.74	-9.21	-9.66	
8	Aug-08	1282.83	1.22	1.21	
703	Sep-50	19.45	5.59	5.44	
704	Aug-50	18.42	3.25	3.20	
705	Jul-50	17.84	0.85	0.84	
706	Jun-50	17.69	-5.80	-5.98	
707	May-50	18.78	4.57	4.46	
708	Apr-50	17.96	3.88	3.80	
709	Mar-50	17.29	0.41	0.41	
710	Feb-50	17.22			
711					

FIGURE 9.1 S&P 500 monthly data and returns.

special attention in order to use them correctly. Otherwise you may have a frustrating experience and waste hours trying to make them work.

The S&P 500 Monthly Return Data

In many examples in this chapter I will use the monthly return data for the S&P 500 shown in Figure 9.1. Column B shows monthly prices from February 1950 to February 2009. (I have hidden most intermediate rows in the figure.) You can download to spreadsheet this data (using the symbol ^gspc) as well as historical daily, weekly, and monthly price and other data for most stocks from the Yahoo! Finance web site.

In column C I have calculated the monthly ordinary (uncompounded) returns using formulas such as =(B2-B3)/B3*100 in C2 and in column D the monthly continuously compounded returns using formulas such as =LN(B2/B3)*100 in D2. As we will discuss in a later chapter, for financial work we generally use continuously compounded returns, although for the purpose of this chapter either return will be fine. You will notice that the ordinary and continuously compounded returns are close but not the same. I have multiplied both returns by 100 to convert them to percentages, primarily for cosmetic reasons. (I could have formatted them as %, in which case the numbers would have looked the same on the worksheet with a % sign next to each, but the underlying numbers would have remained in decimal format.)

Another obvious point is that we can calculate monthly returns starting one month after the date of the first data point, that is, starting in March 1950.

In our examples, we will use the continuously compounded returns (that is, from column D) unless I indicate otherwise.

DESCRIPTIVE STATISTICS

For any data set you often want to calculate certain descriptive statistics such as mean, standard deviation, and median. The Analysis ToolPak offers a tool called Descriptive Statistics that calculates in one step many of the most common descriptive statistics for a data set. In addition there are several functions in Excel's Statistical group to calculate these and other statistics for a data set. In this section we will cover the Descriptive Statistics tool and then various functions for calculating individual statistics that will be useful for modeling.

The Descriptive Statistics Tool

Select the S&P500 Monthly Returns worksheet and open the dialog box for the Descriptive Statistics tool as shown in Figure 9.2. In the Input Range enter the range for returns using the pointing method. Unless you have included in the range the header (title) row, leave the box next to Labels in first row unchecked. Under Output options select New Worksheet Ply. Further down select all the four boxes, enter 95% next to Confidence Level for Mean and 5 in each of the two boxes below it. Click OK. The output (on a new worksheet) would look like Figure 9.3 (after adjusting column widths).

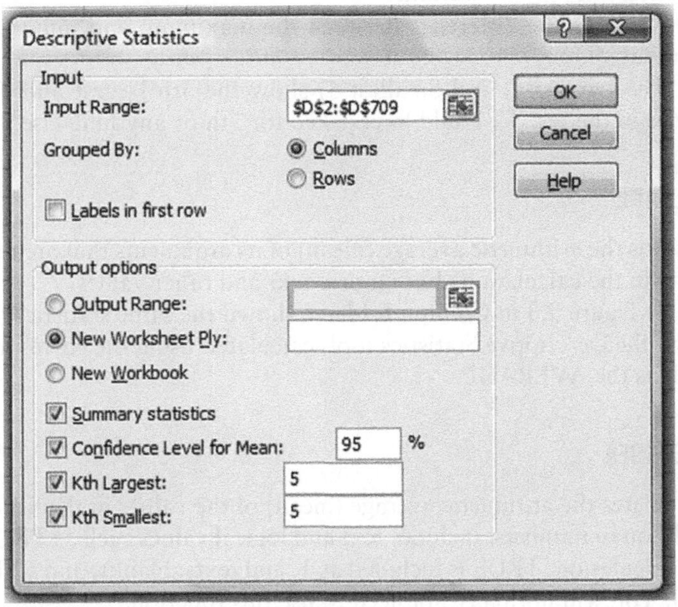

FIGURE 9.2 The Descriptive Statistics dialog box.

	A	B	C	D	E	F
1	*Column1*					
2				**Function used**		
3	Mean	0.535829606		AVERAGE	0.535830	
4	Standard Error	0.157496224		STDEV/SQRT(COUNT)	0.157496	
5	Median	0.88093253		MEDIAN	0.880933	
6	Mode	#N/A				
7	Standard Deviation	4.190701956		STDEV	4.190702	
8	Sample Variance	17.56198289		VAR	17.561983	
9	Kurtosis	2.603994181		KURT	2.603994	
10	Skewness	-0.675240234		SKEW	-0.675240	
11	Range	39.64712482		Max value - Min value	39.647125	
12	Minimum	-24.54280491		MIN	-24.542805	
13	Maximum	15.10431991		MAX	15.104320	
14	Sum	379.3673607		SUM	379.367361	
15	Count	708		COUNT	708.000000	
16	Largest(5)	10.97304475		LARGE	10.973045	
17	Smallest(5)	-12.08813757		SMALL	-12.088138	
18	Confidence Level(95.0%)	0.309216274				
19						
20						

FIGURE 9.3 Descriptive statistics generated by the tool.

In column D I have shown the name of the function that you can use to calculate the same statistic and in column E the same statistics calculated using that function. You are probably already familiar with the descriptive statistics calculated by this tool. For more on some of these statistics see under the corresponding function later in this section.

Range is the difference between the maximum and minimum values in the data set.

The Largest(5) and Smallest(5) show the 5th largest and 5th smallest data values in the set. We could have asked for 7th or anything else.

AVERAGE

Returns the arithmetic average (mean) of its arguments that are numbers. Includes zeros in the calculations but ignores text and other values.

In Figure 9.3 in Column E I have shown the same statistics (as we calculated using the Descriptive Statistics tool) calculated using the corresponding functions such as the AVERAGE.

AVERAGEA

Calculates the arithmetic average (mean) of the values in the list of arguments. In addition to numbers, includes text and logical values such as TRUE and FALSE in the calculation. TRUE is included as 1, and texts, blanks, and FALSE are included as 0. You will normally not need to use this function.

TRIMMEAN

Returns the mean of a data set excluding a specified percentage of highest and lowest values. You should use this function if you think your data set has outliers that you want to exclude from the mean calculation because they would significantly skew it.

The syntax is:

TRIMMEAN(array,percent)

Array is the array or range of values to average.

Percent (expressed in fraction as always) is the percentage of highest and lowest data points to be excluded. If your data set has 100 data points and you specify percent as 0.1, then a total of 10 data points—the top 5 and the bottom 5—will be excluded from the mean calculation.

GEOMEAN

Returns the geometric mean of an array or range of positive numbers. If there are 10 numbers in the data set, they are multiplied and then the 10th root is taken (which is the same as raising it to the power of 1/10).

This function is useful for many financial calculations. For example, if the annual return for an investment for the past three years were 15%, −20%, and 5%, the average or mean return is zero. However, this implies that if you had originally invested $100 in this asset, you would have $100 at the end of the three years. But this is not true. To determine the true average return, you have to calculate the compounded average return over the period by taking the geometric mean of 1.15, 0.8, and 1.05 and subtracting 1. The result will be −1.15%, which correctly reflects the fact that at the end of the 3-year period, the value of your investment would be $96.60 and not $100. Note that there are situations where the ordinary mean (that is, the arithmetic average) is more meaningful. So you have to choose between AVERAGE and GEOMEAN depending on your objective.

The function takes a series of positive numbers or an array or range of such numbers as its argument.

HARMEAN

Returns the harmonic mean of a set of positive numbers. The harmonic mean is the reciprocal of the mean (arithmetic average) of the reciprocals of the numbers in the dataset. You are not likely to use harmonic means in finance.

The function takes a series of positive numbers or reference to an array or range containing such numbers as its argument.

MEDIAN

Returns the median of the given numbers. Ignores texts, logical values, and empty cells but includes zeros. The median is the number in the middle of the data set, that is, half the numbers are greater than the median and half are smaller.

MODE

Returns the most frequently occurring, or repetitive, value in an array or range of data. Ignores texts, logical values, and empty cells but includes zeros.

STDEV

Estimates the population standard deviation assuming the data provided is a random sample. Logical values (such as TRUE and FALSE) and text are ignored. Standard deviation measures how widely the data is dispersed around its mean.

Let me clarify when you should use STDEV versus STDEVP. Most of the time the data set you are working with represents a sample from a larger population. For example the monthly returns for S&P 500 we have been using can be considered a sample from monthly returns for a much longer period. In this case we are interested not in the standard deviation of the sample itself; we want to estimate the standard deviation of the underlying population. The standard deviation we calculated using STDEV is just that: an estimate for the underlying population. STDEVP would calculate the standard deviation for only the data in the sample.

As a practical matter, as the sample size gets larger, the difference between the two kinds of standard deviation gets smaller. So it is important to choose carefully (depending on what you are trying to measure) between the two only when your sample size is small.

STDEVA

Estimates the population standard deviation, assuming the data provided is a random sample. Arguments that contain TRUE evaluate as 1; arguments that contain text or FALSE evaluate as 0 (zero). Most of the time you will want to use STDEV instead of this function.

STDEVP

Calculates standard deviation, assuming that the data provided is the entire population—that is, it calculates sample standard deviation. Logical values (such as TRUE and FALSE) and text are ignored. If logical values and text must not be ignored, use the STDEVPA worksheet function.

See the discussion under STDEV to understand how to decide which function you should use in a particular situation.

STDEVPA

Calculates standard deviation, assuming that the data provided is the entire population—that is, it calculates sample standard deviation. Arguments that contain TRUE evaluate as 1; arguments that contain text or FALSE evaluate as 0 (zero). If the calculation must not include text or logical values, as would generally be the case, use the STDEVP function instead.

VAR

Estimates (population) variance based on a sample. Logical values (such as TRUE and FALSE) and text are ignored. If logical values and text must not be ignored, use the VARA worksheet function.

This function parallels STDEV. See the discussion under STDEV to understand when you should VAR and when VARP.

VARA

Estimates (population) variance based on a sample. Arguments that contain TRUE evaluate as 1; arguments that contain text or FALSE evaluate as 0 (zero). If the calculation must not include text or logical values, which will be the case most often, use the VAR worksheet function.

VARP

Calculates variance assuming that the data provided is the entire population—that is, it calculates sample variance. Logical values (such as TRUE and FALSE) and text are ignored. If logical values and text must not be ignored, use the VARPA worksheet function.

This function parallels STDEVP. See the discussion under STDEV to understand how to choose between VAR and VARP for a particular situation.

VARPA

Calculates variance assuming that the data provided is the entire population—that is, it calculates sample variance. Arguments that contain TRUE evaluate as 1; arguments that contain text or FALSE evaluate as 0 (zero). If the calculation must not include text or logical values, which will be the case most of the time, use the VARP worksheet function instead.

AVEDEV

Returns the average of the absolute deviations (differences) of each data point from the mean of the data set. Like standard deviation, it is a measure of the dispersion of the data around the mean; but the two measure them differently.

The function takes a series of numbers or an array or range of numbers as its argument.

DEVSQ

Returns the sum of the squares of deviation of the data points from their mean.

The function takes a series of numbers or an array or range of numbers as its argument.

SKEW

Returns the skewness of a data set or distribution.

Skewness is a measure of how unsymmetrical a distribution is. Symmetrical distributions have a skewness of zero. Distributions of returns that show frequent small losses and a few extreme gains (that is, with an asymmetrical tail extending toward more positive values) are called positively skewed and have positive skewness. Negatively skewed returns have the opposite characteristics and have negative skewness. The distribution in our example is negatively skewed.

KURT

Returns the kurtosis of a data set or distribution.

Kurtosis is the statistical measure to judge if a distribution is more or less peaked than a normal distribution. For all normal distributions, kurtosis equals 3. As is the case with many statistical packages, Excel's KURT function reports excess kurtosis, which is kurtosis minus 3. Therefore, a positive (excess) kurtosis indicates a distribution more peaked (with fatter tails) than a normal distribution and negative kurtosis indicates a distribution less peaked than a normal distribution.

FREQUENCY DISTRIBUTIONS AND HISTOGRAMS

Frequency distributions are widely used in statistical analysis to visualize how the data is distributed, that is, how many data points lie in various ranges of values. Histograms are graphical representation of frequency distributions.

Note that in addition to the FREQUENCY function and Histogram tool I discuss below, you can also use PivotTable to create more flexible frequency distributions. (See the chapter on analyzing data.)

FREQUENCY

To create a frequency distribution you have to start by specifying the ranges (bins in Excel's language) you want to use for counting. You would generally want the bins to cover the whole range of data (that is, at least from the minimum to the maximum value in your data). Also, generally you will want the bins to be of equal size, although this is not required. Start by finding the maximum and minimum values in your data, and then pick a bin size that will create 10 to 15 bins. Once you have a better understanding of the data after creating your initial frequency distribution, you may want to change the bin sizes or even make them unequal.

In our data the maximum monthly return is 15.10% and minimum is –24.54%—a range of about 40%. (You can find these quickly using the MAX and MIN functions.) So let us start with buckets of size 3% and start creating buckets starting at –25%, and going up to 17%, as shown in B2:B16 in Figure 9.4.

The FREQUENCY function generates an array output because it will count and enter the number of data points in each bucket. Therefore, it will have to be entered as an array formula in an appropriate range of cells, which has to be in the column next to the column that defines the buckets. (If you are not familiar with the basics of array formulas, you should learn them before proceeding.) To enter the FREQUENCY function, select the range C2:C17, and then open the dialog box for the FREQUENCY function. For the Data_array argument enter the range D2:D709 in the data worksheet by pointing so that the proper

	A	B	C	D	E	F
1	Range	Upper limit	Count	Cumulative		
2	Less than -25	-25	0	0		
3	-25 to -22	-22	1	1		
4	-22 to -19	-19	0	1		
5	-19 to -16	-16	1	2		
6	-16 to -13	-13	1	3		
7	-13 to -10	-10	4	7		
8	-10 to -7	-7	25	32		
9	-7 to -4	-4	53	85		
10	-4 to -1	-1	142	227		
11	-1 to 2	2	224	451		
12	2 to 5	5	181	632		
13	5 to 8	8	60	692		
14	8 to 11	11	12	704		
15	11 to 14	14	3	707		
16	14 to 17	17	1	708		
17	More than 17		0	708		
18						
19	Total points		708			
20						

FIGURE 9.4 Frequency distribution created using the FREQUENCY function.

worksheet name is included, and for the Bins_array argument enter B2:B16. Now press Shft+Ctrl+Enter to enter this as an array formula. You will now see the frequency distribution in C2:C17.

Note the following:

- The way Excel requires the buckets to be specified (essentially by the upper limit for each bucket) makes it confusing to interpret the frequency distribution, at least in the beginning. What does the count 25 in C8 mean? Does it mean that there were 25 points in the range −10 to −7 or in the range −7 to −4? Writing out the range for each bucket, as I have done in column A, clears up the confusion. But for obvious reasons Excel will not accept A2:A17 as the Bucket_array argument. So you will have to get used to Excel's way, but you can always add the clarifying column.
- We made sure that the buckets we specify cover the whole range of data. If the first bucket had started at −24 instead of −25, there would have been a non-zero count in C2 because there would be at least one data point with value smaller than −24. Similarly, if there had been any data points with values higher than the value shown for the last bucket (17 in B16), their count would have been shown in C17. This is why, when we entered the FREQUENCY function, we had to enter it in the range C2:C17 and not C2:C16.
- We can now see that most of the data is concentrated in the middle and change the bucket sizes, making them smaller in the middle to better see how the returns are distributed. Excel does not require the buckets to be of equal size.
- It is good practice to sum the total number of points in the different buckets (as in C19) to check that the count matches the number of points in the data array.
- Sometimes it is also useful to create a cumulative count as I have done in column D. (The formula in D9 reads =D8+C9 and so on.) Once again, you have to interpret the numbers carefully: Here 85 in D9 means there are 85 data points with values of −4 or less.

You can also create additional columns showing the counts and cumulative counts as percentages of the total number of data points.

The Histogram Tool

The Analysis ToolPak offers a tool called Histogram, which you can use to create both a frequency distribution and a histogram. It has a few other features as well.

Select the S&P500 Monthly Returns worksheet and open the Histogram dialog box as shown in Figure 9.5. In the Input Range box enter (by pointing) the range for the returns data, and in the Bin Range enter (by pointing) the bin range from the Frequency Distribution worksheet that you created earlier. Under

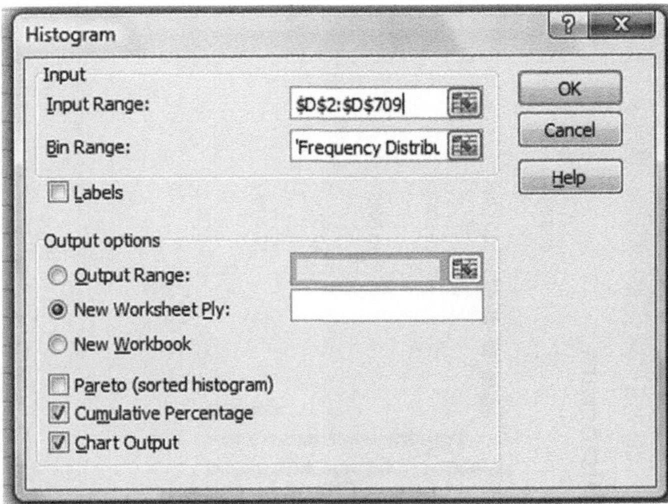

FIGURE 9.5 The Histogram dialog box.

Output options select New Worksheet Ply, and further down check the boxes for Cumulative Percentage and Chart Output. Click OK.

The output (on a new worksheet) will look like Figure 9.6. Actually, it comes out a little squeezed, but you can easily adjust some of the column widths, make the chart larger by dragging its handles, and make other changes.

As with the frequency distribution we created with the FREQUENCY function, here also you can add a column showing the ranges for each bin for clarification. Also, in the Histogram dialog box you can select the Pareto option to have Excel sort the frequency distribution in descending order, with the bin with the largest number of data points at the top and so on. But because the bins are defined with just one number in the frequency distribution table Excel creates, such a sorted table gets confusing. If you want a sorted frequency distribution, create the frequency distribution first, add a column showing the range for each bin, and then sort the table in descending order of the number of data points in each bin using Excel's sort.

COUNTING, RANKING, AND CALCULATING QUANTILES

COUNT

Counts the number of cells that contain numbers. It also counts numbers within the list of arguments.

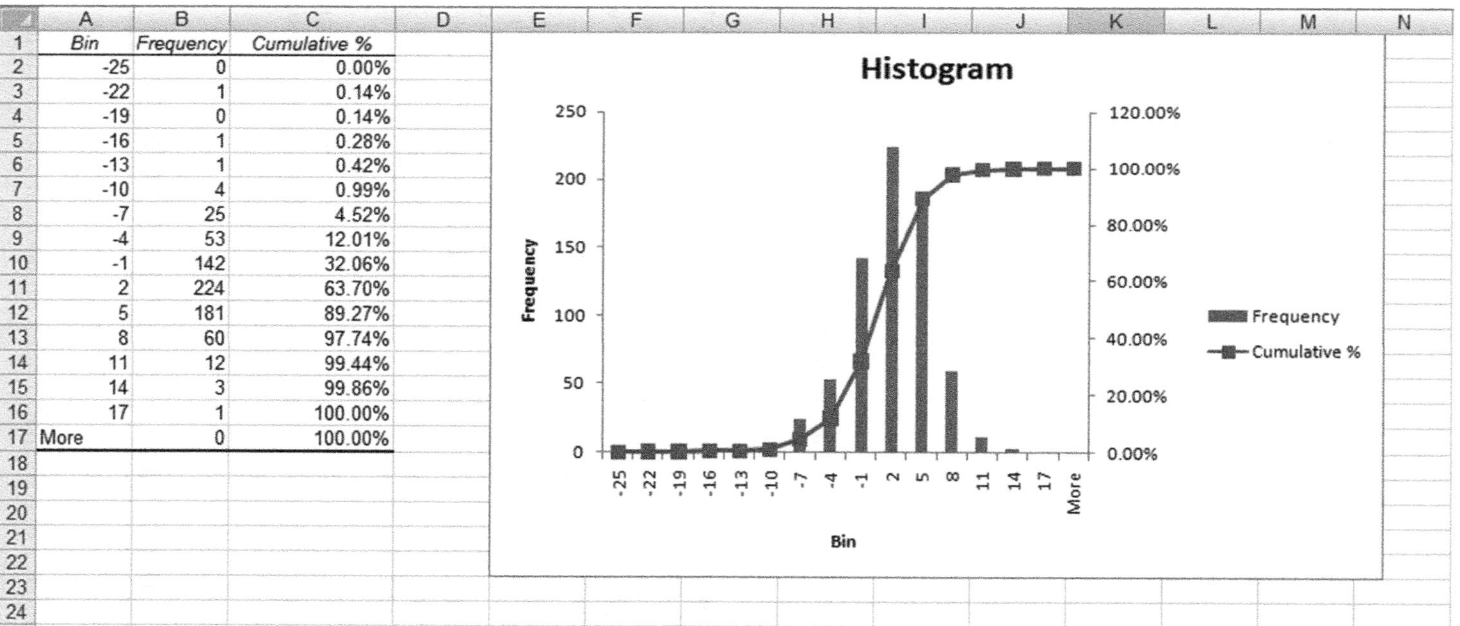
Bin | Frequency | Cumulative %
-25 | 0 | 0.00%
-22 | 1 | 0.14%
-19 | 0 | 0.14%
-16 | 1 | 0.28%
-13 | 1 | 0.42%
-10 | 4 | 0.99%
-7 | 25 | 4.52%
-4 | 53 | 12.01%
-1 | 142 | 32.06%
2 | 224 | 63.70%
5 | 181 | 89.27%
8 | 60 | 97.74%
11 | 12 | 99.44%
14 | 3 | 99.86%
17 | 1 | 100.00%
More | 0 | 100.00%
Histogram
Frequency
250
200
150
100
50
0
120.00%
100.00%
80.00%
60.00%
40.00%
20.00%
0.00%
-25 -22 -19 -16 -13 -10 -7 -4 -1 2 5 8 11 14 17 More
Bin
Frequency
Cumulative %

FIGURE 9.6 Example of histogram.

Arguments that are numbers, dates, or text representations of numbers are counted; arguments that are error values or text that cannot be translated into numbers are ignored. If an argument is an array or reference, only numbers in that array or reference are counted. Empty cells, logical values, text, or error values in the array or reference are ignored. If you need to count logical values, text, or error values, use the COUNTA function.

COUNTA

Counts the number of cells that are not empty and the values within the list of arguments. Includes cells containing logical values, text, or error values in the count.

COUNTBLANK

Counts the number of blank (empty) cells in the specified range of cells.

COUNTIF

Counts the number of cells within a range that meet a specified criterion.

The syntax is:

COUNTIF(range,criterion)

Range is the range of cells from which you want to count cells.

Criterion is to be specified in the form of a number, an expression, or text that defines which cells should be counted. It can be expressed as 53, "53", ">77", or "Male". It can also be a reference to a cell that holds the criterion. You can use the wildcard characters, question mark (?) and asterisk (*), in criteria. A question mark matches any single character; an asterisk matches any sequence of characters. If you want to find an actual question mark or asterisk, type a tilde (~) before the character.

For example, to enter in cell F1 the number of male employees in a list of 1,000 employees where B1:B1000 shows the sex of an employee as Male or Female, you can write the formula =COUNTIF(B1:B1000, "Male") in F1. You can also enter Male in E1 and write the formula in F1 as =COUNTIF(B1:B1000,E1).

SUMIF

Sums the values in a range that meet a criterion you specify. You can also ask to sum the values in a second range based on the results of the test in the first range.

The syntax is:

SUMIF(range,criterion,[sum_range])

Range is the range of cells that you want evaluated. If sum_range is omitted, then the values in this range that meet the criterion are summed.

Criterion is to be specified in the form of a number, an expression, or text that defines which cells should be counted. It can be expressed as 53, "53", ">77", or "Male". It can also be a reference to a cell that holds the criterion. You can use the wildcard characters, question mark (?) and asterisk (*), in criteria. A question mark matches any single character; an asterisk matches any sequence of characters. If you want to find an actual question mark or asterisk, type a tilde (~) before the character.

Sum_range is the range of cells to sum. A cell in this range is included in the sum only if the corresponding cell in range meets the criterion. If sum_range is omitted, then the cells in range that meet the criterion are summed.

Consider the formula =SUMIF(A1:A30,"<50", B15:B44). If the value in A1 is less than 50, then B15 will be included in the summation, and so on.

AVERAGEIF

This is a new function in Excel 2007 and parallels the SUMIF function, except that it averages the cells that are summed by SUMIF.

COUNTIFS, SUMIFS, and AVERAGEIFS

These are new functions added in Excel 2007. They are similar to the corresponding function with IF instead of IFS at the end. These new functions are more powerful and flexible in that you can specify as many criteria as you want and the value in a cell is included in the calculation only if it meets all the criteria.

The syntax for SUMIFS is:

```
SUMIFS(sum_range,criteria_range1,criteria1[,criteria_range2,
criteria2...])
```

Sum_range is the range from which cells are selected for summing. A cell is selected only if all the corresponding criteria specified are met for that cell.

Crtireia_range1, criteria_range2, and so on are one or more ranges in which the associated criteria would be evaluated.

Criteria1, criteria2, and so on are to be specified in the form of a number, an expression, or text that defines which cells should be counted. It can be expressed as 53, "53", ">77", or "Male". It can also be a reference to a cell that holds the criterion. You can use the wildcard characters, question mark (?) and asterisk (*), in criteria. A question mark matches any single character; an asterisk matches any sequence of characters. If you want to find an actual question mark or asterisk, type a tilde (~) before the character.

It is easiest to understand these functions as extended versions of the corresponding functions with IF ending.

AVERAGEIFS has the same syntax, but the syntax for COUNTIFS is slightly different and is as follows:

COUNTIFS(range1,criteria1[,range2,criteria2...])

Here all the cells in the different ranges that meet the corresponding criteria are counted.

LARGE

Returns the *k*th (you specify *k*) largest value in a data set.

SMALL

Returns the *k*th (you specify *k*) smallest value in a data set.

MAX

Returns the maximum value in a list of arguments, ignoring logical values and texts.

MAXA

Returns the largest value in a list of arguments. Text and logical values such as TRUE and FALSE are compared as well as numbers. TRUE values count as 1; FALSE and texts count as 0.

MIN

Returns the smallest value in a list of arguments, ignoring logical values and texts.

MINA

Returns the smallest value in a list of arguments. Text and logical values such as TRUE and FALSE are compared as well as numbers. TRUE values count as 1; FALSE and texts count as 0.

PERCENTILE

Returns the *k*th (you specify *k*) percentile of values in a range. If the 95th percentile value for a set of data is 315, then it means that 95% of the values in the range are equal to or less than 315.

The syntax is:

PERCENTILE(array,k)

Array is the array or range of data that determines the relative standing.
k is the percentile value in the range 0 to 1, inclusive.
For an example, see the discussion under RANK.

PERCENTRANK

Returns the rank of a value in a data set as a percentage of the data set.
The syntax is:

PERCENTRANK(array,x,significance)

Array is the array or range of data with numeric values that determines the relative standing.

x is the value for which you want to know the rank.

Significance is an optional value that specifies the number of significant digits desired in the returned percentage value. A default value of 3 is assumed if this is omitted.

For an example, see the discussion under RANK.

QUARTILE

Returns the specified quartile of a data set.
The syntax is:

QUARTILE(array,quart)

Array is the array or range of numeric values for which you want the quartile value.

Quart indicates which quartile to return. Use 0 (zero) to get the minimum, 1 for the first quartile (25th percentile), 2 for the second quartile (50th percentile), 3 for the third quartile (75th percentile), and 4 for the maximum.

For an example, see the discussion under RANK.

RANK

Returns the rank of a number in a list of numbers. The rank of a number is its size relative to other values in a list. If you were to sort the list, the rank of the number would be its position. You can specify if the rank should be based on ascending or descending order. As is customary with ranking, if two values in the data set are the same, they are assigned the same rank (say, 5) and the next value will be ranked 7.

	A	B	C	D
1	Store	Score	Rank	
2	A	56	7	
3	B	71	4	
4	C	44	9	
5	D	92	1	
6	E	71	4	
7	F	35	10	
8	G	56	7	
9	H	83	2	
10	I	66	6	
11	J	75	3	
12				
13				

FIGURE 9.7 Example of using the RANK function.

You could find the same information by sorting the list of numbers. So this function is useful when for some reason you cannot or do not want to sort the list (or a copy of it).

The syntax of the RANK function is:

RANK(number,ref,order)

Number is the number (value) whose rank you want to find.

Ref is an array of, or a reference to, a list of numbers. (Nonnumeric values in ref are ignored.)

If order is omitted or is 0 (zero), Excel ranks a number as if the list of numbers were sorted in descending order (that is, the largest number will be ranked 1). If order is any nonzero value, Excel ranks a number as if the list of numbers were sorted in ascending order (that is, the smallest number will be ranked 1).

Figure 9.7 shows an example of how you can use this function to determine the rank of ten stores based on their customer satisfaction score in a survey (on a scale of 1 to 100). I wrote the formula =RANK(B2,B$2:B$11) in C2 and copied and pasted in C4:C11. Notice that both store B and store E have the same rank of 4 and there is no store ranked 5.

Figure 9.8 shows a comprehensive example of how the PERCENTILE, PERCENTRANK, QUARTILE, and RANK functions are used. Columns A and B show the ticker symbol and names of a number of mutual funds, and column C shows their total returns in 2006.

In column D we determine the ranks for the funds based on their 2006 returns using the formula =RANK(C2,C$2:C$29) in D2 and copying and pasting it in D3:D29. Note that we have to use absolute reference for the row numbers in specifying the range so that when we copy and paste the formula, the definition of the range does not change.

	A	B	C	D	E	F	G	H	I	J	K
1	Ticker	Name	Return 2006 (%)	Rank	Percent Rank	Quartile	90th percentile?				
2	ARTKX	Artisan International Value	34.46	2	96%	Fourth	Yes		90th percentile	30.50	
3	BDV	BlackRock Dividend Achievers	29.53	5	85%	Fourth					
4	BRAGX	Bridgeway Aggressive Investors 1	7.11	22	22%	First			First Quartile	10.43	
5	BRSGX	Bridgeway Small-Cap Growth	5.31	24	15%	First			Second Quartile	17.74	
6	BRSVX	Bridgeway Small-Cap Value	12.77	20	30%	Second			Third Quartile	27.63	
7	CFIMX	Clipper	15.28	18	37%	Second					
8	CGMFX	CGM Focus	14.92	19	33%	Second					
9	CGMRX	CGM Realty	29.01	6	81%	Fourth					
10	CRMMX	CRM Mid Cap Value Inv	16.95	15	48%	Second					
11	DODFX	Dodge & Cox International Stock	28.01	7	78%	Fourth					
12	DODGX	Dodge & Cox Stock	18.53	14	52%	Third					
13	DODIX	Dodge & Cox Income	5.3	25	11%	First					
14	EGLRX	Alpine International Real Estate	38.74	1	100%	Fourth	Yes				
15	EHSTX	Eaton Vance Large-Cap Value A	18.81	13	56%	Third					
16	ETB	Eaton Vance Tax-Managed Buy-Write Incom	27.5	8	74%	Third					
17	FAIRX	Fairholme	16.72	16	44%	Second					
18	FCNTX	Fidelity Contrafund	11.54	21	26%	Second					
19	FSCOX	Fidelity International Small Cap Opp	25.72	9	70%	Third					
20	GAB	Gabelli Equity	29.56	4	89%	Fourth					
21	GABAX	Gabelli Asset	21.84	11	63%	Third					
22	HABDX	Harbor Bond Instl	3.91	26	7%	First					
23	HAINX	Harbor International Instl	32.69	3	93%	Fourth	Yes				
24	HFCVX	Hennessy Cornerstone Value	20.14	12	59%	Third					
25	HSGFX	Hussman Strategic Growth	3.51	27	4%	First					
26	HSTRX	Hussman Strategic Total Return	5.66	23	19%	First					
27	ICHCX	ICON Healthcare	0.84	28	0%	First					
28	IWB	iShares Russell 1000 Index	15.41	17	41%	Second					
29	IWD	iShares Russell 1000 Value Index	22.48	10	67%	Third					
30											
31											

FIGURE 9.8 Quantile analysis using functions.

In column E we determine the percent rank of the funds using the formula =PERCENTRANK(C$2:C$29,C2) in E2 and copying and pasting it in the other cells.

In column F we want to show for each fund its quartile ranking. For this we have to first determine the quartile boundaries, which we do in J4:J6. The formula in J4 is =QUARTILE(C$2:C$29,1) and so on. Then I used the following formula in F2 to show the quartile of first fund (and copied and pasted it in the other cells in that column):

=IF(C2<=J$4,"First",IF(C2<=J$5,"Second",IF(C2<=J$6,"Third",
"Fourth")))

In column G I wanted to show if a fund is in the 90th percentile. I started by calculating the 90th percentile in J2 using the formula =PERCENTILE (C2:C29,90%), used the formula =IF((C2-J$2)>0,"Yes","") in G2, and used copies of it in the rest of that column.

The Rank and Percentile Tool

The Analysis ToolPak includes a Rank and Percentile tool that can do many of the same analyses you can do using the some of the functions we just discussed. Unfortunately, you can get your output in only one way. If you need what it does, it can be a useful tool. Otherwise you should use the functions we discussed.

Figure 9.9 shows an example of how this tool works. Columns B, C, and D show the same data we used in the previous example. Open the Rank and Percentile tool from the Analysis ToolPak. In the input range enter D2:D29 (by pointing), select the Output Range, and in the box next to it enter H1:K29 and press OK. Excel produces the table shown in that range.

Unfortunately Excel identifies the funds by their point number, which is the serial number of the funds as shown in column A. This is not very useful. So I entered the formula =INDEX(B$2:B$29,H2) in G2 and copied and pasted it in G3:G28. This formula uses the point number in column H (13 in H2) to find the 13th fund's ticker symbol from the range B$2:B$29 and enters it in G2.

The output is a list of the funds sorted by their returns and their percentiles. Note that as with the Rank function if two funds have identical returns they will have the same rank number and the next rank number will be skipped.

NORMAL PROBABILITY DISTRIBUTIONS

You will use the bell-shaped normal probability distribution in many models and calculations. Normal distributions are characterized by just two parameters, the

	A	B	C	D	E	F	G	H	I	J	K	L
1		**Ticker**	**Name**	**Return 2006 (%)**				*Point*	*Column1*	*Rank*	*Percent*	
2	1	ARTKX	Artisan International Value	34.46			EGLRX	13	38.74	1	100.00%	
3	2	BDV	BlackRock Dividend Achievers	29.53			ARTKX	1	34.46	2	96.20%	
4	3	BRAGX	Bridgeway Aggressive Investors 1	7.11			HAINX	22	32.69	3	92.50%	
5	4	BRSGX	Bridgeway Small-Cap Growth	5.31			GAB	19	29.56	4	88.80%	
6	5	BRSVX	Bridgeway Small-Cap Value	12.77			BDV	2	29.53	5	85.10%	
7	6	CFIMX	Clipper	15.28			CGMRX	8	29.01	6	81.40%	
8	7	CGMFX	CGM Focus	14.92			DODFX	10	28.01	7	77.70%	
9	8	CGMRX	CGM Realty	29.01			ETB	15	27.5	8	74.00%	
10	9	CRMMX	CRM Mid Cap Value Inv	16.95			FSCOX	18	25.72	9	70.30%	
11	10	DODFX	Dodge & Cox International Stock	28.01			IWD	28	22.48	10	66.60%	
12	11	DODGX	Dodge & Cox Stock	18.53			GABAX	20	21.84	11	62.90%	
13	12	DODIX	Dodge & Cox Income	5.3			HFCVX	23	20.14	12	59.20%	
14	13	EGLRX	Alpine International Real Estate	38.74			EHSTX	14	18.81	13	55.50%	
15	14	EHSTX	Eaton Vance Large-Cap Value A	18.81			DODGX	11	18.53	14	51.80%	
16	15	ETB	Eaton Vance Tax-Managed Buy-Write Inco	27.5			CRMMX	9	16.95	15	48.10%	
17	16	FAIRX	Fairholme	16.72			FAIRX	16	16.72	16	44.40%	
18	17	FCNTX	Fidelity Contrafund	11.54			IWB	27	15.41	17	40.70%	
19	18	FSCOX	Fidelity International Small Cap Opp	25.72			CFIMX	6	15.28	18	37.00%	
20	19	GAB	Gabelli Equity	29.56			CGMFX	7	14.92	19	33.30%	
21	20	GABAX	Gabelli Asset	21.84			BRSVX	5	12.77	20	29.60%	
22	21	HABDX	Harbor Bond Instl	3.91			FCNTX	17	11.54	21	25.90%	
23	22	HAINX	Harbor International Instl	32.69			BRAGX	3	7.11	22	22.20%	
24	23	HFCVX	Hennessy Cornerstone Value	20.14			HSTRX	25	5.66	23	18.50%	
25	24	HSGFX	Hussman Strategic Growth	3.51			BRSGX	4	5.31	24	14.80%	
26	25	HSTRX	Hussman Strategic Total Return	5.66			DODIX	12	5.3	25	11.10%	
27	26	ICHCX	ICON Healthcare	0.84			HABDX	21	3.91	26	7.40%	
28	27	IWB	iShares Russell 1000 Index	15.41			HSGFX	24	3.51	27	3.70%	
29	28	IWD	iShares Russell 1000 Value Index	22.48			ICHCX	26	0.84	28	0.00%	
30												
31												

FIGURE 9.9 Example of using the Rank and Percentile tool.

mean and the standard deviation. You can do most calculations you need to do for normally distributed variables using the NORMDIST and NORMINV functions.

A normal distribution with a mean of 0 and standard deviation of 1 is called a standard normal distribution. You can, of course, use the functions for normal distributions for standard normal distributions as well. However, because people use standard normal distributions frequently, Excel provides the functions NORMSDIST and NORMSINV specifically for standard normal distributions. They are similar to the two functions for the general normal distributions.

Excel also provides a function called STANDARDIZE, which you can use to calculate how many standard deviations away from the mean a particular observation is. You will rarely use this function.

NORMDIST

Returns the normal cumulative distribution for the specified mean and standard deviation. In other words, if you know the mean and standard deviation of a normal distribution, you can use NORMDIST to find the probability that a random draw from it will have a value less than x. (This probability is equal to the area under the familiar bell-shaped graph of the normal density function to the left of x.)

The syntax of the NORMDIST function is:

NORMDIST(x,mean,standard_dev,cumulative)

x is the value for which you want the cumulative probability.

Cumulative is a logical value that determines the output of the function. If cumulative is TRUE, NORMDIST returns the cumulative probability; if FALSE, it returns the probability mass function.

Because the total area under the graph of a normal density function is 1, the probability that a random draw will have a value greater than x is equal to 1 minus the probability that it will have a value less than x. You can also use this function to calculate the probability that a random draw will have a value between x and y.

Example What is the probability that a random draw from a normal distribution with mean 3 and standard deviation 4 will have a value less than 2? Enter the formula =NORMDIST(2,3,4,TRUE) to get the probability 0.4013. This is the area under the normal density function to the left of the value 2.

Example What is the probability that a random draw from a normal distribution with mean 3 and standard deviation 4 will have a value between 2 and 6? Enter the formula =NORMDIST(6,3,4,TRUE)-NORMDIST(2,3,4,TRUE) to get the probability 0.3721. It is easiest to think of this as the area under the normal density function between 2 and 6.

NORMINV

Returns the inverse of the normal cumulative distribution for the specified mean and standard deviation. Think of NORMINV as the inverse of NORMDIST. If you know x and want to find the probability that a random draw will have a value less than x, you will use NORMDIST. If you know the probability and want to find the corresponding x, you will use the NORMINV function.

The syntax of the NORMINV function is:

NORMINV(probability,mean,standard_dev)

Probability is the probability you want to specify.

If you enter the formula =NORMINV(0.3,3,4) in a cell, you will get a value of 0.9024, which says that for a normal distribution with mean 3 and standard deviation 4, there is a 30% (0.3) probability that a random draw will have a value of 0.9024 or less. As I explained under NORMDIST, you can also say that there is a 70% probability that a random draw will have a value greater than 0.9024.

NORMSDIST

This function, which is designed specifically for standard normal distributions—that is, normal distributions with mean of 0 and standard deviation of 1—works the same way as the NORMDIST function except that it requires only one argument (the x value). The syntax is NORMDIST(x).

NORMSINV

This function, which is designed specifically for standard normal distribution—that is, normal distributions with mean of 0 and standard deviation of 1—works the same way as the NORMINV function except that it requires only one argument (the probability). The syntax is NORMINV(probability).

STANDARDIZE

The STANDARDIZE function returns the distance of an observation, measured in terms of standard deviation, from the mean. This measure, called the Z-value, was used in pre-computer days to look up probabilities from standard normal distribution tables. Now that you can find the probabilities easily using functions like NORMDIST, this function is of limited use.

The syntax of the STANDARDIZE function is:

STANDARDIZE(x,mean,standard_dev)

RANDOM NUMBERS

Excel provides two functions called RAND and RANDBETWEEN as well as a Random Number Generation tool in the Analysis ToolPak to generate random numbers (the same thing as drawing random samples) from a number of common statistical distributions. (Excel includes RAND and RANDBETWEEN in the Mathematical and Trigonometric functions category.)

The RAND and RANDBETWEEN functions can generate random numbers only for uniform distributions, whereas the Random Number Generation tool offers a number of other choices of distribution and some additional flexibilities. Another difference is that the two functions may be called dynamic in the sense that every time the worksheet recalculates, they generate new draws. If you use them in a model such as one that simulates stock prices, then every time the worksheet recalculates—or you force it to recalculate by pressing F9—you will have a new simulation. The Random Number Generation tool generates a set of static draws that are not going to change as your worksheet recalculates or other changes take place. If you want a new set of draws, you will have to generate them by repeating the necessary steps.

RAND

The RAND function returns an evenly or uniformly distributed random number greater than or equal to 0 and less than or equal to 1. Evenly or uniformly distributed means all numbers between 0 and 1 will have equal probability of being drawn. The RAND function does not take any argument, but you still have to include a pair of empty parentheses.

To use it you enter =RAND() in a cell, and every time the worksheet is recalculated RAND will generate a new random number in that cell. (You can force a recalculation and generate new random numbers by pressing F9.) If you need 20 random draws, you have to enter the RAND function in 20 cells, and every time the worksheet recalculates you will have 20 new similar random draws that are independent of one another.

Although the RAND function does not seem very versatile, with a little ingenuity you can make additional uses of it. As I discuss in the section on generating random draws in Chapter 18: Simulating Stock Prices, you can use the RAND function in conjunction with the NORMSINV function to generate random draws from a standard normal distribution (that is, a normal distribution with a mean of 0 and standard deviation of 1). You can further convert this draw into a draw from any other normal distribution by multiplying it by the desired standard deviation and then adding to it the desired mean.

To generate a random real number between any two values (for example, 2 and 8) in a cell, you can use the formula =RAND()*(8–2)+2 in the cell. You can also do the same using the RANDBETWEEN function.

If you want to use RAND to generate a random number but do not want the numbers to change every time the cell is calculated, you can enter =RAND() in the formula bar, and then press F9 to change the formula to a random number.

RANDBETWEEN

The RANDBETWEEN function returns a uniformly distributed random number between the numbers you specify. A new random number is returned every time the worksheet is calculated.

The syntax of the RANDBETWEEN function is:

RANDBETWEEN(bottom,top)

Bottom and top are the lower and upper limits of the range. You use it the same way as the RAND function.

The Random Number Generation Tool

This tool generates one or more columns of random numbers with one of the following distributions: Uniform, Normal, Bernoulli, Binomial, Poisson, and Discrete. (There is a seventh option called Patterned, but it does not generate random numbers.)

Unlike the RAND() function, this tool creates a table of random numbers that will not change when the worksheet recalculates. If you want another set of random numbers, you will have to repeat the steps.

The inputs to the dialog box are:

- **Number of Variables:** Enter the number of columns of values you want to generate. If you do not specify a number, Excel will fill all columns in the output range you specify. If you want 100 random numbers, this gives you an option to specify whether you want them in one column with 100 rows, or 5 columns with 20 rows, or something else. If you opt for the latter, you can also think of the random numbers produced as 20 values for each of 5 different variables with the same distribution. This is why the number of columns is referred to as the number of variables.
- **Number of Random Numbers:** Enter the number of data points you want to see in each column. If you do not specify a number, Excel will fill all rows in the output range you specify.
- **Distribution:** Choose the distribution you want. You will mostly use the Uniform or the Normal distributions, as shown in the examples below. (If you need descriptions of the other distributions or how to use them, click the Help button in the tool's dialog box.)

- **Parameters:** Enter a value or values to characterize the distribution you selected, for example, the minimum and maximum values for uniform distribution or the mean and standard deviation for normal distribution.
- **Random Seed:** You usually leave this blank. However, if you think that in the future you may want to generate the same sequence of random numbers again, enter an integer between 1 and 32,767 and make a note of it. Every time you generate a set of random numbers with the same distribution and parameters and the same seed, Excel will generate the same sequence of random numbers.
- **Output Options:** Choose Output Range and specify a range if you want your output in a specific range in a specific worksheet. Otherwise choose one of the other options. If you are not specifying a range, then make sure that you have specified the number of random numbers you want.

Example To generate 30 random numbers uniformly distributed between 1 and 3, enter 1 for Number of Variables or leave it blank, enter 30 for Number of Random Numbers, choose Uniform for distribution, specify between 1 and 3 in Parameters, and enter a range with 1 column and 30 rows in the Output Range box. Click OK to generate the random numbers. (Uniform distribution means every number in the specified range will have equal probability of being drawn.)

Example To generate 100 random draws for each of two normally distributed variables with a mean of 10 and a standard deviation of 15, enter 2 for Number of Variables, 100 for Number of Random Numbers, choose Normal distribution, and specify a mean of 10 and standard deviation of 15. If you want the output in a new worksheet named Test, select New Worksheet Ply in Output Options and type "Test" in the box next to it. Click OK and Excel will insert a properly named new worksheet and generate two columns of 100 random numbers, each starting in A1 and B1.

Linear Regression and Related Statistics

Linear regression—we will call it just regression because here we will not be involved with non-linear regression—is one of the most widely used tools in statistics. It is also one of the most widely abused. Excel provides a number of functions and one Analysis ToolPak tool for performing regression, which make it very easy to plug in some numbers, do a regression, and get some output. That ease also makes it easy to abuse this powerful statistical tool. Unless you make sure that your data is appropriate for using linear regression and know how to interpret the results using the standard statistics Excel generates with a regression, you can easily draw the wrong conclusions from your analysis.

Here I will discuss how to use the various regression functions and the Regression tool available in Excel, assuming that you have a reasonable grasp of the underlying statistical theory. If you don't, then study at least the basics—and these functions and tool can be very useful to supplement your study of the theory—first.

LINEST

I am starting with LINEST because it is Excel's most comprehensive regression function. It can do both simple regression (one dependent and one independent variable) and multiple regression (one dependent and more than one independent variable). It can also generate the necessary standard statistics for a regression. Because it is so versatile, it is also more complex than the other regression functions, which have more limited abilities; but it can be easier to use in most situations. The advantage of starting with LINEST is that once you understand it, learning the other functions will be easier.

We will discuss the LINEST function in the context of the general multiple regression model:

$$y = m1 \times 1 + m2 \times 2 + b$$

Here y is a set of values for the dependent variable and $\times 1$, $\times 2$, and so on, are corresponding sets of values for the independent variables 1, 2, and so on. For a simple regression we will have a set of values only for $\times 1$. b is called the constant or intercept of the regression and the m's are called the slopes of the regression.

The syntax of the LINEST function is:

LINEST(known_y's, known_x's,const,stats)

Known_y's is the array of the known values for the dependent variable, which can be a single column or single row.

Known_x's is an array of the known independent variables. If there are 3 independent variables, 60 data points, and the known_y's are in a column (a 60 × 1 array), then the array of known_x's would be a 60 × 3 array. If the known_y's are in a row, that is, a 1 × 60 array, then the array of the known_x's would be a 3 × 60 array. For a simple regression with one independent variable, the known_x's will be in a 60 × 1 or 1 × 60 array depending on whether the y values are in a column or row. Needless to say, that they first must correspond to the first set of x's (first row or first column of the array of x's), and so on.

Const is the logical value. If it is FALSE then the constant of the regression, b, is forced to equal 0 (zero). If const is omitted or TRUE then b is calculated normally.

Stats specifies if LINEST should return additional regression statistics. If stats is FALSE or omitted, then LINEST returns an array containing only the b's and m's of the regression. If stats is TRUE, then LINEST returns a larger array containing a number of additional statistics.

	A	B	C	D	E	F	G
1	**Layout of the Output Array from LINEST Function**						
2							
3	m4	m3	m2	m1	b		
4	se4	se3	se2	se1	seb		
5	r2	sey					
6	F	df					
7	ssreg	ssresid					

FIGURE 9.10 Layout of the output array from the LINEST function.

LINEST must be entered as an array formula in an array large enough to hold the statistics you ask for by setting the stats argument to TRUE or FALSE. Figure 9.10 shows the statistics that LINEST returns when stats is TRUE and how they are organized in the output array. The layout is for a multiple regression with four independent variables. As you can see, the output is a 5×5 array in this case. So in this case you will have to enter LINEST as an array formula in a 5×5 array. We will shortly demonstrate how you do that. The array will always have 5 rows and 1 column more than the number of independent variables. So for a simple regression (only one independent variable), you will need a 5×2 array.

Here's what the different statistics in the array are:

m1 to m4 are the slopes of coefficients of the regression.

b is the constant or intercept of the regression.

se1 to se4 are the standard errors for the corresponding coefficients.

seb is the standard error of the intercept b.

r2 is the coefficient of determination.

sey is the standard error for the y estimate.

F is the F-statistic used to judge if the observed relationship between the dependent and independent variables occurred by chance.

df is the degrees of freedom of the regression, which you need to know to find the critical values for the F-statistic for the level of confidence you want in the model.

ssreg is the regression sum of squares.

ssresid is the residual sum of squares.

If you set stats FALSE then you will get only the first row of outputs, that is, the intercept and the slopes of the regression. In that case you will have to enter LINEST in a 1×5 array for multiple regressions with four independent variables.

	A	B	C	D	E	F	G	H	I	J	K	L	M	N
1	**Results of a simple regression**													
2														
3		**Stock (y)**	**Index (x)**		**Output array from LINEST**									
4	1	-0.1299	-0.0767		0.368862721	0.004408241		Slope using SLOPE		0.368862721				
5	2	-0.0763	-0.0895		0.098019964	0.004497464		Intercept using INTERCEPT		0.004408241				
6	3	-0.0738	0.0078		0.126257665	0.044555081								
7	4	-0.1048	-0.0778		14.16121284	98								
8	5	-0.1230	-0.1842		0.028112206	0.194545212								
9	6	0.1134	-0.0966											
10	7	0.0186	0.0121											
11	8	-0.0536	-0.0099											
12	9	-0.1090	-0.0899		**Output from the Regression tool**									
13	10	0.0060	0.0106											
14	11	0.0034	0.0465		SUMMARY OUTPUT									
15	12	-0.0483	-0.0060											
16	13	0.0290	-0.0354		*Regression Statistics*									
17	14	-0.0404	-0.0631		Multiple R	0.355327546								
18	15	0.0106	-0.0087		R Square	0.126257665								
19	16	0.0558	-0.0450		Adjusted R Squ	0.117341927								
20	17	0.1116	0.0147		Standard Error	0.044555081								
21	18	0.0010	0.0352		Observations	100								
22	19	0.0735	0.0128											
23	20	0.0048	-0.0325		ANOVA									
24	21	-0.0001	-0.0180			*df*	*SS*	*MS*	*F*	*Significance F*				
25	22	0.0027	0.0320		Regression	1	0.028112206	0.028112206	14.16121284	0.000285915				
26	23	0.0019	0.0424		Residual	98	0.194545212	0.001985155						
27	24	0.0260	0.0099		Total	99	0.222657418							
28	25	-0.0357	-0.0221											
29	26	0.0005	0.0140			*Coefficients*	*Standard Error*	*t Stat*	*P-value*	*Lower 95%*	*Upper 95%*	*Lower 95.0%*	*Upper 95.0%*	
30	27	0.0266	0.0125		Intercept	0.004408241	0.004497464	0.980161481	0.329419948	-0.004516829	0.013333311	-0.004516829	0.013333311	
31	28	0.0153	0.0163		X Variable 1	0.368862721	0.098019964	3.763138696	0.000285915	0.174345297	0.563380145	0.174345297	0.563380145	
32	29	0.0962	0.0310											
102	99	0.0806	0.0040											
103	100	0.0279	-0.0835											
104														

FIGURE 9.11 Data and output for a simple regression.

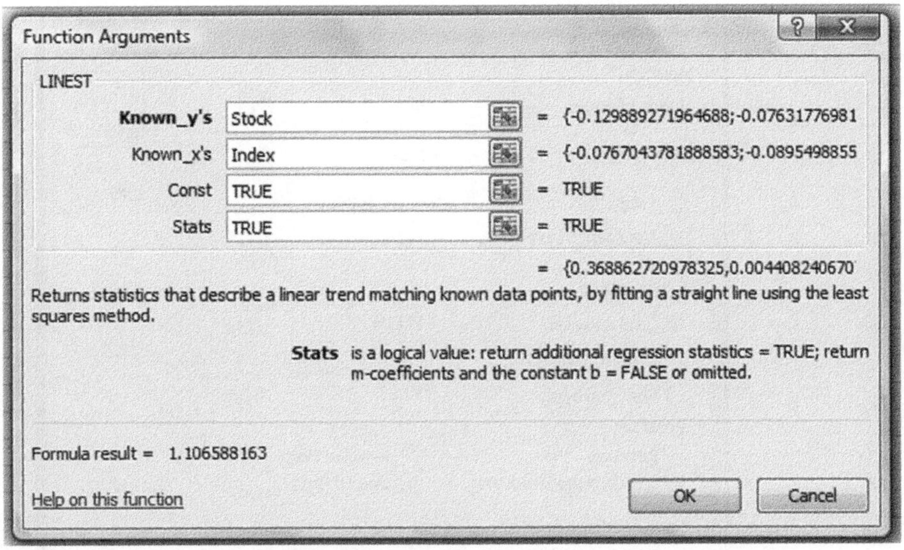

Function Arguments

LINEST

Known_y's Stock = {-0.129889271964688;-0.07631776981

Known_x's Index = {-0.076704378188583;-0.0895498855

Const TRUE = TRUE

Stats TRUE = TRUE

= {0.368862720978325,0.004408240670

Returns statistics that describe a linear trend matching known data points, by fitting a straight line using the least squares method.

Stats is a logical value: return additional regression statistics = TRUE; return m-coefficients and the constant b = FALSE or omitted.

Formula result = 1.106588163

Help on this function OK Cancel

FIGURE 9.12 LINEST inputs for doing regression.

We can now look at an example. We will do a simple regression of the monthly return for a stock (the dependent variable) against the monthly return for an index (the independent variable) to calculate the alpha (the intercept) and beta (slope) for the stock. In Figure 9.11, B4:B103 shows the monthly returns for the stock for 100 months and C4:C103 shows the corresponding values for the index. I have named those ranges Stock and Index, respectively.

Because this is a simple regression, we will have to enter LINEST in a 5 × 2 array to get all the statistics. Select the range E4:F8 and then Formula ⇨ Function Library ⇨ More Functions ⇨ Statistical. Then click on LINEST to open the Function Argument dialog box for it. (See Figure 9.12.) For known_y's enter Stock, for known_x's Index, for Const TRUE and for Stats TRUE. Then press Ctrl+Shft+Enter to enter LINEST as an array function to do the regression. The output you will get is shown in E4:F8.

You will have to interpret the different statistics by referring to the layout of the output array in Figure 9.10 that we discussed. But you will quickly get used to them. For example, the 0.37 (rounded) value in E4 is the slope of the regression or the beta of the stock. The alpha or the intercept of the regression is 0.004 shown in F4, and so on. The R-square of the regression, shown in E6 is only 0.13, which is low.

An important point to note is that the table of statistics is dynamic in that the values will automatically update if you change the input data. This is true of the output of all functions.

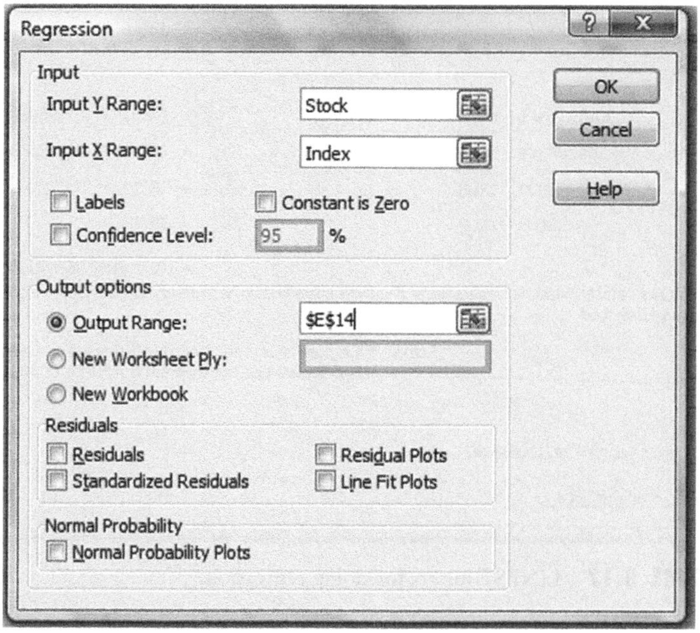

FIGURE 9.13 The dialog box for the Regression tool.

The Regression Tool

The Regression tool in the Analysis ToolPak is another comprehensive tool for doing regression. It also can provide a number of standard statistics for a regression automatically create certain plots. Let us do the same regression again using this tool.

Open the dialog box for the Regression tool as shown in Figure 9.13. Again, enter Stock for Input Y Range and Index for Input X Range. Under output options choose output range and top-left cell where you want the output to start (here E14). And then click OK. You will get the elaborate output shown in Figure 9.11. If you understand regression, the output is self-explanatory because unlike the output of LINEST, this output is very nicely labeled.

As expected, the alpha, beta and other values are the same from both regressions. You can experiment with the other options available in the dialog box for Regression.

Note that the output is not dynamic. If you make any change in the input values, you will have to rerun the Regression tool. This is a key disadvantage of the Analysis ToolPak tools vis-à-vis functions that we discussed when I introduced the Analysis ToolPak.

SLOPE

For simple regressions you can find the slope using this function. This function does not offer any option to force the intercept to be 0.

The syntax is:

SLOPE(known_y's,known_x's)

In Figure 9.11, J4 shows the slope calculated using this function, which agrees exactly with the results from the other two regressions. But the underlying algorithm used in the SLOPE and INTERCEPT functions is different than the underlying algorithm used in the LINEST function. The difference between these algorithms can lead to different results on some rare occasions (when data is undetermined and collinear).

INTERCEPT

For simple regressions you can find the intercept using this function.

The syntax is:

INTERCEPT(known_y's,known_x's)

In Figure 9.11, J5 shows the intercept calculated using this function, which agrees exactly with the results from the other two regressions. But the underlying algorithm used in the SLOPE and INTERCEPT functions is different than the underlying algorithm used in the LINEST function. The difference between these algorithms can lead to different results on some rare occasions (when data is undetermined and collinear).

FORECAST

Most of the time you do a linear regression analysis, which is the same as finding the equation of the straight line that best fits the data, to predict the value of the dependent variable y for some value of the independent variable x. Once you find the slope m and intercept b of the regression line, you can predict the value of other y's as mx+b. Because people do this all the time, Excel includes the function FORECAST, which does that in one function. It does the regression for the data set you provide to find the values of b and m and then returns the value of y for the x you provide.2

The syntax is:

FORECAST(x,known_y's,known_x's)

The first variable, x, is the value for which you want to predict y.

	A	B	C	D	E
1	Predicting Values Using FORECAST and TREND				
2					
3	Year	Revenue	Using FORECAST	Using TREND	
4	2001	50000			
5	2002	54000			
6	2003	62000			
7	2004	66500			
8	2005	69000			
9	2006	76000			
10	2007	77000			
11	2008	87500			
12					
13	2009		90357	90357	
14	2010		95286	95381	
15	2011		99086	100405	
16	2012		105200	105429	
17					
18					

FIGURE 9.14 Predicting values using FORECAST and TREND.

Known_y's and known_x's are as we defined before.

The FORECAST function estimates the b and m the same way as the SLOPE and INTERCEPT functions do. You cannot force the b to be 0. Also, if you want to predict y's for 5 different x's, you will have to enter the function in 5 different cells.

In Figure 9.14, B4:B11 shows the actual revenues of a company for the years 2001 to 2008. To predict the revenue for 2009 from this historical data using linear regression, in C13 enter the formula =FORECAST(A13,B4:B11,A4:A11), and then you can copy and paste it in C14:C16 to predict revenues for 2010 to 2012.

TREND

Like FORECAST, TREND also predicts the values of y's for a set of x's based on a set of known y's and x's. But TREND is a more flexible function in that it can do multiple regression (that is, it can work with more than one independent variable) and you can also force the intercept of the regression to be 0. TREND does the regression the same way as LINEST and then uses the calculated regression coefficients to predict the values of y's for the new x's.

The syntax is:

TREND(known_y's,known_x's,new_x's,const)

Known_y's, known_x's, and const are as we discussed for LINEST.

New_x's must match known_x's, that is, if the latter has values for 3 independent variables and we want to make 5 predictions, then new_x's must be must be a 5 × 3 or 3 × 5 array depending on how the known values are laid out. TREND must be entered as an array formula in an array of suitable dimensions (in this case 5 × 1 or 1 × 5).

To repeat the predictions we made in Figure 9.14 using FORECAST, select D13:D17, open the dialog box for entering the TREND function and enter A4:A11 for known_x's, B4:B11 for known_y's, A13:A16 for new_x's and TRUE for const. Finish by pressing Ctrl+Shft+Enter to enter this it as an array formula.

CORREL

Correlation is a statistic that measures the degree to which two sets of data vary together. Its value lies between –1 and +1. The CORREL function returns the correlation coefficient between two sets of data.

The syntax is:

```
CORREL(array1,array2)
```

Array1 and array2 are two ranges containing numbers.

The Analysis ToolPak has a Correlation tool that does the same calculation.

The Correlation Tool

The Correlation tool in the Analysis ToolPak is a more flexible tool to calculate the pair-wise correlations when more than two variables are involved.

COVAR

Covariance also measures the degree to which two sets of data vary together. The difference between covariance and correlation is that correlation is calculated by dividing the covariance by the product of the standard deviations of the two data sets, so that the correlation statistic always has a value between –1 and +1. The COVAR function returns the covariance between two sets of data.

The syntax is:

```
COVAR(array1,array2)
```

Array1 and array2 are two ranges containing numbers.

The Analysis ToolPak has a Covariance tool that does the same calculation.

The Covariance Tool

You can use this tool in the Analysis ToolPak to calculate covariance among any number of variables. The result is presented in the form of a correlation matrix.

STATISTICAL TESTS

TINV

Returns the t-value of the Student's t-distribution as a function of the probability and the degrees of freedom. The result is generally used to construct confidence intervals. (Remember that the t-distributions are generally used in place of the normal distribution in cases where the sample size is below 30. For larger sample sizes, the normal and t-distributions produce essentially the same results.)

The syntax is:

```
TINV(probability,degrees_freedom)
```

Probability is the probability associated with the two-tailed Student's t-distribution.

Degrees_freedom is the number of degrees of freedom that characterizes the distribution.

The value returned by TINV is the same as the value you look up in a table of the Student's t-distribution. Keep in mind that TINV is the value for a two-tailed test whereas most tables are for a one-tailed test. Therefore, if you want the value corresponding to a 0.05 probability from a one-tailed probability table you will have to enter 2×0.05 or 0.1 in TINV.

Suppose you have a sample mean of 0.5 and sample standard deviation of 0.3 from a sample of 50 data points. You want to create a 90% confidence interval (two-tailed).

To calculate the upper value of the interval you will enter the formula = 0.5+0.3/(SQRT(50)*TINV(0.1,49) to get the value 0.57113. To calculate the lower limit, the formula will be = 0.5–0.3/(SQRT(50)*TINV(0.1,49) and the value will be 0.42887.

TDIST

Returns the percentage points (probability) for the Student t-distribution where a numeric value (x) is a calculated value of t for which the percentage points are to be computed. The result is generally used for hypothesis testing. (Remember that the t-distributions are generally used in place of a normal distribution in cases where sample size is below 30. For larger sample sizes, the normal and t-distributions produce essentially the same results.)

The syntax is:

```
TDIST(x,degrees_freedom,tails)
```

The variable x is the numeric value at which to evaluate the distribution.

Degrees_freedom is an integer indicating the number of degrees of freedom.

Tails specifies the number of distribution tails to return. If tails = 1, TDIST returns the probability assuming a one-tailed test. If tails = 2, TDIST returns the probability assuming a two-tailed test.

TTEST

Returns the probability associated with a Student's t-test. Use TTEST to determine whether two samples are likely to have come from two populations with the same mean.

The syntax is:

TTEST(array1,array2,tails,type)

Array1 and array2 are the two data sets.

Tails should be 1 or 2 to specify if the test should use a one- or two-tailed distribution.

Type indicates the kind of t-test to perform. If type is 1, a paired test is performed. If type is 2, a two-sample equal variance test (homoscedastic) is performed. If type is 3, a two-sample unequal variance (heteroscedastic) test is performed.

Tools to Perform Student's T-tests

The Analysis ToolPak provides three tools for performing the two-sample t-test to draw conclusions about the means for two populations based on two samples. The three tools are:

t-Test: Paired Two-Sample for Mean Use it when both samples come from the same population.

t-Test: Two-Sample Assuming Equal Variances Use this test if you believe that the variances of the populations underlying the two samples are equal.

t-Test: Two-Sample Assuming Unequal Variances Use this test if you believe that the variances of the populations underlying the two samples are unequal.

For details on using these tools look in Excel's Help.

FTEST

Returns the result of an F-test (used to measure the difference in variability). An F-test returns the two-tailed probability that the variances in array1 and array2 are not significantly different. Use this function to determine whether two samples have different variances. For example, given test scores from public and private schools, you can test whether these schools have different levels of test score diversity.

The syntax is:

```
FTEST(array1,array2)
```

FDIST

Returns the F probability distribution. You can use this function to determine whether two data sets have different degrees of diversity. For example, you can examine the test scores of men and women entering high school and determine if the variability in the females is different from that found in the males.

The syntax is:

```
FDIST(x,degrees_freedom1, degrees_freedom2)
```

The variable x is the value at which to evaluate the function.
Degrees_freedom1 is the numerator's degrees of freedom.
Degrees_freedom2 is the denominator's degrees of freedom.

FINV

Returns the inverse of the F probability distribution. If p =FDIST(x,...), then FINV(p,...) =x. The F distribution can be used in an F-test that compares the degree of variability in two data sets. For example, you can analyze income distributions in the United States and Canada to determine whether the two countries have a similar degree of income diversity.

The syntax is:

```
FINV(prob, degrees_freedom1,degrees_freedom2)
```

Prob is the probability associated with the F cumulative distribution.
Degrees_freedom1 is the numerator's degrees of freedom.
Degrees_freedom2 is the denominator's degrees of freedom.

The F-Test Two-Sample for Variance Tool

Use this Analysis ToolPak tool to test using the F-test (based on two samples) if the variance of two populations are roughly the same. The F-test compares two variances, V1/V2, to produce an F statistic. Values close to 1 indicate that the variances are similar. (See details in Help if you need to use this tool.)

CHAPTER 10

Using the Financial Functions

Excel includes numerous financial functions. You can look at them as ready-made mini-models that you can build into your analysis and models. If they were not there, you would have had to create many of them on your own. So learning what is available and learning to use them well will save you a lot of time in doing your analysis and building your models.

In this chapter I cover the functions that you are likely use often in detail and list the others that you may use only in special situations. Instead of using Excel's alphabetical order, I have grouped them by use so that you can see at a glance what different functions are available for each type of use.

Do not look at these functions as "black boxes." As a finance person you must thoroughly understand exactly how a function does its calculations before you use it. Otherwise you may input wrong arguments, and even when you enter the correct arguments you may get wrong answers or not the answers you are looking for.

For a general discussion how to use Excel functions and install and use the Analysis ToolPak see the chapter on advanced Excel features.

ANNUITY FUNCTIONS

Excel provides several functions to do different kinds of calculations for constant annuities, which you can use for both loans and investments. Constant annuities are equal cash flows (either all inflows or all outflows) that take place at equal time intervals. Constant annuities are governed by a set of four variables; if you specify three, then the fourth can be calculated. The Excel functions for calculating these variables are: PV, FV, PMT, RATE, and NPER. These functions actually go one step beyond handling just constant annuities in that in addition to the annuity payment you can also specify a cash flow pv at time 0 and another cash flow fv at the end of the annuity period, that is, nper periods from time 0.

I have also included a few other functions here that Excel provides for annuity-related calculations. However, you will use the five functions I mentioned before much more frequently than these others.

In the annuity functions, the commonly used arguments have the following meanings:

- Rate is the interest rate per period (month, year, etc.). It must be consistent with the measure of period used for specifying nper. You can enter the rate in decimal or percent (that is, as 0.08 or 8%). If you use percent, be sure to include the % symbol.
- Nper is the total number of periods (same as total number of payments) for the annuity. It must be an integer or else it is truncated to an integer.
- Pmt is the annuity amount per period.
- Pv is an additional cash flow now (time 0).
- Fv is an additional cash flow nper periods from now.
- Type is 0 for a regular annuity or annuity in arrears where the first payment occurs one period from now and 1 for an annuity due or annuity in advance where the first payment occurs now. If a function allows a type argument, you can use it to specify whether payments will be made at the beginning or at the end of the periods.

Here are a few things to keep in mind about these functions.

- When you choose type 0, present values are calculated and the pv argument relates to one period before the first cash flow (that is, now). Future values are calculated and the fv argument relates to the time of the last annuity cash flow. For type 1, it works the other way around.
- As we will see in Chapter 14: Time Value of Money, with some modifications you can use constant annuity functions to do calculations for growing annuities. You can also use these functions to calculate present value or future value of a single cash flow by using 0 for pmt.
- You must consistently use the same definition of period in specifying the arguments for a function. If you are measuring period in months then the payments must be monthly payments, the interest rate must be the monthly interest rate, the number of periods must be in number of months, and so on.
- You must specify the signs for the arguments of a function consistently from the point of view of one entity. For example, if you are borrowing money from a bank and specifying signs from your point of view, then the sign for the borrowing will be positive because it is a cash inflow and the signs for the loan payments will be negative because they are cash outflows. By using proper and consistent signs, you can use all these functions both for loans and investments.

PV

The PV function calculates the present value of a constant annuity. You can also include an additional cash flow that will occur at the end of the annuity period. By setting the annuity amount equal to zero, you can use this function to calculate the present value of a future cash flow.

The syntax of the PV function is:

PV(rate,nper,pmt,fv,type)

Fv and type are optional arguments, and if omitted, they are assumed to be zeros.

Example You are told that to pay off a loan that carries an 8% annual interest, you have to make 10 equal annual payments of $1,000 each at the end of each year. What is the loan amount? Enter the formula =PV(0.08,10,–1000,0,0) to get the answer $6,710.08. What if the loan involves an additional payment of $2,000 at the end of 10 years? Enter the formula =PV(0.08,10,–1000,–2000,0) to get the answer $7,636.47.

FV

The FV function calculates the future value of a constant annuity. You can include an additional cash flow that will occur now (time 0). By setting the annuity amount equal to zero you can use this function to calculate the future value of a cash flow that occurs now.

The syntax of the FV function is:

FV(rate,nper,pmt,pv,type)

Pv and type are optional arguments, and if omitted, they are assumed to be zeros.

Example You plan to invest $1,000 every year for 10 years starting a year from now. If you expect to earn a return of 8% per year, how much money will you accumulate at the end of 10 years? Enter the formula =FV(0.08,10,–1000,0,0) to get the answer $14,486.56. What if you can make an additional investment of $2,000 now? Enter the formula =FV(0.08,10,–1000,–2000,0) to get the answer $18,804.41.

Example You have a $10,000 loan at 8% annual interest rate. After you make 10 annual payments of $1,000 starting today, what will be the remaining balance on the loan at the end of 10 years? Enter the formula =FV(0.08,10,–1000,10000,1) to get the answer, –$5943.76. The negative sign indicates that you will have to make a payment of this amount to pay off the loan. Note that this is not the remaining balance immediately after you make the tenth payment at the beginning of the tenth year. Rather, it is the remaining balance a year later at the end of the tenth year, that is, 10 years from now.

PMT

The PMT function calculates the constant annuity payments you will have to make to pay off a loan or to accumulate a certain amount of money.

The syntax of the PMT function is:

PMT(rate,nper,pv,fv,type)

Fv and type are optional arguments, and if omitted they are assumed to be zeros.

Example You have a loan of $10,000 that carries an annual interest rate of 8%. If you want to pay it off in 10 equal annual installments starting a year from now, what will be the annual payment? Enter the formula =PMT(0.08,10,10000,0,0) to get the answer, which is –$1,490.29. What if the lender agrees to let you make a final payment of $2,000 at the end of 10 years to reduce your annual payments? Enter the formula =PMT(0.08,10,10000,–2000,0) to get the answer –$1,352.24.

Example You want to accumulate $10,000 in 10 years by investing in equal annual installments earning returns at the rate of 8% per year. If you start investing a year from now, how much will you have to invest annually? Enter the formula =PMT(0.08,10,0,10000,0) to get the answer –$690.29. If you can invest an additional $2,000 now, how would that reduce the annual investment requirement? Enter the formula =PMT(0.08,10,–2000,10000,0) to get the answer –$392.24.

NPER

The NPER function calculates how many constant annuity payments you will have to make to pay off a loan or to accumulate a certain sum of money.

The syntax of the NPER function is:

NPER(rate,pmt,pv,fv,type)

Fv and type are optional arguments, and if omitted, they are assumed to be zeros.

Example You have a $10,000 loan at an interest rate of 8% per year and you can afford to make annual payments of $1,000 starting a year from now. How many payments will you have to make to pay off the loan? Enter the formula =NPER(0.08,–1000,10000,0,0) to get the answer 20.91. This means that you will have to make 20 full payments and then a final payment smaller than the $1,000. If you think you will be able to pay an additional $4,000 at the end of the period, how would that reduce the number of payments required?

Enter the formula =NPER(0.08,–1000,10000,–4000,0) to get the answer 15.9, which should be interpreted the same as the previous answer. (Note that if you enter an annual payment of less than the annual interest payment, you will not get an answer because at that rate the loan will never be paid off.)

Example You can save $500 per year starting a year from now. If you can earn 8% per year interest on your investment and want to accumulate $10,000, how many years will it take? Enter the formula =NPER(0.08,–500,0,10000,0) to get the answer 12.4. If you can invest an additional $2,000 today, how will it reduce the number of years it will take to reach your goal? Enter the formula =NPER(0.08,–500,–2000,10000,0) to get the answer 8.8.

RATE

The RATE function calculates the periodic interest rate on a loan that can be paid off with a certain number of equal periodic payments. Alternately, it calculates the return you will have to earn in order to accumulate a certain amount of money by making a number of equal periodic investments.

The syntax of the RATE function is:

RATE(nper,pmt,pv,fv,type,guess)

Fv, type, and guess are optional arguments. If fv and type are omitted, they are assumed to be zeros. If guess is omitted, it is assumed to be 10%.

Guess is your guess of what the rate would be. If RATE does not converge, try different values for guess. RATE usually converges if guess is between 0% and 100%.

Example You have a $10,000 loan that can be paid off with 10 annual payments of $1,200 each if you make the first payment one year from now. What is the interest rate on the loan? Enter the formula =RATE(10,–1200,10000,0,0) to get the answer 3.46% per year. What if the loan involves a $2,000 additional final payment? Enter the formula =RATE(10,–1200,10000,–2000,0) to get the answer 5.90%.

Example You want to accumulate $20,000 by making 10 annual investments of $1,000 each. You will make the first payment one year from now. What rate of return would you need to earn? Enter the formula =RATE(10,–1000,0,20000,0) to get the answer 14.69%. What if you can make an additional investment of $2,000 today? Enter the formula =RATE(10,–1000,–2000,20000,0) to get the answer 9.06%.

IPMT

The IPMT function calculates how much of the equal periodic payment you make on a loan in a particular period will be applied towards interest.

The syntax of the IPMT function is:

IPMT(rate,per,nper,pv,fv,type)

Per is the period number for which the interest amount is to be calculated. Fv and type are optional arguments and if omitted, they are assumed to be zeros.

Example You have a $10,000 loan at 8% interest that you will pay off in 10 equal annual installments starting a year from now. How much of the third payment will be applied to interest? To calculate it, enter the formula =IPMT(0.08,3,10,10000,0,0). The answer is –$685.13. If you will pay off the loan with 10 equal payments starting a year from now and a payment of $2,000 at the end of the tenth year, then you will enter the formula =IPMT(0.08,3,10,10000,–2000,0). The answer is –$708.11; it is this amount of the third payment that will be applied to interest. (Note that in these cases Excel internally calculates the equal periodic payments first. For example, they are $1,490.29 and $1,352.24, respectively.)

PPMT

The PPMT function calculates how much of the equal periodic payment you make on a loan in a particular period will be applied towards the loan principal.

The syntax of the PPMT function is:

PPMT(rate,per,nper,pv,fv,type)

Per is the period number for which the principal amount is to be calculated. Fv and type are optional arguments and if omitted, they are assumed to be zeros.

Example For the example under IPMT, to calculate the principal part of the third payment, enter the formula =PPMT(0.08,3,10,10000,0,0) when there is no lump sum payment at the end and the formula =PPMT(0.08,3,10,10000,–2000,0) in the second case. The answers are –$805.16 and –$644.13, respectively. Note that in both cases the interest plus principal payments add up to the equal periodic payments, as they should.

CUMIPMT

The CUMIPMT function calculates the cumulative interest payment you will make on a loan over a number of consecutive periods if you are repaying the loan with equal periodic payments.

The syntax of the CUMIPMT function is:

CUMIPMT(rate,nper,pv,start_period,end_period,type)

Start_period and end_period specify the consecutive periods for which the cumulative principal payment is to be calculated. Note that unlike in the other functions, here type is not optional.

Example You have a $10,000 loan at 8% interest that you will pay off in 10 equal annual installments starting a year from now. How much cumulative interest payment will you make as parts of the third to sixth payments? To find the answer, enter the formula =CUMIPMT(0.08,10,10000,3,6,0). The answer of –$2,333.04 says that for your third through sixth payments, $2,333.04 will be applied toward interest. (Note that here again Excel internally calculates the equal periodic payment first. In this example it is $1,490.29.)

CUMPRINC

The CUMPRINC function calculates the cumulative principal payment you will make on a loan over a number of consecutive periods if you are repaying the loan with equal periodic payments.

The syntax of the CUMPRINC function is:

CUMPRINC(rate,nper,pv,start_period,end_period,type)

Start_period and end_period specify the consecutive periods for which the cumulative principal payment is to be calculated. Note that unlike in some of the other functions, here type is not optional.

Example You have a $10,000 loan at 8% interest that you will pay off in 10 equal annual installments starting a year from now. How much cumulative principal payment will you make as parts of the third to sixth payments? To find the answer, enter the formula =CUMIPMT(0.08,10,10000,3,6,0). The answer of –$3,628.14 says that from your third through sixth payments, $3,628.14 will be applied toward principal. (Note that here again Excel internally calculates the equal periodic payment first. In this example it is $1,490.29. The third to sixth payments would add up to $5,961.18, which equals the sum of the part applied to the principal as calculated here and the part applied to interest as we calculated in the example for CUMIPMT.)

EFFECT

The EFFECT function converts a nominal interest rate to an effective interest rate depending on how frequently interest is compounded.

The syntax is:

EFFECT(nominal_rate,npery)

Nominal_rate is the nominal annual interest rate.

Npery is the number of compounding periods per year. This must be an integer or else it will be truncated to an integer.

If nominal annual interest rate is 10% and interest is compounded annually (npery = 4), then the effective annual interest rate is =EFFECT(10%,4) or 10.3813%.

NOMINAL

The NOMINAL function does the opposite of the EFFECT function. Given an effective annual interest rate and the number of compounding periods per year, it returns the nominal annual interest rate.

The syntax is:

NOMINAL(effect_rate,npery)

Effect_rate is the effective annual interest rate.

Npery is the number of compounding periods per year. Must be an integer or else it will be truncated to an integer.

If the effective annual interest rate is 10.3813% and interest is compounded quarterly then the nominal annual interest rate is =NOMINAL(10.3813,4) or 10%.

INVESTMENT ANALYSIS FUNCTIONS

In addition to the functions that apply specifically to annuities, Excel offers several other time value of money functions that are primarily used for investment analysis.

NPV

The NPV function calculates the net present value of a series of cash flows equally spaced in time with the cash flows taking place at the end of the periods. This means that the first cash flow is assumed to take place one period from now or, equivalently, the net present value is calculated as of one period before the first cash flow.

The syntax of the NPV function is:

NPV(rate,value1,value2,. . .)

Rate is the discount rate per period.

Value1, value2, and so on, are up to 29 arguments representing the cash flows in order (earliest first). They must be equally spaced in time. You can specify both cash inflows and cash outflows by using appropriate signs. You can enter the cash flows as a mix of numbers, individual cell references (that is, cell names or cell addresses), and arrays (ranges). If cash flow in any period is zero, you have to enter it as zero or indicate it with an extra comma.

For example, the formula =NPV(0.1, 1000, A3, −B5,0,C5:C10) specifies a discount rate of 10% and has zero cash flows at the end of period 2 and also at the end of period 5.

An important pitfall to keep in mind is that because the NPV function discounts the first cash flow for one period and so on, you cannot include a cash flow at time 0 (often the initial investment in a business) in the NPV function. You can get around this problem by entering in the NPV function cash flows starting with time 1 and adding to the result the cash flow at time 0. (On the other hand, to calculate the correct internal rate of return using the IRR function, you must include any cash flow at time 0 as the first cash flow argument.)

As discussed earlier, you can also use the PV function to calculate the net present value for some special types of cash flows.

IRR

The IRR function calculates the internal rate of return for a series of cash flows. As is well known, IRR is not always the best way to evaluate a project. In choosing between two competing projects, it can often lead to the wrong choice. Also, some cash flows can have two IRRs, which is confusing. Learn the advantages and shortcomings of IRR before using this function, and keep in mind that NPV is the theoretically correct and best tool for making investment decisions.

To use the IRR function, the cash flows must be equally spaced in time and in order (the first cash flow first, the second cash flow second, etc.), but do not have to be equal. Also, they must include at least one positive and one negative cash flow.

The syntax of the IRR function is:

IRR(values,guess)

Values is an array or range containing the cash flows. You can use this function as =IRR({−100, 110}) where the braces are necessary to convert the cash flows into an array or as =IRR(G6:G7), where G6:G7 is a range (array) containing the cash flows.

Guess is an optional initial guess you provide, but you may need to provide it only if you expect the answer to be unusually large (positive or negative). If you omit it, Excel starts with a guess of 10%.

Excel tries to find an answer accurate to within 0.00001 percent using an iterative technique. If it cannot do so within 20 tries, it returns #NUM!. At that point, or if the answer is far from what you expected, try a different initial guess.

Remember that the answer will be in the unit of time used for the cash flows—that is, if you use monthly cash flows, the internal rate of return will be a monthly rate.

See the discussion under the NPV function to understand why and how you need to handle a cash flow at time 0 differently in the NPV and IRR functions.

MIRR

The MIRR function calculates the modified internal rate of return for a series of cash flows.

The modified internal rate of return is a better measure than the regular IRR for making investment decisions, but NPV is still the theoretically correct and best measure. MIRR overcomes the two shortcomings of IRR. Most of the time in choosing between two competing projects it leads to the same decision as NPV does, whereas IRR can lead to the opposite decision. Also, MIRR cannot lead to confusing multiple results, as IRR does at times.

MIRR assumes that all cash flows of a project are financed or reinvested at some explicit rate, generally the cost of capital, while the regular IRR assumes that the cash flows from each project is reinvested at the project's own IRR. Since reinvestment at the cost of capital or some other explicit rate is generally more correct MIRR is a better indicator of a projects true profitability.

To calculate the MIRR all cash outflows (that is, investments) are present valued to time 0 as a measure of the total investment in the project. All cash inflows (revenues) are future valued to a terminal point, as a measure of total cash generated by the project. The discount rate used for both is generally the same, which can be the cost of capital or some other explicit rate. The MIRR is then calculated as the rate at which the present value of the terminal value of all the cash generated by the project equals the total investment in the project. MIRR is then the effective rate of return the investor earns on the present value of all his investments.

Excel's MIRR function allows you to specify different rates for the cash inflows and the cash out flows.

To use the MIRR function the cash flows must be equally spaced in time and entered in order (the first cash flow first, the second cash flow second, etc.), but do not have to be equal. Also, they must include at least one positive and one negative cash flow.

The syntax of the MIRR function is:

MIRR(values,finance_rate,investment_rate)

Values is an array or range containing the cash flows. You can specify values as {−100,110,35} where the braces are necessary to convert the cash flows into an array or as (G6:G8), where G6:G8 is a range (array) containing the cash flows.

Finance_rate is the interest rate you pay on the money used in the cash flows (that is, on cash outflows or investments you make using financing).

Investment_rate is the interest rate you receive on the cash flows inflows (cash you receive) as you reinvest them.

As with the IRR function (and unlike the convention for the NPV function) you must include in the MIRR function any cash flow (generally a negative cash flow or investment) at time 0.

Before you use this function, make sure that you clearly understand the concept of MIRR.

XNPV

The XNPV function calculates the net present value of a series of cash flows that are not equally spaced in time.

The syntax of the XNPV function is:

XNPV(rate,values,dates)

Rate is the annual discount rate to apply to the cash flows. (Here you cannot use the rate for any other measure of period.)

Values represent the series of cash flows and the dates represent the corresponding dates. The safest way to use this function is to create a table of the dates and cash flows (for example, with the dates in A4:A10 and the cash flows in B4:B10) and use the ranges in a formula as =XNPV(0.1, B4:B10, A4:A10).

The XNPV is calculated as of the first date in the arguments, which also has to be the earliest date. If there is no cash flow on the first date, you still have to enter it with a cash flow of zero so that Excel knows to what date you want everything discounted back. The other cash flows can be in any order because Excel does discounting based on the number of days between the date of a cash flow and the first date. For discounting Excel assumes that the specified rate is the effective annual rate with daily compounding and uses the derived daily rate to calculate the effective rate for each discounting period. (See the formula in Help under the XNPV function.)

XIRR

The XIRR function calculates the internal rate of return for a series of cash flows that are not necessarily periodic. (For periodic cash flows, it is easier to use the IRR function.)

The syntax of the XIRR function is:

XIRR(values,dates,guess)

Values represent the series of cash flows and the dates represent the corresponding dates. The safest way to use this function is to create a table of the dates and cash flows (for example, with the dates in A4:A10 and the cash flows in B4:B10) and use the ranges in a formula as =XIRR(B4:B10, A4:A10). The cash flows must include at least one positive and one negative cash flow.

Guess is an optional initial guess you provide, but you may need to provide it only if you expect the answer to be unusually large (positive or negative). If you omit it, Excel starts with a guess of 10%.

Excel tries to find an answer accurate to within 0.000001 percent using an iterative technique. If it cannot do so within 100 tries, it returns #NUM!. At that point, or if the answer is far from what you expected, try a different initial guess.

Note that the answer you get will be an (effective) annual rate of return.

FVSCHEDULE

FVSCHEDULE calculates the future value of a cash flow today by applying a series of different interest rates for the intervening periods. You can use this function for variable or adjustable rate loans or investments.

The syntax of the FVSCHEDULE function is:

FVSCHEDULE(principal,schedule)

Principal is the cash flow today and schedule is an array of the interest rates to apply. You can use this function as =FVSCHEDULE(100,{0.1,0.05}), where the braces are necessary to convert the interest rates into an array, or as =FVSCHEDULE(100,G6:G7), where G6:G7 is a range (array) containing the interest rates.

Note that here the interest rates do not have to be for periods of equal length because Excel simply compounds the rates as given. One interest rate may be for a three-month period, a second can be for a two-year period, and so forth, as long as together they cover the entire period.

Chances are you will find it easier to write your own formulas to do this type of calculation and, therefore, will rarely use this function.

BOND FUNCTIONS

Excel includes numerous functions to do bond-related calculations. I will discuss the important one in detail and list what else is available so that if you need any of them you can look them up in Help.

PRICE

Returns the price per $100 face value of a bond that pays periodic interest. This is the primary function for pricing regular bonds.

The syntax is:

PRICE(settlement,maturity,rate,yield, redemption,frequency,basis)

Settlement is the bond's settlement date.
Maturity is the maturity date.
Rate is the annual coupon rate.
Yield is the yield to maturity.
Redemption is the redemption value per $100 of face value.
Frequency is the number of coupon payments per year.
Basis is an indicator of the day counting convention to use. Basis is optional. If it is omitted, Excel assumes the 30/360-day convention. For the other available options look in Help.

You can enter the settlement and maturity dates either as text strings with quotation marks (for example, "5/1/1999") or as serial numbers representing the dates using Excel's convention (that is, serial date values). You can also simply enter the dates in cells and use the cell references as arguments.

Most bonds trade with accrued interest, meaning that when you buy a bond you have to pay interest notionally accrued since the last coupon date, and then you will collect the full coupon at the next interest payment date. This results in both the seller and buyer collecting interest correctly for the days for which they hold a bond. Primarily for this reason it is useful to be able to quickly find certain information about the coupon dates. Excel includes the following functions for doing so. All of them require the same four arguments, settlement, maturity, frequency, and basis, that we discussed a little earlier.

YIELD

Returns the yield to maturity for a bond that pays periodic interest.

The syntax is:

YIELD(settlement,maturity,rate,pr,redemption,frequency,basis)

Settlement is the bond's settlement data.
Maturity is the maturity date.
Rate is the annual coupon rate.
pr is the price per $100 of face value.
Redemption is the redemption value per $100 of face value.
Frequency is the number of coupon payments per year.

Basis is an indicator of the day-counting convention to use. Basis is optional. If it is omitted or 0, Excel assumes the 30/360-day convention. For the other available options look in Help.

You can enter the settlement and maturity dates either as text strings with quotation marks (for example, "5/1/1999") or as serial numbers representing the dates using Excel's convention (that is, serial date values). You can also simply enter the dates in cells and use the cell references as arguments.

PRICEMAT

Returns the price per $100 face amount of a security that pays interest at maturity (a zero-coupon bond).

The syntax is:

PRICEMAT(settlement_date,maturity_date,issue_date,
rate_at_date_of_issue,annual_yield,day_basis)

YIELDMAT

Returns the annual yield of a security that pays interest at maturity (zero-coupon bond).

The syntax is:

YIELDMAT(settlement,maturity,issue,rate,pr,basis)

DURATION

Duration is an important concept. For detailed discussion of duration and modified duration refer to the chapter on bonds.

DURATION returns the Macauley duration of a bond.

The syntax is:

DURATION(settlement,maturity,coupon,yield,frequency,basis)

Settlement is the bond's settlement data.

Maturity is the maturity date.

Coupon is the annual coupon rate.

Yield is the yield to maturity.

Frequency is the number of coupon payments per year.

Basis is an indicator of the day-counting convention to use. Basis is optional. If it is omitted, Excel assumes the 30/360-day convention. See Help for other options.

You can enter the settlement and maturity dates either as text strings with quotation marks (for example, "5/1/1999") or as serial numbers representing the dates using Excel's convention (that is, serial date values). You can also simply enter the dates in cells and use the cell references as arguments.

If you are not working with a specific bond but want to calculate the duration of, say, a 10-year bond with a certain coupon, and so on, use two made-up dates 10 years apart (for example, 1/1/1990 and 1/1/2000).

MDURATION

Duration is an important concept. For detailed discussion of duration and modified duration refer to the chapter on bonds.

MDURATION returns the modified duration of a bond.

The syntax is:

MDURATION(settlement,maturity,coupon,yield,frequency,basis)

Arguments for this function are the same as those for DURATION.

Functions for Treasury Bills

Excel provides 3 functions to calculate the bond-equivalent yield, the price, and the yield on a Treasury bill. They all use the same arguments: the settlement and maturity dates, the discount rate, and the price.

TBILLEQ Returns the bond-equivalent yield for a Treasury bill.

TBILLPRICE Returns the price per $100 face value for a Treasury bill.

TBILLYIELD Returns the yield for a Treasury bill.

Functions for Other Price and Yield Calculations

Excel provides 8 other functions to do price and yield calculations for bonds. Not too many people need to use these, but if you do, carefully study the explanations provided in Help first. Some of them require understanding certain conventions of the fixed-income securities markets, and if you use them without knowing these conventions, you may get wrong answers or interpret the answers incorrectly.

These functions mostly use the same four arguments, which are: the settlement date on which you are buying the bond, the maturity date for the bond, the frequency of coupon payment per year, and the day-counting convention to use. The functions for pricing odd-period bonds also require the date of the first or last regular coupon payment.

You can enter dates either as text strings with quotation marks (for example, "5/1/1999") or as a serial number representing the date using Excel's convention (that is, a serial date value). You can also enter a date in a cell and refer to that cell.

ODDFPRICE Returns the price per $100 face value of a bond with an odd (short or long) first period.

ODDFYIELD Returns the yield of a bond that has an odd (short or long) first period.

ODDLPRICE Returns the price per $100 face value of a bond with an odd (short or long) last coupon period.

ODDLYIELD Returns the yield of a bond that has an odd (short or long) last period.

PRICEDISC Returns the price per $100 face value of a discounted security.

PRICEMAT Returns the price per $100 face value of a security that pays interest at maturity.

YIELDDISC Returns the annual yield for a discounted security.

YIELDMAT Returns the annual yield of a security that pays interest at maturity.

Functions for Coupon Dates Calculations

Excel provides six functions to calculate the number of days since the last coupon payment, number of days between two coupon payments, and so on. All the functions use the same four arguments, which are: the settlement date on which you are buying the bond, the maturity date for the bond, the frequency of coupon payment per year, and the day-counting convention to use.

You can enter the settlement and maturity dates either as text strings with quotation marks (e.g., "5/1/1999") or as serial numbers representing the dates using Excel's convention (that is, serial date values). You can also enter the dates in cells and refer to those cells.

COUPDAYBS Returns the number of days from the last coupon payment date to the settlement date.

COUPDAYS Returns the number of days between the last coupon payment date before the settlement date and the next coupon payment date.

COUPDAYSNC Returns the number of days from the settlement date to the next coupon date.

COUPNCD Returns a number (Excel's date serial number) that represents the next coupon date after the settlement date. To view the number as a date, use a date format for the cell.

COUPNUM Returns the number of coupons payable between the settlement date and maturity date, rounded up to the nearest whole coupon.

COUPPCD Returns a number (Excel's date serial number) that represents the previous coupon date before the settlement date. To view the number as a date, use a date format for the cell.

Functions to Convert Dollar Pricing

Excel provides two functions to convert decimal prices of securities to fractional prices and vice versa. You can specify the integer to use or being used in the denominator.

DOLLARDE Converts a dollar price expressed as a fraction into a dollar price expressed as a decimal number. DOLLAR(1.02,16) will produce 1.125.

DOLLARFR Converts a dollar price expressed as a decimal number into a dollar price expressed as a fraction. DOLLARFR(1.125,16) will produce 1.02. If the fraction (the second argument) is not an integer, it is truncated.

DEPRECIATION FUNCTIONS

Excel provides five functions to calculate depreciation using various accounting conventions. One is to calculate depreciation using the straight-line method and the others using different accelerated depreciation methods. The variable declining-balance (VDB) function is a new function and is the most versatile. It looks a little complicated, but is worth learning if you have to calculate depreciation.

SLN

Returns the annual straight-line depreciation of an asset. For straight-line depreciation, the depreciation amount is the same for all years.

The syntax is:

```
SLN(cost,salvage,life)
```

Cost is the initial cost of the asset.

Salvage is expected value of the asset at the end of the depreciation life.

Life is the number of years over which the asset is to be depreciated.

Although life is generally expressed in years, in which case SLN provides the annual depreciation, life can be expressed in other measures of period in which case the depreciation will be per period.

DB

DB returns the annual depreciation under the declining balance method. Under this method the depreciation for each (full) year is calculated as the same percentage of the (declining) book value of the asset at the beginning of the year. The annual percentage depreciation amount is chosen such that at the end of the asset's depreciation life, its book value will decline to the salvage value.

Under this method the annual depreciation (dollar) amount will be the highest in the first year and then decline steadily over the life of the asset. However, if the asset is put on the books partway through the first year, then the first calendar year depreciation, which will be for less than 12 months, may be smaller than the second full year depreciation.

The syntax is:

DB(cost,salvage,life,period,month)

Cost is the initial cost of the asset.

Salvage is the expected salvage value at the end of the depreciation life.

Life is the number of years over which the asset is to be depreciated.

Period is the period for which you want to calculate the depreciation amount (e.g., 3rd year).

Month is the number of months in the first year for which the asset is to be depreciated. If it is omitted, it is assumed to be 12.

The month argument confuses some people. If the asset is put on the books on April 1, then month will be 9 because in the first year the asset should be depreciated for 9 months. The default value of 12 means that if month is not specified, then the asset is assumed to be put on the book on January 1. Also note that if the asset is put on the book partway through the first year, then for an asset with, say, 6 year depreciation life, you will have to calculate 7 depreciation amounts for 7 calendar years, of which the first and the last will be for fractional years.

Column B of Figure 10.1 shows the year-by-year depreciation for an asset whose initial value is $100,000, salvage value is $5,000, and depreciation life is 10 years. The asset is assumed to be put on the books on January 1.

The formula I entered in B11 to calculate the first year depreciation is =DB(B$3,B$4,B$5,A11); then I copied and pasted it for the other years. You have to enter the same formula for every year except that in the second year the period would be 2 and so on. Here this happens automatically as a result of copying and pasting because column A has the year numbers and the reference for year number in the formula (A11) is a relative reference.

As a check you should always calculate the total depreciation amount calculated for the life of the asset as I have done in cell B22. In this case it is slightly different from the correct value of $95,000 because of the way Excel calculates the annual depreciation using this method.

	A	B	C	D	E	F	G
1	**Calculating Depreciation Using Different Functions**						
2							
3	Initial cost	$100,000					
4	Salvage value	$5,000					
5	Depreciation life (yrs.)	10					
6							
7							
8							
9							
10	Year	DB	DDB	SDY	VDB (No switch)	VDB (Switch)	
11	1	$25,900	$20,000	$17,273	$20,000	$20,000	
12	2	$19,192	$16,000	$15,545	$16,000	$16,000	
13	3	$14,221	$12,800	$13,818	$12,800	$12,800	
14	4	$10,538	$10,240	$12,091	$10,240	$10,240	
15	5	$7,809	$8,192	$10,364	$8,192	$8,192	
16	6	$5,786	$6,554	$8,636	$6,554	$6,554	
17	7	$4,288	$5,243	$6,909	$5,243	$5,304	
18	8	$3,177	$4,194	$5,182	$4,194	$5,304	
19	9	$2,354	$3,355	$3,455	$3,355	$5,304	
20	10	$1,744	$2,684	$1,727	$2,684	$5,304	
21							
22	Total depreciation	$95,009	$89,263	$95,000	$89,263	$95,000	
23							
24							
25							

FIGURE 10.1 Calculating depreciation using financial functions.

Note that in this example I have omitted the last argument, month, because the asset is put on the books on January 1, for which the default value of 12 is the correct number. If the asset is put on the books on, say, April 1, you will have to enter 9 for month because the asset has to be depreciated for 9 months in the first year. Note that you have to enter month as 9 not just for the first year but for every year because every time the DB is calculated, Excel has to know that the asset was depreciated for 9 months and not a full year in the first year. This also means that an additional depreciation will have to be calculated for the first 3 months of the 11th year. So you will have to add a line and calculate depreciation for that year. Even after doing everything correctly, most often you will find that the total depreciation will not exactly match the required amount—in this case, $95,000. This again is a result of the way Excel does the DB calculation, and the error gets exaggerated when the first year is a fractional year. However, the difference should be small.

DDB

DDB returns the depreciation of an asset using the double-declining-balance method or a faster or slower method you specify. Under the double-declining-balance method, the annual percentage depreciation rate is double that under the straight-line method (for the same depreciation life), but this percentage rate is applied to the (declining) book value of the asset at the beginning of each year.

If there is no salvage value and this method is applied for the entire life of the asset, the asset value will not get fully depreciated by the end of its life (that is, the remaining value will not go down to zero.) So at some point we have to switch to the straight-line method for the remaining life of the asset to fully depreciate it by the end of its depreciation life. We can do this manually or, as we will see, we can use the VDB function to do the same automatically.

The syntax is:

DDB(cost,salvage,life,period,factor)

Cost is the initial cost of the asset.

Salvage is the expected salvage value at the end of the depreciation period.

Life is the number of years over which the asset is being depreciated.

Period is the period for which you want to calculate the depreciation amount (e.g., 3rd year).

Factor is the number by which the annual straight-line depreciation rate is multiplied to determine the annual depreciation rate to use in DDB. If factor is 2 or omitted, then the double-declining-balance method is used. You can specify other numbers as well, although higher numbers resulting in faster depreciation may not be allowed for tax purposes.

Column C of Figure 10.1 shows the year-by-year depreciation calculated for the same asset using the DDB function. The formula in C11 is =DDB(B$3,B$4,B$5,A11,2), and it is copied and pasted in the other cells. Because A11 is a relative reference, the correct period number is automatically provided to DDB. This example uses the DDB method for all the results, and for the reason I explained before, the total depreciation falls about $6,000 short of the needed amount. We will see shortly under the VDB function how to solve this problem.

The DDB function (and method) does not adjust the annual percentage depreciation rate to account for the salvage value. This means that if the salvage value is high enough, the total depreciation calculated using this method may exceed the required amount, that is, the asset may get depreciated down to an amount smaller than its salvage value. To prevent this from happening, DDB compares the calculated depreciation with the amount remaining to be depreciated to get the asset down to its salvage value. If the remaining depreciation amount is smaller, then DDB outputs that as the depreciation amount for that year and the depreciation for any remaining years will be zero. So, ironically, if there is a large enough salvage value, the calculated total depreciation may turn out to be exactly what is required, although you may not like the effect of the adjustment on last or later years.

Note that the DDB function cannot accommodate partial year depreciations in cases where the asset is put on the books at some point other than January 1, although, if you want, you can calculate quarterly (or even monthly) depreciations for the entire life by expressing depreciation life in quarters and adjusting per accordingly.

SYD

SYD returns the depreciation of an asset using the sum-of-years' digit method. This is a simple method that also ensures that the asset will correctly depreciated down to the exact salvage value by the end of its depreciation life. If the depreciation life is 4 years, then the sum of years' digits is $1 + 2 + 3 + 4 = 10$. SYD depreciates 4/10 of the asset's depreciable value (that is, its initial value less salvage) in the 1st year, 3/10 in the 2nd year, and so on.

The syntax is:

```
SYD(cost,salvage,life,per)
```

Cost is the initial cost of the asset.

Salvage is the expected salvage value at the end of the depreciation period.

Life is the number of years over which the asset is being depreciated.

Per is the period for which you want to calculate the depreciation amount (e.g., 3rd year).

Column D of Figure 10.1 shows the year-by-year depreciation calculated for the same asset using the SYD function. The formula in D11 is =SYD(B$3,B$4,B$5,A11). As expected, the total depreciation turns out to be exactly the required amount—$95,000.

This function also cannot handle fractional years, but if you want you can accommodate fractional years by expressing the depreciation life in quarters or even months and adjusting per accordingly.

VDB

VDB is a more recent and more flexible and powerful depreciation function. It calculates depreciation using the double-declining-balance method, and as with DDB, you can specify a faster or slower rate using 1.5 or something else in place of 2. But VDB gives you the option to choose if you want it to apply the same depreciation method for the entire depreciation life of the asset or switch to the straight line method at an appropriate time so that the asset is depreciated down to its exact salvage value at the end of its depreciation life. Another flexibility is that you can calculate quarterly, monthly, or even daily depreciation.

The syntax is:

```
VDB(cost,salvage,life,start_period,end_period,factor,no-switch)
```

Cost is the initial cost of the asset.

Salvage is the expected salvage value at the end of the depreciation period.

Life is the number of years (or periods) over which the asset is being depreciated.

Start_period is the starting point in time of the period for which you want to calculate the depreciation. It must be in the same unit as life. For the first period start_period would be 0, for the second period 1, and so on.

The end_period is the ending point in time for the period for which you want to calculate the depreciation. It must be in the same unit as life. For the first period end_period would be 1, for the second period 2, and so on.

Factor is the number by which the annual straight-line depreciation rate is multiplied to determine the annual depreciation rate to use in the calculations. If factor is 2 or omitted then the double-declining-balance method is used. You can specify other numbers as well although higher numbers resulting in faster depreciation may not be allowed for tax purposes.

No_switch is a logical value. If it is FALSE or omitted, depreciation calculation will switch to the straight-line method at the point when depreciation under that method will more advantageous, and such a switch will also ensure that the asset is depreciated exactly down to the salvage value at the end of its depreciation life. If it is TRUE, then the deprecation for all years will be exactly the same as under DDB and the problems we discussed under DDB will result. (In this case VDB will also guard against overdepreciating an asset the same way DDB does.)

Columns E and F of Figure 10.1 show the year-by-year depreciation calculated for the same asset using the VDB function. In column E, no_switch is TRUE and depreciation numbers are exactly the same as in column C for DDB. In column F, no_switch is FALSE. Here from year 7 on, depreciation is calculated using the straight-line method and, as a result, the total depreciation comes out exactly right. The formula in E11 is =VDB(B$3,B$4,B$5,A11-1,A11,2,TRUE), and in F11 it is the same except for the last argument, which is FALSE.

As I mentioned earlier, you can use VDB to calculate depreciation exactly, even for a certain number of days, by switching to measuring time in days and switching all arguments to that unit. For example, if you want to calculate depreciation by quarter and an asset is put in service on June 13th, you can calculate the correct depreciation for the rest of the second quarter and for full quarters after that by counting everything in days.

CHAPTER 11

Other Useful Excel Functions

In this chapter, I selectively cover Excel's Mathematical, Date and Time, and Text functions that you are likely to use. Excel has many more functions in these categories, which you can look up as necessary.

For a general discussion on Excel's functions and how to learn and use them, see the chapter on advanced Excel features.

Mathematical Functions

In addition to the functions I discuss here, this category includes a complete set of trigonometric functions and several functions for doing matrix calculations and calculations with arrays. I do not discuss them here because you are not likely to use them much.

TRUNCATING AND ROUNDING NUMBERS

Excel provides several functions for truncating and rounding numbers. The differences among some of them are subtle, and the way they work on negative numbers may be different from what you expect. Be careful about choosing the right function for your application; if in doubt, experiment to make sure you understand how a function will handle negative arguments.

ROUND

Rounds a number to the specified number of digits (the second argument). This function follows the standard mathematical definition of rounding.

ROUND(1.36,1) equals 1.4.
ROUND(-1.36,1) equals –1.4.

ROUNDUP

Rounds a number away from zero to the specified number of digits.

ROUNDUP(1.34,1) equals 1.4.
ROUNDUP(−1.34,1) equals –1.4.

ROUNDDOWN

Rounds a number toward zero to the specified number of digits.

ROUNDDOWN(1.36,1) equals 1.3.
ROUNDDOWN(-1.36,1) equals –1.3.

MROUND

Returns a number rounded to the desired multiple.

The syntax is:

MROUND(number,multiple)

Number is the value to round.

Multiple is the multiple to which you want to round the number.

MROUND rounds up, away from zero, if the remainder of dividing number by multiple is greater than or equal to half the value of multiple.

MROUND(10,3) equals 9, the nearest multiple of 3.
MROUND(−10,03) equals –9.
MROUND(1.3,0.2) equals 1.4.
MROUND(5,–2) returns an error.

EVEN

Rounds a number to the nearest even integer away from zero.

EVEN(1.4) equals 2.
EVEN(–1.4) equals –2.

ODD

Rounds a number to the nearest odd integer away from zero.

ODD(1.4) equals 3.
ODD(–1.4) equals –3.

CEILING

Rounds a number away from zero to the nearest multiple of significance (that is, multiple of a number) you specify.

CEILING(3.41,0.05) equals 3.45.
CEILING(2.4,2) equals 4. CEILING(−2.4,−2) equals –4.

If the number and significance are of different signs, CEILING returns the #NUM! error value. CEILING(−2.4,2), for example, will produce #NUM!.

FLOOR

Rounds a number toward zero to the nearest multiple of significance (that is, multiple of a number) you specify.

FLOOR(2.6,2) equals 2.
FLOOR(−2.6,−2) equals –2.

If the number and significance are of different signs, FLOOR returns the #NUM! error value. FLOOR(−2.4,2), for example, will produce #NUM!.

INT

Rounds a number down to the nearest integer. Positive numbers are rounded toward zero and negative numbers are rounded away from zero.

INT(7.6) equals 7.
INT(−7.4) equals –8.

TRUNC

Truncates a number to the specified number of digits after the decimal point by removing the rest of its fractional part. Note that it is a simple truncation; no rounding takes place. If the number of digits is omitted, it is assumed to be zero and the number is truncated to an integer.

The syntax is:

TRUNC(number,num_digits)

Number is the number you want to truncate.

Num_digits is a number specifying the precision of the truncation (that is, how many digits you want to retain after the decimal point). The default value for num_digits is 0 (zero).

Examples:

TRUNC(7.7) equals 7.
TRUNC(−7.7) equals −7.
TRUNC(7.77,1) equals 7.7.
TRUNC(−7.77,1) equals −7.7.

LOGARITHMS

LN

Returns the natural logarithm of a number. (Note that in VBA the Log function returns the natural logarithm.)

LOG

Returns the logarithm of a number to the base specified. If the base is omitted, it is assumed to be 10. (Note that in VBA the Log function returns the natural logarithm.)

The syntax is:

LOG(number,base)

LOG10

Returns the logarithm of a number to the base 10.

OTHER MATHEMATICAL FUNCTIONS

In Excel's listings, RAND and RANDBETWEEN are included in the Mathematical and Trigonometric Functions category. I have covered them among Statistical Functions.

ABS

Returns the absolute value (that is, the number without its sign) of a number.

COMBIN

Returns the possible number of combinations for a given number of items.

The syntax is:

COMBIN(number,number_chosen)

Number is the number of items.
Number_chosen is the number of items in each combination.

EXP

Returns e raised to a power.

FACT

Returns the factorial of a number.

MOD

Returns the remainder after a number is divided by a specified divisor. The result has the same sign as the divisor.

MOD(3,2) equals 1.
MOD(3,–2) equals –1.
MOD(–3,2) equals 1.
MOD(3,–2) equals –1.

PI

Returns the value of pi. This function does not take any argument, but you still have to write it as PI().

POWER

Returns the result of a number raised to a specified power. The syntax is:

POWER(number,power)

PRODUCT

Multiplies all the numbers or ranges given as arguments and returns the result.

QUOTIENT

Returns the integer portion of the result of a division. The syntax is:

QUOTIENT(numerator,denominator)

RAND, RANDBETWEEN

Returns a random number. See the detailed discussion in the chapter on statistical analysis.

SIGN

Returns the sign of a number: 1 for positive, 0 for zero, and –1 for negative.

SQRT

Returns the positive square root of a number. (The equivalent function in VBA is Sqr.)

SUM

Returns the sum of its arguments.

SUMSQ

Returns the sum of the squares of its arguments.

Date and Time Functions

Excel offers many useful date and time functions, and they are easy to use as long as you understand how Excel stores date and time and in what formats you can provide the arguments for these functions.

In all the date and time functions, you can use date or time as arguments by entering date as a serial number and time as a fraction (of the 24 hour day). You can also express them as texts (that is, enclosed by quotation marks) in one of Excel's date or time formats. For example, you can use DATEVALUE("7/17/2003") or HOUR("3:30:30 PM"). (To see Excel's standard date and time formats, look in the Format Cells dialog box under Date and Time.)

For details on how Excel stores date and time, search in Help. A few key points are:

- Excel stores dates as sequential numbers known as serial values. Excel stores times as decimal fractions because time is considered a portion of a day. Dates and times are values and, therefore, can be added, subtracted, and included in other calculations. For example, to determine the difference between two dates, you can subtract one date from the other. You can view a date as a serial value and a time as a decimal fraction by changing the format of the cell that contains the date or time to General format.
- In its default setting, Excel counts the serial number of dates starting with January 1, 1900, as 1.
- Because the date counting starts from 1/1/1900, Excel cannot store (nor do calculations with) dates prior to this date.
- To be safe, you should always enter the year part of a date as a four-digit number, that is, enter 2003 instead of 03. When you enter a date in a cell and you enter only two digits for the year, Excel interprets 00 through 29 as 2000 through 2029, and 30 through 99 as 1930 through 1999.

- When you enter what looks like a date in a cell, Excel shows it as a date using a date format. If you want to see its serial number, reformat the cell as General or Number with 0 decimal points.

DATE

Returns the serial number of a date when you enter the year, month, and day as separate number arguments. The DATE function is most useful in formulas where year, month, and day are formulas, not constants. You can use this function to manipulate the different parts of a date.

Entering =DATE(2003,7,17) will generate the serial number 37819. To see it, you have to reformat the cell as General.

You must enter the year as a four-digit number because for this function, Excel interprets two-digit year numbers in strange way. (See earlier discussion on this.)

TIME

Returns the decimal number for a particular time entered as numbers representing hour, minutes, and seconds as arguments (that are separated by commas). This function is useful if you want to manipulate the components of time individually. The TIME function is most useful in formulas where hour, minute, and second are formulas, not constants.

The decimal number returned by TIME is a value ranging from 0 to 0.99999999, representing the times from 0:00:00 (12:00:00 A.M., midnight) to 23:59:59 (11:59:59 P.M.).

DATEVALUE

Returns the serial number of a date specified as a text (that is, in quotations) in one of Excel's date formats. For example, you can use DATEVALUE("7/17/2003"), DATEVALUE("17-Aug-2003"), and so on.

TIMEVALUE

Returns the decimal number of the time represented by a text string. The decimal number is a value ranging from 0 (zero) to 0.99999999, representing the times from 0:00:00 (12:00:00 A.M., midnight) to 23:59:59 (11:59:59 P.M.).

DAY

Converts a date argument to a day of the month between 1 and 31.

WEEKDAY

Returns the day of the week corresponding to a date. The day is given as an integer, ranging from 1 (Sunday) to 7 (Saturday), by default. (Other options—for example, counting Monday as 1—are also available.)

MONTH

Returns the month of a specified date value. The month is given as an integer, ranging from 1 (January) to 12 (December).

YEAR

Returns the year corresponding to a specified date. The year is returned as an integer in the range 1900–9999.

HOUR

Returns the hour of a time value. The hour is given as an integer, ranging from 0 (12:00 A.M.) to 23 (11:00 P.M.).

MINUTE

Returns the minutes of a time value. The minute is given as an integer, ranging from 0 to 59.

SECOND

Returns the seconds of a time value. The second is given as an integer in the range 0 (zero) to 59.

DAYS360

Calculates the number of days between two date arguments, based on a 360-day year. This is useful for certain financial calculations.

NOW

Returns the serial number of the current date and time.

TODAY

Returns the serial number of the current date.

EDATE

Returns the serial number that represents the date that is the indicated number of months before or after a specified date. Use EDATE to calculate maturity dates or due dates that fall on the same day of the month as the date of issue.

WORKDAY

Returns a number that represents a date that is the indicated number of working days before or after a specified date. Working days exclude weekends and any dates you specify as holidays.

NETWORKDAYS

Returns the number of whole working days between two specified date values. Working days exclude weekends and any dates you specify as holidays.

EOMONTH

Returns the serial number for the last day of the month that is the indicated number of months before or after a specified date. Use EOMONTH to calculate maturity dates or due dates that fall on the last day of the month.

WEEKNUM

Returns a number that indicates where the week of a specified date falls numerically within a year.

YEARFRAC

Calculates the fraction of the year represented by the number of whole days between two specified dates. Use the YEARFRAC worksheet function to identify the proportion of a whole year's benefits or obligations to assign to a specific term.

Text Functions

CONCATENATE

Joins several text strings into one text string.

EXACT

Compares two text strings and returns TRUE if they are exactly the same, FALSE otherwise. EXACT is case sensitive but ignores formatting differences.

FIND

Finds one text string (find_text) within another text string (within_text), and returns the number of the starting position of find_text from the first character of within_text. You can also use SEARCH to find one text string within another, but unlike SEARCH, FIND is case sensitive and does not allow wildcard characters.

SEARCH

SEARCH returns the number of the character at which a specific character or text string is first found, beginning with a specified position. Unlike FIND, SEARCH is not case sensitive.

REPLACE

Replaces a specific number of characters at a specific position in a text string with a new text string (of any length).

SUBSTITUTE

Substitutes new text for specific old text in a text string.

TRIM

Removes all extra spaces from a text string except for single spaces between words.

LEFT

Returns a specified number of characters from the beginning of a text string.

RIGHT

Returns a specified number of characters from the end of a text string.

MID

Returns a specified number of characters from a text string, starting at a specified position.

LEN

Returns the number of characters in a text string.

LOWER

Converts all uppercase letters in a text string to lowercase.

UPPER

Converts all lowercase letters in a text string to uppercase.

PROPER

Capitalizes the first letter of each word in a text string and converts all other letters to lowercase letters.

FIXED

Rounds a number to the specified number of decimals, formats the number in decimal format using a period and commas, and returns the result as text.

VALUE

Converts a text string that represents a number to a number.

TEXT

Converts a value to text in a specified number format.

REPT

Creates a new text string by repeating a given text string a specified number of times.

CLEAN

Removes all nonprintable characters from text. Use CLEAN on text imported from other applications that contains characters that may not print with your operating system.

Information Functions

CELL

The CELL function returns information about the formatting, location, or contents of a cell whose address is provided as the second argument. CELL takes two arguments. The first argument is a code for the type of information to display. Look in Help for a list of the codes for the various information you can request.

Functions to Determine Type of Data

Excel provides a series of functions that you can use to determine the type of data in a cell or check if the data is of a particular type.

The TYPE function returns a number code indicating the data type of a value provided as argument or referenced in the argument. For the codes that it returns for the different types of data, see the list in Help.

The following functions are available to check if the value provided as argument or referenced in the argument is of a particular data type. They return TRUE if the data type matches and FALSE otherwise: ISBLANK, ISERR, ISEVEN, ISERROR, ISLOGICAL, ISNA, ISNONTEXT, ISNUMBER, ISODD, ISREF, and ISTEXT.

PART Two

Financial Modeling Using Excel

CHAPTER 12

Building Good Excel Models and Debugging Them

In Chapter 1: Introduction to Financial Analysis and Modeling, I discuss the steps to building models using both Excel and VBA and stress that it is best to start developing good model-building habits from the very beginning. In this chapter, I cover three important topics that will help you develop good models efficiently. I then conclude with a discussion of how you should work through the Excel models in the following chapters for maximum benefit.

Attributes of Good Excel Models

While Excel models can be widely different from one another, all good ones need to have certain common attributes. In this section, I briefly describe the attributes that you should try to build into your models. Some of these apply to VBA models as well. I am including them both here and in the similar chapter for VBA so that you can have comprehensive lists of the attributes at both places.

Realistic

Most models you develop will be directly or indirectly used to make some decisions. The output of the model must therefore be realistic. This means that the assumptions, mathematical relationships, and inputs you use in the model must be realistic. For most real-world models, making sure of this takes a lot of time and effort, but this is not a place where you should cut corners. If a model does not produce realistic outputs, it does not matter how good its outputs look or how well it works otherwise.

Error-Free

It is equally important that a model be error-free. You must extensively test a model to make sure of this. It is generally easier to fix a problem when a model just does not work or produces obviously wrong answers; it is much harder to find errors that are more subtle or occur for only certain combinations of input values. See the section on debugging for help on making your models error-free.

Flexible

The more different types of question a model can answer, the more useful it is. In the planning stage, you should try to anticipate the different types of questions the model is likely to be used to answer so that you do not have to make major changes every time someone tries to use it for something slightly different.

Easy to Use

Even if a model does not include a fancy user interface, it should be easy to use. You can do many simple things to make a model easy to use without going the full distance of creating an impressive user interface. For example, a clear description of what the model does and how to run it is useful. Clustering and color coding all input data and clearly labeling them are also helpful. If you visualize how the user will use the model and what problems may arise, you will be able to come up with ideas to make your models easy to use.

Easily Understandable Formulas

Many Excel models—especially large, complex ones—often include formulas that go on for lines. No one other than the person who built the model can decipher and check them, let alone update them.

Avoid writing long formulas whenever you can. Shorten them by using intermediate calculations and other methods. Also, wherever possible use short, descriptive cell and range names to make formulas readable. Do not use long names because they also make formulas difficult to read.

Unfortunately, one of Excel's key strengths is also one of its big weaknesses. To create formulas by copying and pasting, you generally have to use relative and mixed references instead of cell and range names, but this makes formulas difficult to read.

If a model needs to use many long formulas and IF functions nested several layers deep, consider building the model in VBA. In VBA, such formulas are much easier to write, understand, and check. Also, in well-written VBA procedures, the code for any set of calculations has to appear only once. When you want to make changes to a formula, you do not have to worry about forgetting to make them at every place a copy of the formula appears.

Judicious Formatting

Poor, haphazard formatting will not affect the working of your model, but it will reduce its usefulness because it is distracting. Use formatting (fonts, borders, patterns, colors, etc.) judiciously to make your models easier to understand and use.

Appropriate Numbers Formatting

Format numbers with the minimum number of decimal points necessary. Using too many decimal points makes numbers difficult to read and often gives a false sense of precision as well. Make the formatting of similar numbers uniform throughout the model. (Remember that displaying numbers with fewer decimal points does not reduce the accuracy of the model in any way because internally Excel continues using the same number of significant digits.)

Wherever appropriate, make numbers more readable by using special formatting to show them in thousands or millions.

Minimum Hard Coding

Hard-coded values—that is, values embedded in formulas—are difficult to change, especially in large models because there is always the danger of missing them in few places. It is best to set up any value that may have to be changed later as a variable.

Well Organized and Easy to Follow

The better organized a model is, the easier it is to follow. For example, the inputs for a model should be clustered (and possibly color-coded) in one section of the spreadsheet or in a separate input sheet (in large models). Similarly, wherever possible the outputs should be clustered as well. Modularize large models by putting different types of analysis or computations on different sheets. In large models it may also be useful to provide the key outputs in a highlighted summary section.

Another way to make your models easy to follow is to include good titles, headings, and labels. They should be short but informative and self-explanatory—not cryptic.

Good Output Production

A model that does not produce good outputs to get its major results across persuasively is not as useful as it can be. Good models should include built-in reports that any user can produce easily. These reports should be attractive, easy to read, and uncluttered. Avoid trying to squeeze in too much information in one page. If the reports have to include a lot of data, organize them in layers so that people can start by looking at summary results and then dig into additional details as necessary.

Although the phrase "a picture is worth a thousand words" is cliché, it is true. Use Excel's excellent charting features to present a model's output graphically wherever appropriate.

Good Documentation

Good documentation is a must for all but trivial models. For hints on producing good documentation, see the separate section on it later in this chapter.

Data Validations

Making a model bulletproof generally requires a lot of extra work that may not be always justified. But any model that may be used by others should include some data validation to filter out at least the most likely errors in input data.

Documenting Excel Models

Documenting a model means putting in writing, diagrams, flowcharts, and so on, the information someone else (or you yourself in the future) will need to figure out what a model does, how it is structured, what assumptions are built into it, and so forth. With proper documentation, a user can use a model efficiently and effectively and, most important, make changes to (update) it if necessary. It should also include notes of any shortcuts you may have taken for now that should be fixed later and any assumptions or data you have used now that may need to be updated later on.

There is no standard format or structure for documenting a model. So you have to be guided by the objectives mentioned above. There are some common approaches and tools for documenting Excel models. Every model needs to be documented differently and everyone does documentation differently. Over time you will develop your own style.

COMMON WAYS TO DOCUMENT YOUR EXCEL MODEL

One great advantage of Excel is that it makes documenting a model convenient. If your model is well-organized, tables have clear titles, footnotes, and column and row labels, important variables have descriptive names, formulas are easy to read and understand, and so on, then it may require very little additional documentation. Remember that it is easy to make your worksheets show the formula instead of the values in the cells, and it is easy to print out the worksheets in this form. This by itself can constitute a significant part of your documentation provided the formulas are easy to understand and are short. You can supplement it with printouts of a list of all the cell comments and cell and range names and addresses in your workbook.

To have a worksheet show formulas instead of values, select Formulas ⇨ Formula Auditing ⇨ Show Formulas in Excel 2007. In previous versions of Excel, select Tools ⇨ Options. In the View tab, select Formulas under Window options. You can also use Ctrl+' (generally the key above the Tab key) to toggle between Normal view and Formula view. If you print out worksheets with formulas, make sure you choose the printing option to include the row and column headings in your printout. Otherwise, you will have difficulty following the formulas.

Assumptions, Inputs and Outputs

Whenever possible, in a single worksheet model, you should put all the assumptions and inputs of a model in one clearly labeled area of your worksheet. Alternately, you can put them in a properly named separate worksheet in the workbook for larger models, and include necessary explanations about them in adjacent cells. Similarly, you should make the important outputs easy to recognize and understand. These will reduce the need for separate documentation.

Cell Comments

Comments in cells should constitute your next level of documentation. This is an easy and effective form of documentation, and you should insert the comments as you develop your model instead of planning to insert them later. It is wise to insert in cells only those comments that will not need to be updated repeatedly as you progress. Since cell comments generally remain hidden and are spread all over the worksheet or workbook, it is easy to forget to update them when they should be updated, and that can create confusion down the road.

Model Description

For all but very simple models, you should have a worksheet in your workbook called something like "Model Description," and include in it a description of the model. This description should explain what the model does, how it should be run, what underlying theories it is based on, what external files it needs to accesses, and so on.

Version Description

If you are developing a large model and saving different versions of the workbook as I have suggested before, then the workbook should include a worksheet named "Version Description" listing against each version number the major changes you made in that version. Every time you save your work under a new version name, start a new row of description under that version number in the Version Description worksheet and keep adding to it as you make major changes. The key is to do this as you go along and not wait until later when you may forget some of the changes you made. This is essentially the history (log) of the model's development. If you ever want to go back to an earlier stage and go in a different direction from there, this log will save you a lot of time. Also, you may sometimes want to have several different versions of a model. You can document here how they differ from each other.

Other Documentation

For a really big model, you may also need to create a book of formal documentation (which will include information on why and how certain decisions were made, flow charts for the model, etc.) and a user's manual. For most of your work, however, documentation of the type I discussed before should be adequate.

Debugging Excel Models

Debugging is finding and fixing errors in a model. It is a search, and as with any search, you get better and faster at it with experience. It also pays to be systematic and thorough in your search from the beginning. People waste a lot of time searching for errors in their models for the same reason they waste a lot of time looking for something they have misplaced—they look through the same area again and again without breaking up the whole area into smaller pieces and searching each area thoroughly before moving on to the next one.

If your model has an obvious error (for example, one of the cells is showing an error value instead of the expected result), then you should search backward from that point using the tools we will discuss. These errors are generally easier to find. If you only suspect that there may be some errors or you just want to check things, however, you should break down the model or the part of it you want to check into a number of logical components and thoroughly test each component before moving onto the next. Before you leave a component, you should be absolutely sure that it is working correctly.

It will help to divide possible errors into two groups and talk about them separately. The first group I discuss comprises the types of error that Excel generally identifies for you automatically. Excel often suggests solutions for these errors. These are obviously easier to see and fix. The other group of errors I discuss can be subtler and more difficult to find. I will discuss the special tools that Excel provides to help you look for them.

ERRORS EXCEL MAY FIND FOR YOU

Here are the major types of errors that Excel generally identifies and sometimes even offers to fix for you:

Syntax Errors in Formulas

When you enter a formula with a syntax error, Excel will show a dialog box with an error message, and it may even suggest a correction. If you want to accept Excel's proposed correction, simply click OK in the dialog box. Do not accept Excel's suggestion without scrutinizing it, though, because Excel may offer a suggestion that is correct from the point of view of syntax, but it may not produce the formula you meant to write. For example, if you enter a formula that does not have an equal number of left and right parentheses, Excel will propose one or more parentheses that will create the proper matching. However, Excel may suggest entering the parentheses in the wrong places. If you accept its suggestion, the order of calculation, and hence the result, may be wrong.

Formulas That Produce Error Values

If a formula cannot properly evaluate a result, Excel displays an error value in the cell, which provides useful clues to what the problem may be. Here are brief explanations of what the different error values mean. If necessary, you can find more detailed explanations and also help on fixing the problems by searching in Excel 2007 Help for finding, understanding, and correcting formula errors, or in previous versions of Excel for "Error values," and then selecting the specific type of error value.

- #####: The result is wider than the cell. Generally you can solve the problem by widening the column.
- #Value: The formula includes an argument or operand of the wrong type.
- #DIV/0!: The formula is trying to divide by zero or the cell referred to in the denominator is empty.
- #NAME?: The formula uses a name that Excel does not understand. This may be because you misspelled a cell or range name you are trying to use, you forgot to name the range or cell or deleted the name, or the formula includes a text but one of the quotation marks is missing.
- #N/A: A value referred to in the formula or function is not available. This usually happens when a cell or range referred to in the formula is empty.
- #REF: The formula includes a cell reference that is not valid, probably because the cell referred to has been deleted.
- #NUM: There is a problem with the number in a formula or a function.

- #NULL: The formula refers to the intersection of two ranges that do not intersect.

Spelling Mistakes

As in Word, you can have Excel automatically detect spelling mistakes and offer suggestions for fixing them. To use this feature in Excel 2007, select Review ⇨ Proofing ⇨ Spelling (in previous versions of Excel, select Tools ⇨ Spelling, and click the Spelling icon on the toolbar) or press F7. If you want Excel to check only a particular area instead of the entire spreadsheet, select the area before turning on the spellchecker. The spellchecker verifies the spelling in everything (for example, comments and chart title), including hidden rows and columns.

ERRORS YOU WILL HAVE TO FIND YOURSELF

It is impossible to produce a list of all the different errors that may creep into a model and offer suggestions for handling them. Let us look at the ones that occur most often.

Errors in the Financial and Mathematical Aspects of the Problem

These errors may not fall under the traditional category of bugs, but in financial models these may often be the most serious errors. As I have emphasized before, unless you can correctly solve the financial and mathematical aspects of a problem by hand, you are not going to be able to build an error-free model for it.

You have to look for this type of error by checking the model part by part, often using hand calculations and using your understanding of the mathematics and finance of the problem to make sure that the model's results make sense and they change as expected when you change the different inputs.

Errors in Translating the Solution into a Model

Even if you know how to solve the financial and mathematical aspects of a problem correctly, you may make mistakes in translating them into an Excel model. The errors here may be simple ones like writing the wrong Excel formulas for the underlying equations to more complex ones like making logical errors in translating the solution into Excel formulas.

To find and fix this type of error, you have to follow the same approach that I discussed before.

Circular Reference

A circular reference occurs when a formula indirectly refers to its own value. There are times when you will intentionally use a circular reference in a model, and for it to produce the desired results, you must have Excel's iteration turned on. You can, however, also inadvertently create a circular reference that you do not want. If iteration is not on, then entering a circular reference will produce an error message with an offer to help you find and resolve the problem. Unless you are planning to use circular reference intentionally in a model, keep the iteration off. I discuss circular references in detail in Chapter 8: Finding Iterative Solutions.

Using Wrong Names or Cell Addresses in Formulas

In writing formulas with cell and range names, you may sometimes type in the wrong name. If it does not happen to be another valid name, Excel will point it out by showing the error value #NAME? in the cell. If you type in a wrong but valid name, however, Excel will not flag it as an error. Most of the time Excel also does not stop you from entering the wrong cell addresses or wrong type (relative, absolute, or mixed) of cell address in formulas.

In both cases, your first line of defense is to enter cell names or references into formulas by pointing to the cells as opposed to typing in their names or addresses. Beyond that, being careful and double-checking your formulas is the primary remedy. Be particularly careful about using the right type (relative, absolute, or mixed) of cell reference in formulas that you are going to copy and paste. If errors still creep in and some of the results look suspicious, you can also track the errors using Excel's auditing tools.

Using Formula Auditing Tools for Debugging

Excel provides a few special formula auditing tools for debugging that can be especially useful when working with large models. There are two Excel features—Zoom and Go To Special—that are also useful for debugging. These can be used on their own or in conjunction with the auditing tools. Let me briefly discuss them first.

Zoom

You can use the zoom feature to see more of the spreadsheet at a time or to zoom in on smaller parts. In Excel 2007 the easiest way to zoom in or out, that is, to change magnification, is to use the Zoom slider bar located at the right side of the status bar (near the bottom of the screen). Just click and drag the slider. Alternately, select View ⇨ Zoom to open the Zoom dialog box. Then you can select one of the Magnification choices or select Custom and enter your own magnification percentage. You can also zoom in on the current selection by selecting View ⇨ Zoom ⇨ Zoom to Selection.

In previous versions of Excel you can either use the zoom dropdown list box in the Standard toolbar or select View ⇨ Zoom.

Go To Special

You can use the Go To Special feature to select all the cells in the worksheet that meet the specified criterion. For example, you can use it to select all the cells that have formulas in them to quickly locate any cell that is supposed to have a formula but for some reason does not. When you are using this feature you may find it useful to zoom out to see more of the spreadsheet at a time.

To get to the Go To Special dialog box, press Ctrl+G or select Home ⇨ Find and Select ⇨ Go To Special in Excel 2007 (in previous versions of Excel Edit ⇨ Go To and click the Special button at the bottom of the Go To dialog box). The Go To Special dialog box offers a large number of options from which to choose. For an explanation of any of the options that may not be obvious, look in Help.

THE FORMULA AUDITING TOOLS

To understand and use the formula auditing tools, you need to understand what Excel calls the cell precedents and cell dependents.

The cell precedents of a formula cell are the cells that contribute to the result of the formula in the cell. The cells that are used (referred to) in the formula in a cell are called the direct cell precedents of that cell. The indirect cell precedents of a cell are the cells that contribute to the result of the cell indirectly, that, is, through one or more levels of precedents.

The cell dependents of a cell are the formula cells whose results depend on that cell. Cell dependents can also be direct or indirect.

Using the Formula Auditing Tools

If the result of a formula in a cell is wrong, then it can be either because the formula is wrong or because one of the cell's precedents has wrong results. If you cannot find the problem by just examining the formula in the cell with the wrong result, it may be helpful to identify and check the precedents of the cell. For this and other uses, Excel provides several tools to graphically show the precedents and dependents of a cell.

In Excel 2007 these tools are located in the Formula Auditing group in the Formulas tab. In previous versions of Excel select Tools ⇨ Auditing. Then you can click on a specific tool or click Show Auditing Toolbar to bring up a floating toolbar. If you hold the cursor on any of the buttons on the toolbar, you will see what the tool does.

When you select a cell with a formula in it and click the Trace Precedent (or press Ctrl+[) or Trace Dependent (Ctrl+]) buttons, Excel points to the precedents or dependents of the cell with arrows. With every additional click on one of these buttons, Excel reveals one more level of precedents or dependents (if they exist). You can collapse the arrows, one level at a time, by clicking the Remove Precedent (Ctrl+Shift+[) or Remove Dependent (Ctrl+Shift+]) buttons, or you can remove all the arrows at once by clicking the Remove All Arrows button.

The ability to see a cell's precedents can be useful in finding the source of an error in the cell. Similarly, if you are going to make a change in a cell, it is useful to first look at what cells will be affected by it. When using these tools it helps to zoom out to see more of the spreadsheet at a time.

Remember that you can easily have your spreadsheet show the formulas instead of results. The easiest way is to switch between the regular view and formula view of the worksheet by pressing the shortcut key combination Ctrl+'. Sometimes it is helpful to open a second window to see both the normal and formula view of the worksheet at the same time (one above the other).

Learning Modeling Using Excel

You will learn to model with Excel faster if you systematically work through the models in the following chapters of Part Two instead of just browsing through the completed models. (For each model there is a workbook on the CD with all the necessary data and the solution.) If you are comfortable with the topic of a chapter, you can go straight to the models. Otherwise, you can start by going through the "Review of Theory and Concepts" sections to refresh your memory.

Whenever you need to use an Excel feature with which you are not thoroughly familiar, go back to the appropriate chapter and section in Part One to fully understand it before trying to use it in a model. Trying to use a new feature in the middle of a complex model for the first time often makes things unnecessarily frustrating.

THE FOUR LEARNING TRACKS

You can follow four different Learning Tracks (LT) of decreasing challenge—LT 1 most challenging to LT 4 least challenging—to work through the models in the following chapters. The more challenging a track you choose, the faster you will learn. I recommend that you choose the most challenging track you can follow without getting too frustrated.

The model for any problem can be structured in many different ways, and I encourage you to develop your own style over time. Nonetheless, in the beginning you should structure your models more or less along the lines of the examples so that you will start to learn good modeling practices and pick up good modeling habits.

Note that no matter which learning track you choose, in developing a model you should always follow the modeling steps I discussed in Chapter 1: Introduction to Financial Analysis and Modeling. The following descriptions of each track primarily relate to the Step 6 of that process.

Learning Track 1 (Most Challenging)

Read the problem statement thoroughly and, if necessary, refer to the "Review of Theory and Concepts" section for the financial and mathematical aspects of the problem. If the model requires data, make a copy of its workbook, clear everything other than any necessary data, and then develop the model in the same workbook. If after trying for a while you have difficulty getting started, take a look at the structure of the sample solution, but do not look at the formulas unless you are stuck.

After you have completed the model and thoroughly tested it, compare it with the sample solution on the CD. If you are working on this track, you will find it helpful to work on the models in the order I have included them in the chapter because the later models build on what you learn from the earlier ones.

Learning Track 2

Read the problem statement thoroughly, make a copy of the model's workbook, and in it clear everything other than any necessary data and the titles, heading, labels, and so on. This will retain the structure of the model and help you get started because beginners often have the most problems with the structure of a model. After that, read the "Modeling Strategy" section of the model and also refer back to the "Review of Theory and Concepts" section of the chapter if necessary. Finally, try to develop the model following the modeling steps found in Chapter 1: Introduction to Financial Analysis and Modeling.

After you have completed the model and thoroughly tested it, compare it with the sample solution.

Learning Track 3

Read the problem statement thoroughly, make a copy of the model's workbook, and in it clear everything other than any necessary data and the titles, heading, labels, and so on. This will retain the structure of the model. Read the "Modeling Strategy" section of the model and refer to the "Review of Theory and Concepts" section of the chapter if necessary. Try to go through the first 5 steps of modeling discussed in Chapter 1: Introduction to Financial Analysis and Modeling on your own. After that, develop the model following the step-by-step instructions in the section "Building the Model" and test it.

Learning Track 4 (Least Challenging)

Read the problem statement and the Modeling Strategy. Then make a copy of the model from the CD and go through it. You may find it even easier to look through the model following the step-by-step instructions provided in the section "Building the Model."

Even if you follow this track, the more you think through and try to fully understand the "why" of each step, the more you will learn.

CHAPTER 13

Financial Statements Forecasting

The objective of financial statements modeling, that is, creating pro forma financial statements, is to make financial projections for the future that can be used to make decisions. Financial statements models are probably the most widely used type of financial model and they are used extensively in corporate finance for planning, credit analysis, mergers and acquisitions analysis, business valuations, and many other applications. Financial statement models are especially useful to answer "what if" questions. Depending on the application, the models may be created for abbreviated financial statements or they may be created with extensive details including various supporting schedules that feed into the primary financial statements. Even for making minor decisions it is always safer to do projections with financial statement models instead of doing back-of-the-envelope calculations; it significantly reduces the chances of leaving out certain items and making wrong projections.

Review of Theory and Concepts

Financial statement modeling generally involves modeling all the three primary financial statements: the income statement, the balance sheet, and the statement of cash flows. This last one, however, does not have to be modeled independently because it is derived from the other two. The models almost always include a series of financial indicators that can be used to make decisions. It is also customary to prepare a number of sensitivity tables or charts to show how some of the projections (outputs of the model) will change with changes in the values of one or more inputs to the model, and a few scenarios to show what certain key financial indicators of the company may look like under different circumstances in the future.

Although all applications do not call for developing a full-fledged financial forecasting model, it helps to understand what that involves and how it is done so that you can then adapt it to a specific problem at hand. The key steps in developing a financial statement model are:

- Step 1: Understand the expected uses of the model and the required outputs.
- Step 2: Collect historical data for the company, its industry, and its major competitors.
- Step 3: Understand the company's plan and develop a comprehensive set of modeling assumptions.
- Step 4: Build the model and debug it.
- Step 5: Improve the model based on feedback.

STEP 1: UNDERSTAND THE EXPECTED USES OF THE MODEL

Although most financial statements forecasting models are structurally similar, they have to be customized for each application. It is essential to understand up front why the model is being created, what outputs are expected from it, and what types of decisions will be based on those outputs. As with all models, it does not pay to get started unless you know where you are going and why. To take one simple example: if you know what kind of outputs will be required, you can design your spreadsheets accordingly, and when the time comes to create reports you will not have to redo many things.

STEP 2: COLLECT HISTORICAL DATA

Financial statement forecasting models have to start with at least some historical financial statements for the company. While the bare minimum may be last year's balance sheet, it is unlikely that you can produce useful projections based on only this. Try to get historical financial statements for at least three years—five is better—and make sure that they are based on consistent accounting policies. Unlike in some other applications, here nothing needs to be correct to the last dollar or, depending on the size of the corporation, to the last million dollars; however, the statements should be generally consistent. It is also essential that you collect some of the explanatory material (e.g., the footnotes) that goes with the statements. You would need to develop a good understanding of the recent history of the corporation, and much of the useful information is usually buried in the footnotes.

You also need to collect some historical data for the company's industry and its major competitors. You will need the information to create some benchmarks to judge if the company has been doing well or poorly and where there may be room for improvement. If possible, get some industry forecasts for market growth, pricing trends, and so on, and some general economic forecasts for expected GDP growth, interest rate trends, and so forth.

STEP 3: UNDERSTAND THE COMPANY'S PLANS AND DEVELOP A COMPREHENSIVE SET OF MODELING ASSUMPTIONS

This is a key step, but most people tend to skip it. You cannot produce any forecast without knowing what the company's plans are for the future. Sure, you can put together a model, throw in some assumptions, and churn out some numbers. But what good are they going to do for anybody?

For example, a company may be considering building a new warehouse to expand its sales. This will probably require investment in not just the warehouse but in additional working capital and other things. However, the action is expected to increase sales, and the cost of goods sold and other expenses will increase in tandem as well. Unless you have a good handle on these numbers your forecasts will not be useful.

In your model, you will need to forecast each line item in the income statement and balance sheet with the exception of (1) the line items that depend on the other line items, such as subtotals, and (2) the line item or items that you are going to use as the plug. (I will explain what the plug is shortly.) So you need to develop a comprehensive set of assumptions on how you will forecast each of these line items. (In the modeling section I show you an example of what this may look like.) Let us discuss how you create this set of assumptions.

Forecasting Line Items

There is no one right way to forecast any line item; the method you choose depends on your understanding of the business and what you think will produce good forecasts. The one method that people think of right away but which generally does not work well is regression analysis. If you see any obvious trends in the historical data, use them. Usually, however, the number of data points available are so few that you can judge any trend just by looking at the numbers as well as you will be able to do using formal regression analysis.

The method used most often (and the one that you should try first) may be called sales-driven forecasting. For example, in some businesses and for some companies, the ratio of cost of goods sold (COGS) to sales may be a fairly stable number so that you may decide to project cost of goods sold as the same percentage of projected sales. However, you may also believe, based on your analysis of the industry, management's plans, and so on, that the company will be able to improve the ratio over the years, in which case you can build this improvement into your model. In either case you are tying it to sales, and this is sales-driven forecasting.

Many other line items in the financial statements tend to be sales-driven as well, and because of this, most financial statement forecasting models use sales growth rate as the key independent variable. To decide which line items can be projected as percentage of sales, it is customary to create what are known as common size statements, which are simply the regular financial statements in which every line has been divided by the sales for the year.

If you look at the common size statements for a company for the past few years, you will be able to spot some stable relationships as well as some trends, and you can use them at least for the first round of forecasting. You may be able to find some such relationships in other financial indicators as well and use that information to forecast certain line items. You should always try to confirm these relationships using industry data and use a combination of industry numbers and company numbers to decide what specific percentage numbers to use in any forecast.

There is another set of assumptions that may be called policy assumptions that you would need to incorporate in your model. For example, management may have its own target debt to equity ratio, dividend growth rate, and so on. Needless to say, all these assumptions should be documented in your list of assumptions.

The "Plug"

Even if you forecast all the line items reasonably well, at first your balance sheet will not balance (except in rare situations by luck). The amount by which the balance sheet does not balance at first is called the "plug" amount because it is the amount you have to plug into the balance sheet to balance it. Theoretically, the company can balance the balance sheet by changing any line item or combination of line items, that is, by using them as the plug. As a practical matter, though, it has to use line items on which the company has discretion. For example, a company cannot use accounts payable as the plug line because it has very little flexibility to increase that line. (It can, of course decrease it by paying its bills faster, but that would be wasting money.)

Usually, then, one or more of the cash and marketable securities, short-term debt, long-term debt, and equity lines are used as the plug. Because of this, the plug amount is generally called discretionary funding needed (DFN). (There is no universally accepted name, but when you use a term similar to this, everyone understands what you mean.) DFN can be positive or negative.

From the point of view of finance people, determining how big a plug a particular course of action will require and how best to fill that gap are two of the key reasons for doing financial statements modeling. The models give us not just the size of the plug but also the information and tools we need to decide how best to fill it. For example, the model may show us that if we use debt as the plug, it will increase the company's debt ratios to unacceptable levels. In this case, we may want to consider selling new stocks or look for other ways to reduce the size of the necessary plug.

We will also see that instead of just specifying that one particular line item should be used as the plug, we can design the models to meet additional objectives such as maintain a target level of debt to equity ratio or a maximum amount of short-term debt.

STEP 4: BUILD THE MODEL AND DEBUG IT

The best way—maybe the only way—to learn how to build financial statement models is to work through a number of them, and this is what we will do in the modeling section. Let me mention a few things here that you need to keep in mind when building your model.

One of the important advantages of the universally used double-entry bookkeeping system is that it automatically maintains certain essential ties between the income statement and the balance sheet for actual transactions and does not let them get out of line from each other. But because we do not use double-entry bookkeeping in modeling financial statements, we have to consciously maintain these ties. Here are some of them and a few other issues to keep in mind.

Depreciation

The difference between the accumulated depreciation at the beginning and the end of a year should equal the depreciation expense on the income statement. The depreciation expense is generally estimated based on some assumption (for example, as a percentage of sales) or from a depreciation schedule using information on when the depreciable assets were put on the books, their assumed lives, and the depreciation method to use. It therefore should be calculated first and then accumulated depreciation for the end of a year should be calculated as the sum of the accumulated depreciation at the end of the previous year plus the (income statement) depreciation expense for the year. Generally net property, plant and equipment (PP&E) should be calculated as the gross PP&E less the accumulated depreciation.

Retained Earnings

As the name implies, the retained earnings for the end of a year should be calculated as the retained earnings at the end of the previous year plus earnings retained for the year, meaning net income available to holders of common equity less common dividend paid.

Interest Expense

Unlike depreciation and retained earnings, the interest expense does not have to directly tie to any item on the balance sheet or income statement. You can enter almost any interest expense and still create a balanced balance sheet. Nonetheless, interest expense should be calculated based on interest rates and debt balances and not by using a trend in interest expense or some other method. This means that interest expense on long-term debt should be based on the existing rates on them by referring to the long-term debt schedule that all companies maintain. If some long-term debt is projected to be paid off during the forecast period, the reduction in the long-term portion of the interest expense should be based on the interest rates that the maturing debt going off the book carried. Interest expense on short-term debt should be based on projected balances and short-term interest rates.

Interest expense should generally be calculated based on the average debt balance for a year. If debt is used as the plug, as it often is, this will create a circular reference; the debt level will depend on the interest expense and the interest expense will depend on the debt level. Excel can easily handle this.

Sign Convention and Formatting of Financial Statements

In preparing financial statements and associated schedules, you should consciously choose as consistent a sign convention for the various items as possible. Opinions differ on what is consistent, though, and that is why you find people using different conventions. For example, some people prefer to enter cost of sales as a negative number in which case it has to be added to sales to calculate gross operating income. In the models in this book, I have shown cost of sales as a positive number and, therefore, it has to be subtracted from sales. If you follow my approach, selling, general, and administrative expenses and depreciation (on the income statement) should also be shown as positive numbers in order to be consistent. For certain other items, what would be the consistent approach may not be clear. Make sure that you do not add a number that should be subtracted based on the convention you are using and vice versa.

You should put some effort into making your financial statements attractive and easy to read. For statements that you will print out and distribute, it is often best to format them without Excel's grid lines and add lines to indicate subtotals. I will show you in Model 1 one possible approach to making your financial statements look good. If you make a conscious effort, you will have no problem developing even better designs.

STEP 5: IMPROVE THE MODEL BASED ON FEEDBACK

It may not be any exaggeration to say that once you have a model and a set of outputs, the important and fun part of the work begins. You will be surprised to find how flexible, informative, and useful these models can be. Remember that a model is only as good as the assumption built into it. Most of the times you will build a model to help the users make certain decisions, so you will have to get feedback from them and update the model based on different or additional assumptions to make it more realistic and useful. In the models we build, you will see how one can start with a simple model and keep adding more and more information and features into it.

THE LEVEL OF DETAIL IN A MODEL

The level of detail in a model should depend on the application. For example, for regular work you may forecast depreciation using a growth rate, a percentage of sales, or PP&E. For important work, though, it may be appropriate to build a separate deprecation schedule using a schedule of the assets on the books, their expected lives, and the depreciation method that would be actually used. The output from this schedule can then be fed into the depreciation line on the income statement. It is possible to create similar sub-models for many of the other line items, and at times it may be appropriate to do so. Remember, however, that projections are projections, and just using more detail does not automatically improve their quality. As a matter of fact, a good case can be made for starting with a fairly simple model and adding details only as you become convinced that the additions will improve the model's projections.

THE STATEMENT OF CASH FLOWS

While the accrual basis accounting we use has many advantages, its major disadvantage is that it obscures vital information about what is happening with the company on a cash basis. (In this chapter, and most of the time in discussions of financial statements, the word cash refers to not just cash but short-term marketable securities as well because they can be quickly and easily converted into cash at or close to their values on the books.) Cash is the lifeblood of a business. If we do not pay attention to how much cash a company is generating and what it is doing with it, a company may seem to be doing very well on an accrual basis while it slides towards a financial crisis or even bankruptcy.

Because of the importance of cash, the statement of cash flows has become the third primary financial statement. Its objective is to explain the change in the cash account for an accounting period (usually a quarter or year) in terms of other—mostly balance sheet—accounts. In other words, it tries to explain how this change in cash position occurred. Users of financial statements use the statement of cash flows to better understand what is going on with a company and make important decisions.

The Three Categories of Cash Flows

The statement of cash flows classifies cash receipts and payments into operating, investing, and financing activities.

- Operating activities mostly involve income statement items. Net income and depreciation are generally the largest components of cash flow from operating activities.
- Investing activities involve changes in long-term assets. For many companies, capital expenditure is the major component of cash flow for investing activities.
- Financing activities primarily involve cash flows related to borrowings and shareholders' equity.

While everyone breaks down the statement of cash flows into these three categories of activities, the names they use for the three categories vary somewhat.

Modeling the Statement of Cash Flows

The statement of cash flows is the easiest of the three primary financial statements to model. We actually do not have to model it separately; it can be derived from the projected income statement and balance sheet. Somehow many people have difficulty with this statement and end up with statements of cash flows that do not "work," meaning the sum of the cash flows from the three categories of activities does not match the change in cash, as it must.

One way to avoid this problem is to recognize that the statement of cash flows is based on a rearrangement of the basic equation relating assets to liabilities and shareholders' equity, which is:

$$\text{Assets} = \text{Liabilities} + \text{Shareholders' Equity}$$

If we measure each of these variables in terms of changes (Δ), we can rewrite this equation as:

$$\Delta\text{Assets} = \Delta\text{Liabilities} + \Delta\text{Shareholders' Equity}$$

Now if we break down the assets into cash and non-cash assets and rearrange the equation slightly, it becomes:

$$\Delta\text{Cash} = \Delta\text{Liabilities} + \Delta\text{Shareholders' Equity} - \Delta\text{Non-Cash Assets}$$

The change in the cash account (that is, the difference between the end-of-year cash balance minus the beginning-of-year cash balance) must therefore automatically equal the changes on the right-hand side, provided that we remember to put the minus signs in front of the change in the non-cash asset lines (which is equivalent to taking for them the difference between beginning-of-year and end-of-year balances instead of the other way around).

One more thing we have to do is organize these changes in the line items in the three categories of cash flows we use in the statement of cash flows. Sometimes when it is not clear what a line item represents (for example, the ones labeled "other"), it may be difficult to decide which category it should be put in. If it is a relatively large number, you may want to investigate it further to categorize it correctly; otherwise taking your best guess usually works fine.

One question that should come to your mind at this point is: "Where is net income in this equation?" If you mechanically follow this equation, your statement of cash flows will have no net income line because there is no net income line in the balance sheet. All statements of cash flows, however, start with net income. Where does it come from?

The answer is that the net income is a part of the change in shareholders' equity. In a simple situation, the change in shareholders' equity will be the same as the change in retained earnings, which is equal to net income minus dividends paid. So in the statement of cash flows, you will have to break down the change in shareholders' equity into two lines: net income and dividends paid.

In more complex situations where a company has issued or bought back shares during the period, the change in the shareholders' equity will not equal net income minus dividends paid. The difference will be the issuance or repurchase of stocks (or a few other possible transactions or changes). These will become one or more additional lines in the statements of cash flows. Sometimes it may be more informative and, therefore, desirable to break down some of the other line items as well. If you conform to the approach we discussed, the sum of all the cash flows can only equal the change in cash.

FREE CASH FLOW

The regular financial statements, even the statement of cash flows, do not provide a good measure or explanation of the cash that a company is generating or consuming. Free cash flow is the measure generally used for that. Free cash flow is a company's true operating cash flow. It is the total after-tax cash flow generated by the company that is available for distribution to all providers of the company's capital: creditors as well as shareholders. It can be thought of as the after-tax cash flow that would be available to the company's shareholders if the company had no debt. Free cash flow is before financing and, therefore, is not affected by the company's financial structure.

For forecast periods you can also conceptually think of free cash flow as the cash that the company can afford to distribute after providing for all the funds needed to execute its plans. We calculate free cash flow in a few steps, usually starting with the net operating profit after taxes (NOPAT).

NOPAT

As the name implies, NOPAT is the profit from operations less (cash) taxes attributable to it. The definition requires an explanation. First, profits from operations exclude income from any sources that are not considered part of the company's normal operations. For this reason, interest expenses will be excluded from it. Interest income on normal levels of operating cash and marketable securities should be included in NOPAT because the company needs a certain amount of cash for operations. However, if for some reason the company holds cash in excess of what may be needed for operations, then the interest income (and the related taxes) on the excess amount should be excluded from NOPAT.

Second, the tax deducted from NOPAT should reflect only cash taxes that would be due on the pre-tax operating income. The distinction between cash taxes and book taxes need to be made because companies often book taxes that are not paid in cash immediately.

For most purposes, we can back into NOPAT from reported net income. First we should take out any non-operating income (after-tax amounts) from net income. Then we should add back the after-tax amount of interest expense. (We calculate the after-tax amount of interest expense by applying the company's statutory tax rate to the pre-tax interest expense.) Finally, to reflect only cash taxes we should make adjustments for any non-cash taxes. For example, if the company's deferred taxes went up for the year, it usually means that the company booked more taxes than were due in cash. We should therefore deduct any increase in the deferred tax balances on the balance sheet.

Gross Cash Flow

Once we have estimated NOPAT, we should add the depreciation expense to NOPAT to calculate the gross cash flow from operations. The obvious reasoning is that depreciation is a non-cash expense.

Various Investments

From the gross cash flow we have to deduct the various investments the company made during the year. Capital expenditures or increases in gross PP&E are likely to be a major component here. As a company expands, it also has to make additional investments in working capital and other things. All such investments related to operation should be deducted from the gross cash flow to arrive at the free cash flow.

Uses of the Free Cash Flow

Both to understand what the company did with the free cash flow and to make sure that we calculated it correctly, it is good to look at the uses side of the free cash flow. Since the free cash flow, if positive, is the money available for distributions to the providers of the company's capital, most of it is distributed to them. Such distributions would normally include interest payments (the after-tax amount because it is tax deductible), dividend payments, loan repayments, and stock repurchases. Sometimes the company may choose to invest some of the free cash flow in some non-operating assets or even hold part of it as excess cash. We can add up all these uses of free cash flow to make sure that the total matches the available free cash flow.

If a company's free cash flow is negative, it means that the company is consuming more cash than it is generating. We should then ask where the money is going (maybe the company is going through a big expansion phase) and how the company is raising the money (maybe it is borrowing more or drawing down from a non-operating cash balance it had built up).

In the modeling section, we will build a model to calculate free cash flow from standard financial statements.

Free Cash Flow and Business Valuation

Probably the most important application of the concept of free cash flow occurs in business valuation. You have heard it said many times that the value of a company or business is equal to the present value of all its future cash flows. The right cash flow to use in this calculation is the free cash flow because from the investors' point of view, the value of a company should depend on the cash flows that the investors can expect to get from the company over the years. It is the free cash flow that the company will be able to distribute to them.

Incidentally, the discount rate to use in such valuations should be appropriate for the risk of this free cash flow. It turns out that most of the time the after-tax weighted average cost of capital (WACC) for the company is the right discount rate.

Modeling Examples

My approach to presenting the models in this and the following chapters have been influenced by the series of excellent books on spreadsheet modeling by Professor Craig W. Holden of the Kelley School of Business, Indiana University. Over the years, both my students and I have found his approach to presenting spreadsheet models to be very effective. I want to acknowledge my debt to him.

MODEL 1: HISTORICAL FINANCIAL STATEMENTS

The Problem

Historical income statements and balance sheets for Vitex Corp. for 2005–2008 are shown in Figure 13.1. In these statements, identify all the numbers that should

◇	A	B	C	D	E	F
1	**Historical Income Statements and Balance Sheets for Vitex Corp.**					
2						
3	**Income Statement ($ Million)**					
4		Year Ending Dec. 31,				
5		2005	2006	2007	2008	
6	Sales	$1,234.9	$1,251.7	$1,300.4	$1,334.4	
7	Cost of Sales	$679.1	$659.0	$681.3	$667.0	
8	Gross Operating Income	$555.8	$592.7	$619.1	$667.4	
9						
10	Selling, General & Admn. Expenses	$339.7	$348.6	$351.2	$373.3	
11	Depreciation	$47.5	$52.0	$55.9	$75.2	
12	Other net (Income)/Expenses	($11.8)	($7.6)	($7.0)	($8.2)	
13	EBIT	$180.4	$199.7	$219.0	$227.1	
14						
15	Interest (Income)	($1.3)	($1.4)	($1.7)	($2.0)	
16	Interest Expense	$16.2	$15.1	$20.5	$23.7	
17	Pre-Tax Income	$165.5	$186.0	$200.2	$205.4	
18						
19	Income Taxes	$56.8	$64.2	$67.5	$72.6	
20	**Net Income**	**$108.7**	**$121.8**	**$132.7**	**$132.8**	
21						
22	Dividends	$38.3	$38.7	$39.8	$40.1	
23	Addition to Retained Earnings	$70.4	$83.1	$92.9	$92.7	
24						
25	**Balance Sheet ($ Million)**					
26	**Assets**					
27	Cash and Marketable Securities	$25.6	$23.0	$32.1	$28.4	
28	Accounts Receivable	$99.4	$102.9	$107.3	$120.1	
29	Inventories	$109.6	$108.0	$114.9	$116.8	
30	Other Current Assets	$96.7	$91.4	$103.7	$97.5	
31	Total Current Assets	$331.3	$325.3	$358.0	$362.8	
32						
33	Property, Plant and Equipment, Gross	$680.9	$734.3	$820.8	$913.1	
34	Accumulated Depreciation	$244.8	$296.8	$352.7	$427.9	
35	Property, Plant and Equipment, Net	$436.1	$437.5	$468.1	$485.2	
36						
37	Other Non-Current Assets	$203.2	$205.1	$407.0	$456.3	
38	Total Non-Current Assets	$639.3	$642.6	$875.1	$941.5	
39						
40	**Total Assets**	**$970.6**	**$967.9**	**$1,233.1**	**$1,304.3**	
41						
42	**Liabilities and Shareholders' Equity**					
43	Accounts Payable	$82.8	$77.1	$71.8	$80.5	
44	Short-Term Debt	$39.1	$29.7	$79.8	$110.3	
45	Other Current Liabilities	$152.0	$123.8	$172.1	$111.3	
46	Total Current Liabilities	$273.9	$230.6	$323.7	$302.1	
47						
48	Long-Term Debt	$163.5	$145.0	$201.8	$218.1	
49	Deferred Income Taxes	$22.3	$19.6	$15.0	$12.7	
50	Other Non-Current Liabilities	$100.6	$80.1	$115.0	$94.5	
51	Total Liabilities	$560.3	$475.3	$655.5	$627.4	
52						
53	Paid-In Capital	$46.9	$46.1	$38.2	$44.8	
54	Retained Earnings	$363.4	$446.5	$539.4	$632.1	
55	Total Shareholders' Equity	$410.3	$492.6	$577.6	$676.9	
56						
57	**Total Liabilities and Shareholders' Equity**	**$970.6**	**$967.9**	**$1,233.1**	**$1,304.3**	
58						
59						
60	**Other Data**					
61	Stock price (year-end)	$55.50	$65.30	$55.70	$51.40	
62	Average number of shares outstanding (millions)	48.0	47.3	46.8	46.2	
63						
64						

FIGURE 13.1 Model 1: Historical income statements and balance sheets for Vitex Corp.

be calculated based on other numbers in them and replace these numbers with the appropriate formulas. Then reformat the statements to look like Figures 13.2 and 13.3 to make them more attractive and readable. (Start with the statements in the worksheet "Inputs" in the file for this model, which has the statements without the equations in them.)

From these income statements and balance sheets create the corresponding statements of cash flows as shown in Figure 13.4. Create the statements of cash flows on a separate worksheet and link them to the income statements and balance sheets so that none of the numbers in them has to be reentered manually.

Modeling Strategy

Replace all subtotals and totals in both the income statements and balance sheets with equations. In doing so, be consistent with the sign convention I have used. Otherwise you will get wrong answers. For example, I have shown Cost of Sales as a positive number and, therefore, it has to be subtracted from Sales to calculate Gross Operating Income.

To create the statement of cash flows, review the earlier discussion about it if necessary. At the bottom of the statement create an additional section to calculate the difference between the beginning- and end-of-year Cash and Marketable Securities balances to double-check the same number from the statements of cash flows.

Building the Model

1. **Enter formulas to calculate subtotals and totals:** Here are the formulas you have to enter in the income statement for the year 2005:
   - To calculate Gross Operating Income, in B8 enter =B6-B7.
   - To calculate EBIT, in B13 enter =B8-SUM(B10:B12).
   - To calculate Pre-Tax income, in B17 enter =B13-SUM(B15:B16).
   - To calculate Net Income, in B20 enter =B17-B19.
   - To calculate Addition to Retained Earnings, in B23 enter =B20-B22.

   For the 2005 balance sheet, enter the following:

   - To calculate Total Current Assets, in B31 enter =SUM(B27:B30).
   - To calculate Net PP&E, in B35 enter =B33-B34.
   - To calculate Total Non-Current assets, in B38 enter =B35+B37.
   - To calculate Total Assets, in B40 enter =B31+B38.
   - To calculate Total Current Liabilities, in B46 enter =SUM(B43:B45).
   - To calculate Total Liabilities, in B51 enter =B46+SUM(B48:B50).
   - To calculate Total Shareholders' Equity, in B55 enter =B53+B54.
   - To calculate Total Liabilities and Shareholders' Equity, in B57 enter =B51+B55.

   Copy the formulas into the columns for 2006–2008.

Income Statement for Vitex Corp.
Millions of Dollars

	Year Ending Dec. 31,			
	2005	2006	2007	2008
Sales	$1,234.9	$1,251.7	$1,300.4	$1,334.4
Cost of Sales	$679.1	$659.0	$681.3	$667.0
Gross Operating Income	$555.8	$592.7	$619.1	$667.4
Selling, General & Admn. Expenses	$339.7	$348.6	$351.2	$373.3
Depreciation	$47.5	$52.0	$55.9	$75.2
Other net (Income)/Expenses	($11.8)	($7.6)	($7.0)	($8.2)
EBIT	$180.4	$199.7	$219.0	$227.1
Interest (Income)	($1.3)	($1.4)	($1.7)	($2.0)
Interest Expense	$16.2	$15.1	$20.5	$23.7
Pre-Tax Income	$165.5	$186.0	$200.2	$205.4
Income Taxes	$56.8	$64.2	$67.5	$72.6
Net Income	**$108.7**	**$121.8**	**$132.7**	**$132.8**
Dividends	$38.3	$38.7	$39.8	$40.1
Addition to Retained Earnings	$70.4	$83.1	$92.9	$92.7

FIGURE 13.2 Model 1: Example of well-formatted income statements for Vitex Corp.

Balance Sheet for Vitex Corp.
Millions of Dollars

	Year Ending Dec. 31,			
	2005	2006	2007	2008
Assets				
Cash and Marketable Securities	$25.6	$23.0	$32.1	$28.4
Accounts Receivable	$99.4	$102.9	$107.3	$120.1
Inventories	$109.6	$108.0	$114.9	$116.8
Other Current Assets	$96.7	$91.4	$103.7	$97.5
Total Current Assets	$331.3	$325.3	$358.0	$362.8
Property, Plant and Equipment, Gross	$680.9	$734.3	$820.8	$913.1
Accumulated Depreciation	$244.8	$296.8	$352.7	$427.9
Property, Plant and Equipment, Net	$436.1	$437.5	$468.1	$485.2
Other Non-Current Assets	$203.2	$205.1	$407.0	$456.3
Total Non-Current Assets	$639.3	$642.6	$875.1	$941.5
Total Assets	**$970.6**	**$967.9**	**$1,233.1**	**$1,304.3**
Liabilities and Shareholders' Equity				
Accounts Payable	$82.8	$77.1	$71.8	$80.5
Short-Term Debt	$39.1	$29.7	$79.8	$110.3
Other Current Liabilities	$152.0	$123.8	$172.1	$111.3
Total Current Liabilities	$273.9	$230.6	$323.7	$302.1
Long-Term Debt	$163.5	$145.0	$201.8	$218.1
Deferred Income Taxes	$22.3	$19.6	$15.0	$12.7
Other Non-Current Liabilities	$100.6	$80.1	$115.0	$94.5
Total Liabilities	$560.3	$475.3	$655.5	$627.4
Paid-In Capital	$46.9	$46.1	$38.2	$44.8
Retained Earnings	$363.4	$446.5	$539.4	$632.1
Total Shareholders' Equity	$410.3	$492.6	$577.6	$676.9
Total Liabilities and Shareholders' Equity	**$970.6**	**$967.9**	**$1,233.1**	**$1,304.3**

FIGURE 13.3 Model 1: Example of well-formatted balance sheets for Vitex Corp.

	A	B	C	D	E	F
1	**Statements of Cash Flows for Vitex Corp.**					
2	Millions of Dollars					
3						
4		Year Ending Dec. 31,				
5		2005	2006	2007	2008	
6	**Cash Flows from Operations**					
7	Net Income		$121.8	$132.7	$132.8	
8	Depreciation Expense		$52.0	$55.9	$75.2	
9	Decrease/(Increase) in Accounts Receivable		($3.5)	($4.4)	($12.8)	
10	Decrease/(Increase) in Inventories		$1.6	($6.9)	($1.9)	
11	Decrease/(Increase) in Other Current Assets		$5.3	($12.3)	$6.2	
12	Increase/(Decrease) in Accounts Payable		($5.7)	($5.3)	$8.7	
13	Increase/(Decrease) in Other Current Liabilities		($28.2)	$48.3	($60.8)	
14	Increase/(Decrease) in Deferred Income Taxes		($2.7)	($4.6)	($2.3)	
15	Increase/(Decrease) in Other Non-Current Liabilities		($20.5)	$34.9	($20.5)	
16	**Total Cash Flows from Operations**		**$120.1**	**$238.3**	**$124.6**	
17						
18	**Cash Flows from Investing**					
19	(Additions to) Property, Plant & Equipment		($53.4)	($86.5)	($92.3)	
20	(Investment) in Other Non-Current Assets		($1.9)	($201.9)	($49.3)	
21	**Total Cash Flows from Investing**		**($55.3)**	**($288.4)**	**($141.6)**	
22						
23	**Cash Flows from Financing**					
24	From Issuance/(Repayment) of Short-Term Debt		($9.4)	$50.1	$30.5	
25	From Issuance/(Repayment) of Long-Term Debt		($18.5)	$56.8	$16.3	
26	From Sale/(Repurchase) of Equity		($0.8)	($7.9)	$6.6	
27	Cash Dividends Paid to Shareholders		($38.7)	($39.8)	($40.1)	
28	**Total Cash Flows from Financing**		($67.4)	$59.2	$13.3	
29						
30	**Net Change in Cash & Marketable Securities**		**($2.6)**	**$9.1**	**($3.7)**	
31						
32						
33	Beginning Cash & Marketable Securities		$25.6	$23.0	$32.1	
34	Ending Cash & Marketable Securities		$23.0	$32.1	$28.4	
35	**Net Change in Cash & Marketable Securities**		($2.6)	$9.1	($3.7)	
36						
37						

FIGURE 13.4 Model 1: Statements of cash flows for Vitex Corp.

2. **Create formulas for other items:** Accumulated Depreciation for a year should be calculated as Accumulated Depreciation for the previous year plus the Depreciation (expense) for the current year from the income statement. To calculate it for 2006, in C34 enter the formula =B34+C11. Copy the formula into D34:E34 for 2007–2008. (We cannot use the formula for 2005 because we do not have the Accumulated Depreciation for 2004.)

   Retained Earnings for a year would equal Retained Earnings from the previous year plus the Addition to Retained Earnings for the current year. For 2006, in C54 enter the formula =B54+C23 and copy it into D54:E54. As before, we cannot use the formula for 2005.
3. **Create the statement of cash flows:** In a new worksheet, create the headings and labels as shown. Notice how I have labeled each line to clearly indicate what a positive or negative number will mean. For example, Decrease/(Increase) in Accounts Receivable means that a positive number will indicate a

decrease in Accounts Receivable; a negative number will indicate an increase. We want a decrease to appear as a positive number because that will indicate an addition to (or source of) cash and, therefore, it should be added to Net Income and other sources of cash. In creating the formula for this, we have to make sure that a decrease will come out as a positive number. Make sure you fully understand the sign convention indicated for each item by its label.

For Net Income select C7, enter an equal sign, click on the tab for the worksheet IS & BS (or whatever name you gave to the worksheet where you created the income statement and balance sheets), click on C20, and press Enter. You will see the formula ='IS & BS'!C20.

For Depreciation Expense, select C8, enter an equals sing, click the tab for the IS & BS worksheet, click C11, and press Enter.

For Accounts Receivable, select C9, enter an equals sign, click the tab for IS & BS, click B28, insert a minus sign, click C28, and press Enter. In C9 you will see the formula ='IS & BS'!B28-'IS & BS'!C28. As I discussed before, to get the right sign, this equation must be entered as B28-C28, and not the other way around. You have to use the same convention for all assets accounts and the opposite convention for all the liability and shareholders' equity accounts.

Enter similar formulas for all the other lines, being careful about the sign convention.

For subtotals, in C16 enter =SUM(C7:C15), and enter similar formulas in C21 and C28. Finally, to calculate Net Change in Cash & Marketable Securities, in C30 enter the formula =C16+C21+C28.

For a check, in C33 enter the formula ='IS & BS'!B27 and in C34 the formula ='IS & BS'!C27, using the pointing method as usual. Then in C35 enter =C34-C33. The result should match the number in C30 in both magnitude and sign. (Note that the beginning of the year is the same as the end of the previous year.)

Copy all the formulas into the columns for 2007 and 2008. Because we do not have the numbers for 2004, we cannot create the statement of cash flows for 2005.

4. **Create the formatted income statement and balance sheets:** Create these following the examples shown in Figures 13.2 and 13.3 to turn off the regular grid lines.

   If you can come up with other ideas to make your financial statements look better, feel free to use them, but make sure that your statements look at least as good as the example. From here on I will use the regular worksheet formats, but you should use fancier formats like these when handing out any of your important work.

Testing the Model

Because here you have the actual income statements and balance sheets, as long as your numbers agree with them, your model should be correct. For the statement of cash flows, we created an independent check, which is the best way to test all statements of cash flows.

Uses of the Model

This model should enhance your understanding of financial statements and their interconnections. You will find this knowledge useful in both understanding them and building other financial statement models.

MODEL 2: COMMON SIZE STATEMENTS

The Problem

Create common size income statements and balance sheets for Vitex Corp. from the corresponding historical statements for 2005–2008 and then calculate the four-year averages for each line item expressed as percentage of sales.

Modeling Strategy

It is generally convenient and useful to create common size statements in a set of columns next to the regular statements. So start with the spreadsheet you created in Model 1 and work with the same sheet. Some people create the common size statements for each year in the column next to the column for the regular statements for the same year, thereby interspersing the two types of statements. I prefer to create the common size statements as a separate set because then it is easier to calculate averages as we will need to do and it is also easy to hide them if necessary.

Doing the calculations for this model is simple. You need to create just one formula using the right mixed reference and then you can copy it into all the cells for all the years. Calculate the averages in a column next to the common size statements.

Building the Model

1. **Create the headings for the common size statements:** Make a copy of the spreadsheet you created in Model 1 and create the heading for the common size statements in columns G:J as shown in Figure 13.5. Note that in the figure I have hidden the regular statement columns B:E, but I am doing the calculations based on them. You will need them open to write your formulas.
2. **Create the formulas for the common size statements:** In G6 enter the formula =B6/B$6 and then copy it into all the cells for the income statements and balance sheets for all the years. Format them for percentage with one decimal point.

◇	A	G	H	I	J	K	L
1	**Historical Common Size Statements for Vitex Corp.**						
2							
3	**Income Statement**	**Common Size Statements**					
4		Year Ending Dec. 31,					
5		2005	2006	2007	2008	Average	
6	Sales	100.0%	100.0%	100.0%	100.0%	100.0%	
7	Cost of Sales	55.0%	52.6%	52.4%	50.0%	52.5%	
8	Gross Operating Income	45.0%	47.4%	47.6%	50.0%	47.5%	
9							
10	Selling, General & Admn. Expenses	27.5%	27.9%	27.0%	28.0%	27.6%	
11	Depreciation	3.8%	4.2%	4.3%	5.6%	4.5%	
12	Other Net (Income)/Expenses	-1.0%	-0.6%	-0.5%	-0.6%	-0.7%	
13	EBIT	14.6%	16.0%	16.8%	17.0%	16.1%	
14							
15	Interest (Income)	-0.1%	-0.1%	-0.1%	-0.1%	-0.1%	
16	Interest Expense	1.3%	1.2%	1.6%	1.8%	1.5%	
17	Pre-Tax Income	13.4%	14.9%	15.4%	15.4%	14.8%	
18							
19	Income Taxes	4.6%	5.1%	5.2%	5.4%	5.1%	
20	**Net Income**	8.8%	9.7%	10.2%	10.0%	9.7%	
21							
22	Dividends						
23	Addition to Retained Earnings						
24							
25	**Balance Sheet**						
26	**Assets**						
27	Cash and Marketable Securities	2.1%	1.8%	2.5%	2.1%	2.1%	
28	Accounts Receivable	8.0%	8.2%	8.3%	9.0%	8.4%	
29	Inventories	8.9%	8.6%	8.8%	8.8%	8.8%	
30	Other Current Assets	7.8%	7.3%	8.0%	7.3%	7.6%	
31	Total Current Assets	26.8%	26.0%	27.5%	27.2%	26.9%	
32							
33	Property, Plant and Equipment, Gross	55.1%	58.7%	63.1%	68.4%	61.3%	
34	Accumulated Depreciation	19.8%	23.7%	27.1%	32.1%	25.7%	
35	Property, Plant and Equipment, Net	35.3%	35.0%	36.0%	36.4%	35.7%	
36							
37	Other Non-Current Assets	16.5%	16.4%	31.3%	34.2%	24.6%	
38	Total Non-Current Assets	51.8%	51.3%	67.3%	70.6%	60.2%	
39							
40	**Total Assets**	78.6%	77.3%	94.8%	97.7%	87.1%	
41							
42	**Liabilities and Shareholders' Equity**						
43	Accounts Payable	6.7%	6.2%	5.5%	6.0%	6.1%	
44	Short-Term Debt	3.2%	2.4%	6.1%	8.3%	5.0%	
45	Other Current Liabilities	12.3%	9.9%	13.2%	8.3%	10.9%	
46	Total Current Liabilities	22.2%	18.4%	24.9%	22.6%	22.0%	
47							
48	Long-Term Debt	13.2%	11.6%	15.5%	16.3%	14.2%	
49	Deferred Income Taxes	1.8%	1.6%	1.2%	1.0%	1.4%	
50	Other Non-Current Liabilities	8.1%	6.4%	8.8%	7.1%	7.6%	
51	Total Liabilities	45.4%	38.0%	50.4%	47.0%	45.2%	
52							
53	Paid-In Capital	3.8%	3.7%	2.9%	3.4%	3.4%	
54	Retained Earnings	29.4%	35.7%	41.5%	47.4%	38.5%	
55	Total Shareholders' Equity	33.2%	39.4%	44.4%	50.7%	41.9%	
56							
57	**Total Liabilities and Shareholders' Equity**	78.6%	77.3%	94.8%	97.7%	87.1%	
58							
59							

FIGURE 13.5 Model 2: Historical common size statements for Vitex Corp.

3. **Calculate the averages:** Create the column for averages with the proper heading. In K6 enter the formula =SUM(G6:J6)/4 and copy it into the rest of the column.

Testing the Model

There is not much to test in this model. Still, visually check the numbers in just one row to make sure that the formulas have copied over correctly.

Uses of the Model

I discussed the uses of the common size statements earlier. Now you can see by looking across each row and the averages which items can be forecast as percentage of sales and which you will need to forecast using some other approach. These statements give you a lot of insight into the company and point out issues you need to investigate. For example, you may want to investigate how the company has managed to bring down its ratio of Cost of Sales to Sales, is this improvement sustainable, is it now in line with the industry, and so on.

MODEL 3: FINANCIAL INDICATORS

The Problem

From the income statements, balance sheets, and other data provided calculate the financial indicators for Vitex Corp. for 2005–2008 shown in Figure 13.6.

Modeling Strategy

It is usually easiest and most convenient to calculate the financial indicators on the same worksheet and the same columns as the corresponding income statement and the balance sheet. As I pointed out earlier, sometimes different people use slightly different definitions for the same indicator. If one of the numbers shown does not agree with what you get, check below to see what definition I have used here. Also, these are only a few indicators, albeit some of the most important ones. One could calculate many other indicators depending on the intended use.

Building the Model

1. **Create headings and labels:** Create the headings and labels as shown. I am using the worksheet from Model 1, and the same column for each year starting at row 64 for this section.
2. **Calculate the valuation indicators:** Use the following definitions. Enter the formulas in one column for one year, copy them over for the other years, and format the cells appropriately.

	A	B	C	D	E	F
64	**Financial Indicators for Vitex Corp.**	**2005**	**2006**	**2007**	**2008**	
65	**Valuation Ratios**					
66	EPS	$2.26	$2.58	$2.83	$2.87	
67	Dividend per Share	$0.80	$0.82	$0.85	$0.87	
68	P/E Ratio	24.5	25.3	19.6	17.9	
69	P/B (price to book) Ratio	6.5	6.3	4.5	3.5	
70	Dividend Payout Ratio	35%	32%	30%	30%	
71						
72	**Profitability Ratios**					
73	Return on Equity (ROE)		27.0%	24.8%	21.2%	
74	Return on Sales (ROS)	14.6%	16.0%	16.8%	17.0%	
75						
76	**Growth Rates**					
77	EPS Growth Rate		13.7%	10.0%	1.4%	
78	Dividend Growth Rate		2.6%	3.9%	2.1%	
79	Sales Growth Rate		1.4%	3.9%	2.6%	
80	EBIT Growth Rate		10.7%	9.7%	3.7%	
81	Net Income Growth Rate		12.1%	8.9%	0.1%	
82						
83	**Liquidity Ratios**					
84	Current Ratio	1.21	1.41	1.11	1.20	
85	Quick Ratio	0.46	0.55	0.43	0.49	
86						
87	**Operating Efficiency Ratios**					
88	Inventory Turnover Ratio	6.2	6.1	5.9	5.7	
89	Receivable Turnover Ratio	12.4	12.2	12.1	11.1	
90						
91	**Leverage Ratios**					
92	Total Debt to Total Capitalization	33.1%	26.2%	32.8%	32.7%	
93	Long-Term Debt to Total Capitalization	26.7%	21.7%	23.5%	21.7%	
94	Total Debt to Equity	49.4%	35.5%	48.8%	48.5%	
95						
96	**Coverage Ratios**					
97	Times Interest Earned (TIE)	11.1	13.2	10.7	9.6	
98	Cash Coverage Ratio	14.1	16.7	13.4	12.8	
99						
100						

FIGURE 13.6 Model 3: Historical financial indicators for Vitex Corp.

- EPS: Net income divided by the average number of shares outstanding. In B66 enter =B20/B62.
- Dividend per share: Dividend paid divided by average number of shares outstanding. In B67 enter =B22/B62. You generally do not have to calculate the dividend per share because it is known and it is multiplied by the average number of shares outstanding to calculate the total dividend paid.
- P/E ratio: Price divided by EPS. In B68 enter =B61/B66.
- P/B (price to book) ratio: Price divided by book value (that is, total shareholders' equity) per average number of shares outstanding. In B69 enter the formula =B61/B55*B62.

- Dividend payout ratio: Total dividend paid out divided by net income. In B70 enter =B22/B20.

3. **Calculate profitability ratios:** Proceed as before with the following definitions:
   - Return on equity (ROE): Net income divided by average shareholders' equity. Average here means average of the year-end numbers from the previous year and this year. If you use this definition, then you cannot calculate it for 2005. People sometimes calculate ROE based on just the year-beginning equity number as well. In C73 enter the formula =C20/((B55+C55)/2).
   - Return on sales (ROS): EBIT divided by sales. In B74 enter =B13/B6.
4. **Calculate growth rates:** To calculate EPS growth rate, in C77 enter the formula =C66/B66-1. Calculate the other growth rate similarly. Note that dividend growth rate is calculated based on dividend per share even though it is called just dividend growth rate.
5. **Calculate liquidity ratios:** Proceed as before with the following definitions:
   - Current ratio: Current assets divided by current liabilities. In B84 enter the formula =B31/B46.
   - Quick ratio: Cash and marketable securities plus accounts receivable divided by current liabilities. Some people use only cash and marketable securities in the numerator. In B85 enter the formula =(B27+B28)/B46.
6. **Calculate operating efficiency ratios:** Proceed as before with the following definitions:
   - Inventory turnover: Cost of sales divided by inventories. In B88 enter the formula =B7/B29.
   - Receivable turnover: Sales divided by receivables. In B89 enter =B6/B28.
7. **Calculate leverage ratios:** Proceed as before with the following definitions:
   - Total debt to total capitalization ratio: (Short-term debt + long-term debt)/(short-term debt + long-term debt + total shareholders' equity). In B92 enter the formula =(B44+B48)/(B44+B48+B55).
   - Long-term debt to total capitalization: Long-term debt/(short-term debt + long-term debt + total shareholders' equity). In B93 enter =B48/(B44+B48+B55).
   - Total debt to equity: (Short-term debt + long-term debt)/ total shareholders' equity. In B94 enter =(B44+B48)/B55.
8. **Calculate leverage ratios:** Proceed as before with the following definitions:
   - Times interest earned: EBIT divided by interest expense. In B97 enter =B13/B16. Because often only net interest expense, that is, interest expense net of interest income, is available, this is used in the numerator. Here I am using gross interest expense because it is available separately.
   - Cash coverage ratio: (EBIT + depreciation)/ interest expense. In B98 enter =(B13+B11)/B16.

Testing the Model

Here you can check the numbers against those in the figure. Otherwise, though, you have to check them by hand calculations as well as by judging them for reasonableness. For example, ROE up to 30% may be reasonable, but higher values should be double-checked.

Uses of the Model

Although this model does not require much skill, you will calculate and use financial indicators extensively both to evaluate the historical performance of companies and to judge the reasonableness of your projected financial statements and make policy decisions. For these reasons, you should always include a number of key financial indicators in all your financial statements forecasting models.

MODEL 4: FINANCIAL STATEMENT FORECASTING WITH UNBALANCED BALANCE SHEET

The Problem

You have been asked to prepare projected financial statements for Vitex Corp. for 2009–2012 starting with the historical statements for 2005–2008. For your forecast, use the assumptions shown in Figure 13.7 but make your model flexible enough so that a user can easily play "what if" games. Include a set of key financial indicators that the management can use to judge the effects of different decisions.

As indicated in the assumptions, hold the levels of both short-term and long-term debts constant. This will result in an unbalanced balance sheet. Show the difference as the discretionary funding needed in a separate line.

Model characteristics: Both short-term debt (STD) and long-term debt (LTD) are held constant. No plug is used to balance the balance sheet, so it is likely to be unbalanced.

Modeling Strategy

As I have emphasized before, the assumptions are the key to forecasting models like this. For any such model, it is best to create a detailed assumption sheet like Figure 13.7 and keep it in the same workbook so that both you and others can tell quickly how the model is projecting each line item.

Start by going through each assumption in conjunction with the common size financial statements you created in Model 2. In some places you may not quite agree with an assumption, but I have suggested these assumptions in part to stress that there is no one way of forecasting any particular line item. You need to be flexible and use whatever method is likely to work best for an item.

	A	B
1	**Assumptions for Forecasting Model**	
2		
3		**Assumption**
4	**Income Statement**	
5	Sales	Will grow at 5%, based on input from management
6	Cost of Sales	52% of sales, little better than historical average
7	Selling, General & Admn. Expenses	29% of sales, based on expected worsening
8	Depreciation	8% of Gross PP&E, based on analysis of depreciation schedules
9	Other Net (Income)/Expenses	-0.7% of sales, based on historical average
10	Interest Income	Calculate based on average balance and interest rate specified later
11	Interest Expense	For STD calculate based on average balance and interest rate
12		For LTD interest expense will remain unchanged at $13.5 million
13	Income Taxes	35% of pre-tax income
14		
15	**Balance Sheet**	
16	**Assets**	
17	Cash and Marketable Securities	2.1%, of sales based on historical average
18	Accounts Receivable	8.4% of sales, based on historical average
19	Inventories	8.8% of sales, based on historical average
20	Other Current Assets	7.6% of sales, based on historical average
21	Property, Plant and Equipment, Gross	Will grow at 11% per year, based on discussion with management
22	Accumulated Depreciation	Calculated from other items
23	Property, Plant and Equipment, Net	Calculated from other items
24	Other Non-Current Assets	Will grow at 10% per year, based on discussion with management
25		
26	**Liabilities and Shareholders' Equity**	
27	Accounts Payable	6.1% of sales, same as historical average
28	Short-Term Debt	Use to balance the balance sheet (plug)
29	Other Current Liabilities	8.3% of sales, same as 2008
30	Long-Term Debt	Will remain unchanged
31	Deferred Income Taxes	1.4% of sales, based on historical average
32	Other Non-Current Liabilities	7.6% of sales, based on historical average
33	Paid-In Capital	Will remain unchanged
34	Retained Earnings	Calculated from other items
35		
36	**Other Assumptions**	
37	Dividend payout ratio	40%, based on discussion with management
38	Interest on short-term debt	7%, based on economic forecast
39	Interest on long-term debt	Rates embedded in existing debt, annual expense $13.5 million
40	Interest on cash & marketable securities	6%, based on economic forecast
41	Number of shares outstanding	Will remain unchanged
42	P/E ratio	Will decline to 16 in 2009 and then improve to 18, 20, and 22 in the following years
43		

FIGURE 13.7 Model 4: Assumptions for financial statements forecasting.

Build the model on a copy of the workbook from Model 3 and add to it the spreadsheet for the statements of cash flows. In the main spreadsheet (see Figure 13.8), set up the headings for 2009–2012 next to the columns for the historical data and a column for forecasting factor, the ratio, or growth rate you will use to forecast a particular line.

Based on the assumptions sheet, start entering formulas for each line. Do not "hard code" any ratio or growth rate because then they will be difficult to change to ask "what if" questions. For each line, you need to only enter the formula in the cell for the year 2009 and then you should be able to copy it for the other years.

Your projected balance will almost certainly not balance because we are not using any plug here. Set up a line for discretionary funding need (DFN) below the balance sheet and show in it the DFN, calculated as the difference between total asset and total liabilities and total shareholders' equity. We discussed before the implications of the DFN being positive or negative.

Once the income statements and balance sheets are done, you only have to copy and paste their formulas from the previous years to calculate the financial indicators. You can create the statements of cash flows the same way.

Building the Model

1. **Set up the forecast columns:** Start with a copy of the worksheet with the historical financial statements and financial indicators from Model 3. Create the heading for 2009–2012 and add the heading for Forecasting Factor. You may want to separate the forecasting period from the historical period by a heavy border like the one I have created; you may also want to hide the years 2005–2007 so that your working columns will be on the screen.
2. **Create income statement formulas:** Proceed line by line as follows by looking up the assumption for the line and then implementing it in a formula. In most cases you can create the formula for 2009 and then copy it to the other years. In addition, you can copy over all the formulas for subtotals and totals from the historical period.

   In the following instructions I will assume that you have already formatted a particular cell in the Forecasting Factor column so that instead of saying enter 0.05, I will say enter 5%. If you plan to format a cell afterwards then you should enter 0.05 instead of 5%.

   - Sales: The assumption is it will grow at 5%. Enter it in J6 and then in F6 enter the formula =E6*(1+$J$6).
   - Cost of Sales: It should be 52% of Sales. In J7 enter 52% and then in F7 enter the formula =F6*$J$7.
   - SG&A: Assumed to be 29% of sales. In J10 enter 29% and then in F10 enter the formula =F6*$J$10.

◇	A	E	F	G	H	I	J
1	**Income Statement and Balance Sheet for Vitex Corp.**						
2							
3	**Income Statement ($ Million)**						
4			Forecast Period				Forecasting
5		2008	2009	2010	2011	2012	Factor
6	Sales	$1,334.4	$1,401.1	$1,471.2	$1,544.7	$1,622.0	5.0%
7	Cost of Sales	$667.0	$728.6	$765.0	$803.3	$843.4	52.0%
8	Gross Operating Income	$667.4	$672.5	$706.2	$741.5	$778.5	
9							
10	Selling, General & Admn. Expenses	$373.3	$406.3	$426.6	$448.0	$470.4	29.0%
11	Depreciation	$75.2	$81.1	$90.0	$99.9	$110.9	8.0%
12	Other Net (Income)/Expenses	($8.2)	($9.8)	($10.3)	($10.8)	($11.4)	-0.7%
13	EBIT	$227.1	$194.9	$199.8	$204.4	$208.6	
14							
15	Interest (Income)	($2.0)	($1.7)	($1.8)	($1.9)	($2.0)	6.0%
16	Interest Expense	$23.7	$21.2	$21.2	$21.2	$21.2	7.0%
17	Pre-Tax Income	$205.4	$175.5	$180.4	$185.1	$189.4	
18							
19	Income Taxes	$72.6	$61.4	$63.1	$64.8	$66.3	35.0%
20	**Net Income**	**$132.8**	**$114.0**	**$117.3**	**$120.3**	**$123.1**	
21							
22	Dividends	$40.1	$45.6	$46.9	$48.1	$49.2	40.0%
23	Addition to Retained Earnings	$92.7	$68.4	$70.4	$72.2	$73.9	
24							
25	**Balance Sheet ($ Million)**						
26	**Assets**						
27	Cash and Marketable Securities	$28.4	$29.4	$30.9	$32.4	$34.1	2.1%
28	Accounts Receivable	$120.1	$117.7	$123.6	$129.8	$136.2	8.4%
29	Inventories	$116.8	$123.3	$129.5	$135.9	$142.7	8.8%
30	Other Current Assets	$97.5	$106.5	$111.8	$117.4	$123.3	7.6%
31	Total Current Assets	$362.8	$376.9	$395.7	$415.5	$436.3	
32							
33	Property, Plant and Equipment, Gross	$913.1	$1,013.5	$1,125.0	$1,248.8	$1,386.2	11.0%
34	Accumulated Depreciation	$427.9	$509.0	$599.0	$698.9	$809.8	
35	Property, Plant and Equipment, Net	$485.2	$504.6	$526.0	$549.9	$576.4	
36							
37	Other Non-Current Assets	$456.3	$501.9	$552.1	$607.3	$668.1	10.0%
38	Total Non-Current Assets	$941.5	$1,006.5	$1,078.2	$1,157.2	$1,244.4	
39							
40	**Total Assets**	**$1,304.3**	**$1,383.4**	**$1,473.9**	**$1,572.8**	**$1,680.7**	
41							
42	**Liabilities and Shareholders' Equity**						
43	Accounts Payable	$80.5	$85.5	$89.7	$94.2	$98.9	6.1%
44	Short-Term Debt	$110.3	$110.3	$110.3	$110.3	$110.3	
45	Other Current Liabilities	$111.3	$116.3	$122.1	$128.2	$134.6	8.3%
46	Total Current Liabilities	$302.1	$312.1	$322.1	$332.7	$343.9	
47							
48	Long-Term Debt	$218.1	$218.1	$218.1	$218.1	$218.1	
49	Deferred Income Taxes	$12.7	$19.6	$20.6	$21.6	$22.7	1.4%
50	Other Non-Current Liabilities	$94.5	$106.5	$111.8	$117.4	$123.3	7.6%
51	Total Liabilities	$627.4	$656.3	$672.7	$689.9	$707.9	
52							
53	Paid-In Capital	$44.8	$44.8	$44.8	$44.8	$44.8	
54	Retained Earnings	$632.1	$700.5	$770.9	$843.1	$916.9	
55	Total Shareholders' Equity	$676.9	$745.3	$815.7	$887.9	$961.7	
56							
57	**Total Liabilities and Shareholders' Equity**	**$1,304.3**	**$1,401.6**	**$1,488.3**	**$1,577.7**	**$1,669.7**	
58							
59	**Discretionary Funding Need (DFN)**		**($18.2)**	**($14.4)**	**($5.0)**	**$11.1**	
60							
61							

FIGURE 13.8 Model 4: Projected financial statements for Vitex Corp. showing DFN.

- Depreciation: Supposed to be 8% of gross PP&E. Enter 8% in J11 and then in F11 enter =F33*$J$11.
- Other net (income)/expense: Should be –0.7% of sales. Enter –0.7% in J12 and then in F12 enter the formula =F6*$J$12.
- Interest (income): Assumed to be at 6% rate on the average balance. Enter 6% in J15 and then in F15 enter the formula =-$J$15*(E27+F27)/2.
- Interest expense: Is supposed to be $13.5 million for long-term debt plus 7% on average short-term debt balance. In J16 enter 7% and then in F16 enter the formula =13.5+$J$16*(E44+F44)/2.
- Income taxes: Should be 35% of pre-tax income. Enter 35% in J19 and then in F19 enter =F17*$J$19.
- Dividends: Assumed to be 40% of net income. In J22 enter 40% and then in F22 enter =F20*$J$22.

3. **Create balance sheet formulas other than for short-term debt:** Enter the balance sheet formulas as before.
   - Current assets: All the current asset items are calculated as percentages of sales. Enter the appropriate percentage values in J27:J30, in F27 enter the formula =F$6*$J27, and then copy it into the rest of the cells in F27:I30.
   - Gross PP&E: Supposed to grow at 11% per year. In J33 enter 11% and in F33 enter the formula =E33*(1+$J$33).
   - Accumulated depreciation and Net PP&E are calculated as in the historical periods. Copy the formulas from there.
   - Other non-current assets: Expected to grow at 10% per year. Enter 10% in J37 and in F37 enter the formula =E37*(1+$J$37).
   - Accounts payable: Should be 6.1% of sales. Enter it in J43 and then in F43 enter =F6*$J$43.
   - Short-term debt: Based on the assumptions make it the same as the year-end 2008 number for all the years.
   - Other current liabilities: Assumed to be 8.3% of sales. Enter 8.3% in J45 and then in F45 enter =F6*$J$45.
   - Long-term debt: Will remain constant. Enter the same number as in 2008.
   - Deferred taxes and other non-current liabilities: Supposed to be 1.4% and 7.6% of sales, respectively. Enter the formulas for them the same way we have been doing.
   - Paid in capital: Will remain constant. Enter the same number as in 2008.
   - Retained earnings: Calculate as previous year's retained earnings plus current year's addition to retained earnings. In F54 enter the formula =E54+F23 and copy it into the cells for the other years.
4. **Calculate DFN:** Insert 3 lines below the balance sheet and in row 59 enter the label Discretionary Funding Need (DFN). In F59 enter the formula =F40-F57 to calculate the DFN and copy it into G59:I59.

	A	E	F	G	H	I	J
60							
61			Forecast Period				
62		2008	2009	2010	2011	2012	
63	**Other Data**						
64	Stock Price (year-end)	$51.40	$39.50	$45.69	$52.09	$58.64	
65	Average Number of Shares Outstanding (millions)	46.2	46.2	46.2	46.2	46.2	
66							
67	**Financial Indicators**						
68	**Valuation Ratios**						
69	EPS	$2.87	$2.47	$2.54	$2.60	$2.67	
70	Dividend per Share	$0.87	$0.99	$1.02	$1.04	$1.07	
71	P/E Ratio	17.9	16.0	18.0	20.0	22.0	
72	P/B (price to book) Ratio	3.5	2.4	2.6	2.7	2.8	
73	Dividend Payout Ratio	30%	40%	40%	40%	40%	
74							
75	**Profitability Ratios**						
76	Return on Equity (ROE)	21.2%	16.0%	15.0%	14.1%	13.3%	
77	Return on Sales (ROS)	17.0%	13.9%	13.6%	13.2%	12.9%	
78							
79	**Growth Rates**						
80	EPS Growth Rate	1.4%	-14.1%	2.8%	2.6%	2.3%	
81	Dividend Growth Rate	2.1%	13.8%	2.8%	2.6%	2.3%	
82	Sales Growth Rate	2.6%	5.0%	5.0%	5.0%	5.0%	
83	EBIT Growth Rate	3.7%	-14.2%	2.5%	2.3%	2.1%	
84	Net Income Growth Rate	0.1%	-14.1%	2.8%	2.6%	2.3%	
85							
86	**Liquidity Ratios**						
87	Current Ratio	1.20	1.21	1.23	1.25	1.27	
88	Quick Ratio	0.49	0.47	0.48	0.49	0.50	
89							
90	**Operating Efficiency Ratios**						
91	Inventory Turnover Ratio	5.7	5.9	5.9	5.9	5.9	
92	Receivable Turnover Ratio	11.1	11.9	11.9	11.9	11.9	
93							
94	**Leverage Ratios**						
95	Total Debt to Total Capitalization	32.7%	30.6%	28.7%	27.0%	25.5%	
96	Long-Term Debt to Total Capitalization	21.7%	20.3%	19.1%	17.9%	16.9%	
97	Total Debt to Equity	48.5%	44.1%	40.3%	37.0%	34.1%	
98							
99	**Coverage Ratios**						
100	Times Interest Earned (TIE)	9.6	9.2	9.4	9.6	9.8	
101	Cash Coverage Ratio	12.8	13.0	13.7	14.3	15.1	
102							

FIGURE 13.9 Model 4: Projected financial indicators for Vitex Corp.

5. **Calculate the financial indicators:** To be able to match the row numbers in your worksheet to the one shown in Figure 13.9, make sure that you have the label Other Data in row 63 of your worksheet. Copy the same formulas that we used for the historical period. The only exception is the P/E ratios, for which you have to enter 16, 18, 20, and 22 for the four years, and the stock price now has to be calculated from the EPS and the P/E ratios. For the latter, in F64 enter the formula =F69*F71 and copy it into the other cells. Because the balance sheet is not balanced, these numbers will not be quite

	A	E	F	G	H	I	J
1	**Statement of Cash Flows for Vitex Corp.**						
2	Millions of Dollars						
3							
4				**Forecast Period**			
5		**2008**	**2008**	**2010**	**2011**	**2012**	
6	**Cash Flows from Operations**						
7	Net Income	$132.8	$114.0	$117.3	$120.3	$123.1	
8	Depreciation Expense	$75.2	$81.1	$90.0	$99.9	$110.9	
9	Decrease/(Increase) in Accounts Receivable	($12.8)	$2.4	($5.9)	($6.2)	($6.5)	
10	Decrease/(Increase) in Inventories	($1.9)	($6.5)	($6.2)	($6.5)	($6.8)	
11	Decrease/(Increase) in Other Current Assets	$6.2	($9.0)	($5.3)	($5.6)	($5.9)	
12	Increase/(Decrease) in Accounts Payable	$8.7	$5.0	$4.3	$4.5	$4.7	
13	Increase/(Decrease) in Other Current Liabilities	($60.8)	$5.0	$5.8	$6.1	$6.4	
14	Increase/(Decrease) in Deferred Income Taxes	($2.3)	$6.9	$1.0	$1.0	$1.1	
15	Increase/(Decrease) in Other Non-Current Liabilities	($20.5)	$12.0	$5.3	$5.6	$5.9	
16	**Total Cash Flows from Operations**	**$124.6**	**$210.9**	**$206.3**	**$219.2**	**$232.9**	
17							
18	**Cash Flows from Investing**						
19	(Additions to) Property, Plant & Equipment	($92.3)	($100.4)	($111.5)	($123.8)	($137.4)	
20	(Investment) in Other Non-Current Assets	($49.3)	($45.6)	($50.2)	($55.2)	($60.7)	
21	**Total Cash Flows from Investing**	**($141.6)**	**($146.1)**	**($161.7)**	**($179.0)**	**($198.1)**	
22							
23	**Cash Flows from Financing**						
24	From Issuance/(Repayment) of Short-Term Debt	$30.5	$0.0	$0.0	$0.0	$0.0	
25	From Issuance/(Repayment) of Long-Term Debt	$16.3	$0.0	$0.0	$0.0	$0.0	
26	From Sale/(Repurchase) of Equity	$6.6	$0.0	$0.0	$0.0	$0.0	
27	Cash Dividends Paid to Shareholders	($40.1)	($45.6)	($46.9)	($48.1)	($49.2)	
28	**Total Cash Flows from Financing**	$13.3	($45.6)	($46.9)	($48.1)	($49.2)	
29							
30	**Net Change in Cash & Marketable Securities**	**($3.7)**	**$19.2**	**($2.3)**	**($7.9)**	**($14.4)**	
31							
32							
33	Beginning Cash & Marketable Securities	$32.1	$28.4	$29.4	$30.9	$32.4	
34	Ending Cash & Marketable Securities	$28.4	$29.4	$30.9	$32.4	$34.1	
35	**Net Change in Cash & Marketable Securities**	($3.7)	$1.0	$1.5	$1.5	$1.6	
36							

FIGURE 13.10 Model 4: Projected statements of cash flows for Vitex Corp.

correct. However, with the assumptions we are using, the DFN numbers are small and so the indicators are not too far off.

6. **Create the statements of cash flows:** To create the statements of cash flows (Figure 13.10), you only have to create the additional headings for the projection columns and copy over the formulas from the historical data area. Because the balance sheet is not balanced, the change in cash and marketable securities line from your statements of cash flow will differ from the "check" numbers. (The differences are related to the DFNs. See if you can reconcile them.)

Testing the Model

You have to thoroughly check a model like this. First check it line by line making sure you are using the right assumptions and the formulas you have entered are correct. Also make sure that you have copied over all the formulas for subtotals and totals as well as for calculating the retained earnings and accumulated depreciation correctly. After that, look through the financial indicators and make sure that the variations from the historical numbers and among the four projected years seem consistent with the assumptions.

Uses of the Model

Even before we fix the problem that the balance sheet is not balanced it should be obvious that a model like this is essential for planning and other applications that I mentioned earlier. You can change any of the assumptions and see its impact. For example, the current projections paint a fairly bleak picture for the company. What steps can it take to improve things? What will happen if it can tighten up SG&A costs and reduce the ratio of SG&A to sales? You can check this out as well as many other possibilities quickly.

You can make the model even more flexible. For example, here we have assumed that growth rates or ratios to sale remain constant for all the four years. We could easily set up four different forecasting factors for the four years in four different columns and use them in the model. Writing and copying formulas using them will be easy. However, you should not get carried away with building in additional flexibilities. They generally require coming up with more and more assumptions and beyond a certain points these assumptions can just become a numbers game because our ability to see into the future in detail is quite limited. You should always try to use the minimum number of assumptions and not the maximum number.

We can also build into a model like this certain decision rules and constraints to see what the statements will look like under them. We will explore some such possibilities in the next few models.

MODEL 5: FINANCIAL STATEMENT FORECASTING, VERSION 1

The Problem

We saw in Model 4 that most of the time projected balance sheets will be out of balance and will indicate a need for discretionary financing. Modify the model so that it will automatically balance the balance sheet by adjusting the short-term debt, that is, using short-term debt as the plug. Keep all other assumptions the same.

Model characteristics: LTD is held constant and the balance sheet is balanced by varying STD, which can go negative (that is, it is not constrained to being zero or positive).

Modeling Strategy

We cannot just balance the balance sheet by adding the DFN amount to the short-term debt because any change in the short-term debt will change the interest expense, which will change the short-term debt needed to balance the balance sheet and so forth. We have a circular reference here because the interest expense on short-term debt is supposed to be calculated based on the average balance for the year. If the interest expense were to be calculated using the year-beginning balance, which is fixed, then we would not have a circular reference and we would be able to balance the balance sheet by adding the DFN amount to the short-term debt.

You can think of the circular reference in more detail as follows: any change in short-term debt will change the interest expense, which will change the net income, which will change the retained earnings, which will change the short-term debt needed to bring the balance sheet into balance. If you are not familiar with circular reference, look it up in Chapter 4: Advanced Excel Features. As I explain there, to set up a circular reference you do not have to do anything other than turn on iteration and then just write your formulas the normal way. Excel will take care of the rest.

But what formula would you use to calculate short-term debt? It should equal total assets minus the sum of all liabilities and shareholders' equity lines other than the short-term debt line itself.

Because you will start with Model 4, once the income statements and balance sheets are updated, the financial indicators as well as the statements of cash flows will automatically update and will now have the correct numbers.

Building the Model

Start with a copy of Model 4 and make sure that Excel's iteration is on. Even though a circular reference is involved, you do not need to change the way the interest expense is calculated.

Because short-term debt is going to be the plug that balances the balance sheet, it must equal the difference between total assets and all other liabilities and total shareholders' equity. In F44 enter the formula =F40-F55-SUM(F48:F50)-F43-F45. The balance sheets will balance and the DFNs will become zero as in Figure 13.11. If you do a comparison with the balance sheet from Model 4, you will see that the change in the short-term debt (from the previous year-end balance) is a little different from the DFN we had there because of the effect of including the change in debt in the interest expense calculation.

Testing the Model

The only change we have made is in the calculation of the short-term debt. The balanced balance sheet is an indication that the model is working. To check that

◇	A	E	F	G	H	I	J
1	**Income Statement and Balance Sheet for Vitex Corp.**						
2							
3	**Income Statement ($ Million)**						
4			Forecast Period				Forecasting
5		2008	2009	2010	2011	2012	Factor
6	Sales	$1,334.4	$1,401.1	$1,471.2	$1,544.7	$1,622.0	5.0%
7	Cost of Sales	$667.0	$728.6	$765.0	$803.3	$843.4	52.0%
8	Gross Operating Income	$667.4	$672.5	$706.2	$741.5	$778.5	
9							
10	Selling, General & Admn. Expenses	$373.3	$406.3	$426.6	$448.0	$470.4	29.0%
11	Depreciation	$75.2	$81.1	$90.0	$99.9	$110.9	8.0%
12	Other net (Income)/Expenses	($8.2)	($9.8)	($10.3)	($10.8)	($11.4)	-0.7%
13	EBIT	$227.1	$194.9	$199.8	$204.4	$208.6	
14							
15	Interest (Income)	($2.0)	($1.7)	($1.8)	($1.9)	($2.0)	6.0%
16	Interest Expense	$23.7	$20.6	$20.0	$20.5	$21.4	7.0%
17	Pre-Tax Income	$205.4	$176.1	$181.6	$185.8	$189.3	
18							
19	Income Taxes	$72.6	$61.6	$63.6	$65.0	$66.2	35.0%
20	**Net Income**	**$132.8**	**$114.5**	**$118.0**	**$120.8**	**$123.0**	
21							
22	Dividends	$40.1	$45.8	$47.2	$48.3	$49.2	40.0%
23	Addition to Retained Earnings	$92.7	$68.7	$70.8	$72.5	$73.8	
24							
25	**Balance Sheet ($ Million)**						
26	**Assets**						
27	Cash and Marketable Securities	$28.4	$29.4	$30.9	$32.4	$34.1	2.1%
28	Accounts Receivable	$120.1	$117.7	$123.6	$129.8	$136.2	8.4%
29	Inventories	$116.8	$123.3	$129.5	$135.9	$142.7	8.8%
30	Other Current Assets	$97.5	$106.5	$111.8	$117.4	$123.3	7.6%
31	Total Current Assets	$362.8	$376.9	$395.7	$415.5	$436.3	
32							
33	Property, Plant and Equipment, Gross	$913.1	$1,013.5	$1,125.0	$1,248.8	$1,386.2	11.0%
34	Accumulated Depreciation	$427.9	$509.0	$599.0	$698.9	$809.8	
35	Property, Plant and Equipment, Net	$485.2	$504.6	$526.0	$549.9	$576.4	
36							
37	Other Non-Current Assets	$456.3	$501.9	$552.1	$607.3	$668.1	10.0%
38	Total Non-Current Assets	$941.5	$1,006.5	$1,078.2	$1,157.2	$1,244.4	
39							
40	**Total Assets**	**$1,304.3**	**$1,383.4**	**$1,473.9**	**$1,572.8**	**$1,680.7**	
41							
42	**Liabilities and Shareholders' Equity**						
43	Accounts Payable	$80.5	$85.5	$89.7	$94.2	$98.9	6.1%
44	Short-Term Debt	$110.3	$91.8	$95.2	$104.3	$120.4	
45	Other Current Liabilities	$111.3	$116.3	$122.1	$128.2	$134.6	8.3%
46	Total Current Liabilities	$302.1	$293.6	$307.0	$326.8	$354.0	
47							
48	Long-Term Debt	$218.1	$218.1	$218.1	$218.1	$218.1	
49	Deferred Income Taxes	$12.7	$19.6	$20.6	$21.6	$22.7	1.4%
50	Other Non-Current Liabilities	$94.5	$106.5	$111.8	$117.4	$123.3	7.6%
51	Total Liabilities	$627.4	$637.8	$657.5	$683.9	$718.1	
52							
53	Paid-In Capital	$44.8	$44.8	$44.8	$44.8	$44.8	
54	Retained Earnings	$632.1	$700.8	$771.6	$844.1	$917.9	
55	Total Shareholders' Equity	$676.9	$745.6	$816.4	$888.9	$962.7	
56							
57	**Total Liabilities and Shareholders' Equity**	**$1,304.3**	**$1,383.4**	**$1,473.9**	**$1,572.8**	**$1,680.7**	
58							
59	**Discretionary Funding Need (DFN)**		**$0.0**	**$0.0**	**$0.0**	**$0.0**	
60							
61							

FIGURE 13.11 Model 5: Projected financial statements for Vitex Corp. with balanced balance sheets.

the circular reference is working properly, calculate the interest expense by hand using the debt balances from the balance sheet and make sure that it matches the model's result.

Uses of the Model

This model has all the versatilities of Model 4 and it also produces the correct answers in that the balance sheet is balanced and the interest expense ties to the debt levels. However, what if under some changes in assumptions the company generates enough additional cash to pay off all the short-term debt? Under this model we will end up with a negative short-term debt, which makes sense if we think of it as investment of excess funds, but at the very least it may look confusing, and to the extent that interest rate on investments is different from interest rate on debt, the net income will not be exactly right. We will make the necessary modifications in the next model.

MODEL 6: FINANCIAL STATEMENT FORECASTING, VERSION 2

The Problem

In Model 5 we saw that under the assumptions made, Vitex's performance is projected to be weak for 2009–2012. In looking for ways to improve performance, management wants to know what the projections will look like if it can accomplish the following: lower the ratio of cost of sales to sales to 50%, and slow the growth rates of both gross PP&E and other non-current assets to 8% per year.

Model characteristics: Same as Version 1 but with different forecasting factors (input assumptions) that make STD negative in certain years. (LTD is held constant and the balance sheet is balanced by varying STD, which can go negative because it is not constrained to being zero or positive).

Modeling Strategy

Because of the way we have set up the model by using forecasting factors instead of hard coding the different assumptions, making these changes are easy. Reflect the suggested changes in the Assumptions sheet, which you should always do to keep track of things, and then change the three forecasting factors in the Model sheet.

Building the Model

Start with a copy of Model 5 and change the three forecasting factors. The results should match those shown in Figure 13.12.

◇	A	E	F	G	H	I	J
1	**Income Statement and Balance Sheet for Vitex Corp.**						
2							
3	**Income Statement ($ Million)**						
4			Forecast Period				Forecasting
5		2008	2009	2010	2011	2012	Factor
6	Sales	$1,334.4	$1,401.1	$1,471.2	$1,544.7	$1,622.0	5.0%
7	Cost of Sales	$667.0	$700.6	$735.6	$772.4	$811.0	50.0%
8	Gross Operating Income	$667.4	$700.6	$735.6	$772.4	$811.0	
9							
10	Selling, General & Admn. Expenses	$373.3	$406.3	$426.6	$448.0	$470.4	29.0%
11	Depreciation	$75.2	$78.9	$85.2	$92.0	$99.4	8.0%
12	Other Net (Income)/Expenses	($8.2)	($9.8)	($10.3)	($10.8)	($11.4)	-0.7%
13	EBIT	$227.1	$225.2	$234.0	$243.2	$252.6	
14							
15	Interest (Income)	($2.0)	($1.7)	($1.8)	($1.9)	($2.0)	6.0%
16	Interest Expense	$23.7	$18.9	$14.9	$11.3	$7.5	7.0%
17	Pre-Tax Income	$205.4	$207.9	$221.0	$233.8	$247.1	
18							
19	Income Taxes	$72.6	$72.8	$77.3	$81.8	$86.5	35.0%
20	Net Income	$132.8	$135.2	$143.6	$152.0	$160.6	
21							
22	Dividends	$40.1	$54.1	$57.5	$60.8	$64.2	40.0%
23	Addition to Retained Earnings	$92.7	$81.1	$86.2	$91.2	$96.4	
24							
25	**Balance Sheet ($ Million)**						
26	**Assets**						
27	Cash and Marketable Securities	$28.4	$29.4	$30.9	$32.4	$34.1	2.1%
28	Accounts Receivable	$120.1	$117.7	$123.6	$129.8	$136.2	8.4%
29	Inventories	$116.8	$123.3	$129.5	$135.9	$142.7	8.8%
30	Other Current Assets	$97.5	$106.5	$111.8	$117.4	$123.3	7.6%
31	Total Current Assets	$362.8	$376.9	$395.7	$415.5	$436.3	
32							
33	Property, Plant and Equipment, Gross	$913.1	$986.1	$1,065.0	$1,150.2	$1,242.3	8.0%
34	Accumulated Depreciation	$427.9	$506.8	$592.0	$684.0	$783.4	
35	Property, Plant and Equipment, Net	$485.2	$479.4	$473.0	$466.2	$458.9	
36							
37	Other Non-Current Assets	$456.3	$492.8	$532.2	$574.8	$620.8	8.0%
38	Total Non-Current Assets	$941.5	$972.2	$1,005.3	$1,041.0	$1,079.7	
39							
40	**Total Assets**	**$1,304.3**	**$1,349.1**	**$1,401.0**	**$1,456.6**	**$1,516.0**	
41							
42	**Liabilities and Shareholders' Equity**						
43	Accounts Payable	$80.5	$85.5	$89.7	$94.2	$98.9	6.1%
44	Short-Term Debt	$110.3	$45.1	($5.5)	($58.4)	($113.4)	
45	Other Current Liabilities	$111.3	$116.3	$122.1	$128.2	$134.6	8.3%
46	Total Current Liabilities	$302.1	$246.9	$206.3	$164.1	$120.2	
47							
48	Long-Term Debt	$218.1	$218.1	$218.1	$218.1	$218.1	
49	Deferred Income Taxes	$12.7	$19.6	$20.6	$21.6	$22.7	1.4%
50	Other Non-Current Liabilities	$94.5	$106.5	$111.8	$117.4	$123.3	7.6%
51	Total Liabilities	$627.4	$591.1	$556.8	$521.2	$484.2	
52							
53	Paid-In Capital	$44.8	$44.8	$44.8	$44.8	$44.8	
54	Retained Earnings	$632.1	$713.2	$799.4	$890.6	$986.9	
55	Total Shareholders' Equity	$676.9	$758.0	$844.2	$935.4	$1,031.7	
56							
57	**Total Liabilities and Shareholders' Equity**	**$1,304.3**	**$1,349.1**	**$1,401.0**	**$1,456.6**	**$1,516.0**	
58							
59	**Discretionary Funding Need (DFN)**		**$0.0**	**$0.0**	**$0.0**	**$0.0**	
60							
61							

FIGURE 13.12 Model 6: Projected financial statements for Vitex Corp. with negative short-term debt.

Discussion of the Results

As expected, if these operating goals can be achieved, then Vitex's performance will improve significantly over the years. Study the financial statements and the various financial indicators from this version with those from the previous version to see how these changes affect them and if the changes agree with what you intuitively expected. Trying to guess how any change in assumptions will affect the statements and financial indicators and then confirming your intuitions by making the changes in the model is one of the best ways to develop a deeper understanding of financial statements. I strongly recommend that you spend some time playing such "what if" games on your own.

Under the new assumptions, Vitex will generate enough excess cash over the years to pay off all the short-term debt. Because the short-term debt is used as the only line that can be changed to balance the balance sheet (for example, we are not allowing repayment of long-term debt) in the outer years, the excess cash generated actually makes the short-term debt negative. We therefore need to incorporate some additional financial policies in the model to handle this situation.

You will also notice that the dividends increase sharply in 2009 onwards, in part because we have required that 40% of net income is paid out in dividends every year. However, corporations generally prefer to grow dividends at a steady pace instead of allowing them to jump around with earnings. We will see that we can incorporate more sophisticated dividend policies into the model to reflect the way management is likely set dividends in the future.

MODEL 7: FINANCIAL STATEMENT FORECASTING, VERSION 3

The Problem

In the previous model, we saw that under certain circumstances the short-term debt level can go negative because the company generates cash in excess of what can be used to pay off all short-term debt. In practice, this obviously cannot happen, and a company may pursue the following policy: Maintain a specified minimum level of C&MS, use excess cash beyond that to pay off STD, and if all STD is paid off then deposit excess cash in the C&MS account. Modify Model 6 to incorporate this policy. Assume that the desired minimum level for C&MS is zero.

Model characteristics: Builds on Version 2, which has the same modeling logic as Version 1 but a few different input assumptions. STD used as the plug but is not allowed to go negative. Once all STD is paid off, any additional cash is used to build C&MS. Minimum level for C&MS is zero. (LTD is held constant.)

Modeling Strategy

The output of the model is shown in Figure 13.13. The logic to impose the required constraints is somewhat complex and we have to build it up in steps. Let us start by assuming that the C&MS account does not even exist. In this case, we can calculate a value for STD—let us call it P—that will balance the balance sheet. We can calculate P as:

P = Sum of all asset accounts except C&MS − Sum of all liability and shareholders' equity accounts except STD

P will balance the balance sheet (ignoring C&MS), but it can go negative. Let us define STD as:

$$\text{STD} = \text{Max}(P, 0)$$

Once STD is calculated using this condition, the full balance sheet (including the C&MS account) must also balance. Therefore, we can calculate the C&MS using the equation:

C&MS = Total liabilities and shareholders' equity − Sum of all asset accounts except C&MS

The key difference between this equation and the one for P is that here we are using the total liabilities and shareholders' equity including the STD. Make sure you understand the logic, and once you do you can easily implement it starting with a copy of Model 6.

Building the Model

Start with a copy of Model 6.

1. **Calculate STD:** In cell F44, enter the formula =MAX((SUM(F28:F30)+F38)-(F55+SUM(F48:F50)+F43+F45),0). The first argument of the MAX function is the P we defined above. The first part of it relates to the asset side and the second part to the liability side following the definition. Copy and paste the formula into the cells for the other years.
2. **Calculate C&MS:** In cell F27 enter the formula =F57-(SUM(F28:F30)+F38). Copy and paste the formula into the cells for the other years.

Testing the Model

Check to make sure that the balance sheet is balanced and STD does not go negative. You should also check the interest income and interest expense numbers

◇	A	E	F	G	H	I	J
1	**Income Statement and Balance Sheet for Vitex Corp.**						
2							
3	**Income Statement ($ Million)**						
4			Forecast Period				Forecasting
5		2008	2009	2010	2011	2012	Factor
6	Sales	$1,334.4	$1,401.1	$1,471.2	$1,544.7	$1,622.0	5.0%
7	Cost of Sales	$667.0	$700.6	$735.6	$772.4	$811.0	**50.0%**
8	Gross Operating Income	$667.4	$700.6	$735.6	$772.4	$811.0	
9							
10	Selling, General & Admn. Expenses	$373.3	$406.3	$426.6	$448.0	$470.4	29.0%
11	Depreciation	$75.2	$78.9	$85.2	$92.0	$99.4	8.0%
12	Other Net (Income)/Expenses	($8.2)	($9.8)	($10.3)	($10.8)	($11.4)	-0.7%
13	EBIT	$227.1	$225.2	$234.0	$243.2	$252.6	
14							
15	Interest (Income)	($2.0)	($0.9)	($1.1)	($3.8)	($7.1)	6.0%
16	Interest Expense	$23.7	$17.9	$14.0	$13.5	$13.5	7.0%
17	Pre-Tax Income	$205.4	$208.1	$221.1	$233.5	$246.2	
18							
19	Income Taxes	$72.6	$72.8	$77.4	$81.7	$86.2	35.0%
20	**Net Income**	**$132.8**	**$135.3**	**$143.7**	**$151.8**	**$160.0**	
21							
22	Dividends	$40.1	$54.1	$57.5	$60.7	$64.0	40.0%
23	Addition to Retained Earnings	$92.7	$81.2	$86.2	$91.1	$96.0	
24							
25	**Balance Sheet ($ Million)**						
26	**Assets**						
27	Cash and Marketable Securities	$28.4	$0.0	$36.5	$90.8	$147.1	
28	Accounts Receivable	$120.1	$117.7	$123.6	$129.8	$136.2	8.4%
29	Inventories	$116.8	$123.3	$129.5	$135.9	$142.7	8.8%
30	Other Current Assets	$97.5	$106.5	$111.8	$117.4	$123.3	7.6%
31	Total Current Assets	$362.8	$347.5	$401.4	$473.9	$549.4	
32							
33	Property, Plant and Equipment, Gross	$913.1	$986.1	$1,065.0	$1,150.2	$1,242.3	**8.0%**
34	Accumulated Depreciation	$427.9	$506.8	$592.0	$684.0	$783.4	
35	Property, Plant and Equipment, Net	$485.2	$479.4	$473.0	$466.2	$458.9	
36							
37	Other Non-Current Assets	$456.3	$492.8	$532.2	$574.8	$620.8	**8.0%**
38	Total Non-Current Assets	$941.5	$972.2	$1,005.3	$1,041.0	$1,079.7	
39							
40	**Total Assets**	**$1,304.3**	**$1,319.6**	**$1,406.6**	**$1,514.9**	**$1,629.0**	
41							
42	**Liabilities and Shareholders' Equity**						
43	Accounts Payable	$80.5	$85.5	$89.7	$94.2	$98.9	6.1%
44	Short-Term Debt	$110.3	$15.6	$0.0	$0.0	$0.0	
45	Other Current Liabilities	$111.3	$116.3	$122.1	$128.2	$134.6	8.3%
46	Total Current Liabilities	$302.1	$217.4	$211.8	$222.4	$233.6	
47							
48	Long-Term Debt	$218.1	$218.1	$218.1	$218.1	$218.1	
49	Deferred Income Taxes	$12.7	$19.6	$20.6	$21.6	$22.7	1.4%
50	Other Non-Current Liabilities	$94.5	$106.5	$111.8	$117.4	$123.3	7.6%
51	Total Liabilities	$627.4	$561.6	$562.4	$579.6	$597.6	
52							
53	Paid-In Capital	$44.8	$44.8	$44.8	$44.8	$44.8	
54	Retained Earnings	$632.1	$713.3	$799.5	$890.6	$986.6	
55	Total Shareholders' Equity	$676.9	$758.1	$844.3	$935.4	$1,031.4	
56							
57	**Total Liabilities and Shareholders' Equity**	**$1,304.3**	**$1,319.6**	**$1,406.6**	**$1,514.9**	**$1,629.0**	
58							
59							
60							
61							

FIGURE 13.13 Model 7: Projected financial statements for Vitex Corp. with no negative short-term debt.

to make sure that they tie to the balance sheet numbers. Remember that they are being calculated based on the average balances. Even though the C&MS balance at the end of year 2009 is projected to be zero, the average balance is not zero and there is some interest income in 2009.

Uses of the Model

This is a more realistic model. It does not necessarily provide more useful information, but it is better than handing someone a balance sheet with negative debt numbers because that may confuse some people and they may even consider it to be wrong.

MODEL 8: FINANCIAL STATEMENT FORECASTING, VERSION 4

The Problem

In Model 7 we set the minimum level for C&MS at zero. Most corporations, though, would want to have some C&MS in hand. Modify the model so that C&MS will be a minimum of $20 million and will be higher if there is excess cash left after all STD is repaid.

Model Characteristics: Builds on Version 3. STD is used as the plug but is not allowed to go negative. Minimum level for C&MS is $20 million. Once all STD is paid off, any additional cash is used to build C&MS. (LTD is held constant.)

Modeling Strategy

The financial statements for this model are shown in Figure 13.14. The logic for this model is similar to that for Version 3 except that here instead of completely ignoring the C&MS account to start with, we can assume that it has a fixed balance of $20 million. We will therefore add 20 to the asset side in our calculation for P. After that, we can calculate the C&MS account using the same formula as before because the full balance sheet has to balance. Think through the logic and then implement it starting with a copy of Model 7.

Building the Model

Start with a copy of Model 7. In J27 enter 20 as the minimum required balance for C&MS. Then in F44 enter the formula =MAX((SUM(F28:F30)+F38+$J$27)-(F55+SUM(F48:F50)+F43+F45),0).

The only change here is that we are including the minimum required C&MS on the asset side by including the reference to the cell $J$27.

◇	A	E	F	G	H	I	J
1	**Income Statement and Balance Sheet for Vitex Corp.**						
2							
3	**Income Statement ($ Million)**						
4			Forecast Period				Forecasting
5		2008	2009	2010	2011	2012	Factor
6	Sales	$1,334.4	$1,401.1	$1,471.2	$1,544.7	$1,622.0	5.0%
7	Cost of Sales	$667.0	$700.6	$735.6	$772.4	$811.0	50.0%
8	Gross Operating Income	$667.4	$700.6	$735.6	$772.4	$811.0	
9							
10	Selling, General & Admn. Expenses	$373.3	$406.3	$426.6	$448.0	$470.4	29.0%
11	Depreciation	$75.2	$78.9	$85.2	$92.0	$99.4	8.0%
12	Other Net (Income)/Expenses	($8.2)	($9.8)	($10.3)	($10.8)	($11.4)	-0.7%
13	EBIT	$227.1	$225.2	$234.0	$243.2	$252.6	
14							
15	Interest (Income)	($2.0)	($1.5)	($1.7)	($3.8)	($7.1)	6.0%
16	Interest Expense	$23.7	$18.6	$14.7	$13.5	$13.5	7.0%
17	Pre-Tax Income	$205.4	$208.0	$221.0	$233.5	$246.2	
18							
19	Income Taxes	$72.6	$72.8	$77.3	$81.7	$86.2	35.0%
20	**Net Income**	**$132.8**	**$135.2**	**$143.6**	**$151.8**	**$160.0**	
21							
22	Dividends	$40.1	$54.1	$57.5	$60.7	$64.0	40.0%
23	Addition to Retained Earnings	$92.7	$81.1	$86.2	$91.1	$96.0	
24							
25	**Balance Sheet ($ Million)**						
26	**Assets**						
27	Cash and Marketable Securities	$28.4	$20.0	$36.4	$90.7	$147.0	20
28	Accounts Receivable	$120.1	$117.7	$123.6	$129.8	$136.2	8.4%
29	Inventories	$116.8	$123.3	$129.5	$135.9	$142.7	8.8%
30	Other Current Assets	$97.5	$106.5	$111.8	$117.4	$123.3	7.6%
31	Total Current Assets	$362.8	$367.5	$401.3	$473.8	$549.3	
32							
33	Property, Plant and Equipment, Gross	$913.1	$986.1	$1,065.0	$1,150.2	$1,242.3	8.0%
34	Accumulated Depreciation	$427.9	$506.8	$592.0	$684.0	$783.4	
35	Property, Plant and equipment, Net	$485.2	$479.4	$473.0	$466.2	$458.9	
36							
37	Other Non-Current Assets	$456.3	$492.8	$532.2	$574.8	$620.8	8.0%
38	Total Non-Current Assets	$941.5	$972.2	$1,005.3	$1,041.0	$1,079.7	
39							
40	**Total Assets**	**$1,304.3**	**$1,339.6**	**$1,406.6**	**$1,514.8**	**$1,628.9**	
41							
42	**Liabilities and Shareholders' Equity**						
43	Accounts Payable	$80.5	$85.5	$89.7	$94.2	$98.9	6.1%
44	Short-Term Debt	$110.3	$35.7	$0.0	$0.0	$0.0	
45	Other Current Liabilities	$111.3	$116.3	$122.1	$128.2	$134.6	8.3%
46	Total Current Liabilities	$302.1	$237.4	$211.8	$222.4	$233.6	
47							
48	Long-Term Debt	$218.1	$218.1	$218.1	$218.1	$218.1	
49	Deferred Income Taxes	$12.7	$19.6	$20.6	$21.6	$22.7	1.4%
50	Other Non-Current Liabilities	$94.5	$106.5	$111.8	$117.4	$123.3	7.6%
51	Total Liabilities	$627.4	$581.6	$562.4	$579.6	$597.6	
52							
53	Paid-In Capital	$44.8	$44.8	$44.8	$44.8	$44.8	
54	Retained Earnings	$632.1	$713.2	$799.4	$890.5	$986.5	
55	Total Shareholders' Equity	$676.9	$758.0	$844.2	$935.3	$1,031.3	
56							
57	**Total Liabilities and Shareholders' Equity**	**$1,304.3**	**$1,339.6**	**$1,406.6**	**$1,514.8**	**$1,628.9**	
58							
59							
60							
61							

FIGURE 13.14 Model 8: Projected financial statements for Vitex Corp. with minimum cash balance.

Testing the Model

Test it by first making sure that the C&MS balance is 20, but not higher, as long as STD is positive. It should go above that level only when STD drops to zero. To make sure that the logic is working properly, vary the minimum C&MS level and make sure that the model is responding appropriately.

Uses of the Model

This model is even more realistic than the previous model because all corporations would want to keep a minimum balance in the C&MS account. This level does not have to be constant. For example, if the corporation wants to maintain a C&MS level tied to sales, (for example, 2.1% of sales as in the original assumptions), we can enter 2.1% in cell J27 and then in F44 enter the formula =MAX((SUM(F28:F30)+F38+$J$27*F6)−(F55+SUM(F48:F50)+F43+F45),0) and copy and paste it for the other years.

MODEL 9: FINANCIAL STATEMENT FORECASTING, VERSION 5

The Problem

One problem you will notice with the current projections is that because management is willing to go up to a dividend payout ratio of 40% (from 30% in 2008) and EPS is growing, the dividend goes up sharply in 2009. Management generally wants to grow the dividend at a steady pace and so it may want to impose the additional condition that dividend per share will not be increased by more than 10% in any year. Incorporate this additional restriction on the Version 4 model.

Model Characteristics: STD is used as the plug but is not allowed to go negative. Once all STD is paid off, any additional cash is used to build C&MS. Minimum level for C&MS is $20 million. LTD remains constant. Dividend payout can go up to 40% but dividend per share cannot grow more than 10% in any year.

Modeling Strategy

This is another realistic constraint and is easy to implement. In calculating total dividend amount for a year, the model now has to calculate it in two ways, once as 40% of net income and once at a per share dividend rate 10% higher than the previous year and then select the lower of the two.

It is important to remember that the growth rate constraint is on dividend per share and not total dividend. If number of shares outstanding remains the same then the two are the same; but if shares outstanding increase or decrease then they will not be. You have to apply the constraint carefully on the right variable.

Building the Model

Start with a copy of Model 8. In J21, enter 10% to use for the constraint on dividend growth rate. Then in cell F22 enter the formula =MIN(F20*$J$22, E22*(1+$J$21)*F65/E65). The first argument here calculates the total dividend based on the payout ratio constraint as before. The second argument calculates the total dividend for the current year using the maximum growth rate allowable per year. The multiplication by F65/E65 effectively first converts the previous year's total dividend to a per share number, and then converts the maximum allowable per share dividend for the current year to a total dividend number.

Testing the Model

You can check the model by changing some of the numbers to make sure that under different conditions different constraints become binding. You can also look at the dividend growth rates from before (Model 8) and after applying the new constraints (this model) and notice that dividend is now growing at 10% per year whereas it was growing much faster before.

Uses of the Model

This model again shows that once you have the basic structure of a forecasting model, you can easily add conditions to make it more and more realistic.

MODEL 10: FINANCIAL STATEMENT FORECASTING, VERSION 6

The Problem

In practice, long-term debts come due over time. For preliminary planning it is often assumed that as they come due, long-term debt will be paid off and be effectively replaced by STD because it is the balancing account. Modify Model 9 to accommodate a long-term debt repayment schedule. Assume that any long-term debt repaid carries an interest rate of 9% per year.

Model Characteristics: STD is used as the plug but is not allowed to go negative. Once all STD is paid off, any additional cash is used to build C&MS. Minimum level for C&MS is $20 million. LTD is paid off as they mature based on a schedule. Dividend payout can go up to 40%, but dividend per share cannot grow more than 10% in any year.

Modeling Strategy

The projected financial statements for this model are shown in Figure 13.15. If long-term debt level on the balance sheet is reduced as they mature based on the specified schedule, the model as it is set up will automatically make the necessary adjustments to the STD and C&MS accounts and maintain a balanced balance sheet.

You have to reduce the interest expense for the long-term debt that is being paid off. Because we are calculating interest expense based on average balance, the reduction for the first year will have to be calculated on half the repayment in the first year. For the second year it will be on the full repayment for the first year plus half of the repayment for the second year, and so forth. We have to take this somewhat complex approach because our interest expense calculation already includes total interest expense on all the long-term debt that is outstanding at the end of 2008. We are now deducting the reduction in long-term interest expense relative to that.

Building the Model

Start with a copy of Model 9.

1. **Create LTD repayment schedule:** In row 59, enter the label "Long-term debt repayment for the year" and in F59:I59 enter the debt amounts to be repaid in different years.
2. **Adjust long-term debt levels:** In F48 enter the formula =E48-F59 to reduce long-term debt balance from previous year-end by the planned repayment for the projection year. Copy the formula over for the other years.
3. **Adjust interest expense:** In cell J17 enter the long-term interest rate of 9% to be used for repayments. Insert comments in J16 and J17 to explain what the two different rates are.

   In cell F16 enter the formula =13.5+$J$16*(E44+F44)/2-($F59/2)*$J$17. This reduces the interest expense by the interest on half the long-term debt to be repaid during the year.

   In cell G16 enter the formula =13.5+$J$16*(F44+G44)/2-($F59+$G59/2)*$J$17 for reasons explained earlier.

   In cell H16 enter the formula =13.5+$J$16*(G44+H44)/2-($F59+$G59+$H59/2)*$J$17.

   In cell I16 enter the formula =13.5+$J$16*(H44+I44)/2-($F59+$G59+$H59+$I59/2)*$J$17.

Testing the Model

Check that the long-term debt balance is declining by the correct amounts. Check the interest expense numbers by hand calculation. Although it is not necessary to

◇	A	E	F	G	H	I	J
1	**Income Statement and Balance Sheet for Vitex Corp.**						
2							
3	**Income Statement ($ Million)**						
4			Forecast Period				Forecasting
5		2008	2009	2010	2011	2012	Factor
6	Sales	$1,334.4	$1,401.1	$1,471.2	$1,544.7	$1,622.0	5.0%
7	Cost of Sales	$667.0	$700.6	$735.6	$772.4	$811.0	50.0%
8	Gross Operating Income	$667.4	$700.6	$735.6	$772.4	$811.0	
9							
10	Selling, General & Admn. Expenses	$373.3	$406.3	$426.6	$448.0	$470.4	29.0%
11	Depreciation	$75.2	$78.9	$85.2	$92.0	$99.4	8.0%
12	Other Net (Income)/Expenses	($8.2)	($9.8)	($10.3)	($10.8)	($11.4)	-0.7%
13	EBIT	$227.1	$225.2	$234.0	$243.2	$252.6	
14							
15	Interest (Income)	($2.0)	($1.5)	($1.2)	($2.4)	($4.7)	6.0%
16	Interest Expense	$23.7	$18.0	$12.4	$9.1	$6.8	7.0%
17	Pre-Tax Income	$205.4	$208.6	$222.8	$236.5	$250.5	9.0%
18							
19	Income Taxes	$72.6	$73.0	$78.0	$82.8	$87.7	35.0%
20	Net Income	$132.8	$135.6	$144.8	$153.7	$162.8	
21							10%
22	Dividends	$40.1	$44.1	$48.5	$53.4	$58.7	40.0%
23	Addition to Retained Earnings	$92.7	$91.5	$96.3	$100.3	$104.1	
24							
25	**Balance Sheet ($ Million)**						
26	Assets						
27	Cash and Marketable Securities	$28.4	$20.0	$20.0	$60.5	$94.9	20
28	Accounts Receivable	$120.1	$117.7	$123.6	$129.8	$136.2	8.4%
29	Inventories	$116.8	$123.3	$129.5	$135.9	$142.7	8.8%
30	Other Current Assets	$97.5	$106.5	$111.8	$117.4	$123.3	7.6%
31	Total Current Assets	$362.8	$367.5	$384.9	$443.6	$497.1	
32							
33	Property, Plant and Equipment, Gross	$913.1	$986.1	$1,065.0	$1,150.2	$1,242.3	8.0%
34	Accumulated Depreciation	$427.9	$506.8	$592.0	$684.0	$783.4	
35	Property, Plant and Equipment, Net	$485.2	$479.4	$473.0	$466.2	$458.9	
36							
37	Other Non-Current Assets	$456.3	$492.8	$532.2	$574.8	$620.8	8.0%
38	Total Non-Current Assets	$941.5	$972.2	$1,005.3	$1,041.0	$1,079.7	
39							
40	Total Assets	$1,304.3	$1,339.6	$1,390.1	$1,484.6	$1,576.8	
41							
42	Liabilities and Shareholders' Equity						
43	Accounts Payable	$80.5	$85.5	$89.7	$94.2	$98.9	6.1%
44	Short-Term Debt	$110.3	$50.3	$3.1	$0.0	$0.0	
45	Other Current Liabilities	$111.3	$116.3	$122.1	$128.2	$134.6	8.3%
46	Total Current Liabilities	$302.1	$252.1	$214.9	$222.4	$233.6	
47							
48	Long-Term Debt	$218.1	$193.1	$178.1	$158.1	$128.1	
49	Deferred Income Taxes	$12.7	$19.6	$20.6	$21.6	$22.7	1.4%
50	Other Non-Current Liabilities	$94.5	$106.5	$111.8	$117.4	$123.3	7.6%
51	Total Liabilities	$627.4	$571.3	$525.4	$519.6	$507.6	
52							
53	Paid-In Capital	$44.8	$44.8	$44.8	$44.8	$44.8	
54	Retained Earnings	$632.1	$723.6	$819.9	$920.2	$1,024.3	
55	Total Shareholders' Equity	$676.9	$768.4	$864.7	$965.0	$1,069.1	
56							
57	Total Liabilities and Shareholders' Equity	$1,304.3	$1,339.6	$1,390.1	$1,484.6	$1,576.8	
58							
59	Long-term Debt Repayment for the Year		25	15	20	30	
60							
61							

FIGURE 13.15 Model 10: Projected financial statements for Vitex Corp. with declining long-term debt.

do so, as a challenge see if you can reconcile the total debt and C&MS account balances for this Model with those in Model 9. (Hint: You may find it easier to do so if you first set the interest rates to zero.)

Uses of the Model

This is another step in making the model realistic. In practice, a model like this can be tied to a corporation's debt repayment schedule and the interest rate reductions can be based on the interest rates on the actual debts maturing. The assumption that as long-term debts mature they will be replaced by short-term debt may not be completely realistic. Management may want to impose a policy of maintaining a specific relationship between short-term and long-term debt (for example, long-term debt will be 60% of total debt).

MODEL 11: FINANCIAL STATEMENT FORECASTING, VERSION 7

The Problem

Management has decided that, in the projections, it wants to maintain a target capital structure of 30% debt and 70% equity. Within debt, it wants to have 40% short-term debt and 60% long-term debt. Stocks will be issued or bought back as needed at the average price for the year. As before, stock price at the end of each year will be estimated based on the assumed P/E ratios applied to the EPS for the year just ended and calculated using the average number of shares that were outstanding during the year. The interest rate on long-term debt, whether issued or repaid, will be at 9%. Calculate C&MS as 2.1% of sales.

Model Characteristics: Total capitalization is used as plug and target capital structure is maintained. C&MS balance is calculated as percentage of sale. Dividend payout can go up to 40%, but dividend per share cannot grow more than 10% in any year.

Modeling Strategy

The financial statements for this model are shown in Figures 13.16 and 13.17. Start by noting all the changes to be made in the assumptions sheet.

The key difference in this model is that the total capitalization (the sum of short-term debt, long-term debt, and total shareholders' equity) is now the plug. Every year you have to calculate the plug amount as the difference between total assets and the sum of all other liability items, and then allocate it among the three categories of capital in the target proportions.

For simplicity, assume that the paid-in capital remains unchanged—although in practice, if stocks are issued or repurchased, this account will be adjusted. If you had enough information, you could easily allocate any stock issuance or

◇	A	E	F	G	H	I	J
1	**Income Statement and Balance Sheet for Vitex Corp.**						
2							
3	**Income Statement ($ Million)**						
4				Forecast Period			Forecasting
5		2008	2009	2010	2011	2012	Factor
6	Sales	$1,334.4	$1,401.1	$1,471.2	$1,544.7	$1,622.0	5.0%
7	Cost of Sales	$667.0	$700.6	$735.6	$772.4	$811.0	**50.0%**
8	Gross Operating Income	$667.4	$700.6	$735.6	$772.4	$811.0	
9							
10	Selling, General & Admn. Expenses	$373.3	$406.3	$426.6	$448.0	$470.4	29.0%
11	Depreciation	$75.2	$78.9	$85.2	$92.0	$99.4	8.0%
12	Other Net (Income)/Expenses	($8.2)	($9.8)	($10.3)	($10.8)	($11.4)	-0.7%
13	EBIT	$227.1	$225.2	$234.0	$243.2	$252.6	
14							
15	Interest (Income)	($2.0)	($1.7)	($1.8)	($1.9)	($2.0)	6.0%
16	Interest Expense	$23.7	$20.1	$19.4	$20.3	$21.3	7.0%
17	Pre-Tax Income	$205.4	$206.8	$216.4	$224.7	$233.3	9.0%
18							
19	Income Taxes	$72.6	$72.4	$75.7	$78.7	$81.6	35.0%
20	**Net Income**	**$132.8**	**$134.4**	**$140.7**	**$146.1**	**$151.6**	
21							10%
22	Dividends	$40.1	$43.1	$46.0	$49.3	$53.1	40.0%
23	Addition to Retained Earnings	$92.7	$91.3	$94.7	$96.8	$98.6	
24							
25	**Balance Sheet ($ Million)**						
26	**Assets**						
27	Cash and Marketable Securities	$28.4	$29.4	$30.9	$32.4	$34.1	2.1%
28	Accounts Receivable	$120.1	$117.7	$123.6	$129.8	$136.2	8.4%
29	Inventories	$116.8	$123.3	$129.5	$135.9	$142.7	8.8%
30	Other Current Assets	$97.5	$106.5	$111.8	$117.4	$123.3	7.6%
31	Total Current Assets	$362.8	$376.9	$395.7	$415.5	$436.3	
32							
33	Property, Plant and Equipment, Gross	$913.1	$986.1	$1,065.0	$1,150.2	$1,242.3	**8.0%**
34	Accumulated Depreciation	$427.9	$506.8	$592.0	$684.0	$783.4	
35	Property, Plant and Equipment, Net	$485.2	$479.4	$473.0	$466.2	$458.9	
36							
37	Other Non-Current Assets	$456.3	$492.8	$532.2	$574.8	$620.8	**8.0%**
38	Total Non-Current Assets	$941.5	$972.2	$1,005.3	$1,041.0	$1,079.7	
39							
40	**Total Assets**	**$1,304.3**	**$1,349.1**	**$1,401.0**	**$1,456.6**	**$1,516.0**	
41							
42	**Liabilities and Shareholders' Equity**						
43	Accounts Payable	$80.5	$85.5	$89.7	$94.2	$98.9	6.1%
44	Short-Term Debt	$110.3	$122.5	$126.8	$131.4	$136.4	12.0%
45	Other Current Liabilities	$111.3	$116.3	$122.1	$128.2	$134.6	8.3%
46	Total Current Liabilities	$302.1	$324.3	$338.7	$353.9	$369.9	
47							
48	Long-Term Debt	$218.1	$183.8	$190.2	$197.1	$204.6	18.0%
49	Deferred Income Taxes	$12.7	$19.6	$20.6	$21.6	$22.7	1.4%
50	Other Non-Current Liabilities	$94.5	$106.5	$111.8	$117.4	$123.3	7.6%
51	Total Liabilities	$627.4	$634.2	$661.3	$690.0	$720.5	
52							
53	Paid-In Capital	$44.8	$44.8	$44.8	$44.8	$44.8	
54	Retained Earnings	$632.1	$670.0	$694.9	$721.8	$750.7	
55	Total Shareholders' Equity	$676.9	$714.8	$739.7	$766.6	$795.5	
56							
57	**Total Liabilities and Shareholders' Equity**	**$1,304.3**	**$1,349.1**	**$1,401.0**	**$1,456.6**	**$1,516.0**	
58							
59	Stock Issuance/(Buyback) (in dollars)		($53.4)	($69.8)	($69.9)	($69.6)	
60	Stock Issuance/(Buyback) (in millions of shares)		(1.1)	(1.3)	(1.1)	(0.9)	
61							
62							
63	**Other Data**						
64	Stock Price (year-end)	$51.40	$47.67	$57.82	$68.45	$79.90	
65	Average Number of Shares Outstanding (millions)	46.2	45.1	43.8	42.7	41.7	
66							
67	**Financial Indicators**						
68	**Valuation Ratios**						
69	EPS	$2.87	$2.98	$3.21	$3.42	$3.63	
70	Dividend per Share	$0.87	$0.95	$1.05	$1.16	$1.27	
71	P/E Ratio	17.9	16.0	18.0	20.0	22.0	
72	P/B (price to book) Ratio	3.5	3.0	3.4	3.8	4.2	
73	Dividend Payout Ratio	30%	32%	33%	34%	35%	
74							

FIGURE 13.16 Model 11: Projected financial statements for Vitex Corp. with capital structure constraints.

	A	E	F	G	H	I
1	Statement of Cash Flows for Vitex Corp.					
2	Millions of Dollars					
3						
4				Forecast Period		
5		2008	2009	2010	2011	2012
6	Cash Flows from Operations					
7	Net Income	$132.8	$134.4	$140.7	$146.1	$151.6
8	Depreciation Expense	$75.2	$78.9	$85.2	$92.0	$99.4
9	Decrease/(Increase) in Accounts Receivable	($12.8)	$2.4	($5.9)	($6.2)	($6.5)
10	Decrease/(Increase) in Inventories	($1.9)	($6.5)	($6.2)	($6.5)	($6.8)
11	Decrease/(Increase) in Other Current Assets	$6.2	($9.0)	($5.3)	($5.6)	($5.9)
12	Increase/(Decrease) in Accounts Payable	$8.7	$5.0	$4.3	$4.5	$4.7
13	Increase/(Decrease) in Other Current Liabilities	($60.8)	$5.0	$5.8	$6.1	$6.4
14	Increase/(Decrease) in Deferred Income Taxes	($2.3)	$6.9	$1.0	$1.0	$1.1
15	Increase/(Decrease) in Other Non-Current Liabilities	($20.5)	$12.0	$5.3	$5.6	$5.9
16	Total Cash Flows from Operations	$124.6	$229.1	$224.9	$237.1	$249.9
17						
18	Cash Flows from Investing					
19	(Additions to) Property, Plant & Equipment	($92.3)	($73.0)	($78.9)	($85.2)	($92.0)
20	(Investment) in Other Non-Current Assets	($49.3)	($36.5)	($39.4)	($42.6)	($46.0)
21	Total Cash Flows from Investing	($141.6)	($109.6)	($118.3)	($127.8)	($138.0)
22						
23	Cash Flows from Financing					
24	From Issuance/(Repayment) of Short-Term Debt	$30.5	$12.2	$4.3	$4.6	$5.0
25	From Issuance/(Repayment) of Long-Term Debt	$16.3	($34.3)	$6.4	$6.9	$7.4
26	From Sale/(Repurchase) of Equity	$6.6	($53.4)	($69.8)	($69.9)	($69.6)
27	Cash Dividends Paid to Shareholders	($40.1)	($43.1)	($46.0)	($49.3)	($53.1)
28	Total Cash Flows from Financing	$13.3	($118.5)	($105.1)	($107.8)	($110.3)
29						
30	Net Change in Cash & Marketable Securities	($3.7)	$1.0	$1.5	$1.5	$1.6
31						
32						
33	Beginning Cash & Marketable Securities	$32.1	$28.4	$29.4	$30.9	$32.4
34	Ending Cash & Marketable Securities	$28.4	$29.4	$30.9	$32.4	$34.1
35	Net Change in Cash & Marketable Securities	($3.7)	$1.0	$1.5	$1.5	$1.6
36						
37						

FIGURE 13.17 Model 11: Projected financial statements of cash flows for Vitex Corp.

repurchase between paid-in capital and retained earnings. But here do all the adjustments in the retained earnings account because financially it makes no difference. This also means that you will not calculate retained earnings as the sum of the previous year's retained earnings and the current year's addition to it anymore. Instead, after you have calculated the retained earning as discussed (that is, based on the plug), you can calculate the stock issuance or repurchase amount as the difference between last year's retained earnings plus the current year's addition minus the current year's retained earnings.

How many shares you will have to sell or buy back will depend on the stock price, which will involve a circular reference as follows: the average stock price for the year will depend on the year-end stock price, which will depend on the EPS, which will depend on the average number of shares outstanding during the year, which in turn will depend on the number of shares you will have to sell or buy back. As we have seen before, you do not have to do anything special to set up the circular reference. As long as you enter the right formulas in the cells and iteration is turned on, Excel will take care of the rest.

(You can calculate the average number of shares outstanding as the sum of the average number of shares outstanding during the previous year plus the number of new shares issued or minus the number of shares repurchased during the current year. This will be an approximate number. To calculate a better number, you would have to know the number of shares outstanding at the end of the previous year. Try to understand why this is true and how you will calculate the average number of shares outstanding if you know the number of shares outstanding at the end of the previous year.)

The interest expense calculation will also be a little more complex. The base line \$13.5 million expense for long-term debt has to be adjusted by additions to or reductions in long-term debt at the interest rate of 9%. However, this rate will have to be applied to the cumulative change through the end of the previous year plus the average change during the past year.

Notice that now neither short-term nor long-term debt balances can go negative, and you can calculate the C&MS balance independently as 2.1% of sales.

Finally, you will need to reflect the stock issuance or repurchase in the statement of cash flows by changing the formulas there. In the historical period we assumed that the change in paid-in capital reflected stock issuance or repurchase. Now you have to use the stock issuance or repurchase that you calculate in conjunction with the balance sheet.

Building the Model

Start with a copy of Model 10. As always, unless otherwise noted, you can copy the formula for 2009 into the cells for the other years.

1. **Calculate STD:** In J44 enter (30% × 40% =)12% to reflect the percentage of STD in total capitalization. In F44 enter the formula =(F$40-(F$43+F$45+F$49+F$50))*$J44. As discussed, the plug here is the amount of total assets (the first term), less the total of all liabilities other than debt (the second term).
2. **Calculate LTD:** In J48 enter (30% × 60% =)18% to reflect the percentage of LTD in total capitalization. In F48 enter the formula =(F$40-(F$43+F$45+F$49+F$50))*$J48, which is similar to the formula for STD.
3. **Calculate shareholders' equity:** Make the paid-in capital in each year from 2003 to 2006 the same as the year-end 2002 number. To calculate retained earnings, in F54 enter the formula =(F$40-(F$51+F$53)). This is the amount needed to balance the balance sheet, and now that you have calculated STD and LTD based on the specified capital structure, this will automatically make total shareholders' equity the right percentage (70%) of total capital as well.
4. **Calculate stock issuance/(buyback) in dollars:** Enter the appropriate label in A59. In F59 enter the formula =F55-(E55+F23). It calculates the stock repurchase/issuance as the difference between what the retained earnings

would have been without them and what it has been calculated to be. Calculated this way, buybacks will be negative, which is generally the sign convention used.

5. **Calculate the number of stock issuance/(buyback):** Enter the appropriate label in A60. In F60 enter the formula =F59/((E64+F64)/2). This uses the average stock price for the calculation.
6. **Adjust the average number of shares outstanding:** To calculate the average number of shares outstanding during a year, in F65 enter the formula =E65+F60. (As mentioned before, this is approximate.)
7. **Change calculation of C&MS:** In J27 enter 2.1% and then in F27 enter =F6*$J$27 to calculate the C&MS as a percentage of sales.
8. **Calculate interest expense:** In J17 enter 9% for the marginal long-term interest rate and put explanatory comments in J16 and J17. (I am using J17 here because it is a nearby empty cell. Attaching the comment is essential to avoid confusion.)

   To calculate interest expense, in F16 enter =13.5+$J$16*(E44+F44)/2+$J$17*((F48-E48)/2). The last part of the formula calculates the adjustment to the long-term interest expense of $13.5 million (on the long-term debt existing at the end of 2008) that will result from the change in the average balance in long-term debt over the year. Writing the average change in LTD as (F48-E48) takes care of the proper sign of the interest expense adjustment.

   You cannot copy this formula for the other years. In G16 enter the formula =13.5+$J$16*(F44+G44)/2+$J$17*((F48-$E48)+(G48-F48)/2). As discussed, this calculates the cumulative change in LTD through the end of the previous year and adds to it the average change for the current year. This formula can be copied into the other years.
9. **Make changes to statements of cash flows:** The only change needed is in the line "From Sale/(Repurchase) of Equity." In F26 enter the formula =(Model!F54+Model!F53)-(Model!E54+Model!E53+Model!F23) and copy it for the other years. (Use of this formula is instructive, but you could also enter =Model!F59 and so forth.)

Testing the Model

To make sure that the capital structure is on target, check the Leverage Ratios section of the financial indicators. You have to check the calculations related to share repurchase by hand and do the same for the interest expense calculations. The most important test is to look at the numbers that have changed and ask, "Does it make sense?" For example, ask yourself why the model is buying back stocks. To understand why, look at the statement of cash flows to see how the extra cash is being generated and how it is being used to adjust the different components of capital. Since equity is 70% of the capital structure, bulk of the excess cash is going to buying back stock.

Uses of the Model

This model demonstrates how informative and comprehensive such a model can be. If you try to do the calculations by hand instead of taking this systematic approach, it is almost certain that you will miss taking into consideration a number of factors and you will never be sure if the numbers are correct. It also provides lot of flexibility to incorporate additional policies. For example, after looking at the results, management may decide that they want to make the capital structure adjustment slowly over a few years. For this, you will have to set up year-by-year capital structure targets and use them in the model. It is relatively easy to do.

MODEL 12: FINANCIAL STATEMENTS SENSITIVITY ANALYSIS

The Problem

One of the major uses of financial statement forecasting models is to do sensitivity analysis. We can see the effect of making changes in any of the input (independent) variables on the other dependent variable by making the changes in the model. But trying these out one at a time does not provide us a comprehensive picture. Your management wants to see how Net Income, EPS, dividend per share, and stock price will change for 2012 for sales growth rates from 1% to 10% per year over the years. Create a one-input data table to show this information. Also create a two-input data table to show how EBIT for 2009 will depend on cost of sales to sales ratio and sales growth rate in a reasonable range. (Use Model 11 for your analysis.)

Model Characteristics: Total capitalization is used as plug and target capital structure is maintained. C&MS balance is calculated as percentage of sale. Dividend payout can go up to 40%, but dividend per share cannot grow more than 10% in any year.

Modeling Strategy

Once you have a working, fully tested model, choosing the right independent and dependent variables for sensitivity analysis is an important challenge. It is so easy to do these in Excel that the tendency is to drown management with numbers. Instead of taking that easy way out, you need to devote some time to decide which sensitivity analyses will be most informative to look at.

In this case, the problem already specifies the tables to prepare. Data Table is the ideal tool for doing this analysis. Remember that it is easiest to create data tables in the same sheet that has the independent and dependent variables. Start with a copy of Model 11 and set up your data tables at the bottom of the Model sheet. Use appropriate formatting, and so on to make them look attractive. The results are shown in Figure 13.18.

	A	E	F	G	H	I	J
105	**Sensitivity Analysis for Vitex Corp.**						
106							
107			For 2012				
108			Net Income	EPS	Div./Share	Stock Price	
109			$151.6	$3.63	$1.27	$79.90	
110	Sales growth rates per year>	1.0%	$118.6	$2.80	$1.12	$61.52	
111		2.0%	$126.5	$2.99	$1.20	$65.83	
112		3.0%	$134.7	$3.20	$1.27	$70.32	
113		4.0%	$143.0	$3.41	$1.27	$75.04	
114		5.0%	$151.6	$3.63	$1.27	$79.90	
115		6.0%	$160.5	$3.86	$1.27	$84.93	
116		7.0%	$169.6	$4.10	$1.27	$90.11	
117		8.0%	$179.0	$4.34	$1.27	$95.44	
118		9.0%	$188.6	$4.59	$1.27	$100.95	
119		10.0%	$198.5	$4.85	$1.27	$106.61	
120							
121							
122							
123							
124					EBIT for 2009		
125							
126	Cost of sales to sales ratio >		48.0%	49.0%	50.0%	51.0%	52.0%
127	Sales growth rates per year >	1.0%	$240.5	$227.0	$213.6	$200.1	$186.6
128		2.0%	$243.7	$230.1	$216.5	$202.9	$189.2
129		3.0%	$246.8	$233.1	$219.4	$205.6	$191.9
130		4.0%	$250.0	$236.1	$222.3	$208.4	$194.5
131		5.0%	$253.2	$239.2	$225.2	$211.1	$197.1
132		6.0%	$256.3	$242.2	$228.0	$213.9	$199.8
133		7.0%	$259.5	$245.2	$230.9	$216.7	$202.4
134		8.0%	$262.7	$248.2	$233.8	$219.4	$205.0
135		9.0%	$265.8	$251.3	$236.7	$222.2	$207.6
136		10.0%	$269.0	$254.3	$239.6	$225.0	$210.3
137							

FIGURE 13.18 Model 12: Sensitivity analysis based on financial statements for Vitex Corp.

Building the Model

Start with a copy of Model 11.

1. **Create the one-input data table:** Enter the range of values for sales growth rate in E110:E119. Enter the labels in F108:I108. These are only labels; Excel does not understand them. To indicate where Excel should get the Net Income numbers from, in F109 enter =I20, in G109 enter =I69, in H109 enter =I70, and in I109 enter =I64. Select E109:I119 and select Data Table. In Column input cell, enter =$J$6 by pointing to indicate the cell for the sales growth rate, and click OK. Format the table appropriately.
2. **Create the two-input data table:** Enter the sales growth rates in E127: E136 and the cost of sales to sales ratios in F126:J126. In E126 enter =F13 to indicate where Excel should get the values for the EBIT for 2003 from. (Because this looks odd, I have hidden the content of the cell using custom formatting with just a semicolon (;).

Select E126:J136 and select Data ⇨ Data Tools ⇨ What If-Analysis ⇨ Data Table. In Row input cell, enter $J$7 (by pointing) to tell Excel where to substitute the values for cost of sales to sales ratios. In Column input cell, enter =$J$6 by pointing to indicate the cell for the sales growth rate. Click OK. Format the table appropriately.

Testing the Model

It is easiest to test the data tables by checking if they have the right numbers for input values you are currently using on your worksheet. For example, because your worksheet currently uses 5% for sales growth rate and 50% for cost of sales to sales ratio, your current EBIT number for 2009 should match the corresponding number in the data table.

Uses of the Model

These types of sensitivity tables may be considered the fruits of your modeling. This is what management needs to see to make decisions. Of course, you cannot get to this point until you have a correct and realistic model.

MODEL 13: FINANCIAL STATEMENTS SCENARIO ANALYSIS

The Problem

The management also wants to look at a few scenarios for the future because sensitivity analysis of the type that can be done with Data Table can show sensitivity with respect to only one or two input variables per table. Starting with Model 11, do a scenario analysis for an optimistic and pessimistic scenario defined by management as follows:

- Optimistic scenario: Sales growth rate 7% per year, Cost of sales to sales ratio 49%, SG&A to sales ratio 28%, and Gross PP&E growth rate 7% per year.
- Pessimistic scenario: Sales growth rate 3% per year, Cost of sales to sales ratio 51%, SG&A to sales ratio 30%, and Gross PP&E growth rate 9% per year.

In your output, show the values for Net Income, EPS, Dividend per share, ROE, and Times interest earned for both 2009 and 2012.

Model characteristics: Total capitalization is used as plug and target capital structure is maintained. C&MS balance is calculated as percentage of sale.

	A	B	C	D	E	F	G
1							
2		**Scenario Summary**					
3				Current Values:	Optimistic 2012	Pessimistic 2012	
4					Created by Chandan Sengupta on 7/26/2009	Created by Chandan Sengupta on 7/26/2009	
5		Changing Cells					
6			Sales growth rate	5.0%	7.0%	3.0%	
7			Cost of sales to sales ratio	50.0%	49.0%	51.0%	
8			SG&A to sales ratio	29.0%	28.0%	30.0%	
9			Gross PP&E growth rate	8.0%	7.0%	9.0%	
10		Result Cells:					
11		2003					
12			Net income	$134.4	$157.3	$112.2	
13			EPS	$2.98	$3.52	$2.46	
14			Dividend per share	$0.95	$0.95	$0.95	
15			Return on equity	19.3%	22.7%	16.1%	
16			Times interest earned	11.2	13.0	9.5	
17		2006					
18			Net income	$151.6	$195.2	$112.2	
19			EPS	$3.63	$4.84	$2.58	
20			Dividend per share	$1.27	$1.27	$1.03	
21			Return on equity	19.4%	25.6%	14.0%	
22			Times interest earned	11.8	15.5	8.7	
23		Notes: Current Values column represents values of changing cells at					
24		time Scenario Summary Report was created. Changing cells for each					
25		scenario are highlighted in gray.					
26							

FIGURE 13.19 Model 13: Scenario analysis based on financial statements for Vitex Corp.

Dividend payout can go up to 40%, but dividend per share cannot grow more than 10% in any year.

Modeling Strategy

As I discussed before, what output of a model one should look at to make decisions is itself an important decision. Here, of course, you are told what to present, but this is just an example. It takes a good understanding of the business and the model to specify meaningful scenarios and outputs to look at.

The output for this problem is shown in Figure 13.19. Start with a copy of Model 11. You will not be able to have the Scenario Manager create the right row labels. Once you have created the table with the Scenario Manager, you will have to edit the table to make it more understandable.

Building the Model

Start with a copy of Model 11.

Select Data ⇨ Data Tools ⇨ What-If Analysis ⇨ Scenario Manager. Click Add; in Scenario name, enter Optimistic 2006, and in the Changing cells box enter the cell numbers for the independent variables (J6, J7, J10, and J33) by clicking the appropriate cells. Click OK, and then in the boxes for the values enter the values for the optimistic scenario. Click OK. Now click Add again to create the pessimistic scenario the same way and enter the values of the independent variables for it. Click OK.

Back in the Scenario Manager dialog box click Summary. In the Scenario Summary dialog box, make sure that the Scenario summary is selected, and then in the Results cells box enter the cell address for the output variables by pointing—separated by commas (F20, F69, F70, F76, F100, I20, I69, I70, I76, I100)—and click OK.

Excel will create the Scenario Summary table on a separate spreadsheet. Format the table and enter the appropriate row labels.

Testing the Model

By looking at the current values, check that the input and output values are using the right cells, that is, you entered the right cell addresses to set up the scenarios and the outputs.

Uses of the Model

Data Table and Scenario Manager create two different types of tables to provide two different perspectives. Both are important to make real use of the financial statement forecasting models you create. Remember that the summary table created by the Scenario Manager is not dynamic. If you make any changes in your model, the table will not update automatically. You will have to create a new table following the same step. Tables created by Data Table will update automatically.

MODEL 14: CALCULATING FREE CASH FLOW

The Problem

Starting with Model 11, develop a statement to calculate the free cash flow generated by Vitex in both the historical and forecast periods and show how the free cash flow is being used.

Model Characteristics: Total capitalization is used as plug and target capital structure is maintained. C&MS balance calculated as percentage of sale. Dividend payout can go up to 40%, but dividend per share cannot grow more than 10% in any year.

Modeling Strategy

It is best to calculate free cash flow using a format similar to that of the statement of cash flows. You should be able to develop this model based on the earlier discussion in the section "Free cash flow." One problem that often arises is that without additional information it is difficult to judge which accounts with "other" in their title should be considered operating accounts. For simplicity, assume all such accounts for Vitex are operating accounts. The worksheet for this model is shown in Figure 13.20.

Building the Model

Start with a copy of Model 11. I will discuss only the formulas for the year 2006. You can copy them over for the other years. As always, whenever you can, use the pointing method to enter formulas.

1. **Create a template for the calculation:** Make a copy of the existing worksheet for statement of cash flows, change the titles and labels on it and clear all formulas. (We will actually use many of the lines from the regular cash flow statements. If you prefer, you can use them by cutting and pasting them at the right places. I will discuss it here as if we are starting from scratch.)
2. **Enter net income:** In C6 enter =Model!C20.
3. **Calculate interest expense after taxes:** To use the formulas for tax rate, in J7 enter 35%. In C7 enter the formula =Model!C$16*(1-$J$7), which is the interest expense after tax (at the statutory rate).
4. **Make adjustment for deferred taxes:** To eliminate non-cash taxes represented by an increase in deferred tax balance, in C8 enter =Model!C49-Model!B49.
5. **Calculate NOPAT:** To calculate the NOPAT, in C9 enter the formula =SUM(C6:C8).
6. **Enter depreciation and calculate gross cash flow:** For depreciation, in C11 enter =Model!C11. Then, to calculate the gross cash flow, in C12 enter the formula =C9+C11.
7. **Deduct the investments to calculate free cash flow:** To reflect the investment in working capital, in C14 enter =(Model!B31-Model!B43-Model! B45)-(Model!C31-Model!C43-Model!C45). Note that this is a slightly different definition of working capital because it excludes short-term debt, which is part of financing.

   To reflect capital expenditures or investment in PP&E, in C15 enter =Model!B33-Model!C33. You have to use gross and not net PP&E here.

   For investments in the other non-current assets and liabilities, in C16 enter =Model!C50-Model!B50 and in C17 enter =Model!B37-Model!C37.

   Finally, to calculate the free cash flow, in C18 enter the formula =C12+SUM(C14:C17).

	A	C	D	E	F	G	H	I
1	**Free Cash Flow Calculation for Vitex Corp.**							
2	Millions of Dollars							
3								
4			Historical Period			Forecast Period		
5		2006	2007	2008	2009	2010	2011	2012
6	Net Income	$121.8	$132.7	$132.8	$134.4	$140.7	$146.1	$151.6
7	Interest Expense after Taxes	$9.8	$13.3	$15.4	$13.1	$12.6	$13.2	$13.9
8	Increase/(Decrease) in Deferred Income taxes	($2.7)	($4.6)	($2.3)	$6.9	$1.0	$1.0	$1.1
9	Net Operating Profit after Taxes (NOPAT)	$128.9	$141.4	$145.9	$154.4	$154.3	$160.3	$166.6
10								
11	Depreciation Expense	$52.0	$55.9	$75.2	$78.9	$85.2	$92.0	$99.4
12	Gross Cash Flow	$180.9	$197.3	$221.1	$233.3	$239.5	$252.4	$265.9
13								
14	(Increase)/Decrease in Working Capital	($27.9)	$10.3	($56.9)	($4.1)	($8.8)	($9.2)	($9.7)
15	(Additions to) Property, Plant & Equipment	($53.4)	($86.5)	($92.3)	($73.0)	($78.9)	($85.2)	($92.0)
16	Increase/(Decrease) in Other Non-Current Liabilities	($20.5)	$34.9	($20.5)	$12.0	$5.3	$5.6	$5.9
17	(Investment) in Other Non-Current Assets	($1.9)	($201.9)	($49.3)	($36.5)	($39.4)	($42.6)	($46.0)
18	**Free Cash Flow**	**$77.2**	**($45.9)**	**$2.1**	**$131.6**	**$117.7**	**$121.0**	**$124.2**
19								
20								
21	**Uses of Free Cash Flow**							
22	Net Interest Expense after Taxes	($9.8)	($13.3)	($15.4)	($13.1)	($12.6)	($13.2)	($13.9)
23	Issuance/(Repayment) of Short-Term Debt	($9.4)	$50.1	$30.5	$12.2	$4.3	$4.6	$5.0
24	From Issuance/(Repayment) of Long-Term Debt	($18.5)	$56.8	$16.3	($34.3)	$6.4	$6.9	$7.4
25	From Sale/(Repurchase) of Equity	($0.8)	($7.9)	$6.6	($53.4)	($69.8)	($69.9)	($69.6)
26	Cash Dividends Paid to Shareholders	($38.7)	($39.8)	($40.1)	($43.1)	($46.0)	($49.3)	($53.1)
27	**Total Uses of Free Cash Flow**	($77.2)	$45.9	($2.1)	($131.6)	($117.7)	($121.0)	($124.2)
28								
29								

FIGURE 13.20 Model 14: Free cash flow calculations for Vitex Corp.

8. **Enter and sum the uses of free cash flow:** For the uses of free cash flow enter the following (note that uses are negative here):
   - For cash used to pay after-tax interest expense, in C22 enter =-C7.
   - For cash used to pay off short-term debt, in C23 enter =Model!C44-Model!B44.
   - For cash used to pay off long-term debt, in C24 enter =Model!C48-Model!B48.
   - For cash used to repurchase stocks, in C25 enter =(Model!C53+Model!C54)-(Model!B53+Model!B54+Model!C23).
   - For dividends paid, in C26 enter =-Model!C22.

   To calculate the total use of free cash flow, in C27 enter =SUM(C22:C26). Make sure that it is equal to the free cash flow generated. (The signs will be opposite because of the sign convention we are using.)

Testing the Model

The test of the model is that the free cash flow generated must equal the total uses. Beyond this, you should analyze both the components of the free cash flow and its uses line by line in conjunction with the balance sheet both to make sure the numbers are being calculated correctly and that they make sense.

Uses of the Model

A free cash flow statement provides important insight into the operations as well as financing of a business. For example, for Vitex Corp. it shows that the company will generate significantly more free cash flow in 2009 than in 2008 because of a much smaller investment in working capital and so forth. This improvement does not show in net income.

CHAPTER 14

Time Value of Money

Time value of money is a key concept in finance. It is used by almost everyone—knowingly or unknowingly. We use it unknowingly when we intuitively prefer to get paid today and make payments later. We also use it explicitly to make decisions about whether we should buy a house or continue to rent, to make retirement plans, and so forth. Corporations use the concept to make decisions about simple investments and financings to mega-mergers.

Although Excel provides several functions to do various types of time value of money calculations, they are based on certain assumptions that often do not hold in practical situations. You therefore need to learn the underlying theory and concepts well and be able to write your own formulas to do calculations that cannot be done using the built-in functions. You also need to learn the theory and concepts well to clearly understand how the built-in functions work and what their limitations are so that you can take full advantage of them and not use them incorrectly.

While we will use the time value of money concepts and calculations throughout the book, we will use them most heavily in Chapter 17: Bond Pricing and Duration. You may want to view that chapter almost as an extension of this chapter.

Review of Theory and Concepts

PRESENT AND FUTURE VALUES

The essence of the time value of money concept is that a dollar today is worth more than a dollar in the future. If you have the dollar today, you can invest it and earn a return on it so that on any future date you will have more than a dollar. This is the future value of the dollar. If you have PV_0 dollars today and expect to be able to earn a return of r_1 by investing it for one period, then the future value FV_1 of your investment at the end of the period will be:

$$FV_1 = PV_0(1 + r_1)$$

If you consider investing it for several more periods and in successive periods expect to earn returns of r_2, r_3, and so on, then at the end of n periods the future value of your investment will be:

$$FV_n = PV_0(1 + r_1)(1 + r_2)\ldots(1 + r_n)$$

This process of calculating future value is called compounding because it includes earning returns on returns: in every period, you are earning a return not just on your original investment but also on all the returns you have earned until then.

So far we have not imposed any requirement that the periods be equal, just that each return be appropriate for the length of the corresponding period. The first period, then, may be a year, in which case r_1 will have to be an annual return, the second period may be a month, in which case r_2 must be a monthly return, and so forth. This is the general formula for calculating future value over time where the length of each period and the rate of return for it can be different.

If we assume that all the periods are equal in length (for example, one year) and all the expected returns are the same (r), then we can simplify the equation to:

$$FV_n = PV_0(1 + r)^n$$

Assume that instead of asking what a certain amount of money today will be worth at some point in the future, we ask what a certain amount of money in the future is worth today. We then have to reverse the calculations, and the general equation for calculating the present value will be:

$$PV_0 = \frac{FV_n}{(1 + r_1)(1 + r_2)\ldots(1 + r_n)}$$

And if we assume that all the periods are equal in length and all the expected returns are the same, then the equation for present value becomes:

$$PV_0 = \frac{FV_n}{(1 + r)^n}$$

The process of calculating present value is called discounting, which is the inverse of compounding. This also involves earning return on return although it is not as easy to see it here as it was in the case of compounding.

Calculating present and future values can also be viewed as the process of moving an amount of money forward or backward through time. The amounts of money involved are called cash flows because they involve cash as opposed to some accounting measures like earnings. We can write the present value of a cash flow that will occur t periods from now as:

$$PV_0 = \frac{CF_t}{(1+r)^t}$$

It is easy to see that if we are anticipating several cash flows over time, we can calculate the present value of each and then add them together to get the total present value of all of them.

Here are the key points to keep in mind about calculating present and future values and doing time value of money problems:

- The time value of money concept applies only to cash flows because we can earn returns or have to pay returns only on cash we invest or borrow. We cannot calculate present values or future values for net income, operating income, and so on, because they do not represent cash.
- Only cash flows taking place at the same point in time can be compared to one another and combined together. If you are dealing with cash flows that take place at different points in time, you have to move them to the same point in time, that is, calculate their present or future values at the same point in time first before comparing or combining them. For such calculations, most of the time we either present value all cash flows to today or future value them to the farthest point in time the problem involves. However, if it is more convenient in a specific situation, we can move all cash flows to any other point in time as well. Whenever you calculate a present or future value (especially using Excel function) make sure you know which point in time they relate to.
- The simpler formulas we derived as well as most Excel functions can be used only when all the periods are of equal length and the rate of return is the same for all the periods. Otherwise you have to use the longer period-by-period formulas.
- We use the term *compounding* when we calculate future values or move earlier cash flows to a later point in time and the term *discounting* when we calculate present values or move future cash flows to an earlier point in time. However, we often use the term discount rate to refer to the rates of return in both cases.
- The most important thing to remember about the discount rate you choose to apply to one or a series of cash flows is that it must reflect the risk of the

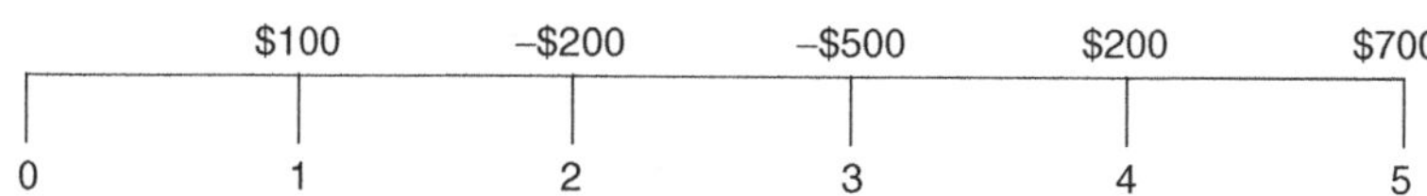

FIGURE 14.1 A timeline for cash flows.

cash flows. It is easy to understand that the discount rate should be higher for more risky cash flows and lower for less risky cash flows. However, estimating the risk of a cash flow and deciding what the appropriate discount rate for it should be is one of the knottiest problems in finance. In the models in this chapter, we will assume that we know what the appropriate discount rate is.

The Importance of Using Timelines

For all but trivial time value of money problems, it is best to use a timeline as shown in Figure 14.1 to minimize the possibility of making mistakes. The primary objectives of a timeline are to show clearly at what point in time each cash flow occurs and whether it is a cash inflow or outflow. Here are the things you need to keep in mind in drawing timelines:

- Today or now is designated as time 0. Other points in time are marked as 1,2,3, and so on, with the distance between each pair of adjacent markings representing equal time periods, which can be month, quarter, year, and so on, depending on the problem. The unit of the time period should be indicated on the timeline. The time period between time 0 and time 1 is the first period and so forth. (If you have a problem where you have to use unequal time periods, you should still use a timeline, but be careful about marking the points in time and discounting for the different lengths of time.)
- All cash flows (except in the rare situation when they are assumed to be continuous) take place at specific points in time and not over a period of time.
- On a timeline cash inflows are shown as positive numbers and cash outflows as negative numbers. A timeline can be drawn from the point of view of only one entity. To keep the signs of the cash flows consistent, you should always keep in mind (and, if necessary, mark on the timeline) from whose point of view the timeline is being drawn. For example, if you borrow $10,000 from a bank today, in a timeline drawn from your point of view this would be a positive cash flow at time 0 because this is an inflow. If you were drawing the timeline from the point of view of the bank, though, this would be a negative cash flow because it is an outflow.

- Unless the discount rates for all the periods are the same, you should also show the discount rate for each period on the timeline. The discount rate and time periods used in a timeline must be in consistent units: If the time markings are one month apart, then the discount rate should be a monthly discount rate and so forth.

If you are entering period-by-period cash flows in a worksheet, then it can serve as your timeline also. Enter in an adjacent row or column, as appropriate, 0, 1, 2, and so on, to indicate at which point in time each cash flow is taking place. You can also indicate in another column (or row) the discount rates, especially if they vary from period to period. Even when you do not need a period-by-period cash flow on your worksheet, you can still decide to create a timeline on the worksheet instead of a separate piece of paper because then it will always be there with your model.

Frequency of Compounding and Effective Rates

The actual return you earn on an investment depends not just on the expected nominal rate of return on the investment but also on how frequently the return will be actually or conceptually paid, that is, how often it is compounded. If the expected return is 8% and it is paid only once a year, then 8% is the return you will earn over a one-year period. However, if it is paid every six months at the same annual rate, then you will be able to reinvest the returns you get every six months and earn additional returns on them to end up with a higher actual return than if the return were paid only once a year.

If the annual interest rate is r and interest is paid m times per year, then you can look at each year as m periods in each of which you will earn a return of r/m. We can then write the future value of a cash flow as:

$$FV_n = PV_0 \left(1 + \frac{r}{m}\right)^{nm}$$

From this we can see that the effective annual interest rate in this case is:

$$\text{Effective annual interest rate} = \left(1 + \frac{r}{m}\right)^m - 1$$

If m is 12, then the interest will be paid monthly; this is called the effective annual interest rate with monthly compounding. Clearly, the more frequently you compound, the higher the effective interest rate will be. But you cannot arbitrarily choose what m is. How often the stated annual return will be compounded is something that is agreed upon upfront between the borrower and the lender.

In the extreme case, if you assume that the annual return will be compounded continuously (that is, will be paid and reinvested at infinitesimally small intervals), then it can be shown that

$$\text{Effective annual interest rate} = e^r - 1$$

This is called the continuously compounded effective annual rate. This rate will be only slightly higher than daily compounding; in practical situations it is not that important. It is used extensively in theoretical analysis, however, because effective interest rate written in this form is much easier to deal with in many mathematical equations and in calculus.

All of the above discussions apply to discounting as well.

To clearly understand what the effective annual interest rate means, let us assume that you are investing $100 at 8% interest. If it is compounded annually, then at the end of the year you will have $108. If you get the interest every six months, then at the end of the first 6 months you will get $4 of interest, which you will reinvest at the same rate. At the end of another six months, this $4 will grow to $4 × 1.04 or $4.16 and you will receive another $4 of interest. So at the end of one year you will have $108.16, a little more than before.

Now suppose you calculate the effective interest rate first, which will be $(1 + 0.08/2)^2 - 1 = 0.0816$. If you apply this rate to your original investment of $100, you get $108.16, the same as the amount you got before. This means that once you calculate the effective interest rate, it tells you what annual return you will actually earn and you can apply it to your investment to calculate your return for one year or many years.

Reinvestment Risk

In calculating future values or effective interest rates, most of the time we assume that the interest rates will remain constant throughout the period so that all interest income can be reinvested at the same rate. In real life, we generally do not know ahead of time at what rates we will be able to reinvest future interest income. This poses an important risk because how much money we accumulate at our investment horizon will very much depend on the reinvestment rates over the years. If you want to use one or several reinvestment rates different from the investment rate over the years, then you will not be able to use either the short formulas or Excel's functions to do the calculations. You will have to create your own model and do a period-by-period analysis. These same considerations apply to discounting or calculating present values as well.

Inflation and the Real Rate of Return

Suppose you expect to earn an annual return of 8% on an investment and expect that inflation rate will be 3% per year. It is tempting to assume that you will earn a real return of $(8\% - 3\%) = 5\%$ per year, that is, your buying power will grow at 5% per year. However, this is not correct. Let us see why.

Let us assume you have \$1,000 to invest for a 10-year period. If you truly earn a real return of 5% per year, then in 10 years your investment should have buying power (in today's dollar) of $\$1,000 \times (1.05)^{10} = \$1,629$.

In 10 years, though, you will actually have $\$1,000 \times (1.08)^{10} = \$2,159$ in nominal dollars, and its buying power in today's dollars will be $\$2,159/(1.03)^{10} = \$1,606$. This clearly is the right answer because we did it exactly the way it will work out if your assumptions about the return on the investment and inflation rate turn out to be right. Although the difference between the two answers looks small, it is significant because it will grow bigger with longer time horizon (for example, \$4,322 versus \$4,146 for a 30-year horizon) and larger investments.

Why did we get the wrong answer? We can say, "Because we did not account for the effect of compounding properly." As we saw, the correct answer is given by $\$1,000 \times (1.08)^{10}/(1.03)^{10}$, which means that the correct real rate of return is $(1.08/1.03) - 1 = 4.9\%$ and not 5%.

Let us generalize this answer. If the nominal rate of return is r, the inflation rate is i, and the real rate of return is k, then we can calculate k from the equation:

$$1 + k = \left(\frac{1 + r}{1 + i}\right)$$

The same reasoning holds the other way around as well. If you evaluate a project's cash flows expressed in nominal dollars, expect an inflation rate of i, and want the project to earn a real return of k, then, from the above equation, the appropriate discount rate for the nominal dollar cash flows is $(1 + i) \times (1 + k) - 1$ and not $i + k$.

In general, it is safer to do calculations in terms of nominal dollars and nominal rates of return than real dollars and real rates of return. This is particularly true if taxes are involved because taxes are assessed on nominal dollars and in many situations accounting for taxes correctly when doing calculations in terms of real dollars becomes overly complex.

INVESTMENT AND PROJECT EVALUATION

Deciding if one should make an investment or undertake a project is one of the most important applications of the time value of money concept.

Net Present Value (NPV)

The sum of the present values of a series of cash flows (for example, all the expected cash flows from a project, including any initial investment) is called its net present value (NPV). It is the key tool in finance to judge if a project is worth investing in or not. It is calculated as:

$$NPV = \sum_{t=0}^{t=n} \frac{CF_t}{(1+r)^t}$$

It is customary to do the analysis from the point of view of the investor so that cash flows representing investments are negative. Often the initial cash flow (at time 0) is the investment in the project and is negative even though there may be additional (net) negative cash flows over the years.

Assuming that the discount rate used is appropriate for the risk of the series of cash flows, a positive NPV indicates that over the years the project will generate more cash than will be needed to pay off, with the necessary returns, all the investments the project will require. Therefore, a project with positive NPV is considered acceptable while one with negative NPV is not. NPV measures in present value terms the excess cash the project would generate.

Internal Rate of Return (IRR)

The internal rate of return (IRR) measures the rate of return of a series of cash flows or project taking into consideration the time value of money. It is the alternate measure used to decide if an investment or project should be accepted. Mathematically speaking, IRR is the rate of return at which the NPV of a project or series of cash flows will equal zero, and it is calculated by iteration (trial and error) from the equation for NPV. If the IRR is greater than the rate of return appropriate for the risk of the project, then the project is considered acceptable (and will have a positive NPV). Otherwise the project should be rejected.

Although many people find the IRR measure intuitively more appealing, it has a few shortcomings, and an alternate measure—modified internal rate of return (MIRR)—has been developed to overcome some of them. In general, though, NPV is the more reliable tool for evaluating projects or investments.

CONSTANT ANNUITIES

A constant annuity is a series of equal cash flows that occur at regular intervals. Learning to do calculations with constant annuities efficiently is important because they occur in many practical situations. In dealing with annuities, we almost always assume that the applicable discount rate is the same for the entire period of the annuity. This happens to be the case in many practical situations and makes it possible to derive compact formulas to do various types of annuity calculations. Keep in mind, however, that this is an assumption, and if it does not apply to a

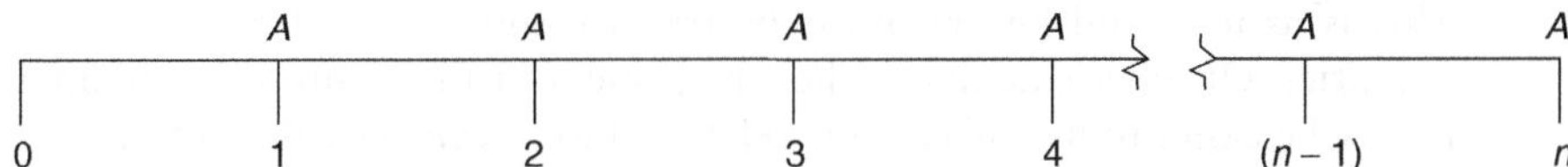

FIGURE 14.2 A timeline for a regular annuity.

problem you are working on, then you should not use the compact formulas in your problem.

Excel has several built-in functions to do various types of annuity calculations, which use the same formulas we will discuss. So you will rarely have to write your own formulas to do annuity calculations. Nonetheless, it is always important to understand how a built-in function does its calculations because that will reduce your chances of using it incorrectly and enable you to find innovative uses of it at times (as we will see when we work with growing annuities.) Remember that all of Excel's built-in annuity functions make the constant discount rate assumption.

Constant Annuities in Arrears

Figure 14.2 shows the timeline for a regular constant annuity where A is the constant periodic cash flow, n is the number of cash flows, and r is the periodic discount rate. Most often the word "constant" is dropped and unless otherwise qualified, an annuity is assumed to be a constant annuity. In a regular annuity, the first annuity payment occurs at time 1, that is, in one period from now or at the end of the first period. Such an annuity is called a regular annuity or an annuity in arrears. We can calculate the present value PVC_0 and future value FVC_n of an annuity in arrears as:

$$PVC_0 = \frac{A}{(1+r)^1} + \frac{A}{(1+r)^2} + \ldots + \frac{A}{(1+r)^n} = A\left[\frac{1 - \dfrac{1}{(1+r)^n}}{r}\right]$$

$$FVC_n = A(1+r)^{n-1} + A(1+r)^{n-2} + \ldots + A = A\left[\frac{(1+r)^n - 1}{r}\right]$$

Make sure (by referring to the timeline) that you understand how the present value and future value for each cash flow is being calculated.

You should also note that the future value of the annuity given by the formula is the same as the future value of the present value of the annuity, that is:

$$FVC_n = PVC_0(1+r)^n$$

This is as it should be and must be true for any series of cash flows, not just annuities. Once we calculate either the present or the future value of an annuity, it may be easier to use this simple relationship to calculate the other.

If this were an annuity in perpetuity, that is, the annuity payments were to go on forever instead of for n periods, the present value would be:

$$PVC_0 = \frac{A}{r}$$

The important points to note about this type of annuity and these formulas are:

- These annuity formulas calculate the present value at a point in time one period earlier than the first annuity payment, and the future value at the same point in time as the last annuity payment. In the calculation for the future value, the last cash flow does not earn any return. (It is important to keep these conventions in mind to avoid making mistakes, especially when using Excel's built-in functions to do annuity calculations.)
- The discount rate you use with any cash flow must be appropriate for its risk. In addition, in doing annuity calculations with these formulas, you have to always use a discount rate that matches the annuity interval. This means that for monthly annuities you must use the discount rate per month and so forth. People sometimes forget this requirement and end up with significant errors. Finally, you must use the effective discount rate for the annuity period: if the cash flows are annual but the interest rate is going to be compounded monthly, then you have to calculate and use the effective interest rate per year.

Constant Annuities in Advance

If everything about the previous annuity remains the same except that the cash flows take place one period earlier as shown in Figure 14.3, then it is called an annuity in advance or annuity due. In this case, both the present value and the

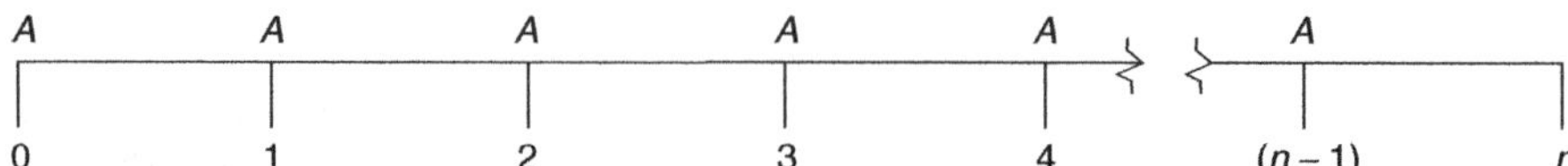

FIGURE 14.3 A timeline for an annuity in advance.

future value will be higher because the cash flows are taking place earlier. The PVC_0 and FVC_n can be calculated as:

$$PVC_0 = A + \frac{A}{(1+r)^1} + \frac{A}{(1+r)^2} + \ldots + \frac{A}{(1+r)^{n-1}} = A(1+r)\left[\frac{1 - \frac{1}{(1+r)^n}}{r}\right]$$

$$FVC_n = A(1+r)^n + A(1+r)^{n-1} + \ldots + A(1+r) = A(1+r)\left[\frac{(1+r)^n - 1}{r}\right]$$

As before, the future value of the annuity given by the formula is the same as the future value of the present value of the annuity.

The present value for an annuity due in perpetuity is:

$$PVC_0 = \frac{A(1+r)}{r}$$

As you can see from the timeline, these annuity formulas calculate the present value at the same point in time as the first cash flow, and the future value at a point in time one period beyond the last cash flow. Here, in the calculation for present value the first cash flow does not get discounted, but in the future value, the last cash flow earns return for one period. (Once again, it is important to keep these conventions in mind to avoid making mistakes, especially when using Excel's built-in functions to do annuity calculations.)

The points I made before about choosing the right discount rate apply here as well.

The System of Four Variables for Constant Annuities

As we can see from the annuity formulas we derived, there are four variables involved here: the present value (or equivalently, the future value), the constant annuity amount A, the number of periods n, and the discount rate r. Given any three of these we can calculate the fourth. For example, assume that I have $100,000 today (the present value) and that I invest earning 10% interest per year (the discount rate). I can calculate the maximum amount I can withdraw every year (the annuity amount) if I want to be able to make 10 withdrawals (the number of periods) starting today.

We can rearrange the present value formulas to calculate the annuity amount or the number of periods when the other variables are given. If the discount rate is the unknown, however, we have to calculate the answer by trial and error (iteration). In any case, you will almost always use Excel's built-in functions to do this type of calculation. You only need to recognize that these four variables are tied to one another and once three of them are specified, the other can be calculated.

As we saw, the present value and the future value are not independent of each other, that is, in any problem specifying one automatically specifies the other. We cannot specify both.

GROWING ANNUITIES

Often in real life we encounter annuities where the annuity amount grows at a constant rate over time instead of remaining constant. For example, if you were planning for your retirement, you would probably want to plan to withdraw annually an amount that grows at the expected rate of inflation instead of remaining constant. Otherwise the buying power of your annual withdrawal and your standard of living will steadily decline. Even at modest-sounding inflation rate like 3%, over the years the buying power of a constant annuity will deteriorate significantly. (This is what makes cost of living adjustments—COLA—in pensions and Social Security payments so valuable.)

It is more complex to derive formulas for growing annuities, and Excel does not provide any built-in functions for them. In your Excel models you can do calculations for growing annuities in one of three ways: (1) You can write your own formulas using the formulas we will derive, (2) you can use Excel's built-in functions for constant annuities using the substitutions we will discuss, or (3) you can enter the growing annuity amounts in a column (or row) in a worksheet, calculate the present value or the future value for each cash flow, and then calculate their sum.

In Excel, the third method may be the simplest and safest one to use and it will work in most situations provided the user knows how to use Goal Seek. In many situations, though, you will have to use Excel's functions for constant annuities with appropriate substitutions, and for that you have to go through the discussions in the next few sections. Also remember that if you have to deal with growth rates that do not remain constant or, for that matter, if any of the other assumptions does not hold (for example, the discount rate changes over time), then you have to build your own model by entering in a column or row the period-by-period cash flows and then discounting or compounding them appropriately.

Growing Annuities in Arrears

For the growing annuity in arrears shown in Figure 14.4 where the first cash flow of $A(1 + g)$ at time 1 grows at the rate of g per period, we can calculate the present value as:

$$PVG_0 = \frac{A(1+g)}{(1+r)} + \frac{A(1+g)^2}{(1+r)^2} + \ldots + \frac{A(1+g)^n}{(1+r)^n}$$

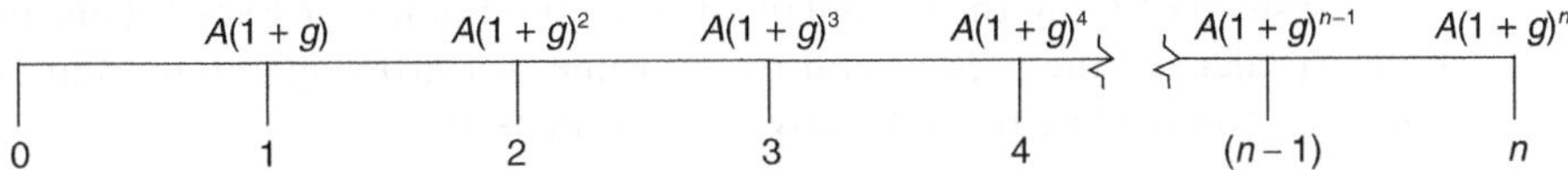

FIGURE 14.4 A timeline for a regualr annuity.

This looks a little more complex than the corresponding constant annuity formula, but notice that if we substitute $(1 + k)$ for $(1 + r)/(1 + g)$ then the formula for PVG_0 becomes the same as the formula for PVC_0 with k substituted for r. So we can use Excel's built-in formulas for a constant annuity in arrears to do calculations for a growing annuity in arrears by substituting a (growth) adjusted discount rate k for the regular discount rate r.

It is important to note that for the equivalence to work, the first cash flow for the growing annuity in arrears has to be $A(1 + g)$ and not A. If in a problem the first cash flow for a growing annuity in arrears is given as \$1,000 and the growth rate is 5%, and you want to use the constant annuity formula or Excel's built-in functions to do the calculations, then in addition to using the adjusted discount rate k, you will have to use \$1,000/1.05 for A.

We can write the future value for the same growing annuity in arrears as:

$$FVG_n = A(1+g)(1+r)^{n-1} + A(1+g)^2(1+r)^{n-2} + \ldots + A(1+g)^n$$

To make this formula look like the formula for the constant annuity in arrears, we have to divide both sides of this equation by $(1 + g)^n$ to get:

$$\frac{FVG_n}{(1+g)^n} = A\frac{(1+r)^{n-1}}{(1+g)^{n-1}} + A\frac{(1+r)^{n-2}}{(1+g)^{n-2}} + \ldots + A$$

As before, if we substitute $(1 + k)$ for $(1 + r)/(1 + g)$ in the right-hand side of this formula, it would look the same as the right-hand side of the corresponding formula for constant annuity in arrears with k substituted for r. So to calculate FVG_n using the formula for constant annuity in arrears or Excel's built-in functions for a constant annuity in arrears, we have to (1) substitute the adjusted discount rate k for the regular discount rate r, (2) use for A the first cash flow divided by $(1 + g)$ (as explained before), and (3) multiply the value for future value we get from the constant annuity formula or Excel function by $(1 + g)^n$ to get FVG_n.

If instead of using the formulas for constant annuity or Excel's built-in functions to calculate the present and future values for growing annuities in arrears, you want to calculate them directly, the formulas are:

$$PVG_0 = A(1+g)\left[\frac{1-\left(\frac{1+g}{1+r}\right)^n}{r-g}\right]$$

$$FVG_n = A(1+g)\left[\frac{(1+r)^n-(1+g)^n}{r-g}\right]$$

As we discussed before, you can also calculate FVG_n as the future value of PVG_0.

If $r = g$, then the present and future values for n-period growing annuities in arrears become:

$$PVG_0 = nA$$
$$FVG_n = nA(1+r)^n$$

The present value of a growing annuity in arrears in perpetuity is

$$PVG_0 = \frac{A(1+g)}{r-g}$$

Remember that for all these the first cash flow for the growing annuity in arrears is $A(1+g)$ and not A.

Growing Annuities in Advance

For a growing annuity in advance, as shown in Figure 14.5 we can write:

$$PVG_0 = A + A\left(\frac{1+g}{1+r}\right) + A\left(\frac{1+g}{1+r}\right)^2 + \ldots + A\left(\frac{1+g}{1+r}\right)^{n-1}$$

$$\frac{FVG_n}{(1+g)^n} = A\left(\frac{1+r}{1+g}\right)^n + A\left(\frac{1+r}{1+g}\right)^{n-1} + \ldots + A\left(\frac{1+r}{1+g}\right)$$

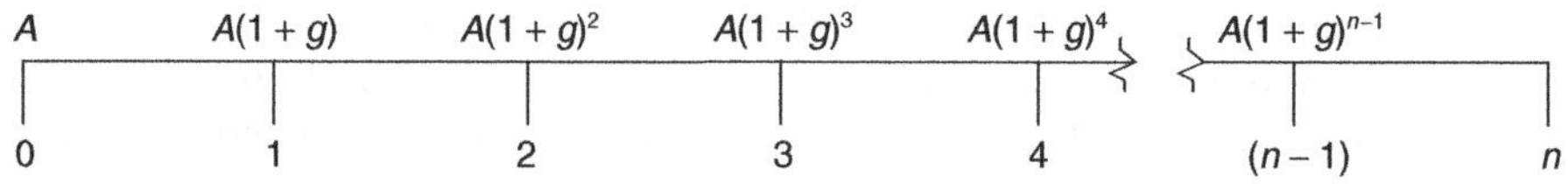

FIGURE 14.5 A timeline for a growing annuity in advance.

As before, with proper substitutions and adjustments, we can use the formulas for constant annuities in advance or Excel's built-in functions for them to do calculations for growing annuities in advance. Here, the first annuity amount is A and not $A(1+g)$ as was the case with growing annuities in arrears.

Here are the compact formulas for growing annuities in advance:

$$PVG_0 = A(1+r)\left[\frac{1-\left(\dfrac{1+g}{1+r}\right)^n}{r-g}\right]$$

$$FVG_n = A(1+r)\left[\frac{(1+r)^n-(1+g)^n}{r-g}\right]$$

If $r = g$, then the present and future values for n-period growing annuities in advance become:

$$PVG_0 = nA$$
$$FVG_n = nA(1+r)^n$$

You may be surprised to see that they are the same as the corresponding formulas for growing annuities in arrears, but the difference is that there the first cash flow was $A(1+g)$ and here it is A.

The present value of a growing annuity in advance in perpetuity is:

$$PVG_0 = \frac{A(1+r)}{r-g}$$

The System of Five Variables for Growing Annuities

We discussed before that constant annuities are governed by a system of four variables. Growing annuities are governed by a system of five variables—the old ones plus the growth rate g—and given any four of these you can calculate the fifth. You should also recognize that a constant annuity is the same as a growing annuity with a growth rate of zero. Most of the other issues I discussed under the system of four variables for constant annuities apply to this system of variables as well.

Modeling Examples

The key to building any time value of money models is to get the timings, signs, and amounts of the cash flows right. Your first step always should be to make sure that you fully understand the cash flows of the problem. The discount rate or the rate of return is also important, but in many cases they will be variables of your model, and users will specify their values.

It is good to keep in mind that you can solve all time value of money problems without using any of Excel's built-in financial functions—as long as you know how to write the formulas for calculating the present and future value of a cash flow, are good at creating formulas by copying formulas written with the right mix of relative and absolute references, and use the power of Goal Seek. An additional advantage of taking this "back-to-the-basics" approach is that if the cash flows are laid out, it is easy to understand and verify them by checking the calculations with a hand calculator. The results from functions are often harder to check.

So, as you go through the following models pay special attention to how these models use the back-to-the-basics approach.

MODEL 1: EFFECT OF COMPOUNDING FREQUENCY

The Problem

You have an opportunity to invest $100,000 for 10 years at a nominal interest rate (also called the annual percentage rate, or APR) of 8%. Create a model to calculate the effective annual interest rate you will earn and the amount your investment will grow to (that is, its future value) for various numbers of compounding periods per year. Set up a one-input data table to show the effective interest rates and the future values of the investment for daily, weekly, biweekly, monthly, quarterly, semiannual, and annual compounding.

Modeling Strategy

The output for this model is shown in Figure 14.6. To calculate the effective annual interest rate, use the formula we discussed earlier, making the nominal interest rate and the number of compounding period variables. To calculate the future value of your investment, use the effective annual interest rate you calculated in conjunction with the future value formula we discussed earlier as well as Excel's FV function to learn doing it both ways. Note that although the FV function is designed primarily to calculate the future value of an annuity, it also lets you include an additional amount of initial investment. You can therefore use the FV function to calculate the future value we need by entering the initial investment as the pv argument and setting the annuity amount as zero.

To set up the data table, specify the number of compounding periods per year as the input variable down a column. Then specify the effective annual interest rate and the future value from the previous part of the model as the dependent variables in two columns of the table.

	A	B	C	D	E
1	**Effect of Compounding Frequency**				
2					
3	Nominal annual interest rate (APR)	8.00%			
4	Number of compounding periods per year	2			
5	Amount of initial investment	$100,000			
6	Length of investment period (years)	10			
7					
8	Effective interest rate	8.16%			
9	Future value of investment (using formula)	$219,112			
10	Future value of investment (using function)	$219,112			
11					
12					
13					
14			**Effective**	**Future**	
15			**Int. rate**	**Value**	
16	**Compounding period**		8.16%	$219,112	
17	Annual	1	8.00%	$215,892	
18	Semi-annual	2	8.16%	$219,112	
19	Quarterly	4	8.24%	$220,804	
20	Monthly	12	8.30%	$221,964	
21	Bi-weekly	26	8.32%	$222,281	
22	Weekly	52	8.32%	$222,417	
23	Daily	365	8.33%	$222,535	
24					
25					

FIGURE 14.6 Model 1: Effect of compounding frequency.

Building the Model

1. **Set up input variables:** Create the labels for the input variables in A3:A6 and format cells B3:B6. Enter the input values for the problem.
2. **Create formula to calculate effective interest rate:** Create the labels in A8:A10. In cell B8 enter the formula =(1+B3/B4)^B4-1 to calculate the effective interest rate.
3. **Set up calculation for future value using formula:** In cell B9 enter the formula =B5*(1+B8)^B6. Note that here you have to use the effective interest rate from cell B8.
4. **Set up formula to calculate future value using FV function:** To enter the FV function, select B10, click the function icon and then select the FV function. In the dialog box, enter the appropriate values to create the formula =FV(B8,B6,0,-B5) in the cell. You have to use the effective interest rate and enter zero for the annuity payment. Also, for the pv argument you have to enter -B5 to have the future value come out positive. You can omit the type argument because it does not matter here.
5. **Set up data table:** Start by entering the labels and values for different compounding periods in cells A17:B23. Also enter the labels in C14:D15. Since the value of the dependent variable effective interest rate is in cell B8, in C16 enter =B8. Similarly, in D16 enter =B9 (or =B10) to indicate that the future

values of the investment for this column are to be obtained from cell B9 (or B10). Now select B16:D23 and select Data ⇨ Table. Since this is a one-input data table with the independent variable number of compounding periods specified down a column, you only need to enter B4 for the Column input cell in the dialog box. Click OK and Excel will complete the data table.

Testing the Model

Check the calculation for effective interest rate by entering 1 in B4, in which case the effective interest rate should be the same as the nominal interest rate in cell B3. Also check the effective interest rate by doing one or two calculations with a hand calculator.

For the future value, you have already done it in two ways. As long as the two values in B9 and B10 agree, your model should be correct.

In the data table make sure that the values of the dependent variables match the numbers in the model. For example, if you enter 365 in B4, then the values in C23 and D23 should match the values in B8 and B9, respectively.

Uses of the Model

You can use the model to calculate the effective interest rate and future value of any amount of investment at any time in the future for any frequency of compounding. The data table clearly shows the effect of more frequent compounding, which becomes more pronounced as the investment period gets longer. Also, since data tables are dynamic, any time you change one of the input variables, the data table will automatically update.

MODEL 2: CONSTANT ANNUITIES

The Problem

You are planning to save $1,000 annually for the next 10 years and invest the money in a mutual fund earning 8% per year interest income on it. Calculate the present value of this annuity and how much money you will have 10 years from now if you make the first investment today and make a total of 10 contributions. Also show how the present value and future value will differ if you make the first investment a year from now. Make the annual saving amount, number of contributions, and the interest rates input variables. Build the model to do the calculations in three different ways: using year-by-year cash flows and no Excel function for discounting or compounding, using formulas we derived earlier, and using Excel's built-in annuity functions.

	A	B	C	D	E	F	G	H	I
1	**Present and Future Values for Constant Annuities**								
2									
3	Annual saving (A)	$1,000							
4	Number of years (n, <= 20)	10							
5	Interest rate (rr, % per year)	8.00%							
6									
7		**Computations using**							
8		Table	Formulas	Functions					
9	**Annuity in arrears**								
10	Present value	$6,710	$6,710	$6,710					
11	Future value	$14,487	$14,487	$14,487					
12									
13	**Annuity in advance**								
14	Present value	$7,247	$7,247	$7,247					
15	Future value	$15,645	$15,645	$15,645					
16									
17									
18		**Table for annuity in arrears**				**Table for annuity in advance**			
19	Time	Cash flow	PV	FV		Cash flow	PV	FV	
20	0					$1,000	$1,000	$2,159	
21	1	$1,000	$926	$1,999		$1,000	$926	$1,999	
22	2	$1,000	$857	$1,851		$1,000	$857	$1,851	
23	3	$1,000	$794	$1,714		$1,000	$794	$1,714	
24	4	$1,000	$735	$1,587		$1,000	$735	$1,587	
25	5	$1,000	$681	$1,469		$1,000	$681	$1,469	
26	6	$1,000	$630	$1,360		$1,000	$630	$1,360	
27	7	$1,000	$583	$1,260		$1,000	$583	$1,260	
28	8	$1,000	$540	$1,166		$1,000	$540	$1,166	
29	9	$1,000	$500	$1,080		$1,000	$500	$1,080	
30	10	$1,000	$463	$1,000					
31	11								
32	12								
33	13								

FIGURE 14.7 Model 2: Present and future values for a constant annuity.

Modeling Strategy

The worksheet for this model is shown in Figure 14.7. Calculating the present and future values of the annuity using the formulas and Excel's built-in functions is straightforward. As long as you write them using the three input values as variables, these values will automatically recalculate when a user changes any of the inputs. However, for the part of the model that uses year-by-year cash flows, you will have to set up the cash flow tables for the maximum number of years (say, 20) for which you want to allow a user to use the model, and then use IF functions to make the cash flows zero for the years beyond the number of years (for example, 10) that the user specifies.

Building the Model

Note that in this model there are formulas in B21:D40 and F20:H39. Parts of these ranges appear blank because I have used a custom formatting to make the cells that are not used and would have zeros in them (depending on the number of years the user enters) appear blank.

1. **Set up input variables and data validation:** Set up the three input variables and name cell B3 A, cell B4 n, and cell B5 rr. (I am using rr for the interest rate because Excel does not let you name a cell r.) Insert a data validation in B4 to limit the number of years to 20. (You can use a higher number as long as you set up the annuity tables accordingly.)
2. **Create formulas using Excel's functions:** Create the necessary labels in A7:D15. Select D10, and click the Paste Function button. In the Paste Function dialog box, find the function PV (under Financial) and double click it. In the Function Arguments dialog box, enter rr for Rate, n for Nper, -A for Pmt, 0 for FV, and 0 for Type. Instead of typing these in you can also enter them by clicking the corresponding cells. According to Excel's conventions, you have to use -A to have the PV come out positive. (You could skip the FV argument by putting in a comma and in this case you could skip the Type, too, because a blank or zero indicates an annuity in arrears.) Click OK and you should have the present value of the annuity.

   Enter the FV function in D11 with the same arguments. Enter PV and FV functions in D14 and D15, but now make sure you enter 1 for Type because these are annuities in advance.
3. **Create formulas using the annuity formulas:** To calculate the present value of the annuity using the formulas we derived, in C10 enter =A*((1-(1/(1+rr)^n))/rr). This is straightforward as long as you use the parentheses in the right places to make sure that Excel does the calculations in the order you want.

   For the other calculations, in C11 enter =A*((1+rr)^n-1)/rr, in C14 enter =A*(1+rr)*((1-1/(1+rr)^n)/rr), and in C15 enter =A*(1+rr)*((1+rr)^n-1)/rr. The results should match the results you got using the Excel functions.
4. **Create the year-by-year annuity tables:** Enter the labels in A18:H19. In A20:A40, create the series of points in time, that is, the timeline 0 to 20. To do so, enter 0 in A20, enter =A20+1 in A21 and then copy the formula down. (You can also use Excel's fill handle.)

   You have to enter the cash flows or the annuity amount in B21:B40. Which cells have actual cash flows and which have zeros will have to depend on the n that the user specifies. In B21 enter =IF(A21>n,0,A) and copy and paste the formula into B22:B40. This will enter the annuity amount in the cells covering the annuity period and zeros beyond that. (Since this part of the table covers annuity in arrears, A20 should be blank.)

   To calculate the present value of each cash flow as of time 0, enter the formula =B21/(1+rr)^A21 in C21. The formula picks up the amount to be discounted from B21 and uses the value in A21 to discount it for the appropriate number of years. Copy the formula into C22:C40.

   To calculate future values to the end of the period specified by the user, enter =B21*(1+rr)^(n-A21) in D21 and copy it into D22:D40.

Create the annuity in advance part of the table similarly, keeping in mind that here the first cash flow takes place at time 0, the last at time n-1, and future values have to be calculated at time n. The formula in F20 is =IF(A20>n-1,0,A), in G21 is =F20/(1+rr)^A20, and in H21 is =F20*(1+rr)^(n-A20). Copy these formulas down to row 39.

5. **Enter the sum of the present and future values in the appropriate cells:** Cell B10 should be the total of the present values in C21:C40. In B10 enter =SUM(C21:C40). Similarly, in B11 enter =SUM(D21:D40), in B14 enter =SUM(G20:G39), and in B15 enter =SUM(H20:H39).
6. **Apply custom formatting to make unused cells in table appear blank:** With the model as entered, cells not used in the table whenever n is less than 20 will have zeros in them. It is preferable to make them look blank. To do so, select B21:D40, select Format ⇨ Cells and then the Numbers tab. For the Category, select Custom and then in the Type box enter $#,##0;; and press OK. This will make positive amounts appear in currency format with zero decimal points while negative and zero amounts will appear as blanks. Apply the same format to F20:H39. (If you do not quite understand this formatting, look up Custom Formatting in Chapter 4: Advanced Excel Features.)

Testing the Model

You have already calculated the present and future values in three ways. If they agree with each other using a range of input values, you do not need to test the model any further. Normally you would do the calculations using only one of these methods. In such situations, you should test the model using one of the other methods or using a hand calculator.

Uses of the Model

This model demonstrates the three common ways of calculating the present and future values of constant annuities. You will rarely use the method that uses the formulas for annuities because the other two are generally easier and safer to use.

As we have discussed, constant annuities are governed by a system of four variables. In this model you can use Goal Seek to calculate any of them given the other three. For example, if you want to know how much you will have to save annually to accumulate $20,000 at the end of 10 years, you should set n equal to 10, and then use Goal Seek. Make any one of the cells B11, C11, or D11 the target cell (Set cell), $20,000 the target value (To value), and enter B3 as the By changing cell. You can also use other Excel functions to solve similar problems.

Limitations of the Model

Users who do not understand the model and do not know Goal Seek will not be able to use it to answer the other types of questions like the one we discussed in the "Uses of the Model" section. For these users, you essentially have to build a separate model depending on which three variables they are going to specify and which will be the answer.

MODEL 3: GROWING ANNUITIES

The Problem

You are planning to save for your retirement in annual installments and you think that every year you will be able to save 4% more than the previous year because your income will grow as well. You will invest the money in a mutual fund earning 8% per year interest income. You plan to start by investing $1,000 now and the future contributions will grow as mentioned. How much money will you accumulate at the end of 20 years? How would the money you accumulate change if, a year from now, you make your first contribution of $1,000 plus the annual contribution growth rate (4%)? In both cases, you will make a total of 10 contributions and you want to calculate the future value of your savings 10 years from today. Make all the important variables of the problem input variables. Use the model to determine how much the initial contributions will have to be in the two cases if you want to accumulate $100,000 in 20 years.

Modeling Strategy

The worksheet for this model is shown in Figure 14.8. This model is similar to the last model. You only have to set up an additional input variable (g) and make some modifications to accommodate the growth in annual savings rate. Calculating the present and future values of the annuity using the formulas is straightforward. You just have to replace the formulas for constant annuities with those for growing annuities. Doing the calculations using Excel's functions will require the substitutions we discussed earlier, and you will have to be especially careful about what to enter in the functions for the payment amounts. For the part of the model that uses year-by-year cash flows, all you have to do is set up the growing annual savings amount properly. Then the same formulas you used for the present value and future value calculations before will work.

Building the Model

It will be easiest to start with a copy of the previous model. Do not try to create this model in the same workbook, however, because the names of the cells will conflict. Start with a copy of the previous workbook.

1. **Set up input variables and data validation:** Add a few rows below row 5 to match the example of this model. Create the labels in A6 and A8 and name

	A	B	C	D	E	F	G	H	I
1	**Present and Future Values of Growing Annuities**								
2									
3	Annual saving (A)	$1,000							
4	Number of years (n, <= 20)	10							
5	Interest rate (rr, % per year)	8.00%							
6	Growth rate (g, % per year)	4.00%							
7									
8	Adjusted interest rate (k, % per year)	3.85%							
9									
10		**Computations using**							
11		Table	Formulas	Functions					
12	**Annuity in arrears**								
13	Present value	$8,173	$8,173	$8,173					
14	Future value	$17,646	$17,646	$17,646					
15									
16	**Annuity in advance**								
17	Present value	$8,488	$8,488	$8,488					
18	Future value	$18,324	$18,324	$18,324					
19									
20		**Table for annuity in arrears**				**Table for annuity in advance**			
21	Time	Cash flow	PV	FV		Cash flow	PV	FV	
22	0					$1,000	$1,000	$2,159	
23	1	$1,040	$963	$2,079		$1,040	$963	$2,079	
24	2	$1,082	$927	$2,002		$1,082	$927	$2,002	
25	3	$1,125	$893	$1,928		$1,125	$893	$1,928	
26	4	$1,170	$860	$1,856		$1,170	$860	$1,856	
27	5	$1,217	$828	$1,788		$1,217	$828	$1,788	
28	6	$1,265	$797	$1,721		$1,265	$797	$1,721	
29	7	$1,316	$768	$1,658		$1,316	$768	$1,658	
30	8	$1,369	$739	$1,596		$1,369	$739	$1,596	
31	9	$1,423	$712	$1,537		$1,423	$712	$1,537	
32	10	$1,480	$686	$1,480					
33	11								

FIGURE 14.8 Model 3: Present and future values for a growing annuity.

the cell B6 g and the cell B8 k. The other input cells are already named A, n, and rr. Because we are going to use k frequently in this model, it is better to calculate its value in a cell (B8) and give the cell the name k. To calculate k, in B8 enter =(1+rr)/(1+g)-1.

2. **Create formulas using Excel functions:** To calculate the present value using Excel functions for the case where you plan to make your contributions in arrears, that is, you plan to make the first contribution a year from now, in D13 enter =PV(k,n,-A,0,0). Note that for the annuity amount you are entering A and not A(1+g) even though the problem says the first contribution will equal A(1+g). We discussed in the section on growing annuities why you have to do this if you want to use a constant annuity function for growing annuities in arrears. If necessary, go back and review that section. You also have to use the growth-adjusted interest rate for the discount rate.

   To calculate the future value for the annuity in arrears, in D14 enter =FV(k,n,-A,0,0)*(1+g)^n. Here again you have to use A instead of A(1+g) and also multiply the value you get using the constant annuity function by $(1+g)^n$. You may want to review the earlier discussion on growing annuities to make sure you understand why you have to do this last multiplication.

For the annuities in advance, in D17 enter =PV(k,n,-A,0,1), and in D18 enter =FV(k,n,-A,0,1)*(1+g)^n.

3. **Create formulas using the annuity formulas:** To calculate the present and future values for the annuity in arrears using the annuity formulas, in C13 enter =A*(1+g)*((1-((1+g)/(1+rr))^n)/(rr-g)) and in C14 enter =A*(1+g)*((1+rr)^n-(1+g)^n)/(rr-g).

   For the annuity in advance, in C17 enter =A*(1+rr)*(1-((1+g)/(1+rr))^n)/(rr-g) and in C18 enter =A*(1+rr)*((1+rr)^n-(1+g)^n)/(rr-g).
4. **Create the year-by-year calculation table:** The only change you have to make here is in the column for cash flows. In B23 enter =IF(A23>n,0,A*(1+g)^A23). As before, for years beyond n, this will make the cash flows zero, but for the earlier years, the cash flows will now grow at the rate of g per year. Copy the formula into B24:B42. (You may have to reapply the custom formatting to hide the formulas in the cells beyond n.)

   For the cash flows for the annuity in advance, in F22 enter =IF(A22>n-1,0,A*(1+g)^A22) and copy it into F23:F41.

Testing the Model

As before, because the model calculates the same values using three different methods, if they agree with one another, there is no need to test further. You can also test this model against the previous model by entering the same values for input variables in both with g = 0 in this model, which effectively converts this into a model for constant annuities.

Uses of the Model

The model shows that if you start your investment today, you will accumulate $18,324 in 10 years versus $17,646 if you start your saving and investment one year from now.

To calculate how much your initial contribution must be in order to accumulate $100,000 in 20 years, you have to use Goal Seek. Enter 20 in B4. If you make your first contribution today (for the annuity in advance) in Goal Seek, use D18 for Set cell, 100000 for To value, and B3 for By changing cell. The answer is $1,500.

To calculate the first contribution if you make it one year from now, use Goal Seek with D14 for Set cell and the same values for the other two inputs as before. In this case, make sure you press OK when Goal Seek has an answer. If you look at cell B3, you will see A = $1,557. However, this is not the first contribution needed. Look at cell B23: it shows the correct first contribution of $1,620, which is 4% higher than the A. Recall that when you use the Excel function for constant annuities for a growing annuity in arrears, the A you enter in the function (or get out of it) is not the first contribution but the first contribution divided by (1+g). You have to remember this or else use the annuity table, which will show you the year-by-year contributions including the first contribution.

As we discussed, growing annuities are governed by a system of five variables and you can specify any four of them and calculate the fifth from this model using the Goal Seek.

Limitations of the Model

As before, users who do not understand the model and do not know Goal Seek will not be able to use it to answer the different types of questions it is capable of answering. For these users, you have to build a separate model depending on which four variables they are going to specify and which answer they want.

MODEL 4: LOAN AMORTIZATION TABLE, VERSION 1

The Problem

Create a model to produce an amortization table for a fixed rate loan. The loan is to be repaid in equal annual installments over its life and the first payment is to be made at the end of the first year. Use Excel's PMT function to calculate the required annual payment. The model should validate the user inputs for appropriateness and ask the user to modify any input that is not appropriate.

Modeling Strategy

The worksheet for this model is shown in Figure 14.9. Look at the model example to see what a loan amortization table looks like and the columns it needs to have. A loan amortization table shows how each annual payment is applied to the declining remaining loan balance to pay off the loan in full by the end of the loan life.

Use data validation to restrict interest rate to less than 20%, loan life to less than 30 years, and the initial loan amount to positive values only. (The first two restrictions are arbitrary and for illustration only.) Calculate the required annual payment amount using Excel's PMT function.

The year-beginning balance for the first year will equal the initial loan balance and in the subsequent years it will equal the year-end balance of the previous year. Each year you will have to split the annual payment into two components: the interest component calculated as the year-beginning balance multiplied by the interest rate, and the principal repayment component, which is the remaining part of the annual payment and is used to repay principal. The year-end balance for a year will equal the year-beginning balance less the principal repayment for the year. You only need to create the formulas for the first year and year-beginning balance for the second year. After that you can copy the formulas into the remaining lines of the table.

It is easier to create an amortization table for a specific loan life because the table can then have a known number of rows filled with the necessary formulas.

	A	B	C	D	E	F	G	H
1	**Loan Amortization Table Using PMT Function**							
2								
3	**Input Data**							
4	Interest rate (rr, % per year)	10%						
5	Loan life (n, years)	15						
6	Initial loan balance (P, $)	$100,000						
7	Required annual payment (APmt, $)	$13,147						
8			**Year**	**Year-beg**	**Annual**	**Interest**	**Principal**	**Year-end**
9				**Balance**	**Payment**	**Component**	**Repaid**	**Balance**
10								
11			1	$100,000	$13,147	$10,000	$3,147	$96,853
12			2	$96,853	$13,147	$9,685	$3,462	$93,391
13			3	$93,391	$13,147	$9,339	$3,808	$89,582
14			4	$89,582	$13,147	$8,958	$4,189	$85,393
15			5	$85,393	$13,147	$8,539	$4,608	$80,785
16			6	$80,785	$13,147	$8,078	$5,069	$75,716
17			7	$75,716	$13,147	$7,572	$5,576	$70,140
18			8	$70,140	$13,147	$7,014	$6,133	$64,007
19			9	$64,007	$13,147	$6,401	$6,747	$57,260
20			10	$57,260	$13,147	$5,726	$7,421	$49,839
21			11	$49,839	$13,147	$4,984	$8,163	$41,675
22			12	$41,675	$13,147	$4,168	$8,980	$32,696
23			13	$32,696	$13,147	$3,270	$9,878	$22,818
24			14	$22,818	$13,147	$2,282	$10,866	$11,952
25			15	$11,952	$13,147	$1,195	$11,952	$0
26			16					
27			17					
28			18					

FIGURE 14.9 Model 4: Loan amortization table using PMT function.

If you create a table for a 20-year loan life and the user wants to use it for a loan with 10-year life, then after the tenth year the numbers that the formulas generate will not be meaningful. To get around this problem, you can write each formula with IF functions to do the calculations during the life of the loan as above but enter zeros in the cells in the years beyond that. This will work, but will generate a table with lots of zeros. To make your table look nicer, you can apply special formatting as we used before to make the cells with zeros appear blank.

Note that since the table has to include both cash flows and balances, each row includes numbers for both the beginning and the end of the year and, therefore, represents two points in time. This is different from other situations when a column also represents a timeline and each row represents only one point in time. When you create tables like this, you have to keep in mind—and, if necessary, note in the table—whether a balance is before or after the cash flow that takes place at the same time. For example, in this case the year-end balance numbers are after the cash flows (that is, the annual payments) that take place at the same time.

Building the Model

1. **Enter labels in worksheet:** Enter the appropriate labels in the worksheet, format the input cells and adjust the column widths.

2. **Name the input cells and set up data validation:** Name the input cells as follows: B4 rr, B5 n, and B6 P. Set up data validation to restrict values in B4 to decimal numbers less than 0.2 (that is, 20%), in B5 to whole numbers less than 31, and in B6 to decimal numbers not less than 0. Enter a set of input values.
3. **Calculate the required annual payment:** In B7 enter the formula =PMT (rr,n, -P) to calculate the required annual payment. Instead of typing in the formula, use the function dialog box to enter it and enter the arguments by pointing to the appropriate cells. This will automatically enter the cell names you have already assigned and make the formula more readable. Note that to have the annual payment come out positive, you have to enter -P for the pv argument. You can omit the last two arguments because you want fv to be zero and this is a regular annuity. Name the cell B7 APmt.
4. **Create the formulas for the first year:** In C11:C48 enter 1 to 30 for the years. In D11 enter =P because the beginning balance would equal the initial loan amount. In E10 enter the formula =IF(C11>n,0,APmt). For the first year you could make it just =APmt, but in subsequent years you would need the IF function to enter 0 if the year is beyond the life of the loan based on the test condition of the IF. It is better to use the IF in the first year as well to keep the formulas uniform.

   In F11 enter the formula =IF(C11>n,0,D11*rr) to calculate the required interest payment for the year. In G11 enter =IF(C11>n,0,E11-F11) to calculate how much of the annual payment will be applied towards repayment of principal. Finally, in H11 enter =IF(C11>n,0,D11-G11) to calculate the year-end balance after applying the payment for the year.
5. **Create formulas for the rest of the table:** The only difference for year 2 is that the year-beginning balance should equal the balance at the end of the previous year. In D12 enter =IF(C12>n,0,H11). To complete the other cells for year 2, copy E11:H11 into E12:H12. All the other years should be same as the second year. Copy D12:H12 into D13:H40 (for a 30-year table).
6. **Apply custom formatting to make unused portion of table blank:** Select D11: H40 and enter the custom format $#,##0;; to make cells with 0 look blank.

Testing the Model

If the model is working properly, then the final balance at the end of the loan life should be zero because the loan should be exactly paid up by that point.

Uses of the Model

The most important use of this model is to visualize how an amortizing loan gets paid off over the years with the equal annual payments. In the early years, most of the payments go towards paying interest and the remaining loan balance declines slowly. However, as you get closer to the end of the loan life, larger and larger portions of the payment are freed up to pay off principal.

Because of the way we calculated the annual payment by setting the FV argument in the PMT function as zero, this model pays off the loan using equal annual payments. It is easy to modify it to accommodate equal annual payments followed by a final lump sum payment, also called a balloon payment. For example, if the loan has a final balloon payment equal to 20% of the initial loan amount, we can modify the formula in B7 to read =PMT(rr,n,-P, 0.2*P). This will produce an amortization table with the final balance equal to the balloon payment.

It is also easy to convert the table for periodic payments other than annual payments, (for example, to accommodate monthly payments for a mortgage). You just have to use monthly interest rate and loan life in months, and increase the number of rows in the table as necessary.

Limitations of the Model

This model will work only if the interest rate remains fixed for the entire loan life and all the annual payments are equal. As we will see later, for loans with changing interest rates or changing monthly payments, we have to use a somewhat more complex model.

MODEL 5: LOAN AMORTIZATION TABLE, VERSION 2

The Problem

Create a model to produce an amortization table for a fixed rate loan. The loan is to be repaid in equal annual installments over its life and the first payment is to be made at the end of the first year. Instead of using any of Excel's built-in financial functions, use Goal Seek to calculate the required constant annual payment. The model should validate the user inputs for appropriateness and ask the user to modify any input that is not appropriate.

Modeling Strategy

The worksheet for this model is shown in Figure 14.10. You can create this model by making a simple modification to the previous model. Instead of calculating the required annual payment using the PMT function, enter any guess in the cell for it. The amortization table will be automatically updated based on this annual payment, but the final balance will not be zero. Since for the right annual payment the final balance should be zero, you can use Goal Seek with the annual payment

	A	B	C	D	E	F	G	H
1	**Loan Amortization Table Using Goal Seek**							
2								
3	**Input Data**							
4	Interest rate (rr, % per year)	10%						
5	Loan life (n, years)	15						
6	Initial loan balance (P, $)	$100,000						
7	Required annual payment (APmt, $)	$13,147						
8			**Year**	**Year-beg**	**Annual**	**Interest**	**Principal**	**Year-end**
9				**Balance**	**Payment**	**Component**	**Repaid**	**Balance**
10								
11			1	$100,000	$13,147	$10,000	$3,147	$96,853
12			2	$96,853	$13,147	$9,685	$3,462	$93,391
13			3	$93,391	$13,147	$9,339	$3,808	$89,582
14			4	$89,582	$13,147	$8,958	$4,189	$85,393
15			5	$85,393	$13,147	$8,539	$4,608	$80,785
16			6	$80,785	$13,147	$8,078	$5,069	$75,716
17			7	$75,716	$13,147	$7,572	$5,576	$70,140
18			8	$70,140	$13,147	$7,014	$6,133	$64,007
19			9	$64,007	$13,147	$6,401	$6,747	$57,260
20			10	$57,260	$13,147	$5,726	$7,421	$49,839
21			11	$49,839	$13,147	$4,984	$8,163	$41,675
22			12	$41,675	$13,147	$4,168	$8,980	$32,696
23			13	$32,696	$13,147	$3,270	$9,878	$22,818
24			14	$22,818	$13,147	$2,282	$10,866	$11,952
25			15	$11,952	$13,147	$1,195	$11,952	$0
26			16					
27			17					
28			18					

FIGURE 14.10 Model 5: Loan amortization table using Goal Seek.

as the independent variable, the final balance as the dependent or target variable, and zero as the target value to calculate the required annual payment.

Building the Model

Start with a copy of the previous model in a different workbook to avoid any conflict because of the named cells.

1. **Change annual payment to an input value:** In B7, enter an arbitrary guess for annual payment—for example, $1000. This will overwrite the formula that was there to calculate the annual payment and make it an input variable. The amortization table will update based on this number.
2. **Determine the required payment using Goal Seek:** Open the Goal Seek dialog box. For Set cell, enter the cell address of the final balance, for To value enter 0, and for By changing cell enter B7. Click OK and then click OK again in the Goal Seek Status dialog box to accept the answer.

Testing the Model

If the model is working properly, then the final balance at the end of the loan life should be zero because the loan should be exactly paid up by that point.

Uses of the Model

This model does not do anything more than the previous model but as we will see, it can be extended to accommodate loans with varying interest rates and changing annual payments.

It is easy to use this model for a loan with a balloon payment at maturity. To calculate the required annual payment for such loans, use Goal Seek as before. This time, in the To value box of the Goal Seek dialog box, enter the amount of the balloon payment instead of zero.

Limitations of the Model

One limitation of this model is that to use it a user must know how to use Goal Seek. You cannot automate Goal Seek in Excel, but we will see later that you can automate Goal Seek using VBA so that users can work with this model even without knowing how to use Goal Seek.

This model also works only if the interest rate remains fixed for the entire loan life and all the annual payments are equal. However, as we will see next, it can be easily extended to accommodate more complex situations.

MODEL 6: LOAN AMORTIZATION TABLE FOR CHANGING INTEREST RATE

The Problem

Create a model to produce an amortization table for a variable rate loan for which the interest rate can change in two steps over its life, that is, the loan life is broken down into three interest rate periods with different interest rates specified for the three periods. The loan is to be repaid in equal annual installments over the life of the loan and the first payment is to be made at the end of the first year. The user will provide the lengths of the three interest rate periods (in years) and the interest rates for each of them. The model will have to calculate the appropriate equal annual payment.

Modeling Strategy

The worksheet for this model is shown in Figure 14.11. You cannot calculate the required equal annual payment for this model using any of Excel's built-in functions. But you can create it as an extension of the previous model, where you use for each year the interest rate appropriate for it based on the inputs the user provides. One approach is to create an additional column of interest rates in the amortization table and use a formula with nested IF functions in each cell of this column to select the interest rate appropriate for a year. Then use the interest rate from this column to do the other calculations for a year. Finally, as before,

	A	B	C	D	E	F	G	H
1	**Loan Amortization Table for Changing Interest Rate**							
2								
3	**Input Data**							
4	Initial loan balance (P, $)	$100,000						
5								
6		Length (yrs)	Int Rate					
7	Period 1	5	6.00%					
8	Period 2	3	8.00%					
9	Period 3	7	9.00%					
10								
11	Loan life (yrs)	15						
12	Required annual payment (APmt, $)	$10,961						
13								
14								
15	**Year**	**Year-beg**	**Annual**	**Interest**	**Principal**	**Year-end**	**Interest**	**Year**
16		**Balance**	**Payment**	**Component**	**Repaid**	**Balance**	**Rate**	
17								
18	1	100,000	10,961	6,000	4,961	95,039	6.00%	1
19	2	95,039	10,961	5,702	5,258	89,781	6.00%	2
20	3	89,781	10,961	5,387	5,574	84,208	6.00%	3
21	4	84,208	10,961	5,052	5,908	78,300	6.00%	4
22	5	78,300	10,961	4,698	6,263	72,037	6.00%	5
23	6	72,037	10,961	5,763	5,198	66,840	8.00%	6
24	7	66,840	10,961	5,347	5,613	61,226	8.00%	7
25	8	61,226	10,961	4,898	6,062	55,164	8.00%	8
26	9	55,164	10,961	4,965	5,996	49,168	9.00%	9
27	10	49,168	10,961	4,425	6,535	42,633	9.00%	10
28	11	42,633	10,961	3,837	7,124	35,509	9.00%	11
29	12	35,509	10,961	3,196	7,765	27,744	9.00%	12
30	13	27,744	10,961	2,497	8,464	19,281	9.00%	13
31	14	19,281	10,961	1,735	9,225	10,056	9.00%	14
32	15	10,056	10,961	905	10,056	0	9.00%	15
33								16

FIGURE 14.11 Model 6: Loan amortization table for changing interest rate.

use Goal Seek to determine the equal annual payment that makes the final loan balance zero.

Building the Model

Start with a copy of Model 5 in a different workbook to avoid any conflict because of the named cells. Delete all cell names.

1. **Set up data input cells and labels for them:** Enter appropriate labels for the data input cells and name the cell B4 as P, the cells B7, B8, B9 as Ln1, Ln2, and Ln3, and the cells C7, C8, C9 as rr1, rr2, rr3.
2. **Calculate total loan life:** In cell B11 enter the formula =B7+B8+B9 to calculate the total loan life from the lengths of the three periods entered by the user.
3. **Set up column of year numbers:** To make the model flexible, in the previous models we allowed loan life of up to 30 years and extended the amortization table to 30 years. We then wrote out formulas in such a way that the cells

for the years beyond the loan life had zeros in them, and we used special formatting to make them look empty. We could not do this for the Year column, though, and so the years extended up to 30 no matter what the loan life. This did not look good.

To hide years beyond the loan life, create a second year column in column H (it can be hidden later) and in H18:H47 enter the year numbers 1 to 30. In cell A18 enter the formula =IF(H18>Lnt,0,H18). This formula will enter zeros in the cells beyond the loan life and you can now use custom formatting in this column to make the cells with zeros look empty.

4. **Choose interest rate for each year:** Enter the appropriate heading in G15:G16 to make the column G the interest rate column. Now you have to create a formula to choose the right interest rate for each year. The formula should be general so that you copy it into the cells for all the years in this column. In G18 enter the formula =IF(H18<=Ln1,rr1,IF(H18<=(Ln1+Ln2), rr2,IF(H18<=Lnt,rr3,0))). Using three nested IF functions, this formula checks which period the year number for the current row (H18) falls in and accordingly chooses the appropriate interest rate for the year.

   If the current year number (H18) is less than or equal to Ln1, then this year falls into period 1 and the appropriate interest rate is rr1. If the current year number is not in period 1, then the next IF function checks if it is in period 2. If it is then the interest rate is rr2. Otherwise the third IF function checks if it is within the loan life. If it is, then the interest rate is rr2. For years beyond the loan life the interest rate is zero.

   Now copy this formula into G19:G47 and format the cells in this column using the format we have been using.
5. **Calculate the interest component:** You now have to use the interest rate from column G to calculate the interest component for each year. In cell D18 enter the formula =IF(H18>Lnt,0,B18*G18) and copy it into cells D19:D37.
6. **Determine the required payment using Goal Seek:** Open the Goal Seek dialog box. For Set cell, enter the cell address of the final balance, for To value enter 0, and for By changing cell enter B12. Click OK and then again click OK in the Goal Seek Status dialog box to accept the answer.

Testing the Model

If the model is working properly, then the final balance at the end of the loan life should be zero because the loan should be exactly paid off by that point.

Uses of the Model

You can use this model for loans for which the interest rate does not remain constant for the entire life. In this case we have allowed only 3 different interest rates, but we could use this model even if the interest rate changed every year.

In such a case, we would make the cell G18:37 input cells and let the user enter the different interest rates directly into them.

It is also easy to use this model if the loan has a balloon payment at maturity. To calculate the required annual payment for such loans, use Goal Seek as before but in the To value box of the Goal Seek dialog box enter the amount of the balloon payment instead of zero.

Limitations of the Model

This model works only for constant annual payments, but with a simple modification we can use it for changing annual payments as well.

MODEL 7: LOAN AMORTIZATION TABLE FOR CHANGING ANNUAL PAYMENT

The Problem

Create a model to produce a loan amortization table for a fixed rate loan for which the annual loan payment can change in two steps during the loan life. The first payment is to be made at the end of the first year. The user will provide the year numbers when the annual payments will change and the percentages by which they will change in each instance. The model will have to calculate the first annual payment.

Modeling Strategy

The worksheet for this model is shown in Figure 14.12. You cannot create this model using any of Excel's built-in functions. However, you can use essentially the same strategy as we used in the last model except that here the interest rate remains constant and you have to change the annual payments using formulas with nested IF functions. Finally, as before, you must use Goal Seek to determine the first annual payment that makes the final loan balance zero.

Building the Model

Start with a copy of Model 5 in a different workbook to avoid any conflict because of the named cells. (You may want to change the Year column the same way we changed it in the previous the model.)

1. **Set up data input cells and labels for them:** Enter appropriate labels for the data input cells and name the cell B4 as P, cell B5 as rr, B6 as Lnt. Also name B9 and B10 as Ln1 and Ln2, and C9 and C10 as Inc1 and Inc2.

	A	B	C	D	E	F	G
1	**Loan Amortization Table for Changing Annual Payment**						
2							
3	**Input Data**						
4	Initial loan balance	$100,000					
5	Interest rate (%)	9.00%					
6	Loan life (yrs)	15					
7							
8		Year no	Increment				
9	Payment increment: Step 1	5	10.00%				
10	Payment increment: Step 2	11	20.00%				
11							
12	Required initial annual payment	$11,231					
13							
14							
15	**Year**	**Year-beg**	**Annual**	**Interest**	**Principal**	**Year-end**	Year
16		**Balance**	**Payment**	**Component**	**Repaid**	**Balance**	
17							
18	1	100,000	11,231	9,000	2,231	97,769	1
19	2	97,769	11,231	8,799	2,431	95,338	2
20	3	95,338	11,231	8,580	2,650	92,688	3
21	4	92,688	11,231	8,342	2,889	89,799	4
22	5	89,799	12,354	8,082	4,272	85,528	5
23	6	85,528	12,354	7,697	4,656	80,871	6
24	7	80,871	12,354	7,278	5,075	75,796	7
25	8	75,796	12,354	6,822	5,532	70,264	8
26	9	70,264	12,354	6,324	6,030	64,234	9
27	10	64,234	12,354	5,781	6,573	57,662	10
28	11	57,662	14,824	5,190	9,635	48,027	11
29	12	48,027	14,824	4,322	10,502	37,525	12
30	13	37,525	14,824	3,377	11,447	26,078	13
31	14	26,078	14,824	2,347	12,477	13,600	14
32	15	13,600	14,824	1,224	13,600	0	15
33							16

FIGURE 14.12 Model 7: Loan amortization table for changing annual payment.

2. **Create formula to change annual payment:** In C18 enter the formula =IF(G18>Lnt,0,APmt). The formulas in the other cells in the Annual Payment column will need to change the annual payments at the specified years. To do this, in C19 enter =C18*IF(G19>Lnt,0,IF(G19=Ln1,1+Inc1, IF(G19=Ln2,1+Inc2,1))). This formula makes the current year's annual payment same as the previous year's by using a multiplier of 1 except in the two years when it is supposed to change to a different level. At these junctures the IF functions change the multiplier to the values specified by the user. Once you fully understand this formula, copy it into C20:C47.
3. **Determine the required payment for the first year using Goal Seek:** Open the Goal Seek dialog box. For Set cell, enter the cell address of the final balance, for To value enter 0, and for By changing cell enter B12. Click OK and then again click OK in the Goal Seek Status dialog box to accept the answer.

Testing the Model

If the model is working properly then the final balance at the end of the loan life should be zero because the loan should be exactly paid off by that point.

Also check to see that the annual payment amounts are changing by the right amounts in the right years.

Uses of the Model

You can extend this model to loans for which not just the annual payment but the interest rate also changes over the years.

It is also easy to use this model if the loan has a balloon payment at maturity. To calculate the required annual payment for such loans, use Goal Seek as before but in the To value box of the Goal Seek dialog box enter the amount of the balloon payment instead of zero.

MODEL 8: THE CONDOMINIUM PROJECT

The Problem

A condominium wants to start an annual program of collecting and saving money for a future capital project. A total of ten collections will be made, with the first collection made today. The parameters of the problem are: (1) the project's cost, if done today, is $100,000, (2) the project will be undertaken and paid for 10 years from today, (3) the cost of the project will grow at an expected inflation rate of 5% per year, (4) interest rate that can be earned by investing the accumulated balance over the years is 8% per year, and (5) the annual collection will be increased once a year at a constant growth rate of 3%. Make all of the above parameters input variables in your model.

Create a model that will use the Goal Seek function to calculate the necessary amount of the first annual collection. Create an additional model that will use Excel's built-in PMT functions to calculate the necessary amount of the first annual collection. The model should use the FV argument of the PMT function. In other words, you will use the future value of an annuity.

Modeling Strategy

The worksheet for this model is shown in Figure 14.13. The annual collections represent a growing annuity. You can set up a model using year-by-year cash flows as we did before and then use Goal Seek to calculate the required collection for the first year. Remember that the future value of the growing annuity will have to equal the future cost of the project.

Because the annual collection will grow at a fixed rate, to create a model using the PMT function you have to use a growth-adjusted interest rate. You will also have to adjust the future cost of the project by the growth rate as discussed in the section on growing annuities.

	A	B	C	D	E	F	G
1	**The Condominium Project**						
2							
3	**Input data**				Annual	Accumulated	
4	Cost of project today (CNow)	$100,000		Time	Collection	Balance	
5	Inflation rate (Infl)	5.00%		0	$9,253	$9,253	
6	Return on investment (Ret)	8.00%		1	$9,530	$19,524	
7	Collection growth rate (Grth)	3.00%		2	$9,816	$30,902	
8	Years till construction (NYrs)	10		3	$10,111	$43,485	
9				4	$10,414	$57,378	
10	Adjusted rate of return (AdjRet)	4.85%		5	$10,727	$72,695	
11	Future cost of project (FutCost)	$162,889		6	$11,048	$89,558	
12	Adjusted future cost of project (AdjFutCost)	$121,205		7	$11,380	$108,103	
13				8	$11,721	$128,472	
14	Required first collection (using PMT)	$9,253		9	$12,073	$150,823	
15				10		$162,889	
16	Required first collection (using table)	$9,253					
17							
18							

FIGURE 14.13 Model 8: The condominium project.

Building the Model

1. **Set up data input cells and labels for them:** Create the labels for the data input cells and name the data cell as follows: B4 CNow, B5 Infl, B6 Ret, B7 Grth, and B8 NYrs. Also create the label in A16 and enter an arbitrary number ($1,000) in B16 as an initial guess for the required collection for the first year.
2. **Calculate future cost of project:** Enter the label in cell A11 and in B11 enter the formula =CrntCost*(1+Infl)^NYrs to calculate the future cost of the project based on the assumption that it will grow at the expected inflation rate. Name the cell B11 FutCost.
3. **Set up year-by-year cash flow table:** Create the labels for the year-by-year cash flow table. In the Time column, enter 0 through 10. In E5 enter the formula =B16 for the first collection. In E6 enter the formula =E5*(1+Grth) to grow the previous year's collection by the specified growth rate. Copy the formula in E6 into the cells E7:E14. Because there are going to be 10 collections starting today, the last collection takes place at time 9, that is at the beginning of the tenth year. There is no collection at time 10.

   In F5 enter the formula =E5 because it is the accumulated balance at time 0 and no interest will be collected at that point. In F6 enter the formula =F5*(1+Ret)+E6 to calculate the accumulated balance at time 1 as the accumulated balance at time 0 plus the interest earned on it plus the new contribution made at time 1. This is a general formula for accumulated balance that you can now copy into cells F7:F15.

   Note that the last collection takes place at time 9 (that is, at the beginning of the tenth year) but the project is to be undertaken at time 10 (that is, at the end of the tenth year). In all time value problems, getting the timing of all cash flows right is critical.

4. **Run Goal Seek to calculate required first collection:** The tenth-year accumulated balance in the table will correspond to the initial guess for the first collection ($1,000). To determine the first year collection that will be required to accumulate a balance equal to the future cost of the project at time 10, use Goal Seek as follows: Open the Goal Seek dialog box. For Set cell, enter the cell address of the final accumulated balance F15, for To value enter the future cost of the project, and for By changing cell enter B16. Click OK and then again click OK in the Goal Seek Status dialog box to accept the answer.
5. **Calculate the growth-adjusted rate of return:** Enter the label in cell A10. Name the cell B10 AdjRet and enter in it the formula =(1+Ret)/(1+Grth)-1 to calculate the growth-adjusted rate of return.
6. **Calculate adjusted future cost of the project:** As we saw during our discussion of using functions for constant annuities for growing annuities, the future value we have to use is not the future value we want but a future value adjusted by the growth rate. In cell A12 enter the appropriate label, name the cell B12 AdjFutCost. In B12 enter the formula =FutCost/(1+Grth)^NYrs to calculate the growth-adjusted future cost of the project. If the reason for doing this is not clear, review the section on growing annuities.
7. **Calculate the required first collection using the PMT function:** Enter the label in A14 and in B14 enter the formula =PMT(AdjRet,NYrs,0,-AdjFutCost,1). (It is easier and safer to use the dialog box for PMT.) You have to use the adjusted interested rate and adjusted future cost of the project. Also, because the first payment takes place today and not one period in the future, this is an immediate annuity; you have to enter 1 for the last argument to indicate this.

Testing the Model

You have created two separate models for the same problem. If their answers agree, then it is almost certain that both models are working properly. Test the models by changing some of the inputs to see that you get the same answers using both models. (Remember to run Goal Seek every time you change an input.) Also, the year-by-year cash flow table shows exactly how the money will accumulate; you should do a few hand calculations to spot check some numbers on the table.

Two Important Points

It is possible to create a model for this problem in present value instead of future value terms. But it gets more complicated and the chances of making mistakes go up. If your objective is to accumulate a certain amount of money at a future point in time, then it is best to solve problems like this in terms of future values at that point in time as we have done here.

One final note: In many situations like this, it is possible to create an elegant, compact model using PMT and other functions. However, it is generally safer to create the year-by-year cash flow balance accumulation table and use it to solve the problem; it is then much easier to check your model with hand calculations. Also, as we saw, if the growth rate of the cash flows is not constant, you cannot use the built-in functions.

CHAPTER 15

Financial Planning and Investments

Many of the financial decisions that individuals have to make in their personal lives such as choosing a mortgage, investing their savings, and planning for retirement require using financial models. However, the models are developed and used most of the time by others (for example, financial planners) on their behalf. In this chapter we will develop a few such versatile models. They illustrate additional applications of the concept of the time value of money and also involve investing and taxation.

Review of Theory and Concepts

Let us start by reviewing a few basic issues that many personal finance models involve. We will then discuss two alternate approaches to retirement planning and an approach to structuring investment portfolios that we will use to develop several models.

SOME BASIC ISSUES

Inflation

Inflation is one of the key factors that has to be incorporated in many models for making personal finance decisions, especially when long-term planning is involved. If you are saving money to buy a car three years from now, inflation may not be an important factor. But if you are 30 now, plan to retire at age 65, and expect to live until you are 90, inflation must be factored into the models you use. For example, it is impossible for any of us to guess how much we will need in nominal dollars per year during retirement—it may be 35 years away. However, we may be able to say more comfortably that we will need in today's dollars (also called constant dollars or buying power) an amount equal to 80% of our current expenses.

Long-term planning has to be done in one of two ways. We can do the analysis in constant or real dollars, which makes the computations easy, but then we cannot reflect taxes realistically because taxes have to be paid on nominal dollar income and investment returns, not on real dollar amounts. Alternately, we can do all calculations in nominal dollars but carefully reflect in them the impact of anticipated inflation. For example, if we anticipate inflation to be 3% per year, we can decide to grow the necessary living expenses at the same rate or at a higher or lower rate tied to the rate of inflation. Similarly, we may also want to assume that we will be able to save a growing amount (at least in nominal terms) over the years; assuming that we can only save a fixed dollar amount in nominal terms over the years actually implies that we will be saving less and less per year over time. This requires starting with a much higher savings rate today, which most of us cannot afford. To some extent, inflation also must be factored into the rates of return we assume. For example, we may want to assume that on our investments we will be able to earn a return 4% higher than the rate of inflation.

Taxes

We generally have to factor in three types of taxes into our models: taxes on ordinary income (also called ordinary income tax), taxes on dividends, and taxes on capital gains.

Taxes on ordinary income apply to wages, salaries, and other income, as well as most interest income except income from investment in municipal bonds, which are tax-free. This tax is charged at different rates depending on one's income level or tax bracket. Unless we want to calculate income taxes in detail by taking into consideration different rates for the different tax brackets, we should generally use the marginal tax rate in our models, that is, the tax rate that will apply to the next dollar of income. For most people, it is in the range of 25% to 30%, especially when state income taxes are factored in.

The tax rate on most dividend income is currently 15%; these taxes have to be paid as the dividends are received.

Capital gains are defined as the appreciation in the value of an investment asset. You pay taxes at the special capital gains tax rate when an asset is held for more than one year before it is sold. Currently, the rate for most people is 15%. One important point to keep in mind is that capital gains taxes have to be paid only when the asset is sold; until then no taxes have to be paid, even if the asset's value keeps growing.

Tax Basis and Calculating Taxes on Sales over Time

When we buy and sell assets over time in tranches, the calculation of the capital gains taxes can get somewhat complicated. We need a simple approach to handle capital gains taxes in models in such situations, and for that we need to understand tax basis.

The tax basis (often just called basis) of a stock or any other asset is the price at which you bought it. If you buy \$100 of stocks, then your basis for all of the stocks you bought is \$100. If you sell all of them at the same time at \$120, then you will apply or use the entire basis to calculate the capital gains tax. Your capital gain is (\$120 − \$100) = \$20 and the tax on this gain is (\$20 × 15%) = \$3.

If you sell \$90 of stocks when the value of the total portfolio is \$120, then you will be selling (\$90/\$120 × 100) = 75% of your portfolio and you will use 75% of your original basis to calculate the capital gain on your sale. The capital gains will be (\$90 − 75% of \$100) = \$15 and the capital gains tax will be (15% of \$15) = \$2.25. Since you used up \$75 of tax basis, your remaining tax basis will be \$25. You will use this remaining tax basis against future sales.

Every time you buy additional stocks, what you pay gets added to your tax basis. Every time you sell stocks, you use up a portion of the tax basis and deduct it from the tax basis you had before the sale.

Note that this approach is good for making calculations for projections. Computations of actual tax bills are based on the purchase price of the specific lot of stocks you sold, which you can designate at the time of sale.

In developing models, we will also have to address the reverse question: How much of an asset do we have to sell to be left with a certain amount of after-tax money? Here is how we can calculate the amount of stock (X) you have to sell to generate A amount of after-tax proceeds:

Let:

X = before-tax stock sale
A = after-tax proceeds from the stock sale
S = value of stock portfolio (before sale)
B = tax basis of stock portfolio (before sale)
T = capital gains tax rate

Then:

$$\text{Tax on sale} = (X - B \times X/S) \times T$$
$$A = X - ((X - B \times X/S) \times T)$$
$$X = A/(1 - (1 - B/S) \times T)$$

Reinvestment Income

Many stocks pay dividends, generally quarterly, and most fixed income investments (bonds, for example) provide ongoing interest income. Unless these investments are in tax-deferred accounts, we have to pay taxes on these returns before reinvesting the funds at rates available at that time. Because the taxes and the reinvestment rates we assume can significantly affect actual returns earned over time, our models should explicitly incorporate them and let the user specify the tax rates as well as reinvestment rates.

When we buy a bond, it is tempting to assume that if we reinvest the interest income as we receive it, over time we will earn on our original investment a return equal to the yield to maturity at which we bought it. Because of the intermediate taxes and potentially different reinvestment rates, the actual return generally turns out to be quite different. In addition, if you want to take into consideration the inflation rate for the intervening period and ask what real return we will earn or we earned, the answer can be very different from the original yield to maturity. We will build a model to calculate return, taking into consideration the intermediate taxes, the reinvestment rate, and the inflation rate.

Taxable versus Tax-Deferred Accounts

To encourage saving for future needs, tax laws provide certain opportunities to defer or even to never pay taxes on the returns on some of our savings. The advantage of not having to pay taxes on investment returns is obvious. The opportunity to defer taxes, especially for a long time, can be a great advantage, too, because then we can earn additional returns on the taxes we are deferring. To take advantage of any of these opportunities, you must meet certain eligibility criteria.

In building models, we have to know whether we are dealing with taxable accounts where taxes on returns have to be paid annually, tax-deferred accounts (for example, IRAs, profit-sharing plans, etc.), or tax-free accounts where no taxes will have to be paid (for example, Roth IRAs). Also remember that interest income on municipal bonds is tax-free, and capital gains taxes do not become due until an asset is sold, which provides great opportunities to defer the capital gains taxes for long time periods.

Sometimes we can develop models that will work for both taxable and tax-deferred accounts or even tax-free accounts. For taxable applications, the user has to input the appropriate tax rate. For tax-deferred or tax-free accounts, the user will set the tax rates to zero. However, not all models can be built with this flexibility, and you should always document any tax-related limitation of a model.

SAVING AND INVESTING FOR RETIREMENT

Almost everyone has to save and invest for future needs. The needs may be short-term (such as the down payment for a house or car) or long-term (such as retirement and children's educations). The analysis and modeling required to answer questions in all of these areas are similar; we can address them by focusing on retirement planning.

Some of the questions people ask most often about retirement are:

- How much do I have to save and invest per month if I want to accumulate a certain amount of money by the time I retire?
- If during retirement I anticipate needing a certain amount of money per year, how much do I have to save and invest until retirement to be able to afford that?
- If I retire with a certain amount of money in savings, how much can I expect to be able to withdraw annually without running out of money in my lifetime?

Addressing questions like these fall under the general heading of retirement planning. Let us look at two approaches to retirement planning, one in real dollars and one in nominal dollars.

Real Dollar Retirement Planning

Whenever you do analysis or modeling in real dollars, you have to specify real or fixed dollars of what point in time you mean. Using real dollars of today is different from using real dollars of 10 years back or 10 years into the future. If nothing is specified, then real dollars of today are assumed.

If you want to have a retirement income of $40,000 per year in real dollars, that is, $40,000 in today's dollars in the first year of retirement growing at the rate of inflation in each subsequent year, how big a nest egg will you need at the time of retiring? The answer, of course, depends on your life expectancy and the return you expect to earn on your investments over the years.

Although it may be adequate to assume that you will live until age 90 or 95, you can never be sure. You may live longer, and if you do and run out of money, you will be in a difficult situation. Many experts therefore advise that you should plan for retirement assuming you will live forever. If you plan for retirement assuming that you will live forever instead of until age 90 or 95, you will probably need about a 20% larger initial nest egg. Planning for this additional amount will provide a margin of safety and peace of mind.

In this analysis we are talking about real return, for which, based on historical data, 2% to 5% is the recommended range. Your specific choice will depend on how conservative or aggressive you want to be with your assumption.

If you assume a 4% real return, then based on the perpetuity formula we developed for annuities, the nest egg you will need is $40,000/0.04 or $1 million (in today's dollars). Remember that the $40,000 is the before-tax real dollar annual withdrawal you will be able to afford from the $1 million nest egg, and you probably have to pay taxes on most or all of it. So you have to estimate your annual requirement accordingly.

If you are 35 now, how much must you save and invest every month to have that $1 million nest egg when you retire at 65? You can do the calculations using the annuity formulas assuming an appropriate real rate of return. If the answer you get is $1,200 per month in real dollars, it means that you have to save an amount increasing at the rate of inflation every month, starting with $1,200 in the first month.

This is a simple and useful way to do retirement planning. We will develop a model to do the calculations for this approach and see how the monthly real savings requirement changes depending on the return assumptions both during the saving and the retirement years.

Nominal Dollar Retirement Planning

In our discussion of retirement planning in real dollars as well as retirement planning in general, a key assumption we make is that your investments will earn the assumed return uniformly over the years, and that during retirement you will sell a certain amount of your investment in stocks every year irrespective of market conditions. As we know, stock market returns do not come in a uniform stream over the years—the market goes through long up-and-down periods. If you get unlucky and hit a few years of down period during the early years of retirement and keep selling the assumed (in your retirement plan) dollar amount of stocks every year, then you will significantly increase the chances of running out of money during retirement—even if in the long run the stock market provides a return equal to your assumption. The reason is that if you sell a lot of stocks in a depressed market in the early years, then when the market recovers and provides much higher returns, you will not have a large enough investment in the stock market to make up for the earlier losses.

One possible way around this problem is to not sell stocks when the market is depressed. To be able to do this, you should have enough money in safe investments by the time you retire, that is, in good quality, short-term fixed income investments, to cover your needs for a 10- to 15-year period. I call this the security horizon. You should pick a security horizon in the 10- to 15-year range. Then, during years in which the stock market does poorly, you should draw your annual living expenses from the safe investments and not sell any stocks. And, in years when the stock market does well, you should sell stocks to cover your expenses and also to build up your safe investment reserves to the level required by your security horizon. This approach can significantly reduce your risk of running out of money during retirement.

As you can imagine, if you want to follow this strategy, calculating what size nest egg you will have to build by the time you retire gets somewhat complex because we do not know ahead of time in which years the market will provide above-average returns and in which years it will do poorly. The conservative approach is to assume that you will start retirement with enough of your nest egg in safe investments to cover your planned withdrawals for the next 14 years (assuming you have chosen a security horizon of 15 years and have already withdrawn the money for the current year) and invest the rest in stocks. For modeling purposes, you then assume that every year you will sell enough stocks to maintain a level of safe investments adequate to cover the expenses for the next 14 years. Finally, you will start drawing down your safe investments when you run out of stocks to sell. As you will see, this will happen 15 years before your assumed life expectancy, and you will run out of money in the assumed last year of life.

Let me emphasize that the above is a conservative modeling assumption about when and how much stock you will sell. In real life, as discussed before, you will not sell stocks in bad years and you will sell more stocks than necessary in good years. This is one of many available approaches to retirement planning.

We will build a model to calculate how big a nest egg you will need under this approach, using various assumptions about security horizon, returns on safe investments and stocks, taxes, and so on.

STRUCTURING PORTFOLIOS

For long-term investment success, it is essential that an investor creates and maintains a properly structured portfolio. A portfolio is generally structured at three levels.

First, the investor has to choose the broad asset classes (for example, stocks, bonds, etc.) in which to invest and decide how much of the portfolio to invest in each asset class. This is generally called the portfolio's asset allocation. Studies have shown that a portfolio's asset allocation has the largest impact on its long-term return.

Second, the investor has to choose within each asset class the categories of securities in which to invest. For stocks, the categories may be large-cap stocks, small-cap value stocks, and so on. For bonds, these may be short-term bonds, long-term bonds, foreign bonds, and so on. The investor then must decide what percentage of his allocation to each asset class he wants to allocate to each category within that class.

Finally, within each category of securities the investor has to choose specific securities and mutual finds and decide how much to invest in each of them. To make this decision, the investor will probably start with a select list of stocks or funds in each category and then do an allocation among them.

Although both financial theory and analysis of historical data provide some guideline for portfolio structuring, there is quite a bit of leeway in choosing the allocation at each level. There is no perfect answer, and even for the same person the "right" portfolio will change over the years as family circumstances change (for example, children go to and then finish college, the couple approaches retirement, and so forth). Although most people think that they should adjust their portfolios at least periodically in response to changing market outlook, market history shows that no one can reliably predict what the market will do in the future and which stocks will do better than the others over the years. Contrary to what most people believe, then, the structure and holdings of a portfolio should not be influenced much by anyone's views on the market outlook.

It is best to structure a portfolio systematically as described above and the best way to do so is by using a portfolio-structuring model. We will develop one such model in the modeling section.

Modeling Examples

MODEL 1: RETURN WITH CHANGING REINVESTMENT RATES

The Problem

Build a model to calculate how much money you will accumulate over time if you invest in bonds in a taxable account, taking into consideration the taxes on the coupon income, the reinvestment rate, and any capital gains taxes that will be due when the bonds mature. Build the model under the following assumptions, but make all the key variables input variables so that the user can change them.

On January 1, you invested in a taxable account $100,000 in 8% coupon (paid semi-annually) bonds with 20-year remaining life at $900 per bond. There was no accrued interest involved because you bought the bonds right after a coupon payment. You expect to be able to reinvest all interest received during the first 10 years (20 coupons) at an interest rate of 6% per year (APR) and during the remaining 10 years at an interest rate of 5% per year (APR), paid semiannually. Using the model, answer the following questions:

- What is the APR yield to maturity on the bonds?
- If your assumptions about the reinvestment rates turn out to be true, what effective annual rate of return with annual compounding will you earn on your investment over the 20-year period? (Ignore all taxes for this calculation.)
- If your ordinary income tax rate is 35% and the capital gains tax rate is 15% and you have to pay ordinary income taxes on the interest income as you receive them, what effective annual after-tax rate of return will you earn on your investment over the 20-year period?
- If you expect 3% per year inflation over the 20-year period, recalculate your before-tax and after-tax effective real annual rates of return over the period.

Modeling Strategy

The worksheet for this model is shown in Figure 15.1. Start by calculating how much face amount of bond you will be able to buy with your initial investment. To calculate the yield to maturity, you can use Excel's RATE function. (If you are not familiar with yield to maturity, see Chapter 17: Bond Pricing and Duration.)

To calculate the money that you will accumulate over the years, you have to do a period-by-period calculation by setting up a table to keep track of what the interest income on the bonds as well as on all the reinvestments will be. On all interest income, you will have to calculate the taxes and deduct it before reinvesting the money at the specified reinvestment rates.

Base your calculation of the rate of return over the years on the total amount of money you will have at the end of the 20-year period after paying all taxes. This will include all accumulated after-tax interest income plus the face amount

	A	B	C	D	E	F
1	**Return with Changing Reinvestment Rate**					
2						
3	**Inputs**					
4	Initial investment	$100,000				
5	Bond price	$900				
6	Bond coupon rate	8.00%				
7	Expected annual inflation rate	3.00%				
8	Remaining life of bond (years)	20				
9	Reinvestment rate for first period	6.00%				
10	Reinvestment rate for remaining years	5.00%				
11	Length of first period (years)	10				
12	Ordinary income tax rate	35.00%				
13	Capital gains tax rate	15.00%				
14						
15	Face amount of bonds purchased	$111,111				
16						
17	Yield to maturity (APR)	9.09%				
18	Final balance after all taxes	$273,489				
19	Effective annual rate of return (nominal)	5.16%				
20	Effective annual rate of return (real)	2.10%				
21						
22						
23			**Accumulated interest income**			
24		Period-beg	Coupon	Other interest	Income tax	Period-end
25		Balance	Received	Received	Paid	Balance
26	Semi-annual periods					
27	1	$0	$4,444	$0	$1,556	$2,889
28	2	$2,889	$4,444	$87	$1,586	$5,834
29	3	$5,834	$4,444	$175	$1,617	$8,837
30	4	$8,837	$4,444	$265	$1,648	$11,898
31	5	$11,898	$4,444	$357	$1,680	$15,019
63	37	$142,700	$4,444	$3,567	$2,804	$147,908
64	38	$147,908	$4,444	$3,698	$2,850	$153,200
65	39	$153,200	$4,444	$3,830	$2,896	$158,578
66	40	$158,578	$4,444	$3,964	$2,943	$164,044
67						

FIGURE 15.1 Model 1: Return with changing reinvestment rate.

of the bonds less any capital gains taxes you will have to pay on the face amount at that time.

Calculate the real rate of return from the nominal rate of return using the relationship: (1 + real rate of return) = (1 + Nominal rate of return)/(1 + rate of inflation). This relationship works if the rate of inflation is constant over time. Otherwise you have to convert the final wealth into constant dollars of the initial period and then calculate the real return using that with the initial investment amount.

Note that even though the problem calls for both pre-tax and after-tax analysis, you do not need to build two separate models. You can build the model incorporating taxes and do any pre-tax analysis by setting the tax rates equal to zero.

Building the Model

1. **Set up input variables:** Create labels for the input variables in A4:A13. If you want, you can also name the cells for at least the important input variables.
2. **Calculate amount of bond purchased and yield to maturity:** To calculate the face amount of bond purchased, in B15 enter the formula =B4*1000/B5. To calculate the yield to maturity at the purchase price, in B17 enter the formula =RATE($B$8*2,–1000*B6/2,B5,–1000)*2.
3. **Set up table to calculate accumulated interest income:** The table has to be set up by interest payment period (that is, six months) and not yearly.

   The first column of the table shows the accumulated interest income at the beginning of the period. This would be zero for the first period and equal to the balance at the end of the previous period (after payment of taxes) for all other periods. In B27 enter 0, in B28 enter =F27, and copy it into the remaining columns in the table.

   The coupon received will depend on the face amount of bonds purchased and not on the initial investment of $100,000. In C27 enter the formula =$B$15*$B$6/2 and copy it into the rest of the column in the table.

   The other interest received is the interest on the accumulated interest income at the beginning of the year based on the reinvestment rate at the time. To calculate it, in D27 enter the formula =B27*IF(A27<= $B$11*2,$B$9/2,$B$10/2). Here, the IF function chooses the appropriate reinvestment rate based on the specified length of the first period. Copy the formula into the rest of the cells in the column.

   Income tax at the ordinary income tax rate will have to be paid on all—coupon and other—the interest income earned during the period. To calculate it, in E27 enter the formula =(C27+D27)*$B$12. Copy the formula in the remaining cells in the column.

   The period-end balance is the period-beginning balance plus interest received during the period less taxes paid. To calculate it, in F27 enter the formula =B27+C27+D27–E27 and copy it down the column.

4. **Calculate the rates of return:** To calculate the rates of return, you first have to calculate the final balance after all taxes. In F66, you already have the accumulated interest income after taxes. When you receive the face amount of the bond on maturity, if you have a capital gain, you will have to pay capital gains taxes. However, if you have a capital loss, we will assume that there is no tax benefit. To calculate the total after-tax amount of money at the end of 20 years, in B18 enter the formula =IF(B15>B4,$B$15–($B$15–$B$4)*$B$13,$B$15)+F66. Here, the IF function checks if there is a gain or a loss on the bonds. If there is a gain, then the capital gains taxes are deducted from the face amount to calculate the net proceeds at maturity. If there is a loss (that is, you bought the bonds at a premium), then the proceeds equal the face amount received. The accumulated after-tax interest income is then added to the balance.

   Calculate the actual annual rate of return using the final balance, the initial investment and the number of years. To do so, in B19 enter the formula =((B18/B4)^(1/B8)–1.

   To calculate the real rate of return, in B20 enter the formula =(1+B19)/(1+B7)–1.

Testing the Model

The model has to be mostly tested using hand calculations or side calculations using Excel itself. For example, if you set the purchase price at $1,000, the reinvestment rate equal to the coupon rate, and the tax rates equal to zero, the effective annual interest rate on the bond should be equal to the effective annual rate of return from the model. You should do some testing by changing one input at a time to ensure that the results are changing as anticipated.

Uses of the Model

Because we have set up most variables as input variables, the model can be used to answer a wide range of questions. For example, if you want to assume that the investment is in a tax-deferred account, you can set the tax rates to zero. You can, of course, change the reinvestment rates. It is interesting to see the effect of taxes on the actual return you earn over time. It is also interesting to note that on a bond paying 8% coupon that you even bought at a discount, the real rate of return you can expect to earn over the years after taxes is only 2.1%.

Limitations of the Model

You should be able to easily use the model for maturities other than 20 years by expanding or contracting the table and making a few other minor changes. However, someone who does not understand the model and is less familiar with

Excel will not be able to do this. With some additional work, you can make this model more versatile. It is easier, however, to develop a more versatile model in VBA.

MODEL 2: SAVING FOR RETIREMENT

The Problem

Assume that you are 30 years old now. Starting today, you want to save enough money to accumulate $1 million (after all taxes) in today's dollars by the time you retire at 65. You will do this in 35 growing annual installments. You expect to be able to save every year an amount that is 2% more than the previous year. You currently have $100,000 saved, and you plan to invest this money and all new savings in a stock fund that is expected to return 8% per year, of which 2% will be dividends and 6% will be capital gains. All the money will be in taxable accounts, so you will have to pay income taxes at a 15% rate on the dividend incomes as you earn them at the end of each year. You will reinvest the rest of the dividends. In addition, assume that you will sell all holdings at the time you retire and pay the necessary capital gains taxes at the rate of 15% and the inflation rate will average 3% per year over the period.

How much money will you have to save in the first year?

Set this up as a model so that a user can input other values (different tax rates, for example) to do similar calculations for his own situations.

Modeling Strategy

The worksheet for this model is shown in Figure 15.2. The calculations here are similar to those in Model 1, and you will have to do a year-by-year analysis. Because you do not know how much you will have to save in the first year, start by assuming $1,000. At the beginning of every year, add the new (growing) saving for the year to the accumulated investment balance. At the end of the year, calculate the dividend you will get; then calculate and deduct the dividend tax. Add the after-tax dividend amount and the capital appreciation for the year to the balance at the beginning of the year to calculate the end-of-year balance. This becomes the balance for the beginning of the next year.

To calculate the capital gains tax when you sell all your holdings at age 65, you will have to keep track of your tax basis, that is, the amount of money you are investing in stocks. Using the accumulated tax basis, calculate the capital gains tax you will have to pay at the end of the 35 years and the final after-tax savings balance. You want this balance to equal the equivalent of $1 million in today's dollars. Calculate this target amount and then use Goal Seek to determine what your first year savings will have to be to reach this target.

	A	B	C	D	E	F	G
1	**Saving for Retirement**						
2							
3	**Inputs**						
4	Target balance (in today's dollars)	$1,000,000					
5	Current savings balance ($)	$100,000					
6	Expected annual inflation rate (%)	3.00%					
7	Planned savings increment rate (%)	2.00%					
8	Expected annual dividend income (%)	2.00%					
9	Expected annual capital appreciations (%)	6.00%					
10	Ordinary income tax rate on dividends (%)	15.00%					
11	Capital gains tax rate (%)	15.00%					
12	Current age	30					
13	Retirement age	65					
14							
15	Required first year annual saving	**$8,240**	**Remember to run Goal Seek**				
16	Number of installments of savings	35					
17	Target balance in future dollars	$2,813,862					
18	Final after-tax balance less target balance	$0					
19							
20							
21		Yr-beg bal	Annual	Dividend	Capital	Yr-end bal	Tax
22		(Pre saving)	Saving	Income	Appreciation	After div tax	Basis
23							
24	1	$100,000	$8,240	$2,165	$6,494	$116,575	$110,081
25	2	$116,575	$8,405	$2,500	$7,499	$134,604	$120,610
26	3	$134,604	$8,573	$2,864	$8,591	$154,202	$131,618
27	4	$154,202	$8,745	$3,259	$9,777	$175,493	$143,133
55	32	$2,261,621	$15,225	$45,537	$136,611	$2,452,163	$903,297
56	33	$2,452,163	$15,529	$49,354	$148,062	$2,657,705	$960,777
57	34	$2,657,705	$15,840	$53,471	$160,413	$2,879,408	$1,022,067
58	35	$2,879,408	$16,157	$57,911	$173,734	$3,118,524	$1,087,449
59							

FIGURE 15.2 Model 2: Saving for retirement.

Building the Model

1. **Set up input variables:** Label the input variable cells and name them as follows: B4 as TarBal, B5 as CurBal, B6 as InflRate, B7 as SavIncr, B8 as DivRet, B9 as CapRet, B10 as DivTax, B11 as CapTax, B12 as CurAge, and B13 as RetAge. Also name B15 AnlSav and enter $1,000 as an initial guess.
2. **Set up year-by-year calculation table:** Starting in cell A24, label the rows 1 to 35 to indicate the years. In B24 enter =CurBal as the initial savings balance. In C24 enter the formula =AnlSav as the first installment of savings deposited at the beginning of the year.

   To calculate the dividend amount at the end of the year, in D24 enter the formula =(B24+C24)*DivRet. In E24 enter the formula =(B24+C24)*CapRet to calculate the capital appreciation for the year. To calculate the year-end balance, in F24 enter the formula =(B24+C24+E24)+D24*(1-DivTax). Finally, to keep track of the tax basis for the savings, in G24 enter the formula =B24+C24+D24*(1-DivTax). This sums the initial investment, the new contributions made at the beginning of the year, and the after-tax dividend amount reinvested.

   For the second year, in B25 enter the formula =F24 because the initial balance will equal the ending balance from the previous year. In C25 enter the formula =C24*(1+SavIncr) to calculate the new savings amount. In G25 enter the formula =G24+C25+D25*(1-DivTax). All other formulas will be the same. Copy them from the first year and copy the row for the second year into all the remaining years in the table.

3. **Calculate first installment of savings required:** In B16 enter the formula =RetAge-CurAge to calculate the number of savings contributions you will make. In B17, enter the formula =TarBal*(1+InflRate)^NumSav to convert the target balance into dollars of the year when you will retire. To calculate the difference between the after-tax projected balance and the target balance at the time of retirement, in B18 enter the formula =F58-(F58-G58)*CapTax-B17. The first part of this equation calculates the after-tax projected balance as the difference between the projected balance before the payment of capital gains taxes and the amount of the capital gains taxes.

   To calculate the required amount of first-year contribution, run Goal Seek with Set cell as B18, To value as 0, and By changing cell as B15.

Testing the Model

You have to check the model using a combination of two approaches. Make the values of several input variables zero simultaneously and change the values of the others to make sure that the values in the table are changing as expected. Also check them with hand calculations.

Uses of the Model

This model can be used to do calculations for a wide range of circumstances and is not limited to use only for retirement savings. For example, if all the investments are going to be in tax-deferred accounts, then you can do the analysis by setting the tax rates to zero. If you want to assume that you will not sell all stocks at the time of retirement, set the capital gains tax rate as zero. If you want to consider fixed income investment, make the dividend rate equal to interest rate, capital appreciation rate equal to zero, and the dividend tax rate equal to ordinary income tax rate.

Limitations of the Model

The model will not work as built for different numbers of years until retirement. You will have to manually make a few changes. Also, every time you change a variable, you will have to manually rerun Goal Seek. This model is therefore not suitable for users who do not understand it or know Excel. We will develop a VBA model that will overcome these limitations.

MODEL 3: RETIREMENT PLANNING IN REAL DOLLARS

The Problem

Develop a model to calculate how much you will have to save monthly in real dollars if you want a certain amount of real dollar income forever after retirement. Make the following the input variables of the model: number of years until retirement, expected real returns on investments until and after retirement, and the annual real income you desire. Create a data table to show how the annual savings requirement changes with the years-until-retirement variable and the assumed real rate of return during the savings years. (All real dollars refer to today's dollars.)

Modeling Strategy

The worksheet for this model is shown in Figure 15.3. As we discussed before, the nest egg you will need at the time of retirement is the desired annual income divided by the anticipated real rate of return on investments during the retirement years. Calculate this required amount. Then calculate the amount you will have to save annually in real dollars using the PMT function. Use the nest egg amount as the future value and the expected real rate of return during the savings years as the rate.

	A	B	C	D	E	F	G	H	I
1	**Retirement Planning in Real Dollars**								
2	Uses different rates during saving and withdrawal years								
3									
4	Real annual portfolio return during saving years	5%							
5	Real annual portfolio return during retirement	4%							
6	Years till retirement	20							
7	Real annual withdrawal target	$50,000							
8									
9	Nest egg needed	$1,250,000							
10	Monthly portfolio return during saving years	0.41%							
11	Required real monthly saving	$3,080							
12									
13									
14		**Required monthly saving for $50,000 annual withdrawal (in today's dollars)**							
15									
16			**Real annual portfolio return during saving years**						
17		$3,080.30	2%	3%	4%	5%	6%	7%	
18		5	$19,835	$19,356	$18,888	$18,433	$17,989	$17,557	
19		10	$9,427	$8,964	$8,521	$8,098	$7,694	$7,308	
20		15	$5,969	$5,525	$5,109	$4,720	$4,357	$4,018	
21	**Years till retirement**	20	$4,248	$3,824	$3,436	$3,080	$2,757	$2,463	
22		25	$3,223	$2,819	$2,457	$2,134	$1,848	$1,596	
23		30	$2,544	$2,160	$1,824	$1,533	$1,283	$1,069	
24		35	$2,065	$1,700	$1,389	$1,128	$910	$730	
25		40	$1,709	$1,363	$1,077	$843	$655	$506	
26									
27									

FIGURE 15.3 Model 3: Planning for retirement in real dollars.

Building the Model

1. **Set up the input variables:** Create the labels for the input variables and enter a set of reasonable values for them.
2. **Calculate nest egg and monthly savings requirements:** To calculate the nest egg you will need at the time of retirement, in B9 enter the formula =B7/B5.

   To calculate the monthly return rate during the saving years, in B10 enter the formula =(1+B4)^(1/12)-1. This assumes that the specified annual real rate of return is an effective rate. If you assume it is an annual percentage rate, then the monthly rate will be the annual rate divided by 12.

   To calculate the monthly savings requirement, in B11 enter the formula =PMT(B10,B6*12,0,-B9).
3. **Create the data table:** To create the data table, in B18:B25, enter a series of numbers for years until retirement. In C17:H17, enter a range of real returns for the saving years. In B17 enter the formula =B11. Select B17:H25 and then open the Data Table dialog box. In Row input cell, enter B4 and in Column input cell, enter B6. Click OK.

Testing the Model

This model is easy to test. You can test it with some calculations using a hand calculator or by doing some side calculations in Excel.

Uses of the Model

Although this is a simple model, it can be quite useful for retirement planning because it requires only a few inputs. It works best if you assume that before retirement all the investments will be in tax-deferred accounts and after retirement full taxes will have to be paid on all withdrawals. In this case, you can treat the withdrawals as the before-tax amounts and calculate an after-tax amount by applying an average tax rate to it. (The average tax rate will be appropriate if you assume this will be the bulk of your income. Otherwise a marginal tax rate may be more appropriate.)

MODEL 4: RETIREMENT PLANNING IN NOMINAL DOLLARS

The Problem

A friend of yours who is close to retirement has asked for your advice on how he should invest his assets and manage his withdrawals during retirement. He will need to withdraw a specific amount of money (growing at the rate of inflation) every year for living expenses. He wants you to develop a model for him. This model should estimate how much money your friend can expect to withdraw annually during retirement under various assumptions from a nest egg of certain size. It should also estimate what size nest egg he will have to accumulate by the time of retirement to be able to withdraw a certain inflation-adjusted amount annually. (All of the money is invested in taxable accounts.)

You explain to him the retirement planning approach we discussed earlier under "Nominal Dollar Retirement Planning" and he agrees to follow that approach. Build him a model that he can use to address his two concerns. The input variables for the model are: returns on fixed income and equity investments, ordinary income and capital gains tax rates, inflation rate, funds available for initial investment, initial annual withdrawal, and security horizon.

Modeling Strategy

You will have to set up the model to do year-by-year calculations as shown in the worksheet for the model in Figure 15.4. Let us use SH for your friend's security horizon.

In your model at the beginning of every year, you will first withdraw the money for the current year. You will then calculate how much money has to be invested in safe investments to provide for the withdrawal needs for the next SH −1 years. For the rest of that year, this amount of money will be invested in fixed income and the rest of the money will be invested in stocks.

You will find at the beginning of every year (other than the first year) that when you do the calculations and make the portfolio adjustments, you will need to sell some stocks to replenish the safe investment holdings to the required level. One complication you will face is that when you calculate how much stock you will need to sell to replenish the safe investment holdings, you will have to calculate how much in capital gains taxes you will have to pay on the sales and take this into account. For this, you will have to keep track of the tax basis of the stock holdings and use the approach we discussed earlier to calculate capital gains taxes that will be due on the sales.

You must do the calculations the same way every year until you run out of stocks to sell. At that point, you will have to start drawing money from the safe investments. Making this switch in Excel is difficult. You will see that you can use an Excel model without the switch to answer the two retirement planning questions posed in the problem, but it is much easier to do so using a similar model in VBA.

This is a somewhat complex model. You may want to use a template for the model that you can create by copying the model and then deleting all the formulas in it. Make sure you clearly understand what each column in the table represents.

Building the Model

1. **Set up the input variables:** Set up the input variables as shown and name the input cells as follows: C3 as FR, C4 as SR, C5 as TO, C6 as TC, C7 as InflR, C8 as IB, C9 as AD, and C10 as SH. Enter the input values as shown.

	A	B	C	D	E	F	G	H	I	J	K	L	M	N	O
1	**Planning for Retirement in Nominal Dollars**														
2															
3	Return on fixed income		6%												
4	Return on stocks		12%												
5	Tax rate (ordinary)		25%												
6	Tax rate (cap. gains)		15%												
7	Inflation rate		3%												
8	Initial balance		$1,300,000												
9	Initial annual withdrawal		$65,000												
10	Security horizon (years)		15												
11															
12															
13	Year	Total Bal.	FI Holding	After-tax	Stock Hold.	Annual	Int Income	Return on	Stock Hold.	FI Holding	Total Bal.	Tax basis	Basis	CG Tax	Check on
14		Year-beg.	Year-beg	Stock Sales	Year-beg	Withdrawal	After Tax	Stock	Year-end	Year-end	Year-end	of Stock	Used	Paid	Tax paid
15															
16	1	$1,300,000	$817,873		$417,127	$65,000	$36,804	$50,055	$467,182	$854,677	$1,321,860	417,127			
17	2	$1,320,966	$842,409	($54,682)	$411,607	$66,950	$37,908	$49,393	$461,000	$880,317	$1,341,318	367,507	49,621	$893	$893
18	3	$1,339,551	$867,681	($56,322)	$402,911	$68,959	$39,046	$48,349	$451,260	$906,727	$1,357,987	321,198	46,309	$1,767	$1,767
19	4	$1,355,366	$893,712	($58,012)	$390,627	$71,027	$40,217	$46,875	$437,502	$933,929	$1,371,431	278,040	43,158	$2,621	$2,621
20	5	$1,367,975	$920,523	($59,752)	$374,294	$73,158	$41,424	$44,915	$419,209	$961,947	$1,381,156	237,870	40,170	$3,456	$3,456
21	6	$1,376,885	$948,139	($61,545)	$353,394	$75,353	$42,666	$42,407	$395,801	$990,805	$1,386,606	200,525	37,345	$4,271	$4,271
22	7	$1,381,539	$976,583	($63,391)	$327,343	$77,613	$43,946	$39,281	$366,624	$1,020,529	$1,387,154	165,842	34,683	$5,066	$5,066
23	8	$1,381,310	$1,005,880	($65,293)	$295,488	$79,942	$45,265	$35,459	$330,946	$1,051,145	$1,382,091	133,664	32,179	$5,844	$5,844
24	9	$1,375,487	$1,036,057	($67,252)	$257,090	$82,340	$46,623	$30,851	$287,941	$1,082,679	$1,370,620	103,834	29,829	$6,604	$6,604
25	10	$1,363,272	$1,067,138	($69,269)	$211,323	$84,810	$48,021	$25,359	$236,682	$1,115,160	$1,351,842	76,205	27,629	$7,348	$7,348
26	11	$1,343,764	$1,099,153	($71,347)	$157,257	$87,355	$49,462	$18,871	$176,128	$1,148,615	$1,324,742	50,633	25,573	$8,078	$8,078
27	12	$1,315,948	$1,132,127	($73,488)	$93,846	$89,975	$50,946	$11,261	$105,107	$1,183,073	$1,288,180	26,978	23,654	$8,794	$8,794
28	13	$1,278,681	$1,166,091	($75,693)	$19,916	$92,674	$52,474	$2,390	$22,306	$1,218,565	$1,240,871	5,112	21,866	$9,499	$9,499
29	14	$1,230,678	$1,201,074	($77,963)	-$65,851	$95,455	$54,048	($7,902)	($73,753)	$1,255,122	$1,181,369	-15,091	20,203	$10,193	$10,193
30	15	$1,170,491	$1,237,106	($80,302)	-$164,933	$98,318	$55,670	($19,792)	($184,725)	$1,292,776	$1,108,050	-33,749	18,657	$10,879	$10,879
31	16	$1,096,493	$1,274,219	($82,711)	-$278,994	$101,268	$57,340	($33,479)	($312,473)	$1,331,559	$1,019,086	-50,971	17,222	$11,557	$11,557
32	17	$1,006,857	$1,312,446	($85,193)	-$409,895	$104,306	$59,060	($49,187)	($459,082)	$1,371,506	$912,423	-66,863	15,892	$12,230	$12,230
33	18	$899,525	$1,351,819	($87,748)	-$559,729	$107,435	$60,832	($67,167)	($626,897)	$1,412,651	$785,754	-81,521	14,659	$12,898	$12,898
34	19	$772,190	$1,392,374	($90,381)	-$730,842	$110,658	$62,657	($87,701)	($818,543)	$1,455,030	$636,488	-95,038	13,517	$13,564	$13,564
35	20	$622,259	$1,434,145	($93,092)	-$925,864	$113,978	$64,537	($111,104)	($1,036,968)	$1,498,681	$461,714	-107,499	12,461	$14,229	$14,229
36	21	$446,819	$1,477,169	($95,885)	-$1,147,747	$117,397	$66,473	($137,730)	($1,285,477)	$1,543,642	$258,165	-118,983	11,484	$14,894	$14,894
37	22	$242,604	$1,521,484	($98,762)	-$1,399,799	$120,919	$68,467	($167,976)	($1,567,775)	$1,589,951	$22,176	-129,565	10,582	$15,561	$15,561
38	23	$5,945	$1,567,129	($101,724)	-$1,685,731	$124,547	$70,521	($202,288)	($1,888,019)	$1,637,650	($250,369)	-139,313	9,748	$16,231	$16,231
39	24	($267,274)	$1,614,143	($104,776)	-$2,009,700	$128,283	$72,636	($241,164)	($2,250,864)	$1,686,779	($564,085)	-148,292	8,979	$16,905	$16,905

FIGURE 15.4 Model 4: Planning for retirement in nominal dollars.

2. **Set up the year-by-year analysis table:** Set up the headings for the year-by-year analysis table. Read the column headings carefully to clearly understand what will go into each column. If necessary, read the comments I have attached to some of the column headings.
3. **Calculate the total balance at the beginning of the year:** In the first year, the beginning balance is equal to the initial balance. In B16 enter the formula =IB. For all other years, it is equal to the sum of the fixed income balance, equity balance, and the money withdrawn. To calculate this, in B17 enter the formula =E17+C17+F17. Note that the total balance at the beginning of the year is less than the total balance at the end of the previous year because I am assuming that the capital gains taxes on the necessary stock sales are paid (or set aside) in the interim.
4. **Calculate required safe holding at the beginning of the year:** The fixed income holding at the beginning of each year will equal the amount necessary to cover the future withdrawals for a number of years equal to the security horizon minus one year. (The subtraction of one year is necessary because the specified security horizon is assumed to include the current year, but the withdrawal for the current year is being handled separately.) This is a growing annuity with a growth rate equal to the rate of inflation. Its rate of return is equal to the after-tax return on fixed income. To calculate this amount, in C16 enter the formula =PV((1+FR*(1-TO))/(1+InflR)-1,SH-1,-F16,0). (If the formula is not clear, review the section "Growing Annuities" in Chapter 14: Time Value of Money. Copy this formula down the column.
5. **Calculate the amount of stock to sell:** At the beginning of each year, you will have to sell enough stocks to bring up the level of investment in fixed income securities to the required level shown in column C. This will equal the required fixed income balance less the fixed income balance at the end of the previous year less the amount of withdrawal for the year. To do this calculation, in D17 enter the formula =J16-C17-F17. There will be no sales involved in the first year.
6. **Calculate the amount of stock holding at the beginning of the year:** In the first year, it is equal to the initial balance less the withdrawal and the allocation to fixed income investment. In E16 enter the formula =B16-C16-F16.

   In the subsequent years, this will equal the stock holdings at the end of the previous year less the (before-tax) amount of stock sold to build up the fixed income holdings to the required level. To do this calculation, in E17 enter the formula =I16+D17/(1-TC+TC*L16/I16). Here, the second part is the amount of stock you will have to sell to be left with the necessary after-tax amount shown in column D. This formula is based on the earlier discussions related to tax basis. (The sign is + because a sale in column D is shown as a negative number.)
7. **Calculate the annual withdrawal:** This will start at the specified amount and grow at the rate of inflation. In F16 enter the formula =AD and in F17,

the formula =AD*(1+InflR)^(A17-1). Copy the second formula down the column.

8. **Calculate the interest income after tax:** To calculate this, in G16 enter the formula =C16*FR*(1-TO) and copy it down the column.
9. **Calculate the return on the stock investment:** In H16 enter the formula =E16*SR to calculate the return on the stock part of the portfolio. Copy the formula down the column.
10. **Calculate the year-end stock holding:** This is equal to the year-beginning stock holding (after any stock sale) plus the return on stocks. In I16 enter the formula =E16+H16 and copy it down the column.
11. **Calculate the year-end fixed income holding:** This is equal to the fixed income holding at the beginning of the year plus the after-tax return on fixed income.
12. **Calculate the total year-end balance:** In K16 enter the formula =I16+J16.
13. **Calculate the tax basis for stocks:** To calculate the taxes you will have to pay when you sell any stock, you have to keep track of the tax basis of the stock holdings. We discussed this in an earlier section. In cell L16 enter the formula =E16 because the initial tax basis equals the amount of stocks bought at the beginning. To keep track of the remaining tax basis in the subsequent years, in cell L17 enter the formula =L16*E17/I16 and copy it down the column.
14. **Calculate the tax basis used in the current year:** In M17 enter the formula =L16-L17 and copy it down the column.
15. **Calculate the capital gains taxes paid:** In N17 enter the formula =(I16-E17-M17)*TC and copy it down the column.
16. **Check the capital gains taxes paid:** To double-check the capital gains tax calculations, calculate it a second way as the difference between the total balance at the end of a year and at the beginning of the next year. By design, the capital gains taxes are assumed to be paid between the points in time when these two calculations are made.

Testing the Model

You will have to check the model by doing hand calculations for the first year and in a few columns for the second year where the formulas are different from the first year. Beyond that the formulas are the same. You can also do some reasonableness tests. For example, if you reduce the rates of return, you should run out of money earlier. Similarly, reducing the tax rates should have predictable impacts.

Uses of the Model

For the input data used in the model, how long will the money last? It is not obvious. The year-beginning total balance first goes negative in the twenty-fourth year, but this does not mean that the money will last for 24 years. If you look closely, you will notice that the stock holding first goes negative in year 14, which really means that the model does not work (with this set of inputs) after year 13 because year 14 calls for selling more stock than is available at that point. In the row for year 13, however, the model has already provided for the necessary withdrawal for that year and has also set aside enough money for the next 14 years (security horizon of 15 years less one year). In addition, there is still some investment left in stocks at that point.

To do the analysis correctly, the model should sell off the remaining stock in the fourteenth year as well as any necessary amount of safe investments to cover the withdrawal for that year. Thereafter, it should start drawing down the money in safe investments. However, this is not easy to do in Excel, in part because the stock holdings will go negative in different years depending on the inputs.

In this case, the money will last 13 years (the year before the stock holdings go negative) plus 14 years (based on the safe investment holdings at that point) plus a fraction of a year. This fraction depends on the stock balance at the end of the thirteenth year.

Given any set of input data, the model can tell how long the money will last. (You may have to add more lines to the table.)

You can also use the model to estimate what size nest egg is needed to provide for a certain life expectancy. For example, if the life expectancy is 30 years, you will want the stock balance to remain positive through (30 – 14) = 16 years and go negative in the seventeenth year. You can find the necessary initial balance by changing the initial balance in steps until the stock balance goes negative in the seventeenth year.

We will see that in VBA you can create a model that will automatically switch to drawing down the safe investment once the investment in stocks is used up.

MODEL 5: PORTFOLIO STRUCTURING

The Problem

Create a model that an investor can use to structure a portfolio using the three-level approach discussed earlier. The user will input the total portfolio size as well as his allocations at the levels of asset class, categories within each asset class, and specific mutual funds within each category. The portfolio output should show the amount of money that will be invested in each mutual fund.

Modeling Strategy

The worksheet for this model is shown in Figure 15.5. The key to creating a useful model in this case is to structure a worksheet that will work well for both data input and data output. The worksheet shown is one possible approach.

	A	B	C	D	E
1	Portfolio Structuring				
2					
3		**Total portfolio value**			**$1,000,000**
4			**Allocations**		
5			By fund	By asset &	
6				category	
7					
8		**Asset allocation**			
9		Money market		**10%**	
10		Stocks		**60%**	
11		Bonds		**30%**	
12					
13					
14	**MK**	**Money market**		**10%**	
15	VUSXX	Vanguard Admiral Treasury Money Market	10%		$10,000
16	VMSXX	Vanguard Tax-Exempt Money Market	90%		$90,000
17					
18					
19		**Stocks**		**60%**	
20		**Domestic stocks**			
21	**LC**	**Large cap**		18%	
22	VFINX	Vanguard 500 Index, Investor shares	50%		$54,000
23	VTSMX	Vanguard Total Stock Market Index	50%		$54,000
24					
25	**LV**	**Large cap value**		28%	
26	VIVAX	Vanguard Value Index	100%		$168,000
27	PRFDX	T. Rowe Price Equity Income			$
28					
29	**SC**	**Small cap**		8%	
30	VEXMX	Vanguard Extended Market Index	40%		$19,200
31	NAESX	Vanguard Small-Cap Index	60%		$28,800
32					
33	**SV**	**Small cap value**		16%	
34	VISVX	Vanguard Small-Cap Value Index	100%		$96,000
35					
36	**RE**	**REIT**		10%	
37	VGSIX	Vanguard REIT Index	100%		$60,000
38					
39	**SO**	**Other special categories**		0%	
40					
41		**International stocks**			
42	**IT**	**International developed markets**		20%	
43	VDMIX	Vanguard Developed Markets Index	100%		$120,000
44	VPACX	Vanguard Pacific Stock Index			
45					
46	**IE**	**Emerging markets**		0%	
47	VEIEX	Vanguard Emerging Market Stock Index	100%		
48					
49		Check: Total % allocation to stock categories		100%	
50					
51		**Bonds**		**30%**	
52	**SB**	**Short term bonds**		70%	
53	VBISX	Vanguard Short-Term Bond Index	30%		$63,000
54	VFSTX	Vanguard Short-Term Corporate			
55	VFISX	Vanguard Short-Term Treasury	70%		$147,000
56					
57	**IB**	**Intermediate-term bonds**			
58	VFIIX	Vanguard GNMA			
59	VFIJX	Vanguard Intermediate Bond Index			
60					
61	**LB**	**Long-term bonds**			
62					
63	**TB**	**Total return bonds**		30%	
64	FBDFX	Fremont Bond	40%		$36,000
65	DODIX	Dodge & Cox Income	60%		$54,000
66					
67	**IB**	**Inflation-protected bonds**			
68	VIPSX	Vanguard Inflation-Protected Securities Fund			
69					
70	**JB**	**Junk bonds**			
71	**FB**	**Foreign bonds**			
72					
73		Check: Total % allocation to bond categories		100%	
74					
75		**Check: Total portfolio value**			$1,000,000
76					

FIGURE 15.5 Model 5: Portfolio structure based on allocations provided by user.

The user will enter the total portfolio size as well as the desired asset allocations near the top. Use three asset classes: money market, stocks, and bonds. Within each asset class, the worksheet provides for several asset categories. The user can add more categories within any asset class rather easily or delete some of the categories provided. Similarly, the user can add more individual securities within each category.

Instead of asking the user to show his allocation to each category as a percentage of the entire portfolio, have him enter the allocation as a percentage of the asset class to which it belongs. For example, if the user indicates that he wants 20% of his equity (stock) investments to go into large-cap value funds, then the allocation to each category within it will change as he changes his allocation to stocks (as it should). The allocations to all the categories within each asset class should add up to 100%. Similarly, allocations to individual funds within each category should be expressed as a percentage of the category and not the asset class. The allocations to funds in each category should add up to 100%. This structure of the model has the following advantage: any change in allocation at a higher level will cascade down to the lower levels.

The user will provide all of this input and will have the opportunity to ask "what if" questions by changing the allocations at any of the three levels. Create a column to show the actual dollar investment in each fund based on the allocations specified. Provide a sum of the investment in all the funds so that the user can make sure that there are no mistakes in the allocations.

The calculations are straightforward. The dollar allocation to a fund is the dollar size of the portfolio multiplied by the percent allocations to the fund's asset class, its category (except in the case of money market, which has no categories in it), and to the fund.

Building the Model

1. **Set up the input area:** Columns A through D comprise the input area for the model. Set this up as shown. Name the following cells: E3 as PortVal, D9 as MPrcnt, D10 as SPrcnt, and D11 as BPrcnt.

   At the asset class level, it may be better to let the user provide allocations for only two (here, money market and stocks) and have the model calculate the third (the formula in D11 is =1-MPrcnt-SPrcnt). It is useful to provide totals (in D49 and D73) of the percentage allocations to the various categories in stocks and bonds so that the user can easily see that the allocations for each asset class add up to 100%. The formula in D49 is =SUM(D21:D46) and in D73 is =SUM(D52:D71).
2. **Create column of dollar allocations to each fund:** For each fund in the money market asset class, calculate the dollar investment by multiplying the portfolio size by the allocation to money market and the allocation to the fund. To do

so, in E15 enter the formula =PortVal*MPrcnt*C15 and copy it into the other money market fund cells.

To calculate the dollar investment in each stock and bond fund, multiply the total portfolio value by the asset class allocation, then by the category allocation, and finally by the fund allocation. In E23 enter the formula =PortVal*SPrcnt*$D$21*C22 and create similar formulas for all stock and bond funds.

3. **Format fund dollar investment cells to suppress 0 values:** Custom format the dollar investment cells for all the funds with "$#,##0;;". This will make a cell appear blank if there is no allocation to a fund.
4. **Create a sum for the portfolio:** For verification purposes, in E75 enter the formula =SUM(E15:E71) to calculate a total for the portfolio.

Testing the Model

If the total portfolio value that the model calculates at the bottom matches the specified portfolio value, then you can be reasonably sure that the model is working properly. It is also easy to visually check the percentage and dollar allocations to the categories and funds.

Uses of the Model

This model is very useful for structuring different portfolios. One advantage of this design is that the user can add more funds in each category or even add more categories, although doing so requires some knowledge of Excel.

Limitation of the Model

One problem with this model is that the output will look cluttered, especially if there are many funds in each category and the user uses only a few of them. It is, of course, possible to manually hide the rows for the unused funds, but this creates additional work every time a new set of allocations is made. We will see that it is easy to create a model in VBA that can work with many funds and still automatically create a clearer output sheet that shows only the funds with investments in them.

CHAPTER 16

Analyzing Market History

In investing, we often want to measure and show the performance of various asset classes both over time and relative to each other and compare their risks. In this chapter, we develop a number of models to do such analysis and plot the results in a few different types of charts commonly used to display them.

Review of Theory and Concepts

INDEXES

The historical returns for various asset classes such as stocks and bonds are generally measured using indexes. For example, historical returns on stocks are most often measured using the S&P 500 index, which represents the average price of (approximately) the 500 largest U.S. stocks. An index represents the average for its components; we use it to talk about what happened to the components on average.

In the S&P 500 index, stocks are not weighted equally; rather, they are weighted by their market values. The effect is that a 10% change in the price of the stock of a larger company has a larger impact on the index vis-à-vis a 10% change in the price of the stock of a smaller company. Another way to visualize this is to think of the S&P 500 as the value of a portfolio of 500 stocks, in which the money is distributed among the different stocks in proportion to their market values and not equally.

Because the S&P 500 index is based on approximately the 500 largest stocks and is further weighted by the market values of the component stocks, it primarily represents the performance of the stocks of the very large companies. There are other indexes that measure the performance of other groups of stocks. For example, the Russell 2000 stock index, based on the smallest 2,000 of the largest

3,000 stocks, is widely used as the indicator of the performance of small stocks. The Dow Jones Wilshire 5000 stock index is based on the prices of all the stocks regularly traded in the U.S. stock market. These two indexes are also weighted for market value.

In using these indexes to measure the historical performance of stocks, you should keep in mind that they are based only on the prices of the component stocks and do not include the dividends paid by them. As we will see, we must calculate the total returns on these indexes by assuming reinvestment of the dividends before we can use them to analyze historical returns on stocks or compare return on stocks to other assets. Some historical data you look at may already be based on total returns and not just price. Before using any historical data you have to know what the data represent.

There are also many bond indexes used to represent performance of bonds. A key difference is that most bond indexes already represent total returns with interest reinvested.

MEASURING RETURNS

Total return is the measure used most often to calculate the historical performance of an asset. In analyzing and comparing performance, we use year-by-year total returns as well as cumulative and annualized total returns over different periods of time. It is also customary to look at and display total return over different periods of time to see how an initial $1 investment in an asset would have grown in value over the period.

Total Return

Suppose a stock is selling at $100 per share and does not pay any dividend. You bought one share of the stock for $100 and its price went up to $107 in a year. You earned a 7% annual return on your investment, and we call this a capital gain or capital appreciation. If the price goes up next year by another $10, then the return for the second year would be $10/$107 = 0.0935 or 9.35%, and the annualized return for the two-year period would be ($117/100)$^{0.5}$ − 1 = 0.0817 or 8.17%.

Now suppose the stock pays a quarterly dividend of $1 and you received 4 dividend payments during the first year. What return did you earn during the first year? You may say that it was 11%—$7 of capital gains plus $4 of dividend income divided by the $100 initial investment. This assumes that you simply held on to these dividends in cash and did not reinvest the money. Assume that someone else made the same investment but reinvested the dividends, earning 10% annual return on them. At the end of the first year, this individual ended up with more than $111 and earned a return higher than 11% for the year. These two different return numbers may be correct for the two slightly different situations, but as is now clear, the return depends on what assumption one makes about reinvesting the dividends. More generally, if an investment provides intermediate returns like dividends, the actual return an investor earns will depend on how she reinvests these intermediate returns.

It is useful to be able to provide a unique measure of return. For this, it is customary to define the total return on an investment as the return earned assuming that all intermediate returns received in cash are reinvested in the same asset on the day that those returns are received at the price of the asset at that time.

Using our example, assume that the price of the stock was \$103 on the day that the first dividend of \$1 was paid. We then assume that the \$1 was used to buy an additional \$1/\$103 or 0.00971 shares of the same stock. On the next dividend date, the amount of the dividend received was \$1.00971 and not \$1 because the dividend was received on 1.00971 shares, not 1 share. We assume that this dividend was reinvested in additional shares at the stock price at the time the second divided was paid. Suppose that by repeating the same calculation through the end of the year, we end up with 1.05 shares at the end of the year. Because the stock price at this point was \$107, the total value of the holdings would have been 1.05 × \$107 = \$112.35. We can then say that the total return on the stock for the first year (with dividend reinvested) was 12.35%.

This definition of total return on investment is used widely because it makes intuitive sense and provides the same answer no matter who is doing the calculation. Note that here we are also assuming that all of the dividends or other intermediate returns are available for reinvestment; none of it has to be paid in taxes. This may not be realistic in some situations (for example, if the investment is in a taxable account), but we make this simple assumption because then we do not have to deal with the different tax rates that different people face. In calculating total return, we also assume that we can buy the stock in fractional amounts. In real life, we cannot do this with individual stocks; however, we can do it with investments in mutual funds.

In calculating total returns for bonds, we assume that the intermediate interest coupons are reinvested at the interest rate available at the time those coupon payments are received.

Total Return versus IRR

There is another way we can calculate a unique return on an investment: we can calculate the internal rate of return (IRR) for the cash flows involved. For the first year of investment in the stock, this would involve an outflow of \$100 at the beginning followed by four dividend inflows and a (conceptual) inflow equal to the year-end price of the stock. This will produce a different return for the year because it implicitly assumes that the dividends are reinvested at the internal rate of return. However, the total return calculation is considered more realistic. It is almost universally used because we can actually reinvest the dividends in the stock, whereas there is no practical way of reinvesting them earning a return exactly equal to the IRR. It is likely that no one would be interested in doing that, either.

Real versus Nominal Returns

Most of the time we measure returns in nominal terms, that is, we ignore the effect of inflation. Such returns can be deceptive, however. If an asset provides a return of 5% during a period when inflation is 7%, then an investment in the asset will actually reduce our buying power. Because the objective of investment is to preserve and grow buying power, it is important to look at returns both in nominal and real (inflation-adjusted) terms.

The inflation adjustment is generally done using the consumer price index (CPI), which measures the changing average price of goods and services over time. Since it is an index, its value can be arbitrarily set equal to 100 at a particular point in time. If the average price then goes up by 3% over the next year, the index value will be 103 at the end of the year.

Measuring the CPI is a highly complex undertaking. The objective is to measure how the cost of living for the "average" consumer is changing. This means that we have to first decide what goods and services in what quantities the "average" consumer buys (called the basket of goods and services) and then survey their prices and recalculate the index value periodically. The Bureau of Labor Statistics (BLS) does all of this and publishes the CPI every month. People almost always use the CPI to convert nominal returns into real returns. However, it is important to recognize that, for many people, the actual change in price level they experience may be significantly different from the change in the CPI because they may be consuming a very different basket of goods and services.

The current series of CPI uses 1982 to 1984 as the base period, meaning that the index is set at 100 at the average price level for that period. This is, however, not particularly important to know. What you have to recognize is that the index measures the relative price change over time; CPI values of 176.7 for December 2001 and 180.9 for December 2002 tell us that during 2002, average prices went up by $(180.9 - 176.7)/176.7 = 2.38\%$. We can use the CPI both to inflate and deflate prices over time to constant dollars of any point in time, not just the 1982–1984 base period.

For example, assume that we made an investment of \$10,000 in December of 2001 and it grew to \$11,000 by December, 2002. This final value of the investment can then be converted to constant dollars of December 2001 either by using the formula $\$11{,}000 \times (176.7/180.9)$ or the formula $\$11{,}000/(1 + 0.0238)$. It is easy to see that these approaches are equivalent, both conceptually and mathematically.

There are also two equivalent ways to convert nominal returns to real returns. As we discussed in Chapter 14: Time Value of Money, if the nominal rate of return is r, the inflation rate is i, and the real rate of return is k, then we can calculate k from the equation:

$$1 + k = \left(\frac{1+r}{1+i}\right)$$

We can use this equation for single periods or for multiple periods (using annualized returns and inflation rates).

A second (and often safer) method is to express the initial and final values of an investment in dollars of the same point in time (for example, beginning of the period). One can then calculate the return from these values. Both methods will become clearer when we use them in models.

Cumulative and Annualized Returns

If the annual (or periodic) returns for an asset for years 1, 2, ... n are given by r_1, r_2, ... r_n, then we can calculate the return over the n periods, called the cumulative return, and the compounded average annual return, called the annualized return, over the n years as:

$$\text{Cumulative return} = (1+r_1)(1+r_2)\ldots(1+r_n) - 1$$
$$\text{Annualized return} = (1 + \text{Cumulative return})^{(n/1)} - 1$$

We can calculate the real cumulative and annualized returns by first converting the nominal annual returns into real annual returns (as discussed before) and then using them in these same equations. Alternately, we can first calculate the final value of an investment over the period in nominal dollars, convert it to constant dollars of the initial period, and then calculate cumulative and annualized returns using the initial and the final values.

Growth of $1

It is often easier to visualize the performance of an asset over time if we display how an initial investment in it of $1 would have grown over the years. The computation is simple. If the total return on an asset was 5% in year 1 and 7% in year 2, then an initial investment of $1 at the beginning of year 1 would have grown to $1 × 1.05 = $1.05 by the end of year 1 and to $1.05 × 1.07 = $1.1235 by the end of year 2.

If these are nominal total returns, then we have calculated the growth of an initial $1 investment in nominal terms. However, we should also look at the growth of the $1 investment in real terms. Assume that the CPI was 130 at the beginning of year 1 and 133 and 137, respectively, at the ends of years 1 and 2.

The real values of the investment (in dollars of the beginning of year 1) would then be $1.05 × 130/133 = $1.0263 at the end of year 1 and $1.1235 × 130/137 = $1.0661 at the end of year 2.

Rolling Period Returns

Sometimes we want to know how an asset performed over a particular length of time (10 years, for example). We can, of course, pick a specific 10-year period to look at, but that may not be representative because we cannot tell what period should be considered representative. So we often pick a length of period, like 10 years, and ask how investment in the asset performed in every possible ten-year window over the whole or part of a longer period for which we have data available. For example, if we have data for 1980–2000 and want to consider 10-year rolling periods, we would look at periods like 1980–1989, 1981–1990, and so on. This type of analysis is useful for individual assets as well as for comparing two or more assets because then we can make statements like "In 80% of the possible ten-year windows, stocks outperformed bonds." These are called rolling period returns. As we will see, such rolling period returns can reveal much about the historical risk and return of assets.

RISK

The two common measures of an asset's risk are its beta and its volatility (or standard deviation) of its returns. Beta measures the systematic risk of an asset, whereas standard deviation of its returns measures the total risk. Although beta is the measure of risk one should use in a portfolio context, the volatility or standard deviation measure is often easier to visualize. For example, if we say that stocks have historically provided an annualized return of 10% with a standard deviation of 20%, then we can infer that approximately 70% of the time the annual return on stocks was between −10% and 30%. When looking at historical returns on an asset, it is also meaningful to look at the maximum and minimum annual returns as a more intuitive (albeit less rigorous) measure of risk.

Modeling Examples

MODEL 1: CALCULATING TOTAL RETURNS

The Problem

Given the monthly price and dividend data for a large-cap stocks index for the period 1990–1995 and the corresponding CPI values, calculate the nominal and real cumulative and annualized returns over the period. Assume that the prices shown are per (notional) share at the beginning of the month, the dividends are paid monthly at the end of the month and are shown annualized (monthly values times 12), and the CPI values are for the beginning of the month. (Stocks generally pay quarterly dividends. However, since indexes comprise many stocks that pay dividends at different times, indexes are generally assumed to pay dividends on a monthly basis.)

Modeling Strategy

The spreadsheet for this model is shown in Figure 16.1. To calculate the total returns in nominal terms, use the definition of total return in the following steps: Start with an initial investment of $1,000 and calculate how many shares you will be able to buy with that money. At the end of the month, calculate the dividend you will receive on the shares you bought, and then calculate how many additional shares you will be able to buy at the stock price of the beginning of the next month using the dividend received. This will give you the number of shares you will own at the beginning of the next month, and then you can repeat the steps all the way to the end of the period.

	A	B	C	D	E	F	G	H	I
1	**Calculating Nominal and Real Total Returns**								
2									
3									
4								**Nominal**	**Real**
5						Final portfolio value		$2,155.15	$1,778.28
6						Cumulative return: 1990-95		115.52%	77.83%
7						Annualized return: 1990-95		13.65%	10.07%
8									
9									
10									
11		Large cap	Div/share	CPI		Shares held	Shares bought	Portfolio value	Portfolio value
12		Price	Annual				with dividend	Nominal $	Constant $
13		Mo-beg	Mo-end	Mo-beg		Mo-beg	Mo-end	Mo-beg	Mo-beg
14									
15	1990.01	339.97	11.14	127.4		2.9414	0.0083	$1,000.00	$1,000.00
16	1990.02	330.45	11.23	128.0		2.9497	0.0082	$974.73	$970.16
17	1990.03	338.46	11.32	128.7		2.9579	0.0083	$1,001.12	$991.00
18	1990.04	338.18	11.44	128.9		2.9661	0.0081	$1,003.08	$991.40
19	1990.05	350.25	11.55	129.2		2.9742	0.0079	$1,041.71	$1,027.19
82	1995.08	559.11	13.51	152.9		3.4744	0.0068	$1,942.57	$1,618.60
83	1995.09	578.77	13.58	153.2		3.4812	0.0068	$2,014.79	$1,675.48
84	1995.10	582.92	13.65	153.7		3.4879	0.0067	$2,033.17	$1,685.27
85	1995.11	595.53	13.72	153.6		3.4946	0.0065	$2,081.12	$1,726.14
86	1995.12	614.57	13.79	153.5		3.5011	0.0065	$2,151.66	$1,785.80
87	1996.01	614.42	13.89	154.4		3.5076		$2,155.15	$1,778.28
88									
89									
90									

FIGURE 16.1 Model 1: Comparing nominal and real total returns.

At the end of the period, calculate the market value of the stocks you end up with and calculate the cumulative return over the period using this final value of your investment and the initial investment of $1,000. Then calculate the annualized return, remembering that the cumulative return is for a period of 6 years. (Note that you could start with any initial investment. The $1,000 is an arbitrary initial investment I am using.)

To calculate the real return, convert the portfolio values at the end of each month to constant dollars of the beginning of 1990 using the CPI values. Use the final portfolio value in constant dollars to calculate the cumulative and annualized real returns for the 6-year period. (For the problem as specified, you do not have to calculate the constant dollar value of the portfolio for every month. You only need the constant dollar value at the end of the period, that is, at the beginning of 1996. However, if you want to calculate the year-by-year total returns as well, then you would need some of these intermediate values.)

Building the Model

The input data for this model is in A11:D87. Carefully read the labels for the column to understand the data.

1. **Enter the labels for output table:** You could set up the table somewhat differently as well. Make sure that the columns are labeled clearly, because keeping track of which numbers are for the beginning of the month and which are for the end of the month is critical.
2. **Enter the formulas for the first month:** Enter in H15 the initial investment amount of $1,000. Enter in F15 the formula =1000/B15 to calculate the initial number of shares purchased. To calculate the number of shares purchased with the dividend received at the end of the month, in G15 enter the formula =F15*C15/12/B16. Because the given dividend rate is annualized, you have to divide it by 12 and use the price for the beginning of the next month to calculate how many shares you will be able to buy with the dividend.

   Finally, to calculate the value of the portfolio at the beginning of the month in constant dollars of the beginning of 1990, in I15 enter the formula =H15*D$15/D15. To calculate the portfolio value at any time in constant dollars of the beginning of 1990, the first CPI value in this formula must always refer to the beginning of 1990. This is why you have to use the mixed reference in the first D$15: when you subsequently copy the formula into other cells in the same column, its row reference will not change.
3. **Enter the formulas for the second month:** To calculate the number of shares owned at the beginning of the second month, in F16 enter the formula =F15+G15. To calculate the value of the portfolio at the beginning of the month, in H16 enter the formula =F16*B16. In G16 and I16, copy the formulas from the rows above.

4. **Fill the rest of the table:** Fill up the rest of the table by copying and pasting the formulas from F16:I16. However, you will not need to calculate the number of shares you could buy at the end of the last month, so clear the cell G87.
5. **Set up table for cumulative and annualized returns:** Create the labels for the table for calculating the cumulative and annualized returns. (Since this is the more important table, it is better to put it in the more prominent spot, above the other one.)
6. **Calculate the cumulative and annualized total returns:** Copy the final nominal and constant dollar values of the portfolio into H5 and I5 by entering in them the formulas =H87 and =I87. To calculate the nominal cumulative total return, in H6 enter the formula =H5/H15-1, and to calculate the nominal annualized total return for the period, in H7 enter the formula =(H6+1)^(1/6)-1. The corresponding formulas for real returns are: =I5/I15-1 in I6 and =(I6+1)^(1/6)-1 in I7. These formulas give the real returns because they use the constant dollar final value of the portfolio.

Testing the Model

The best way to test the model is to verify the numbers in the first two rows using hand calculations. If these are right, then the rest of the table should be correct.

Uses of the Model

The model is useful for grasping the concept of total return with dividend reinvested, and it can be used for longer or shorter periods by extending or contracting the table. Note that individual stocks generally do not pay monthly dividends. However, the model can still be used for them. The difference is that the dividend numbers for certain months will be zeros.

Limitations of the Model

In practice, you may often have many years of data and want to calculate the total returns for various subperiods. This model can be adopted for that, but it can get cumbersome at times. As we will see, you can create a more flexible and easier-to-use model to do the same things using VBA.

MODEL 2: COMPARING RETURNS ON SEVERAL ASSETS

The Problem

Given the annual total return data for three indexes for small-cap stocks, large-cap stocks, and bonds for the period 1982 to 2002, show in a chart how a $1 investment in each asset class at the beginning of 1982 would have grown over the years through the end of 2002. Plot the results in a chart. Also calculate the compounded average annual return for each asset class over this period.

Modeling Strategy

The worksheet for this model is shown in Figure 16.2. Start with an investment of $1 in each asset at the beginning of 1982. The value of the investment in an asset at the beginning of each subsequent year will equal the value at the beginning of the previous year plus the total return earned during the previous year. This is the same as the value at the beginning of the previous year multiplied by 1 plus the total return for the previous year. Calculate the annualized return for the period using the ending value of each $1 investment and 21 as the number of years.

Building the Model

The data for this model is shown in the table in A27:D50 of the worksheet.

1. **Enter the labels for output table:** Enter the appropriate labels for the table in G27:I28. To avoid any possible confusion, indicate in the label that the values in the table are for the beginning of the years.
2. **Enter formulas to calculate the values of the investments for each year:** Start by entering $1 in G30:I30. To calculate the investment value at the beginning of 1983 for small-cap stocks, in G31 enter the formula =G30*(1+B30). Now copy the formula into H31 and I31 and then copy G31:I31 into all the rows down to row number 51. Even though your data ends in 2002, your table needs to extend to 2003 because that row represents the values of the investment for the beginning of 2003 (equivalent to the end of 2002).
3. **Calculate the average annual returns:** To calculate the average annual return for the small-cap index, in G24 enter the formula =(G51/G30)^(1/21)-1. Note that the period 1982–2002 covers 21 years, not 20. Copy the formula into H24 and I24.
4. **Create chart:** Create an XY chart with the yearly values for the three assets along the Y-axis and the years along the X-axis. Appropriately format and label the chart.

Testing the Model

Check the computed values for 1983 using hand calculations. Because you just copied the same formulas in the other rows, if these values are correct then the rest of the table and the chart should also be correct.

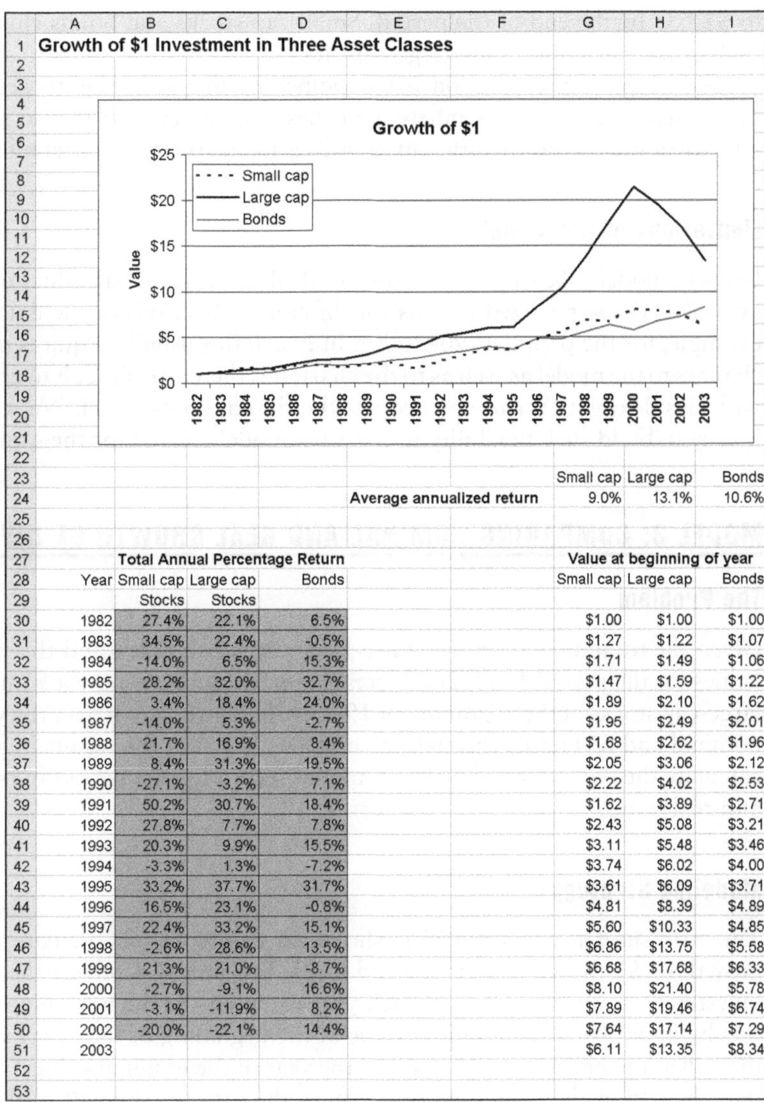

	Small cap	Large cap	Bonds
Average annualized return	9.0%	13.1%	10.6%

	Total Annual Percentage Return			Value at beginning of year		
Year	Small cap Stocks	Large cap Stocks	Bonds	Small cap	Large cap	Bonds
1982	27.4%	22.1%	6.5%	$1.00	$1.00	$1.00
1983	34.5%	22.4%	-0.5%	$1.27	$1.22	$1.07
1984	-14.0%	6.5%	15.3%	$1.71	$1.49	$1.06
1985	28.2%	32.0%	32.7%	$1.47	$1.59	$1.22
1986	3.4%	18.4%	24.0%	$1.89	$2.10	$1.62
1987	-14.0%	5.3%	-2.7%	$1.95	$2.49	$2.01
1988	21.7%	16.9%	8.4%	$1.68	$2.62	$1.96
1989	8.4%	31.3%	19.5%	$2.05	$3.06	$2.12
1990	-27.1%	-3.2%	7.1%	$2.22	$4.02	$2.53
1991	50.2%	30.7%	18.4%	$1.62	$3.89	$2.71
1992	27.8%	7.7%	7.8%	$2.43	$5.08	$3.21
1993	20.3%	9.9%	15.5%	$3.11	$5.48	$3.46
1994	-3.3%	1.3%	-7.2%	$3.74	$6.02	$4.00
1995	33.2%	37.7%	31.7%	$3.61	$6.09	$3.71
1996	16.5%	23.1%	-0.8%	$4.81	$8.39	$4.89
1997	22.4%	33.2%	15.1%	$5.60	$10.33	$4.85
1998	-2.6%	28.6%	13.5%	$6.86	$13.75	$5.58
1999	21.3%	21.0%	-8.7%	$6.68	$17.68	$6.33
2000	-2.7%	-9.1%	16.6%	$8.10	$21.40	$5.78
2001	-3.1%	-11.9%	8.2%	$7.89	$19.46	$6.74
2002	-20.0%	-22.1%	14.4%	$7.64	$17.14	$7.29
2003				$6.11	$13.35	$8.34

FIGURE 16.2 Model 2: Growth of $1 investment in three asset classes.

Uses of the Model

As you can see both from the table and the chart, this type of analysis provides a very compelling comparison of the behavior of the different asset classes over time. For example, it is clear that despite all the ups and downs in the individual years, large-cap stocks provide an excellent return over the period: a $1 investment grew to $13.35 by the end of the period. Small-cap stocks and bonds closely matched each other, but both trailed large-cap stocks.

This type of presentation is so compelling that it is easy to get misled and fail to recognize the risks inherent in these investments. It is also important to remember that choosing different periods is likely to lead to different conclusions.

Limitations of the Model

Users of models like this often want to calculate the terminal values of investment as well as the annualized returns for different subperiods of the data period (for example, for the period 1990–2000). In Excel, this usually requires making some changes to the model as well as to the chart. It is therefore difficult to create a model with this flexibility for use by people who do not know Excel. We will see that it is easy to build such flexibility into a VBA model created for the same analysis.

MODEL 3: COMPARING NOMINAL AND REAL GROWTH OF INVESTMENT

The Problem

Given the total annual returns for a large-cap stock index and the year-end CPI values for the period 1982–2002, create a model to show how a $1 investment in large-cap stocks at the beginning of 1982 would have grown over the years in both nominal and real terms through the end of 2002. Plot the results in a chart. Also calculate the compounded average annual return for the period in both nominal and real terms.

Modeling Strategy

The worksheet for this model is shown in Figure 16.3. Calculate the nominal growth of $1 the same way you did in the last model. Convert the value of the investment at the beginning of each year to dollars of the beginning of 1982; do this by multiplying the nominal value at the beginning of the year by the ratio of the CPI at the beginning of 1982 and the year of the nominal value. (This assumes that the CPI at the beginning of a year is the same as the CPI at the end of the previous year.)

Building the Model

The data for this model is shown in the table in A28:C51 of the worksheet.

1. **Enter the labels for output table:** Enter the appropriate labels for the table. To avoid any possible confusion, make sure that you indicate that the values in the table are for the beginning of the years.

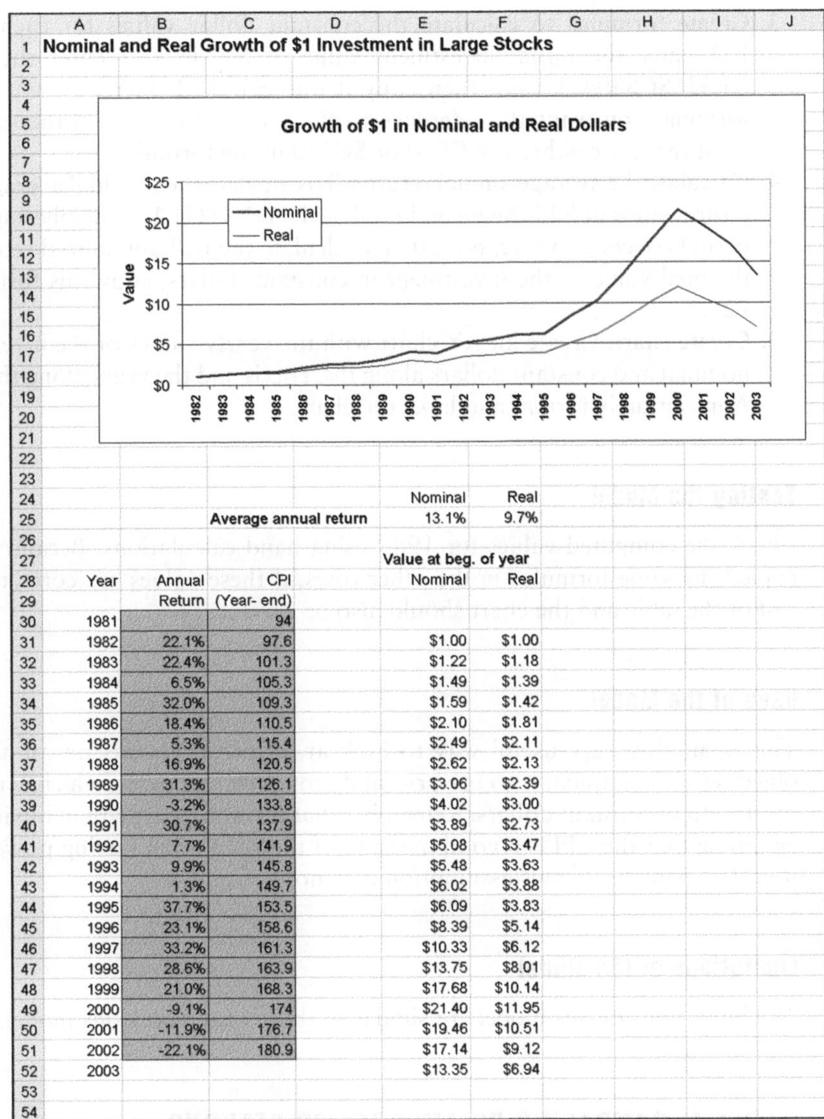

	Nominal	Real
Average annual return	13.1%	9.7%

Year	Annual Return	CPI (Year- end)	Value at beg. of year Nominal	Value at beg. of year Real
1981		94		
1982	22.1%	97.6	$1.00	$1.00
1983	22.4%	101.3	$1.22	$1.18
1984	6.5%	105.3	$1.49	$1.39
1985	32.0%	109.3	$1.59	$1.42
1986	18.4%	110.5	$2.10	$1.81
1987	5.3%	115.4	$2.49	$2.11
1988	16.9%	120.5	$2.62	$2.13
1989	31.3%	126.1	$3.06	$2.39
1990	-3.2%	133.8	$4.02	$3.00
1991	30.7%	137.9	$3.89	$2.73
1992	7.7%	141.9	$5.08	$3.47
1993	9.9%	145.8	$5.48	$3.63
1994	1.3%	149.7	$6.02	$3.88
1995	37.7%	153.5	$6.09	$3.83
1996	23.1%	158.6	$8.39	$5.14
1997	33.2%	161.3	$10.33	$6.12
1998	28.6%	163.9	$13.75	$8.01
1999	21.0%	168.3	$17.68	$10.14
2000	-9.1%	174	$21.40	$11.95
2001	-11.9%	176.7	$19.46	$10.51
2002	-22.1%	180.9	$17.14	$9.12
2003			$13.35	$6.94

FIGURE 16.3 Model 3: Nominal and real growth of $1 investment in stocks.

2. **Enter formulas to calculate the nominal values of the investment for each year:** Start by entering $1 in E31. To calculate the investment value at the beginning of 1983, in E32 enter the formula =E31*(1+B31). Copy the formula into E33:E52. Even though the data ends in 2002, the table needs to extend to 2003 because that row represents the value of the investment for the beginning of 2003 (equivalent to the end of 2002).

3. **Create formulas to calculate the constant dollar values for each year:** In F31 enter the initial investment value of $1. In F32 enter the formula =E32*$C$30/C31 and then copy it into F33:F52. Here, as you copy the formula, you want the reference to the cell C30 to remain the same. You must therefore either use C$30 or $C$30 in the formula.
4. **Calculate the average annual returns:** To calculate the nominal average annual return, enter in E25 the formula =(E52/E31)^(1/21)-1, remembering that the period covers 21 years, not 20. To calculate the real annualized return using the final value of the investment in constant dollars, copy this formula into F25.
5. **Create chart:** Create an XY chart with the yearly values of the investment in nominal and constant dollars along the Y-axis and the years along the X-axis. Appropriately format and label the chart.

Testing the Model

Check the computed values for 1983 using hand calculations. Because you just copied the same formulas in the other rows, if these values are correct then the rest of the table and the chart should also be correct.

Uses of the Model

This is another very useful way to look at historical returns on an asset. The objective of investment is to preserve and grow buying power, which is measured by growth in constant dollars. Remember that this shows growth in buying power assuming that the CPI is a good measure of the changes in buying power for the user; for many users, this assumption may not be valid.

Limitations of the Model

The limitations of this model are similar to those of the previous model.

MODEL 4: COMPARING ROLLING PERIOD RETURNS

The Problem

Given the total annual returns for large-cap stocks and the year-end CPI values for the period 1946–2002, create a model to calculate the cumulative nominal and real returns for all possible rolling 15-year windows (periods) starting at the beginning of each year. Plot the results in a bar chart to provide a visual comparison of nominal and real returns. Also calculate the nominal and real compounded average annual returns for the rolling 15-year periods and plot them in a separate chart.

Calculate the maximum, minimum, mean, and median values as well as the standard deviation for each type of return to provide measures of risk.

Modeling Strategy

The outputs of this model are shown in Figures 16.4, 16.5, and 16.6. Start by adding 1 to the returns for each year. Then use the formula discussed earlier to calculate the cumulative nominal return for the first 15-year window (starting on the first year), using the data for the first 15 years. To multiply the 1 plus return numbers for the 15 years, use Excel's PRODUCT function. Use the same method to calculate the cumulative return for each subsequent 15-year window.

To calculate the real cumulative returns, remember that when you multiply 1 + the annual return numbers for the 15 years, you actually get the final value of an initial $1 investment. You can therefore express the final value in constant dollars of the beginning of the period using the values of the CPI for the beginning of the period and the end of the period. Then use it (remembering that the implicit initial investment is $1) to calculate the real cumulative return for the 15-year window. Use the same method for all the other 15-year windows.

Calculate the nominal and real annualized returns for each window from the corresponding cumulative returns using the formulas discussed earlier.

Use Excel's MAX, MIN, AVERAGE, MEDIAN, and STDEV functions to calculate the maximum value and so on for each type of rolling 15-year return over the data period. Note that I am recommending using the STDEV instead of the STDEVP function to calculate the standard deviation, because these 15-year returns can be considered to be a sample from all possible 15-year returns. We want to estimate the standard deviation for the population and not the sample. If we want to calculate the standard deviation of the sample, we would use the STDEVP function.

Building the Model

The input data for this model is shown in A10:C70 of the worksheet.

1. **Enter the labels for output table:** Enter the appropriate labels for the tables for cumulative and annualized returns.
2. **Calculate cumulative returns:** To calculate 1 + return for the first year, in E14 enter the formula =B14+1. Copy it into E15:E70 to calculate the same for all the other years. To calculate the nominal cumulative return for the first 15 years, in F14 enter the formula =PRODUCT($E14:$E28)-1. The PRODUCT function multiplies the 1+ return values for the first 15 years. Copy this formula into F15:F56 to calculate the cumulative returns for the

	A	B	C	D	E	F	G	H	I	J
1	**Rolling Period Nominal and Real Returns**									
2										
3						**15 year**			**15 year**	
4						**Cumulative return**			**Annualized return**	
5					Max	1245.6%	741.9%		18.9%	15.3%
6					Min	89.0%	-8.0%		4.3%	-0.6%
7					Mean	519.4%	262.5%		12.0%	7.4%
8					Median	506.4%	225.3%		12.8%	8.2%
9					Std. Dev.	312.7%	228.5%		4.1%	5.1%
10		**Data**								
11		Large cap	CPI			**Window returns**			**Window returns**	
12		Stocks	Year-end		(1+Ret)	Nominal	Real		Nominal	Real
13	1945		18.2							
14	1946	-9.3%	21.5		0.91	599.9%	327.4%		13.9%	10.2%
15	1947	4.9%	23.4		1.05	884.4%	605.5%		16.5%	13.9%
16	1948	5.3%	24.1		1.05	756.1%	558.9%		15.4%	13.4%
17	1949	18.2%	23.6		1.18	897.1%	677.6%		16.6%	14.7%
18	1950	32.7%	25.0		1.33	883.8%	644.2%		16.5%	14.3%
19	1951	23.5%	26.5		1.23	734.2%	555.8%		15.2%	13.4%
20	1952	18.9%	26.7		1.19	506.4%	388.4%		12.8%	11.2%
21	1953	-1.7%	26.9		0.98	532.9%	398.5%		13.1%	11.3%
22	1954	52.6%	26.7		1.53	614.9%	441.7%		14.0%	11.9%
23	1955	31.4%	26.8		1.31	329.6%	204.3%		10.2%	7.7%
24	1956	6.5%	27.6		1.06	240.3%	129.1%		8.5%	5.7%
25	1957	-11.1%	28.4		0.89	264.9%	145.1%		9.0%	6.2%
26	1958	43.8%	28.9		1.44	389.3%	227.0%		11.2%	8.2%
27	1959	13.0%	29.4		1.13	190.1%	81.5%		7.4%	4.1%
28	1960	0.2%	29.8		1.00	89.0%	7.1%		4.3%	0.5%
29	1961	27.6%	30.0		1.28	159.0%	39.1%		6.5%	2.2%
30	1962	-8.8%	30.4		0.91	151.6%	29.7%		6.3%	1.7%
31	1963	22.6%	30.9		1.23	155.8%	25.2%		6.5%	1.5%
32	1964	16.7%	31.2		1.17	122.2%	1.4%		5.5%	0.1%
33	1965	12.5%	31.8		1.13	126.1%	-8.0%		5.6%	-0.6%
34	1966	-10.3%	32.9		0.90	166.3%	-1.9%		6.7%	-0.1%
35	1967	24.1%	33.9		1.24	182.0%	-1.3%		7.2%	-0.1%
36	1968	11.0%	35.5		1.11	177.4%	-3.7%		7.0%	-0.2%
37	1969	-8.3%	37.7		0.92	205.8%	7.2%		7.7%	0.5%
38	1970	4.1%	39.8		1.04	255.1%	27.1%		8.8%	1.6%
39	1971	14.2%	41.1		1.14	350.3%	64.0%		10.6%	3.4%
40	1972	19.1%	42.5		1.19	367.0%	73.7%		10.8%	3.7%
41	1973	-14.8%	46.2		0.85	312.9%	52.1%		9.9%	2.8%
42	1974	-26.4%	51.9		0.74	466.0%	117.0%		12.2%	5.3%
43	1975	37.3%	55.5		1.37	910.0%	315.7%		16.7%	10.0%
44	1976	24.0%	58.2		1.24	612.3%	195.4%		14.0%	7.5%
45	1977	-7.3%	62.1		0.93	650.6%	216.8%		14.4%	8.0%
46	1978	6.5%	67.7		1.07	771.8%	281.5%		15.5%	9.3%
47	1979	18.8%	76.7		1.19	799.4%	317.6%		15.8%	10.0%
48	1980	32.5%	86.3		1.32	667.0%	293.0%		14.5%	9.6%
49	1981	-5.0%	94.0		0.95	697.3%	348.3%		14.8%	10.5%
50	1982	22.1%	97.6		1.22	932.7%	512.0%		16.8%	12.8%
51	1983	22.4%	101.3		1.22	1026.4%	581.6%		17.5%	13.6%
52	1984	6.5%	105.3		1.06	1083.5%	631.5%		17.9%	14.2%
53	1985	32.0%	109.3		1.32	1245.6%	741.9%		18.9%	15.3%
54	1986	18.4%	110.5		1.18	826.7%	482.1%		16.0%	12.5%
55	1987	5.3%	115.4		1.05	589.5%	331.2%		13.7%	10.2%
56	1988	16.9%	120.5		1.17	409.9%	225.3%		11.5%	8.2%
57	1989	31.3%	126.1		1.31					
58	1990	-3.2%	133.8		0.97					
59	1991	30.7%	137.9		1.31					
60	1992	7.7%	141.9		1.08					
61	1993	9.9%	145.8		1.10					
62	1994	1.3%	149.7		1.01					
63	1995	37.7%	153.5		1.38					
64	1996	23.1%	158.6		1.23					
65	1997	33.2%	161.3		1.33					
66	1998	28.6%	163.9		1.29					
67	1999	21.0%	168.3		1.21					
68	2000	-9.1%	174.0		0.91					
69	2001	-11.9%	176.7		0.88					
70	2002	-22.1%	180.9		0.78					
71										
72										

FIGURE 16.4 Model 4: 15 year rolling period nominal and real returns.

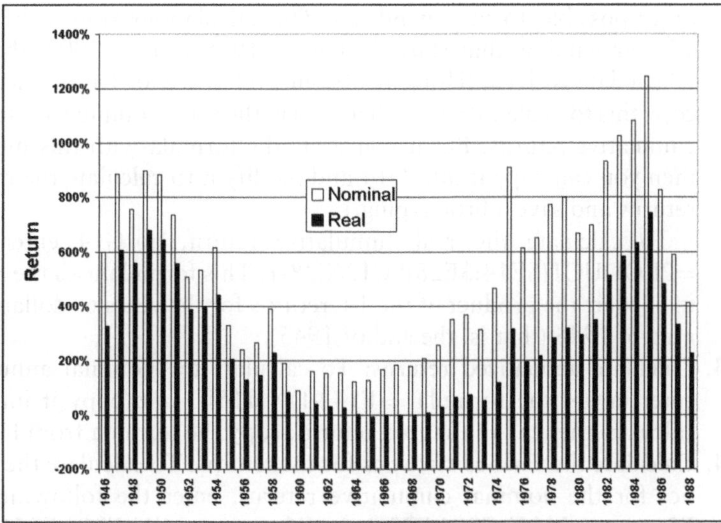

FIGURE 16.5 Model 4: 15 year rolling period nominal and real cumulative returns.

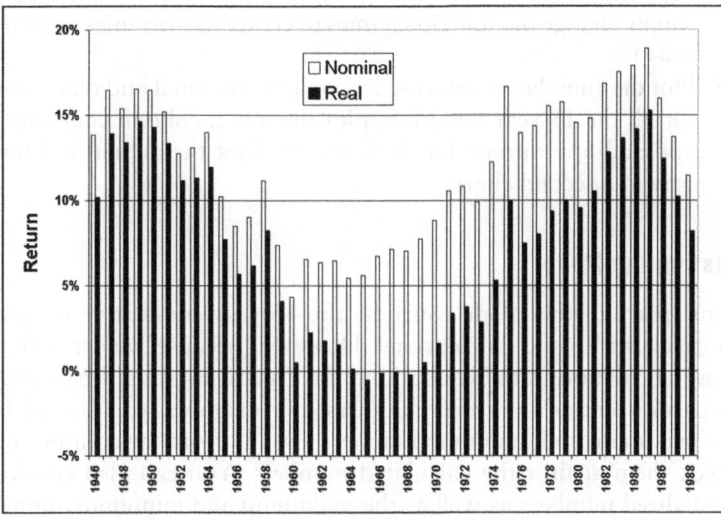

FIGURE 16.6 Model 4: 15 year rolling period nominal and real annualized returns.

other possible 15-year windows. The calculations stop in F56 because the 15-year window that starts in F56 or 1988 ends in 2002, the last year for which data is given. (Using an absolute reference for E is not necessary here to copy this formula into the other cells in the same column to calculate nominal cumulative returns. But if you write the formula with this mixed reference, then you can copy it into G14 and modify it to calculate the real cumulative returns and save a little typing.)

To calculate the real cumulative return, in G14 enter the formula =PRODUCT($E14:$E28)*C13/C28-1. This formula uses the ratio C13/C28 to convert the product of the 1+ returns for the years to dollars of the beginning of 1946 (that is, the end of 1945).

3. **Calculate annualized returns:** To calculate the nominal annualized return, enter in I14 the formula =(F14+1)^(1/15)-1 and copy it into I15:I56. To calculate the real annualized returns, copy the formula from I14 to J14:J56.
4. **Calculate the various statistics for the returns:** To calculate the various statistics for the nominal cumulative returns, enter the following formulas: in F5 enter =MAX(F$14:F$56), in F6 enter =MIN(F$14:F$56), in F7 enter =AVERAGE(F$14:F$56), in F8 enter =MEDIAN(F$14:F$56), and in F9 enter =STDEV(F14:F56). To duplicate these formulas for the other returns, copy F5:F9 into G5:G9, I5:I9, and J5:J9. (Here again, it is not essential to use the absolute references in the formulas. I used them because then I can copy the formula in the maximum cell into the minimum and other cells and simply change the function names to create the formulas appropriate for those cells.)
5. **Plot the cumulative returns:** To compare nominal and real cumulative returns for all the 15-year windows, plot them in a column chart, format the chart, and add appropriate labels as shown. Plot the annualized returns the same way in a second chart.

Testing the Model

Some parts of this model, such as the 15-year cumulative returns, are difficult to check with hand calculations. However, because we are using functions for most calculations, double-checking the arguments should be sufficient. It is easy to check some of the other numbers. For example, you should be able to find the maximum and minimum numbers visually from the columns of numbers and check them against the calculated numbers. You can also check the individual annualized numbers as well as the maximum and minimum annualized numbers against the cumulative numbers with hand calculations. The mean and median values should be close to each other though not the same. Similarly, the annualized mean, median, and standard deviation numbers you can calculate by hand from the corresponding cumulative numbers. They should be close to the numbers from the model; they will not be the same, however.

Uses of the Model

A model like this, but especially the charts, are very useful to get a feeling for the level of return one may expect from the stock market for long-term investments. The statistics also give useful information. For example, we can see that over a 15-year investment horizon, stocks historically provided nominal annualized returns of 12% per year with a standard deviation of 4.1%. The maximum was 18.9% and the minimum was 4.3%.

You can also modify the model to do calculations for other window lengths to see how the standard deviation goes up, that is, how much the risk increases for shorter investment horizons. However, one of the limitations of this model is that you cannot do the calculations for other rolling periods by changing just one input number; you have to change the formulas. We will see later that you can create similar models in VBA where the user can easily change the window length as well as the period of data (for example, 1980 to 2000) to use in the analysis.

CHAPTER 17

Bond Pricing and Duration

Bonds are key instruments used by corporations, governments, and various other entities for financing, and the bond market is a major part of our capital market. Bonds come in bewildering varieties, but they can be distinguished from one another and priced on the basis of a few characteristics. Because the bond market is so huge and bonds are used in one form or another by most players in the financial markets—from individuals to institutions—how bonds are priced and how the price should vary as interest rate and other factors change is of great interest.

In this chapter we will develop a few basic models to understand bonds and their characteristics. Excel has a number of built-in functions for valuing bonds and studying their characteristics, some of which are similar to the models we will develop. It is likely that in the future you will use these functions more often for bond analysis. Nonetheless, you will develop a much better understanding of bonds by working through these models. In addition, they will enhance your understanding of the concept of time value of money and help you improve your modeling skills.

Review of Theory and Concepts

A bond is a contract or instrument under which the issuer borrows money from lenders and agrees to make one or more payments of interest and principal on specific dates to the holder of the bond. The issuers of bonds range from the U.S. Treasury to corporations, municipalities, and others.

KEY CHARACTERISTICS OF BONDS

Although all bonds have certain common characteristics, these may differ because of different contractual provisions. Following are the primary characteristics of a bond that determine its price, both initially and over time.

Par Value

Par value is the stated value of the bond. Most bonds are originally issued at or close to the par value, and bonds promise to repay the par amount. For most bonds, the par value is $1,000. Some bonds have par values that are some multiple of $1,000, but irrespective of this, bond analysis is almost always done on the basis of $1,000 par value and bonds are generally quoted as a percentage of par value.

Coupon Interest Rate

Most bonds promise to pay periodically (typically every six months) a fixed number of dollars of interest called the coupon payment. When coupon payment is expressed as a percentage of the bond's par value and annualized by multiplying by the number of periods per year (for example, a semiannual payment would be multiplied by 2), it is called the bond's coupon interest rate or coupon rate. Note that the coupon rate, which is an annualized number, does not reflect any compounding. A bond with an 8% coupon rate and semiannual payment will therefore actually provide an effective interest rate somewhat higher than 8%.

Some bonds pay a variable or floating interest rate over the years. Another special type of bond, called zero-coupon bonds pay no interest or coupons over the years. They are initially sold below—generally well below—par value, and when the par amount is paid at maturity it constitutes the return of the capital as well as payment of all the interest accumulated over the intervening years.

Maturity Date

Bonds generally have a specified maturity date on which the par value must be repaid. Because this date remains fixed, the remaining life of the bond decreases over time. In most bond analysis, we use remaining life rather than original maturity because it is the remaining maturity of a bond that matters.

Call Provision

Most corporate bonds have a call provision that gives the issuer the right to call or redeem the bonds after a few years. For example, the issuer may have the right to call an issue of bonds at any time after five years at par value. Alternately, there may be a declining schedule of redemption price such that the issuer pays 105% of par value to call during the sixth year, 104% to call in the seventh year, and so forth. Calls provide the issuers a degree of protection against interest rate risk: if interest rates go down sufficiently, they can call and replace the bonds with new ones or other forms of debt at a lower rate. A compensation for this protection is built into the interest rate on a bond.

Credit Risk

Credit risk is another important characteristic of a bond, but it cannot be quantified precisely like the other characteristics. It is reflected in bond analysis in the required return on a bond. We will discuss it more later.

BOND VALUATION

Like all other financial assets, the value of a bond is the present value of its expected future cash flows discounted at a rate appropriate for its risk—that is, the risk of those cash flows. A typical bond that promises to pay a fixed coupon rate of $C/2$ every six months and repay the par amount FV at maturity represents an annuity plus one additional payment at maturity and can be valued as such. The current price P of such a bond is:

$$P = \sum_{t=1}^{t=n} \frac{C/2}{(1 + r/2)^t} + \frac{FV}{(1 + r/2)^n}$$

Here, $r/2$ is the appropriate semiannual discount rate and n is the remaining life of the bond measured in the unit of the coupon payment period (six months).

This is the bond valuation equation. All the values on the right-hand side except the discount rate are known, and the discount rate can be estimated by looking at comparable bonds. With these values we can use the PV annuity function to calculate the price of a bond.

The System of Five Bond Variables

From the bond valuation equation we can see that the five key bond variables—price, par value, coupon rate, remaining life, and discount rate—are tied together, and any four of them determine the fifth. We can also see how these variables affect one another. For example, the price of a bond will go down if the discount rate goes up and vice versa (if the other variables remain constant). We will explore these relationships when we build models using this equation.

EAR versus APR

In bond analysis, it is important to keep in mind the distinction between the effective annual rate (EAR) and the annual percentage rate (APR). The annual percentage rate is the periodic discount rate multiplied by the frequency of coupon payments per year. In the bond valuation equation as written, the coupon is paid semiannually and by using a semiannual discount rate of $r/2$, we have implicitly assumed that the appropriate annualized discount rate, expressed as APR, is r.

If we were told that the appropriate annualized discount rate expressed as EAR is r, then we would have used a semiannual discount rate k calculated as:

$$(1+k)^2 = (1+r) \quad \text{or} \quad k = (1+r)^{0.5} - 1$$

Unless otherwise indicated, the APR convention should be assumed in bond analysis because it is used more often.

Current Yield

The current yield of a bond is its annualized coupon rate, that is, the periodic coupon rate multiplied by the frequency of payment per year divided by the current price of the bond.

Yield to Maturity

If a bond is selling at a price other than par, then its current yield does not fully reflect the actual return a buyer will earn by buying the bond at the current price and holding it until maturity. For example, if a bond is currently selling at $950, then in addition to collecting the coupons over the years, the buyer will also realize a capital gain of $50 at maturity. This will make the overall return a little higher than the current yield.

This is captured in the yield to maturity (YTM) measure. The yield to maturity is the discount rate that makes the discounted value of the expected future cash flows of a bond equal to its current price. It is the interest rate that the buyer will actually earn if the bond is held to maturity and there is no default.

To calculate the YTM, we substitute all the other values in the bond valuation equation and by trial and error determine the discount rate at which the two sides of the equation become equal. This analysis will give us a semiannual interest rate for a bond that pays a semiannual coupon. Under the APR convention, we would double it to get the annualized YTM.

The YTM is used the other way around as well. To determine the appropriate price of a bond, we can estimate what its YTM should be by looking at the YTMs for comparable bonds. We can then use our estimate of the right YTM for the bond to calculate its price from the bond valuation equation.

Yield to Call

If a bond has call provisions, we can also calculate a yield to call (YTC) the same way we calculate yield to maturity. We simply use the bond valuation equation and assume that the bond will get called at the call price once it becomes callable. If a bond is selling above the call price, then YTC rather than YTM may be a more realistic measure of what return a buyer is likely to earn by holding the bond.

RISKS OF BOND INVESTING

Bond investors assume three types of risk: interest rate risk, reinvestment risk, and credit risk. These are important for understanding bonds as well as for investing in them.

Interest Rate Risk

Interest rate risk is the risk that a bond's price will fall if interest rates rise. (The reverse is also true.) We do not know when interest rates will go up or down; it is therefore important to know how much risk we are taking before investing in a bond, that is, how much the price of a bond will change in response to fluctuations in interest rates. As we will soon see, we use a bond's modified duration as a measure of its interest rate risk.

Reinvestment Risk

What we do with the coupon payments we receive from a bond affects what actual return we earn on our initial investment in a bond over the years. In calculating yield to maturity, we implicitly assume that we will be able to reinvest all the coupons earning returns equal to the yield to maturity. If interest rates go down over time, this may not be possible, and if we have to reinvest the coupons at lower rates then we will earn a lower return over time. This uncertainty is called a bond's reinvestment risk.

Zero-coupon bonds do not have any reinvestment risk because they do not pay any coupons that have to be reinvested. So, if held to maturity, zero-coupon bonds provide a return exactly equal to their YTM at the time of purchase. However, if they are sold before maturity then the return realized may be higher or lower than the YTM at the time of purchase (depending on the price received).

Credit Risk

Credit risk is the risk that because of financial problems of the issuer, part or all of the interest or principal due on a bond may not be received. Bonds issued by the U.S. Treasury have no credit risk because the U.S. Government can always make payments by printing more money. The required return or discount rate on U.S. Treasury bonds is thus always the lowest of any bond of equivalent maturity. The required return on all other bonds is estimated by adding an appropriate premium to the interest rate on Treasury bonds of comparable maturities.

While we are all free to make our own assessment of the credit risk of a bond and decide what the premium should be, this is not an easy undertaking. Most people use what is called a bond's credit rating assigned by rating agencies like S&P and Moody's. The ratings range from AAA or Aaa (for the most creditworthy bonds) to D (for bonds that are in default). To determine the appropriate interest rate premium over U.S. Treasuries of equivalent maturity or the discount rate for a bond, people generally start with the YTM of bonds with a comparable credit rating and maturity and make adjustments to it if necessary. Incidentally, the credit premiums for bonds of the same rating vary widely over time for several reasons and, therefore, a bond's price can vary even if its credit rating and U.S. Treasury interest rates remain the same.

BOND DURATION

What is the effective average life of an investment in a bond? It is tempting to think that it is equal to its maturity or half of its maturity. This is generally not true, however. Why? Because bonds make coupon payments over the years, and even though all the coupon payments are generally equal in amount, the present values of the distant coupon payments are much smaller than those of the earlier ones. Also, the present value of the final principal payment is less than its nominal value. So we have to measure the effective average life, taking the time value of money into consideration.

Macauley Duration

Macauley duration (also called simply duration) is the average life of a bond's payments calculated using the present value of the coupon and principal payments as the weights. If annual interest rate is r, then for a bond that pays annual coupon of C, has remaining life of n years, and has a current price of P, the duration can be calculated as:

$$D = \frac{1}{P}\sum_{t=1}^{n}\frac{tC}{(1+r)^t} + \frac{1}{P}\left(\frac{nFV}{(1+r)^n}\right)$$

Modified Duration

It can be shown that for a bond,

$$\frac{dP}{P} = -D\frac{dr}{1+r} \quad \text{or} \quad \frac{dP}{P} = -D'dr$$

The significance of this equation is that if we define $D' = D/(1+r)$ to be the modified duration of a bond, then the modified duration measures the interest rate sensitivity of a bond's price for small changes in interest rate. For example, if the modified duration of a bond is 10 years, then a 0.25% increase in interest rate will reduce the bond's price by 2.5%. Because of this simple relationship, modified duration is widely used as a measure of the interest rate risk of bonds. Keep in mind that the relationship holds strictly only for small changes in interest rates because the modified duration itself changes with the interest rate. Nonetheless, it is always true that bonds with longer modified durations have higher interest rate risk.

Although the modified duration is the correct measure of interest rate risk, the duration itself is often used as an approximate measure of interest rate risk as well. Since zero-coupon bonds pay no intermediate coupons, their duration is always equal to their remaining life, and, therefore, they have much higher interest rate risk than coupon bonds of equal maturity.

In the models we develop we will be able to see these properties in more detail.

THE YIELD CURVE AND FORWARD RATES

Even casual observations show that interest rates depend both on maturity and the credit risk of the borrower. Generally the longer the maturity of a loan, the higher the interest rate the borrower has to pay (although at times this relationship gets inverted). As mentioned before, it is customary in the credit market to determine the appropriate interest rate for different borrowers by adding suitable premiums to the equivalent U.S. Treasury rate because Treasuries have no credit risk. Therefore, the interest rates on Treasuries of various maturities are watched closely.

Yield Curve

The yield curve is a plot (or table) of the interest rates on U.S. Treasuries as a function of their maturities at any point in time. Generally, interest rates for a few months to up to 30 years are included. The yield curve is customarily based on the interest rates on zero-coupon Treasuries because zero coupons have no reinvestment risk. To emphasize the point, such yield curves are often called zero-coupon yield curves. The yield curve generally slopes upward, meaning interest rates tend to be higher for longer maturities. There is no law that says it has to be that way, though, and over time yield curves take on all kinds of shapes. Sometimes they are even downward-sloping (called inverted).

Forward Rates

If we find from the yield curve that the five-year interest rate is 6% and the six-year interest rate is 7%, can we say anything about what the interest rate should be for a one-year borrowing 5 years from now? We can actually determine exactly at what rate we should be able to enter into a contract today to borrow one-year money in five years. This is called the forward rate, and it is exactly determined by the five- and six-year rates because otherwise there will be opportunity to make arbitrage or riskless profit. However, recognize that forward rates tell you at what rate you can enter into a contract today to borrow money in the future. They do not tell you what the rate will be at that time, and if instead of entering into a contract today you wait five years, the rate for borrowing one-year money at that time will probably be much different.

We can show that if y_t represents t year interest rate and $f_{t,T}$ represents the forward rate for borrowing money for (T-t) years t years in the future, then:

$$f_{t,T} = \left(\frac{(1+y_T)^T}{(1+y_t)^t}\right)^{1/(T-t)} - 1$$

Bond Pricing Using the Yield Curve

Earlier I mentioned that bonds can be priced using yield to maturity. However, this actually provides only an approximate value because in such valuations we discount all future cash flows—no matter when they take place—at the same rate. Now we know that this cannot be appropriate unless the yield curve happens to be flat. Bonds can be more accurately valued by discounting each coupon and the par amount by maturity-matched discount rates based on the yield curve. Maturity-matched discount rate means the zero-coupon U.S. Treasury interest rate for the particular maturity plus the appropriate credit risk premium for the rating of the bond we are pricing. However, depending on the shape of the yield curve at the time, this may or may not make a big difference vis-à-vis YTM–based valuation.

Modeling Examples

MODEL 1: YIELD CURVE AND FORWARD RATES

The Problem

Using the Treasury zero-coupon rates provided, plot a yield curve. Also calculate and plot the forward rates for the various periods.

Modeling Strategy

The worksheet for this model is shown in Figure 17.1. For the yield curve, express all maturities in years and then plot a chart with the interest rate on the Y-axis and the maturity on the X-axis.

For the forward rates, use the equation we discussed earlier. Recognize that when you use 15- and 20-year rates in the equation, you are calculating the

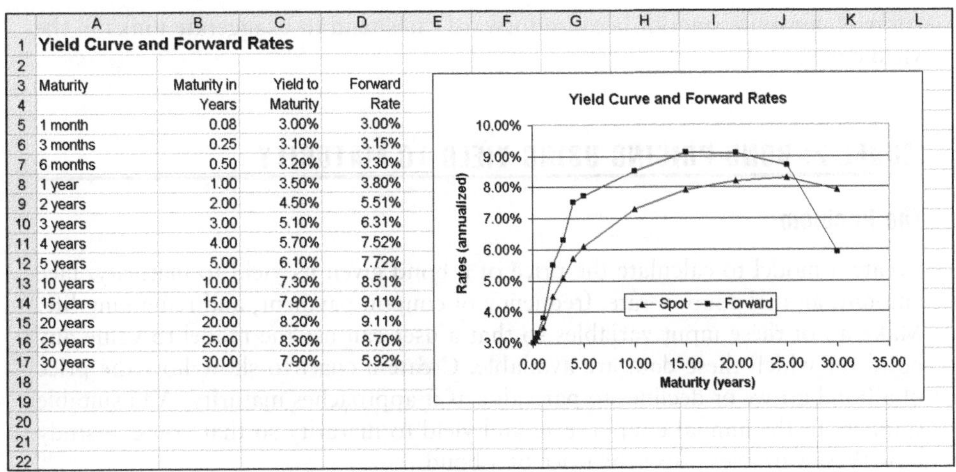

	A	B	C	D
1	**Yield Curve and Forward Rates**			
2				
3	Maturity	Maturity in	Yield to	Forward
4		Years	Maturity	Rate
5	1 month	0.08	3.00%	3.00%
6	3 months	0.25	3.10%	3.15%
7	6 months	0.50	3.20%	3.30%
8	1 year	1.00	3.50%	3.80%
9	2 years	2.00	4.50%	5.51%
10	3 years	3.00	5.10%	6.31%
11	4 years	4.00	5.70%	7.52%
12	5 years	5.00	6.10%	7.72%
13	10 years	10.00	7.30%	8.51%
14	15 years	15.00	7.90%	9.11%
15	20 years	20.00	8.20%	9.11%
16	25 years	25.00	8.30%	8.70%
17	30 years	30.00	7.90%	5.92%

FIGURE 17.1 Model 1: Yield curve and forward rates.

annualized forward rate for the five-year period between year 15 and year 20. So although all the forward rates are annualized rates, they are not for the same lengths of period and, therefore, are not exactly comparable. This is the best you can do, however, with the data given and generally available.

Building the Model

1. **Calculate forward rates:** It is easiest to understand the equation for the forward rate for year 1. In cell D8 enter the formula =((1+C8)^B8/(1+C7)^B7)^(1/(B8-B7))-1 and analyze it by substituting in it the actual values. What it says is that a one-year interest rate today combined with a one-year forward rate one year from now must produce the two-year interest rate today. Once you understand the equation, copy it into the other cells.
2. **Plot the chart:** Create the XY chart using the data from columns B, C, and D and format and label it properly.

Testing the Model

Check the forward rates with a hand calculation. This will also help you better understand forward rates.

Uses of the Model

The model is useful for creating updated yield curves and forward rates quickly. An interesting benefit of plotting forward rate is that it points out where the yield curve is not quite smooth because forward rates tend to exaggerate kinks in the yield curves.

MODEL 2: BOND PRICING USING YIELD TO MATURITY

The Problem

Create a model to calculate the price of a bond given its yield to maturity, face amount, annual coupon rate, frequency of coupon payment, and remaining life. Make all of these input variables so that a user can use the model to value any bond for which these data are available. Create a chart to show how the price of a bond grows or declines to par value as it approaches maturity. Add suitable spinners to the annual coupon rate and yield to maturity so that you can study how these variables affect the price of a bond.

Modeling Strategy

The worksheet for the model is shown in Figure 17.2. Use the bond valuation equation to calculate the bond price. Remember that the calculations are to be done in units of coupon payment period. So the appropriate discount rate would be the yield to maturity divided by the coupon payment frequency (assuming APR convention).

To draw the chart, first create a one-input data table with the remaining life as the independent variable and the bond price as the dependent variable.

Building the Model

1. **Set up input variables:** Create the labels for the input variable cells as shown and name the input variable cells as follows: Cell B4 CR, B5 y, B6 Cpns, B7 f, and B8 Face. Add the spinners to cells C4 and C5 using the Control Toolbox. For the spinner in C4, make D4 the linked cell and set Min at 0 and Max at 200. For the spinner in C5, make D5 the linked cell and Set Min at 0 and Max at 200. In B4 enter the formula =D4*0.001 and in B5, the formula =D5*0.001.
2. **Calculate bond value:** To calculate the discount rate per coupon payment period, in B10 enter the formula =y/f and name the cell Disc. To calculate the coupon amount per payment, in B11 enter the formula =Face*CR/f and name the cell cPmt. To calculate the remaining life in years, in B12 enter the formula =Cpns/f and name the cell Life.

   Finally, to calculate the bond price using the PMT function, in B14 enter the formula =IF(CR=B5,Face,PV(Disc,Cpns,-CPmt,-Face)). The formula makes the bond price equal to the face value if the yield to maturity is equal to the

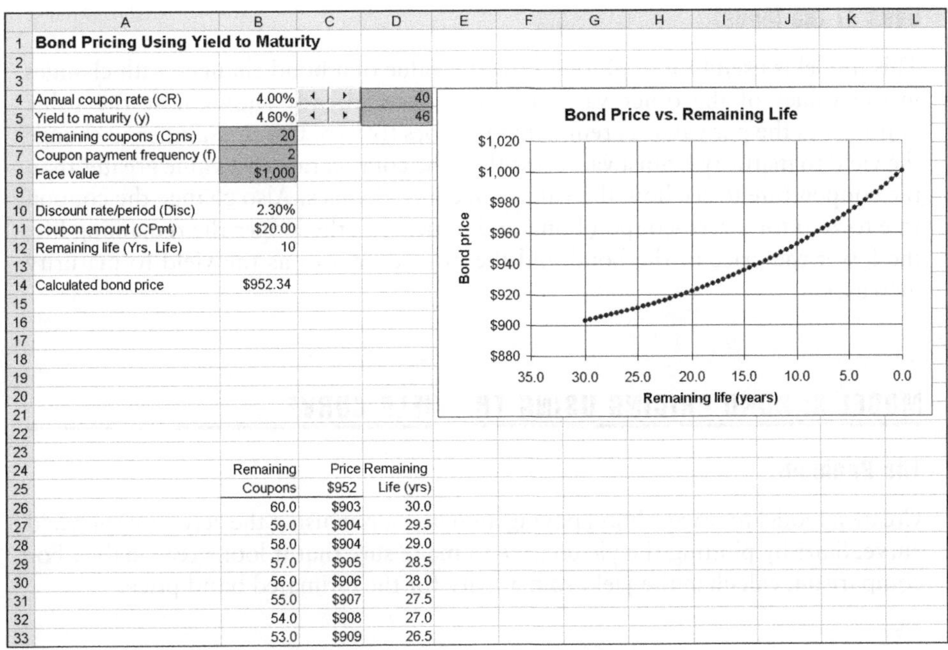

	A	B	C	D
1	**Bond Pricing Using Yield to Maturity**			
2				
3				
4	Annual coupon rate (CR)	4.00%		40
5	Yield to maturity (y)	4.60%		46
6	Remaining coupons (Cpns)	20		
7	Coupon payment frequency (f)	2		
8	Face value	$1,000		
9				
10	Discount rate/period (Disc)	2.30%		
11	Coupon amount (CPmt)	$20.00		
12	Remaining life (Yrs, Life)	10		
13				
14	Calculated bond price	$952.34		
24		Remaining	Price	Remaining
25		Coupons	$952	Life (yrs)
26		60.0	$903	30.0
27		59.0	$904	29.5
28		58.0	$904	29.0
29		57.0	$905	28.5
30		56.0	$906	28.0
31		55.0	$907	27.5
32		54.0	$908	27.0
33		53.0	$909	26.5

FIGURE 17.2 Model 2: Pricing a bond using yield to maturity.

coupon rate. Otherwise it calculates the value from the PMT function using the face value as an additional future payment.

3. **Create data table:** We cannot set up the data table to show the remaining life starting at the specified remaining life. So make the remaining life 60 semiannual periods. Enter in B27 the formula =B26-1. Then copy it into B28:86 to get the remaining life down to zero. The purpose of setting up the series in reverse order is to have the X-axis in the chart go from higher numbers on the left to 0 on the right. In C25 enter =B14 and select B25:C86. Open the Data Table dialog box. In the Column input cell box, enter $B$6 (by clicking the cell) and click OK.

   Because the chart should be preferably set up with remaining life in years, in D26 enter the formula =B26/f and copy it down the column.
4. **Create the chart:** Create the chart using data from C26:D86 and properly format and label it.

Testing the Model

You can test the bond value calculated using Excel's bond valuation functions or a hand calculator.

Uses of the Model

This model is useful for exploring how the value of a bond changes with changes in the values of the other variables. The chart already shows how the value approaches the par value as remaining life goes to zero. Use the spinner to change the yield to maturity from a value less than the coupon rate to a value greater than the coupon rate to see how the valuation curve changes. Also change the coupon rate to zero for a zero-coupon bond and notice that the longer the remaining life, the lower the price of the bond and the price decreases as the yield to maturity increases.

MODEL 3: BOND PRICING USING THE YIELD CURVE

The Problem

Create a model to price a bond paying annual coupon using the zero-coupon yield curve. Start by plotting the yield curve to make sure that it looks reasonable. For comparison, calculate the yield to maturity for the estimated bond price.

Modeling Strategy

The worksheet for the model is shown in Figure 17.3. Here you have to discount each cash flow from the bond, that is, the coupon payments as well as the final principal payment, using maturity-matched discount rates. Note that in practice all bond issuers have to pay interest rates higher than the yield curve because of credit risk and other factors. The appropriate discount rate, then, would be the yield curve rate plus a premium, which may be constant or may vary with maturity.

Building the Model

1. **Set up input cells:** Create the labels for the input cells and name them as follows: B4 CR, B5 Life, and B6 Face.
2. **Create yield curve:** Enter the yield curve data in C25:D35 and properly label the columns. Plot the yield curve.
3. **Create bond cash flows:** To create the bond cash flows, in E26 enter the formula =Face*CR and copy it into E27:E34. In E35, enter the formula =Face+Face*CR.
4. **Calculate bond value:** To calculate the present value of each cash flow, in F26 enter the formula =E26/(1+D26)^C26 and copy it into F27:F35. To calculate the value of the bond, in B8 enter the formula =SUM(F26:F35).

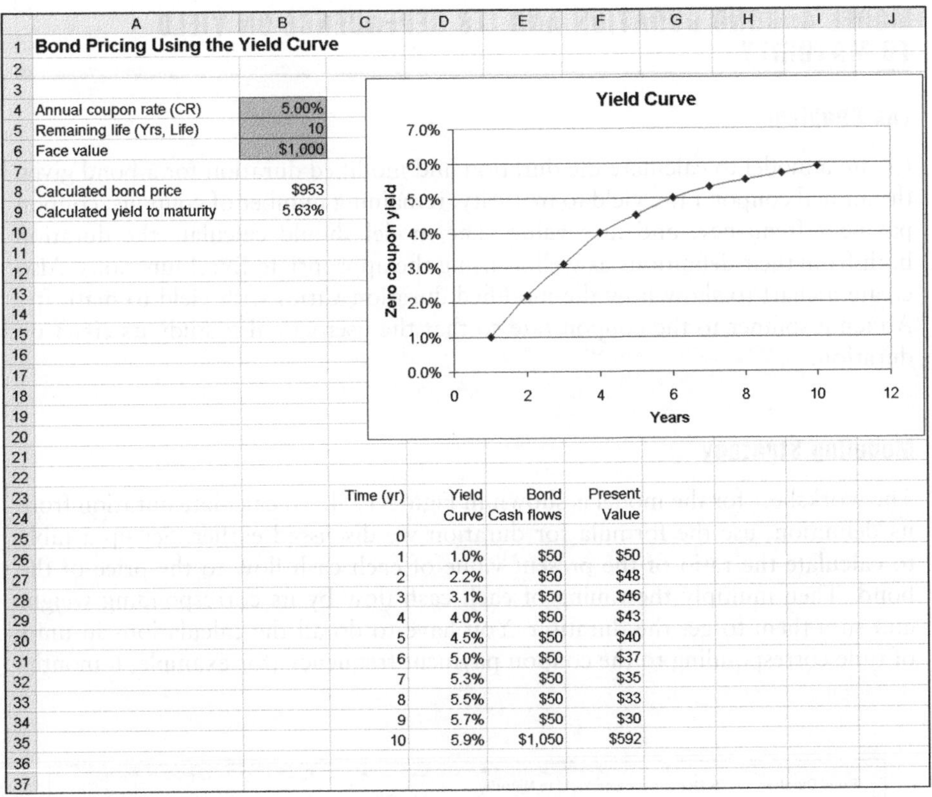

	A	B
1	**Bond Pricing Using the Yield Curve**	
4	Annual coupon rate (CR)	5.00%
5	Remaining life (Yrs, Life)	10
6	Face value	$1,000
8	Calculated bond price	$953
9	Calculated yield to maturity	5.63%

Time (yr)	Yield Curve	Bond Cash flows	Present Value
0			
1	1.0%	$50	$50
2	2.2%	$50	$48
3	3.1%	$50	$46
4	4.0%	$50	$43
5	4.5%	$50	$40
6	5.0%	$50	$37
7	5.3%	$50	$35
8	5.5%	$50	$33
9	5.7%	$50	$30
10	5.9%	$1,050	$592

FIGURE 17.3 Model 3: Pricing a bond using the yield curve.

5. **Calculate the yield to maturity:** To calculate the yield to maturity, in B9 enter the formula =RATE(Life,-Face*CR,B8,-Face).

Testing the Model

The easiest way to test this model is by doing some hand calculations.

Uses of the Model

This model produces a more realistic valuation for a bond. However, as mentioned before, the appropriate discount rates would be the rates from the yield curve plus some premium. Notice that the yield to maturity is significantly different from most of the yields and is lower than the 10-year yield even though this is a 10-year bond. The reason, of course, is that the yield curve here is very steep.

MODEL 4: BOND DURATION AND ITS DEPENDENCE ON YIELD TO MATURITY

The Problem

Create a model to calculate the duration and modified duration for a bond given the annual coupon rate, yield to maturity, remaining number of coupons, coupon payment frequency, and face value. The model should calculate the duration both from their definitions as well as using the appropriate Excel functions. Also create a chart to show how the modified duration varies with yield to maturity. Attach a spinner to the coupon rate so that the user can also study its effect on duration.

Modeling Strategy

The worksheet for the model is shown in Figure 17.4. To calculate duration from its definition, use the formula for duration we discussed earlier. Set up a table to calculate the ratio of the present value of each cash flow to the price of the bond. Then multiply the timing of each cash flow by its corresponding weight and sum them to get the duration. You have to do all the calculations in units of time corresponding to the coupon payment frequency (for example, 6 months

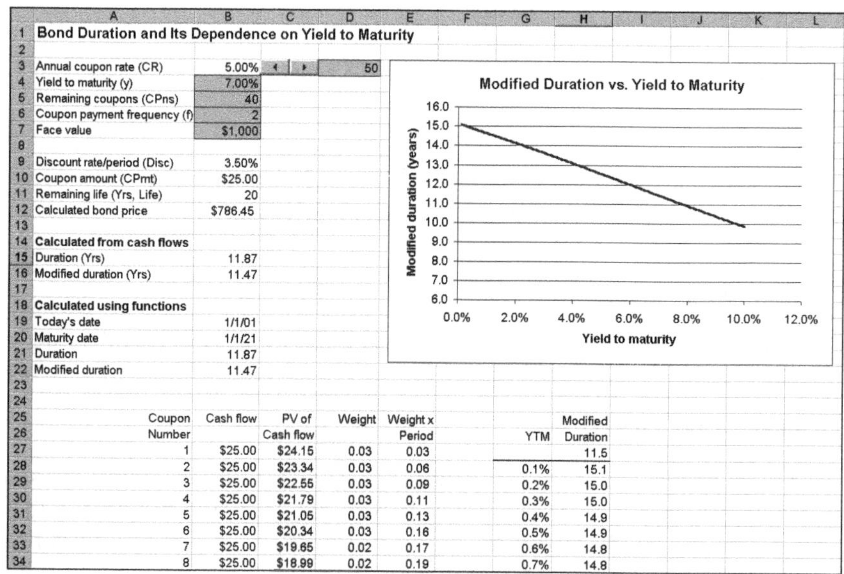

FIGURE 17.4 Model 4: Bond duration and its dependence on the yield to maturity.

for frequency 2). To convert the calculated duration into years, multiply it by the frequency of coupon payment.

To calculate the modified duration, divide the regular duration by 1 plus the discount rate. Remember to use the discount rate used in the calculations and not the annual discount rate.

To calculate the durations using Excel's functions, use DURATION and MDURATION with made-up settlement and maturity dates.

Building the Model

1. **Set up input variables:** Create the labels for the input variables and name the input cells as follows: B3 CR, B4 y, B5 Cpns, B6 f, and B7 Face. Insert a spinner at C3 and make D3 the linked cell. In B3 enter the formula =D3/1000 for proper scaling.
2. **Calculate intermediate values:** Label the cells A9:A12. In cell B9 enter the formula =y/f to calculate the discount rate per period and name the cell Disc. In B10 enter the formula =Face*CR/f to calculate the periodic coupon payment amount and name the cell CPmt. In B11 enter the formula =Face*CR/f and name it Life. Finally, in B12 enter the formula =IF(CR=B4,Face,PV(Disc,Cpns,-CPmt,-Face)) to calculate the bond price. The IF makes the bond price the same as the face value when the yield to maturity equals the coupon rate.
3. **Create table to calculate duration:** Enter the heading in A25:E26. Because there are 40 coupons left, enter 1 through 40 in A27:A66 and enter another 40 in A67 for the principal repayment. You could also include the principal repayment with the last coupon. For the coupon payments, in B27 enter =CPmt, copy it into B28:B66, and in B67 enter =Face.

   To calculate the present values, in C27 enter the formula =B27*(1+Disc)^-A27 and copy it into C28:C67. To calculate the weights, in D27 enter the formula =C27/$B$12 and copy it into D28:D67. Finally, in E27 enter the formula =A27*D27 to multiply the timing of a cash flow by the weight. Copy it into E28:E67.
4. **Calculate durations:** To calculate the duration, in B15 enter the formula =SUM(E27:E67)/f. You have to divide by the frequency of payment, f, to express the duration in years. To calculate the modified duration, in B16 enter the formula =B15/(1+Disc).
5. **Calculate durations using functions:** In B19 and B20 enter two arbitrary dates 20 years apart. To calculate the duration, in B21 enter the formula =DURATION(B19,B20,CR,y,f) and to calculate the modified duration, in B22 enter the formula =MDURATION(B19,B20,CR,y,f).
6. **Create chart:** To draw the chart, you need to calculate the duration for a range of values for yield to maturity and it is easiest to do it with a data table. In G28:G127 create a series of yields from 0.1% to 10% in 0.1% intervals.

In H27 enter =B22 to indicate where the value for the dependent variable is. Select G27:H127, and then Data ⇨ Table. For Column input cell, enter B4 and click OK to complete the data table.

Use the data from the two columns of the data table to create the chart and format and label it.

Testing the Model

Because you have calculated the durations in two different ways, if the results agree then your model is working properly.

Uses of the Model

Notice how the modified duration goes down as the yield to maturity goes up. Why is this? Because as the yield to maturity goes up, the present values of the distant cash flows become smaller and therefore their timings count less in the duration calculation. Use the spinner to study the effect of the coupon rate (relative to the yield to maturity) on duration.

This model lacks flexibility in that the duration calculation from the formulas will work only for a fixed life of 40 periods or 20 years. You could make it more flexible by using some IF functions. To the extent that Excel has the built-in functions that can handle bonds of any maturity, however, trying to make the model more flexible is not very important. If Excel did not offer the duration functions, you could, of course, create your own in VBA.

MODEL 5: DEPENDENCE OF BOND DURATION ON REMAINING LIFE

The Problem

Create a model to show the dependence of the modified duration of a bond on the bond's remaining life in the form of a chart. Make all of the key bond variables input variables so that the user can specify them.

Modeling Strategy

The worksheet for the model is shown in Figure 17.5. This model is similar to Model 4. As we saw in Model 4, though, if we calculate durations by creating a table of year-by-year cash flows, and so on, it is difficult to make the remaining life a variable because that requires making the number of rows depend on the remaining life. To calculate modified duration, you therefore have to use Excel's modified duration function (with an arbitrary settlement date and the maturity date calculated by adding the remaining life to it). Alternately, you can use a

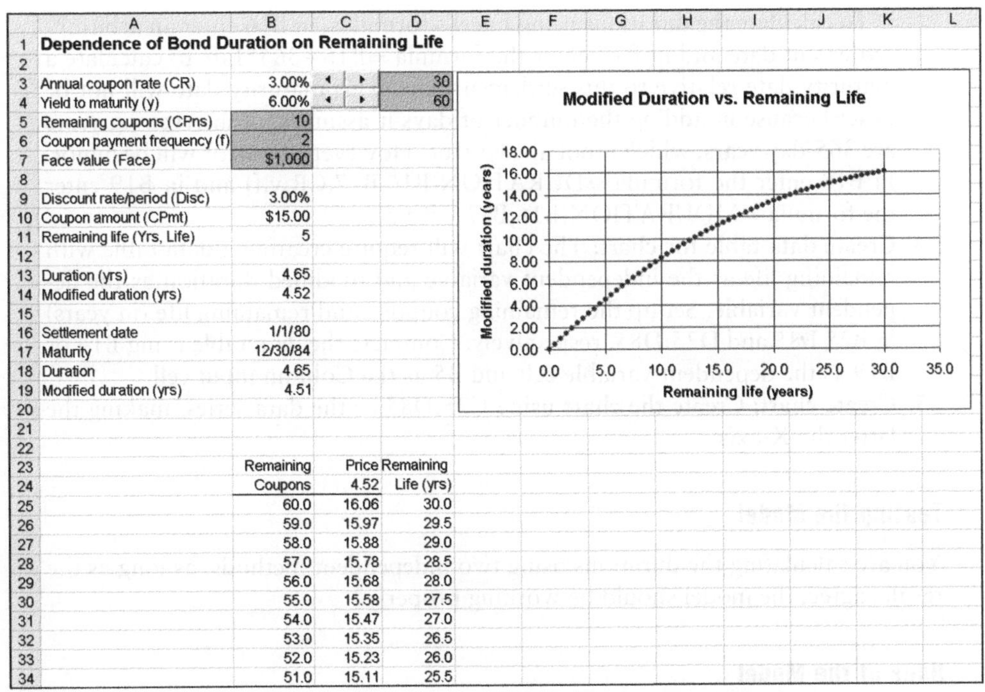

	A	B	C	D
1	**Dependence of Bond Duration on Remaining Life**			
2				
3	Annual coupon rate (CR)	3.00%		30
4	Yield to maturity (y)	6.00%		60
5	Remaining coupons (CPns)	10		
6	Coupon payment frequency (f)	2		
7	Face value (Face)	$1,000		
8				
9	Discount rate/period (Disc)	3.00%		
10	Coupon amount (CPmt)	$15.00		
11	Remaining life (Yrs, Life)	5		
12				
13	Duration (yrs)	4.65		
14	Modified duration (yrs)	4.52		
15				
16	Settlement date	1/1/80		
17	Maturity	12/30/84		
18	Duration	4.65		
19	Modified duration (yrs)	4.51		
20				
21				
22				
23		Remaining	Price	Remaining
24		Coupons	4.52	Life (yrs)
25		60.0	16.06	30.0
26		59.0	15.97	29.5
27		58.0	15.88	29.0
28		57.0	15.78	28.5
29		56.0	15.68	28.0
30		55.0	15.58	27.5
31		54.0	15.47	27.0
32		53.0	15.35	26.5
33		52.0	15.23	26.0
34		51.0	15.11	25.5

FIGURE 17.5 Model 5: Dependence of bond duration on remaining life.

compact formula for duration that does not require setting up a table of cash flows, and so on.

Building the Model

1. **Set up input variables:** Enter the labels for the input variables and name the cells for the input variables as shown. Add the spinners for annual coupon rate and yield to maturity, making D3 and D4 the linked cells for them. For proper scaling, in B3 enter the formula =D3/1000 and in B4 the formula =D4/1000.
2. **Calculate intermediate variables:** Enter the labels in A9:A11. In B9 enter the formula =y/f, in B10 the formula =Face*CR/f, and in B11 the formula =Cpns/f.
3. **Calculate durations:** To calculate duration with a formula, in B13 enter the formula =((1+Disc)/(Disc*f)-(1+Disc+Cpns*(CR/f-Disc))/(CR*((1+Disc)^Cpns-1)+Disc*f)). We have not derived this formula, but it can be derived from the basic definition of duration. To calculate the modified duration, in B14 enter the formula =B13/(1+Disc).

To calculate the durations using Excel's formulas, in B16 enter an arbitrary settlement date and in B17 enter the formula =B16+365*Life to calculate a maturity date relative to this settlement date. This maturity date will not be exact because in adding the number of days it assumes all intervening years are 365-day years, which is not always true. However, the error will be minor. In B18 enter the formula =DURATION(B16,B17,CR,y,f) and in B19 enter the formula =MDURATION(B16,B17,CR,y,f).

4. **Create data table for chart:** The chart will require creating a data table with remaining life as the independent variable and modified duration as the dependent variable. Set up the remaining coupons and remaining life (in years) in B25:B85 and D25:D85, respectively. Complete the data table using B14 or B19 as the dependent variable cell and B5 as the Column input cell.
5. **Create chart:** Create the chart using C25:D85 as the data series, making the latter the X-axis.

Testing the Model

You are calculating the durations using two independent methods; as long as the results agree, the model should be working properly.

Uses of the Model

The model is useful for studying how modified duration varies with changes in the different bond variables. For example, you will notice that the modified duration gets longer as the coupon rate declines while for zero-coupon bonds it is close to remaining life.

CHAPTER 18

Simulating Stock Prices

In most of finance, especially in analysis of derivatives, we assume that asset prices are unpredictable and follow a geometric Brownian motion. Most people find it difficult to grasp exactly what this means, but having a good understanding of it is essential to do any work with derivatives. In this chapter we will build a few models that will help you understand exactly what a geometric Brownian motion is, what it implies for future prices of stocks, and how we can use it to simulate stock prices. Such simulations form the basis for Monte Carlo simulations, which is one of the three approaches used widely to price derivatives.

Review of Theory and Concepts

We will explore geometric Brownian motion starting with some preliminaries and a simple model of stock prices. After we discuss geometric Brownian motion and its implications, we will discuss how to estimate the necessary parameters from historical data to simulate stock prices.

Simulation

Simulating the price of a stock means generating price paths that a stock may follow in the future. (The price path of a stock is the graph of its price against time.) If the price of a stock were predictable, then there would be only one possible future price path for it, and there would be no need to simulate it. However, if a stock's price is not constrained by any rule, then it might follow any price path we can imagine or draw. In this case, it is meaningless to talk about simulating the stock's price. We therefore talk about simulating stock prices only because future stock prices are uncertain (called stochastic), but we believe they follow, at least approximately, a set of rules that we can derive from historical data and our other knowledge of stock prices. This set of rules is called the model for stock prices.

These rules produce an infinite number of possible future price paths for a stock, and we cannot tell which path the stock will actually follow. However, we can simulate as many of them as we want, and we can also make probabilistic statements about future stock prices such as "There is only a 5% chance that this stock's price will be below $15 a year from now." Simulating stock prices and being able to make such probabilistic statements can be very useful, especially in working with derivatives.

To start with, let us look at a simple example to understand what we mean by stock prices being uncertain, why we can still make probabilistic statements about future stock prices, and how we can simulate stock prices once we choose the rules (or model) they follow.

A Simple Model for Stock Prices

Consider a stock whose price today is $20 and that trades only once a day. It follows the simple rule that every day, its price can either go up or down by $1 with equal probability. We can see that we will never be able to tell what the price of the stock will be tomorrow or at any time in the future. We can say, however, that the expected (mean) price of the stock is $20. This is true no matter how many days ahead we look, although the price can vary widely from this mean. We can also calculate the standard deviation of the stock's price on any day in the future and make probabilistic statements about the future price of the stock.

We can simulate the price of this stock using a coin. We will flip the coin once to represent each day. If the coin comes up heads, we will assume that the stock price goes up by $1 for that day; if it comes up tails, the stock price goes down by $1 for that day.

Suppose the first coin flip representing the first day is heads. Then the result of our simulation is that the price of the stock will be $21 at the end of the first day. If we get heads again, then the simulated price at the end of the second day will be $22. We can simulate the stock price for as many days as we want by repeating the process, and if we plot our results on a chart (with the day number along the X axis and stock price along the Y axis), we will have one simulated price path.

Note that the simulation depends on our model for the stock price and the price path we generated with the first set of coin flips is one of many possible price paths. The number of possible price paths will increase rapidly with the number of days for which we run our simulation. We can start over as many times as we want to generate additional price paths and if we do the simulation for a large number of days, then most of the price paths will be different from one another.

In this case, it is easy to mathematically calculate the expected value, standard deviation, and so on, of the stock price for any time horizon (for example, 100 days). We could also run a few thousand simulations to get a distribution of what the stock price would be at any time horizon and calculate the expected value, standard deviation, and so on, from those values. In pricing derivatives, simulations are particularly useful when we cannot derive exact mathematical formulas for the price.

Clearly, the model we used for stock price is not realistic because it does not conform to many things we know about stock prices, an obvious one being that stock prices do not change exclusively in $1 steps. This brings up another key point about simulations: a simulation will be realistic only if the underlying model is realistic. The model must reflect our understanding of stock prices and conform to historical data.

The Geometric Brownian Motion Model

Based on extensive analysis of historical data and other considerations, we generally assume in finance that prices of stocks that do not pay any dividend follow a special type of stochastic process known as *geometric Brownian motion.* The geometric Brownian motion model assumes or implies the following properties for stock prices:

- They are continuous in time and value.
- They follow a Markov process, meaning that only the current stock price is relevant for predicting future prices; in this respect, the stock's price history is irrelevant.
- The proportional return for a stock over a very short period of time is normally distributed.
- The price of a stock is lognormally distributed.
- The continuously compounded return for a stock is normally distributed.

The model also implies that the longer we plan to hold a stock, the more uncertain we become about the stock's final price, that is, the more widely the actual final price may vary from the expected final price. However, the longer we plan to hold a stock, the more certain we can be about earning the expected rate of return. These may sound contradictory, but we will see why they are not.

We know that the first assumption about stock prices—that they are continuous in time and value, meaning that stock prices can be observed at all times and they change continuously—does not strictly hold. Markets are closed during nights and weekends, and stock prices can change only in steps of multiples of full cents. Nonetheless, this is a reasonable assumption and it makes modeling stock prices easier.

The second assumption—that stock prices follow a Markov process—is essentially the same as the weak form of the efficient market hypothesis, which says that the future price of a stock cannot be predicted based on its price history. For example, whether a stock's price was up or down yesterday (or a minute ago) or by how much tells us nothing about what is going to happen to it in the future.

If a stock has been going up for a few days, it does not mean that it has gained some momentum and is now more likely to go up for the next few days as well.

This, of course, contradicts the claims of most Wall Street experts, especially the chartists, that stock prices can be predicted by analyzing their price history in various sophisticated ways. There is overwhelming evidence to show that these claims are erroneous with maybe a few minor exceptions. The support levels, resistance levels, momentum and so forth that are discussed with so much passion and conviction on Wall Street do not really help to predict future stock prices.

Let us now discuss the other three properties in some details.

Proportional Returns on Stocks Are Normally Distributed

Because stock prices follow geometric Brownian motion, we can write the proportional return—change in the stock price divided by its initial value—over a short interval of time as:

$$\frac{\Delta S}{S} = \mu \Delta t + \sigma \varepsilon \sqrt{\Delta t}$$

Here, ΔS is the change in the stock's initial price S over a very short period of time Δt. From the equation, we see that the proportional return is made up of two components. The first is a certain component and the second is an uncertain component, which makes the proportional return uncertain or random.

- In the first component, μ is the expected rate of return (per unit of time, generally year) for the stock for very short time intervals. It is also called the drift rate per unit of time. The first component represents the return that the stock will earn at that rate over the short period of time Δt. If the price of a stock were not uncertain, that is, the uncertain second component did not exist, then the stock price would grow over time at the rate of μ continuously compounded (assuming μ remains constant over the time period). Under this assumption, if the price of the stock today is S_0, then its price S_T at time T in the future would be:

$$S_T = S_0 \exp(\mu T)$$

- In the second component, which is stochastic or random, ε is a random draw from a standard normal distribution, that is, a normal distribution with a mean of zero and standard deviation of 1. If you have difficulty conceptualizing what this means, think of it as something similar to the coin flip example discussed earlier. The difference is that here you can get any value from minus infinity to infinity, with values closer to zero much more likely to be drawn than values far from zero. (We will see later how you can make random draws from a standard normal distribution in Excel.) σ is called the volatility of the stock. The effect of multiplying ε by $\sigma\sqrt{\Delta t}$ is that this random component of the stock's return is effectively drawn from a normal distribution with a mean of zero and standard deviation $\sigma\sqrt{\Delta t}$. (We will give an intuitive definition of σ or volatility later.)

- Because the standard deviation of the second component is not constant but is proportional to the square root of the length of the time interval, it implies that the longer a time interval we consider, the more variable the return will become.
- When the two components are added together, the proportional return on the stock over a short time interval becomes a variable that is normally distributed with a mean of $\mu\Delta t$ and standard deviation of $\sigma\sqrt{\Delta t}$, which is written as:

$$\frac{\Delta S}{S} \sim \phi\left(\mu\Delta t,\ \sigma\sqrt{\Delta t}\right)$$

It will be easier to understand the implication of this assumption (or model) if we look at an example. Let us assume that the current price of a stock is \$10, μ is 12% per year, σ is 40% per year, and the small time interval we want to consider is 1 day or 0.004 years. (Empirical work shows that in these types of models we get better results if we count days in trading days instead of calendar days. Because there are about 250 trading days per year, 1 day equals 0.004 years.)

To calculate the second component we will need ε, which is a random draw from a standard normal distribution. Let us say that the value we get for ε by making such a draw is 0.8. (We will see later how we can make such draws.) Then we can calculate the two components of the proportional return on the stock as follows:

$$\text{First component} = \mu\Delta t = 0.12 \times 0.004 = 0.00048$$
$$\text{Second component} = \varepsilon\sigma\sqrt{\Delta t} = 0.8 \times 0.4 \times 0.0632 = 0.0202$$

The proportional return for the stock over a one-day interval (for this draw) is then the sum of the two components, that is, 0.0207 or 2.07%.

We have to remember that the model is not predicting that the return will be 2.07%. What it is saying is that the return will be normally distributed with a mean of 0.00048 and standard deviation of $0.4 \times 0.0632 = 0.0253$ and one of a possible infinite number of returns is 2.07%. We can get many other possible returns by drawing new values for ε and using them in the equation. Because the draws for ε will be negative half of the time, the second component will also be negative about half of the time. So the proportional return can be positive as well as negative.

If we consider an interval of 10 days, the mean of the return will be 10 times as large, that is, 0.0048, but the standard deviation will not be 10 times as large because it equals $\sigma\sqrt{\Delta t}$ and not $\sigma\Delta t$. The standard deviation will be 0.08, and if our first draw for ε again happens to be 0.8, the return over the 10 day period will be 0.0688 or 6.9%.

Let me emphasize that the equation for the proportional return we have been using holds strictly only for infinitesimal intervals of time. So while using it for a 1-day period may be acceptable, although not strictly correct, using it for a 10-day interval certainly is not acceptable. I used it for the 10-day interval only to make the point that as we look at longer intervals, the variability of the proportional return increases, but not in direct proportion to time. We will see soon how we handle finite intervals, whether they be 1 day, 10 days, or something else.

Stock Prices Are Lognormally Distributed

Another implication of our assumption that stock prices follow a geometric Brownian motion is that stock prices are lognormally distributed, that is, the natural logarithm of stock prices are normally distributed. If S_0 is the stock price now and S_T the price at time T, we can write:

$$\ln\frac{S_T}{S_0} \sim \phi\left[\left(\mu - \frac{\sigma^2}{2}\right)T,\ \sigma\sqrt{T}\right]$$

and

$$\ln S_T \sim \phi\left[\ln S_0 + \left(\mu - \frac{\sigma^2}{2}\right)T,\ \sigma\sqrt{T}\right]$$

Note that the mean of the distribution for the logarithm of the stock price ratio is not μ but $\mu - \sigma^2/2$, which is important.

Because the stock price itself is lognormally distributed, we cannot calculate the expected value or the variance of the stock price at time T directly from the above distribution. For example, the expected value of the stock price is given by:

$$E(S_T) = S_0 \exp(\mu T)$$

From this we can get an intuitive understanding of how stock prices evolve under the geometric Brownian motion assumption. The expected value of the stock price grows at the rate of μ, continuously compounded, and an uncertainty component is superimposed on it to generate the fluctuating stock price we observe.

Unlike a normal distribution, a lognormal distribution is not symmetrical. Also, a lognormally distributed variable has a minimum value of zero and maximum value of infinity, whereas a normally distributed variable has a minimum value of minus infinity and maximum value of infinity. Because stock prices cannot have a value less than zero, they can be represented by a lognormal distribution but not by a normal distribution. (Remember that we really do not know the true distribution of stock prices. What we are saying here is that based on historical data and other things we know about stock prices, it is reasonable to assume that stock prices are lognormally distributed. We will see in one of the models we develop what lognormal distributions look like.)

Because T can be any time interval, we can use the lognormal distribution of stock prices to simulate the price of a stock at time $t + \Delta t$ given its price at t, where Δt is a short time interval (for example, a day). The forms of the equation we will use extensively to simulate stock prices and estimate volatility are:

$$\ln\left(\frac{S_{t+\Delta t}}{S_t}\right) = k\Delta t + \sigma\varepsilon\sqrt{\Delta t}$$

and

$$S_{t+\Delta t} = S_t \exp\left(k\Delta t + \sigma\varepsilon\sqrt{\Delta t}\right)$$

Here, for simplicity, I have substituted k for $\mu - \sigma^2/2$.

Let us see how we can use the second equation to simulate stock prices. Assume that the current price of a stock is \$10, k is 12% per year, and σ is 40% per year. Consider a small time interval of one day and assume also that our first draw from the standard normal distribution is 0.8. Then, as before, the value of the term inside the parentheses is 0.0207. Substituting this value and the initial stock price of \$10 in the equation gives us the stock price a day later as \$10.29. We can simulate subsequent days the same way by starting every day with the previous day's price and making a new draw from the standard normal distribution for each day. Remember that the price path we generate this way is just one of the possible infinite number of price paths, and if we start all over again we will get a different price path.

As I pointed out before, because the standard deviation is not constant but is proportional to the square root of the length of the time interval, the longer a time interval we consider, the more variable a stock's price will be. The variability is less than what it would have been, though, if the standard deviation had been proportional to time.

The Continuously Compounded Rate of Return Is Normally Distributed

The last important implication of the geometric Brownian motion assumption is that the continuously compounded rate of return η per year for a stock is normally distributed, and we can write:

$$S_T = S_0 \exp(\eta T)$$

where

$$\eta \sim \phi\left(\mu - \frac{\sigma^2}{2}, \frac{\sigma}{\sqrt{T}}\right)$$

These equations tell us two important things about stock prices. First, the standard deviation of η declines as we consider longer time intervals. This means that if we hold a stock for a short time, our actual return may vary significantly from the expected return, but the longer we hold a stock, the more likely we are to earn a return close to the expected return. This is one of the reasons stock investors are advised to follow a "buy and hold" strategy.

Second, we have called σ the volatility of a stock but have yet to give it an intuitive definition. Now we can. Notice that when $T = 1$, the standard deviation of the stock return equals σ. We can therefore say that the volatility of a stock is the standard deviation of the distribution of its continuously compounded return over a one-year time horizon. This means that if a stock's expected return is 12% per year and volatility is 40% per year, then—based on well-known properties of normal distributions—we can say that about 70% of the time the realized return will be between (12% − 40%) = −28% and (12% + 40%) = 52% and so forth.

Clearly, the higher the volatility of a stock, the more risky it is (considering total risk as opposed to just systematic risk). Stocks generally have volatilities in the range of 20% to 60%. You can see, then, that holding stocks for the short term can be very risky. You can reduce your risk by holding stocks for the long term and also by diversifying, that is, by holding a large number of stocks instead of one or a few stocks.

The Two Expected Returns

In our discussions, we have used two different expected returns for stocks, μ and k (or $\mu - \sigma^2/2$). How do they differ from each other?

μ is the expected rate of return per year for the stock for infinitesimal intervals of time, whereas k is the expected continuously compounded rate of return per year for finite intervals of time like days or years. This is why we have to use k and not μ in simulations.

We also saw that the expected price of a stock grows at the continuously compounded rate of μ and we can write:

$$E(S_T) = S_0 \exp(\mu T)$$

What this means is that k, the expected continuously compounded rate of return per year for a stock, is not the same as the rate of return we would calculate from the expected future price of the stock (unless volatility is 0). To put it in another way, we cannot get the expected future price of the stock by growing its current price at the expected continuously compounded rate of return per year. If two stocks have the same price today and the same μ, then their expected prices at any time in the future will be the same. The stock with the higher volatility, however, will have a lower continuously compounded expected rate of return. This may seem confusing, but it turns out this way because natural logarithm is a nonlinear function and stock price is lognormally distributed whereas the continuously compounded annual return for a stock is normally distributed.

How do we estimate and specify the value of k for simulation? As we know from experience, we cannot reliably estimate the expected rate of return for stocks from historical returns. We can use estimates from analysts and other sources, but these are usually not reliable, either. Fortunately, most of the time we would want to simulate the price of a stock to work with derivatives on it, and for that we do not need estimates of the expected return for the stock.

Estimating Volatility

We defined the volatility of a stock as the standard deviation of the distribution of its continuously compounded return over a one year time horizon. It is a measure of our uncertainty about a stock's return.

To simulate a stock's price or do many other calculations (for example, estimate price of options on the stock), we need to estimate the future volatility of a stock. Many different approaches are used to estimate future volatility. A common one is to base it on a stock's historical volatility calculated from its daily prices for a certain number of days. Here is how this is done using the following equation we discussed earlier:

$$\ln\left(\frac{S_{t+\Delta t}}{S_t}\right) = k\Delta t + \varepsilon\sigma\sqrt{\Delta t}$$

Define:

$n+1$: Number of observations

S_i: Stock price at end of the ith interval ($i = 0,1,\ldots n$)

τ: length of observation time interval in years

and let

$$u_i = \ln\left(\frac{S_i}{S_{i-1}}\right)$$

The estimates of mean and standard deviation of the returns are given by:

$$\overline{u} = \frac{1}{n}\sum_{i=1}^{i=n} u_i$$

$$s = \sqrt{\frac{1}{n-1}\sum_{i=1}^{i=n}(u_i - \overline{u})^2}$$

Alternately, we can also write:

$$s = \sqrt{\frac{1}{n-1}\sum_{i=1}^{i=n} u_i^2 - \frac{1}{n(n-1)}\left(\sum_{i=1}^{i=n} u_i\right)^2}$$

Note that we use the divisor $(n - 1)$ instead of n to get unbiased estimates of volatility.

Because we are using observations at intervals of τ measured in years, the estimate of the annualized volatility will be:

$$\hat{\sigma} = \frac{s}{\sqrt{\tau}}$$

If we use daily prices and assume that there are 250 trading days in a year, then the time interval is 1/250 years. To annualize the daily volatility, we have to multiply it by $\sqrt{250}$. (Empirical work has shown that we get better estimates of annual volatility if we use the number of trading days per year instead of 365 days to annualize the daily volatility.)

Volatility is generally estimated using 90 to 180 days of price history, but it is always a judgment call. The more data we use, the more accurate our estimate will be—provided volatility remained constant for the entire period. Volatility of any stock fluctuates a lot over time, however. Using longer periods therefore may not be meaningful. The period of 90 to 180 days is a reasonable compromise. We are, of course, mostly interested in what volatility will be in the future and not what it was in the past. So other techniques are also used to improve volatility estimates for the future. As we will see in Chapter 19: Options and Option Portfolios, one alternate method used widely is to estimate (implied) volatility from the price of options on the stock.

GENERATING RANDOM NUMBERS

For stock price simulations, you will need random draws from a standard normal distribution, which is the same as saying you will need to generate random numbers with a standard normal distribution. (A standard normal distribution has a mean of 0 and standard deviation of 1.) You can do this in two ways in Excel.

The first is a two-step approach using the RAND and NORMSINV functions. The RAND function returns an evenly distributed random number greater than or equal to 0 and less than or equal to 1. To use it, you enter =RAND() in a cell, and every time the worksheet is recalculated, RAND will generate a new random number in that cell. (You can force a recalculation and generate a new random numbers by pressing F9.) If you need 20 random draws, you have to enter the RAND function in 20 cells. Every time the worksheet recalculates, you will have 20 new random draws that are independent of one another.

To convert a uniformly distributed random number between 0 and 1 into a random draw from a standard normal distribution, you have to use the random draw from the uniform distribution as the argument of the NORMSINV function. This function returns the inverse of the standard normal cumulative distribution. You can do the calculation in one cell by entering =NORMSINV(RAND()) in it. Alternately, you can enter the RAND function in one cell and enter the NORMSINV function in another cell, with the first cell as its argument. If you need 100 draws, you will use 100 cells or 100 pairs of cells, depending on which approach you are taking. (To understand why this works, see the discussions of the RAND and NORMSINV functions.)

The alternate approach is to use the tool for Random Number Generation from the Analysis ToolPak. You can use this tool to directly generate the desired number of random draws from a standard normal distribution.

The key difference between the two approaches is that if you use the first approach, your random draws will change every time the worksheet recalculates. Therefore, if you have developed a model for simulating stock prices and want to see many new price paths quickly, you will use the first approach. To generate a new price path, you will simply press F9. However, if you want to generate one or more paths but do not want them to change as your worksheet recalculates for any reason, you will use the second approach. You may call a model that uses the first approach a dynamic model, and one that uses the second approach a static model.

While both these approaches work for simple demonstrations, they have two shortcomings for serious practical applications of simulations. First, if you want to generate thousands of paths, you may find both these approaches to be too slow. Second, if you want to do some calculations with the paths you are successively generating (for example, to estimate the mean stock price a year from now), you will not be able to do it in Excel using either approach. You can write VBA programs that overcome both problems.

Modeling Examples

MODEL 1: ESTIMATING A STOCK'S VOLATILITY, VERSION 1

The Problem

Create a model to calculate the annualized volatility for a stock based on the last 254 and 125 days of daily closing price data. Do the calculations in two ways: using the formula for volatility and using Excel's built-in functions for calculating standard deviation.

Modeling Strategy

The worksheet for this model is shown in Figure 18.1. We discussed the necessary formulas in the earlier section on estimating volatility. To calculate the

	A	B	C	D	E	F	G
1	Estimating a Stock's Volatility Using Daily Data						
2							
3							
4		Using formulas		Using Excel functions			
5	Number of days of data	254	125	254	125		
6	Number of daily returns	253	124	253	124		
7	Mean daily return	-0.0011	0.0000				
8	Daily variance	0.0016	0.0016				
9	Daily standard deviation	0.0403	0.0404	0.0403	0.0404		
10	Volatility (annualized SD)	63.65%	63.95%	63.65%	63.95%		
11							
12							
13							
14							
15	Date	Closing	Price	Daily	Squared deviation		
16		price	relative	return	254 days	125 days	
17	2-Jan-03	13.64	1.0412	0.0404	0.0017	0.00163	
18	31-Dec-02	13.10	1.0100	0.0100	0.0001	1E-04	
19	30-Dec-02	12.97	0.9969	-0.0031	0.0000	9.4E-06	
20	27-Dec-02	13.01	0.9931	-0.0069	0.0000	4.7E-05	
21	26-Dec-02	13.10	0.9813	-0.0189	0.0003	0.00036	
22	24-Dec-02	13.35	0.9933	-0.0067	0.0000	4.5E-05	
23	23-Dec-02	13.44	1.0128	0.0127	0.0002	0.00016	
24	20-Dec-02	13.27	1.0208	0.0206	0.0005	0.00042	
25	19-Dec-02	13.00	0.9834	-0.0168	0.0002	0.00028	
26	18-Dec-02	13.22	0.9678	-0.0327	0.0010	0.00107	
27	17-Dec-02	13.66	0.9971	-0.0029	0.0000	8.4E-06	
28	16-Dec-02	13.70	1.0224	0.0221	0.0005	0.00049	
29	13-Dec-02	13.40	0.9497	-0.0516	0.0026	0.00266	
30	12-Dec-02	14.11	1.0188	0.0186	0.0004	0.00035	
31	11-Dec-02	13.85	0.9943	-0.0058	0.0000	3.3E-05	
32	10-Dec-02	13.93	1.0319	0.0314	0.0011	0.00098	
33	9-Dec-02	13.50	0.9520	-0.0491	0.0023	0.00241	

FIGURE 18.1 Model 1: Estimating volatility of a stock from daily prices for fixed number of days.

continuously compounded rate of daily return, first calculate the price relative of the stock (today's price divided by yesterday's price) for every day and then take its natural logarithm. Use these daily rates of return in the appropriate formulas to calculate the daily standard deviation. Then annualize it assuming 250 trading days per year.

To calculate the volatility using Excel's built-in functions, use the calculated daily returns in Excel's STDEV function and then annualize the result. You should use the STDEV function because it provides an unbiased estimate of population standard deviation from a random sample.

Building the Model

Start with the daily stock price data in columns A and B, starting in row 17 as shown.

1. **Set up output area:** Enter the labels in A5:A10 and B4:E4.
2. **Calculate daily price relatives and daily returns:** In C17 enter the formula =B17/B18 to calculate the daily price relatives. Copy the formula into all the cells below C17 in column C up to one day before the last day for which data is given. (Entering it in the cell for the last day will result in a division by 0.)

   To calculate the continuously compounded daily return, in cell D17 enter the formula =LN(C17).
3. **Calculate daily standard deviation:** Enter the number of days in cells B5:E6 as shown. The number of daily return is one less than the number of days of data to be used.

   To calculate the mean daily returns, in B7 enter the formula =SUM ($D17:$D269)/(B$6) and in C7 enter the formula =SUM($D17:$D140)/(C$6).

   To calculate the squared deviation from the mean, in E17 enter the formula =(D17-$B$7)^2 and in F17, enter the formula =($D17-$C$7)^2. Since you are going to copy these formulas in the cells below and all calculations in a column will have to use the same mean return, the cell references for the mean returns have to be made absolute. Copy the formula in E17 into E18:E269 and the formula in F17 into F18:F140.

   To calculate the daily variance, in B8 enter the formula =SUM ($E17:$E269)/(B$6-1) and in C8 enter the formula =SUM($F17:$F140)/(C$6-1). Notice that to get an unbiased estimate of the daily variances in both cases the divisor used is one less than the number of data points used.

   Calculate the daily standard deviation by entering in B9 the formula =SQRT(B$8). Copy the formula into C9.
4. **Annualize the daily standard deviation:** To calculate the annualized volatility, in B10 enter the formula =B$9*SQRT(250) and copy the formula in C10.

5. **Calculate the annualized volatility using Excel functions:** In D9, enter the formula =STDEV($D17:$D269), which will calculate the daily standard deviation from the daily returns. Copy the formula into E9.

   To annualize the volatilities, in D10 enter the formula =D$9*SQRT(250) and copy it into E10.

Testing the Model

Because you have calculated the annual volatilities in two ways, if the answers from the two calculations are identical then they should be correct.

Uses of the Model

Models like this are used all the time to calculate the volatility of a stock's price from historical data. Notice that, as expected, the estimates depend on how many days of data you use. In this case the difference is minor, but often they can be significantly different.

Limitations of the Model

In this model, the user cannot easily change the number of days of data to be used for making the estimate. We will create this flexibility in the next model.

MODEL 2: ESTIMATING A STOCK'S VOLATILITY, VERSION 2

The Problem

Create a model to calculate the annualized volatility for a stock based on daily closing price data. The user should be able to specify how many days of data, going backward from the last day, the model should use for the estimate. Do the calculations in two ways: using the formula for volatility and also using Excel's built-in functions for calculating standard deviation.

Modeling Strategy

The worksheet for this model is shown in Figure 18.2. This model has to do the same calculations as Model 1 except that the number of days of data to use is not fixed. This means that the calculations have to ignore the data for the days beyond the number of days specified.

For calculating volatility with the formulas, one simple approach is to use IF functions to make the daily returns and squared deviations 0 for the days to be ignored so that even though the calculations will be done including all the days for which data is available, the data for the days beyond the number of specified days will have no effect on the results.

	A	B	C	D	E	F	G	H	I
1	**Estimating a Stock's Volatility Using Daily Data**								
2									
3		**Using**	**Using**						
4		**Formula**	**Function**						
5	Number of days of data	200							
6	Number of daily returns	199							
7	Mean daily return	-0.0008							
8	Daily variance	0.0017							
9	Daily standard deviation	0.0410	0.0410						
10	Volatility (annualized SD)	64.83%	64.83%						
11									
12									
13									
14							For formula		For function
15	Date	Closing	Price	Daily	Squared		Daily	Squared	Daily
16		price	relative	return	deviation	Day No.	return	deviation	return
17	2-Jan-03	13.64	1.0412	0.0404	0.0017	1	0.0404	0.0017	0.0404
18	31-Dec-02	13.10	1.0100	0.0100	0.0001	2	0.0100	0.0001	0.0100
19	30-Dec-02	12.97	0.9969	-0.0031	0.0000	3	-0.0031	0.0000	-0.0031
20	27-Dec-02	13.01	0.9931	-0.0069	0.0000	4	-0.0069	0.0000	-0.0069
21	26-Dec-02	13.10	0.9813	-0.0189	0.0003	5	-0.0189	0.0003	-0.0189
22	24-Dec-02	13.35	0.9933	-0.0067	0.0000	6	-0.0067	0.0000	-0.0067
262	11-Jan-02	20.21	0.9624	-0.0383	0.0014	246	0.0000	0.0000	Extra
263	10-Jan-02	21.00	1.0072	0.0072	0.0001	247	0.0000	0.0000	Extra
264	9-Jan-02	20.85	0.9952	-0.0048	0.0000	248	0.0000	0.0000	Extra
265	8-Jan-02	20.95	1.0205	0.0203	0.0004	249	0.0000	0.0000	Extra
266	7-Jan-02	20.53	0.9856	-0.0145	0.0002	250	0.0000	0.0000	Extra
267	4-Jan-02	20.83	1.0034	0.0034	0.0000	251	0.0000	0.0000	Extra
268	3-Jan-02	20.76	1.0796	0.0766	0.0060	252	0.0000	0.0000	Extra
269	2-Jan-02	19.23	1.0618	0.0600	0.0037	253	0.0000	0.0000	Extra
270	31-Dec-01	18.11							
271									
272									

FIGURE 18.2 Model 2: Estimating volatility of a stock from daily prices for specified number of days.

For calculating volatility with Excel's STDEV function, make use of the fact that the function ignores any argument that is not a number. You can again use IF functions to make the daily return cells show text for the days to be ignored. With this change, daily returns for all the days for which data is available can be used in the STDEV function.

Building the Model

It may be easier to start with a copy of Model 1 and modify it than to start fresh. I will discuss primarily the changes you have to make.

1. **Set up data input and output area:** Enter the labels in A5:A10 and B3:C4. B5 is the cell for the number of days that the user will specify.
2. **Create day count:** Clear all columns beyond E. To number the days, in F17 enter 1, in F18 enter the formula =F17+1, and copy it into all the cells in column F to the end of the data range.

3. **Create new columns for daily returns and squared deviations:** In cell G17 enter the formula =IF(F17>$B$5-1,0,D17). This will copy the daily return into this cell, but in cells beyond the number of days specified by the user (as determined by the condition) it will enter 0 in the cell. Copy the formula into G18:G269.

   To do the same for squared deviation, in H17 enter the formula =IF(F17>$B$5-1,0,E17) and copy it into H18:H269.
4. **Create new column for daily return for use with the STDEV function:** In I17 enter the formula =IF(F17>$B$5-1,"Extra",D17). This is similar to the formula we entered in G17. Here, however, in cells beyond the number of days specified, the IF function will enter the text "Extra" instead of 0. Entering 0 would not have worked because the cells would have been counted as legitimate data and would have produced wrong results.
5. **Calculate volatility using formulas:** The calculations are the same as before except that you have to use the data from the columns G and H. Enter the formulas as follows: in B6, enter =B$5-1. In B7, enter =SUM($G17:$G269)/(B$6). In B8 enter =SUM($H17:$H269)/(B$6-1). In B9 enter =SQRT(B$8). In B10 enter =B$9*SQRT(250).
6. **Calculate volatility using STDEV:** Here you have to use the data from column I. In C9, enter the formula =STDEV($I17:$I269) and in C10, the formula =C$9*SQRT(250).

Testing the Model

As long as the results from the two different methods of calculation agree exactly, your model should be correct. You can also check it against the results from the previous model.

MODEL 3: SIMULATING STOCK PRICES

The Problem

Develop a model to simulate the price of a stock given its current price, expected return, volatility, and the simulation step size. Make all of these input variables so that the user can change them. The user should also be able to generate new price paths easily. Create a chart to show the simulated price paths for the stock and its certain and uncertain components.

Modeling Strategy

The worksheet for this model is shown in Figure 18.3. Use the equations discussed earlier to calculate the stock price at the end of a step (based on the price at the beginning of the step) and repeat the process for each step. To simulate the price for each step, you will need a random draw from a standard normal distribution.

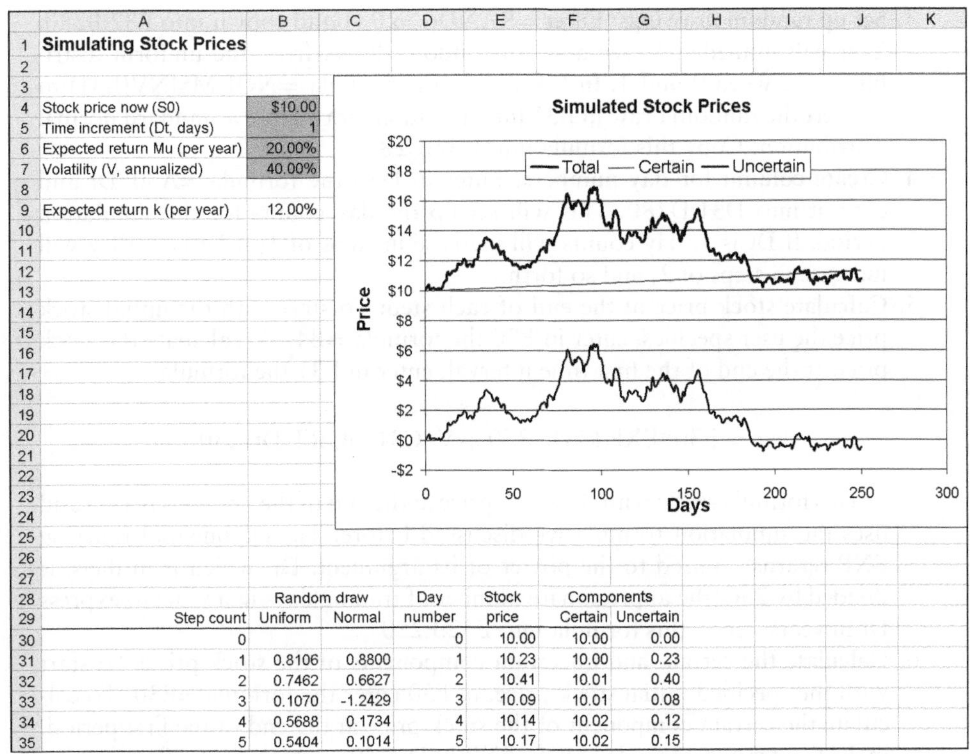

Simulating Stock Prices

	A	B
4	Stock price now (S0)	$10.00
5	Time increment (Dt, days)	1
6	Expected return Mu (per year)	20.00%
7	Volatility (V, annualized)	40.00%
9	Expected return k (per year)	12.00%

		Random draw		Day	Stock	Components	
	Step count	Uniform	Normal	number	price	Certain	Uncertain
30	0			0	10.00	10.00	0.00
31	1	0.8106	0.8800	1	10.23	10.00	0.23
32	2	0.7462	0.6627	2	10.41	10.01	0.40
33	3	0.1070	-1.2429	3	10.09	10.01	0.08
34	4	0.5688	0.1734	4	10.14	10.02	0.12
35	5	0.5404	0.1014	5	10.17	10.02	0.15

FIGURE 18.3 Model 3: Simulation of a stock's price.

As explained earlier, you can use the RAND function to draw a random sample between 0 and 1 from a uniform distribution and then use the NORMSINV to convert it into a random draw from a standard normal distribution. You use this approach here instead of using the Random Number Generation tool because using RAND allows the user to get a new set of draws and create a new simulation by simply pressing F9.

Building the Model

1. **Set up data input area:** Set up the data input area as shown and name B5 Dt, B6 Mu, and B7 V. To calculate k, enter the formula =Mu-V^2/2 in B9. Name B9 k and enter an appropriate label in A9.
2. **Create column for step count:** Enter 0 in A30 and 1 in A31, select the two cells and, by dragging the corner handle, fill cells A32:A280 to create step counts up to 250. This will provide for 250 steps of simulation. You can use fewer or more steps. The user specifies Dt. With Dt of 1, it will cover about one year of simulation for trading days; with Dt of 2, about 2 years, and so on.

3. **Set up random drawings:** Enter =RAND() in B31 and copy it into B32:B280. You will immediately see a set of random draws from the uniform distribution between 0 and 1. In C31, enter the formula =NORMSINV(B31) to convert the random draw in B31 into a random draw from a standard normal distribution. Copy this formula into C32:C280.
4. **Create column for day numbers:** Enter in D30 the formula =A30*Dt and copy it into D31:D280. This will set up the day counts for the simulation period. If Dt is 1, day counts will increase in steps of 1; if Dt is 2, they will increase in steps of 2, and so forth.
5. **Calculate stock price at the end of each step:** To start with the initial stock price the user specifies, enter in E30 the formula =B4. To calculate the stock price at the end of the first time interval, enter in E31 the formula

   = E30*EXP(k*Dt/250 + V*C31*SQRT(Dt/250))

   This formula starts with the stock price at the end of the previous period and uses the simulation formula we discussed before. The exponential function EXP returns e raised to the power of its argument. Dt, which is in days, is divided by 250 (the approximate number of trading days in a year) to express Dt in years. Copy this formula into E32:E280
6. **Calculate the certain and uncertain components of the stock price:** To start with the specified initial stock price, in F30 enter the formula =E30. To calculate the certain component of the stock price at the end of the first period, in F31 enter the formula =F30*EXP(k*Dt/250), which is the first part of the formula we used before. Copy this formula into F32:F280. The uncertain component is the simulated stock price less the certain component. To calculate it, in G30 enter the formula =E30-F30 and copy it into G31:G280.
7. **Create chart:** Select D30:G280 and use the Chart Wizard to create an embedded chart. (Use Chart type XY.) Properly format and label the chart. Try different simulations (by changing the input values and also by pressing F9). You will notice that the scale for the Y-axis will keep changing and it may make it difficult get a good feel for the simulation results. Instead of letting Excel automatically choose the appropriate scale for the Y-axis for different simulations, I have set the minimum value at −2 and the maximum value at 20. I have also specified that the X-axis cross the Y-axis at −2. These settings make it easier to see the simulated stock price and its two components. However, if you fix the scale, then you may have to change the scale manually again for a much different initial price.

Testing the Model

You can test the model's output against hand calculations. For any row, calculate the simulated stock price starting with the previous price and use the random draw from column C. Also change the input variables and make sure that the changes taking place seem reasonable.

Uses of the Model

This model is very useful for visualizing how stock prices develop under the geometric Brownian motion assumption. As you can observe by pressing F9 repeatedly to generate different price paths, the simulated price paths look remarkably similar to the price history of individual stocks and stock indexes. This should convince you that all the patterns in the historical price charts that chartists see are mostly illusions, because prices generated through this stochastic process generate similar patterns as well.

You can also see the effect of volatility by changing it from 0 to high numbers. In this model, μ is an input. Therefore, if you hold it constant and increase volatility, the expected continuously compounded rate of return (k) will get smaller with the effect that the line showing the certain component will become flatter. The variations around it, however, will become more pronounced.

Limitations of the Model

Although it is not a limitation of the model itself, it is somewhat disappointing that such an elegant model is of very little help in making investment decisions. However, if playing around with the model convinces you that trying to pick winning stocks is a loser's game, then you will have learned a valuable lesson.

MODEL 4: LOGNORMAL DISTRIBUTION OF STOCK PRICES

The Problem

Create a model to show in a chart the lognormal distribution of a stock's price at some point in time in the future. The user should be able to specify the stock's current price, expected annual return and volatility, and also the time horizon.

Modeling Strategy

The worksheet for this model is shown in Figure 18.4. This model requires a good understanding of the geometric Brownian motion model of stock prices and probability distributions. If you are not comfortable with them, you may want to skip this model. Also note that this model produces an approximate distribution of stock prices at the specified time horizon.

You have to start by deciding what range of stock prices the chart should cover. We will assume that it will be enough to cover a range of 4 standard deviations above and below the mean stock price at the horizon. Break down the chosen range into 200 equidistant stock prices, and for each stock price chosen

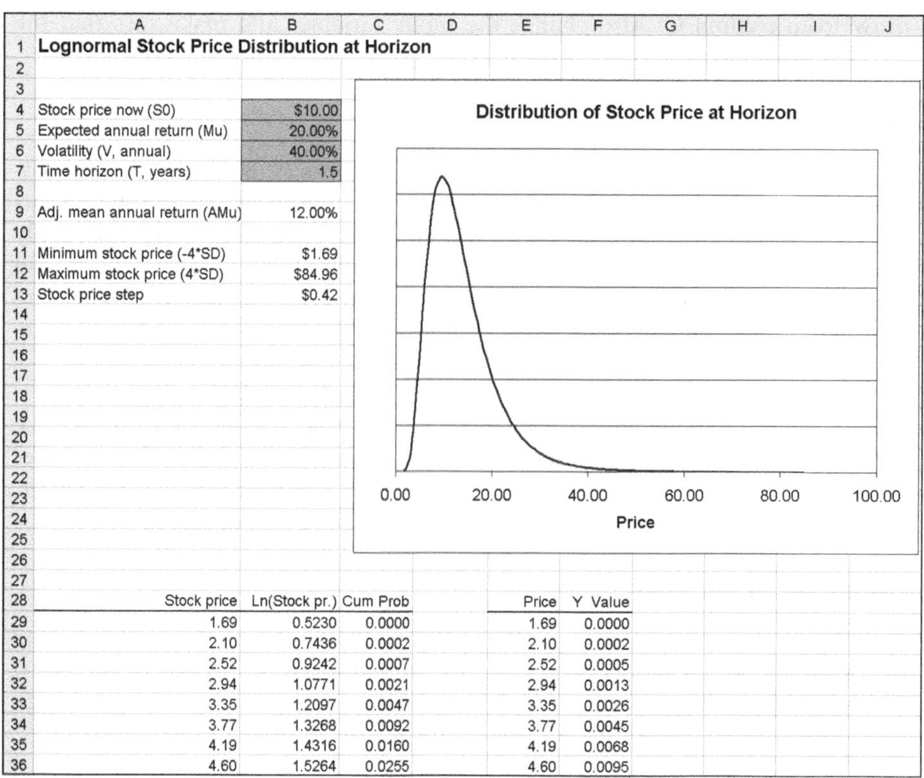

Lognormal Stock Price Distribution at Horizon
Stock price now (S0) $10.00
Expected annual return (Mu) 20.00%
Volatility (V, annual) 40.00%
Time horizon (T, years) 1.5
Adj. mean annual return (AMu) 12.00%
Minimum stock price (-4*SD) $1.69
Maximum stock price (4*SD) $84.96
Stock price step $0.42
Distribution of Stock Price at Horizon
0.00
20.00
40.00
60.00
80.00
100.00
Price
Stock price Ln(Stock pr.) Cum Prob
1.69 0.5230 0.0000
2.10 0.7436 0.0002
2.52 0.9242 0.0007
2.94 1.0771 0.0021
3.35 1.2097 0.0047
3.77 1.3268 0.0092
4.19 1.4316 0.0160
4.60 1.5264 0.0255
Price Y Value
1.69 0.0000
2.10 0.0002
2.52 0.0005
2.94 0.0013
3.35 0.0026
3.77 0.0045
4.19 0.0068
4.60 0.0095

FIGURE 18.4 Model 4: Lognormal distribution of stock price at horizon.

calculate the cumulative probability. To plot the chart, you need the probability of the stock price falling between each pair of adjacent stock prices. Calculate this as the difference between the cumulative probabilities for each pair of prices. Plot the chart using the stock prices in the X-axis and the probability of the stock price falling between that price and the price below it in the Y-axis.

Building the Model

1. **Set up data input cells:** Create the data input cells with the proper labels and name them as shown
2. **Calculate adjusted mean annual return:** To calculate this, in B9 enter the formula =Mu-(V^2)/2. Name the cell B9 AMu.
3. **Calculate minimum and maximum stock prices to use:** To calculate the minimum stock price to use in the chart, in B11 enter the formula =EXP((LN(S0)+AMu*T)-4*V*SQRT(T)). The first two terms in the formula

relates to the mean stock price at the horizon and the last part subtracts from it 4 standard deviations. This is based on the equation in the section entitled "Stock prices are lognormally distributed."

To calculate the maximum stock price for the chart in B12 enter the formula =EXP((LN(S0)+AMu*T)+4*V*SQRT(T)). This is 4 standard deviations above the mean.

4. **Calculate stock price step and stock price series:** To calculate the stock price step, in B13 enter the formula =(B12-B11)/200. This will break down the chosen stock price range into 200 equal steps. The selection of 200 is arbitrary, but for the chart to look good you need a large number of steps.

   To create the series for stock prices, in A29 enter the formula =B11, in A30 the formula =A29+$B$13, and then copy this formula into A31:A229.
5. **Calculate cumulative probability for each stock price:** Calculate the logarithm of each stock price by entering the formula =LN(A29) in B20 and then copying it into B30: B229.

   To calculate the cumulative probability in C29 enter the formula =NORMDIST(B29,LN(S0)+AMu*T,V*SQRT(T),TRUE). The NORMDIST function calculates the cumulative probability for the logarithm of the stock price (B29), which is normally distributed with the mean given by the second argument and standard deviation by the third argument.
6. **Calculate the probability for the range between each pair of price:** In F29 enter the formula =$C29. In F30, enter the formula =$C30-$C29. This calculates the probability of the price falling in the range between $1.32 and $1.93 as the difference between the cumulative probabilities. Copy the formula into F31:F229.
7. **Create the chart:** For convenience, duplicate in E29:E229 the stock prices in A29:A229. Plot an XY chart using the data from the columns E and F. Format and label it appropriately.

Testing the Models

There is no simple way to test the model other than double-checking the formulas. It can also be checked by testing that the distribution is changing as expected as the different input variables are changed.

Uses of the Model

The model is useful for developing an intuitive feeling for how the future price distribution of a stock will change with the various variables that influence it. For example, by changing the volatility you can see how the distribution becomes essentially symmetrical at low volatilities and increasingly skewed at higher volatilities. Similarly, the distribution is nearly symmetrical for short time horizons but becomes increasingly skewed as the time horizon gets longer.

CHAPTER 19

Options and Option Portfolios

In the last three decades, derivative securities—meaning securities whose prices depend on the prices of other securities or assets—have become one of the most important segments of the financial markets. They are used for both speculating and hedging, but a key use is to create portfolios with characteristics that meet the wide range of needs and tastes of the millions of participants in the financial markets.

Options constitute one of the most important classes of derivative securities, and it is now recognized that many real life problems have "option-like characteristics." In this chapter, we will develop several models to estimate the prices and the Greeks for options. We will also demonstrate some of their properties and will develop a model for a portfolio of stocks and options that can be used to study various option-trading strategies.

Review of Theory and Concepts

Some of the theory and mathematics related to the pricing of options is fairly complex and beyond the scope of this book. For details on them, you can refer to any of the standard books on derivatives. An excellent book on the subject is *Options, Futures, and Other Derivatives* by John C. Hull (6th edition); some of the material in this chapter parallels his presentations.

OPTION BASICS AND TERMINOLOGY

Options can be created on almost any asset, and they are now actively traded on a wide range of assets such as stocks, bonds, and currencies. It is easiest to learn the basics of options by looking at options on stocks. The concepts can then be extended to options on other kinds of assets.

There are two types of options: *calls* and *puts*. A call option on a stock gives the buyer or holder the right (but not the obligation) to buy the stock at a particular price within a specified period of time. For example, if you buy a 3-month call option on General Electric (GE) stock with an exercise price of $30 for a price of $3, you will have the right to buy from the option's seller (also called the writer) one stock of GE for the exercise price of $30 anytime during the 3-month period, irrespective of the stock's price at that time.

In options terminology, the GE stock is called the underlying security or asset, the $30 price at which you have the right to buy the stock is called the exercise or strike price, and the $3 you paid to buy the call option is called the option or call premium. Since the right the call gives you is valid for a period of 3 months, the call is said to have a life or time until expiration of 3 months. The process of purchasing the GE stock by paying the $30 exercise price, if and when you choose to do so, is called exercising the call.

If you have the right to exercise an option at any time during its life (as we have been assuming), then it is called an American option. If, however, you have the right to exercise an option only at the end of its life, then it is called a European option. (If you have difficulty remembering which is which, use this mnemonic: *A*merican *A*lways, *E*uropean at *E*xpiration.)

If instead of a call option you had bought an American put option on a GE stock under the same terms, then you would have the right to sell a GE stock at any time during the 3-month period at $30 irrespective of the price of the stock at that time. (All other terminology remains the same.)

Although almost all options people trade are American options, it is easier to first analyze European options and then consider American options as an extension. This is the approach we will take.

Why would you buy a call option? Suppose the GE call you bought was a European call and GE stock goes up to $50 at the time the call expires. Then you will be able to exercise your call to buy the stock for $30 and immediately sell it in the market for $50. This will produce a gross profit of $20, or a net profit of $17, after deducting the call premium you paid. The $20 is called the call's payoff.

For you to make money on the call, GE stock will have to be above $33 at the time of the call's expiration. Beyond that, the higher the price of GE stock at the call's expiration, the higher your profit will be. Theoretically, your profit potential is unlimited. However, if GE stock price is below $30 at the call's expiration, then you will not exercise the call because you do not have any obligation to do so and you would not want to buy GE stock at $30 if it is available in the market for less. Your maximum loss is therefore limited to the $3 premium you paid.

It should now be clear that people buy call options because they offer highly leveraged opportunities to profit from the rise in a stock's price with the downside risk limited to the premium paid. Because puts work exactly the opposite way, they offer highly leveraged opportunities to profit from the fall in a stock's price, with the downside risk limited to the premium paid. So if you expect a stock to go up, you will buy calls, and if you expect it to go down, you will buy puts.

What we mean by highly leveraged is that on equal dollar investments, an option investor has the potential to make significantly higher profits on the options than on the underlying asset. This applies to losses as well, except that the loss on an option is limited to the premium paid. (You will be able to see all of this clearly using some of the models we will develop.)

One other difference between calls and puts, mostly of theoretical interest, is that there is no limit on a call's profit potential because there is no limit on how high a stock's price can go. A put's profit potential is limited because a stock's price can never fall below zero.

Here are a few other option terms you should be familiar with. Whenever an option's exercise price equals the stock price, the option is said to be *at-the-money*. If the exercise price is lower than the stock price, then a call option is said to be *in-the-money* and a put option is said to be *out-of-the-money*, because you could make a profit by immediately exercising the call but not the put. When the exercise price is above the stock's price, then the call is out-of-the-money and the put is in-the-money. Over its life, a call or a put can fluctuate among these different stages as the price of the stock fluctuates, but you would exercise an European call only if it is in-the-money at the time of expiration. If an option is in-the-money, the (gross) amount of money you can make by exercising it immediately is called the option's *intrinsic value*. At other times, the intrinsic value is zero. Most of the time during its life, an option sells for more than its intrinsic value.

PAYOFFS OF OPTIONS AT EXPIRATION

Let us consider a call option—European or American—with exercise price K and assume the stock price is S at the time of the call's expiration. If S is less than or equal to K, the call holder will let the call expire and the payoff of the call will be zero. If S is greater than K, the call holder will exercise the call for a payoff of $S - K$. The results for a put holder are obvious. We can express the payoffs for options at expiration as:

$$\text{Payoff to call holder} = \text{Max}(0, S - K)$$
$$\text{Payoff to put holder} = \text{Max}(0, K - S)$$

In developing option models, we will find that in many situations we can use exactly the same equations for calls and puts if we define an option type indicator, OptType, with values of 1 for calls and −1 for puts. We can then write one equation for option payoff as follows:

$$\text{Payoff to option holder} = \text{Max}\{0, \text{OptType} \times (S - K)\}$$

The option holder's profit will be equal to the payoff less the total premiums paid for the options.

If instead of an option an investor buys the stock at K and at some point in the future the stock price is S, then we can calculate the profit or payoff (for stocks they are the same) at that point as:

$$\text{Profit of stockholder} = (S - K)$$

In this case, the investor will have a profit if the stock price is above the purchase price and a loss if the stock price is below the purchase price. If instead of buying the stock, the investor sells the stock short, then the situation will be reversed. (Selling short means the investor sold stocks that he did not own. He borrowed the stocks from someone and delivered them to the buyer, and at some point in the future he will have to buy an equal number of stocks to return them to the lender.)

THE BLACK-SCHOLES-MERTON EQUATION FOR OPTION VALUATION

As we saw, it is easy to calculate the payoffs for options at expiration. To eliminate arbitrage opportunities, the value of an option at expiration must equal its payoff. But what should be the values of options before expiration? Black, Scholes, and Merton (BSM) showed that values of European options depend on five variables: S, the price of the stock; K, the exercise price; r, the continuously compounded risk-free interest rate per year; q, the continuous dividend yield per year; T, the time until expiration (in years); and σ, the stock's annualized volatility. (We discussed volatility in Chapter 18: Simulating Stock Prices. The three economists also showed that, with these symbols, the price of an European call option, c, and put option, p, are given by the following equations:

$$c = Se^{-qT}N(d_1) - Ke^{-rT}N(d_2)$$

and

$$p = Ke^{-rT}N(-d_2) - Se^{-qT}N(-d_1)$$

where

$$d_1 = \frac{\ln(S/K) + (r - q + \sigma^2/2)T}{\sigma\sqrt{T}}$$

$$d_2 = \frac{\ln(S/K) + (r - q - \sigma^2/2)T}{\sigma\sqrt{T}} = d_1 - \sigma\sqrt{T}$$

The notation $N(d)$ stands for the cumulative standard normal probability distribution function for value d. In other words, $N(d_1)$ is the probability that a random sample you draw from a standard normal distribution (that is, a normal distribution with a mean equal to zero and standard deviation equal to 1) will have a value less than or equal to d_1. Because the normal distribution is symmetrical with a mean equal to zero, $N(-d) = 1 - N(d)$, which will simplify modeling the equation for puts once we have modeled the equation for calls.

Let us note a few points about these equations:

- The equations give the values of only European options. Values of American options are always greater than or equal to those of their European counterparts because they offer the holders all the rights of European options as well as the right to exercise them at any time, not just at expiration. In some situations, this additional right makes no difference, that is, the holder of an American option does not have an opportunity to make any more money than the holder of a similar European option. In these situations, the values of American options are the same as those of their European counterparts. In most situations, American options provide slightly better payoff potential than their European counterparts and, therefore, have slightly higher values than similar European options. We will discuss later how to estimate the values of American options.
- A key assumption of the BSM equations is that the stock price follows the geometric Brownian motion we discussed earlier.
- The original option-pricing equations, which are generally referred to as the Black-Scholes equations, applied only to stocks that pay no dividends. Merton extended those equations as above to dividend-paying stocks, and we will refer to these as the BSM equations. We can get the original equations by substituting zeros for q. An advantage of the equations in this form is that they can be used not just for options on dividend-paying stocks but for a number of other types of options, such as options on currencies.
- The equations assume that the stock has a constant continuous dividend yield, which does not strictly apply to any stock because stocks pay only discrete (generally quarterly) dividends that change in steps. However, it is easy to convert such discrete dividends to equivalent constant continuous dividend yields and use them to price options with minor errors. Also, if the dividend yield is not constant for the life of the option, the equations can still be used with q equal to the average annualized dividend yield during the life of the option.
- If in the equation for the call value we multiply S, K, d_1, and d_2 by the option type indicator (optType) we discussed earlier, then for optType = 1, we get the equations for the call value and for optType = −1, we get the equations for the put value. This property can be used in both Excel and VBA models for these equations.

An Apparent Puzzle

You may, and most people do, find it puzzling that the price of an option does not depend on the expected return on the stock. In other words, how well the stock is expected to do does not matter in pricing the option. How can this be?

The reason is that the stock's price already reflects how well it is expected to do, and because we calculate the price of the option in terms of the price of the underlying stock, the expectation about the stock's price does not have to be taken into consideration again.

Put-Call Parity

As you would guess, the values of two otherwise identical European put and call options are related. The relationship, expressed by the following equation, is called *put-call parity*.

$$c + Ke^{-rT} = p + Se^{-qT}$$

If we know or can calculate the value of an European put or call, then we can use the put-call parity to calculate the value of its counterpart.

Implied Volatility

Of the variables on which the price of an option depends, the only one that cannot be observed directly—and therefore has to be predicted to value an option—is the volatility of the price of the underlying stock. Naturally, the volatility predictions and the estimate of an option's value of different market participants will vary.

Since we can observe the prices of options on a stock in the market, it is possible to ask the question *What forecast of volatility of the stock price would justify this option price?* As we will see, this volatility can be calculated from the BSM equations using a trial and error approach, that is, by iteration. It is called the implied volatility of the option. We can view this as the market's opinion or prediction of the stock's volatility. Ideally, the implied volatility calculated from all options on a stock expiring at the same time would be the same. In practice, however, they are not, and we can attribute this to various reasons. The most likely explanation is that stock prices over time do not behave exactly the way we assume them to behave in most theoretical analyses like the derivation of the BSM equations. Market participants generally monitor the average implied volatility calculated from the actively traded options on a stock, believing that it provides useful information about the stock's future price movement.

The Effect of Dividends

How do dividends on a stock affect the price of options on it? We can calculate that from the BSM equations, but it is worthwhile to develop an intuitive understanding of it. Let us consider two otherwise identical stocks, one of which pays dividends and the other does not. At least theoretically, both stocks should provide the same total returns over time. So as the dividend-paying stock pays dividends, its stock price will fall behind the price of the other stock and the potential payoffs from call options on it will be lower and from put options will be higher than those from options on the stock that pays no dividends. Dividends on the underlying stock therefore have the effect of reducing the price of call options and increasing the price of put options on it. These effects are already reflected in the BSM equations through q.

THE GREEK LETTERS

Since the price of an option depends on several variables, it will change with changes in the value of any of those variables. Option investors and traders as well as those who use options to hedge their portfolios need to understand and measure the impact of changes in the different variables on the price of options. At the simplest level, the holder of an option wants to know how much the value of his option will change if the stock price changes by one dollar or how fast the value of his option will deteriorate with the passage of time. At more complex levels, these sensitivities are used to measure and control the risks of large portfolios with respect to the different variables. For example, financial institutions who hold large portfolios that include enormous positions in derivatives need to estimate how the values of their portfolios would change if volatility went up or down sharply and decide how much of that risk they should hedge and how they should do so.

In mathematical terms, these sensitivities are measured by partial derivatives of the option price with respect to the different variables that determine option prices, and they are represented by certain Greek letters. This is why they are generally referred to as the Greek letters or simply "the Greeks." If you do not understand what partial derivatives are, what you need to know and must remember is that all these measures quantify the sensitivities only for very small changes in the underlying variables, while the other variables remain unchanged. I will explain this a little more in the next section on deltas.

A good way to develop some appreciation for the magnitudes and the behaviors of the Greeks is to look at charts that show how the price of an option changes with changes in the values of the different variables. We will be able to create such charts using some of the models we develop.

In the following sections, we will define the various Greeks and the equations to calculate their values for European options on dividend-paying stocks, which can be derived from the BSM equations. Note that the Greeks apply to portfolios of derivatives as well, and are most often used to measure the risks of portfolios and to hedge those risks.

Delta

Delta represents the sensitivity of the price of an option (or portfolio) to changes in the price of the stock. The delta for European calls on dividend-paying stocks is given by:

$$\Delta = e^{-qT} N(d_1)$$

For puts, it is:

$$\Delta = q^{-qT}[N(d_1) - 1]$$

This means that when the delta of an option is 0.5, a small change in the stock's price (say, a 10-cent change) will change the option's price by about 5 cents. Since this holds true only for small changes, this relationship will hold more closely for a 1-cent change in stock price and will be less accurate for a $1 change in the stock price. What happens is that the value of delta itself changes as the stock price changes. Therefore, to better estimate the change in an option's price for a larger change in the stock's price, you may have to estimate and take the difference between the prices of the option at the two prices of the stock instead of trying to estimate it using delta. As a practical matter, we will see that we can create models to easily estimate the effects of larger changes in the stock's price to the extent that the BSM equations hold.

Theta

Theta measures how the price of an option changes with time. You can use it to estimate how fast an option will lose value with the passage of time. The theta for call options is:

$$\Theta = -\frac{SN'(d_1)\sigma e^{-qT}}{2\sqrt{T}} + qSN(d_1)e^{-qT} - rKe^{-rT}N(d_2)$$

where

$$N'(x) = \frac{1}{\sqrt{2\pi}}e^{-x^2/2}$$

For a put option, it is:

$$\Theta = -\frac{SN'(d_1)\sigma e^{-qT}}{2\sqrt{T}} + qSN(-d_1)e^{-qT} + rKe^{-rT}N(-d_2)$$

Gamma

As I mentioned when discussing delta, the delta of an option changes with changes in the stock price. Since delta is one of the most important measures of an option's risk, it is important to measure how delta itself changes with changes in the price of the stock. This is what gamma measures.

Gamma is the sensitivity of a stock's delta to the stock price. It has the same value for both call and put options and is given by:

$$\Gamma = \frac{N'(d_1)e^{-qT}}{S\sigma\sqrt{T}}$$

Vega

Vega is the rate of change of the value of an option with respect to the volatility of the stock's price. Since option prices are quite sensitive to changes in volatility and volatility can fluctuate widely over time, this is another important measure of risk. The vega for both call and put options is given by:

$$\text{vega} = S\sqrt{T}N'(d_1)e^{-qT}$$

Rho

Rho measures the sensitivity of the price of an option with respect to the risk-free interest rate. For a call option, it is given by:

$$\text{rho} = KTe^{-rT}N(d_2)$$

For a put option, it is:

$$\text{rho} = -KTe^{-rT}N(-d_2)$$

The d_2 here has the same definitions as in the BSM equations.

Option Leverage

Although it does not belong among the Greek letters, option leverage is another sensitivity that investors often consider. Leverage is the percentage by which an option's price changes for a 1% change in the stock price. One reason investors buy options is that options are highly leveraged investments: if the stock moves in their favor, investors could earn much higher percentage returns on their investments in options than they would on investments in the underlying stock. Leverage, of course, cuts both ways and makes options highly risky as well, although the maximum possible loss on the investment in options is limited to the price paid.

As you would guess, the leverage of an option is related to its delta and equals the delta times the ratio of the stock price to the option price. Substituting for the values of delta, we get:

$$\text{Leverage of calls} = e^{-qT} N(d_1) \frac{S}{C}$$

$$\text{Leverage of puts} = e^{-qT} [N(d_1) - 1] \frac{S}{P}$$

We will develop a model to see how large these leverages are and how they vary with time and other factors.

VALUING AMERICAN OPTIONS

One thing that makes valuing European options somewhat easier is that they can be exercised only at expiration—we know with certainty exactly when they will be exercised, if they are exercised at all. American options are more difficult to value because they can be exercised at any time. If at any point along the way it is optimum to exercise an American option because the holder will make more money by doing so than by holding onto it until expiration, then a rational holder will exercise it early (that is, before expiration).

We can, therefore, make two observations about the values of American options. First, since an American option offers all the rights of an otherwise identical European option and then some, the value of an American option will always be at least as much as that of its European counterpart. Second, if it can be shown that it may be optimal to exercise an American option early, then the value of the option will be higher than that of its European counterpart. How much higher is, of course, the key issue.

It can be shown that the only American options that are never optimal to exercise early are call options on stocks that do not pay any dividend. In theory, then, identical European and American calls on such stocks would have the same values. In all other cases—that is, for put options on non-dividend–paying stocks and for both call and put options on dividend-paying stocks—under certain circumstances it may be optimum to exercise American options early and, therefore, they cannot be valued using the BSM equations.

It turns out that it is not possible to come up with BSM–type exact equations to value American options. They are generally valued using binomial trees, which we will discuss in the next chapter. While the BSM equations are valuable for the insights they provide into option values, binomial trees and other numerical methods are used in the real world more often to value options because most options traded in the financial markets are American options.

OPTION ON OTHER ASSETS

The BSM equations are quite versatile and can be used to value European options on a number of other classes of assets. They can be used to value European options on stock indexes, with q representing the average dividend yield on the stocks comprising the index. (Since indexes are generally based on a large number of stocks, compared to individual stocks, dividends on them are inherently closer to being continuous.)

The BSM equations can also be used to value European options on currencies by substituting the foreign risk-free rate for q.

Finally, they can be used to value European options on the futures of various assets by replacing q with the domestic risk-free interest rate. Options on futures of several assets are now traded extensively.

So even though all the models we will develop in this chapter are for stocks, you will be able to use them for a wide range of options on other assets without much modification.

As with stocks, valuing American options on any of the other assets gets more complex and generally requires use of binomial trees and other numerical methods.

OPTION PORTFOLIOS

Investors, speculators, and hedgers generally combine positions in puts, calls, and the underlying stock to create portfolios of various characteristics to suit their risk preference. They can then take advantage of their expectations about of the stock's price. Over the years, investors and traders have created a large number of trading strategies, some of which are quite complicated and can be confusing for a beginner. As long as a portfolio consists of European options and positions on just one stock, it is relatively easy to model it to predict its values at various points in time for any range of stock prices or other variables by valuing the positions separately and then adding them together. We will develop a versatile model for such portfolios, which you will be able use to explore and understand the myriad option-trading strategies.

Institutions and large investors, however, hold portfolios of dozens or even hundreds of different assets and options and derivatives on them. Modeling such portfolios gets highly complex, in part because of the interdependence of the various instruments in the portfolios. We will not get into the modeling of these types of portfolios. However, what you learn here are the essential building blocks for these more complex portfolio models.

Modeling Examples

MODEL 1: OPTION PAYOFFS AT EXPIRATION

The Problem

You have bought 500 GE stocks at $25 each; you have also bought 3 put and 2 call option contracts on GE stocks for $5.80 and $1.30 per share, respectively. All the options have an exercise price of $30 and expire in 6 months. Create a model to calculate (separately) the payoffs and profits for all the positions at the time the options expire if the price of the GE stock at that time is $40. Make your model general so that a user can use it to calculate payoffs and profits on other long and short stock-and-option positions. In addition to the two separate model components for puts and calls, create a component that can be used for both puts and calls using the appropriate value for an option type indicator, optType, as discussed before. (Note that an option contract on a stock represents options on 100 shares of the stock. Also, stock positions are often quantified in lots of 100 shares.)

Modeling Strategy

This model involves implementing the equations we discussed in the section "Payoff of Options at Expiration." The worksheet for this model is shown in Figure 19.1.

Building the Model

1. **Set up worksheet:** Create a worksheet with labels for the inputs as shown and enter the input values.
2. **Create formula for payoff on calls:** You have to calculate the terminal stock price minus the call exercise price. If this is positive, then the payoff is equal to terminal stock price less the exercise price. If the difference is negative, then the payoff is zero. So the payoff is the higher of zero and the difference between terminal stock price and exercise price. In B10 enter =MAX(0,B8-B4)*B6*B7 to implement this. The function MAX picks the largest of the arguments provided. Notice that the sign of the position—positive if you bought the calls and negative if you sold the calls—automatically produces the payoff with the right sign.

	A	B	C	D	E	F
1	**Payoffs and Profits at Expiration for Stock and Option Positions**					
2						
3	**Payoff of call positions at expiration**			**Profit of stock positions**		
4	Exercise price	$30.00		Purchase price/share	$25.00	
5	Premium/share	$1.30		Number of lots bought/(sold)	5	
6	Number of contracts bought/(sold)	2		Shares/lot	100	
7	Shares/contract	100		Price on future date	$40.00	
8	Stock price at options expiration	$40.00				
9				Profit/(loss)	$7,500	
10	Payoff	$2,000				
11	Profit/(loss)	$1,740		**Payoff of option positions at expiration**		
12				Option type indicator, Call = 1, Put = -1	-1	
13				Exercise price	$30.00	
14	**Payoff of put positions at expiration**			Premium/share	$5.80	
15				Number of contracts bought/(sold)	3	
16	Exercise price	$30.00		Shares/contract	100	
17	Premium/share	$5.80		Stock price at options expiration	$40.00	
18	Number of contracts bought/(sold)	3				
19	Shares/contract	100		Payoff	$0	
20	Stock price at options expiration	$40.00		Profit/(loss)	-$1,740	
21						
22	Payoff	$0				
23	Profit/(loss)	-$1,740				
24						
25						

FIGURE 19.1 Model 1: Payoffs and profits at expiration for options and stock.

3. **Create formula for profit on calls:** Profit on the call position is equal to the payoff less the premium paid for the calls. In B11 enter =B10-B5*B6*B7 to calculate the profit.
4. **Create formula for payoff on puts:** Puts payoff if the stock price ends up below the exercise price—the opposite of calls. In B22 enter =MAX(0,B16-B20)*B18*B19 to calculate put payoff.
5. **Create formula for profit on puts:** In B23 enter =B22-B17*B18*B19.
6. **Create formula for profit on stocks:** The profit on stocks is the terminal stock price less the price you paid. In E9 enter =(E7-E4)*E5*E6.
7. **Set up data validation for opt type:** To make sure that the user cannot enter anything other than 1 or −1 in E12, select E12, then select Data ⇨ Validation to bring up the Data Validation dialog box. Click the Settings tab. For Allow, choose List, and in the box for Source enter 1, −1. Make sure that neither Ignore blank nor In-cell dropdown is selected. In the Error Alert tab, type an appropriate message in the Error message box. (This message shows up if the user tries to enter anything other than what you specified earlier.) Click OK to complete.
8. **Create single formula for payoff of both puts and calls:** Name E12 optType by selecting the cell and then typing the name in the name box (at the left end of the formula bar). In E19 enter =MAX(0,optType*(E17-E13))*E15*E16. (If you do not understand the formula, see the earlier discussion in the section "Payoff of Options at Expiration.")
9. **Create formula for profit on puts and calls:** In E20 enter =E19-E14*E15*E16.

Testing the Model

To test the model, enter positive and negative positions and terminal prices higher and lower than exercise prices and check model outputs against hand-calculated results.

MODEL 2: PROFIT OF OPTION PORTFOLIOS AT EXPIRATION

The Problem

Develop a model to calculate the projected profits of a portfolio of up to 10 positions in stocks, calls, and puts at the time of expiration of the options for a range of terminal stock prices (that is, stock prices when the options expire). All the positions are on the same stock and all the options expire at the same time. For each position, the user should be able to enter the position type (stock, put, or call), exercise price or stock purchase price, position size, and premium paid (if option). Create a chart to show the projected portfolio profits (values) for a range of terminal stock prices.

Modeling Strategy

The worksheet for this model is shown in Figure 19.2. Use the method of the last model to calculate the payoffs for each position for each terminal price depending on the type of the position. Then, for each terminal price, sum the payoffs of all the positions and subtract the total premium paid to calculate the portfolio profit for that terminal price.

Building the Model

1. **Set up data input area and data validation:** Set up the data input area as shown and name D24 cSize. In A13, set up a data validation to ensure that the user can only enter C, P, or S. Copy it into A14:A22 using the validation option in Paste Special.
2. **Create column of terminal prices:** Instead of using fixed terminal prices, we want to let the user specify them by indicating in D25 the lowest terminal price he wants to see and in D26 the step size at which the terminal price should increase. In B35 enter =$D$25 and in B36 enter =B35+$D$26. Then copy the formula in B36 into B37:B64.
3. **Create links to input cells:** To be able to create one formula that you can copy into all the relevant cells to calculate the payoff for each position for all the terminal stock prices, we need to duplicate the input data for position type, exercise price, and position size in F31:O33. Also, as we will see, to make the payoff formula shorter, it will be convenient to have the position types

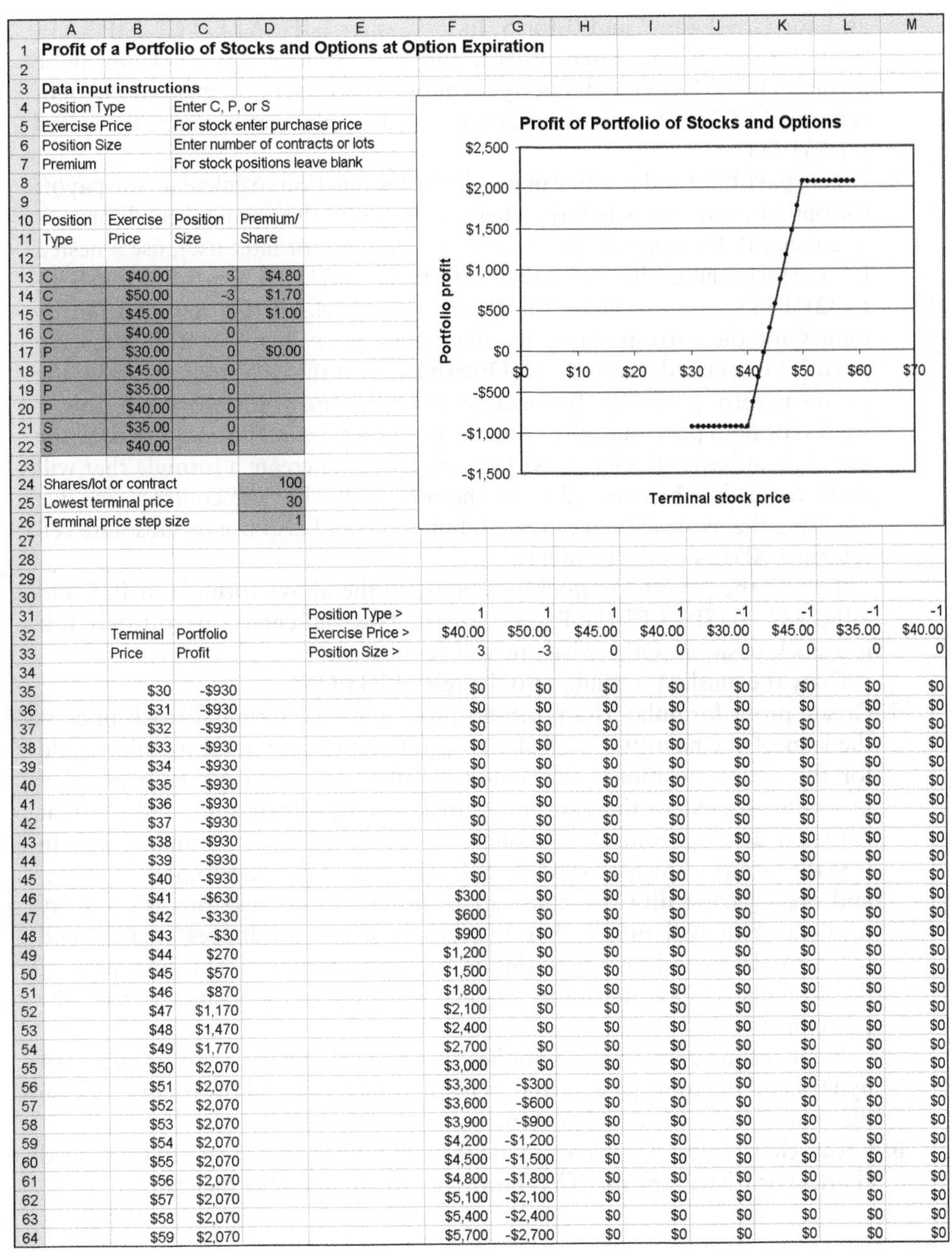

Profit of a Portfolio of Stocks and Options at Option Expiration

Data input instructions

Position Type	Enter C, P, or S
Exercise Price	For stock enter purchase price
Position Size	Enter number of contracts or lots
Premium	For stock positions leave blank

Position Type	Exercise Price	Position Size	Premium/ Share
C	$40.00	3	$4.80
C	$50.00	-3	$1.70
C	$45.00	0	$1.00
C	$40.00	0	
P	$30.00	0	$0.00
P	$45.00	0	
P	$35.00	0	
P	$40.00	0	
S	$35.00	0	
S	$40.00	0	

Shares/lot or contract	100
Lowest terminal price	30
Terminal price step size	1

Terminal Price	Portfolio Profit									
		Position Type >	1	1	1	1	-1	-1	-1	-1
		Exercise Price >	$40.00	$50.00	$45.00	$40.00	$30.00	$45.00	$35.00	$40.00
		Position Size >	3	-3	0	0	0	0	0	0
$30	-$930		$0	$0	$0	$0	$0	$0	$0	$0
$31	-$930		$0	$0	$0	$0	$0	$0	$0	$0
$32	-$930		$0	$0	$0	$0	$0	$0	$0	$0
$33	-$930		$0	$0	$0	$0	$0	$0	$0	$0
$34	-$930		$0	$0	$0	$0	$0	$0	$0	$0
$35	-$930		$0	$0	$0	$0	$0	$0	$0	$0
$36	-$930		$0	$0	$0	$0	$0	$0	$0	$0
$37	-$930		$0	$0	$0	$0	$0	$0	$0	$0
$38	-$930		$0	$0	$0	$0	$0	$0	$0	$0
$39	-$930		$0	$0	$0	$0	$0	$0	$0	$0
$40	-$930		$0	$0	$0	$0	$0	$0	$0	$0
$41	-$630		$300	$0	$0	$0	$0	$0	$0	$0
$42	-$330		$600	$0	$0	$0	$0	$0	$0	$0
$43	-$30		$900	$0	$0	$0	$0	$0	$0	$0
$44	$270		$1,200	$0	$0	$0	$0	$0	$0	$0
$45	$570		$1,500	$0	$0	$0	$0	$0	$0	$0
$46	$870		$1,800	$0	$0	$0	$0	$0	$0	$0
$47	$1,170		$2,100	$0	$0	$0	$0	$0	$0	$0
$48	$1,470		$2,400	$0	$0	$0	$0	$0	$0	$0
$49	$1,770		$2,700	$0	$0	$0	$0	$0	$0	$0
$50	$2,070		$3,000	$0	$0	$0	$0	$0	$0	$0
$51	$2,070		$3,300	-$300	$0	$0	$0	$0	$0	$0
$52	$2,070		$3,600	-$600	$0	$0	$0	$0	$0	$0
$53	$2,070		$3,900	-$900	$0	$0	$0	$0	$0	$0
$54	$2,070		$4,200	-$1,200	$0	$0	$0	$0	$0	$0
$55	$2,070		$4,500	-$1,500	$0	$0	$0	$0	$0	$0
$56	$2,070		$4,800	-$1,800	$0	$0	$0	$0	$0	$0
$57	$2,070		$5,100	-$2,100	$0	$0	$0	$0	$0	$0
$58	$2,070		$5,400	-$2,400	$0	$0	$0	$0	$0	$0
$59	$2,070		$5,700	-$2,700	$0	$0	$0	$0	$0	$0

FIGURE 19.2 Model 2: Profit of a portfolio of stocks and options at option expiration.

as 1 for C, −1 for P and 0 for S. In F31, enter =IF($A13="C",1,IF($A13 ="P",−1,0)), in F32 enter =$B13, and in F33 enter =$C13. Copy these formulas to G31:O33 and modify them one at a time to tie them to the right cells in A14:C22. (As a challenge, try to find a simpler way to create the values for F31:O33.)

4. **Create payoff formula:** You can use the MAX function to calculate the payoff for option positions as before, where in each row the terminal stock price is in column B. However, to enhance your skill (and for later use), use a nested If statement here. In F35 enter =IF(F$31*($B35-F$32)>0,F$31*($B35-F$32)*F$33*cSize,0). Here, the IF function checks if the option is in-the-money for the corresponding terminal stock price. If it is TRUE, then the payoff is calculated and entered. Otherwise, or if this is a stock position, the payoff is zero. Study the IF function to make sure you understand how it works for both puts and calls using the position type in F31. Also analyze the use of the mixed cell references. The objective is to create a formula that will work correctly when copied to all the other cells. For the contract size, we are using the name cSize we created, but you could also use the absolute cell reference $D$24 in the formulas.

   To add the payoff for stock positions, to the above formula in F35 add +IF(F$31=0,($B35-F$32)*F$33*cSize,0). This will enter a payoff only if it is a stock position. Otherwise this will equal zero.

   Copy the finished formula into the rest of F35:O64.

5. **Create profit formula:** The portfolio profit for each terminal stock price is the sum of the payoffs for all the 10 positions less the total premium paid for the option positions. You could calculate the latter for each position in a column next to the data input area, calculate their sum, and use that here. To develop your skill, though, try using an array formula. Type in C35 the formula =SUM(F35:O35)-SUM($C$13:C$22*$D$13:$D$22*cSize) and press Ctrl+Shift+Enter instead of just Enter because this is an array formula. You will notice that Excel puts a pair of braces ({}) around the formula to indicate that this is an array formula. The first part of the formula simply sums the payoffs for all the 10 positions from the 10 columns.

   In the second part, Excel multiplies C13 by D13 and the contract size, C14 by D14 and the contract size, and so forth. It then sums all the results because the results are inside the SUM function.

6. **Create chart:** Select B35:C64 and use the Chart Wizard to create an embedded chart. (For Chart type use XY.) Properly format and label the chart.

Testing the Model

To test the model, first check that the terminal prices in B35:B64 are properly reflecting the lowest terminal price and the terminal price step size.

Next, enter a set of input data for all 10 positions and make sure that the values in F31:O33 are reflecting them correctly. Change some of the input data to see that the values in F31:O33 are changing the way they should.

Now create just one call position in A13:D13 of size 1 and enter zeros for all other position sizes. Look at F35:F64 as well as C35:C64 to make sure that both payoffs and the profits are correct. (Check them using hand calculations.)

Try the same for one put and one stock position. If all the positions work individually, then create 3 positions and make sure that the total profit is being calculated properly.

Uses of the Model

This model is ideal to understand the payoffs and profits from individual puts and calls as well as to explore various option-trading strategies. To see the payoffs and profits from individual puts and calls, create single positions and study the chart.

To study any trading strategy, create a portfolio of stocks and options reflecting it and study the model output and the chart. For example, a bullish call spread involves buying one or more calls at one strike price and selling an equal number of calls at a higher strike price. To see the profit characteristics of a bullish call spread, enter C, \$40, 3, and \$4.80 in A13:D13 and C, \$50, −3, and \$1.70 in A14:D14. Make sure that all other position sizes are zeros. Enter \$30 in D25 and \$1 in D26 (to focus on the relevant terminal price range).

Notice that at terminal stock prices of \$40 and less, you will have a loss of \$930 because all the calls will expire worthless and you will lose the net premium you paid. At terminal stock prices of \$50 and more, you will have a profit of \$2,070. You will break even at a terminal stock price of about \$43. Above this, your profit will grow steadily up to the maximum value at the terminal stock price of \$50.

Remember that to see realistic results, you need to enter realistic option premiums; you cannot just make them up. You can either use actual data for a particular stock and options on it (from newspapers, quote machines, etc.) or theoretical option premiums from an option-pricing model like the BSM model we will develop later. Also remember that in this model you always have to use options on the same stock and with the same expiration date.

Limitations of the Model

The important limitations of the model are:

- The model can handle different positions entered at different times. However, for the model to work, all of the option positions must expire at the same time, because the model can calculate the payoff of an option position only at the time of expiration. It cannot show the payoffs and profits at any earlier point in time. (We will create a different model for that later.)

- In this type of model, you want to create formulas that will work properly when you copy them into a large number of cells; as such, you must mostly use cell references (with the right combination of relative, mixed, and absolute references) instead of cell names. This makes the formulas difficult to read and check, and creates a lot of room for making mistakes. Be sure to test your models thoroughly.
- The model can handle positions in only one stock and options on it. Creating a realistic model for a portfolio with positions in different stocks and options on them gets lot more complicated.

MODEL 3: PROFIT OF OPTION PORTFOLIOS AT EXPIRATION (USING ARRAY FORMULAS)

The Problem

In Model 2, we calculated the payoff for each position in a separate column, summed them up for each terminal stock price, and subtracted from the sums the total premium paid to calculate the portfolio profit for each terminal stock price. Develop a more compact model for the same problem using array formulas to do all the calculations in just one column. (If you want to get good at writing array formulas, creating this model will be excellent practice for you and you will get a good feel for the advantages and disadvantages of using array formulas. If you are not interested in array formulas, you can go on to the next model.)

Modeling Strategy

The overall strategy is essentially the same as before. The difference is in how you write the formulas. The worksheet for this model is shown in Figure 19.3.

Building the Model

Instead of trying to create the key formula in C35 on your own for the first time, look through the finished model carefully using the following guidelines and then try to recreate it.

1. **Set up data validation:** Same as in Model 2.
2. **Create column of terminal prices:** Same as in Model 2.
3. **Convert position types:** As before, for calculations we need to convert the position types to 1 for C, −1 for P and 0 for S. In E13 enter

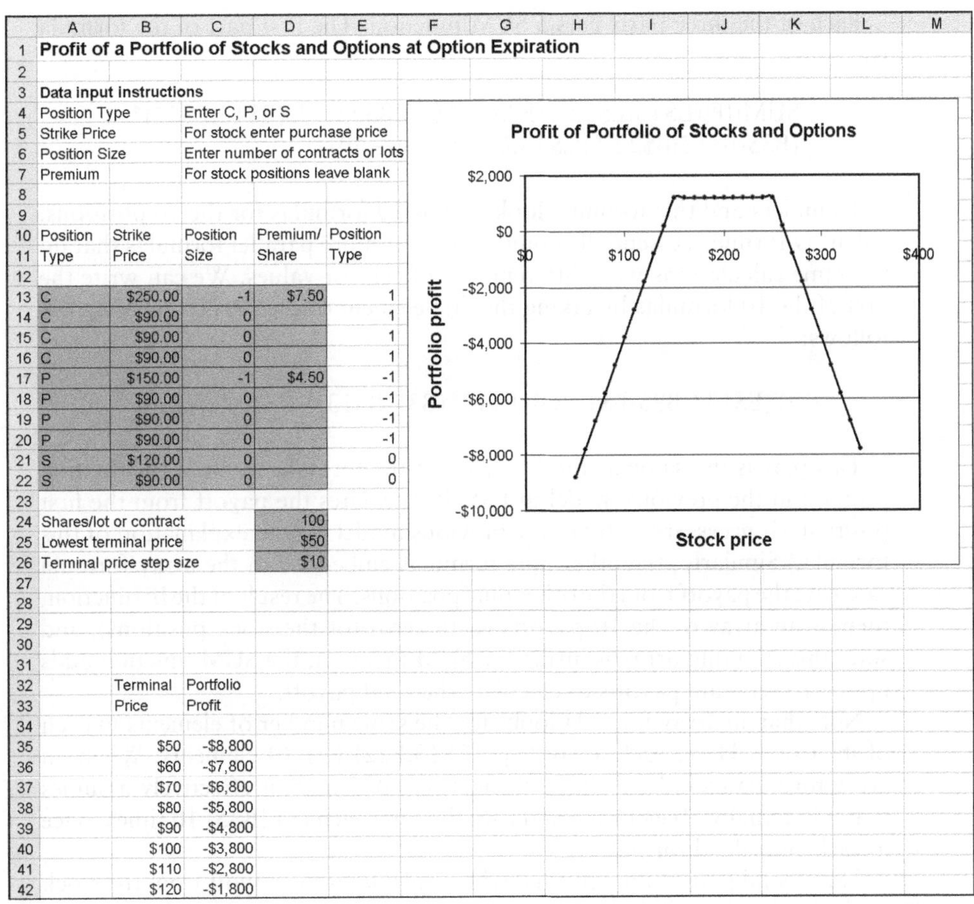

Profit of a Portfolio of Stocks and Options at Option Expiration

Data input instructions

Position Type	Enter C, P, or S
Strike Price	For stock enter purchase price
Position Size	Enter number of contracts or lots
Premium	For stock positions leave blank

Position Type	Strike Price	Position Size	Premium/ Share	Position Type
C	$250.00	-1	$7.50	1
C	$90.00	0		1
C	$90.00	0		1
C	$90.00	0		1
P	$150.00	-1	$4.50	-1
P	$90.00	0		-1
P	$90.00	0		-1
P	$90.00	0		-1
S	$120.00	0		0
S	$90.00	0		0

Shares/lot or contract	100
Lowest terminal price	$50
Terminal price step size	$10

Terminal Price	Portfolio Profit
$50	-$8,800
$60	-$7,800
$70	-$6,800
$80	-$5,800
$90	-$4,800
$100	-$3,800
$110	-$2,800
$120	-$1,800

FIGURE 19.3 Model 3: Profit of option portfolio at option expiration using array formulas.

=IF(A13="C",1,IF(A13="P",−1,0)), which is essentially the same as the formula we used before to do the conversion. Copy the formula into E14:E22.

4. **Create the formula for calculating profit:** For C35, you have to create the formula for calculating the total profit for all the positions for the terminal stock price in B35. The formula should also be such that it can be copied into C36:C64 without any modification. The formula has three parts:

Total profit = Payoff from all option positions + Profit from all stock positions − Total premium paid on all option positions

Each of the three parts uses a SUM function. The first part of the formula is:

SUM(IF((E$13:E$22)*(B35 – B$13:B$22)>0, (E$13:E$22)*(B35-B$13:B$22)*(C$13:C$22)*cSize, 0))

To understand this formula, look at it as 10 formulas for the 10 positions. All array formulas essentially combine two or more parallel formulas that do the same calculations with different sets of cells or values. We can write the first of the 10 formulas by taking the first element of each array (or range) as follows:

IF(E$13*(B35-B$13)>0, E$13*(B35-B$13)* C$13*cSize,0)

This part is the same as the first part of the formula we used for the first position in the previous model in F35. It calculates the payoff from the first position. (If necessary, refer to the previous model for the explanation of this formula.) Similarly, the other nine formulas embedded in the array formula calculate the payoff from the other nine positions. The result of the IF function, then, is an array of the 10 payoffs (with zeros for the stock positions), and since this resulting array is inside the SUM function, the SUM function adds up the 10 separate payoffs to calculate the total payoff.

Note that an array formula looks for the same number of elements in each of its arrays. Here, each array (e.g., E$13:E22) has 10 elements. When an array formula includes a single element like B35 here, it effectively assumes that it is actually 10 elements and uses the same element (B35) 10 times, once in each embedded formula.

The second part of the formula, which calculates the payoff from the stock positions is:

SUM(IF((E$13:E$22)=0,(B35-B$13:B$22)*C$13:C$22)*cSize,0)

Analyze it by breaking it down as before and, if necessary, look at the discussion under the previous model. (It is the second part of the formula in F35 there.) Note that here again the array formula has 10 embedded formulas and it calculates 10 payoffs, but the condition of the IF function makes the payoffs for the option positions zeros.

The third part of the formula, which calculates the total premium paid, is:

SUM($C$13:C$22*$D$13:$D$22*cSize)

We used the same formula in C35 in the previous model and discussed it there.

5. **Copy the formula in C35 into C36:C64:** This is an easy step, provided the formula uses the right mix of cell references to make it work properly in all the cells.
6. **Create chart:** Create the chart as in Model 2.

Testing the Model

You have to test the model the same way you tested the previous model, that is, using one position at a time. Although you do not have a separate column for each position anymore, when you test one position at a time, the results in C35:C64 are for that position only.

(As a challenge, try to make the formulas shorter by using a simpler condition to check if a position will expire in-the-money or out-of-the-money for a particular terminal price.)

Limitations of the Model

The model shows what is good and bad about array formulas. Array formulas allowed us to squeeze 10 columns of calculations into one column. However, the resulting formula is long and most people find formulas like this difficult to understand and debug. In situations like this, you may want to avoid array formulas and create the model in 10 columns as before.

This model works essentially the same way as the previous version and does not overcome any of the limitations of that version.

MODEL 4: BSM MODEL AND THE GREEK LETTERS

The Problem

Develop a model to calculate the price and the Greek letters for European puts and calls on dividend-paying stocks based on the Black-Scholes-Merton (BSM) model. Also verify that the put-call parity relationship holds.

Modeling Strategy

The worksheet for this model is shown in Figure 19.4. This model involves direct implementation of the BSM equations and the equations for the Greek letters discussed before. You can write your formulas for this model using cell addresses, but it will make them difficult to read and check. (Try this out for yourself.) Use named cells instead. Also, calculate values for important intermediate variables separately instead of trying to do all the calculations in the cells for the output variables.

	A	B	C	D	E	F	G
1	**BSM Values and Greek Letters for European Options on Dividend Paying Stocks**						
2							
3					Call	Put	
4	Stock price (S)	$50.00		Price	$5.93	$5.19	
5	Exercise price (K)	$50.00		Delta	0.57	-0.42	
6	Dividend yield (q)	1.00%		Theta (per year)	-6.13	-4.67	
7	Time to maturity (T, years)	0.5000		Gamma	0.03	0.03	
8	Volatility (V)	40.00%		Vega	13.77	13.77	
9	Interest rate (rr)	4.00%		Rho	11.39	-13.12	
10							
11	**Intermediate variables**			Put from put-call parity		$5.19	
12	Exp(-rT) (ert)	0.9802					
13	Exp(-qT) (eqt)	0.9950					
14	(r-q+0.5*V^2) (radj)	0.1100					
15							
16	d1(dOne)	0.1945					
17	N(d1) (NdOne)	0.5771					
18	N(-d1) (NmdOne)	0.4229					
19							
20	d2(dTwo)	-0.0884					
21	N(d2) (NdTwo)	0.4648					
22	N(-d2) (NmdTwo)	0.5352					
23							
24	Exp(-(d1^2)/2)/(2*Pi)^0.5 (NpdOne)	0.391471					
25							
26							

FIGURE 19.4 Model 4: BSM Values and Greek letters for European options.

To check that the put-call parity relationship holds, calculate the put value using the calculated call value in the put-call parity equation. Then compare the answer to the put value you get by calculating it directly from the BSM equation.

Building the Model

If you want to use the same cell names I have used (and I think you should), make sure you build this model in a new workbook. Otherwise you will have problems with duplicate names. (You can get around this problem by using worksheet-level names, but that will create unnecessary additional complications.)

Set up the labels for the input variables in your worksheet and then name the cells for their values using names that are as close to the symbols used in the BSM equations as possible. In the label cell for each variable in the model's worksheet, I have shown in parentheses the name I am using for the cell that holds the value of that variable. Note that I am using rr for the interest rate because Excel does not allow naming a cell r, and for volatility or sigma I am using V.

As you write the formula for each intermediate variable, write it using the cell names. When you finish it, give the cell an appropriate name so that you can use it in the subsequent formulas.

You will need to use the following Excel functions in your formulas: EXP for the exponential function, SQRT for square root, NORMSDIST to calculate the cumulative probability for a standard normal distribution, and PI for the constant π. (Note that even though the PI function does not require any argument, you must include a pair of empty parentheses in it.)

In your formulas, use parentheses wherever you think there may be room for misinterpretation to make sure that calculations are done in the order you want. Without them, Excel may do calculations in a different order and come up with wrong answers.

Testing the Model

The only practical way to test this model is to compare its outputs with those from other models. In this case, you can compare the output of your model with the model I have provided. In theory, you could check your model against hand-calculated answers, but for some of these equations doing hand calculations correctly is not easy.

Uses of the Model

This is a very useful model for developing an understanding of how the different input variables affect the price of a European option and the values of its Greek letters. For example, you can change the stock price while holding all the other variables constant to see how the price of a call option and the different Greek letters change as the call moves from being out-of-the-money to at-the-money to more and more in-the-money. These relationships become even easier to appreciate when you see them in graphical forms. We will do so in later models.

Limitations of the Model

The model has the same limitations as the BSM equations. Also note that you cannot use the model for $T = 0$, for example, to calculate the price of an option at expiration. However, we have already seen how to create a model to calculate option prices at expiration. To get values of the options and the Greek letters for $T = 0$, enter a very small number for T, such as 0.00001.

Estimating Implied Volatility

As we discussed earlier, because the volatility of a stock is not directly observable, it is often useful to estimate the volatility implied in the observed price of an option. The BSM equations cannot be explicitly solved for volatility. The only way to estimate the implied volatility is by trial and error. You cannot automate the process in Excel, but you can use Goal Seek with a model like this one to manually estimate the implied volatility, given the price of a stock and the values of all the other variables that are needed for the BSM equations.

For example, let us assume that the values of all the variables other than volatility are as shown in Figure 19.4 and the observed call price is $10. To estimate the implied volatility, select Tools ⇨ Goal Seek, and then in the dialog box enter E4 for Set cell, 10 for To value, B8 for By changing cell, and click OK to get the implied volatility of 69.8%.

For various reasons, implied volatilities calculated from the observed prices of options with different strike prices maturing at the same time vary from one another. It is therefore customary to create plots of the implied volatilities of options with different strike prices. Such plots are called volatility smiles; they can be created automatically in VBA but not in Excel.

MODEL 5: VARIATION OF OPTION PRICE WITH STOCK PRICE

The Problem

Develop a model and a chart to show how the value of a European put or call option on a dividend-paying stock varies with the price of the underlying stock. Make the chart dynamic by allowing the user to change all of the other variables that affect the price of the option.

Modeling Strategy

The worksheet for this model is shown in Figure 19.5. You have to first rebuild (or copy) part of the last model to calculate the prices of the puts and calls for this model. In the model, you should add spinners to all the input variables other than the stock price so that the user can easily change these variables in reasonable steps. Then you have to calculate the price of a put or a call for a range of stock prices, preferably using a one-variable data table. Finally, you have to create a chart to plot the price of an option against the price of the stock.

Building the Model

1. **Create template:** Start with a new copy of the workbook for the previous model. In the model worksheet, clear the cells you do not need anymore (for example, those for calculating the Greeks). To move the intermediate variables out of the way (as I have done in the sample model), Cut and Paste A11:B22 into A62:B73. (Note that if you Copy and Paste, the names of the cells will not move; they will remain associated with the original cells, which is not what you want.) Also Cut and Paste the cells for option values in the locations I have them in this model. Now using the same values for input variables in the previous model and this one, make sure that the new one is working properly.

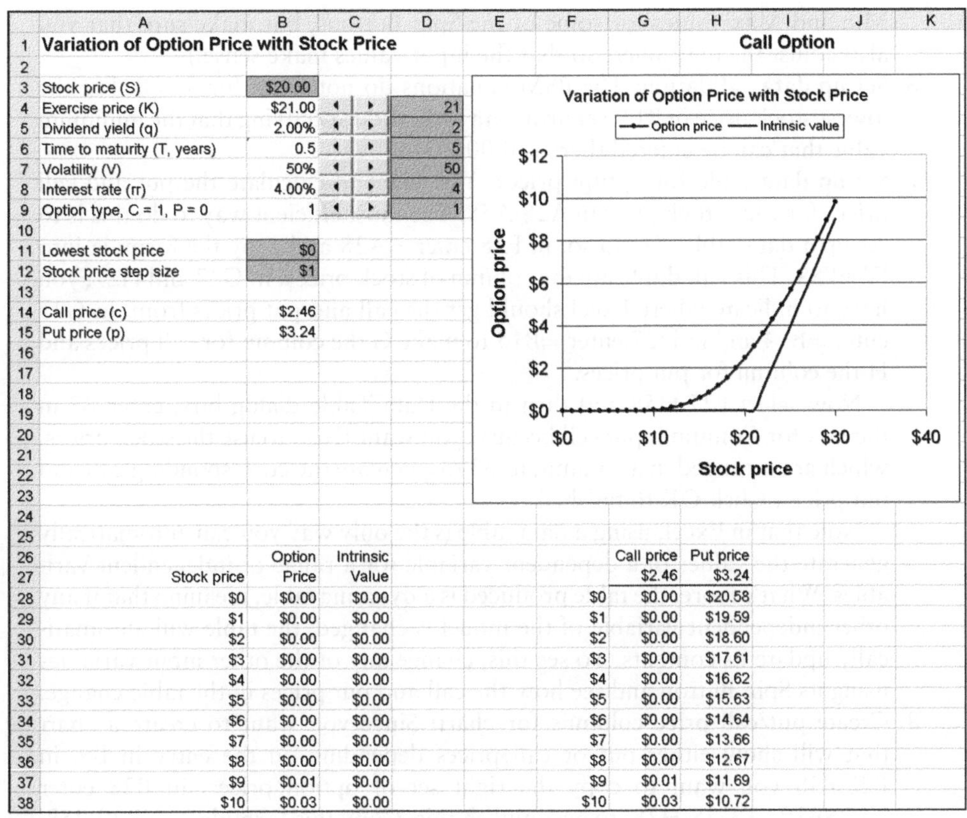

	A	B	C	D
1	Variation of Option Price with Stock Price			
3	Stock price (S)	$20.00		
4	Exercise price (K)	$21.00		21
5	Dividend yield (q)	2.00%		2
6	Time to maturity (T, years)	0.5		5
7	Volatility (V)	50%		50
8	Interest rate (rr)	4.00%		4
9	Option type, C = 1, P = 0	1		1
11	Lowest stock price	$0		
12	Stock price step size	$1		
14	Call price (c)	$2.46		
15	Put price (p)	$3.24		

	Stock price	Option Price	Intrinsic Value		Call price	Put price
27					$2.46	$3.24
28	$0	$0.00	$0.00	$0	$0.00	$20.58
29	$1	$0.00	$0.00	$1	$0.00	$19.59
30	$2	$0.00	$0.00	$2	$0.00	$18.60
31	$3	$0.00	$0.00	$3	$0.00	$17.61
32	$4	$0.00	$0.00	$4	$0.00	$16.62
33	$5	$0.00	$0.00	$5	$0.00	$15.63
34	$6	$0.00	$0.00	$6	$0.00	$14.64
35	$7	$0.00	$0.00	$7	$0.00	$13.66
36	$8	$0.00	$0.00	$8	$0.00	$12.67
37	$9	$0.01	$0.00	$9	$0.01	$11.69
38	$10	$0.03	$0.00	$10	$0.03	$10.72

FIGURE 19.5 Model 5: Variation of option price with stock price.

2. **Create other input cells:** Create the labels for Option type, Lowest stock price and Stock price step size.
3. **Create column of stock prices:** Instead of using a fixed range of stock prices, we want to let the user choose them by indicating in B11 the lowest stock price he wants to see and in B12 the step size at which the stock price should increase. In A28 enter =B11 and in A29 enter =A28+$B$12. Then copy the formula in A29 into A30:A58.
4. **Add spinners and set properties:** Add Spin Buttons to C4:C9. In the Properties dialog box for each, link it to the cell on the right (in the D column) and set the Min and Max values as follows: K, 0 and 1000; q, 0 and 20; T, 1 and 100; V, 0 and 100; rr, 0 and 20; Option type, 0 and 1.
5. **Link input cells:** Link B4:B9 to corresponding cells in D4:D9 with proper multipliers. For example, the formula in B4 is =D4*1. The multipliers for q, V, and rr are 0.01, for T, 0.1, and for Option type, 1. (You can use different

Min and Max values for some of the Spin Buttons, but make sure that you also adjust the multipliers so that the input values make sense.)

6. **Set up data validation:** The BSM equations do not work for S = 0. For the lowest stock price in B11, set up a data validation specifying that the minimum value that can be entered there is 0.00001.
7. **Set up data table for option prices:** You want to calculate the put and call prices for each stock price in A28:A58. The most efficient way to do this is to set up a data table. To do so, in F28 enter =A28 and copy the formula into F29:F58. This will duplicate the column of stock prices. In G27 and H27, you have to indicate where Excel should get the call and put prices from. In G27 enter =B14 and in H27 enter =B15 to make G the column for call prices and H the column for put prices.

   Now select F27:H58 and then in the Data Table dialog box, enter B3 in the box for Column input cell because you want Excel to use the stock prices, which are arranged in a column, in B3 to calculate the corresponding call and put prices. Click OK to finish.

   Note that in Excel, using a data table is the only way you can automatically generate the values of a dependent variable for a range of independent variables. What's more, the table produced is a dynamic table, meaning that if any other independent variable of the model is changed, the table will automatically update its contents. To see this, change any of the other input variables using its Spin Button and see how the call and put prices in the table change.
8. **Create put/call price columns for chart:** Since you want to create a chart that will show either put or call prices depending on the entry in B9, in B28:B58 you want to copy the right set of option prices. In B28 enter =IF($B$9=1,G28,H28) to accomplish this. Copy this formula into B29:B58.
9. **Calculate intrinsic values:** It will also be useful to show the intrinsic values of the options for the various stock prices. To set up a column of intrinsic values, in C28 enter =IF($B$9=1,MAX(0,A28-K),MAX(0,K-A28)). (The intrinsic value is the payoff if an option is exercised immediately.) Copy the formula into C29:C58.
10. **Create chart:** You now have all the necessary data for the chart in A28:C58. Select this range and create an embedded chart as shown in the model. (For Chart type, use XY.) Format and label the chart appropriately.
11. **Create option type label for chart:** To show whether a chart is for calls or puts—which is determined by the input in B9—in H1 enter =IF(B9=1, "Call Option", "Put Option") and format it properly.

Testing the Model

You can check that the model is calculating the right option prices by comparing its results with the output from the previous model. Make sure that the intrinsic values are being calculated correctly and that the chart is plotting the right values for both puts and calls.

Uses of the Model

This model is an excellent tool for developing an understanding of how the different input variables affect the price of a European option. It shows the relationship between an option's price and the price of the stock most clearly. You can also use the various spin buttons to see the effect on the option price of the other variables. When experimenting with the chart, make sure you choose a relevant range of stock prices by selecting the appropriate lowest stock price and stock price step in B11 and B12. If you are looking at an option with a $20 exercise price and you use a stock price range of, say, 0 to 200, everything will be squeezed into one end of the chart and you will not be able to see the necessary details.

You can use this model to explore another important issue: When might it be optimal to exercise an option early? Of course, the European options we are discussing here can be exercised only at expiration. However, as we discussed, if it is optimal to exercise a particular option early, then the American version of it will be more valuable than its European counterpart, because only the American version can take advantage of that opportunity.

I mentioned that it is never optimal to exercise a call option on a non-dividend-paying stock early. To see this, in the model set $q = 0$, and see if you can get the call price line to cross the intrinsic value line by changing any of the variables in any way. You will not be able to. (You would want to exercise an option if its value falls below its intrinsic value, because you can collect the intrinsic value by exercising it right away.)

To see if it is optimal to exercise a call on a dividend-paying stock early and increase the q to a fairly high value—say, 10%—and you will see that the call price line will fall below the intrinsic value line when the call gets deep in-the-money. Therefore, it may be optimal to exercise calls on such a stock early and American calls on such stocks will be more valuable than their European counterparts.

Now try the same things with puts. Here, the important variables are the risk-free rate and remaining life. You will see that for high risk-free rates and long remaining life, the put option line will fall below the intrinsic value line whether the stock pays dividends or not. So early-exercise may be optimal for puts on both dividend-paying and non-dividend-paying stocks, and American put options may be more valuable than their European counterparts. Just how much more, though, is a more difficult question to answer.

If you want to develop a fuller understanding of options, try to explain why early exercise may be optimal in the circumstances we just saw.

Limitations of the Model

The model has the usual limitations of the BSM model. In addition, it shows the variation of the option price with the stock price much more clearly than it shows the variations with the other variables. We will explore that in the next model.

MODEL 6: VARIATION OF OPTION PRICE WITH VOLATILITY

The Problem

Develop a model and a chart to show how changes in volatility impact the price of a European put or call option on a dividend-paying stock. Make the chart dynamic by allowing the user to change all of the other variables on which the price of the options depends.

Modeling Strategy

The worksheet for this model is shown in Figure 19.6. This model is very similar to the last one. You can therefore start with a copy of the last model and effectively swap volatility and stock price to have this model show how changes in volatility impact prices of options.

Building the Model

Since this model is very similar to the last one, you should not need detailed step-by-step instructions to build it. Start with a copy of the last model and follow these steps:

- Swap volatility with stock price. Remember to use Cut and Paste and not Copy and Paste to keep the cell names V and S tied to the right cells.
- Change the properties of the spinner next to stock price in its new position to Min of 0 and Max of 1000. Change B8 to =D8*1.
- Change A12:A13 to Lowest volatility and Volatility step size.
- Change the data table in F27:H58 (if necessary).
- Clear the intrinsic values in E26:C58 and create a new chart.

Testing the Model

Test the model the same way you tested the last model.

Using the Model to Calculate Implied Volatility

As discussed earlier, market participants often derive the volatility from the market price of actively traded options by asking the question, *What volatility would justify this price of the option?* This is called the implied volatility of the option.

You can use this model to calculate the implied volatility of an option. One way to do so would be to first enter the values for the other variables such as stock price in their respective input cells (D5:D10). (Note that even though when you use the spinners to set these values, you can change them only in steps you have

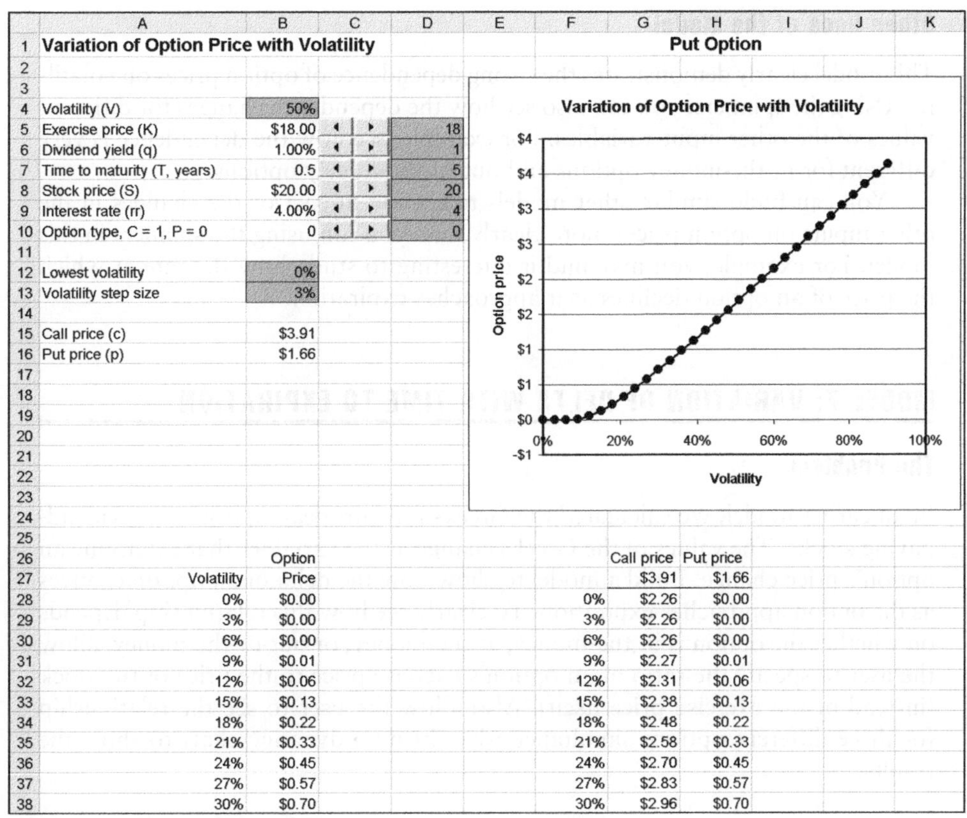

Variation of Option Price with Volatility
Put Option
Volatility (V) 50%
Exercise price (K) $18.00 18
Dividend yield (q) 1.00% 1
Time to maturity (T, years) 0.5 5
Stock price (S) $20.00 20
Interest rate (rr) 4.00% 4
Option type, C = 1, P = 0 0 0
Lowest volatility 0%
Volatility step size 3%
Call price (c) $3.91
Put price (p) $1.66
Variation of Option Price with Volatility
Option price
Volatility
Volatility
Option Price
Call price
Put price
0% $0.00 0% $2.26 $0.00
3% $0.00 3% $2.26 $0.00
6% $0.00 6% $2.26 $0.00
9% $0.01 9% $2.27 $0.01
12% $0.06 12% $2.31 $0.06
15% $0.13 15% $2.38 $0.13
18% $0.22 18% $2.48 $0.22
21% $0.33 21% $2.58 $0.33
24% $0.45 24% $2.70 $0.45
27% $0.57 27% $2.83 $0.57
30% $0.70 30% $2.96 $0.70

FIGURE 19.6 Model 6: Variation of option price with volatility.

set up; you can type into these cells any value you want.) You can then look in the call or put column in the table G28:H58 to find the value closest to the price of the option for which you want to estimate the implied volatility and look up the volatility in the left column.

If you want a more accurate estimate, you can use Goal Seek. As before, enter the appropriate values for all the inputs other than volatility and then in the Goal Seek dialog box, for Set cell enter B15 for call or B16 for put, in the To value box enter the option value for which you want to calculate implied volatility, in the By changing box enter B4, and click OK to see the calculated implied volatility.

Note that in Excel you have to calculate implied volatility "manually" using Goal Seek. You cannot create a model to automatically calculate the implied volatilities for a series of options even though that is something that option users have to do all the time. As we will see later, you can do so easily using VBA.

Other Uses of the Model

This model clearly demonstrates the strong dependence of option prices on volatility. Using the spinners, you can also see how the dependence changes for different values of the other input variables. For example, see how the dependence is very different for in-the-money options and out-of-the-money options.

You can build similar other models to see the impact of the changes in the other inputs on option prices more clearly than you can using the spinners in this model. For example, you may find it interesting to study how the rate at which the price of an option declines as it approaches expiration.

MODEL 7: VARIATION OF DELTA WITH TIME TO EXPIRATION

The Problem

In an earlier model, we calculated the Greeks for European options on dividend-paying stocks. The values of the Greeks change as the variables that determine an option's price change. Build a model to show how the delta of an option changes as the option approaches expiration. To clearly see how this relationship depends on whether the option is in-the-money, at-the-money, or out-of-the-money, allow the user to specify the ratio of an option's exercise price to the price of the stock (instead of the exercise price itself). Also allow the user to see the relationship for three different options simultaneously. Create a dynamic chart to show the results.

Modeling Strategy

The worksheet for this model is shown in Figure 19.7. This model is similar to the previous models with two important differences. First, you have to replace exercise price with the ratio of exercise price to stock price as one of the input variables. Second, the model has to calculate three values of the dependent variable simultaneously instead of just one as in the previous models. This will require using a two-input instead of a one-input data table.

Building the Model

1. **Set up the input variables:** It may be easiest to start with a copy of the Model 5, but you can start from scratch, too. Move (using Cut and Paste) the cells for Exercise price and its label out of the input area to A23:B23. You will still need it, but it will not be an input anymore. In A3:B3, create a new input cell for the ratio of exercise price to stock price. To calculate exercise price from the input variables, in B23 enter =S*B3.

	A	B	C	D
1	**Variation of Delta with Time to Expiration**			
2				
3	Exercise price/Stock price	1.00		
4	Time to maturity (T, years)	0.50		
5	Dividend yield (q)	1.00%		1
6	Volatility (V)	50%		50
7	Stock price (S)	$50.00		50
8	Interest rate (rr)	4.00%		4
9	Option type, C = 1, P = 0	1		1
10				
11	Exercise price/Stock price			
12	For 1st series	1.20		
13	For 2nd series	1.00		
14	For 3rd series	0.80		
15				
16				
17	Shortest time	0.00		
18	Time step	0.06		
19				
20	Call delta	0.58		
21	Put delta	-0.41		
22				
23	Exercise price (K)	$50.00		

Call Deltas

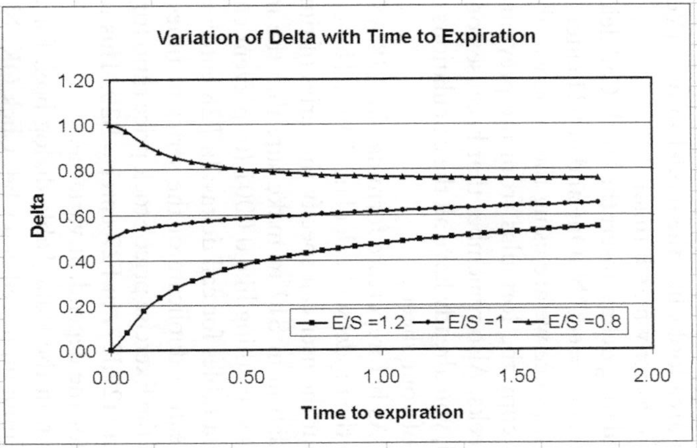

Variation of Delta with Time to Expiration

Delta: 0.00, 0.20, 0.40, 0.60, 0.80, 1.00, 1.20

Time to expiration: 0.00, 0.50, 1.00, 1.50, 2.00

E/S =1.2 — E/S =1 — E/S =0.8

	A	B	C	D
27	Time	E/S =1.2	E/S =1	E/S =0.8
28	0.00	0.00	0.50	1.00
29	0.06	0.08	0.53	0.97
30	0.12	0.17	0.54	0.92
31	0.18	0.23	0.55	0.88
32	0.24	0.28	0.56	0.85
33	0.30	0.31	0.57	0.84
34	0.36	0.34	0.57	0.82
35	0.42	0.36	0.58	0.81
36	0.48	0.38	0.58	0.80
37	0.54	0.39	0.59	0.79
38	0.60	0.41	0.59	0.79

	F	G	H	I
26			Call Delta	
27	0.58	1.20	1.00	0.80
28	0.00	0.00	0.50	1.00
29	0.06	0.08	0.53	0.97
30	0.12	0.17	0.54	0.92
31	0.18	0.23	0.55	0.88
32	0.24	0.28	0.56	0.85
33	0.30	0.31	0.57	0.84
34	0.36	0.34	0.57	0.82
35	0.42	0.36	0.58	0.81
36	0.48	0.38	0.58	0.80
37	0.54	0.39	0.59	0.79
38	0.60	0.41	0.59	0.79

	K	L	M	N
26			Put Delta	
27	-0.41	1.20	1.00	0.80
28	0.00	-1.00	-0.50	0.00
29	0.06	-0.92	-0.47	-0.03
30	0.12	-0.83	-0.46	-0.08
31	0.18	-0.77	-0.45	-0.12
32	0.24	-0.72	-0.44	-0.14
33	0.30	-0.69	-0.43	-0.16
34	0.36	-0.66	-0.42	-0.18
35	0.42	-0.64	-0.42	-0.19
36	0.48	-0.62	-0.41	-0.19
37	0.54	-0.60	-0.41	-0.20
38	0.60	-0.59	-0.40	-0.21

FIGURE 19.7 Model 7: Variation of delta with time to expiration.

In A12:B14, create 3 input variables for the user to specify the ratios of exercise price to stock price that he wants to explore. (At this point, this just means typing the labels in A11:A14.).

Label A17:A18 as Shortest time and Time step; you are now going to focus on time to expiration as the primary independent variable.

Make sure your input area looks like the model shown. (You may have to insert/delete some rows to exactly match this.)

2. **Create formulas for calculating deltas:** Insert the labels Call delta and Put delta in A20:A21. Then in B20 enter =eqt*NdOne and in B21 enter =eqt*(NdOne-1) to calculate the deltas. (Since we are using the same variable names in all models, you could also copy the formulas from the previous model where we calculated all the Greeks. Also remember that because you started with a copy of an earlier model, you already have all the calculations of intermediate variables at the bottom of your sheet.)
3. **Set up column for time:** As before, create formulas in A28:A58 to create the series of times for which the model will calculate deltas. These, of course, will be tied to B17:B18 so that the user can specify the series of times he wants to use. Include a data validation in B17 to make sure that the minimum value the user can enter here is something like 0.0001 (to prevent entering 0).
4. **Create the two-input data tables for call deltas:** In F28 enter =A28 and copy the formula down to create a duplicate of the series of times. In G27 enter =B12 to create a copy of the Exercise price/Stock price ratio for the first series. Enter similar formulas in H27:I27. In F27 enter =B20. This tells Excel from where to get the values for the dependent variable.

   Select F27:I58 and then in the Data Table dialog box, for the Row input cell enter B3 and for Column input cell enter B4. Click OK. Now you should have the table of values for call deltas.
5. **Create the two-input data table for put deltas:** Create the table of values for put deltas by essentially repeating Step 4.
6. **Set up table for creating chart:** Since the user will specify in D9 whether he wants a chart of call or put deltas, you have to create the table B28:D58 to select which values of delta to chart. To do so, enter =IF($B$9=1,G28,L28) in B28 and then copy it into the rest of the table. To set up the legends for your chart, in B27 enter ="E/S ="&G27, and copy the formula into C27:D27. (The &, called the concatenation operator, attaches the value in G27 to the text enclosed in the quotations.)
7. **Create chart:** Create the chart using data from A27:D58. Label and format the chart properly.

Testing the Model

First test if the model is working properly using the ratio of exercise price to stock price instead of exercise price as an input variable. For this, enter a set of values in the input cells (including B3) and check the values of call and put deltas in this model against the model for the Greeks. Remember that in the models for the Greeks you will have to use the exercise price in B23.

Next, check if the data tables for the call and put deltas are calculating the right values. You can enter any value in B3 to see the right values for call and put deltas in B20:B21 and check if the tables have the same values.

Make sure that the table in B28:D58 is picking up the right values of call or put deltas depending on the input in D9.

Finally, check the chart against the table B28:D58 to make sure that it is plotting the right values.

Uses of the Model

You can use the model to study how the deltas depend on the time to expiration as well as if and how far an option is in-the-money or out-of-the-money. For example, you can see that as an option gets closer to expiration, the delta of an in-the-money option approaches 1, of an at-the-money option approaches 0.5, and of an out-of-the-money option approaches zero. See if you can explain to yourself why this happens. Also make sure you understand why deltas for put options have negative signs.

You saw in this model how to use a two-input data table to show the impact of two independent variables on a dependent variable. You can create the same type of model for any of the other Greek letters.

MODEL 8: LEVERAGE OF OPTIONS

The Problem

One reason investors buy options is that options provide high leverage, that is, if the stock moves in their favor, the percentage return on the option investment is likely to be many times the percentage return on an investment in the stock. Create a model to show how the leverage changes as an option approaches expiration and also how it depends on the ratio *X/S*, that is, on how much in-the-money or out-of-the-money the option is.

Modeling Strategy

The worksheet for this model is shown in Figure 19.8. This model is very similar to the previous model, except that here we want to calculate and chart the leverage instead of delta.

Building the Model

1. **Calculate option prices and leverage:** Start with a copy of the previous model and create the cells for the option prices and leverages. (You will have to

	A	B	C	D	E	F	G	H	I	J	K	L	M	N
1	**Leverage of European Options**							**Call Leverage**						
2														
3	Exercise price/Stock price	1.10												
4	Time to maturity (T, years)	0.60												
5	Dividend yield (q)	0.00%		0										
6	Volatility (V)	50%		50										
7	Stock price (S)	$50.00		50										
8	Interest rate (rr)	4.00%		4										
9	Option type, C = 1, P = 0	1		1										
10														
11	Exercise price/Stock price													
12	For 1st series	1.20												
13	For 2nd series	1.00												
14	For 3rd series	0.80												
15														
16	Shortest time	0.04												
17	Time step	0.02												
18														
19	Call price (c)	$6.25												
20	Put price (p)	$9.94												
21	Call leverage	4.033												
22	Put leverage	2.495												
23														
24	Exercise price (K)	$55.00												
25														
26														
27								Call leverage					Put leverage	
28	Time	E/S =1.2	E/S =1	E/S =0.8		4.03	1.20	1.00	0.80		2.50	1.20	1.00	0.80
29	0.04	25.73	12.95	4.91		0.04	25.73	12.95	4.91		0.04	4.81	12.13	28.35
30	0.06	18.92	10.65	4.78		0.06	18.92	10.65	4.78		0.06	4.57	9.83	20.33
31	0.08	15.36	9.28	4.64		0.08	15.36	9.28	4.64		0.08	4.34	8.46	16.18
32	0.10	13.14	8.34	4.50		0.10	13.14	8.34	4.50		0.10	4.13	7.53	13.61
33	0.12	11.60	7.65	4.37		0.12	11.60	7.65	4.37		0.12	3.95	6.84	11.85
34	0.14	10.47	7.12	4.25		0.14	10.47	7.12	4.25		0.14	3.78	6.30	10.56
35	0.16	9.60	6.69	4.13		0.16	9.60	6.69	4.13		0.16	3.64	5.87	9.57
36	0.18	8.90	6.33	4.03		0.18	8.90	6.33	4.03		0.18	3.51	5.51	8.78

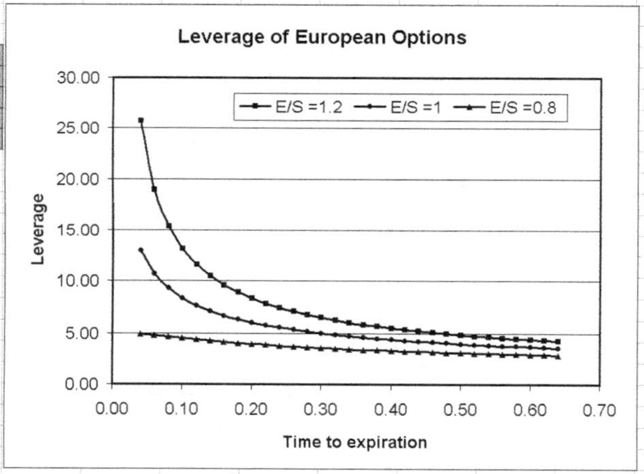

FIGURE 19.8 Model 8: Leverage of European options.

add some rows.) From one of the earlier models, copy into B19:B20 the formulas for calculating the option prices. In B21 enter =eqt*NdOne*S/B19 to calculate the call leverage and in B22 enter =eqt*(1-NdOne)*S/B20 to calculate the put leverage. (Note that for the put option leverage, I have effectively dropped the negative sign to show both call and put leverages as positive numbers.)

2. **Create two-variable data tables for call and put leverages:** To change the data tables, in F28 enter =B21 and in K28 enter =B22. Now set up the data tables as before.
3. **Label the chart properly:** Change the labels on the chart.

Testing the Model

You can check the option values against previous models. You can also check the leverages through hand calculations using the previous model. Make sure the chart is reflecting the values from the table properly.

Uses of the Model

Notice that the leverage for out-of-the-money options goes up sharply as the options approach expiration because the value of the option, which is in the denominator of the leverage calculation, becomes very small. The more out-of-the-money an option is, the higher its leverage (and risk of expiring worthless). (Make sure that the minimum value for time in your chart and tables is at least 0.01, because the leverage calculations closer to expiration for out-of-the-money options are not very meaningful. They will just distort the vertical scale of your chart.)

MODEL 9: PROFIT OF OPTIONS PORTFOLIO AT ANY TIME

The Problem

Model 2 shows the profit of a portfolio of stocks and options only at the time the options expire. We now have models to calculate the values of options not just at expiration, but at any time before that. Create a model to show the values of a portfolio of stocks and European options on dividend-paying stocks for different stock prices at any time. All the options will be on the same stock and expire at the same time.

Modeling Strategy

The worksheet for this model is shown in Figure 19.9. You will now have to calculate the price of each option in the portfolio using the option-pricing model

Row	A	B	C	D
1	**Profit of a Portfolio of Stocks and Options at Any Time**			
2				
3	Position	Exercise	Position	Premium/
4	Type	Pirce	Size	Share
5	Position 1: Call	$50.00	1	$7.14
6	Position 2: Call	$60.00	-2	$13.14
7	Position 3: Call	$70.00	1	$1.92
8	Position 4: Put	$50.00	0	$1.00
9	Position 5: Put	$50.00	0	$1.00
10	Position 6: Put	$50.00	0	$1.00
11	Position 7: Stock	$30.00	0	
12	Position 8: Stock	$40.00	0	
13				
14	Volatility (V)	40%		40
15	Dividend yield (q)	1.00%		1
16	Time to maturity (T, years)	0.5		50
17	Interest rate (rr)	4.00%		4
18				
19	Stock price (S)	$50.00		
20	Exercise price (K)	$70.00		
21	Shares/lot or contract	100		
22				
23	Lowest stock price	$0		
24	Stock price step	$3		
25				
26	Call price (c)	$1.05		
27	Put price (p)	$19.91		
28				
29				
30				

Profit of a Portfolio of Stocks and Options

Portfolio value: $1,700, $1,750, $1,800, $1,850, $1,900, $1,950, $2,000

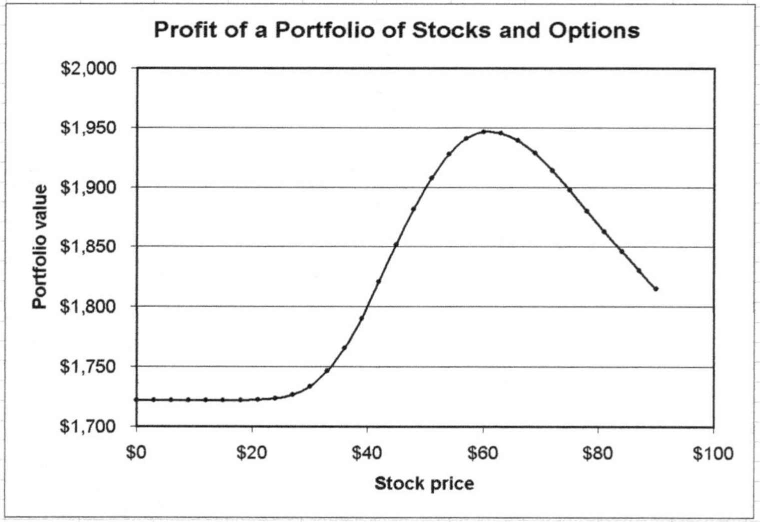

Stock price: $0, $20, $40, $60, $80, $100

Row	A	B	E	F	G	H	J	K	L	M	O	P	Q
31				Position 1	Position 2	Position 3		Position 4	Position 5	Position 6		Position 7	Position 8
32		Portfolio	Size >	1	-2	1	Size >	0	0	0	Size >	0	0
33	Stock price	Value	$1.05	$50.00	$60.00	$70.00	$19.91	$50.00	$50.00	$50.00		$30.00	$40.00
34	$0	$1,722	$0	$0.00	$0.00	$0.00	$0	$49.01	$49.01	$49.01	$0	-$30	-$40
35	$3	$1,722	$3	$0.00	$0.00	$0.00	$3	$46.02	$46.02	$46.02	$3	-$27	-$37
36	$6	$1,722	$6	$0.00	$0.00	$0.00	$6	$43.04	$43.04	$43.04	$6	-$24	-$34
37	$9	$1,722	$9	$0.00	$0.00	$0.00	$9	$40.05	$40.05	$40.05	$9	-$21	-$31
38	$12	$1,722	$12	$0.00	$0.00	$0.00	$12	$37.07	$37.07	$37.07	$12	-$18	-$28

FIGURE 19.9 Model 9: Profit of a portfolio of stocks and options at any time.

for every stock price the user specifies. In the previous model, we allowed up to 10 positions and they could be anything (that is, stock, call, or put). To make creating the model easier, use a total of 8 positions here, the first three of which can only be calls, the second three only puts, and the last two only stocks. You will have to use two-variable data tables to calculate these values from the call or put pricing equations.

Building the Model

1. **Set up input variables:** It may be easiest to start with a copy of Model 5 which already has the call and put pricing equations built into it. Make changes to it to make the input area look like the example for this model (A3:D27).
2. **Create stock price series:** Create the stock price series in A34:A64, tying it to B23 and B24.
3. **Set up a two-variable data table to calculate call prices:** Duplicate the stock price series in E34:E64 by entering =A34 in E34 and then copying the formula into E35:E64.

   Tie the cells in F32:H33 to duplicate the input data in B5:C7 (that is, in F32 enter =C5 and so forth). For clarity, label the cells F31:H31.

   To create the necessary two-variable data table, in E33 enter =B26, select E33:H64, bring up the Data Table dialog box for the data table, enter B20 for Row input cell and B19 for Column input cell, and click OK.
4. **Set up a two-variable data table to calculate put prices:** Repeat the procedure in Step 3.
5. **Calculate values of stock positions:** Set up the table for the values of the stock positions in O31:Q64. The value of any stock position (per share) is the current stock price less the price paid. So to calculate the values of the stock positions, in P34 enter =O34-P$33 and copy it into the rest of the table.
6. **Calculate portfolio value:** For this, you have to multiply the per option or per share values of each call, put, and stock in the tables you just created by the corresponding sizes of the positions and the contract size, and then subtract the total premium paid for the options. To create the formula in B34, enter:

$$\begin{aligned}&= \text{cSize}^*(\text{F\$32}^*\text{F34} + \text{G\$32}^*\text{G34} + \text{H\$32}^*\text{H34})\\&+\text{cSize}^*(\text{K\$32}^*\text{K34} + \text{L\$32}^*\text{L34} + \text{M\$32}^*\text{M34})\\&+\text{cSize}^*(\text{P\$32}^*\text{P34} + \text{Q\$32}^*\text{Q34})\\&-\text{cSize}^*\text{SUM}(\text{C\$5:C\$10}^*\text{D\$5 : D\$10})\end{aligned}$$

The first part is for the call options, the second for the put options, and the third for the stock positions. The last part is an array formula similar to the ones we have used before to calculate the total premium paid for the options. Since this makes the whole formula in B34 an array formula, you have to press Ctrl+Shift+Enter to enter it. Make sure you understand and have properly entered the mixed cell references, and then copy the formula into B35:B64.

7. **Create chart:** Create the chart using data from A34:B64. Properly format and label the chart.

Testing the Model

You have to test the model using a procedure similar to the one we used for Model 2, that is, by entering only one position at a time and checking that the model is working properly for it. In this case, you can check the values against the option values in B26 and B27, but make sure that you compare them only against the values in the tables corresponding to the values in B19 and B20. You can check the values of the stock position by simple hand calculations.

Make sure that the sign and size of the positions are being properly reflected in the final table. Then check the chart to make sure that it is properly reflecting the final table of portfolio values.

Uses of the Model

This is one of the most useful models. You can use it to study a wide range of option-trading strategies and see how the value of your portfolio will change with time or changes in any of the other variables. You should spend some time experimenting with this model to improve your understanding of options and option portfolios.

Limitations of the Model

Its key limitations are those of the BSM model and also that all the options in the portfolio have to expire at the same time. You can create a model in Excel to value portfolios with options expiring at different times, but it will get quite a bit more complex. (Think about how you would do it.) If you want to build in more flexibility than exists in this model, it would be better to create it in VBA. Also recognize that portfolios with more than one underlying asset and derivative on them are significantly more difficult to model.

CHAPTER 20

Binomial Option Pricing

In Chapter 19: Options and Option Portfolios, we saw that the Black-Scholes-Merton (BSM) equations can be used to calculate prices for European options. They cannot, however, be used to price most American options or many other types of options. In this chapter, I discuss a versatile and popular technique for pricing not just any type of option, but any type of derivative security. It involves creating binomial trees and using them in conjunction with the risk-neutral valuation method. I will discuss only what you need to know to develop the models in this chapter. My review parallels the discussions in *Options, Futures, and Other Derivatives* by John C. Hull (6th edition), and you can refer to that book or any other books on derivatives for additional details.

Review of Theory and Concepts

It is generally easier to understand binomial trees and their uses by working through some examples, and that is what we will do when we build the models later in the chapter. If you are new to binomial trees and do not fully understand everything in the following theoretical discussions, read through them once and go on to the modeling section. Things will become clearer once you start working on the models.

Binomial Trees

A binomial tree represents the different possible paths that the price of a stock or other security can follow over time. Binomial trees have to be built following certain rules so that the paths they generate are realistic.

Let us assume that if the price of a stock is S_0, over a short interval of time (step 1) it can either move up to a new level S_0u or down to a new level S_0d as shown in Figure 20.1. Here, $u > 1$ and $d < 1$ and $u - 1$ and $1 - d$

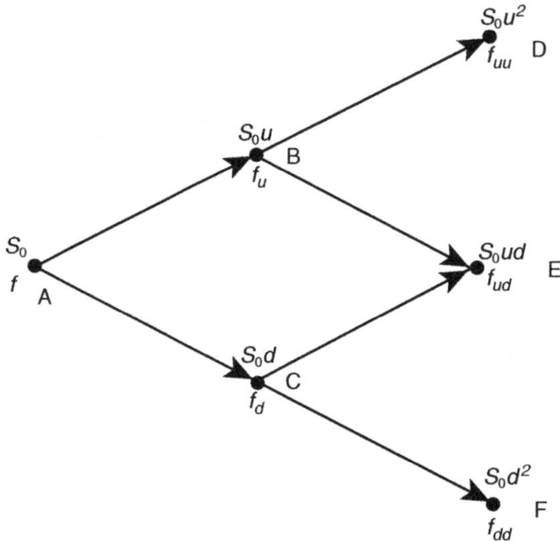

FIGURE 20.1 Stock and option prices in a two-step binomial tree.

represent the proportional increase and decrease in the stock's price over the interval (for example, up 10% or down 8%). If the stock is assumed to always behave the same way, then at the end of the next interval (step 2), the stock can take on 3 possible values and it can take 4 possible paths to get to them (see Figure 20.1).

This is a two-step binomial tree. It may seem simplistic, but by choosing the values for u and d properly and making the steps smaller and smaller, a binomial tree can be made to closely approximate the paths a stock may follow over any period of time.

Risk-Neutral Valuation

So far we have not said anything about the probabilities of the up and down movements. It turns out that we can choose these probabilities in such a way that we can value options and all other derivatives using binomial trees—assuming that we are living in a risk-free world. The assumption of "risk-free world" means all cash flows can be discounted using the risk-free rate of return. This is very convenient because determining the right discount rate for various cash flows is one of the most difficult problems in finance.

This method of valuing derivatives assuming a risk-free world is called risk-neutral valuation. It is important to understand that it is the proper choice of the probabilities of the up and down movements that makes the risk-neutral valuation possible. And once we value something using this approach, the valuation is valid not just in the imaginary risk-free world but in the real world as well.

Valuing European Options

Let us understand the use of binomial trees and risk-neutral valuations by calculating the value of a European call option that expires in two periods (intervals). We can easily calculate the value of the call at each of the three possible stock prices (called nodes) at the end of the two periods. For example, if the strike price of the call is k, then at node D the value of the call will be the higher of 0 and $(S_0u^2 - k)$. We represent this by f_{uu}.

What will be the value of the call at node B? It will be its expected value based on the values at the two nodes (D and E) at the end of step 2 that can be reached from B discounted by the risk-free rate, provided we use the appropriate probabilities. Let us assume that the right probability is p for the up movement and $(1 - p)$ for the down movement, the annual risk-free rate of return is r, and the length of each interval is δt. Then the value of the call at B, C, and A can be calculated as follows:

$$f_u = e^{-r\delta t}\left[pf_{uu} + (1 - p)\,f_{ud}\right]$$
$$f_d = e^{-r\delta t}\left[pf_{ud} + (1 - p)\,f_{dd}\right]$$
$$f = e^{-r\delta t}\left[pf_u + (1 - p)\,f_d\right]$$

We can thus calculate the value of the call option at time 0 by starting with the easily calculated values at each node at expiration and then calculate its values at each intermediate node moving backwards as we just did. We can do it for 2 steps, 200 steps, or more. We can increase the accuracy of the estimated option price by choosing more and more steps because the smaller each interval, the more realistically the binomial tree will represent the possible future paths for the stock. Fifty or 100 steps are usually enough to produce accurate estimates, and on a PC it takes almost no time to do the necessary calculations.

The value of a European put can be calculated similarly. The key difference from the call will be in the values at the time of expiration, which will propagate backwards to produce a different value for the put.

Valuing American Options

American options can be exercised at any time. At expiration, the value of an American option will be the same as that for the corresponding European option. But for American options at every earlier node, we have to also estimate the payoff from exercising the option at that point. If the payoff from immediate exercise is higher than the value calculated at that node as before, then we will have to assume that the value at that node will be equal to the payoff. (We do not have to consider this possibility for European options because they cannot be exercised at any of the earlier nodes.) Such differences will propagate backwards, affecting the price of the option at time 0. So if at one or more nodes early exercise turns out to be more profitable than holding the option to expiration, then the value of an American option will be higher than that of a similar European option.

It turns out that under certain circumstances it can be optimal to exercise put options on non–dividend-paying stocks and both call and put options on dividend-paying options before expiration. Under these circumstances, American options are more valuable than similar European options.

Valuing Options on Stocks with Known Dividend Yield

The BSM equations can be used to value European options on stocks with known dividend yields. As we will see, a known dividend yield can be incorporated in the up and down movement probabilities for risk-neutral valuation. With that adjustment, binomial trees can be used to value both European and American options on dividend-paying stocks the same way we discussed using them for valuing options on stocks that pay no dividend.

Valuing Options on Stocks with Known Dollar Dividends

In the case of individual stocks, it is often more realistic to assume that the stock will pay known dollar amounts of dividends at specific times in the future instead of providing a continuous known dividend yield over time. This can be handled with a minor modification to the binomial tree.

Suppose we know that a stock will pay only one dividend within the period for which we are building a binomial tree. We can calculate the present value of the dividend (using the risk-free rate of return as usual), subtract it from the initial price of the stock, and treat the remaining part of the stock price as its uncertain component. We can then build a tree as before for just the uncertain component of the stock price. Finally, we can create a tree for the total stock price by adding to the uncertain component at each node (from the previous tree) the present value of the dividend at that point in time. The present value will get larger as we step closer to the time of the dividend payment, and, of course, no adjustment for the dividend will have to be made at nodes beyond the time of the dividend payment. This same approach can be used if there are more than one dividend payments during the time covered by the tree.

Option or other derivative prices can be calculated as before using the tree for the total stock price.

Specifying the Parameters for Binomial Trees

Cox, Ross, and Rubinstein (CRR) have shown that if we choose the parameter for a binomial tree and probability of up movement as follows, then the tree will closely match the mean and variance of the stock's price over short time intervals and we can use risk-neutral valuation.

$$u = \exp\left(\sigma\sqrt{\delta t}\right)$$
$$d = \frac{1}{u}$$
$$p = \frac{a-d}{u-d}, \quad \text{where } a = \exp\left[(r-q)\delta t\right]$$

Here σ is the volatility of the stock, q is the constant dividend yield, and δt is the length of each step, that is, it equals the time-length of the tree (for example, time to expiration for the option for a tree for option valuation) divided by the number of steps we choose for the tree. For stocks that do not pay any dividend, q would be 0. Trees built using these parameters are called CRR trees, and we will use CRR trees in all our models. A few other alternate sets of parameters are also used to build other types of binomial trees, such as the Jarrow-Rudd tree, but the trees are still built the same way.

Modeling Examples

MODEL 1: EUROPEAN OPTIONS ON STOCKS WITH KNOWN DIVIDEND YIELD

The Problem

Develop a model to estimate the price of European options (both puts and calls) on stocks with known dividend yields using a 9-step Cox, Ross, and Rubinstein (CRR) binomial tree.

Modeling Strategy

The worksheet for this model is shown in Figure 20.2. Most people find it difficult to build their first binomial tree. Instead of discussing the modeling strategy at length, then, I will make a few observations and suggest that you build this first model following the step-by-step instructions in the next section. Start by studying the worksheet of the model closely (Figure 20.2) and try to understand as much

	A	B	C	D	E	F	G	H	I	J	K
1	**Binomial Pricing of European Options for Stocks with Known Dividend Yield**										
2											
3											
4	Option type (C=1, P=-1)	-1			Step (dt)	**0.0556**					
5	Stock price (S)	$50.00			u	**1.0483**	Up movement multiplier				
6	Exercise price (K)	$50.00			d	**0.9540**	Down movement multiplier, = 1/u				
7	Interest rate (rr, annual)	8.00%			p	**0.5177**	Risk-neutral probability of up movement				
8	Dividend yield (q, annual)	3.00%			emrdt	**0.9956**	Discount factor per step, = Exp(-rr*dt)				
9	Volatility (sig, annual)	20.00%									
10	Time to maturity (T, years)	0.5									
11	Number of steps (n)	9									
12											
13											
14											
15											
16	**Step**	**0**	**1**	**2**	**3**	**4**	**5**	**6**	**7**	**8**	**9**
17	**Time**	**0.00**	**0.06**	**0.11**	**0.17**	**0.22**	**0.28**	**0.33**	**0.39**	**0.44**	**0.50**
18											
19	**Stock price**	$50.00	$52.41	$54.94	$57.60	$60.38	$63.29	$66.34	$69.55	$72.90	$76.42
20			$47.70	$50.00	$52.41	$54.94	$57.60	$60.38	$63.29	$66.34	$69.55
21				$45.50	$47.70	$50.00	$52.41	$54.94	$57.60	$60.38	$63.29
22					$43.41	$45.50	$47.70	$50.00	$52.41	$54.94	$57.60
23						$41.41	$43.41	$45.50	$47.70	$50.00	$52.41
24							$39.50	$41.41	$43.41	$45.50	$47.70
25								$37.68	$39.50	$41.41	$43.41
26									$35.95	$37.68	$39.50
27										$34.29	$35.95
28											$32.71
29											
30	**Put price**	**$2.25**	$1.35	$0.68	$0.26	$0.06	$0.00	$0.00	$0.00	$0.00	$0.00
31			$3.24	$2.07	$1.14	$0.48	$0.12	$0.00	$0.00	$0.00	$0.00
32				$4.53	$3.10	$1.85	$0.88	$0.25	$0.00	$0.00	$0.00
33					$6.11	$4.46	$2.91	$1.55	$0.53	$0.00	$0.00
34						$7.93	$6.17	$4.39	$2.66	$1.11	$0.00
35							$9.88	$8.14	$6.30	$4.35	$2.30
36								$11.84	$10.19	$8.44	$6.59
37									$13.73	$12.16	$10.50
38										$15.54	$14.05
39											$17.29
40											
41											

FIGURE 20.2 Model 1: Binomial pricing of European options with known dividend yield.

of it as you can based on our earlier review of the theory behind the binomial tree method.

In spreadsheets it is usually more convenient to build a binomial tree in the shape of a triangle rather than the tree shape we used for discussions. A 9-step tree will occupy a triangular half of a 10×10 rectangle, and the values can either occupy the upper triangular half or the lower triangular half of the rectangle. If you use the upper triangular half, then the up-movement values are shown in the same row as the previous value and the down-movement values are shown in the row below. Both are, of course, shown in the next column. The columns represent the successive steps and are numbered starting with 0 (now). The length of each step equals the time to expiration divided by the number of steps.

If the tree is built using the bottom triangular half of the rectangle, then the down-movements are shown in the same row in the next column and the up-movements are shown in the row above in the next column. In addition to the alternate shapes of trees, there are also a few alternate approaches available for generating the values for them. The combination one uses is mostly a matter of taste. I will illustrate only one approach, which beginners generally find easiest to follow.

As we saw earlier, the only difference in calculating the price of a call and a put option using binomial trees occurs at the nodes at expiration. This difference can be handled easily with an OptType indicator with values of +1 and –1 for calls and puts. We do not need to create separate models for puts and calls.

Building the Model

1. **Set up the input cells:** Label the input cells as shown and name the cells as indicated in their labels. The option type cell is named OptType.
2. **Calculate the parameters for the tree:** To calculate the necessary parameters for a CRR binomial tree, enter formulas as follows:
   - For the time step, dt, in cell F4 enter the formula =T/n.
   - For the up-movement multiplier, in cell F5 enter the formula =EXP (sig*SQRT(dt)).
   - For the down-movement multiplier, in cell F6 enter the formula =1/F5.
   - For the risk-neutral probability of up-movement, in cell F7 enter the formula =(EXP((rr-q)*dt)-d)/(u-d).
   - For the discount factor per step, in F8 enter the formula =EXP(-rr*dt).
3. **Create the labels for the tree:** In B16:K16 enter the step numbers. In B17 enter the formula =B16*dt and copy it into C17:K17 to show the point in time to which each step corresponds.

   Enter the labels in A16, A17, A19. You can also enter "Option price" in A30. However, if you want a label that says Call Price or Put Price depending on the OptType specified, enter in A30 the formula =IF(OptType=1, "Call", "Put") & "price".
4. **Build the first step of the stock price tree:** In B19 enter the formula =S to start the tree. In column C, we have to show the up- and down-movements from this starting value. As discussed earlier, we will show values for up-movements in the same row. In C19 enter the formula =B19*u.

   In C20 you could enter B19*d for the value for the down-movement and copy and paste this formula in all the cells of the rectangle (except for the first row, row 19). But we want the bottom triangular half of the rectangle to appear blank because these cells are off the tree. So in C20 enter the formula =IF(ROW()-ROW($B$19)>C$16,"",B19*d). This formula, when copied down, can correctly calculate the down-movement values for all rows. We want only 2 rows in step 1, 3 rows in step 2, and so on. The IF function takes care of this. ROW() returns the row number for the cell where the formula is and the IF function compares it with the row number for the first row of the tree, ROW($B$19). If in a cell the difference exceeds the step number, then that cell is off the tree and should be blank. This is what happens when the condition of the IF is satisfied because the resulting double quotes ("") make the cell blank.

Copy this formula into C21:C28. All of these cells will appear blank because they are off the tree.

This is an important formula for building a tree. Make sure you fully understand it.

5. **Build the rest of the stock price tree:** Copy C19:C28 into the rest of the rectangle, D19:K28. Note that as a result, all the cells in the first row will have one formula and the rest of the rectangle will have a different formula. You should now have a tree with values identical to those shown in the figure.
6. **Create the last column of the option price tree:** The option price tree has to be built backwards, starting at expiration. Based on the prices of the stock at the different nodes at expiration, we can easily calculate the values of the option at these final nodes. In K30 enter the formula =MAX(0,OptType*(K19-K)) to calculate the value of the option at that node. To understand the formula, think in terms of a call for which OptType is 1. The value of the call is the price of the stock at the node K19 less the exercise price, except that, if it is negative, the value is 0. This is what the formula calculates using the MAX function. Now think it through for a put with OptType = −1. Copy this formula into K31:K39 to complete the last column of the tree.
7. **Create the formulas to calculate the option prices at the earlier nodes:** For a European option, the value at any node is its expected value in the next step (calculated using the risk-neutral probabilities of up- and down-movements) discounted by the risk-free rate. To calculate the option value at J30, enter the formula =IF(J19="","",(p*K30+(1-p)*K31)*emrdt). The second part of the formula calculates the value of the option. It is meaningful, however, only when a node is on the tree. An easy way to test this is to check if the corresponding cell in the stock price tree is blank or has a value. This is what the IF function does, and it makes cells that are off the tree blank. (You can also use the method we used earlier to decide which cells are off the tree.)

   Copy this formula first into J31:J39 and then copy J30:J39 into the rest of the rectangle, B30:I39. This should produce the value of the option in B30 as shown.

Testing the Model

You have to check the model doing some hand calculations for both the stock and option price trees. You can also check the option prices it generates against prices calculated using the Black-Scholes-Merton (BSM) equations. Recognize, however, that the price calculated by the tree will not match the BSM value unless you use a tree with many more (probably 100 or more) steps. For example, the BSM value for the option shown is $2.18.

Uses of the Model

The most important use of this model is for understanding how to build binomial trees. Because we can use the BSM equations to calculate the exact prices for European options for stocks with known dividend yields, we do not need binomial trees for them. Expanding the tree to many more steps is relatively easy because it primarily involves copying and pasting formulas. Still, expanding or contracting trees—that is, changing the number of steps to use—is more cumbersome in Excel than doing so in VBA.

MODEL 2: AMERICAN OPTIONS ON STOCKS PAYING NO DIVIDEND

The Problem

Develop a model to estimate the price of American options (both puts and calls) on stocks that pay no dividend using a 5-step Cox, Ross, and Rubinstein (CRR) binomial tree. Simultaneously calculate the values of the equivalent European options and highlight the differences in the values between the trees to show where the price differences arise.

Modeling Strategy

The worksheet for this model is shown in Figure 20.3. The key difference between calculating the price of American and European options is that American options can be exercised at any time. So we have to test at every node if exercising before expiration will have a higher payoff than the expected return from holding the option to maturity. As we will see, for stocks that do not pay any dividends, it is never optimal to exercise calls early, but it may be optimal to exercise puts early. In our models, therefore, we will expect call prices for American and European options to be identical, but prices of American puts may be higher than their European counterparts.

Among the tree parameters, for the risk-neutral probability of up-movement, you can either use the formula we used in Model 1 with $q = 0$ or drop the q from the equation. Generate the stock price tree as before. Then start two separate trees for the American and European options. For both, calculate the values at expiration as before. For the European option, generate the rest of the tree as before. For the American options, at each node in the earlier steps, compare the value as we calculated earlier (that is, the value of the European option) with the

◇	A	B	C	D	E	F	G	H	I	J
1	**Binomial Pricing of American Options on Stocks Paying No Dividend**									
2										
3										
4	Option type (C=1, P=-1)	-1			Step (dt)	**0.1200**				
5	Stock price (S)	$60.00			u	**1.0717**	Up movement multiplier			
6	Exercise price (K)	$60.00			d	**0.9331**	Down movement multiplier = 1/u			
7	Interest rate (rr, annual)	4.00%			p	**0.5174**	Risk-neutral probability of up movement			
8	Volatility (V, annual)	20.00%			emrdt	**0.9952**	Discount factor per step, = Exp(-rr*dt)			
9	Time to maturity (T, years)	0.6								
10	Number of steps (n)	5								
11										
12										
13										
14										
15										
16	**Step**	**0**	**1**	**2**	**3**	**4**	**5**			
17	**Time**	**0.00**	**0.12**	**0.24**	**0.36**	**0.48**	**0.60**			
18										
19	**Stock price**	$60.00	$64.30	$68.92	$73.86	$79.16	$84.84			
20			$55.98	$60.00	$64.30	$68.92	$73.86			
21				$52.24	$55.98	$60.00	$64.30			
22					$48.74	$52.24	$55.98			
23						$45.48	$48.74			
24							$42.43			
25										
26	**American put price**	**$3.28**	**$1.55**	$0.45	$0.00	$0.00	$0.00			
27			**$5.18**	**$2.75**	$0.93	$0.00	$0.00			
28				**$7.84**	**$4.72**	$1.93	$0.00			
29					**$11.26**	**$7.76**	$4.02			
30						**$14.52**	$11.26			
31							$17.57			
32										
33	**European put price**	$3.17	$1.52	$0.45	$0.00	$0.00	$0.00			
34			$4.98	$2.68	$0.93	$0.00	$0.00			
35				$7.49	$4.58	$1.93	$0.00			
36					$10.69	$7.48	$4.02			
37						$14.24	$11.26			
38							$17.57			
39										
40										

FIGURE 20.3 Model 2: Binomial pricing of American options on stocks that pay no dividend.

payoff that will be realized by exercising the option immediately. The value of the American option at that node would be the higher of the two.

Using conditional formatting, bold the values in the American option tree that are different from the corresponding values on the European option tree.

Building the Model

1. **Set up the input values and calculate the tree parameters:** This part is essentially the same as in Model 1. Either use dividend yield q = 0, or as I have done, delete q from both inputs and the formula for the risk-neutral probability for up-movement.
2. **Generate the stock price tree:** This is the same as in Model 1.

3. **Create the labels for the trees:** Create the labels as before. To insert the word "put" or "call" into the label depending on the OptType, in A26 I used the formula ="American" & IF(OptType=1,"call", "put") & "price".
4. **Generate the American option pricing tree:** As before, start with the last column. In G26 enter the formula =MAX(0,OptType*(G19-K)) to calculate the value of the option at expiration. Copy it into G27:G31.

   To calculate the value in the earlier steps, in F26 enter the formula =IF(F19="","",MAX(MAX(OptType*(F19-K),0),(p*G26+(1-p)*G27)*emrdt)). It is easier to analyze this formula starting from the inside and working your way out.

   The last portion of the formula is the same as before and calculates the value of the option as the present value of the expected payoffs. The inner MAX function calculates the payoff from immediately exercising the model as the higher of zero and the difference between the stock price at the corresponding node and the exercise price. The multiplication by the OptType handles puts and calls appropriately. The outer MAX function then calculates the value of the American option as the higher of the two values estimated. The IF function checks if the cell is on or off the tree by checking if the corresponding cell in the stock price tree is blank. If it is off the tree then the IF makes the cell blank.

   Once you understand the formula, first copy it into F27:F31, and then copy F26:F31 into the rest the rectangle B26:E31. Cell B26 will show the value of the American option.
5. **Generate the European option price tree:** This is identical to the tree in Model 1.
6. **Bold the cells that are different in the American option tree:** Select F26 and then use conditional formatting based on the formula =ABS(F33-F26)>0.001 to show the cell value as bold when the condition is satisfied. The condition will be satisfied if the value of the American option is different from the corresponding value of the European option by more than 0.001, in which case Excel will make the value of the American option bold. (I used 0.001 instead of 0 in the test because sometimes rounding makes a very small difference between the American and European values, which is not meaningful.)

   Using Paste Special, copy and paste the conditional formatting into the rest of the cells in the American option tree.

Testing the Model

Check to see that the model produces identical values for American and European calls. The values of American puts may be higher. But since we do not know how much higher, you have to do some hand calculations for a few cells in the American option tree to make sure that it is making the right choice between exercising an option immediately and holding on to it, and calculating the payoff from immediate exercise correctly. The rightmost bold cells (for example, F29) show where the option is being exercised immediately and you can check that the value is correct.

Uses of the Model

Binomial trees provide a convenient way to calculate values of American options. To get an accurate value, you need to use a large number of steps (for example, over 50). It is not difficult to expand the Excel tree for this many steps, but as we will see, it is much easier to do so for binomial models in VBA.

MODEL 3: AMERICAN OPTIONS ON STOCKS WITH KNOWN DIVIDEND YIELDS

The Problem

Develop a model to estimate the price of American options (both puts and calls) on stocks with known dividend yields using a 9-step Cox, Ross, and Rubinstein (CRR) binomial tree. Simultaneously calculate the values of the equivalent European options and highlight the differences in the values between the trees to show where the price differences arise.

Modeling Strategy

The worksheet for this model is shown in Figure 20.4. The only difference between this model and Model 2 is that here options are on stocks with known dividend yields. We calculated values for European options on similar stocks in Model 1. You therefore have to effectively combine Models 1 and 2, that is, calculate the risk-neutral probability of up-movement, including the dividend yield. Then, in valuing the American options at all but the nodes at the time of expiration, you have to check if immediate exercise will provide a higher payoff than holding on to the American option.

Building the Model

It will be easier to start with a copy of the workbook for Model 1. I focus only on the necessary modifications here.

1. **Set up the input values and calculate the tree parameters:** This part is the same as Model 1.
2. **Generate the stock price tree:** This is the same as in Model 1.
3. **Create the labels for the trees:** Create the labels as before. To insert the word "put" or "call" into the label depending on the OptType, in A30 I used the formula ="American" & IF(OptType=1,"call", "put") & "price".

	A	B	C	D	E	F	G	H	I	J	K
1	Binomial Pricing of American Options on Stocks with Known Dividend Yield										
2											
3											
4	Option type (C=1, P=-1)	-1			Step (dt)	0.0556					
5	Stock price (S)	$50.00			u	1.0733	Up movement multiplier				
6	Exercise price (K)	$50.00			d	0.9317	Down movement multiplier, = 1/u				
7	Interest rate (rr, annual)	7.00%			p	0.5020	Risk-neutral probability of up movement				
8	Dividend yield (q, annual)	2.00%			emrdt	0.9961	Discount factor per step, = Exp(-rr*dt)				
9	Volatility (sig, annual)	30.00%									
10	Time to maturity (T, years)	0.5									
11	Number of steps (n)	9									
12											
13											
14											
15											
16	Step	0	1	2	3	4	5	6	7	8	9
17	Time	0.00	0.06	0.11	0.17	0.22	0.28	0.33	0.39	0.44	0.50
18											
19	Stock price	$50.00	$53.66	$57.60	$61.82	$66.34	$71.21	$76.42	$82.02	$88.03	$94.48
20			$46.59	$50.00	$53.66	$57.60	$61.82	$66.34	$71.21	$76.42	$82.02
21				$43.41	$46.59	$50.00	$53.66	$57.60	$61.82	$66.34	$71.21
22					$40.44	$43.41	$46.59	$50.00	$53.66	$57.60	$61.82
23						$37.68	$40.44	$43.41	$46.59	$50.00	$53.66
24							$35.11	$37.68	$40.44	$43.41	$46.59
25								$32.71	$35.11	$37.68	$40.44
26									$30.48	$32.71	$35.11
27										$28.40	$30.48
28											$26.46
29											
30	American put price	**$3.78**	**$2.28**	**$1.17**	**$0.45**	$0.10	$0.00	$0.00	$0.00	$0.00	$0.00
31			**$5.32**	**$3.42**	**$1.89**	**$0.81**	$0.21	$0.00	$0.00	$0.00	$0.00
32				**$7.28**	**$4.99**	**$3.00**	**$1.43**	$0.42	$0.00	$0.00	$0.00
33					**$9.63**	**$7.04**	**$4.60**	**$2.46**	$0.84	$0.00	$0.00
34						**$12.32**	**$9.56**	**$6.80**	**$4.12**	$1.69	$0.00
35							**$14.89**	**$12.32**	**$9.56**	**$6.59**	$3.41
36								**$17.29**	**$14.89**	**$12.32**	$9.56
37									**$19.52**	**$17.29**	$14.89
38										**$21.60**	$19.52
39											$23.54
40											
41	European put price	**$3.66**	$2.23	$1.15	$0.45	$0.10	$0.00	$0.00	$0.00	$0.00	$0.00
42			$5.13	$3.33	$1.86	$0.80	$0.21	$0.00	$0.00	$0.00	$0.00
43				$6.99	$4.85	$2.94	$1.41	$0.42	$0.00	$0.00	$0.00
44					$9.20	$6.81	$4.50	$2.43	$0.84	$0.00	$0.00
45						$11.68	$9.19	$6.62	$4.05	$1.69	$0.00
46							$14.27	$11.86	$9.26	$6.45	$3.41
47								$16.82	$14.58	$12.17	$9.56
48									$19.20	$17.13	$14.89
49										$21.44	$19.52
50											$23.54
51											
52											

FIGURE 20.4 Model 3: Binomial pricing of American options on stocks with known dividend yield.

4. **Generate the American option pricing tree:** This step is similar to that in Model 2. Start with the last column. The formula in K30 is =MAX(0,OptType*(K19-K)). Copy it in the rest of the cells in that column.

   To calculate the option price at the earlier steps, in J30 enter the formula =IF(J19="","",MAX(MAX(OptType*(J19-K),0),(p*K30+(1-p)*K31)*emrdt)). This is the same as the formula we used in Model 2.

5. **Generate the European option price tree:** This is identical to the tree in Model 1.
6. **Bold the cells that are different in the American option tree:** Do it the same way you did it in Model 2.

Testing the Model

For dividend-paying stocks, even the values of calls for otherwise identical American and European options can be different. So you have to check the model by doing hand calculations for a few cells in the American option tree to make sure that it is making the right choice between exercising an option immediately and holding on to it, and calculating the payoff from the immediate exercise correctly. The rightmost bold cells (for example, J35) show where the option is being exercised immediately; you can check that the value is correct.

Uses of the Model

Binomial trees provide a convenient way to calculate values of American options. To get an accurate value, you need to use a large number of steps (for example, over 50). It is not difficult to expand the Excel tree for this many steps, but as we will see, it is much easier to do so for binomial models in VBA.

MODEL 4: AMERICAN OPTIONS ON STOCKS WITH KNOWN DOLLAR DIVIDENDS

The Problem

Develop a model to estimate the price of American options (both puts and calls) on a stock that will pay a known dollar amount of dividend at a known time in the future. Use a 5-step Cox, Ross, and Rubinstein (CRR) binomial tree for the calculation. Simultaneously calculate the values of the equivalent European options.

Modeling Strategy

The worksheet for this model is shown in Figure 20.5. To build this model, follow the earlier discussion on valuing options on stocks with known dollar dividends.

Start with a copy of the workbook for Model 2, which already has three trees built into it. Above the current stock price tree, build a new tree for the uncertain component of the stock price using the uncertain component of the initial stock price as its starting point. Then convert the existing stock price tree into one for the total stock price by entering new formulas in it to reflect the present value of the future dividend at each node prior to the dividend payment. The option value trees should work without any modifications because they already work off the tree that you will convert into the total stock price tree.

◇	A	B	C	D	E	F	G	H	I	J
1	**Binomial Pricing of American Options on Stocks with Known Dollar Dividend**									
2										
3										
4	Option type (C=1, P=-1)	-1			Step (dt)	**0.1200**				
5	Stock price (S)	$55.00			u	**1.1486**	Up movement factor			
6	Exercise price (K)	$50.00			d	**0.8706**	Down movement multiplier = 1/u			
7	Interest rate (rr, annual)	8.00%			p	**0.5001**	Risk-neutral probability of up movement			
8	Volatility (sig, annual)	40.00%			emrdt	**0.9904**	Discount factor per step, = Exp(-rr*dt)			
9	Time to maturity (T, years)	0.6000								
10	Number of steps (n)	5								
11	Dividend amount	$2.00								
12	Time to ex-dividend date	0.25								
13										
14										
15										
16	**Step**	**0**	**1**	**2**	**3**	**4**	**5**			
17	**Time**	**0.00**	**0.12**	**0.24**	**0.36**	**0.48**	**0.60**			
18										
19	**Stock price (uncertain part)**	$53.04	$60.92	$69.98	$80.38	$92.32	$106.04			
20			$46.18	$53.04	$60.92	$69.98	$80.38			
21				$40.20	$46.18	$53.04	$60.92			
22					$35.00	$40.20	$46.18			
23						$30.47	$35.00			
24							$26.53			
25										
26	**Stock price (total)**	$55.00	$62.90	$71.98	$80.38	$92.32	$106.04			
27			$48.16	$55.04	$60.92	$69.98	$80.38			
28				$42.20	$46.18	$53.04	$60.92			
29					$35.00	$40.20	$46.18			
30						$30.47	$35.00			
31							$26.53			
32										
33	**American put price**	**$4.27**	**$1.88**	$0.46	$0.00	$0.00	$0.00			
34			**$6.75**	**$3.33**	$0.94	$0.00	$0.00			
35				**$10.29**	**$5.79**	$1.89	$0.00			
36					**$15.00**	**$9.80**	$3.82			
37						**$19.53**	$15.00			
38							$23.47			
39										
40	**European put price**	**$4.07**	$1.82	$0.46	$0.00	$0.00	$0.00			
41			$6.40	$3.21	$0.94	$0.00	$0.00			
42				$9.71	$5.55	$1.89	$0.00			
43					$14.05	$9.32	$3.82			
44						$19.05	$15.00			
45							$23.47			
46										
47										

FIGURE 20.5 Model 4: Binomial pricing of American options on stocks with known dollar dividend.

Building the Model

Start with a copy of the workbook for Model 2.

1. **Set up input variables and calculate the tree parameters:** There is nothing new here except that you have to add the new input variables for the dividend amount and the time until the dividend payment. Name cell B11 div and cell B12 exdiv. Make sure that the copy you are using does not include dividend yield, q.

2. **Build the tree for the uncertain component of the stock price:** Build this tree as before. The only difference is that here in cell B19 you have to use the formula =(S-div*EXP(-rr*exdiv)), where the second part is the present value of the dividend div to be paid at time exdiv.
3. **Build the tree for the total stock price:** To add the present value of the dividend at each node before the ex-dividend time, in B26 enter the formula =IF(B19="","",IF(B$17<exdiv,B19+div*EXP(rr*(B$17-exdiv)),B19)). The long part in the middle of the formula calculates the present value of the dividend at a node using the difference between the ex-dividend time and the time of the node. It then adds this value to the corresponding stock price from the first tree. The inner IF function makes sure that this calculation is done only in nodes prior to the ex-dividend time. After that time, the total stock price is the same as the price on the first tree. This is accomplished by the FALSE leg of the IF function. The outer IF function ensures that only prices for nodes that are on the tree are entered; the other cells are made blank.

   Copy and paste the formula in all the remaining cells of the rectangle.
4. **Build the tree for the American options:** This is built the same way as before based on the tree for the total stock price. In G33 enter the formula =MAX(0,OptType*(G26-K)) and copy it into the rest of the column. In F33 enter the formula =IF(F26="","",MAX(MAX(OptType*(F26-K),0),(p*G33+(1-p)*G34)*emrdt)) and copy it into the rest of the rectangle.
5. **Build the tree for the European option:** This is also built the same way as before using the second stock price tree. The formula in G40 is =MAX(0,OptType*(G26-K)). Copy it into the rest of the column. In F40 enter the formula =IF(F19="","",(p*G40+(1-p)*G41)*emrdt) and copy it into the rest of the rectangle.

Testing the Model

Check the second tree by hand calculating the price at one or two nodes before ex-dividend time to make sure that the present value of the dividend is being added properly. Also check that the prices on both the stock price trees are the same after the ex-dividend time. Test the American and European option trees as before. Also check that the value of the American option is always greater than or equal to that of the European option.

Uses of the Model

This model can be easily extended to accommodate several dividends of known dollar amount. Also, for improved accuracy it can be extended to larger number of steps.

PART Three

VBA for Financial Modeling

CHAPTER 21

Introduction to VBA

Visual Basic for Applications (VBA) is a programming language that is built into Excel and other Microsoft Office applications. It is important for you to remember that VBA is a language and try to learn it the same way you learned your mother tongue—by imitating how others use it to say different things instead of by memorizing the rules of grammar, studying vocabulary lists, and so on. You will then be able to learn VBA faster with less work than if you try any of the other methods people use.

But what is a program and why do we need special languages to write programs?

A program is a recipe, that is, a set of step-by-step instructions that a computer can follow to do what you want done. These instructions have to be written in one of a group of specially designed languages, called programming languages, because computers do not understand and cannot follow instructions written in English or any of the other languages we generally use to communicate with one another. Since we have been using these languages for years, we do not realize that all of them are overly complex. For example, they all have huge vocabularies, and in all of them we can say the same thing in many different ways and use the same words, phrases, and so on, to mean different things in different contexts. These are the complexities that make a language like English so rich. These are the same complexities, however, that make it so difficult to design computers that can understand English or any of the other common languages.

VBA is one of many programming languages that have been developed over the years to write programs that computers can follow. Although most people are intimidated by the idea of learning a programming language, they are by design much simpler and much easier to learn than the languages we speak and use all the time. For example, programming languages have small vocabularies and simple, rigid syntaxes. The key to learning computer languages efficiently is to follow the right method. It should also be encouraging to know that once you learn any one programming language, learning others gets much easier because there are many similarities among all programming languages.

That was the good news. The bad news (if you want to look at it this way) is that you have to always use a programming language exactly the right way—the way it was designed to be used. You cannot take any liberties with it. For example, people just learning English may sometimes say "Rice I eat" or "Eat I rice." Although these sentences are syntactically wrong, anyone who knows English will understand that the speaker means "I eat rice." The message of the sentence is still clear. If you make similar mistakes in a programming language, however, the computer does not understand what you mean. But programming languages follow simple rules; so using them precisely is not much of a problem. What's more, if you make a mistake, most of the time the computer will either fix it for you or tell you that you made a mistake.

Keep in mind that even though a programming language uses English words and some of its syntax may be similar to English syntax, the two are very different. When you speak a foreign language that you do not know well, if you get stuck you can often manage to get your thoughts across by slipping in a few English words or phrases. This does not work with programming languages.

WHY LEARN VBA?

Why should you learn VBA? This actually encompasses two questions. Why should you learn programming, that is, writing programs? And, if you decide to learn programming, why should you choose VBA instead of the many other programming languages available? Let me address the two questions separately and in some detail.

Benefits of Learning Programming

In our context of financial modeling, a simple answer to the question, "Why learn programming?" is "To be able to create models that either cannot be created in Excel or will be overly complex if created in Excel." Over the years, Excel has evolved into a highly flexible modeling tool, and with some ingenuity you can create highly complex and powerful models using Excel. Nonetheless, because of certain limitations inherent in the way all spreadsheet programs work, it is essentially impossible to get Excel models to do certain things, including certain fairly simple things. Most people start learning a programming language primarily for this reason.

While this may be the most important reason from your point of view as well, there are a few other equally important reasons that you may fully appreciate only after you have been modeling with both Excel and VBA for some time. Let me briefly mention just three of them here:

- In many complex Excel models, the formulas in some cells can become very long and extend to several lines. What's more, since many of these formulas are designed to be copied to many different cells, they generally have to use many cell addresses with relative or mixed references and cannot use recognizable names for those cells. The formulas in some large models can therefore become difficult (if not impossible) to understand and check. In VBA, such formulas can be made easy to understand and check by breaking them down into shorter formulas and writing them with variables with descriptive names.

- In large Excel models, the same formula may be copied into dozens or even hundreds of cells. So every time such a formula is changed, it has to be recopied into many cells with the possibility of your missing some of them. Also, if the formulas in a few cells get inadvertently damaged during the updating process, for example, the problem may go unnoticed. In VBA, the same formula usually appears only once. Updating formulas and making sure that they do not get inadvertently damaged are much easier in VBA than they are in Excel.
- Because VBA programs provide step-by-step instructions in the logical sequence in which the computer is supposed to execute a model, it is generally easy to follow VBA models even if they have limited documentation. With complex Excel models, the sequence of calculation and the logic are often not easily discernable. Unless there is good documentation, anyone other than the person who created them may have great difficulty understanding and updating them.

Another way of answering the question, "Why learn programming?" may be with the question, "Why not?" Most people avoid trying to learn programming not because they are not interested or because they are skeptical about the advantages of programming. They never try because they think programming is difficult. They are intimidated. Learning enough to write a program to run an airline's reservation system can be intimidating indeed. However, learning enough to create most financial models in a programming language, especially for your own use, is not that difficult—provided you learn it the right way and focus on learning what you really need to know instead of getting distracted by the hundreds of other things a programming language can do. Once you get over the initial hurdle of learning something new, you will often find yourself writing programs to do even things that you could do with Excel because of some of the advantages I mentioned.

Benefits of Choosing VBA

So far I have been assuming that if you learn a programming language, you will opt for VBA. Let me now make the case for it. VBA—in this case, Excel VBA—is designed to work seamlessly with Excel. In a way, it represents the best of both worlds: you can enjoy the power of a programming language and you can also take advantage of most of the attractive features of Excel. For example, with most programming languages, creating attractive outputs (especially different types of charts and graphs) can take quite a bit of knowledge and a lot of work. With VBA, you can start looking like a professional fairly quickly because you will have access to all the charting power of Excel. Here are a few other advantages:

- VBA is already built into Excel. You do not have to buy a separate program, spend time installing it, or get frustrated when it does not work properly because of conflicts with other programs.
- VBA offers dozens of built-in functions, including many financial functions, to simplify the work of building models. These functions work like the Excel functions, and you can also use most Excel functions in VBA. You therefore get a lot of power with little additional work.
- Microsoft offers a version of VBA with each of its Office applications, such as Word and Access. Because each VBA is designed to work closely with its associated application, there are some differences among the different versions. Nonetheless, all of these are essentially the same programming language, and once you learn Excel VBA, it will take little additional effort to learn any of the other versions. (In this book I cover only the Excel version of VBA, although for simplicity I mostly refer to it as just "VBA" instead of "Excel VBA.")
- Programs written in Excel VBA can be run only from inside Excel and, therefore, only in PCs that have Excel installed in them. However, VBA is closely related to Visual Basic (VB), which is a widely used and more powerful general programming language. Programs written in VB can be run on any PC. So, as with the other versions of VBA, once you learn Excel VBA, it will be easier for you to step up to VB, or for that matter, any other programming language for additional flexibility and power. Also, the programs you write in VBA can be converted to VB with limited modifications.

What is the downside of learning VBA and developing models in VBA? The only one that comes to mind is that because many more people know Excel than VBA, if you pass on an Excel model to a colleague, chances are he will be able to look inside it, understand it, and even modify it if necessary. Most of your friends and colleagues probably do not know VBA. So they may be able to run a VBA model you give them, but they will not be able to understand and modify it. Then again, being one of the few people who knows VBA can be a great advantage, too.

Versions of Excel's Programming Language

Excel VBA, in its current form, was introduced in Excel 97. Earlier versions of Excel included different programming languages. The VBA language in Excel 97 and all later versions including Excel 2007 are essentially the same, and the discussions in this book apply to all these versions of Excel, but not to the earlier ones. Over these later versions of Excel, Microsoft has made only minor changes to VBA, primarily in the peripheral areas like the online Help.

UNDERSTANDING PROGRAMS

I defined a program as a recipe, that is, a set of step-by-step instructions that a computer can follow to do what you want done. The process of writing or creating a program is called programming. Here are a few things that are special about a program:

- It has to be written in a programming language like VBA. For a computer to be able to understand and run a program written in VBA, it must have Excel installed in it. Programs written in some other languages like VB can be run on all PCs, although this takes some additional work.
- A program must be precise and complete to the minutest detail. Remember that although computers can do incredibly complex things, they actually have no intelligence or ability to think. They can only follow instructions exactly as they are given. So while in a cooking recipe "add salt to taste" may be a perfectly adequate instruction, similar vague instructions in a program will not work. (Some advanced computers and programming languages can overcome some of these limitations, but VBA is not one of them.)
- When running a program, the computer generally carries out the instructions in the exact order they are given. Most of the time, then, the order of the instructions matter and must be correct. (However, as we will see, sometimes the program itself can instruct the computer to jump forward or backward a few steps out of order.)
- A program has to be absolutely error-free to produce right results under all circumstances. Most errors will not allow a program to run at all or will stop the program when it reaches the point where the error occurs. Some other errors will not stop the program from running through to the end but will produce wrong results. And then there are errors that may not show up for a long time until certain combinations of input values trigger them. At this point the program may stop working or produce wrong results. Hunting for and fixing errors in programs, called debugging, is a crucial but often time-consuming and frustrating step in programming and developing models. (It is called debugging because errors in programs are generally called bugs.)

The key point you have to remember is that the computer will not do any thinking for you. You have to fully understand a problem, figure out exactly how to solve it, and then lay out the method of solution in minute details in precise steps. All of this comes before you actually start translating your solution into the programming language to create a program.

Most beginners have a lot of problem with translating the method of solution into a series of precise steps because they are not used to thinking in such an organized manner. Unless you can translate your solution into precise steps, however, you will not be able to convert it into a program. In programming, developing the skill to think in orderly steps is as important and as much of a challenge as anything else.

As you will see, writing a program is somewhat like writing a story using a word processor. You will always have the opportunity to go back and rewrite parts, reorganize paragraphs, and so forth. However, you must start with at least a good sketch of the story in mind, and ultimately you will have to get every sentence and every word right.

The Different Names for Programs

Programs are also called procedures, codes, and macros. Some people make some distinctions among these different names; others use them more or less interchangeably, and this is what I will do in this book as well. However, as we will see a little later, you can create only certain types of programs by recording them with Excel's Macro Recorder, and Microsoft specifically calls these recorded programs macros.

In VBA you will write only two kinds of programs: Sub procedures and Function procedures. The names *program, code,* and *macro* are generally not used in this context, that is, Sub procedures are not called Sub codes, Sub macros, and so on. It should be noted, however, that Sub procedures that do not have arguments are also called macros (not Sub macros), in part because they show up in the list of macros in the Macro dialog box.

From time to time, I also call a VBA program "the model" or "the VBA model," although this is not common terminology. In any case, none of it should be confusing.

Example of a VBA Model

A picture is worth a thousand words, as the saying goes. Similarly, looking at an actual program is worth dozens of pages of discussions about programs. Let me introduce you to VBA, then, by walking you through an actual VBA model for a simple problem for which we already created an Excel model in Chapter 14: Time Value of Money. (If you have not covered that chapter yet but feel confident that you know how to solve this problem, then you are ready to go. Otherwise, go through the earlier discussion of this model first.)

The Problem

Create a model to produce an amortization table for a fixed rate loan. The loan is to be repaid in equal annual installments over its life and the first payment is to be made at the end of the first year.

RUNNING THE MODEL

The VBA model for the problem is provided on the CD. To look at it, close all open workbooks (not essential), copy the workbook for this model from the CD to your hard disk, and double-click the file to open it. You will see a message box, which will come up every time you open a workbook that has a macro in it. Read the message once and then click Enable Macros. This will internally enable the macros in the workbook, but you will not see them yet. Select the worksheet "Loan Amort." This is both the input and output sheet for this model. It is shown in Figure 21.1.

The input area is at the top left corner, and B2, B3, and B4 are the input cells. The sheet also shows the amortization table created by the VBA model for the current set of input data. Take a few minutes to look through the table to understand it and visualize how the numbers in it are calculated. Now select any of the cells in the table and notice that there is no formula behind any of the numbers. This is different from Excel where the formulas that calculate the cell values reside in the cells themselves. In VBA, calculations are most often done in the program and only the output values are entered in the cells.

	1	2	3	4	5	6	7	8
1	**Input Data**							
2	Interest rate (annual %)	5.00%	Can't be greater than 15%					
3	Loan life (in years)	10	Must be whole numbers					
4	Initial loan amount (in $)	$200,000	Can't be negative					
5								
6			**Year**	**Year-beg**	**Annual**	**Interest**	**Principal**	**Year-end**
7				**Balance**	**Payment**	**Component**	**Repaid**	**Balance**
8								
9			1	$200,000	$25,901	$10,000	$15,901	$184,099
10			2	$184,099	$25,901	$9,205	$16,696	$167,403
11			3	$167,403	$25,901	$8,370	$17,531	$149,872
12			4	$149,872	$25,901	$7,494	$18,407	$131,465
13			5	$131,465	$25,901	$6,573	$19,328	$112,137
14			6	$112,137	$25,901	$5,607	$20,294	$91,843
15			7	$91,843	$25,901	$4,592	$21,309	$70,535
16			8	$70,535	$25,901	$3,527	$22,374	$48,160
17			9	$48,160	$25,901	$2,408	$23,493	$24,668
18			10	$24,668	$25,901	$1,233	$24,668	$0
19								
20								
21								
22								

FIGURE 21.1 The worksheet for the loan amortization example.

To run the model for a different set of input values, change one or more of the input values, and then press Ctrl+y. This will run the VBA model with the new input values and create a new amortization table almost instantaneously. The Ctrl+y is called the Shortcut key of a program and is assigned by the programmer at his discretion. If a program has a Shortcut key, then using it is one way of running the program.

To run the program another way, select Developer ⇨ Code ⇨ Macros (in previous versions of Excel, Tools ⇨ Macro ⇨ Macros) to open the Macro dialog box, click `Loan_Amortization`, the name of this macro, and then click the Run button to run the macro.

I have indicated in cell C2 that the interest rate you enter cannot be greater than 15%. What happens if you make it greater than 15%? Try it. Enter 17% in cell B2 and run the macro. You will see a message box warning you that interest rate cannot be greater than 15%. Models in both Excel and VBA often include such checks—called data validation—to make sure that the input data being entered is acceptable. In this case there is no particular reason why interest rate greater than 15% should not be acceptable. I imposed this constraint just to make the point. Click OK in the message box and the program will stop. You can enter an acceptable interest rate and run the program again.

Cell C3 indicates that the loan life you enter must be in whole years. What happens if you enter, say, 10.1? Try it. This time you will not see any message box and the program will run through to the end instead of stopping. Notice, however, that the loan does not get fully paid off by the end of the last year. Given the way the problem is defined, fractional loan lives do not make sense here, and a careful programmer would put in a data validation here as well. But I did not, to make the point that simply putting in a note of caution may not always be adequate. It often depends on who is going to use a model. If it is a "quick and dirty" model that only you will use, then such reminders may be good enough. If others are going to use the model as well, then you have to anticipate mistakes they may make and build in safeguards. Good modeling requires attention to such details.

ANALYZING THE MODEL

Now that you have learned two of the ways to run a model and have seen what this model does, it is time to look inside the VBA program to see how it creates the amortization table. For that we have to go to the Visual Basic Editor (VBE), which is where you will do most of your work with VBA. The VBE is part of Excel, but it does not open automatically when you start Excel; you have to start it separately by pressing Alt+F11. This opens the VBE window as shown in Figure 21.2. You can go back and forth between the worksheets in the workbook and the VBE by clicking the appropriate minimized window icon in the Windows task bar at the bottom of the screen. Alternately, you can cycle through all the open windows in your computer by repeatedly pressing Alt+Tab and stop at the

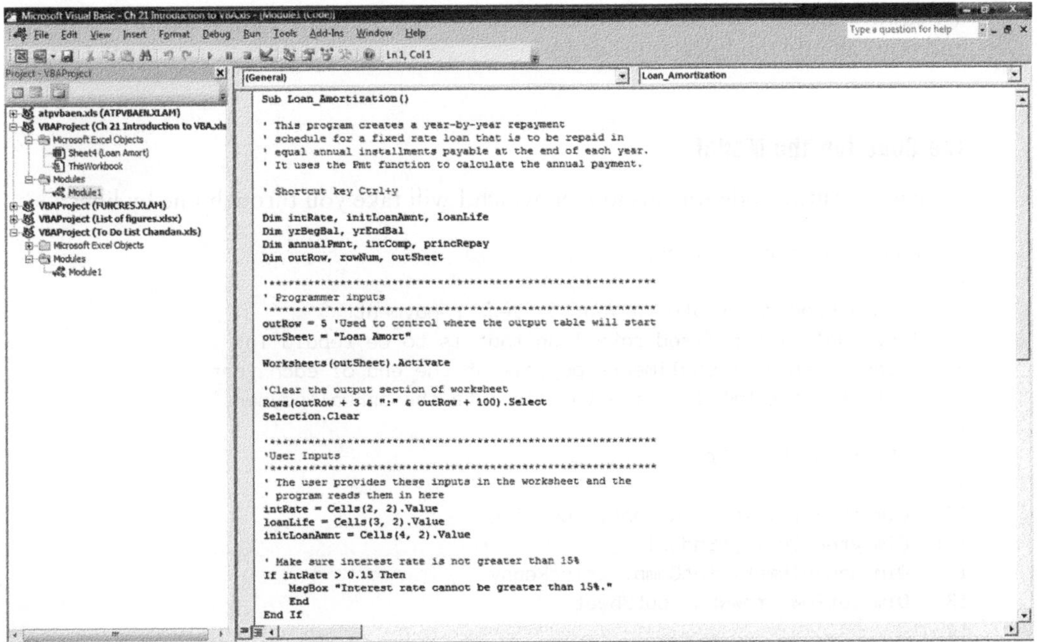

FIGURE 21.2 The Visual Basic Editor.

window you want to activate. (You can hold down the Alt key and press the Tab key as many times as you need.)

The VBE has many components and features. At the moment we only need to make sure that the Code window and the Project Explorer window are open. The Code window is the large window that takes up most of the right-hand side of the VBE window. If the first line in the Code window reads `Sub Loan_Amortization ()` then you already have the right code open. Otherwise you will have to find it using the Project Explorer. In either case, you may want to go through the following steps to learn how the Project Explorer works because you will use it extensively.

The Project Explorer window is a narrow long window along the left side of your screen with the title "Project" in its title bar. If you do not see it, press Ctrl+R to open it. In the Project Explorer window, each open workbook is considered a project and is listed (along with a few other things) in a tree diagram. Find "VBAProject (Ch 21 Introduction to VBA.xls)" in the list and if there is a + to its left, click on it to show all its components. (If the sign is − then the components are already showing.) Find the node titled Modules and if it has a + next to it, click on it to show all the modules and then double-click Module1. If necessary, maximize the window that opens. Make sure that the first line in the code window reads `Sub Loan_Amortization ()`. You have just opened the module that holds the code for the model we want to examine. (Modules in VBA are similar to the worksheets in Excel in that you store your VBA codes in them and you can add modules as needed.)

The Code for the Model

Here is the entire code for this model, which I will take you through line by line:

```
Sub Loan_Amortization()

' This program creates a year-by-year repayment
' schedule for a fixed rate loan that is to be repaid in
' equal annual installments payable at the end of each year.
' It uses the Pmt function to calculate the annual payment.

' Shortcut key Ctrl+y

 Dim intRate, initLoanAmnt, loanLife
 Dim yrBegBal, yrEndBal
 Dim annualPmnt, intComp, princRepay
 Dim outRow, rowNum, outSheet

 '**********************************************************
 ' Programmer inputs
 '**********************************************************
 outRow = 5 'Used to control where the output table will start
 outSheet = "Loan Amort"

 Worksheets(outSheet).Activate

 'Clear the output section of worksheet
 Rows(outRow + 3 & ":" & outRow + 100).Select
 Selection.Clear

 '**********************************************************
 'User Inputs
 '**********************************************************
 ' The user provides these inputs in the worksheet and the
 ' program reads them in here
 intRate = Cells(2, 2).Value
 loanLife = Cells(3, 2).Value
 initLoanAmnt = Cells(4, 2).Value

 ' Make sure interest rate is not greater than 15%
 If intRate > 0.15 Then
    MsgBox "Interest rate cannot be grater than 15%."
    End
 End If
```

```

'*************************************************************
' Compute and output results
'*************************************************************
' Calculate annual payment
annualPmnt = Pmt(intRate, loanLife, -initLoanAmnt,, 0)

' Initialize beginning balance for year 1
yrBegBal = initLoanAmnt

' Loop to calculate and output year-by-year amort. table
For rowNum = 1 To loanLife

    intComp = yrBegBal * intRate
    princRepay = annualPmnt - intComp
    yrEndBal = yrBegBal - princRepay

    Cells(outRow + rowNum + 3, 3).Value = rowNum 'Year number
    Cells(outRow + rowNum + 3, 4).Value = yrBegBal
    Cells(outRow + rowNum + 3, 5).Value = annualPmnt
    Cells(outRow + rowNum + 3, 6).Value = intComp
    Cells(outRow + rowNum + 3, 7).Value = princRepay
    Cells(outRow + rowNum + 3, 8).Value = yrEndBal

    yrBegBal = yrEndBal

Next rowNum

'*************************************************************
' Format the output data in the table
'*************************************************************
Range(Cells(outRow + 4, 4), Cells(outRow + loanLife + 3, 8) _
    ).Select
Selection.NumberFormat = "$#,##0"

End Sub
```

(You cannot show line numbers in front of the code lines in VBE's Code window and you also cannot print out the code from VBA with line numbers. I added the line numbers in Word. However, if you place the cursor on any line in the code, the line number shows up in a window at the center of the tool bar.)

Analysis of the Code

This is far from a beginner's code. So it will take a little perseverance to go through it. You do not have to understand every detail in the first reading. I simply want you to get an overall impression of programming and VBA.

Let me start by making a few general comments about how programs are organized and executed:

- A program comprises a series of statements or instructions, which are analogous to sentences in English. Each statement represents one step of the program "recipe." (A statement may be one or more lines long.)
- Remember that the program is written in the VBA language and these sentences follow the syntax of VBA. They may seem a little strange now, but you will get used to them soon.
- When you run the program, VBA executes one statement at a time, starting at the top and moving down sequentially—unless it is instructed by the program itself to jump ahead or backward.
- In VBA an equals (=) sign instructs the computer to evaluate the part of the statement on its right and assign the result to whatever is on its left. This is why in VBA it is called the assignment operator; it is not an equals sign in the sense we normally use it.

Now to the details:

Line 1: The word `Sub` at the beginning indicates that this is a Sub procedure. All Sub procedures must start with a statement like this one. (The only other kind of procedure in VBA is called a Function procedure.) The word `Sub` is followed by the name of the program that the programmer makes up following a few simple rules. The two parentheses at the end are required. A Sub procedure ends with an `End Sub` statement (line 76 in this program).

Line 2: VBA ignores all blank lines. You can insert them anywhere in your code to make it easier to read.

Lines 3–6: In VBA, an apostrophe signals the beginning of a comment: VBA ignores whatever follows the apostrophe. The comment lines here provide a description of what this program does. It is good practice to include such a description at the beginning of all programs.

Line 8: Comment to document that the Shortcut key for this program is Ctrl+y. (The comment itself does not make this the Shortcut key for this program. You will learn later how that is done.)

Lines 10–13: These are called `Dim` statements and they tell the computer what variables I will use in this program. (We will learn about variables a few lines later.) You have to start each of these lines with the word `Dim` and then list the variables separated by commas. I could have included all these variable names in one very long line. However, long lines that extend beyond the right end of the screen become hard to read. To avoid this, I broke up the list into several separate Dim statements and grouped related variables together.

Lines 15–17: Comment lines. I am using this design to break up the program into several sections and include a brief heading for each section. In this section, I am entering a few inputs the program will use. I am putting them in one place so that it will be easy to find them if I want to make any changes.

Line 18: Creates a variable called `outRow` and assigns to it the value 5. Models primarily manipulate data, which have to be stored somewhere. In Excel we store them in cells in worksheets. In VBA we can also store them in the cells of one or more worksheets. But there is a better alternative. We can create a variable, as we are doing here, by simply choosing a unique name and then assigning to it a piece of data or value. Once we have created it, we can use a variable like `outRow` in any statement, and VBA will use its value to evaluate the statement. We can also change its value anywhere in the program (hence the name variable). This is similar to giving a cell a name in Excel and then using the cell name (instead of the cell address) in formulas to make formulas more readable. We will see later why I am creating this particular variable. (Note that I have included an explanation in the same line using an apostrophe to indicate that the rest of the line is a comment.)

Line 19: Creates another variable called `outSheet`, but instead of a number it stands for a string of characters (generally referred to as string or text) Loan Amort, which is the name of the worksheet I use for the input and output data for this model. As you can see here, string or text data have to be enclosed in quotation marks, but the corresponding variable names do not require quotation marks.

Line 21: VBA substitutes the current values of all variables used in a statement before evaluating or executing it. In this statement, VBA first substitutes Loan Amort for `outSheet`. This statement tells VBA to make the worksheet named Loan Amort the active sheet. This means that whenever the program is asked to do anything with a worksheet (for example, read in data from) without specifying which worksheet, it will assume that this is the worksheet it has to use.

Line 23: This comment line indicates that in the next few statements the numbers in the amortization table from the previous run will be cleared to get ready for making a new run. (I do not clear the column headings of the table or input area because they are needed.)

Line 24: Since VBA first substitutes the current values for all variables, this statement becomes `Rows(8 & ":" & 105).Select` and in VBA language it says "select rows 8 through 105."

Line 25: Clears the selected area—in this case, rows 8 through 105. This deletes the old numbers in the amortization table. (To be safe, I clear many more rows than is necessary.)

Line 32: Reads in the interest rate from cell B2 of the worksheet and assigns it to the variable `intRate`. Here `Cells (2, 2).Value` means value of that cell, which is the input interest rate. Cell B2 translates to `Cells (2, 2)` because VBA generally uses Excel's R1C1 convention (that is, both rows and columns are referred to by numbers, with the row number coming first).

Lines 33–34: Reads in the input data for loan life and initial loan amount and assigns them to appropriate variables.

Line 37: This is one form of `If` statement in VBA. If the input interest rate is greater than 15%, then lines 38 and 39 will be executed. Otherwise VBA will skip those lines and jump to the line following the last line of the `If` statement (line 40, `End If`)—line 41.

Line 38: Displays the message box with the warning message, because if control reaches this point then the input interest rate is greater than 15%.

Line 39: Terminates the program, because if control reaches this point then the input interest rate is greater than 15%.

Line 40: Marks the end of the `If` statement.

Line 46: Calculates the annual payment for the loan using the `Pmt` function and stores it in the variable `annualPmnt`. This is similar to using built-in functions in Excel and, as in Excel, the arguments for a function can be values or variable names.

Line 49: Creates a new variable called `yrBegBal` and makes its value equal to the initial loan amount for use as the loan balance at the beginning of the first year.

Line 52: Beginning of a `For` loop, which ends in Line 67 with the statement `Next rowNum`. A loop is an important tool in all programming languages and is used to repeat a group of statements (here Lines 52 through 67) to do the same things many times with different values for one or more variables. The variable that follows the `For`, (here `rowNum`) is called the counter of the loop and a range of values is specified for it after the equals (=) sign. The loop is repeated with each value in this range. When control gets to this line for the first time, `rowNum` is set equal to 1, the lowest value of the range, and then control moves on to the next line.

Line 54: Calculates the interest due for the year based on the loan balance at the beginning of the year and the interest rate.

Line 55: Calculates how much of the annual payment will remain after paying the interest for the year. This is the principal repayment for the year and is used to reduce the loan balance.

Line 56: Calculates the new loan balance at the end of the year by subtracting the amount available for principal repayment from the year-beginning loan balance. This completes the calculations for the year.

Line 58: This statement is essentially the reverse of the type of statement in line 32. There I was reading in the value of a variable from a cell in the worksheet. Here I am writing out the value of the variable `rowNum` into a cell in the worksheet. For the first run through the loop, `rowNum` is 1, and this value is entered into the cell in the worksheet whose address is given by row number (1 + 5 + 3 =) 9 and column number 3.

Lines 59–63: Fills out the other columns in the amortization table using the values calculated in lines 54–56 and elsewhere.

Line 65: Sets the new year-beginning balance for the next year equal to the year-end balance for the current year. (Notice that I had to write out the year-beginning balance for the current year before updating it for the next year, because assigning a new value to a variable overwrites its old value.)

Line 67: This statement, which marks the end of the loop, sends control back to the beginning of the loop (line 52) where the value of `rowNum` is now incremented by 1 to 2. All the in-between steps are repeated with that value and the updated value for the year-beginning balance. The looping goes on up to `rowNum = loanLife`, that is, the last year, because that is the upper end of the range specified for `rowNum` in line 52. Control then passes onto the line following this line.

Lines 72–73: Selects the range covering the amortization table for formatting. The range is specified by indicating the cell numbers for the range's upper left corner and lower right corner. Check this out by substituting the values for `outRow` and `loanLife` in the statement. The underline (_) character after a space at the end of line 72 indicates that the statement of line 72 continues to line 73. VBA treats the two lines as one statement.

Line 74: Formats the selected range, that is, the table, as currency with zero decimal points (indicated by the string "`$#,##0`").

Line 76: Indicates the end of the Sub procedure.

THE ORDER OF STATEMENTS

Earlier I made the point that most of the time the order of the statements in a code matters and must be correct. We can now use this model to understand more clearly when the order matters and when it does not. In lines 32–34, where I was reading in the input data, the order within those few lines did not matter. I could have read in the loan life before the interest rate and so forth and could have even moved the User Inputs section ahead of the Programmer Input section. On the other hand, I had to read in the input data before using them in any calculation. Also, I could not change the order of the calculations in lines 54–56 because I needed the results of the earlier calculations to do the later calculations. These are the things that determine where order matters and where it does not.

Recording Macros

Excel provides a tool called the Macro Recorder that you can use to automatically record your keystrokes in VBA, that is, actions you take to do something in Excel, and create a macro that you can run to repeat those actions. The best way to familiarize yourself with the Macro Recorder is to record a macro.

In Excel 2007 open a blank workbook and select Developer ⇨ Code ⇨ Record Macro. In earlier versions of excel you can use the Visual Basic toolbar to work with the Macro Recorder efficiently. Open a blank workbook and while you are in Excel, open the Visual Basic toolbar by selecting View ⇨ Toolbar, then clicking Visual Basic. Click the Record Macro button (the small circle) on the VB toolbar to open the Record Macro dialog box. (You can also open the dialog box by selecting Tools ⇨ Macro ⇨ Record Macro.)

Excel automatically assigns the macro a name in the Macro name window. Change it if you want and type in the letter a in the box next to Ctrl+ to assign it a Shortcut key. For the moment you want to leave the Store macro in option as This workbook. Click on the arrow next to it to see that you can also choose to store the macro in a New Workbook or in the Personal Macro Workbook. The latter is an interesting choice that we will discuss later. If you want, you can also enter a description of the macro in the text box labeled Description. Now click OK to close the dialog box. In Excel 2007 the Macro Recorder will now be ready to start recording any action you take. Notice that the Record Macro icon now changes to Stop Recording.

In previous versions of Excel, clicking OK to close the dialog box will bring up a small floating Stop toolbar and prepare the Macro Recorder to start recording any action you take now. Check to make sure that the larger button in the Stop toolbar (called the Relative Reference button) does not look "pressed in." If it does, click it to make it look normal.

Now for your test, select cell H13, type in 123, and then, to finish recording the macro, in Excel 2007, click Stop Macros, or in the previous versions of Excel, click the stop button (the small black square) in the Stop toolbar.

To use the macro you just recorded, clear the cell H13, select any other cell, and press Ctrl+a (the Shortcut key you assigned to the macro). The macro will select the cell H13 and enter in it 123, repeating your action. You can also run the macro by selecting Developer ⇨ Code ⇨ Macros (or the Run Macro button in previous versions) to bring up the Macro dialog box, selecting the name of the macro in the list of macros, and then pressing the Run button. Pressing Alt+F8 also brings up the Macro dialog box. (In previous versions of Excel, selecting Tools ⇨ Macro ⇨Macros will also do the same thing.)

To see the code that the Macro Recorder generated, open the VBE by pressing Alt+F11, and open Module1 if it is not already open. You will see a code similar to the following:

```
1:  Sub Macro1()
2:  '
3:  ' Macro1 Macro
4:  ' Macro recorded 12/15/2002 by Chandan Sengupta
5:  '
6:  ' Keyboard Shortcut: Ctrl+a
7:  '
8:      Range("H13").Select
9:      ActiveCell.FormulaR1C1 = "123"
10:      Range("H13").Select
11:  End Sub
```

Look through the code, but do not worry for now if you do not understand all of it.

Uses of the Macro Recorder

The Macro Recorder is useful for recording and then automatically repeating a series of tasks—especially long ones—that you perform often (for example, formatting particular ranges and entering headings for tables). It is particularly useful for recording formatting because writing codes for formatting can be tedious. Typically you record the formatting, and then cut and paste the relevant part of the recorded code (lines 8–10 in the example) into other codes you are writing. The Macro Recorder can also produce excellent code and save a lot of work when what you are doing involves using a lot of menu commands (for example, creating a chart).

Another important use is to learn or remember how to write code for certain things. If it is something you can do in Excel, you can always turn on the Macro Recorder and record the action. Even if the recorded code is not exactly what you need, most of the time it will help you with useful clues. In all cases, you will probably want to edit the generated code to make it more concise and also to improve and generalize it.

Limitations of the Macro Recorder

Since the Macro Recorder can record only your actions, it cannot generate codes for some of the most powerful tools used in codes such as looping and If statements. So what it can do is limited. Also, as we will see later, the Macro Recorder often generates large and inefficient codes with lots of superfluous statements. But once you are familiar with VBA, you will be able to edit the generated code to what you really need and then use the macro by itself or cut and paste part or all of it into your other codes. A safe way to trim a code is to "comment out" the lines you think you do not need by putting apostrophes in front of them, test the macro to make sure that those lines are really redundant, and then delete them. (See more on this use of comment in Chapter 22: VBA Essentials.)

Absolute and Relative Reference

You recorded the test macro using absolute reference, meaning that whenever you run it, it will perform the recorded actions exactly in the same locations (in this case, cell H13) irrespective of which cell is active (that is, selected) immediately before you run the macro. This is probably what you want most of the time. Sometimes, though, you may want the macro's actions to take place in relative locations, which you can accomplish using relative reference during recording. It is easier to understand what this means by looking at an example.

Select cell A1 and get ready to record a new macro following the steps we used before, but with these changes: assign Ctrl+b as the Shortcut key and before starting the actions to record, click Developer ⇨ Code ⇨ Use Relative References in Excel 2007 (or, in previous versions, click the Relative Reference button in the Stop toolbar to make it look pressed). Now enter X in cell A2, Y in A3, and Z in A4, and then stop recording.

To test the macro, select cell B5 and press Ctrl+b. The letters X, Y, and Z will now appear in cells B6, B7, and B8 because they have the same relationship to the cell B5—which was active when you ran the macro—as the cells A2, A3, and A4 had to the cell A1, which was active immediately before you recorded the macro. This is how a macro works when you record it with relative reference.

Here is what the recorded macro looks like. As before, do not worry if you do not understand it all at this point.

```
Sub Macro1()
'
' Macro1 Macro
' Macro recorded 3/24/2003 by Chandan Sengupta
'
' Keyboard Shortcut: Ctrl+b
'
    ActiveCell.Offset(0, 1).Range("A1").Select
    ActiveCell.FormulaR1C1 = "X"
    ActiveCell.Offset(0, 1).Range("A1").Select
    ActiveCell.FormulaR1C1 = "Y"
    ActiveCell.Offset(0, 1).Range("A1").Select
```

```
    ActiveCell.FormulaR1C1 = "Z"
    ActiveCell.Offset(1, 0).Range("A1").Select
End Sub
```

If you want a macro to always repeat your actions at the same locations—the locations used during recording—you should use absolute reference to record it. On the other hand, if you are recording a macro, for example, to add headings to a table that may be at different locations at different times, then you should record the macro with relative reference.

You can also mix absolute and relative references in the same macro by turning on and turning off the Relative Reference button at the appropriate points during recording. Remember that relative is always with respect to the cell that is active just before you turn on the Relative Reference button and is not the cell that was active immediately before you started recording the macro.

If you find absolute and relative references a little confusing, practice using them in a few other made-up examples to understand how the two work.

Assigning Shortcut Keys to Macros

As we saw, you can assign a Shortcut key to a macro at the time of recording it. To assign a Shortcut key afterwards to any macro, recorded or otherwise, or to change one previously assigned, open the Macro dialog box (use Alt+F8). Select the macro in the list, click the Options button, and then enter a Shortcut key. Shortcut keys are case sensitive. You can use Ctrl+b and Ctrl+B (which will be shown as Ctrl+Shift+B) for two different macros. Of course, to run the macro associated with the latter you will have to press Shift as well.

In assigning Shortcut keys to macros, you have to avoid the Ctrl+ key combinations that Excel uses for certain actions (for example, Ctrl+c for Copy). Otherwise, your macro will override the Excel action that key combination normally performs. Note that even though the key combinations that Excel uses as Shortcut keys are shown with capital letters in the menus (for example, see next to Copy in the Edit menu), they actually work with small letters and you do not have to press Shift to use them. If you use capital C in assigning the Shortcut key to a macro (which will be shown as Ctrl+Shift+C), for example, this will not interfere with Excel's Copy.

Unfortunately, Excel does not give you any warning when you make the mistake of using a key combination that Excel uses. You will discover the problem only when one of Excel's standard Shortcut key combinations stops working the way it is supposed to. So be careful in choosing Shortcut keys.

The Personal Macro Workbook

Earlier we saw that at the time of recording a macro, you have the option to save it in the Personal Macro Workbook. This is a hidden workbook, named

Personal.xlsb in Excel 2007 and Personal.xls in previous versions, which is created automatically when you save the first macro in it. The macros in it are accessible from all workbooks, meaning you will see them (preceded by Personal.xlsb! or Personal.xls!) in the list of available macros in the macro dialog box in any workbook. If you record any macro that you may use often with different workbooks, you should consider saving it in this workbook.

To edit or delete any macro you save in this workbook, you have to first unhide it. In Excel, select View ⇨ Windows ⇨ Unhide (or Windows ⇨ Unhide) and then select the workbook. Then you can open the relevant module to edit or delete the macro. To store in the Personal.xlsb any macro you recorded or VBA procedure you wrote in any other workbook, unhide the Personal.xlsb, open the VBE, and cut and paste the procedure into a module in this workbook.

If you unhide and do some work in the Personal.xlsb and then close it, the macros and programs in it will not be available anymore. You will have to reopen it to use those macros and programs. It will also open automatically the next time you start Excel.

Using VBA's Help

VBA provides extensive and excellent online Help, which works very much like the online Help in Excel. So you should be able to use most of it right away. (If you did not take the time to learn to use Excel's online Help well, this may be a good time to review the earlier discussion of it. Learning to take full advantage of VBA's Help will considerably increase your efficiency in working with VBA.

FINDING HELP IN EXCEL 2007

Select Developer ⇨ Code ⇨ Visual Basic. On the Help menu, click Microsoft Visual Basic Help. In the Type words to search for box, type the method, property, function, statement, or object for which you want help, or type a query.

FINDING HELP IN PREVIOUS VERSIONS OF EXCEL

Here are the two most useful ways to access the online Help in the previous versions of Excel.

Using the Office Assistant

The fastest way to find help on any topic is through the Office Assistant. To get Help with VBA you must access the Office Assistant from the VBE and not from Excel. As with Excel, you often have to know the right keyword to find help on a topic. However, this is generally less of a problem in VBA because most of the time you will be looking for help on a VBA language element or function, which the Office Assistant will recognize. Note that in many cases you can get both a description and an example of the topic you are researching.

Using the Full Help Window to Get Help

You can get to the full Help window (which has two panes, one with three tabs) in at least two ways. Exactly how you get there determines what you will see in the Contents tab. The best way to get to the highest level of Help in the Contents tab (meaning the level from which you can access help on everything) is to use the following approach: While you are in VBE, in the Office Assistant type in "Help Method," click Search, and select "Help Method (Excel)" in the list of topics that come up. This will bring up one panel of the Help window. Now click on the Show icon at top left (it looks like a page with a left arrow pointing to the left attached to it) to bring up the second pane of the Help window with three tabs. The Help window should look like Figure 21.3. (You can get to this Contents tab in many ways. However, because VBA's Help is context sensitive, if you get to it in some other way, you may see only a part of the Contents.)

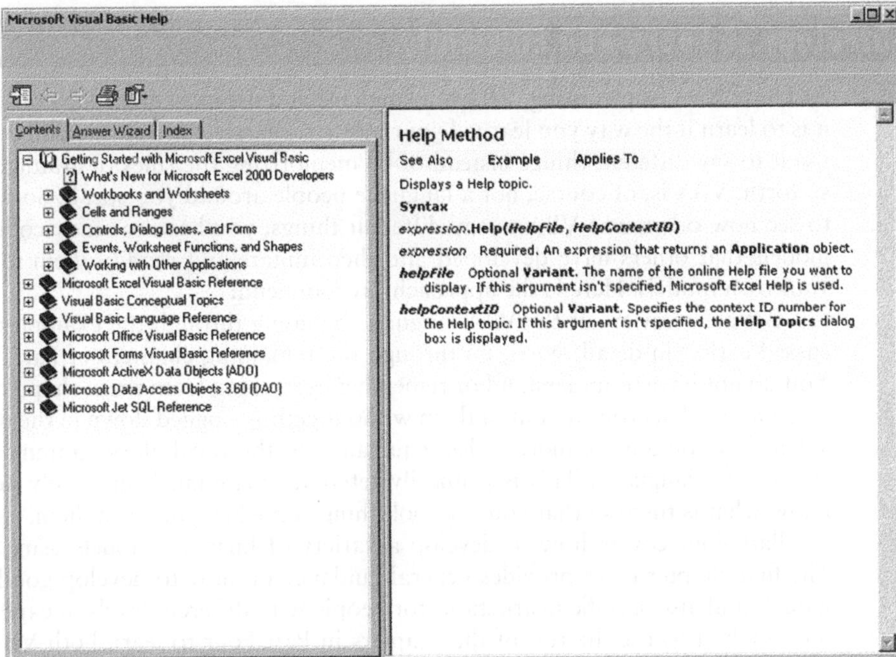

FIGURE 21.3 The Visual Basic Help window.

In the Contents tab the help topics are arranged like chapters in a book with each chapter marked with a book icon and descriptive name. To open the list of topics included in a chapter, you can either double-click the book icon for the chapter or click on the plus sign on its left. A chapter may also include sections marked with additional book icons, which work the same way. (You can collapse the list of sections and topics in a chapter by clicking on the minus sign next to its book icon.)

This tab is particularly helpful if you are trying to learn about some aspect of VBA and not looking for help on something specific. Also, if you have not been able to find help on something through the Office Assistant because you probably did not use the right keyword, you may be able to find it through this tab by guessing which chapter and section has what you need.

The Answer Wizard and Index tabs work the same way as they do in Excel.

Other Ways to Access Help

You can access anything in VBA's online Help in one of the two ways I just described. However, there are ways to get context-sensitive help even faster when you are working with VBA. I will cover them in later chapters.

The Strategy to Learn VBA Efficiently

As I have been emphasizing, VBA is a language and the most efficient way to learn it is to learn it the way you learned your mother tongue—by imitating how others use it to say different things instead of by memorizing the rules of grammar and so forth. VBA is, of course, not a language people around you speak. So for you to see how others use VBA to say different things, you have to study codes and models that others have developed and then imitate and modify them to write your own models. Here is the approach I recommend:

Get an overview of the VBA language by going through the examples I discussed earlier in detail. Next, go through the remaining chapters of Part Three. You do not have to understand or remember everything from these chapters. Try to get as much as you can out of them without getting bogged down in the details. What they contain are more or less equivalent to the vocabulary, grammar, and syntax of a language. This is primarily reference material. You mostly need to know what is there so that you can look things up when you need them.

Part Four covers how to develop a variety of financial models using VBA. The first chapter there provides general guidance on how to develop good VBA models and also specific instructions for people with different levels of experience on how best to use the rest of the chapters in Part Four to learn both VBA and modeling with it.

You should also study VBA codes written by others (for example, from other books) and start creating your own library of VBA code snippets and other information you think you will find useful to write your own codes.

Let me offer one final word of caution. VBA can do hundreds if not thousands of things, and it can do many things in several different ways. If you try to learn it all, you will drive yourself crazy and get nowhere. Your mission, especially early on, should be to stay focused on what you need to know to develop the most common types of financial models. I have selectively covered in this book only the VBA features you will need to do this. Limit yourself early on to only what I have covered here. You can then learn additional VBA features as you need them.

CHAPTER 22

VBA Essentials

A VBA procedure is a recipe or an organized set of statements written in the VBA language to carry out certain tasks. The statements or instructions that make up the recipe are analogous to sentences in English. In this chapter, I discuss the vocabulary and syntax of the VBA language that you need to know to write the statements; I also cover the rules for organizing them into procedures that VBA can follow to do what you want done.

You do not necessarily have to read everything in this chapter right away. You may want to familiarize yourself with the contents and then refer to specific sections as you need them. The best way to learn most of this material is to use them in models. The sooner you start developing models, the faster you will master this material.

An Overview of VBA

You have already had an overview of how VBA works from the example in the previous chapter. Let me reiterate a few points for emphasis.

In both Excel and VBA, you perform actions. These actions are mostly calculations with numbers, but they can also be creating charts, formatting worksheets, and so forth. In VBA, you perform actions by executing VBA code, which is a series of VBA instructions or statements. Unlike in Excel, the actions do not take place as you write the instructions. After you write them, you have to execute them to perform the actions.

You organize the instructions in one of two kinds of VBA procedures for logical and other reasons. A model can be comprised of one, two, or even dozens of procedures, which interact with one another when the model is run (that is, executed). You store the procedures in modules, which are similar to worksheets and are stored in the same workbook. As with worksheets, you can store all your procedures in one module or you can spread them out over several modules.

Two Key Differences between Excel and VBA

There are two key differences between Excel and VBA that you need to pay special attention to while you are learning VBA. Afterwards it will become second nature.

First, in Excel almost everything happens only once and each cell represents only one thing. For example, we looked at a loan amortization problem in both Excel (in Part Two) and VBA (in the previous chapter). In the Excel version, we have a separate cell for the year-beginning balance for each year. Each value is calculated only once and stored in its own cell. In VBA, we often use the same variable again and again, as we did with `yrBegBal` to calculate the year-beginning balance for all the years. If we want to preserve the intermediate values, either because we will need them in later calculations or for some other reasons, we have to write them down or store them somewhere before we calculate the value of the variable again. VBA does not do this automatically; you have to include instructions in the code to do it. (In the example from the previous chapter, we wrote it down in the spreadsheet.)

Second, you do not have to tell Excel specifically in what order the actions have to be carried out; Excel figures out the correct sequence itself, although to us it looks like everything is happening simultaneously. You have to tell VBA in what order you want the actions to be carried out. VBA will not figure it out on its own; it will follow your instructions. Also, in any calculation VBA will always use the latest value of a variable, and this matters in specifying the order of the actions. For example, if in the last example you wanted to do something in the seventh year with the year-beginning balance of the first year, you could not use the variable `yrBegBal` for the calculation in the seventh year because by that time the value stored in it would be the value for the seventh year. So before calculating the value of `yrBegBal` for the second year, you (that is, VBA following your instructions) would have to store it in some other variable for use in the future. This is one of the reasons why the order of the instructions matters.

In VBA, before you calculate anything, you have to make sure that the right values for all the variables necessary for the calculation are already available. Before you overwrite the value of any variable, you have to think if you are going to need it again. In Excel, this is not an issue—each variable (that is, cell) is used to hold only one value that does not change (unless you change the input values or make other changes in your spreadsheet model).

The Visual Basic Editor

The Visual Basic Editor (VBE) and all of VBA are exactly the same in Excel 2007 and the earlier versions of Excel (back to Excel 97) except for the way you access certain VBA features from the Excel screen. In Excel 2007, the Ribbon includes a tab called Developer, which has all of the icons necessary to access the VBA features that can be accessed from the Excel screen. In the previous versions of

Excel the access to VBA from the Excel screen is in the form of the old menu and toolbars. The VBE in Excel 2007 is the same as in the previous versions: It retains the old menu and toolbars approach.

(If, in Excel 2007, you do not see the Developer tab in the Ribbon, select Office ⇨ Excel Options ⇨ Popular. Place a checkmark to the left of Show Developer Tab in the Ribbon, and then back out.)

From your point of view, the Visual Basic Editor (VBE) is the heart of VBA—you will use it to do almost everything with VBA. The VBE is part of Excel, but it does not open automatically when you start Excel. The easiest way to start the VBE is by pressing Alt+F11 once you have Excel running. If you forget this combination, in Excel 2007 you can select Developer ⇨ Code ⇨ Visual Basic. (In previous versions of choose Tools ⇨ Macro ⇨ Visual Basic Editor.)

The VBE opens in its own window. You can go back and forth between the worksheets in the workbook and the VBE by clicking the appropriate minimized icon in the Windows task bar at the bottom of your screen. Alternately, you can cycle through all the open windows in your computer by holding down the Alt key and then repeatedly pressing the Tab key.

THE VBE WINDOW

The VBE window has several parts with which you need to become familiar.

Menu Bar

VBE's menu bar is similar to the menu bars in the previous versions of Excel and all other Microsoft Office applications, and you use it the same way. The shortcut key available for any menu command is shown next to it. You can also bring up a context-sensitive shortcut menu by right-clicking any part of the VBE window.

Toolbar

The toolbar below the menu bar also works the same way the Excel toolbar does. To see all the toolbars available, click View ⇨ Toolbar. You should always have the Standard and Edit toolbars open. To see a description of the tools on each toolbar, search in Help under "Standard Toolbar," for example. If you do not understand the use of any of the tools, wait until we need to use it, at which point it will become clearer.

Project Explorer Window

The Project Explorer window is the narrow long window along the left side of the VBE window with the word Project in its title bar. If you cannot find this or any of the other windows in VBE, click View and then click on the name of the window you want to open. You can also use the shortcut keys shown next to them.

In VBE, every open workbook is considered a project and the Project Explorer window lists all the projects (along with a few other things) in a tree diagram. As with all tree diagrams, a + sign on the left of an item indicates that it has additional items underneath and you can click on the + to see a list of them. Conversely, you can collapse a list of items by clicking the – sign on the left of its parent. If at any time your Project Explorer window looks too crowded, collapse all open lists other than the ones you need.

Code Window

This is the large window that takes up most of the right-hand side of the VBE window. It holds the modules in which you work with and store your codes. Modules are similar to worksheets and are saved in the same workbook. As with worksheets, you can add new modules as needed and remove (delete) any module you do not need anymore. If the Code window shows several modules tiled, you can maximize the module you want to work with (and hide all the others) by clicking on its Maximize button. You can switch among the different modules using the Project Explorer.

Other Windows

VBE has four other windows you can open as needed: Properties Window, Immediate Window, Locals Window, and Watch Window. You can open them from the View menu. I will discuss the Properties and Immediate Windows elsewhere, but I will not discuss the Locals and Watch Windows because I do not find them useful. If you are curious, check in VBA's Help for information on them. In any case, unless you are using them, keep them closed (use the Close button at the upper right corner of each) to make your Code and Project Explorer windows as large as possible and easier to use.

USING THE PROJECT EXPLORER WINDOW

You will primarily use the Project Explorer window to activate a module you want to work with or to add or remove modules.

To see a list of modules in a workbook (project), expand the project in the Project Explorer by clicking the + sign on its left. If the project has any modules, there will be a Modules node. Expand it to see the list of modules. To open a particular module in the Code window, double-click the module (preferably the icon on the left of the name). A single click will select the module but will not open it, which can be deceptive. To know for sure which module is open, look in the title bar of the VBE window. (Every project will also have a node titled Microsoft Excel Objects. Generally you will not use anything in it; keep it collapsed.)

Adding a New Module

To add a new module, right-click the name of the project to open its shortcut menu and choose Insert ⇨ Module. You can also select the project's name and then choose Insert ⇨ Module from the menu bar.

Renaming a Module

To rename a module you have to use the Properties window in VBE. To open it, in VBE press F4 or choose View ⇨ Properties Window. It is a narrow window that opens below the Project Explorer window. To be able to see all its parts, you may have to make it taller. Put your pointer on the border between it and the Project Explorer window, move it around a little until its shape changes, and then hold down the left mouse button and drag the border upward.

Now open the module you want to rename. If its name is Module2, the title bar for the Properties window should read Properties – Module2. Make sure that the Alphabetic tab in the Properties window is selected. The first line in the properties area will read (Name) Module2. Delete the Module2 next to the Name, type in the new name, and then press Enter or click anywhere outside the window. (The name has to follow normal naming conventions; for example, it must start with a letter and cannot have an embedded space in it.)

Removing a Module

To remove a module, open the module to make sure this is the module you want removed and then right-click its name in the Project Explorer window. In the shortcut menu, choose Remove Module xx. You will see a message box with the message "Do you want to export Module xx before removing it?" Generally your answer will be "No," in which case the system will permanently remove (delete) the module. At this point you can also choose to export the module to a file (see the next section for more on this).

Note that when you remove a module, VBE does not renumber the remaining modules; they retain their original numbers.

Exporting and Importing Modules

To export a module to a file, right-click it in the Project Explorer window and in the shortcut menu click Export. The Export File dialog box will open where you can give the file a name (retaining the .bas extension) and save it in the appropriate directory. Exporting keeps the original module where it was and saves a copy of the module in the file.

To import a saved file—you can import only files previous created with Export—right-click the project into which you want to import it. In the shortcut menu, click Import, in the dialog box choose the file you want to import, and then click OK. Notice that VBE gives the file a Module xx name even if you had saved it under some other name. (The File menu also offers the same Import and Export options.)

If you just want to create a copy of a module in another project instead of exporting and importing, you can drag it in the Project Explorer to the project in which you want the copy. Also, you can always select part or all of the code in a module and copy and paste it into any other module.

USING THE CODE WINDOW

You will use the Code window to open and work with your modules. For convenience, you always want to keep both your Code window and the window of the module you are currently working with maximized. To see more of a module, you can make the code window expand to the full screen size by closing all the other windows in VBE. It is generally more convenient, however, to keep at least the Project Explorer window open at all times and open the other windows only when you need them.

SETTING VBE OPTIONS

VBE offers many options for your convenience. There are several toolbars you can choose from (through the View menu) depending on what you are doing. You should have the Standard and Edit toolbars open at all times. To access most of your other options, select Tools ⇨ Options to open the Options dialog box, which has four tabs. For a full explanation of the options in each tab, select the tab and then click the Help button at bottom right. Choose the following options at first. You can change them later if necessary, and at appropriate places I will discuss some changes you may want to make.

Editor Tab

Check all boxes and set the Tab Width at 4.

Editor Format Tab

Leave all Code Colors in Auto, Font in Courier New (Western), Size at 10, and check the box for Margin Indicator Bar.

General

Check all boxes other than Notify Before State Loss and select Break on All Errors under Error Trapping.

Docking

Check all boxes other than the one for Object Browser.

Some Basics

Many of the code examples used in this and subsequent sections are available in the Excel workbook for this chapter on the CD.

ENTERING CODE

To create a new VBA Sub procedure (the basic unit of a VBA code), open the VBE, insert a new module or open an existing module you want to add the procedure to, and type the following line:

```
Sub procedurename ()
```

Once you press Enter, VBA will add the line `End Sub`, and now you can start adding statements between those beginning and ending lines. (I will discuss the other kind of procedure, called the Function procedure, later.) Note that VBA will not recognize a series of statements as a Sub procedure unless the statements are enclosed by the above pair of statements. If you want to try out some of the examples of statements I discuss here or statements you write, at the very least you have to convert them into a simple Sub procedure with the proper beginning and ending statements.

For entering code, the VBE works very much like a word processor except that it does a lot of editing for you. Once you press return at the end of a statement, VBE tries to convert whatever you have typed into legitimate VBA statements by properly capitalizing VBA key words, putting spaces where needed, and so forth (unless the line starts with an apostrophe to indicate that it is a comment). If what you have typed is not a proper VBA statement and VBE cannot fix it, it will give you an error message, which is generally (but not always) helpful.

In addition to typing in code, you can add code by copying and pasting from other codes you have written or from code you have recorded with the Macro Recorder.

During the process of entering code, the Undo button can sometimes be a lifesaver. It is a good idea to play around with it to understand exactly how it works.

RUNNING PROCEDURES

There are many different ways to run a Sub procedure that does not require any arguments, that is, has an empty pair of parentheses after the procedure name as in the earlier example. (Arguments are variable names that go into the parentheses following the procedure names, as with Excel functions. I will discuss them later.) Here are the three ways to run (execute) a Sub procedure you will use most often:

- If you assigned a Shortcut key (for example, Ctrl+a) to a procedure, press that key combination.
- In Excel, open the Macros dialog box by pressing Alt+F8. Then select in the list the macro you want to run and click the Run button.
- In VBE, put your cursor anywhere in the procedure and then press F5, click the Run Sub/UserForm button on the toolbar or select the Run menu and then click Run Sub/UserForm.

I will discuss methods for running the other kinds of procedures later.

If during execution your procedure stops because of an error, VBA will display a dialog box with some information about the nature of the error, which may or may not be helpful. After reading the error message, click Debug. This will close the dialog box, highlight the line containing the error in yellow, and move the cursor to that line. If you can find the error, correct it, click the Reset button (a dark square) in the toolbar, which will remove the yellow highlight and then run the procedure again.

Simple Debugging

Finding and fixing errors in your code, called debugging, can be a simple to a very time-consuming and frustrating process because errors come in bewildering varieties. You get better at debugging only with practice. I discuss debugging along with the special VBA tools available for debugging in a later chapter. Here I briefly discuss a few simple debugging methods that, used well, can be very effective.

Remember that many bugs are simple typing errors. Look for them first, but remember that they are often not easy to see. If this does not work, try these two simple debugging methods:

- Insert one or a few `MsgBox` functions (discussed later) at strategic points in the procedure to display the values of a few key variables at certain points in your procedure and check the results using hand calculations or other methods to determine if the procedure is working properly up to those points. Then, if necessary, move the `MsgBox` functions to earlier or later points and repeat the procedure to zero in on the source of the problem.

- In the VBE, put your pointer in the gray margin (the left edge of the code window) on the left of a statement at a strategic point in the procedure and click. This will set a breakpoint in the code at that statement, which will be indicated by a dark circle in the margin and the statement itself will be highlighted. Now when you run the procedure, execution will be suspended when it gets to the breakpoint and you will be able to see the current value of any variable that has been read in or calculated so far by resting your cursor on it. Using hand calculations and other methods you can then find the problem or decide that the code is working properly up to the current location of the breakpoint. You can run the rest of the code by clicking the Run button or stop execution by clicking the Reset button (on the toolbar). To remove the breakpoint, point at the dark circle in the left margin and click. If necessary, you can set another breakpoint earlier or later in the code and repeat the steps.

  Note that you can set more than one breakpoint at the same time, in which case when you click Run after one break, execution will be suspended at the next breakpoint. This way you can check through the program in small sections.

Ultimately, how quickly you find a bug will mostly depend on how well you understand the logic of your code, because in searching for a bug you are always asking the question "Is this the right value for this variable at this point in the execution of the code?"

ORGANIZING PROCEDURES IN MODULES

VBA procedures are stored in modules, which are similar to worksheets and are stored in the same workbook file. You access and work with the modules in the VBE. You can add and delete modules as needed, and you can copy a procedure from one part of a module to another or from one module to another. A module can hold any number of procedures, but you should keep your procedures organized by putting into each module only those procedures that are related. How you organize your procedures may also depend to some extent on if you will call (that is, execute) one procedure from another. To understand how best to organize such procedures, see the discussion of procedures in the next chapter.

LINE CONTINUATION

VBA will let you make a statement as long as you want. But once a code line extends beyond the right end of the code window, it becomes difficult to read and work with. Also, if you ever want to print out your code, long lines create problems. You should therefore break down long statements into two or more lines to keep all of it fully visible within the code window.

You can continue a statement in the next line by putting a space followed by an underscore (_) at the end of it. When VBA encounters this continuation character, it interprets the statement in the following line as part of the same statement. You can extend a statement into as many lines as you want with a continuation character at the end of all but the last line. Although you do not have to include any special character at the beginning of the second and subsequent lines, it is common practice to indent them by two spaces relative to the first line to make it easier to recognize that any lines after the first are part of the same statement. Here is an example:

```
If termPrice > posStrk Then posVal = (termPrice - posStrk) _
  Else posVal = 0
```

Try to break statements at points that will not affect readability. For example, in this example, breaking the statement the way I have makes it more readable than if I had broken it after the second `termPrice`.

Another point to keep in mind is that if a statement gets too long and you have to continue it into several lines, it may become difficult to follow. You may want to consider breaking up such statements into two or more statements, for example, by calculating an intermediate value in a shorter statement and then using it in the next statement.

MULTIPLE STATEMENTS IN ONE LINE

Although most often you will put each VBA statement in your code in a separate line, if you want to, you can put more than one statement in a line using a colon (:) as a separator. You should use this option only if you think it will enhance the readability of your code in a particular situation. For instance, it may make sense in the following example where each statement is very short (although I would just as soon put these in three lines).

```
intRate1 = 0.05: intRate2 = 0.075: intRate3 = 0.1
```

In some special situations, this option can be useful in writing single-line `If` statements (see later), but even there you can find better alternatives. I primarily mentioned this option so that you will understand what it means if you see it in someone else's code.

ADDING COMMENTS

Comments are notes and reminders you include at various places in your VBA code to make it easier to understand and modify it in the future. Comments are an important part of the overall documentation of a project. For large projects, the documentation may include other elements like flow charts, whereas for small projects comments may be all the documentation you need.

You indicate a comment by an apostrophe. Except when it occurs in texts within quotation marks, VBA interprets an apostrophe as the beginning of a comment and ignores the rest of the line. So you can use an entire line or blocks of line for comments. Alternately, you can put a comment after a statement in a line (for example, to explain something about the statement). Here are two examples:

```
' This is an example of using an entire line for comment
intRate = 0.045 'Based on 3 month Treasury rate in Jan '02
```

I will discuss comments later in more detail when I talk about how to document your models.

An Additional Use of Comments

Let us assume that you want to test a procedure without a particular statement or block of statements, perhaps to try an alternative. Instead of deleting the original statement or block, you can just disable it by inserting an apostrophe at the beginning of the line, that is, by turning it into a comment. Later you can make it active again by deleting the apostrophe.

You can use VBA's Comment Block and Uncomment Block tools on the Edit Toolbar to do this efficiently. To convert a block of statements into comments, select the block and click on the Comment Block button. To reverse the process, select the block of comments and click the Uncomment Block button. (To identify these or any other buttons, rest your cursor on each for a few seconds to bring up its name.)

INDENTING CODE LINES

You can make your code much easier to read and understand by indenting selected code lines or blocks of code lines by different amounts instead of starting all lines flush with the left margin. It is easiest to learn how to indent effectively by looking at examples. You should pay attention to the examples in this and other books to develop your own indenting style.

To make sure that the indents are uniform and that your code looks good, always use the tab key to indent your code, not the space bar. You can use Shift + Tab to "unindent" a line of code. If you want to indent or "unindent" a block of code lines at once, select the block and use the same keys. (Note that you can use the Backspace key to "unindent" one code line, but if you try to "unindent" a block of code lines with it, it will delete the lines. So be careful about using the Backspace for "unindenting.")

VBE offers a useful option to do indenting automatically. In the VBE menu bar, choose Tools ⇨ Options to go to the Options dialog box and then click the Editor tab. Select the Auto Indent box, set Tab Width at 4, and click OK. (You may already have this option selected.) Now every time you press Tab with the cursor at the beginning of a line, you will be indenting the line by 4 spaces. What's more, if you are in an indented line, when you press Enter to start a new line, VBE will automatically indent the new line by the same amount as the previous line to create indented blocks. (When you no longer want the new line to be indented by the same amount, use Tab, Shift + Tab or Backspace to change the amount of indentation.)

OPERATORS

VBA offers the same operators as Excel does, and the order of precedence for them in calculations is also the same. However, there are some important differences in the way some operators are used in VBA statements and Excel formulas. (See the section called "Working with Text" later for the concatenation operator.)

The Assignment Operator

In VBA the equals sign (=) is used as the assignment operator. What this means is that when a statement has an equals sign in it, VBA first evaluates whatever is on the right-hand side of it and then assigns the result to whatever is on the left-hand side. This sounds a lot more complex than it is. For example, the statement `totSales = salesA + salesB + salesC` tells VBA to add up the three sales numbers on the right hand side and store the value in the variable `totSales`. This is straightforward.

But a statement like `x = x + 1`, which you will see all the time in VBA, can be a little confusing if you try to interpret it algebraically. What this means in VBA is add 1 to the current value of `x` and make that the new value of `x`.

Mathematical Operators

VBA uses mathematical operators the same way they are used in Excel. The symbol * is used for multiplication, ^ for exponentiation, < = for less than or equal to, and so forth.

Logical Operators

VBA offers a full set of logical (or Boolean) operators, the most common ones being `And`, `Or`, and `Not`. Excel offers the same choices, but in the form of functions so that they have to be written a bit differently. Here is how these are used in VBA:

```
If loanSize > 1000000 And credRat = 1 Then intRate = 0.08
If loanSize > 1000000 Or credRat = 1 Then intRate = 0.08
```

As in Excel, when you create a compound condition using several `And` operators, it will compute to `True` only if each component is `True`. Conversely, if you create a compound condition using several `Or` operators, then it will compute to `True` as long as at least one of the component conditions is `True`. As in Excel, if you are creating complicated conditions using logical operators, it is safer to clarify them (at least for the user) with parentheses even if they may not be absolutely necessary for VBA.

WORKING WITH TEXT

In VBA, it is easy to work with texts (also called *strings*, meaning strings of characters), such as names and addresses, headings for tables, and messages you want to display once you understand a few simple principles. To use any text several times or to manipulate it in a procedure, it is generally more convenient to first store it in a variable the same way we store numbers. (Variables, which we will discuss in detail later, are essentially names we give to pieces of data such as numbers and text. A variable you intend to use for storing text must be of `Variant` or `String` data type.) Here is an example of creating two text variables:

```
firstName = "John"
lastName = "Smith"
```

The first thing you should note is that texts always have to be enclosed in quotation marks, but you do not put quotation marks around a variable name even though it looks like text. These statements assign the texts on the right to the corresponding variable names. Whenever you subsequently use the variable `firstName` in a statement, VBA will substitute the text in its place before evaluating the statement. Because this confuses many beginners, let me emphasize that when you use `firstName` in a statement, you do not have to put quotations marks around it because it is not a text but a text variable, that is, the name of some text.

The key operator you will use to manipulate text in VBA is the ampersand (`&`), which is called the concatenation operator. It joins the texts stored in the variables on its two sides. (Whenever you use this operator in an expression, make sure you put a space before and after it. Otherwise it sometimes confuses VBA and it will not work properly.) Here are two ways in which you can create a variable called `fullName` using the concatenation operator:

```
fullName = "John " & "Smith"
fullName = firstName & " " & lastName
```

The ampersand does not add any space when it joins texts; you have to provide any space you want. This is why in the first statement I included a space at the end in `"John"` to provide the normal separation between a first name and a last name. In the second statement, to do the same, I had to concatenate a space to the variable `firstName` (because it did not have any trailing space built into it) before concatenating the variable `lastName`.

It is also possible to create new text variables and messages by concatenating texts with numerical variables and numbers (see under the `MsgBox` and `InputBox` functions later). Once you get used to the concept that VBA always substitutes the values for all variables before evaluating a statement, you will find it easy to manipulate text variables in many different ways.

Both Excel and VBA also offer many built-in functions to manipulate text variables. For example, you can create a new variable `shortName` with the first 3 characters of `firstName` using the function `Left()` to extract them as follows:

```
shortName = Left(firstName, 3)
```

THE MSGBOX FUNCTION

Although I will later discuss using Excel's and VBA's built-in functions in codes, I am discussing the `MsgBox` and `InputBox` functions here because you will use them extensively from the very beginning.

The `MsgBox` function displays a dialog box and offers a simple way to provide the user a message and some short outputs, often to show intermediate results and to get simple user responses, if desired. It is also a useful debugging tool because you can insert `MsgBox` functions at strategic points in your code to see intermediate values of variables that can help you track down a problem. VBA displays the dialog box when during the running of a program it gets to a statement that includes the `MsgBox` function.

The syntax of the `MsgBox` function is:

```
MsgBox (prompt[, buttons][, title][helpfile, context])
```

The argument `prompt` is required. It is the message you want displayed. The *`buttons`* argument, which is optional, allows you to specify which buttons (for example, OK) you want your dialog box to show to get the user's response. The optional *title* argument lets you specify a title for the dialog box. You will probably never use the other two optional arguments.

Here is a simple example of how the MsgBox function is used.

```
1:  Sub MsgBox_Test()
2:
3:  intRate = 0.05
4:  MsgBox ("Interest rate is" & intRate * 100 & "%")
5:
6:  End Sub
```

When you run this procedure, VBA will display a dialog box with the message "Interest rate is 5%" (without the quotation marks). Notice that to create the message, I concatenated a text with the variable intRate. I also multiplied the variable by 100 to convert the interest rate into a percentage and concatenated the percentage symbol to the result. Since I did not specify any button, VBA displays the dialog box with the default OK button. Execution is suspended when VBA gets to line 4 and displays a dialog box with the message. When the user clicks the OK button in the dialog box, execution resumes with line 5.

Functions in VBA work the same way as they do in Excel: You provide the parameters; they provide an answer. You may be surprised, then, to see that this function is not providing any answer. We have so far used the MsgBox function in the special way you are likely to use it most often. To use it truly like a function, we have to provide the buttons argument. You can provide the buttons argument either as a constant (which really is VBA's name for a built-in number) or as a number.

For example, if you want the dialog box to display a Yes button and a No button, the buttons argument can be the constant vbYesNo or the number 4, which are equivalent, but the vbYesNo is easier to remember. In this case, the MsgBox truly works as a function and will produce the answer 6 if the user clicks Yes and the answer 7 if the user clicks No. (There is no answer to the question "Why 6 and 7?" It is a choice that Microsoft has made.) The answer that the function produces indicates which button the user clicked and you can use it to take different actions. Here is an example:

```
Sub MsgBox_Test2()

loanAmount = 100000
intRate = 0.05
msgReply = MsgBox("Do you want to increase the interest rate of " _
   & intRate * 100 & "% by 1%?", vbYesNo)
If msgReply = 6 Then intRate = intRate + 0.01
intExpense = loanAmount * intRate
MsgBox ("Interest expense is $" & intExpense)

End Sub
```

In this example, I am calculating the interest expense on a loan using an interest rate that depends on the user's answer to a dialog box. The `MsgBox` in line 5 will display a dialog box with the message "Do you want to increase the interest rate of 5% by 1%?" and a Yes and a No button. If the user clicks Yes, then the `MsgBox` function will produce the answer 6 and assign it to the variable `msgReply`. In line 7, the `If` statement checks if the value of `msgReply` is 6, and if it is `True`, then it increases the interest rate by 1%; otherwise the interest rate remains 5%. Line 8 calculates the interest expense and line 9 uses another `MsgBox` to display the result. Type in the procedure in a module and see how the answer varies depending on whether you click Yes or No in the first dialog box.

Note that in line 7, instead of testing for `msgReply = 6`, you can also test for `msgReply = vbYes` because VBA has a built-in constant `vbYes` with a value of 6. Similarly, there are built-in constants for `vbNo`, `vbAbort`, and so on (corresponding to the various buttons you can specify) that you can use in similar situations to test which button the user clicked. You can then take appropriate action.

For more on the `MsgBox` function and the various options for the buttons, search in VBA's Help under `MsgBox`.

THE INPUTBOX FUNCTION

The `InputBox` is the other function you will use extensively from the very beginning to get inputs from the user (or you may provide the inputs) during the testing phase. It also displays a dialog box in which you can provide a message, most often to explain what kind of input the user should provide in the text box. The result of the `InputBox` function is the input the user provides.

The syntax of the `InputBox` function is:

```
InputBox(prompt[, title] [, default] [, xpos] [, ypos]
  [, helpfile, context])
```

The required argument `prompt` is the message you want to display. The optional argument *`title`* lets you specify a title for the dialog box and the optional argument *`default`* lets you specify a string that will be displayed in the text box as a default option. (The user can accept it or overwrite it.) You are not likely to use the other arguments. Here is an example of how the InputBox function is used:

```
Sub InputBox_Test()

loanAmount = 100000
intRate = InputBox("Enter interest rate in %.",, 5)
msgReply = MsgBox("The interest rate you entered is" _
   & intRate & "%." & "Is this OK?", vbYesNo)
If msgReply = vbNo Then End
intExpense = loanAmount * intRate / 100
```

```
9:  MsgBox ("Interest expense is $" & intExpense)
10:
11: End Sub
```

Type in the procedure in a module and run it to see how it works. Here in line 4 the user is asked to provide the interest rate in percent. He is shown a default value of 5 in the text box of the dialog box, which he can accept or change. When he clicks OK to close the dialog box, whatever is in the text box is assigned to the variable `intRate`. The `MsgBox` then displays the interest rate he has entered and asks him to verify it. If the user clicks Yes, then the interest expenses is calculated and displayed. (Notice the division by 100 to convert the interest rate in percent into decimals.) If the user clicks No, the program is terminated.

The `InputBox` function is good for getting a few inputs, each of which requires its own statement. If there are many input variables or if you are going to run the program repeatedly, this can get tedious. In this case, it is better to create an input area in a spreadsheet (or even a dedicated input spreadsheet) where the user can provide the inputs and the program can read them in from there.

Also, since the user can make all sorts of mistakes in entering the input data, you should include some code to validate the input from an `InputBox` before using it. For example, you can have the user confirm it, as he is asked to do here, or you can provide checks within the program to make sure the input value is of the right type, lies within an acceptable range, and so forth.

THE STOP AND END STATEMENTS

By itself, an `End` statement put anywhere in a code will immediately terminate execution of the code. For example, you can use it to terminate execution if a particular type of error occurs during execution. The `End` statement closes all open files, resets all variables, and so forth, so that execution cannot be restarted from the point where it ended. You can use a `Stop` statement instead to suspend execution (for example, to check the current values of some variables) and then you can restart execution by clicking the Run Sub button on the toolbar. The `Stop` statement is similar to setting a breakpoint in the code except that you build it into the code.

(Another group of `End` statements available in VBA are: `End Function`, `End If`, `End Property`, `End Select`, `End Sub`, `End Type`, and `End With`. All of these are the required statements to indicate the end of the corresponding statement blocks in a code and they work quite differently from the `End` or `Stop` statement. You will encounter them later.)

Variables, Constants, and Arrays

Variables are used to store and manipulate data. You should always store data in variables, that is, give your data names, and then use the names instead of the data themselves in your statements and computations. This makes your statements easier to read, makes it easier to change the data later, and reduces your chances of making mistakes. You can also store data in cells on a worksheet, but it will make your code more cumbersome and will slow down the execution of your code because getting data to and from worksheets takes longer. Using variables to store data gives you more flexibility and is preferable.

The simplest way to create a variable is to just choose a variable name and assign a value to it. A simple statement like `intRate = 0.05` will create the variable `intRate` and store in it the value 0.05. As we will see, however, it is preferable to declare a variable first before starting to use it.

NAMING VARIABLES

The most important thing to remember about naming variables is that, except in special situations (see later in this section), you should always use short but descriptive names. For example, if you use `janSales` instead of names like `JS` or `S1` for January sales, it will be easier for you to remember the name as you write your code and you will not have to keep looking up what name you are using for January sales. It will also be easier for you and others to read your code. At the same time, keeping names short is important to save typing time and reduce typing mistakes, and also to make your code more readable. Long names are generally harder to read, and they can make your statements go on for lines, making everything more cumbersome.

Generally you should not use one- or two-letter names because you will find it hard to remember what they stand for. There are some situations, though, where they can actually make your code easier to enter and read. For example, if you are coding a widely used financial equation like an option pricing equation, you may want to use the standard symbols used in the model as your variable names as well. Also, sometimes if you are using a variable just as a counter or to store an intermediate value for immediate use, you may find it more convenient to use just a one- or two-letter name.

Over time you will develop your own naming style. It is therefore worthwhile to consciously develop a style with which you are comfortable. Another thing to keep in mind is that if you are working on a big project with many variables, then you should first create and write down a variable-naming convention for the project before you start coding. This will save you a lot of time later.

Here are the important rules and some additional suggestions for naming variables:

- Names must start with an alphabetic character and can use all alphabetic characters, numbers, and certain punctuation characters. I recommend that you use only the punctuation character underscore (_) in names to join different pieces of it. For example you can use `jan_Sales` instead of `janSales`, but I prefer the latter because it requires less typing. The only place I use the underscore is in naming my procedures. (Incidentally, the same rules apply to naming procedures, constants, and arguments.)

- You cannot use a space, period (.), exclamation mark (!), or the characters @, &, $, and # in names.
- In variable names, VBA does not distinguish between upper and lower cases: `JanSales` and `jansales` are interchangeable. You can thus make your names more readable by judiciously using capital letters within your names. I usually prefer to start all variable names with a small letter and start each subsequent part of it with a capital letter, such as in `janSales`. This distinguishes the variable names from words and names used by VBA. (As I will explain in the section "Forcing variable declaration," using one or more capital letters in your names can also help you catch typing mistakes right away.)
- You cannot use names identical to the names and words used by VBA. If you do, you will get a syntax error message, although sometimes the message can be cryptic and not very helpful in locating the problem. The easiest solution is to avoid using any name that sounds like one that VBA may be already using. However, you can use these words as part of a longer name. For example, you cannot call a variable `True`, but a name like `trueVal` is fine.

CHANGING VARIABLE NAMES

You do not get stuck with a name you have used for a variable in your code. At times, you may want to change a name because you want to use a new naming convention. You can make such a change at any time. Of course, you have to change the name at every place it appears in your code. Do not try to do it manually one at a time because you may miss a few incidences of the old name. Instead, use Edit ⇨ Replace in the VBE to find and replace all the incidences of the old name with the new name in one step.

DATA TYPES

In VBA, data type refers to the type of data that a variable holds. The three types of data you will use most often in your models are numbers, strings (of characters such as names and addresses, also called texts), and dates. If you choose to do so, you can totally ignore the fact that different variables in your VBA code may hold different types of data. You can create variables as you go along and store any type of data in them. You do not have to specify what type of data a variable will hold, nor do you have to name variables differently to hold different types of data.

But VBA also lets you specify, from an assortment of built-in data types, what type of data each variable will hold. The primary advantages of doing so are that VBA can then use the computer's memory more efficiently and your code will run faster. If you do not specify the data type for a variable, VBA allocates a relatively large space for it. With modern PCs, the sacrifice of memory and speed will not matter most of the time; however, if you are dealing with a large program or speed is important to you, then you should declare the data types for your variables. (See later for how.)

VBA offers a choice of the following data types: `Byte`, `Boolean`, `Integer`, `Long`, `Single`, `Double`, `Currency`, `Decimal`, `Date`, `Object`, `String`, `Variant` (default), and `User-Defined`. The data type can also be the specific type of object a variable will hold (for example, Worksheet). To find out more about any specific data type such as `Double`, search in VBA's Help under "Double." If you want an overview of all data types, click on See Also when the panel with the explanation of the Double Data Type opens, and then choose Data Type Summary.

`Variant` is the most flexible data type. Variables declared as `Variant` can store any type of data, and if you do not specify the data type for a variable, VBA automatically uses `Variant` data type for it. You can almost always get away with declaring all your variables as `Variant` data type or not declaring any data type at all subject to the memory and speed considerations I mentioned earlier. If you take this easy way out, do not use the same variable to hold different types of data in different places in your code (for example, for numbers in one place and for a string of characters in another); it can sometimes produce unexpected results.

To find out more about any of the data types, look them up in VBA's Help.

Working with Numbers

A variable declared as `Integer` can hold whole numbers from −32,768 to 32,767. To handle larger whole numbers, you can declare the variable as `Long` data type. Note that if you declare a variable as `Integer` or `Long`, you should be careful about assigning real numbers to it or using it in mathematical operations because you may get unexpected results.

For real numbers, you can use the `Single` data type or, if you want to carry a larger number of significant digits, the `Double` data type. (For all internal calculations, Excel effectively uses the `Double` data type and then stores the result as `Single` if that is what you specify.)

Working with Dates

To store dates or time in a variable, they have to be enclosed between two number signs (#). You can use any recognizable date literal, but if you want to do date mathematics (for example, find the number of days between two dates), make sure you use Date or Variant variables and not String variables. Here is an example:

```
Sub Date_Example()

issueDate = #2/15/1998#
maturityDate = #2/15/2002#
numDays = maturityDate - issueDate

MsgBox numDays

End Sub
```

This procedure calculates the number of days between the issueDate and the maturityDate.

Determining the Data Type

You can use VBA's TypeName function to determine the data type of a variable. If you declared the variable as a particular data type, then the function will return a string with the name of that data type. However, if the variable's data type is a Variant, then the data type TypeName returns will depend on the data the variable is holding at that point in the code; it can be different at different points in the code. Here is how you use it:

```
myDataType = TypeName (VariableName)
```

DECLARING VARIABLES

You generally declare the data type of a variable using the Dim statement at the beginning of a procedure before any executable statement. (We will talk about a few exceptions later.) You have to declare the data type of each variable separately, but you can declare several variables in one Dim line by separating them by commas. Here are some examples:

```
Dim mrtgRate as Single, mrtgLife as Integer
Dim myName as String * 20, myAge as Variant, myCity, myState
```

Notice that since I have not specified any data type for myCity or myState, VBA will assume them to be Variant. Conversely, I have not just specified myName as a String data type, I have also specified that it will hold a maximum of 20 characters by putting * 20 after it. Specifying the length of a String variable is optional. Sometimes you do it to guard against possible errors. For example, if a variable is not supposed to be more than two characters long, then specifying that will make sure that a longer text cannot be assigned to it by mistake.

When declaring variables, it is good practice to group related variables together to make it easier to find them later.

A Special Reason to Declare All Variables

Unless you want to specify the data type of a variable, you generally do not have to declare it. However, there is an important advantage of declaring every variable in a code: it can help you catch almost immediately any typing mistake that you make in entering variable names in your code. Otherwise, these little mistakes can sometimes be difficult to find. You may waste hours trying to figure out why your code is not working when the problem is just a misspelled variable name.

Here is how this works. Name all your variables using mixed case (for example, `intRate` instead of `intrate`) when declaring them. Then whenever you use variable names in your code, type them with lower case letters only. When you press Enter at the end of a statement, VBA will properly capitalize all the variables that you have declared, but it will not recognize and capitalize misspelled variables. You can therefore immediately see and fix the variables that do not get properly capitalized. Once in a while, the problem may be that you did not declare the variable or did not declare it with mixed case. However, these are much simpler problems to fix.

Forcing Variable Declaration

An even safer approach is to force yourself to declare all variables because that will catch all misspelled variables. To force variable declaration, include the statement `Option Explicit` as the first statement in every VBA module. This will make your program stop and display an error message during execution if VBA encounters any variable you have not declared. Because to VBA a misspelled variable looks like a variable you have not declared, it will flag it.

This can save you a lot time and frustration. If you do not require variable declaration and have misspelled variables in your code, VBA will ignore them and go on without flagging them. This, of course, will produce wrong results in many situations, and you may have to spend a lot of time finding the problem.

You can have VBA automatically enter this statement at the top of every new module by selecting Tools ⇨ Options and then selecting Require Variable Declaration in the Editor tab. However, you will have to still manually enter `Option Explicit` in any module that existed before you turned on this option. I recommend that you always keep this option selected.

SCOPE OF VARIABLES

Scope refers to in what parts of a project and at what times during execution a variable and its value will be available. Depending on how you declare a variable, it can be available only to one procedure, all procedures in a module, or all procedures in a project (that is, all the modules in the workbook). In large projects, especially those extending over many modules, specifying the right scope for your variables is important. But even in shorter projects comprising a few procedures within the same module, specifying the right scopes may be important. Otherwise, the correct value of a variable may not be available at the point in the code where it is needed.

Procedure-Level Variables

If you declare a variable using a `Dim` statement inside a procedure (that is, after the name of the procedure) then it becomes a procedure-level variable. The variable can be used and its value is available only within that procedure. Once the procedure ends, the variable ceases to exist and its value is not available anymore. (If you do not explicitly declare a variable, then VBA treats it as a procedure-level variable.)

Let us clarify this further. If you call a procedure from another procedure then once control is returned to the calling procedure, the values of the procedure-level variables in the called procedure will not be available anymore, for example, for use during the next call.

Also, you can use the same variable names for procedure-level variables in different procedures within a module or different procedure of the same project (in one or more modules). However, for the sake of clarity, you should generally avoid such use.

To understand the above clearly, let us look at the following example. (If you are not yet familiar with how one procedure can be called from another, you may have difficulty understanding the above discussion and the following example right now. You may want to come back here after you have familiarized yourself with that material.)

```
Sub Calling_Routine()
Dim testCount As Integer

testCount = 1
Call Called_Routine(testCount)
testCount = 2
Call Called_Routine(testCount)

End Sub

Sub Called_Routine(rcvdCount)
Dim testCount As Integer
```

```
If rcvdCount = 1 Then testCount = 0
testCount = testCount + 1
MsgBox testCount

End Sub
```

First note that the variable name testCount is used in both procedures. As you can see, this looks confusing although it does not confuse VBA. To VBA these are two different variables because they are procedure-level variables in two different procedures.

Second, when you run this code from the calling procedure, you will see a message both times the Called_Routine is called showing the value of testCount as 1. Here is why: After control is returned to the calling procedure after completing the first call, the value of testCount in the called procedure is not retained. So during the second call, in the called procedure, testCount is assumed to be 0 before it is increased by 1.

Static Variables

To make the value of a procedure-level variable available as long as the code (project) is running (even after the particular procedure has ended), declare the variable within the procedure—but with a Static rather than Dim statement. The two statements have the same syntax.

Let us see the effect of this. In the previous example, change the second line in the called procedure to Static testCount As Integer. Now if you run the code from the calling procedure, the first message you see will show a value of 1 for testCount and the second message will show a value of 2. Since testCount is now declared as Static, it retains its value of 1 even after control is returned after the first call. Its value then becomes 2 during the second execution of the called procedure.

Module-Level Variables

If you want to make a variable available to all procedures in a module (but not to all the other modules, UserForms, etc., in the project) then you should declare it using a Dim or a Private statement before the first procedure of the module. The Dim and the Private statements have the same syntax. The value of a module-level variable remains available as long as the code (project) is running.

Project-Level Variable

To make a variable available to all the procedures in a project (that is, to all modules, UserForms, etc.), declare it using a Public statement at the beginning of one of the VBA modules of the project before the first procedure of the module.

The Public statement has the same syntax as a Dim statement. A project-level variable remains available as long as the code (project) is running. (Note that a Public variable must be declared in a standard VBA module and not in any of the other types of code modules that can be used in a project.)

CONSTANTS

If you need to use some constant values in your procedures, you can give them meaningful names using the Constant statement and then use the names throughout your code. This will make your code easier to read, and in case you need to change one of the values, you will have to make it in only one place. You could accomplish the same thing by storing the values in variables and making sure that you never change them in your code. But defining a constant is a safe way to avoid accidentally changing the value in the code.

As with variables, the scope of a constant depends on where you declare it. If you declare a constant using a Constant statement within a procedure, then it will be available only to that procedure. If you place the Constant statement before the first procedure of a module, then it will be available to all procedures in that module only. To make a Constant available to all procedures in a project, use the statement Public Constant instead of just Constant and put it in any standard VBA module of the project before the module's first procedure.

Here are some examples:

```
Constant intRate = 0.05, myName as String = "Jim Smith"
Public Constant busSgmnts as Integer = 6
```

ARRAYS

The variables we have discussed so far can be called single-element variables in that each of them holds only one piece of data at a time. If you have a large quantity of related data such as 300 days of price history for a stock, you will need 300 single-element variables to store and manipulate them, which is cumbersome and inefficient.

VBA offers a second kind of variable, called array variable or just array, that can hold any quantity of data under the same name. You refer to a specific element of the array by the array name and one or more index numbers enclosed in parentheses. For example, you can store the 300 days of stock price history in an array called stkPrice with 300 elements and refer to the data for the first day as stkPrice (1) and so forth. If the price on the first day was 30.2, then you will store it in the array using a statement like stkPrice (1) = 30.2 and refer to it by that name in other statements. (Since arrays are also variables, technically it may be more correct to talk about scalar or single-element variables and array variables. However, we commonly refer to single-element variables as just variables and array variables as just arrays.)

As we will see, arrays make it possible to store and manipulate large quantities of data efficiently using very compact codes. Although VBA arrays are somewhat similar to arrays and named ranges in Excel, a key difference is that unlike in Excel, we can easily refer to and manipulate individual elements of a VBA array. In Excel, we almost always have to deal with an array or a named range as a whole. The additional flexibility makes VBA arrays a lot more useful; arrays are used a lot more in VBA.

Array Dimension

The dimension of an array refers to the way that data is (conceptually) organized in an array. A one-dimensional array (like the one we talked about for storing 300 days of stock price history) can be viewed as a row or column of data. As we saw, it requires one index number to refer to its individual elements.

If you had 300 days of price data for 5 different stocks, you could store them all in a one-dimensional array with 1,500 elements or five different arrays with 300 elements each. If you were storing the data in an Excel spreadsheet, you would probably store them in 5 columns with 300 rows each because that would be a better organization for the data. You can do the same with a two-dimensional VBA array. A two-dimensional array is similar to an Excel spreadsheet. You need two index numbers—a row number and a column number—to refer to its individual elements. For example, you would refer to the price of the third stock on the 100th day as `stkPrice (100, 3)`. By convention, the first index is called the row number and the second index the column number of the element.

If instead of just the closing price you had 4 different prices (open, high, low, close) for each stock for each day, then you could use a three-dimensional array to store the data, with the first index referring to the day of the data, the second to the data type (1 for open, 2 for high, etc.) and the third to the stock number. Thus `stkData (51,2,3)` could refer to the 51st day's high price for the third stock.

You could have the second index refer to the stock number and the third to the data type also. The choice is yours, but you should try to organize your data in a way that makes it easy to visualize where they reside in the array. For example, it is easiest to visualize a three-dimensional array as an Excel workbook with a number of worksheets, with the third index referring to the different worksheets or pages. If you were storing the data in a workbook, it is likely that you would store all the data for each stock on a separate worksheet. This is why having the third dimension, which is generally called the page index, refer to the different stocks seems more natural than having it refer to the different types of price.

Recognize that what really makes the `stkData (51,2,3)` the 51st day's high price for the third stock is that this is the element where you enter or store that particular piece of data. You have to tell VBA where to store every individual piece of data in an array.

You can create and use arrays of higher dimensions. But you will rarely need to use arrays with more than three dimensions, and visualizing and handling them get overly complex.

Also, VBA will not prevent you from storing totally unrelated data in the same array. However, to make your code easier to write and understand, you should store in each array only those data that are related in some way and use separate arrays for unrelated data.

Declaring Arrays

As with variables, you can declare (specify) the data type for an array or leave the data type unspecified, in which case VBA will assume the data type to be `Variant`. You must declare the size of an array, though, so that VBA knows how much memory it must allocate for the array.

You declare an array the same way as other variables using the `Dim`, `Static`, `Private`, or `Public` statements, except that in the case of an array you generally specify the size of the array at the same time. Here are a few examples (from different procedures):

```
Dim stkPrice(1 To 300, 1 To 5) As Single, tkrSym(1 To 5)
Dim stkPrice(300, 5) As Single, tkrSym(5)
Dim annlSales(1990 To 2005)
```

The first example declares a two-dimensional array called `stkPrice` with 300 rows and 5 columns and data type `Single`. The second array, which is for storing the ticker symbols of the stocks, is a one-dimensional array with 5 elements. Since the data type for it is not specified, VBA will assume it to be `Variant`. We could have specified the data type for it as `String`.

You can also specify only the upper bound of an array index as in the second example, but you have to be careful. If you do not specify the lower bound of an index (as we did in the first example), VBA assumes by default that the lower bound of the index is 0 and not 1. So the `stkPrice` array in the second example is a two-dimensional array with 301 rows going from 0 to 300. If you prefer to have the index values start at 1 and not 0, you can either follow the first example or you can include the following statement before any procedure in the module:

```
Option Base 1
```

If you want to, you can also specify lower bounds other than 0 and 1 for an index as shown in the third example. In this case, the array will hold sales numbers for years 1990 to 2005, and if you dimension it as shown, you will be able to refer to the sales for a particular year more easily by using the year number as the index, such as in `annlSales (2001)`.

Dynamic Arrays

If the size of an array is not known at the time of writing the code (for example, the size will depend on some input data) or you want to specify and change it during the execution of the code, then you can set up the array as a dynamic array. Here, you declare the array as usual but with a blank set of parentheses as follows:

```
Dim stkPrice() As Single
```

Before you use the array in your code, you must specify its dimensions using the ReDim statement and the dimensioning conventions we discussed. You can ReDim an array in your code any number of times, but if you want to preserve the values in the array when you ReDim it, you have to use the ReDim Preserve statement instead of ReDim; otherwise the data in the array will be lost.

A Few Helpful Functions for Use with Arrays

There are three VBA functions that you will find useful when working with arrays, although you do not absolutely need any of them. These are: LBound, UBound, and Erase.

When you use arrays in a procedure, you often need to know the smallest and largest subscript for each dimension of the array—for example, to use it in a For...Next loop. You can, of course, look up these subscripts from the array's Dim or ReDim statements and insert them in your code. However, if you change the range of subscripts for an array and forget to make the necessary corrections at all the places in your code, your code may not work or you may get wrong answers. You can use the LBound and UBound functions to find the lowest and highest subscripts (that is, boundaries) for each dimension of an array. The syntax, which is the same for both, is:

```
LBound (arrayname [, dimension])
```

For the argument dimension you enter 1,2, and so on, to indicate if you want the lowest subscript for the first dimension (row), second dimension (column), and so on. If you skip the argument dimension, VBA assumes it to be 1. For dynamic arrays, these functions will, of course, provide the current dimensions.

Here is an example to show how you use the LBound and UBound functions in code to reinitialize an array to 0.

```
Sub Method1()
Dim myArray(6, 20) As Single
Dim rowCnt, colCnt
```

```
For rowCnt = LBound(myArray, 1) To UBound(myArray, 1)
    For colCnt = LBound(myArray, 2) To UBound(myArray, 2)
        myArray(rowCnt, colCnt) = 0
    Next
Next

End Sub
```

You could use the Erase function to do the same more compactly. When used with a fixed-size array, the Erase function reinitializes numeric arrays to 0, text arrays to a zero-length string (""), and a Variant type array to Empty. You can rewrite the previous code as:

```
Sub Method2()
Dim myArray(6, 20) As Single

Erase myArray

End Sub
```

If you use the Erase function with a dynamic array, it will completely remove the array from memory and you will have to ReDim the array before using it again. In large codes, you may want to use Erase this way to free up memory when you no longer need the values in a dynamic array. For the type of codes you will be writing, however, this is generally not necessary.

Scope of Arrays

You can control the scopes of arrays using the conventions we discussed in the section "Scope of variables." You can also use the conventions for variables to make arrays Constant or Static.

Objects, Properties, and Methods

VBA is an object-oriented programming language. *Objects*, *properties*, and *methods* are three key concepts of all object-oriented languages. Most people find these concepts confusing, though, at least until they have been programming for some time, and many of them give up on learning VBA after wrestling with these concepts for a while.

One way of thinking about these concepts is to recognize that you write VBA programs to manipulate the properties of and apply methods to objects. This statement probably does not mean anything to you right now. After you finish reading this section, it may become clearer and help you remember the relationships among objects, properties, and methods. If not, it will not matter much.

You can learn to develop even large, complex financial models using VBA without ever thinking much about any of these concepts. You can learn how to write VBA statements or instructions, that is, how to "say" things in VBA, simply by imitating and modifying the statements you will see in the examples of procedures in this and other books. There are probably no more than 50 statement structures you have to learn.

OBJECTS

You can think of objects as "things" you work with in VBA, such as ranges, worksheets, workbooks, and charts. What you really need to know about objects is how you tell VBA which object or "thing" you want to manipulate. That's about it.

This is somewhat like giving someone your home address. You have to list the names of the country, city, street, and then the house number or name, which, if you notice, is arranged in a hierarchy. When you give an address, you separate these different pieces of information by commas (if you put them on the same line); in VBA you separate (or connect) them by periods, which is called the dot operator.

Most objects are parts of a collection of similar objects. For example, all open workbooks belong to the Workbooks collections, all worksheets belong to the Worksheets collection, and so forth. When you give someone the name of your city as part of your address, you usually do not have to say City: New York because most of the time it is obvious. However, if you include the name Sales in the "address" of an object, VBA does not know if you mean a workbook named Sales, a worksheet named Sales, or something else. You have to always clarify it by stating to which collection Sales belongs. If it is the name of a workbook, for example, you will say Workbooks ("Sales").

To make it possible to tell VBA exactly which "thing" you want to work with, the collections are further organized in a number of obvious hierarchies. As with your home address, you have to give the "address" of an object following its hierarchy as well, starting at the top of the hierarchy.

The hierarchy that you will probably work with most often is the workbook-worksheet-range hierarchy. To specify or give the "address" of a particular range (a cell is a range with one element) in a worksheet, you have to tell VBA the address of the range, the worksheet it belongs to, and the workbook that the worksheet belongs to. You do so as follows:

```
Workbooks("myBook").Worksheets("mySheet").Range("A1:C3")
```

Here are some important things to note about this expression or format of giving an "address," which you will use all the time:

- If you include actual names of the workbook and the worksheet (as in the example), you have to enclose them in quotation marks because they are texts.

You can also use text variables containing the names, in which case you do not use the quotations.

- The `Range` has to be specified in A1 convention, enclosed in quotations. You cannot use R1C1 convention.
- To refer to just one cell like `A1`, you will use `Range ("A1")` in the above expression. (Here `Range` is the collection of all possible ranges in the specific worksheet.)
- An alternate way to address just one cell is to use `Cells(rowNumber, columnNumber)` in place of the `Range` in the above expression. This parallels the R1C1 convention and is generally more convenient to use. Remember that you cannot use `Cells` to refer to more than one cell at a time. (Here, `Cells` is the collection of all cells in the specific worksheet.)
- If you do not specify the workbook, VBA assumes it to be the one where the code is running. So most of the time you can omit it.
- If you do not specify a worksheet, VBA assumes it to be the active worksheet. The worksheet that is selected before you run a procedure is the active worksheet until you change it from within the procedure. If the right worksheet happens to be the active worksheet when you run the procedure, you can omit the worksheet specification. This can be dangerous, however, because sometimes you may have a different worksheet active before running a procedure, and then your program may not work. If most of your work is going to be done on just one worksheet, then you can activate it early in your procedure (you will learn how later) and then skip the worksheet reference in the rest of your procedure except where you mean a different worksheet.
- If you want to refer to a worksheet instead of a range, you will drop the `Range` part of the expression, and you may not have to specify the workbook as well.

All other objects are also arranged in various hierarchies, and to refer to anything in these hierarchies (for example, a chart or some component of it) you have to use similar expressions. Since all these objects or "things" belong to Excel, Excel—referred to as `Application`—is at the pinnacle of all these hierarchies and is the collection of everything. Technically, then, all "addresses" should start with `Application` and then go down the hierarchy. Since there is no possibility of confusion, though, you can almost always safely omit it. (There is one situation where you have to include it, which I will point out later.)

If you are curious to see how all the objects are organized in Excel, in VBE's Help search for "Objects" and then choose "Microsoft Excel Objects." To see the additional details under Worksheets and Charts (which are of most interest to you), click the arrows next to them in the diagram that comes up.

Let me remind you again that your objective is to be able to tell VBA which object you want it to work with at that moment, that is, you are to provide the "address" of the object. In the VBA Quick Reference sheet (Appendix B and also on the CD), I have shown you how to do this for the objects you are likely to use most often. As you go along, you will work with other objects and figure out how to "address" them, and you will also find alternate ways to "address" the same objects. You may want to keep adding this information to the list to create your personalized reference sheet.

PROPERTIES

Properties are attributes of objects; much of the time your VBA program will be manipulating properties of objects. For example, the property of a cell you will deal with most often is its `Value`. When you store data in a cell, you are setting the `Value` property of the cell object. When you read data from a cell, you are reading its `Value` property. Most objects have many different properties, but you will be dealing with only a handful.

You refer to a particular property of a particular object by attaching the name of the property to the object's address with a period. Here are a few simple examples:

```
Worksheets ("Sales").Cells (3,5).Value = 100
Range ("F20: K35").Name = "East"
Range ("G35").Formula = "= C5 + C6"
```

The first statement will set the `Value` property of the cell in row 3, column 5 of the worksheet `Sales` at 100. In simple English, it means it will enter 100 in that cell. The second statement names the range `East`. The third statement enters the formula on the right-hand side into the cell G35. (In the last two statements, I omitted the `Worksheets` part of the object specification. So VBA will use the active worksheet as the default.)

You will generally deal with only a few properties like `Value` most of the time. One time that you have to work with many different properties is when you are formatting a cell or a range of cells. For this, however, you will generally find it easier to record a macro while you do the formatting. You can edit it, then copy and paste it into your procedure.

As with objects, I have listed some of the properties you will use most often in the VBA Quick Reference sheet (Appendix B and on the CD). You can add to the list as you go along.

METHODS

Methods are actions that you perform with objects. (Think of Methods as the verbs in a sentence.) You create statements by attaching a method to an object with a period. Here are two examples:

```
Range("B5:C10").Clear
Cells(3, 5).Copy Cells(7, 9)
```

The first statement will clear the specified range. (`Clear` will clear everything in the cell, formats, contents, and so on. If you want to clear only the contents, you would use `ClearContents`.) The second statement shows that methods can sometimes require arguments. This statement will copy the contents of the first cell and paste it into the second cell, which is an argument of the `Copy` method.

You will probably use even fewer methods than you will properties, and sometimes the easiest way to find the appropriate method is to record a macro while you do what you want to code (for example, record clearing a cell). Then you can use the recorded code for clue. In the VBA Quick Reference sheet (Appendix B and on the CD). I have listed some of the methods you will use most often. You can expand the list as you go along.

Branching

The statements in a VBA procedure are generally executed line by line, starting at the top. However, if VBA procedures were constrained to doing just this, then VBA's power would be quite limited. This is the only way recorded Macros can run, and it is one of the reasons they have limited power.

In VBA procedures that you write, you can include statements that will make execution jump forward or backward over one or more lines of statements. This action is dependent upon whether certain conditions you specify are satisfied. This is called *branching*. You can also make VBA repeat a group of statements until or while certain conditions are satisfied. This is called *looping*. These two abilities give procedures in any programming language (not just VBA) a lot of their power and flexibility. In this section, I cover the statements that you use for branching, and in the next section I will cover looping.

IF STATEMENTS

`If` statements are the most commonly used branching or decision-making statements in VBA. Conceptually, VBA's `If` statements are similar to the IF function of Excel, but VBA's `If` statements can be used to create much more complex and powerful decision structures. What's more, complex nested `If` statements in VBA are much easier to structure and read than nested IF functions in Excel.

If...Then...Else...Statement

The simplest `If` statement in VBA is the single-line `If...Then...Else` statement, which has essentially the same structure as the IF function in Excel. The syntax of the statement is:

```
If condition Then true_statement [Else false_statement]
```

If the `condition` is satisfied, then the `true_statement` is executed; otherwise the `false_statement` is executed. The `condition` can be a simple condition or you can create a complex condition using logical operators. The `Else` part of the statement is optional. If you omit it then the `true_statement` will be executed if the condition is satisfied; otherwise control will move on to the next statement.

Suppose you want to estimate the interest expense for a loan whose interest rate depends on the size of the loan. If the interest rate is 8% for a loan size up to (but not including) $1,000,000 and 10% for a loan size of $1,000,000 and above, then you can use a simple single-line `If` statement as follows to assign the appropriate interest rate:

```
If loanSize < 1000000 Then intRate = 0.08 Else intRate = 0.1
```

If the 10% interest rate applies to a loan size up to (but not including) $2,000,000 and is 11% for a loan size of $2,000,000 and above, then you can handle it using three single-line `If` statements as follows:

```
If loanSize < 1000000 Then intRate = 0.08
If loanSize >= 1000000 And loanSize < 2000000 Then _
  intRate = 0.1
If loanSize >= 2000000 Then intRate = 0.11
```

In a single-line `If` statement, you can include more than one statement in the `true_statement` as well as in the `false_statement` by putting additional statements in the same line separated by colons, as in the following example:

```
If A > 5 Then A = A + 5 : B = C + D
```

However this can make the line long and the statement hard to read. VBA offers a number of better alternatives. You may want to use the single-line `If` statement exclusively for cases where you have only one `true_statement` and only one `false_statement` to execute.

If...Then...End If Statement

You can use the block `If...Then...End If` statement if you want to execute more than one statement when a condition is satisfied. The syntax of the statement is:

```
If condition Then
    true_statements
End If
```

You can put any number of statements between the first and the last lines. If the condition is not satisfied, all the intermediate lines will be skipped and control will pass to the line following the `End If` line.

If...Then...Else...End If Statement

If you want to execute one block of statements when a condition is `True` and a second block of statements when it is `False`, then you can use the following `If` structure:

```
If condition Then
    true_statements
Else
    false_statements
End If
```

Note that in a structure like this, only one of the two blocks of statements will be executed and then control will pass on to the statement following the `End If` statement.

Here is how you can use this structure in a situation where only two different interest rates are possible:

```
If loanSize < 1000000 Then
    intRate = 0.08
Else
    intRate = 0.1
End If
```

You can include additional `If` statements of any type in both the *true_statements* and the *false_statements* blocks to create nested `If` statements. As is obvious, additional `If` statements must be completely embedded either in the *true_statements* block or in the *false_statements* block. For the situation where three interest rates are possible, you can use the following structure:

```
If loanSize < 1000000 Then
    intRate = 0.08
Else
    If loanSize < 2000000 Then
        intRate = 0.1
    Else
        intRate = 0.11
    End If
End If
```

Analyze this structure to understand how control passes when the different conditions are satisfied. For example, if loan size is less than $1,000,000, the interest rate will be set at 8% and control will move directly on to the statement following the outer `End If` statement. Note how proper indenting makes the structure easier to follow.

If Structures Using ElseIf

You can also create a nested `If` structure using `ElseIf` as follows:

```
If condition1 Then
    1true_statements
ElseIf condition2 Then
    1false_2true_statements
Else
    1false_2false_statements
End If
```

The example with the three possible interest rates can be written using this structure as follows:

```
If loanSize < 1000000 Then
    intRate = 0.08
ElseIf loanSize < 2000000 Then
    intRate = 0.1
Else
    intRate = 0.11
End If
```

You can also use the following slightly different structure for the same situation:

```
If loanSize < 1000000 Then
    intRate = 0.08
    ElseIf loanSize < 2000000 Then intRate = 0.1
    ElseIf loanSize >= 2000000 Then intRate = 0.11
End If
```

As you can see, VBA lets you create a wide variety of `If` structures. Always try to make your `If` structures easy to read and understand. You also must test your `If` structures thoroughly because it is the only sure way to find logical errors that can easily creep into even simple-looking `If` structures. For example, to test the various `If` structures I demonstrated for the interest rate problem, I embedded them in the following brief procedure and then executed the procedure for different loan sizes ($500,000, $1,000,000, and $2,000,000) to see if I would get the correct interest rates.

```
Sub If_Test()
Dim loanSize, intRate

loanSize = 500000

If loanSize < 1000000 Then
    intRate = 0.08
```

```
ElseIf loanSize < 2000000 Then intRate = 0.1
ElseIf loanSize >= 2000000 Then intRate = 0.11
End If

MsgBox intRate

End Sub
```

SELECT CASE...END SELECT STATEMENT

When you want to execute one of several groups of statements based on the value of an expression, you can use VBA's `Select Case...End Select` statement, which is often easier to read than the corresponding `If` statement. The syntax is as follows:

```
Select Case testexpression
    [Case expressionlist-n
        [statements-n]...
    [Case Else
        [elsestatements]
End Select
```

Here is how the example with three interest rates looks when written with the `Select Case...End Select` statement:

```
Select Case loanSize
    Case Is < 1000000
        intRate = 0.08
    Case Is < 2000000
        intRate = 0.1
    Case Else
        intRate = 0.11
End Select
```

The *testexpression* is generally an expression that can be evaluated as a number (for example, 4*loanSize) or a `string` variable.

The *expressionlist-n* can have one of the following forms:

expression as in: `Case 1000`

expression `To` *expression* as in: `Case 1 to 9`

`Is` *comparisonoperator expression* as in `Case Is < 1000000*6`

The *expressionlist-n* can also combine these forms, separated by commas as follows:

```
Case 500, 1000, 1 to 9, Is < 1000000
```

The Case Else clause is optional, but if you include it then the *elsestatements* will be executed if no match is found in one of the other Case selections.

As with If statements, you can nest Select Case statements, and you can combine If and Select Case statements to create intricate decision structures. For all decision structures (especially intricate ones), remember to use proper indentations in your code. Otherwise, these structures can become difficult to follow.

GOTO STATEMENT

You use a GoTo statement to transfer program control to an earlier or later line in a procedure (instead of the next line). The line you want control to jump to must be a line that has only a label, which is a text string that starts with a letter and ends with a colon (:). From there, control will again start moving line by line. The label can also be a number (with no colon), but using labels that are descriptive text strings will make your code more readable. Of course, you want a GoTo statement to be executed only when some condition is met. GoTo statements are therefore almost always used in conjunction with some kind of If statement.

Here is an example that uses a GoTo statement to prevent the user from entering an interest rate higher than 15%:

```
Sub GoToExample()
Dim intRate As Single, intExp As Single

intRate = InputBox("Enter interest rate in %.")
If intRate > 15 Then GoTo RateTooHigh
intExp = 100000 * intRate / 100
MsgBox "Interest expense is $" & intExp
Exit Sub

RateTooHigh:
MsgBox ("Interest rate cannot be greater than 15%.")

End Sub
```

The GoTo statement is so simple that most beginning programmers are tempted to use it a lot. However, GoTo statements make codes difficult to understand and modify because control jumps around instead of moving in an orderly manner. So you should try to use GoTo statements only for VBA's special error-handling procedure, and in almost all other situations you can and should use the other branching alternatives like If statements or Select Case statements.

Here is what the same example may look like if you rewrite it with a block If statement:

```
Sub AlternateTo_GoToExample()
Dim intRate As Single, intExp As Single
```

```
intRate = InputBox("Enter interest rate in %.")

If intRate > 15 Then
    MsgBox ("Interest rate cannot be greater than 15%.")
Else
    intExp = 100000 * intRate / 100
    MsgBox "Interest expense is $" & intExp
End If

End Sub
```

This code is not just shorter; it is easier to follow as well.

Looping

In financial models, you often want to evaluate the same formulas many times with different values for one or more of the variables involved. In Excel, you do it by writing the formulas with relative or mixed references for some of the cell addresses in them and then copying and pasting them into a series of cells. In VBA you do it by creating loops. Loops are lot more flexible and powerful than Excel's copy-and-paste approach. For example, with loops you can repeat a whole set of instructions instead of just one formula, you can repeat them thousands of times if necessary with just a few lines of instruction, and you can audit and modify your instructions much more easily. Loops are one of the most powerful tools in all programming languages, not just VBA

In VBA, you create loops using either `For...Next` or `Do...Loop` statements, and you can either specify exactly how many times a loop will be repeated or you can have looping stop when a condition or one of several conditions you specify is met.

FOR...NEXT STATEMENT

The `For...Next` loop is the simplest and most widely used loop and has the following syntax:

```
For counter = startValue to endValue [Step stepValue]
    [Statements]
    [Exit For]
    [Statements]
Next [counter]
```

The *counter* is a numeric variable you have to specify. It is called the counter of the loop. The first time the loop is executed, the value of the counter is set equal to `startValue` and then every time the loop is repeated the value of the counter is increased by the `stepValue`. If you omit the `Step stepValue` part of the first line, then VBA assumes that `stepValue` is 1.

Here are a few other things you need to know about the `For...Next` loop:

- Although you will often use positive integers for `startValue`, `endValue`, and `stepValue`, you can also use negative integers and numbers with decimal points for any of them. For example, you may want to repeat the loop 12 times to do a set of calculations for all the months of the year. If so, you can specify `startValue` = 1 and `endValue` = 12 and omit the `Step stepValue` portion. But if for some reason you want to, you can specify `startValue` = 12, `endValue` = 1, and `stepValue` = −1.
- Every time VBA loops back to the first line (the `For` line), it calculates the new value for the counter and compares it to the `endValue`. If the `stepValue` you have specified is positive or 0, then the loop is repeated as long as `counter` is < = `endValue`. If the `stepValue` is negative, then the loop is repeated as long as `counter` is > = `endValue`. This means that when looping stops, the value of `counter` will not be equal to `endValue` but will be one step larger or smaller than `endValue` depending on whether `stepValue` is positive or negative. The statements within the loop, though, will not be calculated with this final value. If you want to use the final value of `counter` in any subsequent calculation, you should keep this in mind and make any necessary adjustment to it before using it.
- You can use the same variable as the loop counter in as many loops as you want, except in some situations dealing with nested loops (see the section "Nested Loops"). Whether you do or not depends on what will make your code easier to understand and more consistent. For example, if in several different loops the loop counter refers to years 1950 to 2000, then you may want to use the same loop counter in all of them.
- Although you are allowed to do so, do not write any statement inside the loop to change the value of the `counter`. It will make reading and debugging the code more difficult.
- You may also want VBA to exit the loop before all the repetitions (implied by the `startValue`, `endValue` and `stepValue`) have been completed if certain conditions are met. You can do so by including one or more `Exit For` statements in the loop in a way that control will reach one of them only when one of the conditions—as specified by an `If...Then` or some other statement—is met. When VBA reaches one of these statements, control is transferred to the statement immediately following the last line (the `Next` line) of the loop. (If possible, it is even better to use a `Do...Loop`, as discussed below, for such situation.)
- You do not have to include the `counter` after the `Next` in the last line of the loop. However, if you have several `For...Next` loops in your code, then

including the *counter* in the last line makes it easier to recognize where a particular loop begins and ends (that is, which Next goes with which For). Otherwise, the Next for all the loops look the same and it becomes more difficult to read the code.

Here is an example of how you can use a For...Next loop to calculate how many months it will take to save $1,000 if you save $1 in the first month and in every subsequent month save $3 more than the previous month. (You do not earn any interest on your savings.)

```
Sub SavingCalculation_A()

Dim mnthlySav As Integer, mnthlyIncrease As Integer
Dim savTarget As Integer, totSav As Integer
Dim mnthNum As Integer

mnthlySav = 1 'Saving in first month
mnthlyIncrease = 3 'Increase over previous month
savTarget = 1000 'Saving target
totSav = 0 'Used to total savings

For mnthNum = 1 To 1000
    totSav = totSav + mnthlySav
    If totSav >= savTarget Then Exit For
    mnthlySav = mnthlySav + mnthlyIncrease
Next mnthNum

MsgBox "In " & mnthNum & "months savings will total $" & totSav

End Sub
```

DO...LOOP STATEMENTS

There are four different syntaxes available for the Do...Loop statement. A Do...Loop does not have a loop counter. Instead, you can—but do not have to—include a condition in the Do or Loop part of the statement to specify that the loop will repeat while or until that condition is met. You can also use one or more Exit Do statements within the loop to exit under additional conditions. Make sure to specify at least one condition that will end execution of the loop. Otherwise, the loop will keep repeating. (If during the execution of a program something seems to have gone wrong and the program keeps running, you can stop execution by pressing the Esc key several times.)

The four syntaxes available for the Do...Loop are:

```
Do [While condition]
    [Statements]
    [Exit Do]
    [Statements]
Loop
    [Statements]
    [Exit Do]
    [Statements]
Loop [While condition]

Do [Until condition]
    [Statements]
    [Exit Do]
    [Statements]
Loop

Do
    [Statements]
    [Exit Do]
    [Statements]
Loop [Until condition]
```

One advantage of a Do...Loop is that a condition for exiting the loop included in the Do or Loop line is more visible than one or more Exit For statements embedded within a For...Next loop. However, if you need to exit a loop under several different conditions then you will end up including Exit Do statements in the Do...Loop as well.

Here is what the loop of the previous example would look like if we were to write it with a Do...Loop without any condition in the Do or Loop line. Note that since we do not have a loop counter anymore, we have to keep track of the number of months by keeping count of it within the loop. (We will also need a mnthNum = 0 statement before the loop to set the right initial value for mnthNum.)

```
Do
    mnthNum = mnthNum + 1
    totSav = totSav + mnthlySav
    If totSav >= savTarget Then Exit Do
    mnthlySav = mnthlySav + mnthlyIncrease
Loop
```

We can write the same loop with a While *condition* attached to the Do as follows:

```
Do While totSav < savTarget
    mnthNum = mnthNum + 1
    totSav = totSav + mnthlySav
```

```
    mnthlySav = mnthlySav + mnthlyIncrease
Loop
```

Finally, the condition will have to be changed if we write the loop with Until instead of While:

```
Do Until totSav >= savTarget
    mnthNum = mnthNum + 1
    totSav = totSav + mnthlySav
    mnthlySav = mnthlySav + mnthlyIncrease
Loop
```

Whether you use While or Until is generally a matter of taste, except that in some situations the condition written with one or the other may be easier to understand, giving the syntax a slight edge.

When you use While, you will use the same condition whether you include it in the Do or the Loop line. Most of the time it makes no difference which option you choose, but if the condition you specify is satisfied even before entering the loop then it may make a difference. In the two syntaxes, the condition will be tested at different points in time. If you include it in the Do line then in the special situation mentioned, the statements within the loop will never be executed; if you include it in the Loop line, however, those statements will be executed at least once. Sometimes this may affect your results. (The same comments apply to including Until in the Do or the Loop line.)

NESTED LOOPS

You can include large blocks of statements within any loop, and you can also include one or more loops within other loops. Loops within loops are called nested loops and are very useful. To create nested loops you can use For...Next statements and Do...Loop statements in any combination—with two restrictions. The restrictions are necessary in order to avoid possible confusion during execution.

- Every inner loop must be fully contained within all outer (meaning higher-level) loops, that is, the Next or Loop line of an inner loop always has to come before similar lines of outer loops.
- You cannot use the same loop counter in two loops, one of which is nested within the other.

Here is an example of how nested loops can be used to initialize two arrays.

```
Sub InitializeArrays()

Dim Array1(1 To 5, 1 To 10, 1 To 20) As Integer
Dim Array2(1 To 5, 1 To 15) As Integer
Dim i As Integer, j As Integer, k As Integer
```

```
For i = 1 To 5

    For j = 1 To 10 ' Initialize Array1 to 1
        For k = 1 To 20
            Array1(i, j, k) = 1
        Next k
    Next j

    For j = 1 To 15 ' Initialize Array2 to 2
        Array2(i, j) = 2
    Next j
Next i

End Sub
```

It should be obvious now why the `Next k` line, which belongs to an inner loop, must come before the `Next j` line of an outer- or higher-level loop. It should also be easy to understand why we cannot use `j` as the loop counter in the loop that currently uses `k`—they are nested. However, we can use the same loop counter `j` in two different loops that are not nested within each other. Note how using proper indentation and line spacing as well as including the loop counter in the `Next` line make it easier to understand the nesting structure.

You can use `GoTo` statements to create loops and exit from a loop when certain conditions are met (that is, in place of `Exit For` and `Exit Do` statements). Both, though, will make your code more difficult to understand and modify. You can almost always find alternatives in VBA to using `GoTo` statements; you should find and use such alternatives.

FOR EACH. . .NEXT STATEMENT

You mostly use a `For...Next` statement with a numerical counter to repeat a group of statements for a series of values for the counter. If instead you want to repeat a group of statements for each element in an array or collection, you will use the `For Each...Next` statement with the following structure.

```
For Each element In group
    [Statements]
    [Exit For]
    [Statements]
Next [element]
```

The group can be the name of an array or an object collection. For example, if you want to enter the name of each worksheet in the active workbook into cell A1 of that worksheet, you can use the `For Each...Next` loop as follows:

```
Sub ForEachNext_Example()

Dim mySheet As Worksheet

For Each mySheet In ActiveWorkbook.Worksheets
    Worksheets(mySheet.Name).Cells(1, 1).Value = mySheet.Name
Next mySheet

End Sub
```

Note that here `mySheet` is an Object variable that refers to worksheets. You therefore have to `Dim` it either as `Worksheet` (that is, the type of object it is) or as `Variant`. When you want to use the name of the worksheet `mySheet` is referring to at any time, you have to use the Name property of the object `mySheet`.

THE EXIT STATEMENTS

You use an `Exit` statement to exit from the middle of a block of `Do...Loop`, `For...Next`, `Function`, `Sub`, or `Property` code blocks most often because a particular condition has been satisfied. VBA offers the following Exit statements: `Exit Do`, `Exit For>`, `Exit Function`, `Exit Property`, and `Exit Sub` to exit the different types of code blocks. You could use a `GoTo` statement in place of any of these `Exit` statements, but it is preferable to use the appropriate `Exit` statement because it will make your code easier to follow and debug.

When VBA encounters one of these `Exit` statements, control is transferred to the line immediately following the last line of the block. In a `For...Next` block, the control will jump to the statement following the `Next` statement. In a `Function` procedure, `Exit Function` will return control to the statement the `Function` was called from.

WITH...END WITH STATEMENT

The `With...End With` structure looks like a looping structure, but its purpose is to let you shorten your statements when you are repeatedly dealing with the same object. It also speeds up the execution of the code. The structure of the statement is as follows:

```
With object
    Statements
End With
```

For example, if you have a series of statements—all of which refer to the same worksheet—but do not want to make that the active worksheet, then you can use the With...End With structure as follows:

```
1:  Sub With_Test()
2:
3:  With Worksheets("Sheet2")
4:  .Cells(1, 2).Value = 20
5:  .Cells(2, 2).Value = 30
6:  .Cells(3, 1).Value = "Total"
7:  .Cells(3, 2).Formula = "=B1 + B2"
8:  End With
9:
10:  End Sub
```

Here, using the With...End With structure made it possible to omit the object Worksheets("Sheet2") in front of Cells in lines 4 to 7. You may not use it much in codes you write, but recorded macros use this structure extensively.

Using Built-In Functions

VBA offers dozens of built-in functions that you use in VBA statements essentially the same way you use Excel functions in cell formulas. Many of these are similar or identical to Excel functions, but there are two things you need to keep in mind about using built-in functions in VBA.

First, you can use Excel functions in VBA, but when you do, you have to precede the function name by Application or WorksheetFunction followed by a period (.). For example, to use Excel's Average function in VBA you will use Application.Average or WorksheetFunction.Average.

Second, you cannot use an Excel worksheet function in VBA if VBA has an equivalent function. To see a list of all the Excel functions you can use in VBA, search in VBA Help under "Function" and then choose "List of Worksheet Functions Available to Visual Basic." You can also type WorksheetFunction followed by a period (.) anywhere in a module. In the list that pops up, functions are preceded by green icons. (If the list does not pop up in VBE, choose Tools ⇨ Options and then in the Editor tab of the Options dialog box make sure that Auto List Members is selected.)

You can see a similar list of all VBA built-in functions by typing VBA followed by a period (.). To see a list with full descriptions of these functions, look under Function in VBA Help's Contents tab.

Appendix C: Excel and VBA Built-In Functions includes a categorized list of selected Excel and VBA functions available, with descriptions and also indicates which Excel functions have equivalent VBA functions.

Using the Object Browser to Insert Functions

You can use VBA's Object Browser to search for and insert VBA and Excel functions in your code.

To do so, position the insertion point at the point in the code where you want to use the function. Now open the Object Browser window by pressing F2 or by selecting View ⇨ Object Browser. For VBA functions, open the list in the top left dropdown window (called the Project/Library dropdown list) and select VBA. From the list in the Classes window, select the function category (for example, DateTime) you need. This will bring up a list of all functions in this category in the large window to the right titled Members of "DateTime." When you select one of the functions in this list, its syntax will appear at the bottom of the Object Browser window. To insert the function name in your code, click the Copy button in the Object Browser, close the Object Browser and click the Paste button in VBE's toolbar. If you want to copy the arguments of the function as well, select with your mouse the function and its arguments at the bottom of the Browser Window and then copy and paste it.

To choose from the list of Excel functions available in VBA, open the Object Browser window and in the Project/Library drop-down list select Excel. In the Classes window, select WorksheetFunction. This will bring up a list of all available Excel functions in the right window. You can select and the copy and paste any function from the list as before.

Using Analysis ToolPak Functions in VBA

In the previous versions of Excel, you can also use the functions available in the Analysis ToolPak in VBA. However, you have to set this up first. In Excel, select Tools ⇨ Add-ins and check the box next to Analysis ToolPak—VBA. Click OK. Now in VBE select Tools ⇨ References, check the box next to `atpvbaen.xls`, and click OK. You can now use the Analysis ToolPak functions in VBA code just like any other built-in VBA functions (that is, you do not have to precede them by `Application` or `WorksheetFunction`).

In Excel 2007, Analysis ToolPak does not have any functions in VBA.

CHAPTER 23

Sub and Function Procedures

Earlier I defined a VBA procedure as a recipe or an organized set of statements written in the VBA language to carry out certain tasks. There are only two types of VBA procedures: Sub procedures and Function procedures. A Sub procedure performs a number of actions, but does not return a value. A Function procedure is similar to a Sub procedure in that it can also perform actions, but in addition it can return a value, which can be a single value or an array.

A model may contain any number of procedures. You may view procedures as the way to organize in logical, manageable groups all the instructions VBA will need to do what the model is supposed to do.

You need to learn to develop and use both types of procedures, and this is what I will cover in this chapter.

Sub Procedures

A Sub procedure can perform a number of actions but cannot return a value.

THE STRUCTURE OF SUB PROCEDURES

A somewhat simplified structure of a Sub procedure is:

```
Sub Procedure_Name([argumentlist])
    [Statements]
    [Exit Sub]
    [Statements]
End Sub
```

The first line is called the declaration line of the procedure; it and the last line are required. As a matter of fact, after you type in the first line in a module to start a new Sub procedure and press Enter, VBA will automatically enter the last line. Then you can insert statements in between. Every Sub procedure must have a name. As with variables, short but descriptive names are best. I prefer to use names that use a few descriptive words connected by underscores.

Like the built-in functions, Sub procedures can take various types of arguments such as constants, variables (including arrays), literals (meaning numbers or texts enclosed in quotation marks), or expressions passed by another procedure that they then use in their actions and calculations. These are represented by a list, generally of variables, separated by commas within the parentheses following the procedure name. If a Sub procedure has no argument, its name must be followed by an empty pair of parentheses.

You can include any number of `Exit Sub` statements in a Sub procedure to cause immediate exit from the procedure. If the Sub procedure was called from another Sub procedure (see next section) then this will return control to the statement following the calling statement. Otherwise this will terminate execution.

(For a discussion of the complete Sub statement with explanation of all its parts, search for "Sub statement" in VBA's Help.)

USING SUB PROCEDURES

Sub procedures that do not have any argument can be run directly using one of the methods I discussed before (for example, in VBE by placing the cursor anywhere in the procedure and then clicking the Run Sub button). However, since arguments have to be passed to Sub procedures that require arguments, they can only be run by calling them with arguments from other procedures. This involves including a statement like the following at the appropriate point in the calling Sub procedure:

```
Call Format_Output(firstRow, numRows)
```

When control reaches this statement, the Sub procedure `Format_Output` will be run with the values of the arguments passed, and then control will return to the line following this call line in the calling procedure.

The call has to be a statement by itself and cannot be part of a longer statement. The keyword `Call` is optional, that is, you can drop the Call from the above statement and it will still work the same way. But you should always use it, because it makes the code easier to read. (If you want to omit the keyword `Call`, then search for "Call statement" in VBA's Help for some important additional information.)

Why Call Sub Procedures?

It is important to understand why VBA (and programming languages in general) provides for calling one procedure from another and writing Sub procedures with arguments. Conceptually even the longest and most complex model can probably be written as one very long Sub procedure. Such a procedure, however, would be difficult to understand, debug, and maintain. Also, if it involves doing some things many times, the same block of code may have to be repeated in several places in the procedure. You may forget to make the changes in one or more places.

Being able to call one procedure from another makes it possible to organize a model somewhat like the management structure of a business. In a business the CEO has access to different departments like sales, production, and finance. Each department has its own expertise, and the CEO calls on the departments for help as needed. Similarly, in a large model, you can have a main Sub procedure orchestrate things. It can call special-purpose Sub procedures, each of which does just one thing: a particular type of calculation, formatting of output, and so on, as needed.

Such a structure makes it much easier to understand, debug, and maintain a model. For example, under such a structure, if we want to make a change to a particular set of calculations, we will have to make it at only one place—in the Sub procedure where that set of calculations is done. Even if the model requires doing those calculations dozens of times at various points during execution, they will all be done by calling this one Sub procedure.

Often you may use the same set of calculations in different models. If the calculations are done in a Sub procedure that only does that set of calculations, then that same Sub procedure can be used in all the models, which will save programming and program maintenance time. If you think about it, you will recognize that the built-in functions are based on this same philosophy.

Most experienced programmers prefer to modularize large models by combining many small Sub procedures, each of which has one narrow function. You should start doing the same as your models get bigger. Structurally, such a model may look like this:

```
Sub Main()
    Call Get_User_Input(arguments)
    Call Validate_User_Input(arguments)
    Call Get_Data(arguments)
    Call Do_Calculations(arguments)
    Call Draw_Chart(arguments)
End Sub
```

Each of these called Sub procedures may call other procedures if necessary.

It should also be clear now why we have to be able to pass arguments to some Sub procedures. If we are going to call a Sub procedure to do the same set of calculations on different sets of data, we must have a way to pass these data to it. This is what arguments allow us to do.

Passing Arguments between Procedures

For a called Sub procedure to work properly, you have to understand and follow a set of rules about passing arguments to it and use them properly in writing Sub procedures. Let me discuss them in the context of the following examples:

```
Sub Caller()
Dim R1, R2

R1 = 10
R2 = 20
Call Called(R1, R2)
MsgBox R1

End Sub

Sub Called(D1, D2)
Dim Total

D1 = D1 * 10
Total = D1 + D2
Worksheets("Sheet1").Cells(3, 5).Value = Total

End Sub
```

You will execute this model by running `Caller` using one of the direct methods. In this example, the called Sub procedure does some calculations with the arguments passed, assigns the result to `Total`, and enters the value of `Total` in a worksheet cell.

Here are the rules and some observations:

- Although it is possible to make some of the arguments of a Sub procedure optional, all the arguments will be required in almost all Sub procedures that you write. This means that if the called Sub procedure has 2 arguments, then the calling statement must also provide 2 arguments. (See later for discussion of optional arguments.)
- As shown in our example, you generally do not use the same names for the argument being passed (`R1` and `R2`) and the arguments in the declaration line of the Sub procedure being called (`D1` and `D2`). When called as in this example, VBA passes the memory address of `R1` to `D1` and so forth.
- You do not have to (actually you cannot) declare the data type of the arguments of a called Sub procedure using `Dim` statements within that Sub procedure. Generally they are determined by the data type of the arguments being passed. Since in the example `R1` and `R2` are `Variant` (by default), `D1` and `D2` will be the same.

- If you want to specify the data types of the arguments of a Sub procedure, you have to do so in its declaration line. In our example, you can use `Sub Called (D1 as Integer, D2)`. In this case, `R1` will also have to be `Integer` data type. Otherwise you will get an error message.
- Passing arguments the way this example does is a two-way street. When the execution of the `Called` Sub procedure ends, the current values of `D1` and `D2` are effectively passed back to `R1` and `R2`. (This happens because during the execution of the `Called` Sub procedure, `R1` and `D1` use the same memory location as `R2` and `D2`.) You can verify this by running `Caller`. The message will show that after `Called` is executed, the value of `R1` changes to 100 from the initial 10.
- If you do not want a called Sub procedure to change the value of an argument (say, `R1`) in the calling procedure, you will have to change the declaration statement to `Sub Called(ByVal D1, D2)`. The `ByVal` signals to VBA that it should pass the value of `R1` to `D1` and not its memory location. So when the calculations change the value of `D1`, `R1` is not changed. You can verify this by running `Caller` with this change in the declaration line. The message will now show that the value of `R1` is still 10 even after `Called` is executed.
- The arguments can be arrays as well. In this case, the dimensions of the array being passed will determine the dimensions of the array in the called Sub procedure. As with the data type, you cannot specify in the called procedure the dimensions of an argument array.

So a called Sub procedure can do two things. It can take some actions: as we saw here, it entered the value of `Total` in a cell in `Sheet1`. It can also pass back new values for one or more arguments, as in this case where `R1` changes to 100 after control returned from the `Called` Sub procedure.

Making Arguments Optional

You can make one or more arguments of a Sub procedure optional by preceding the name of the argument by the keyword `Optional`, and you can also specify a default value for the argument in the procedure definition. Here is an example:

```
Sub ArgExample(A, B as Variant, Optional C Default = 0)
```

Here are a few things to keep in mind:

- In calling Sub procedures with optional arguments, you have to provide commas to indicate missing arguments as you do when using built-in functions.
- Be careful in handling missing optional arguments in your code for which you did not provide default values.
- In the argument list of the procedure's Sub statements, the optional arguments must appear after the required arguments.

Another Way to Pass Values

If you want to pass only a few variables back and forth, then doing so through arguments, as we have seen, works fine. If, however, you are going to call several Sub procedures to work on the same variables (including arrays), you can also expand the scope of the corresponding variables to `Private` or `Public` (as I mentioned during our discussion of variables in the previous chapter) and let the Sub procedures work directly with them.

However, remember that a Sub procedure that only works with the variables passed through arguments is generally more versatile: you will be able to use it with different models more easily. Sub procedures that work directly with data that other procedures also use become specialized and often need careful modification before being used in other models.

Scope of a Sub Procedure

As with variables, procedures also have scope that determine from where a procedure can be accessed (called). Unless labeled as `Private`, a procedure is considered `Public` and can be accessed from any module in the workbook. A `Public` procedure does not have to be labeled as such, but if you want, you can insert the word `Public` before the word Sub in the first line.

If you want a procedure to be accessible only to other procedures in the same module, you can do so by including the word `Private` before Sub in its declaration line. Note that `Private` Sub procedures and Sub procedures that require one or more arguments do not show in the list of macros in the Macro dialog box.

You can also use Sub procedures from other workbooks in any workbook. I will explain how later.

Function Procedures

A Function procedure is similar to a Sub procedure in that it can perform actions, but it can also return a value, which can be a single value or an array.

THE ADVANTAGES OF FUNCTION PROCEDURES

A popular use of Function procedures is to design custom functions that can be used in worksheet formulas exactly like Excel's built-in functions. They show up in the list of available functions (under the User Defined category) in the Paste Function dialog box and can be used in formulas like the built-in functions. Here are some of the reasons why this is a popular and attractive use of Function procedures:

- You can create custom financial functions that can do things beyond what Excel's built-in financial functions can do.
- Since custom functions can utilize all the powerful VBA programming tools such as branching and looping, they can be designed to do calculations that may be difficult or impossible to do in worksheets using Excel alone.
- You can use custom functions to automate any set of Excel calculations that you do frequently. This will save time and reduce the chances of making mistakes in the future.
- Custom functions will help you create cleaner worksheets, because many of the formulas that do the calculations will be moved from worksheets to Function procedures in modules.
- You can help others who do not know VBA take advantage of its power by creating custom functions for their use. From their point of view, custom functions can be even more useful than Sub procedures that you may write for them. They can use custom functions to build their own spreadsheet models whereas they can only run Sub procedures "as is."

One disadvantage of custom functions, from the point of view of users who do not know VBA, is that to the user they look like black boxes; users cannot see exactly how the calculations are being done. The built-in functions, of course, have the same limitation.

While Function procedures are generally designed to return a value, like Sub procedures, they can also perform actions and be called from other procedures. You will write many Function procedures that you will call from other Sub and Function procedures to create more modularized models as we discussed earlier.

THE STRUCTURE OF FUNCTION PROCEDURES

A somewhat simplified structure of a Function procedure is as follows:

```
Function FunctionName([argumentlist])[As datatype]
   [Statements]
   [Exit Function]
   [Statements]
End Function
```

As with Sub procedures, once you type in the declaration line of a Function procedure, VBA will automatically enter the `End Function` statement and you can start entering statements in between. Since you will use the name of a Function procedure in expressions as well as in worksheet formulas, it is preferable to keep it short. Still try to make it at least somewhat descriptive.

Like Sub procedures, Function procedures can use various types of arguments such as constants, variables (including arrays), literals, or expressions passed by the calling procedure that it then uses in its actions and calculations. These are represented by a list, generally of variables, separated by commas within the parentheses following the procedure name. If a Function procedure has no argument, its name must be followed by an empty pair of parentheses.

You can include any number of `Exit Function` statements in a Function procedure to cause immediate exit from it. Program execution will continue with the statement following the statement that called the Function procedure.

(For a discussion of the complete Function Statement with an explanation of all its parts, search for "Function statement" in VBA's Help.)

USING FUNCTION PROCEDURES

Let us look at a simple example to understand how Function procedures are created and used.

```
Sub UseFunction()
Dim R1, R2, answer

R1 = 10
R2 = 20
answer = SpclSumSqrs(R1, R2)
MsgBox ("Answer = " & answer)
MsgBox ("R1 = " & R1)

End Sub

Function SpclSumSqrs(D1, D2)

D1 = D1 * 2
D2 = D2 * 3
SpclSumSqrs = D1 ^ 2 + D2 ^ 2

End Function
```

In this example, the Function procedure `SpclSumSqrs` calculates a special type of sum of squares using the two variables passed. Here are the things we can learn about Function procedures from this example:

- If you want a Function procedure to return a value (which is what most Function procedures are designed to do), you have to assign the value to the name of the Function procedure at least once somewhere in the procedure. You can assign values to the name many times within the Function procedure (for example, there may be several possible values that depend on some `If` statements). The most recent value will be returned to the calling procedure or worksheet formula.

- Function procedures (even those without arguments) cannot be run on their own. In VBA they have to be used in expressions in another Sub or Function procedure (as shown here in the `UseFunction` Sub procedure), the same way as the built-in functions. Even though this is sometimes referred to as calling the function, it works differently from calling Sub procedures and the keyword Call is not used. When control returns from a Function procedure, if a value was assigned to the name of the function, that value is substituted for the Function in the calling statement and then execution continues.
- Function procedures, with one exception that I discuss later, can also be used in worksheets the same way as Excel's built-in functions—that is, in formulas. To try this, enter the Function procedure of our example in any module of a workbook. Then select any cell in a worksheet, click the Paste Function button to open the Paste Function dialog box, find the function `SpclSumSqrs` in the User Defined category, and double-click it. Once you enter values for the two arguments and click OK, the answer will appear in the cell.
- If you want a Function procedure to return a value of particular data type, you can specify that at the end of the declaration line for the procedure as shown in the syntax for that line. (Watch out for possible errors due to data type mismatch.)
- Since you cannot run a Function procedure by itself, if you want to test one, you have to create a small Sub procedure to run it from (like the one in the example). If it is the type that can be used in worksheets, then test it in cell formulas.

An Important Restriction

When used in a worksheet formula, a Function procedure cannot do anything with the worksheet other than provide the value of the function to the formula in which it is being used. To check this, enter the statement `Cells(3, 5).Value = D1` anywhere in the `SpclSumSqrs` Function procedure and try to use it in a cell in the worksheet as before. The function will not work because it involves entering a value in a cell in the worksheet. However, you can use this modified function in other VBA procedures as before. For example, if you run the `UseFunction` procedure again, it will work fine and this time the `SpclSumSqrs` function will also enter the value of `D1` in the cell R3C5 of the worksheet. If you are writing a function that you intend to use in worksheets, keep this restriction in mind.

Scope and Passing Arguments

The discussions under Sub procedures of scope, optional arguments, and passing arguments apply to Function procedures as well. If you make a function `Private`, then it will not show up in the list of functions in the Paste Function dialog box. So if you do not want a function to be used in worksheets, make it `Private`.

Functions That Return Arrays

Like some built-in functions, a Function procedure can also be designed to return an array instead of a single value. Here is a simple example to demonstrate how such functions work:

```
Function ArrayOut(numRows, numCols)
Dim tempArray()
Dim i, j

ReDim tempArray(1 To numRows, 1 To numCols)

For i = 1 To numRows
For j = 1 To numCols
tempArray(i, j) = i + j
Next j
Next i

ArrayOut = tempArray

End Function
```

This function returns a two-dimensional array with the number of rows and columns specified by the user as `numRows` rows and `numCols` columns. The function assigns to each element a value equal to the sum of its row and column numbers.

To see how this function works, copy the Function procedure into a module in a workbook. In a worksheet in the same workbook, select a range of the same size as the size of the array you want to create. Now click the Paste Function button. In the Paste Function dialog box find the `ArrayOut` function in the User Defined category and double-click it. Enter the arguments in the dialog box that opens, making sure that they match the size of the range you selected. Since you are entering an array formula, you cannot enter it by clicking OK. Instead, press Ctrl+Shift+Enter to enter it. The range will be filled with the appropriate numbers. Notice that any cell you select in the range shows the same formula, which is enclosed in braces to indicate that this is an array formula. (If you need to, look up the discussion of arrays and array formulas in Part One.)

A few observations about the procedure itself: You cannot dimension `ArrayOut` and enter values directly into its elements. Instead, you have to create an array of the desired size (`tempArray` here), fill it with the appropriate values, and then assign it to `ArrayOut`. Since the size of `tempArray` depends on user inputs, you have to declare it as a dynamic array to start with and then `ReDim` it using the user inputs. Note that I have chosen to specify that the index values for the array start at 1 instead of the default value of 0.

Adding Description to a Custom Function

You can add descriptions similar to those for built-in functions to custom functions you create. Open the workbook that contains the function and then the Macro dialog box by pressing Alt+F8 or using the menu. Type the name of the function in the Macro name box and click the Options button. In the Macro Options dialog box that opens, enter the description of the function in the Description box and click OK when finished.

When pasting one of Excel's built-in functions, you can get help, that is a description, for each argument. You cannot provide similar help for individual arguments of custom functions you create. As an alternative, you can include brief help information (that is, description) for each argument or selected arguments in the description of the function itself.

Using Functions from Other Workbooks

A simple way to make a Function or Sub procedure in one workbook available in another (both in worksheets and VBA procedures) is to copy and paste it into a module in the other workbook. One disadvantage of this approach is that if you modify the function, you may forget to update all copies of it.

If you have a Function procedure in workbook A that you want to use in a worksheet in workbook B, you can easily do so as long as workbook A is open and stays open. If you use the Paste Function button to insert the function in a cell formula in workbook B, the Paste Function dialog box will list the function in the User Defined category (with a workbook reference in front) and you will be able to paste it like any other function. If you want to type in the function in a cell formula, include a reference to the workbook in the following format:

```
WorkbookName.xls!FunctionName(arguments)
```

Remember that unless workbook A is open when you use workbook B, you may get errors with the pasted function.

So for functions that you intend to use in various workbooks, a better option is to save them in the Personal Macro Workbook with the file name "Personal.xls." This is a hidden file that opens automatically and remains open whenever you have Excel open. To save a procedure in this workbook, first unhide it by selecting in Excel Windows ⇨ Unhide. Then select it. Now cut and paste the Function procedure into a module in this workbook. The function will now be accessible from all workbooks and will always work.

(The Personal.xls workbook is not created until you record your first macro in it. If you cannot find it when you try to unhide it, you have to create it first. To do so, record a small macro making sure that in the Record Macro dialog box you choose to store the macro in Personal Macro Workbook. After you have added one or more procedures to this workbook as described above, you can delete the macro you recorded to create this workbook.)

CHAPTER 24

Debugging VBA Codes

Codes rarely run flawlessly the first few times: they may not run at all, they may stop in the middle, or they may run through but produce wrong or suspicious results. Errors in code are called bugs, and the process of finding and fixing them is called *debugging*. Like every modeler, you will have to spend time tracking down and fixing the bugs that invariably slip into almost all models. The good news is that most bugs are relatively easy to find and fix (unless you are working on a huge model with complex logic).

VBA provides several special tools to help with debugging, and learning at least some of them will help. But how fast you can debug a code will mostly depend on your experience, ingenuity, and understanding of the finance and mathematics of the problem. For beginners, debugging often becomes the most frustrating part of developing models. Rest assured that your skill at debugging will improve rapidly with experience.

It has been my experience that you can debug a code much faster by using a few tools systematically instead of trying to use all the different tools VBA offers in a haphazard manner. The few selected tools I discuss here are the ones you are likely to find most useful. I will not discuss VBA's Watch, or Locals Windows, which can be used for debugging, because I do not find them useful. I also do not discuss error handling, which involves including code in your models that notify the user when certain types of errors occur and then continue execution instead of ending it. If you are curious, you can look up these tools in the Help or in books devoted exclusively to programming with VBA.

Break Mode

To debug VBA codes you need to understand VBA's break mode, because you will often have to work in that mode. When a VBA code is running you cannot temporarily stop it, look at the values of the different variables, and interact with the code. You can do all of these things, however, if VBA is in the break mode. In the break mode, execution is suspended at a particular point, and from there on you can control the execution of the code and track what the code is doing. If you are looking for the cause of a runtime or logical error (defined later), for example, you may want to put execution in break mode and then, in slow motion, analyze what is happening. I will discuss later how you can enter the break mode and then proceed in step-by-step slow motion.

THE FOUR BASIC TYPES OF BUGS

The bugs you are likely to encounter can be classified into four broad types:

Syntax Errors

VBA, like all other programming languages, uses a rigid syntax. If a statement you write does not conform to VBA's syntax, you will get a syntax error message. After you finish writing or editing a statement and press return or move the cursor away, VBA immediately checks the statement for syntax errors and automatically fixes the errors if possible. You will therefore get the syntax error message only if there are errors that VBA cannot fix. Most of the time the problem is just a typing error, a misspelled word, or something fairly obvious that you will be able to spot and fix easily.

Compiler Errors

Before it can run a code, VBA has to compile it. Compiling code roughly means translating the code into a language that the computer understands. Certain types of bugs that do not show up during the process of checking syntax show up at this stage and you get a compile error message. These bugs are also generally easy to spot and fix with the help of the messages that VBA provides. Many of these errors may also originate in typing mistakes. For example, if you are using Option Explicit but forget to declare a variable in a `Dim` statement, VBA will highlight it as a variable not defined. This may truly be a variable you forgot to define, but many times it is a variable you misspelled that VBA cannot recognize.

As I recommended in the last chapter, you should always force yourself to declare all variables by specifying Option Explicit. Otherwise, misspelled variable names may affect your results in unpredictable ways and you may have to waste a lot of time finding the bug. (See the discussion of this in Chapter 22 in the section "Declaring Variables.")

Runtime Errors

Runtime errors occur when during the execution of a program VBA cannot evaluate or execute a statement. For example, if the value of the denominator in a division happens to be zero, you will get a runtime error message. When a runtime error occurs, VBA displays a dialog box with an error code (number) and a brief description of the error. You can find a more detailed description of the error in the Help, but often these descriptions are cryptic and not very helpful. (To find a list and descriptions of all the VBA error codes, search in Help under "Err object." In the panel for it, click on See Also and then from the list select "Trappable Errors.")

The dialog box generally has three active buttons. If you click the Debug button, VBA will highlight the code line where execution stopped and go into break mode, which is helpful for debugging. (I will discuss break mode later.) Clicking the End button will end execution, and clicking the Help button will display the online help topic for the particular runtime error.

The good thing about runtime errors is that the code will not run until you find the problem (unless you have included special error handling procedures). Your errors will not go undetected; generally you can find the problem quickly using one of VBA's special debugging tools.

Logical Errors

Logical errors are caused by errors in the programmer's reasoning. This type of error may not stop the code from running through to the end, but instead may produce wrong results or do the wrong things. Worse yet, the problems may occur only under certain circumstances and so they may go undetected in the debugging stage. Some VBA tools will help you search for the logical problems, but your understanding of the finance and mathematics of the problem may be the most important tools here.

THE VBA DEBUGGING TOOLS

You do not need any special tools to deal with syntax and compile errors. VBA will point out where the problem is and it may even give you helpful hints on what the problem may be. Even if VBA's message is not helpful, you will generally be able to see and fix the problem easily, especially as you gain experience. Most of the time it is either a typing mistake or a mistake in the structure of a statement. For example, you may not have included all the required arguments in a built-in function you are using or have not included all the required elements in a `For` statement.

Debugging runtime and logical errors generally require finding out where the problem is occurring and then backtracking from there to find the source. In essence, you have to follow the calculations that VBA is doing and the actions it is taking by tracking the values of a few key variables to figure out where things are going wrong. This is where some of the special debugging tools come handy.

MsgBox

As I discussed in the section titled "Simple Debugging" in Chapter 22, the `MsgBox` function is not designed specifically as a debugging tool. However, it can be used as a simple and effective debugging tool. (See the discussion there.)

The most important advantage of using the `MsgBox` is that you do not have to learn and remember anything new. It works fairly well for simple codes. It is not very useful, though, if you need to monitor the values of several variables—especially during the execution of a loop. You will have to keep clicking OK and you may have to keep writing down the values. In such situations, you may want to use the Immediate Window (discussed later) or have your code output (write out) these values on a separate spreadsheet the same way it writes out the values of the output variables.

Breakpoint

I discussed briefly in Chapter 22 how you can insert breakpoints in the code to enter the break mode. To set a breakpoint in your code, in the VBE put your pointer in the gray margin (the left edge of the code window) on the left of a statement at a strategic point in the code and click. The breakpoint will be indicated by a dark circle in the margin and the statement itself will be highlighted. You can also set a breakpoint at any executable statement by putting the cursor on it and then pressing F9 (or clicking the Toggle Breakpoint button on the toolbar). All these methods work as toggles, meaning you can remove a breakpoint by repeating the same steps.

When you run the procedure, execution will be suspended when it gets to the breakpoint and you will be able to see the latest value of any variable that has already been calculated by resting your cursor on it in the code. You can then use hand calculations and other methods to find the problem or decide or decide that the code is working properly up to the current location of the breakpoint. You can run the rest of the code from the breakpoint by clicking the Run Sub button or you can stop execution by clicking the Reset button (on the toolbar).

As we will see soon, however, you also have the option of executing the code one step at a time from that point on, which is often useful. You generally want to put a breakpoint a few steps ahead of the statement that you suspect is causing the problem, examine the values of key variables, and then move step by step toward the suspect statement while monitoring the changing values of the key variables.

You can set as many breakpoints in the code as you want. The advantage is that every time you click Run Sub after execution is suspended at a breakpoint, the code will execute to the next breakpoint and enter break mode again. You can move through large codes quickly by combining such big steps with step-by-step execution.

Stop

The Stop statement is an alternative to breakpoints. Breakpoints remain in effect only during the current session, whereas if you enter a Stop (by itself in a line) in a code it becomes a permanent breakpoint until you remove it. As with breakpoints, executions enter break mode when VBA encounters a Stop statement. Then you can do the same things as you would with breakpoints. In a long code or a code that you are debugging over several sessions, it may be more convenient to use Stop statements instead of breakpoints.

Note that the Stop statement is different from the End statement. When VBA encounters the latter, execution is ended. You cannot restart execution from that point nor can you see the last values of any of the variables because they are automatically reset.

Stepping

If none of the simpler tools discussed so far helps, then you may need to step through the code in order to find the bug. You can step through a code starting either at the beginning or from a point where VBA has entered the break mode. With a little practice you will be able to figure out how you can combine the stepping tools with breakpoints and Stop statements to step through only selected parts of your code. In this way, you will not waste time in stepping line by line through parts that do not seem to have any problems.

To step through the code you may want to use the Debug toolbar. To open it, in VBE select View ⇨ Toolbars and then click Debug. You will use the three buttons on it named Step Into, Step Over, and Step Out.

To see how the tools work, open the code for the loan amortization example we reviewed in Chapter 21: Introduction to VBA. Put the cursor anywhere in the code and click the Step Into button. VBA will highlight the declaration statement (the first line), indicating it is ready to execute that line. Now every time you click Step Into, VBA will execute one statement, highlight it, and stop at the next executable statement. (You can also start stepping when your code is in break mode.)

Click Step Into and line 18 will be highlighted because none of the intermediate lines is executable. Rest your cursor on outRow and a little box will pop up with the message outRow = Empty. This shows that VBA has not executed this statement yet; rather, execution is suspended at this point. Click Step Into again and VBA will execute line 18 and highlight line 19. If you rest your cursor again on outRow again you will see that it now has a value of 5. This is how you can check the current values of all the variables that have been assigned values so far.

You can now keep stepping through the rest of the code, but you have two other options. If you want VBA to execute the code down to a later statement without stopping at each intermediate statement, put your cursor on that statement. Then, on the menu bar select Debug ⇨ Run to Cursor. The intermediate statements will be executed and VBA will highlight and stop at the selected line. (There is no Run to Cursor button on the Debug toolbar.)

The other option is to click the Continue button on the Debug toolbar. VBA will then execute the code down to the next breakpoint or `Stop` (or to the end of the Sub procedure if there is no breakpoint or `Stop`).

You will use the Step Over and Step Out buttons only if your code calls other Sub procedures or Function procedures. If you are confident that a particular Sub procedure or Function procedure is working properly, then you do not need to step through every line of it. When you get to the statement that calls one of them, click Step Over instead of Step Into and VBA will execute the called procedure at normal speed, stopping at the statement that follows the call statement.

If you Step Into a Sub or Function procedure and do not want to go through it step by step beyond a certain point, click the Step Out button to get back to the statement following the calling statement in the calling procedure.

As you saw, you can execute the stepping commands from the Debug toolbar or Debug menu. You can also use their shortcut keys shown in the Debug menu.

Immediate Window

The Immediate Window is one of the special windows available within the VBE that can be used in a few different ways. You may use it to monitor the values of one or more variables as your code runs.

To open the Immediate Window, select View ⇨ Immediate Window or press Ctrl+G. It will open across the bottom of the code window. You can close it by clicking the Close button at the top right corner.

Suppose in the loan amortization example you want to monitor the value of the variable `yrBegBal` as the code runs through the `Do` loop. Enter the following line of code below line 65:

```
Debug.Print "Year beginning balance " & yrBegBal
```

Now run the code and the value of `yrBegBal` with the text from the statement as a label will be printed out in the Immediate Window every time the code runs through the loop. If you are monitoring just one variable then providing the identifying label for it is not necessary. If you are monitoring several variables simultaneously, however, you should add short labels to them as you just did to be able to identify them.

Whether you want to monitor values of variables during debugging using the `MsgBox`, the Immediate Window, or by printing them out to a worksheet is partly a matter of taste and partly a matter of circumstances.

PART Four

Financial Modeling Using VBA

CHAPTER 25

How to Build Good VBA Models

In Chapter 1: Introduction to Financial Analysis and Modeling I discussed the steps one takes to build models using both Excel and VBA and stressed that it is best to start developing good model building habits from the very beginning. In this chapter I cover three important topics that will help you start developing good models efficiently from the beginning. I then conclude with a discussion of how you should work through the models in this book for maximum benefit.

Attributes of Good VBA Models

While VBA models can be widely different from one another, all good ones need to have certain common attributes. In this section I briefly describe the attributes that you should try to build into your models. Some of these apply to Excel models as well. I am including them both here and under Excel so that you can have comprehensive lists of the attributes at both places.

Realistic

Most models you develop will be directly or indirectly used to make some decisions. The output of the model must therefore be realistic. This means that the assumptions, mathematical relationships, and inputs you use in the model must be realistic. For most "real-world" models, making sure of this takes a lot of time and effort, but this is not a place where you should cut corners. If a model does not produce realistic outputs, it does not matter how good its outputs look or how well it works otherwise.

Error-Free

It is equally important that a model be error-free. You must test a model extensively to make sure of this. It is generally much easier to fix a problem when a model just does not work or produces obviously wrong answers. It is much harder to find errors that are more subtle and occur for only certain combinations of input values. See the chapter on debugging for help on making your models error-free.

Flexible

The more different types of question a model can answer, the more useful it is. In the planning stage, you should try to anticipate the different types of questions the model is likely to be used to answer. You then do not have to make major changes every time someone tries to use it for something slightly different.

Easy to Provide Inputs

Most VBA models need inputs from the user, and the easier it is for the user to provide the inputs, the better. Generally a VBA model can get inputs either through input dialog boxes (that is, through the `InputBox` function) or by reading them in from a spreadsheet (or database).

Using input dialog boxes to get input data works well when there are only a few inputs—probably five or less. If the model needs more inputs, it is better to set up an input area in a spreadsheet (or, for large models, even a separate input spreadsheet) where the user can enter the input data before running the model. This approach is particularly helpful if the user is likely to change only one or two inputs from one run to the next. If a model uses a large number of input dialog boxes, the user will have to enter data in each of them every time he runs the model—even if he wants to change only one or two inputs. However, if the user has to provide some input (based on some intermediate outputs) while a procedure is running, then using input dialog boxes is the only option.

If the model uses input dialog boxes, the prompt should provide enough specific information to help the user enter the right data in the right format. Similarly, if the input data is to be provided in certain cells in a spreadsheet, then there should be enough information in the next cell (or nearby) to help the user enter the right data in the right format.

Good Output Production

A model that does not produce good outputs to get its major results across persuasively is not as useful as it can be. Producing reports with VBA models is generally a two-step process: the model produces outputs on spreadsheets and then parts or all of the spreadsheets have to be printed out. For printed outputs good models should include built-in reports (in Excel) that any user can produce easily. The spreadsheet outputs produced by a VBA model should be such that they do not require too much manipulation before creating printed reports. These reports should be attractive, easy to read, and uncluttered. Avoid trying to squeeze in too much information on one page. If a report has to include a lot of data, organize it in layers so that people can start by looking at summary results and then dig into additional details as necessary.

One of the advantages of VBA compared to other programming languages is that it can produce excellent graphical outputs using Excel's charting features. VBA models should include graphical outputs wherever they will enhance the usefulness of the models.

Another thing to keep in mind is that unlike an Excel model, the VBA model does not show intermediate results (unless either through message boxes or through spreadsheet outputs or charts). The modeler should therefore anticipate what output—intermediate and final—the user may want to see and provide for them in the model.

Data Validations

It is generally more important to provide thorough data validation in VBA models than it is in Excel models. If the user accidentally enters invalid data, most of the time the model simply will not run, but it will not provide any useful information on what the problem is and leave the user in a helpless situation.

You can, of course, have the VBA code check input data for various possible errors before using them. A simple alternate approach is to have the input data read in from spreadsheets and provide data validation to the input cells on the spreadsheet using Excel's Data Validation feature. (To keep the codes short and to avoid repeating the same lines of codes, I have generally omitted data validation in the models in this book. Instead of writing data validation codes repeatedly, you can create and keep a few Sub procedures for the type of data validation you need to do for the type of models you work with most often and call them as needed.)

Judicious Formatting

The formatting here refers to formatting of the model's output. Poor, haphazard formatting reduces a model's usefulness because it is distracting. Use formatting (fonts, borders, patterns, colors, etc.) judiciously to make your model's outputs easier to understand and use. (As much as possible, create the formatting parts of the code by recording them with the Macro Recorder.)

Appropriate Numbers Formatting

In the model's outputs, you should format numbers with the minimum number of decimal points necessary. Using too many decimal points makes numbers difficult to read and often gives a false sense of precision as well. Make the formatting of similar numbers uniform throughout the output. (Remember that displaying numbers with fewer decimal points does not reduce the accuracy of the model in any way because internally Excel and VBA continue using the same number of significant digits.)

Wherever appropriate make numbers more readable by using special formatting to show them in thousands or millions.

Well Organized and Easy to Follow

The better organized a model is, the easier it is to follow and update.

The key to making your code organized is to break it down into segments, each of which carry out one distinct activity or set of computations. One way to accomplish this is to use separate Sub procedures and Function procedures for many of such segments, especially the ones that will be repeated many times. In the extreme, the main Sub procedure may simply consist of calls to other Sub procedures and Function procedures. An additional advantage of this approach is that you can develop a number of Sub procedures and Function procedures to do things that you often need to do and incorporate them in other codes as needed. (For more on this, see the section "Why Call Sub Procedures?" in Chapter 23: Sub and Function Procedures.)

Using structured programming also makes a code easier to follow. In a structured program, the procedure is segmented into a number of stand-alone units, each of which has only one entry and one exit point. Control does not jump into or exit from the middle of these units.

The proper visual design of a code can also make it easier to follow. For example, statements should be properly indented to show clearly how they fit into the various `If`, `For`, and other structures. Similarly, each major and minor segment of the code should be separated by blank lines and other means and informatively labeled. (The easiest way to learn these techniques is by imitating well-written codes.)

Statements Are Easy to Read and Understand

Experienced programmers try to make their codes as concise as possible, often using obscure features of the programming language. Such codes may be admired by other experienced programmers, but they often baffle beginners.

With the high speed of modern PCs, codes do not usually have to be concise or highly efficient. It is best to aim for codes that are easy to understand, even if that means that it has more lines of code than is absolutely necessary.

Avoid writing long equations whenever you can. Break them up by doing long calculations in easily understandable steps.

Make all variable names short but descriptive and not cryptic. If in a large model you decide to use a naming scheme, try to make it intuitive and provide an explanation of the scheme in the documentations.

Robust

"Robust" here refers to a code that is resistant to "crashing." It often takes significant extra work to make a code "bulletproof," and that time and effort may not be justified for many of the codes you will write. Nonetheless, the code should guard against obvious problems. For example, unless specified otherwise, a VBA code always works with the currently active spreadsheet. So throughout a code you should make sure that the right worksheet is active at the right time or else precede cell addresses, and so on, by the appropriate worksheet reference.

Using effective data validation for the input data is another way of making your code robust.

Minimum Hard Coding

Hard-coded values are difficult to change, especially in large models because there is always the danger of missing them in a few places. It is best to set up any value that may have to be changed later as a variable and use the variable in all equations.

Even for values that are not going to change it is better to define and use constants. Then use them in the equations. This makes equations easier to read and guards against possible mistakes of typing in the wrong number.

Good Documentation

Good documentation is key to understanding VBA models and is a must for all but trivial ones. For hints on producing good documentation, see the next section.

Documenting VBA Models

Documenting a model means putting in writing, diagrams, flowcharts, and so on, the information someone else (or you in the future) will need to figure out what a model does, how it is structured, what assumptions are built into it, and so forth. A user can then make changes to (update) it if necessary. It should also include, for example, notes on any shortcuts you may have taken for now that should be fixed later and any assumptions or data you have used now that may need to be updated later.

There is no standard format or structure for documenting a model. You have to be guided by the objectives mentioned above. Here are some common approaches to documenting your VBA models. Every model needs to be documented differently and everyone does documentation differently. Over time you will develop your own style.

Including Comments in the Code

The most useful documenting tool in VBA is comments. Comments are notes and reminders you include at various places in the VBA code. You indicate a comment by an apostrophe. Except when it occurs in texts within quotation marks, VBA interprets an apostrophe as the beginning of a comment and ignores the rest of the line. You can use an entire line or blocks of line for comments or you can put a comment after a statement in a line (for example, to explain something about the statement).

You should include in your code all the comments that may be helpful, but do not go overboard and include comments to explain things that are obvious. Including a lot of superfluous comments can make codes harder rather than easier to read. Here are some ideas on what types of comments you may want to include in your code:

- At the beginning of a procedure include a brief description of what the code does. At times it may also be useful to list the key inputs and outputs and some other information as well.
- Every time significant changes are made to the code, insert comments near the beginning of the code below the code description to keep track of the change date, the important changes made at that time, and who made the changes. Sometimes it also helps to insert additional comments above or next to the statement(s) that has been changed to explain what was changed and why. Also record who made the change and when.
- If the procedure uses a particular variable naming scheme, then use comments to explain it.
- Use distinctive comment lines (for example, '*********) to break down long procedures into sections, and at the beginning of each section include a short name or description of the section.
- Use comments next to a variable to explain what it stands for, where its value came from, and anything else that may be helpful.
- You can get more ideas about what kind of comments to include in your code from the examples in this and other books. Over time you will develop your own style of providing comments in code.

Make sure you insert comments as you code. If you put it off until later, your comments may not be as useful, inserting them may take longer because you may have to spend time trying to remember things, and worst of all, you may never get around to it. If you do not include good comments in your code, modifying it a few months later may take much longer.

Documenting Larger Models

If you are developing a large model and saving different versions of the workbook as I have suggested, then the workbook should include a worksheet titled

"Version Description." In this worksheet, list against each version number the major changes you made to the code in that version. Every time you save your work under a new version name, start a new row of description under that version number in the Version Description worksheet and keep adding to it as you make major changes. The key is to do this as you go along and not wait until later when you may forget some of the changes you made. This is essentially the history (log) of the model's development. If you ever want to go back to an earlier stage and go in a different direction from there, the log will save you a lot of time. Also, you may want to have several different versions of a model. You can document here how they differ from each other.

For large models, you may also need to create a book of formal documentation (which will include information on why and how certain modeling decisions were made, flow charts for the model, etc.) and a user's manual. For most of your work, however, documentation of the type I discussed should be adequate.

Learning Modeling Using VBA

You will learn to model with VBA faster if you systematically work through the models in the following chapters of Part Four instead of just browsing through the codes. (For each model there is a workbook on the CD with all the necessary data, the outputs, and the VBA codes.)

I also believe you can learn modeling with VBA faster if you start with problems for which you have already developed Excel models. Then you do not get bogged down in the finance and mathematics of the problem and can focus on the VBA aspect of it. For any chapter you have already worked through the models in the corresponding chapter in Part Two, you can go straight to the models. Otherwise, you may want to first go through the "Review of Theory and Concepts" section of the corresponding chapter in Part Two and even the Excel models. It depends on how comfortable you are with the topic.

SKETCHING THE VBA CODE

In Excel models, the modeler does not have to specify in what order Excel will execute the model; Excel figures it out on its own. A VBA code is different. VBA will execute a code in order except when the programmer asks it to do otherwise using `If` statements, loops, and so on. It is therefore advisable, if not essential, that you create a sketch of the VBA model before starting to write codes. Large, complex models require preparing elaborate flow charts with lots of details. For simpler models you should try to visualize the major blocks of your code, write down briefly what each block of code will do, and decide in what order the blocks should be included in the code. (This is part of Step 5 in the steps I discussed for creating models.)

THE THREE LEARNING TRACKS

You can follow three different Learning Tracks (LT) of decreasing degree of difficulty—LT 1 (most challenging) to LT 3 (least challenging)—to work through the models in the following chapters. The more challenging a track you choose, the faster you will learn. However, for everyone but those who have some previous experience in writing VBA code, LT 1 and LT 2 maybe too difficult and frustrating. If you are new to VBA, start by following LT 3 for your first few models, and as you gain experience try to move onto LT 2 and LT 1.

All models can be structured in many different ways. While simple VBA codes written by two different programmers may be quite similar, their coding for more complex models will be very different and will reflect their personal coding styles. I encourage you to develop your own coding style over time. In the beginning, however, you should structure your models more or less along the lines of the examples so that you will start to learn good coding practices and pick up good coding habits.

No matter which learning track you choose, in developing a model you should always follow the modeling steps of the process I discussed in Chapter 1: Introduction to Financial Analysis and Modeling. The following descriptions of each track primarily relate to Step 6 of that process. Also, work on the models in the order I have included them in each chapter because the later models in a chapter often build on the codes of the earlier models.

Learning Track 1 (Most Challenging)

Read the problem statement thoroughly and then try to develop the model on your own following the modeling steps I discussed in Chapter 1: Introduction to Financial Analysis and Modeling. If necessary, review the corresponding Excel model (if there is one) and refer to the Review of Theory and Concepts. If the model requires data, copy the data into a new workbook and then develop the model in it. If after trying for a while you have difficulty getting started, take a look at the structure of the sample code, but do not look at the details of the statements unless you are stuck.

After you have completed the model and have thoroughly tested and debugged it, compare it with the sample code. If any part of the sample code is not clear, refer to the explanation of it in the "Analysis of the Code" section. For at least the first number of models, you should go through the analysis of the code. It may include suggestions and explanations that you did not consider.

Learning Track 2

Read the problem statement thoroughly, make a copy of the model's workbook, and in it clear everything other than any necessary data and the titles, heading, labels, and so on, of the input and output worksheets. You can use the latter as formatted output worksheets or you can use them for guidance in structuring the model and writing code. Read the "Modeling Strategy" section of the model; if necessary, review the corresponding Excel model (if there is one) and refer to the Review of Theory and Concepts. Finally try to write the code for the model. If after trying for a while you have difficulty getting started, take a look at the structure of the sample code, but do not look at the details of the statement unless you are stuck.

After you have completed the model and have thoroughly tested and debugged it, compare it with the sample code. If any part of the sample code is not clear, refer to the explanation of it in the "Analysis of the Code" section. For at least the first number of models, you should go through the analysis of the code because it may include suggestions and explanations that you did not consider.

Learning Track 3 (Least Challenging)

Read the Problem statement and the Modeling Strategy. Then make a copy of the model from the CD and go through the code step by step using the explanations in the "Analysis of the Code" section.

Once you fully understand the code, start with a new workbook, copy any necessary input data into it, and write the entire code on your own. Then run it, test it, and debug it. This step is absolutely essential. You are not going to learn how to create VBA models by just reading someone else's code. Also remember that the more you think through and try to fully understand the "why" of each step, the faster you will learn.

CHAPTER **26**

Time Value of Money

In this chapter we will develop several models for time value of money problems using VBA. These models are important because time value of money problems are probably the most common type of problems in finance. But the models in this chapter are important for another reason. The early ones are designed to provide a practical introduction to the most common aspects of VBA. I use them to demonstrate how you utilize many of the features of VBA we discussed earlier to write procedures and create actual models.

I have already discussed the underlying theory and concepts for time value of money problems in the parallel chapter in the Excel part of the book, Chapter 14: Time Value of Money. If you have not covered that chapter yet, you may want to do so before tackling this one. The only new concept I discuss here is the concept of iteration.

Review of Theory and Concepts

A good part of the power of any programming language derives from its ability to solve problems using the method of iteration. It is therefore important to learn both the concept of iteration and how to apply it to solve practical problems.

SOLVING PROBLEMS BY ITERATION

Solving a problem by iteration means solving it by systematic trial and error. There are many problems in finance for which it is not possible to write the variable we want to calculate explicitly in terms of the other variables of the problem, even though we know the relationships among them. In such cases, we have to find the answers by iteration.

For example, we can write the following equation to calculate the NPV of a series of cash flows:

$$NPV = \sum_{t=0}^{t=n} \frac{CF_t}{(1+r)^t}$$

If we know the cash flows and the discount rate, we can easily calculate the NPV. However, we cannot solve this equation explicitly for r to directly calculate the discount rate at which the present value of a given series of cash flows equals a specified NPV. Instead, we have to calculate the value on the right-hand side for many different trial values of r until we find the value of r that produces the target NPV. This is solving the equation by iteration.

The type of problems you can solve using iteration is not limited to the ones for which you can write an equation like the one for NPV. For example, if you are doing financial planning for a company and have modeled the future financial statements, then you can use iteration to find what sales growth rate will be necessary to reduce debt to a certain level. Another way of looking at it is to recognize that any problem you can solve using Goal Seek can be solved using iteration as well—Goal Seek itself uses iteration.

If you try different values of r at random in our example, it may take a long time to find the answer—or you may never find it. To get to an answer that is accurate to a specified margin of error quickly, the iteration has to be a systematic search for the answer. A number of sophisticated mathematical techniques are available to do fast systematic searches, and I will describe one of them later. However, because modern computers can do computations very fast, we can often devise intuitive iteration methods that work quite well, and it is useful to understand how you devise such methods.

The Intuitive Approach

To do a systematic search for an answer, we need to start with a guess for the answer, a step size by which we will change the guess in each iteration to get closer to the answer, and a measure of how accurate we want the answer to be.

It is easier to understand the iteration process with an example. Let us say we want to calculate the internal rate of return, IRR, for a series of cash flows. This means that in the earlier equation for NPV, we have to find the discount rate for which the NPV is zero. If we represent the right-hand side of the equation as $f(r)$, then the equation becomes NPV $= f(r)$ and we have to find the r for which $f(r) = 0$. This is also called finding the roots of the equation because r is called a root. (An equation may have more than one root, although we may be interested in only the one that falls within a particular range.)

We will start by substituting our initial guess for r, say r_0, in the function and calculate its value. If the value is positive, we may guess that we need a higher r. We can then try $r_1 = r_0 + h$, where h is the chosen step size, and calculate the value of $f(r_1)$. If the value is still positive but smaller than the previous value then we will keep taking forward steps until we get a negative value for $f(r)$. The IRR will be somewhere between the last two values of r we try, and we can take either value or their average as the answer. (Note that here we are assuming that we will start with a value of r that is smaller than the IRR, which will produce a positive NPV, and as we try larger and larger values of r, the NPV will get smaller. In some problems, things are reversed and then we have to reduce instead of increase the trial value in each step.)

This simple approach has two problems. First, it may not produce as accurate an answer as we want. If our step size is, say, 0.1%, then we will get an answer that is within 0.1% of the actual IRR. If we want an answer that is accurate to within 0.01%, we will have to make the step size that small, and that will require about 10 times as many iterations. Second, the further our initial guess is from the actual IRR, the more iterations we will need to get to the answer, and smaller steps will further increase the required number of iterations.

Intuitively we can see that we will get to the answer faster if we can start with an initial guess that is closer to the answer and use step sizes that are large in the beginning and get smaller as we get closer to the answer.

If we use step sizes that get smaller with each iteration, we also have to provide some measure of the accuracy we want to achieve. In this example, we may specify that we will stop the iteration when the NPV gets to less than $1, or we can specify that we will stop when the step size becomes smaller than 0.01%.

How good an initial guess and scheme for adjusting the step size we can come up with often depends on our understanding of the problem. In some situations we may not be able to come up with a scheme for adjusting the step size that will get us to the answer with the desired accuracy.

The reality is that with modern PCs, for most problems each calculation of $f(r)$ takes almost no time and you can get away with specifying almost any reasonable initial guess and a very small constant step size. Only when you have a problem where each calculation of $f(r)$ takes some time (or you are going to solve the problem hundreds or even thousands of times for different sets of values for the other variables) will you need to find an intuitive way to find a good initial guess. Even more important is a good scheme for adjusting the step size for successive iterations. We will see an example of this in one of the models we develop.

The Bisection Method

This is a popular and conceptually simple mathematical method for iteration that gets to an answer quickly using the concept of starting with a relatively large step and reducing the step size as we get closer to the answer. It is a two-stage method;

in the first stage, the relatively large step size remains constant and in the second stage, the step size is halved (bisected, hence the name) with each iteration.

Even though this is a conceptually simple method, in the beginning some people find it a little confusing. If you do not quite understand it in your first reading through the following description, it will become clear when we develop a model later using this method.

This method works with two guesses at a time instead of one, although in each step we change only one of the guesses. In the first stage, the objective is to quickly find two guesses such that the actual answer lies in the interval between them.

For example, let us assume that in our IRR example, the actual answer is 6.55%, our initial guess is 3%, and the initial step size is 1%. We will first try 3% and 3% + 1% = 4% as our initial pair of guesses; we will have to decide whether the answer lies in this interval or not. How do we do this? We can calculate the NPV for both 3% and 4%, and in this case both of these will be positive because both guesses are smaller than the actual answer of 6.55%. Once we realize through this calculation that the answer does not lie in this interval, we will make 4% to 4% + 1% = 5% our new interval and we will ask the same question again. With two more tries we will conclude that the answer lies between 6% and 7% because for 6% the NPV will be positive but for 7% it will be negative. This is the end of the first stage.

Since the objective of the first stage is to rapidly find an interval that contains the answer, and the size of the interval does not matter much, here we can use a fairly large step, and the step remains constant until we get to the end of the first stage. As a matter of fact, using too small a step in this stage can slow things down.

Then comes stage two. In this stage in each iteration, we halve the interval between the two guesses (that is, pick a new guess that is halfway in-between) for each iteration, find which of the two newly created intervals contains the answer, halve that interval again, and keep repeating the process.

In our example where the two guesses at the end of the first stage are 6% and 7%, we will use a new guess of 6.5% and ask the question "Does the answer lie between 6% and 6.5% or between 6.5% and 7%?" To answer this question we will calculate the NPV for 6.5%, which will be positive, and from our previous calculation we will already know that the NPV for 7% is negative. This will tell us that the answer lies between 6.5% and 7%, and we will then try a new guess of 6.75% and ask the same question again.

In order for this method to work, at every step we have to make sure that the answer is in the interval we are choosing to keep. We choose it by requiring that the values of the function (NPV here) have opposite signs at the two ends of the interval. We generally check this by multiplying the values of the function at the two ends of an interval: In other words, if we multiply the values at the two ends of an interval and get a positive number then the answer does not lie in that interval. If we get a negative number, then the answer lies in that interval. This is the criterion used in programming the bisection method.

Since we cut the step size and, therefore, the length of the interval in half in each step of stage two, the interval rapidly gets smaller with each iteration and we get closer to the answer because it is contained in that interval. Whenever we stop we can take either of the latest two guesses or their average as the answer. The maximum error at any step will be equal to the size of the latest interval. We can stop the iteration when it gets smaller than our desired margin of error.

Using Excel's Goal Seek

You can also use Goal Seek to solve the same type of problems without knowing much about iteration. In this case, though, all the formulas necessary to calculate the target dependent variable for different values of the independent variable must be in the worksheet and cannot be in your VBA code. We will see how you can create these formulas in the worksheet using VBA, although using Goal Seek may not be the best way to solve the problem if you are not going to create the formulas in the worksheet anyway.

We saw before that another problem of using Goal Seek in Excel models is that you cannot automate its use by embedding it in a formula in the worksheet. It has to be used manually, and a user who does not know how to use Goal Seek will not be able to use the model. As we will see, you can program Goal Seek into a VBA model that the user can run and he will not even have to know that he is using Goal Seek.

Modeling Examples

The models in this chapter are designed to provide a solid introduction to VBA. They demonstrate how to use many of the features of VBA we discussed earlier to write procedures and create actual models. We want to keep our focus on learning VBA instead of getting distracted by the complexities of the underlying financial theory or mathematics. As such, all of these models handle the same problem of creating a loan amortization table and use it to calculate the required equal periodic payments for an amortizing loan. We developed several versions of this model in Excel and we looked at the basic version of it in VBA in Chapter 21: Introduction to VBA. So you are already familiar with the theory and the general outline of such models. The different versions deliberately use different features of VBA to demonstrate how some of the most common features of VBA work. I recommend that you study them carefully and then try to reproduce them on your own, making modifications and improvements of your own design.

	1	2	3	4	5	6	7	8
1	**Input Data**							
2	Interest rate (% per year)	10%						
3	Loan life (years)	10						
4	Initial loan balance ($)	$100,000						
5								
6			Year	Year-beg	Annual	Interest	Principal	Year-end
7				Balance	Payment	Component	Repaid	Balance
8								
9			1	$100,000	$16,275	$10,000	$6,275	$93,725
10			2	$93,725	$16,275	$9,373	$6,902	$86,823
11			3	$86,823	$16,275	$8,682	$7,592	$79,231
12			4	$79,231	$16,275	$7,923	$8,351	$70,880
13			5	$70,880	$16,275	$7,088	$9,187	$61,693
14			6	$61,693	$16,275	$6,169	$10,105	$51,588
15			7	$51,588	$16,275	$5,159	$11,116	$40,472
16			8	$40,472	$16,275	$4,047	$12,227	$28,245
17			9	$28,245	$16,275	$2,825	$13,450	$14,795
18			10	$14,795	$16,275	$1,480	$14,795	$0
19								
20								
21								

FIGURE 26.1 Model 1: Loan amortization table using Pmt function.

As I introduce new VBA features, I discuss them here only briefly. Please refer to Chapter 22: VBA Essentials, for more details as necessary.

MODEL 1: LOAN AMORTIZATION TABLE, VERSION 1

The Problem

Create a model to produce an amortization table for a fixed rate loan. The loan is to be repaid in equal annual installments over its life and the first payment is to be made at the end of the first year. Use dialog boxes to get the user inputs. The program should validate the user input for reasonableness and ask the user to modify any input that is not appropriate. For output, use a worksheet predesigned with the necessary labels, table headings, formatting, and so on. The output sheet should look like Figure 26.1.

Modeling Strategy

This model is similar to the one we looked at in Chapter 21: Introduction to VBA. One difference is that instead of having the user input data in the worksheet, which the program then reads in, this model uses the `InputBox` function to get user data through input dialog boxes. Also, if an input fails validation, instead of stopping as before, the program will tell the user why the data is unacceptable and ask him to enter new data.

The Code for the Model

```
Option Explicit
Sub Loan_Amort_V1()

' This program creates a year-by-year repayment
' schedule for a fixed rate loan that is to be repaid in
' equal annual installments payable at the end of each year.
' It uses the Pmt function to calculate the annual payment.
' The worksheet must already have proper headings and labels;
' the program does not create them or do their formatting.

Dim intRate, initLoanAmnt, loanLife
Dim yrBegBal, yrEndBal
Dim annualPmnt, intComp, princRepay
Dim outRow, rowNum, outSheet

'***********************************************************
' Programmer inputs
'***********************************************************
outRow = 5 'Used to control where the output table will start
outSheet = "Loan Amort"

Worksheets(outSheet).Activate

'Clear previous data
Rows(outRow + 4 & ":" & outRow + 300).Select
Selection.Clear
Range("B2:B4").Select
Selection.ClearContents

'***********************************************************
'Get user inputs
'***********************************************************
' The user provides these input data through dialog boxes.
' Input data not meeting specified criteria are not accepted

Do
   intRate = InputBox("Enter interest rate in percent" _
    & " without % sign. It must be between 0% and 15%")

   If intRate < 0 Or intRate > 15 Then
      MsgBox ("Int. rate must be between 0% and 15%.")
   Else
      Exit Do
   End If
Loop
```

```
intRate = intRate / 100

Do
    loanLife = InputBox("Enter loan life in years." _
     & " Loan life must be a whole number.")

    If loanLife < 0 Or (loanLife - Round(loanLife) <> 0) Then
     MsgBox ("Loan life must be a whole number.")
    Else
       Exit Do
    End If
Loop

GetLoanAmnt:
initLoanAmnt = InputBox("Enter loan amount." _
  & " Loan amount must be a positive whole number.")

If initLoanAmnt < 0 Or (initLoanAmnt - Round(initLoanAmnt) _
  <> 0) Then
    MsgBox ("Loan amount must be a positive whole number.")
    GoTo GetLoanAmnt
End If

'**********************************************************
' Write out the input data on the output sheet
'**********************************************************
Cells(2, 2).Value = intRate
Cells(3, 2).Value = loanLife
Cells(4, 2).Value = initLoanAmnt

'**********************************************************
' Compute and output results
'**********************************************************
' Calculate annual payment
annualPmnt = Pmt(intRate, loanLife, -initLoanAmnt,, 0)

' Initialize beginning balance for year 1
yrBegBal = initLoanAmnt

' Loop to calculate and output year-by-year amort. table
For rowNum = 1 To loanLife

    intComp = yrBegBal * intRate
    princRepay = annualPmnt - intComp
    yrEndBal = yrBegBal - princRepay

```

```
93:        Cells(outRow + rowNum + 3, 3).Value = rowNum 'Year number
94:        Cells(outRow + rowNum + 3, 4).Value = yrBegBal
95:        Cells(outRow + rowNum + 3, 5).Value = annualPmnt
96:        Cells(outRow + rowNum + 3, 6).Value = intComp
97:        Cells(outRow + rowNum + 3, 7).Value = princRepay
98:        Cells(outRow + rowNum + 3, 8).Value = yrEndBal
99:
100:       yrBegBal = yrEndBal
101:
102:    Next rowNum
103:
104:    '**********************************************************
105:    ' Format the output data in the table
106:    '**********************************************************
107:    Range(Cells(outRow + 4, 4), Cells(outRow + loanLife + 3, 8) _
108:      ).Select
109:    Selection.NumberFormat = "$#,##0"
110:
111:    End Sub
```

Analysis of the Code

(If you are in front of your computer, you may find it easier to refer to the actual code in the VBE as you follow the analysis of the code instead of in the listing here. However, you cannot get VBA to show the line numbers in VBE next to each line. To see the line number of any line you have to put your cursor in the line and look in the middle area of the tool bar.)

Line 1: You can either type in Option Explicit as the first line in a module or, if you have the appropriate option turned on, VBA itself will add this line to all new modules. Once Option Explicit is specified, VBA requires that all variables be declared, generally using a `Dim` statement. As we discussed earlier, even if you decide to leave all variables as `Variant` data type, you can catch a lot of your typing errors by naming variables with one or more embedded capital letters if you specify Option Explicit. I recommend that you always use this feature.

Line 2: Required `Sub` declaration statement.

Line 3: Blank line to make code more readable. VBA ignores blank lines.

Lines 4–9: Brief description of the program using comment lines.

Lines 11–14: `Dim` statements with related variables grouped under separate `Dim` statements. If we want to declare the data type for any variable, this is where it has to be done. Since I have not done so for any of the variables, VBA makes all of them `Variant` data type, that is, they can hold any type of data.

Lines 16–26: Essentially the same as the previous model.

Lines 27–28: Clears the range B2:B4 in the output sheet because instead of reading in input data from here, the code will later enter into these cells the inputs data that the user provides through dialog boxes. Line 27 selects the range and line 28 clears the contents of the selection. VBA will not let you do this using a single statement like `Range("B2:B4").ClearContents`.

Lines 36–45: This is a `Do...Loop` that does two things. First, in lines 37–38 it uses the `InputBox` function to ask for the interest rate input using a dialog box. The only argument of the function I have used is the prompt that is displayed in the dialog box to help the user. (To keep the code lines short, I had to split the prompt into two parts and connect them with the concatenation operator `&`. VBA does not allow the use of a line continuation sign inside quotation marks.) The `InputBox` function takes a few more arguments that you can use to further customize it. The input the user provides is assigned to the variable `intRate`.

Second, lines 40–44 contain an `If...Else...End If` structure that does data validation. If the interest rate is lower than 0% or higher than 15%, then control enters the `True` leg of the `If` structure, executes the `MsgBox`, and generates a dialog box to alert the user that the data falls outside the acceptable range. When the user clicks OK in the dialog box, control jumps to the `Loop` statement in line 45 and the `Do` loop is repeated giving the user another chance to enter the interest rate. On the other hand, if the interest rate is within the acceptable range, control transfers to the `Else` in line 42 and then executes the `Exit Do` statement in the next line. This transfers control to line 47 (because line 46 is blank), ending the `Do` loop.

Line 47: Here I divide the interest rate in percent by 100 to express it in decimals for use in later calculations. Remember that the equals sign stands for assignment: the value calculated on the right is assigned to the variable on the left.

Lines 49–58: Another `Do...Loop` structure similar to the one in lines 36–45. It gets the life of the loan from the user and validates it. Here I want to make sure that the loan life entered is a positive whole number. I check for this in line 53 where I use the `Round` function to round the `loanLife` the user enters. If the loan life entered is negative or `loanLife - Round(loanLife)` is not equal to zero (<> stands for "not equal to"), indicating that the `loanLife` entered is not a whole number, control will enter the `True` leg of the `If` structure. If the loan life is acceptable, then control will transfer to the `Else` statement. After that, things work as in the previous `Do` loop. Note this simple way to check whether a number is a whole number. You will probably use it often.

Lines 60–68: I am using the code here to get the value for the initial loan amount and validate it. This slightly different approach simply demonstrates an alternative.

Line 60: This is a label. When control gets here, it just moves on to the next line.

Lines 61–62: Used to get the initial loan amount from the user.

Lines 64–68: I am using this `If` structure to check the initial loan amount for the same criteria I used for loan life, although there is no reason why the initial loan amount has to be a whole number. The data is checked in line 64 and if it is acceptable control jumps to line 69 beyond the end of the `If` structure and goes on from there. If the data is not acceptable, control will enter the `If` structure, generate a warning message box, and then in line 67 it will follow the instruction to jump back to line 60 because that has the indicated label.

Some people, especially beginners, often find using the combination of `GoTo` statements and labels to be a simpler way to control program flow than using the `Do` loops, `For` loops, or other formal structures. In all but short programs like this one, however, it is preferable to use the more formal structures because they make programs easier to understand.

Lines 73–75: These lines write out the input values that the user entered into the appropriate cells in the output worksheet.

Line 77–111: The rest of the program is the same as the version I discussed in Chapter 21: Introduction to VBA.

Testing the Model

To test the model, run it and enter both acceptable and unacceptable input values to make sure that the program forces you to change unacceptable data. Then look at the output worksheet to check that the program is writing out the correct input values in the appropriate cells. To check if the numbers in the amortization table are correct, run the program with some simple numbers like the ones I have used in the example. Check to see that the final balance is zero. If not, the program is not working properly. Then check the numbers in the different columns to make sure that they make sense, because sometimes the columns can get interchanged. For example, if you are using an interest rate of 10%, you can easily see if the number in the Interest Component column is 10% of the number in the Year-beginning Balance column for the same year. The numbers in the Annual Payment column should be the same for all years, and the numbers in the Principal Repaid column in each year should equal the annual payment minus the interest component. Finally, the year-beginning balance for each year should equal the year-end balance for the previous year.

Although in this program changing the inputs should not affect the program's running, you should test it by running the program with a few different sets of inputs.

Modifying the Program

You can easily modify the program to handle loans with monthly payments and create a monthly amortization table. To do so, you only need to multiply the `loanLife` by 12 and divide the `intRate` by 12. But where in the program should you make these modifications? You may be tempted to do each one right after the corresponding input has been validated. For example, you may want to divide the right-hand side of the statement in line 47 by 12. If you do so, however, then when in line 73 the program writes out the interest rate in the output worksheet, it will write out the monthly interest rate number, which the user may not recognize. You have to always remember that at every stage the computer works with the latest value of a variable. Where in a program you change a variable's value therefore matters a great deal.

In this case, you can add the following two lines after line 75.

```
intRate = intRate / 12
loanLife = loanLife * 12
```

What else do you have to do? You need to change the description of the program in the initial comment lines, change some of the headings in the output table, and in lines 25–26, you may want to clear 500 instead of 300 rows because a monthly amortization table will have many more rows of data. It is important to keep in mind that whenever you modify a program you must carefully check to make sure that you have made all the necessary changes and not just the obvious ones.

Adding Table Headings, Labels, and So On

So far in this model we worked with a worksheet that already has the necessary labels (for example, in the input area), table headings, and so on, entered and properly formatted. How would you change the program if we wanted it to enter the labels, headings, and so on, and do all the formatting as well so that we can start with a blank worksheet?

This is relatively easy to do with the help of the Macro Recorder. Go to a blank worksheet, turn on the Macro Recorder, and then enter the labels (for example, enter "Input Data" in A1), headings, and so on, and do all the formatting you want to do exactly the way you would have done it for setting up the worksheet. When you are done, stop the recorder and find the module in the VBE where VBA recorded your macro. You can then copy the relevant portion of the code from this macro and append it to the program we had before.

Let us now look at this closely. Module2 in this model's workbook has the macro I recorded for this purpose. I will not go into the line-by-line details here because most of them are obvious; if you do not fully understand all of the details it will not matter greatly. It is precisely because you do not need to or want to get into the details of writing code for formatting, and so on, that you use the Macro Recorder to do them for you. Here is the broad outline of the macro. (Refer to it in VBE.)

Lines 11–40: Code to enter the labels and headings.

Lines 42–44: Code to bold the text in the appropriate cells.

Lines 45–53: Ignore.

Lines 54–58: Code to set column widths.

Lines 58–67: Code to format the numbers in the different cells.

For practice you should record your own macro, but you do not have to do things in the same sequence.

To add this macro to the original program, copy the entire original program into a new module (Module3 here), rename it, delete lines 107–109 (which were being used to format the data in the table), and then append below line 106 the entire working portion of the code (lines 11–67) from the recorded macro.

To make sure that the new program works, you need to test it on a blank sheet. To do this, add a new sheet to the workbook, say, Sheet1. In line 20 of the code, change the name of the worksheet to Sheet1 and then run the program.

Note that I have modified the comments at the beginning of this new program and also changed the comment in line 105 to reflect the changes I have made. You should always remember to make such changes as you modify a program and not put them off until later.

MODEL 2: LOAN AMORTIZATION TABLE, VERSION 2

The Problem

Create a model to produce an amortization table for a fixed rate loan. The loan is to be repaid in equal annual installments over its life and the first payment is to be made at the end of the first year. Determine the required annual payment amount by iteration instead of using VBA's `Pmt` function. The output sheet should look like Figure 26.2 and show the number of iterations used to arrive at the solution.

Modeling Strategy

In this model you will learn how to use iteration to solve a problem. You want to determine the constant annual payment that will pay off the loan at the end of its

	1	2	3	4	5	6	7	8
1	**Input Data**							
2	Interest rate (% per year)	10%						
3	Loan life (years)	10						
4	Initial loan balance ($)	$100,000						
5								
6			**Year**	**Year-beg**	**Annual**	**Interest**	**Principal**	**Year-end**
7				**Balance**	**Payment**	**Component**	**Repaid**	**Balance**
8								
9			1	$100,000	$16,300	$10,000	$6,300	$93,700
10			2	$93,700	$16,300	$9,370	$6,930	$86,770
11			3	$86,770	$16,300	$8,677	$7,623	$79,147
12			4	$79,147	$16,300	$7,915	$8,385	$70,762
13			5	$70,762	$16,300	$7,076	$9,224	$61,538
14			6	$61,538	$16,300	$6,154	$10,146	$51,392
15			7	$51,392	$16,300	$5,139	$11,161	$40,231
16			8	$40,231	$16,300	$4,023	$12,277	$27,954
17			9	$27,954	$16,300	$2,795	$13,505	$14,449
18			10	$14,449	$16,300	$1,445	$14,855	-$406
19								
20								
21								
22	No. of iterations =	64						
23								
24								

FIGURE 26.2 Model 2: Loan amortization table using simple iteration.

life. Start with a guess for the annual payment, and do the necessary calculations to see how much (if any) balance remains unpaid at the end of the loan life. If there is a residual balance, increase the guess by a predetermined amount, and try again. Repeat the process until you find the annual payment for which the final loan balance becomes zero or negative.

Although ideally you want the final balance to equal zero, it is rather difficult to achieve this. To keep things simple for now, start with an initial guess that you know for sure is less than the actual required payment so that the remaining final balance for the first iteration will definitely be positive. You can use an initial guess for annual payment equal to the loan amount divided by the loan life. If the interest rate is zero, this will be the exact required annual payment. Otherwise, this will always be smaller than the required annual payment, which has to include something more to cover interest. So this is a safe initial guess.

Make the step size by which you will increase the annual payment in successive iterations equal to initial loan amount divided by 1,000.

To calculate the residual final balance, for each iteration use the code from the previous model to create an amortization table and look at the balance at the end of the last year. Use a `Do` loop to repeat all the steps (with a the slightly larger guess for each iteration) until the final balance becomes negative.

Since the previous model does a lot of what you have to do in this model, it may be easiest to start with the code of the previous model and make the necessary changes to create this model.

The Code for the Model

```
Option Explicit
Sub Loan_Amort_Ver2()

' This model calculates the annual payment amount
' using an iterative procedure. It starts with a safe guess
' for the annual payment amount and then keeps changing it
' in equal steps until the balance remaining
' at the end of the last year becomes negative.

Dim intRate As Single, initLoanAmnt As Single
Dim yrBegBal As Single, yrEndBal As Single
Dim intComp As Single, princRepay As Single
Dim annualPmnt As Single, annualIncr As Single
Dim loanLife As Integer, outRow As Integer
Dim rowNum1 As Integer, numOfIterations As Integer
Dim outSheet As String

'************************************************************
' User inputs
'************************************************************
' Read in from data entered on worksheet
intRate = Cells(2, 2).Value 'In decimals
loanLife = Cells(3, 2).Value 'in full years
initLoanAmnt = Cells(4, 2).Value 'initial loan balance

'************************************************************
' Programmer inputs
'************************************************************
annualIncr = initLoanAmnt / 1000 'Step size for payment guess
outSheet = "Loan Amort"
outRow = 8 'row below which repayment schedule will start

'************************************************************
' Preliminaries
'************************************************************
' Make the outSheet the active sheet
Worksheets(outSheet).Activate

' Clear previous data
Rows(outRow + 1 & ":" & outRow + 300).Select
Selection.Clear

'************************************************************
' Computations
'************************************************************
```

```
annualPmnt = initLoanAmnt / loanLife ' Initial guess
numOfIterations = 0 ' Counter for number of iterations

' This Do loop controls the iteration
Do While Cells(outRow + loanLife, 8).Value >= 0

   ' Initialize balance at the beginning of year 1
   yrBegBal = initLoanAmnt

   ' Loop to calculate and output year-by-year data
   For rowNum1 = 1 To loanLife
      intComp = yrBegBal * intRate
      princRepay = annualPmnt - intComp
      yrEndBal = yrBegBal - princRepay

      Cells(outRow + rowNum1, 3).Value = rowNum1
      Cells(outRow + rowNum1, 4).Value = yrBegBal
      Cells(outRow + rowNum1, 5).Value = annualPmnt
      Cells(outRow + rowNum1, 6).Value = intComp
      Cells(outRow + rowNum1, 7).Value = princRepay
      Cells(outRow + rowNum1, 8).Value = yrEndBal

      yrBegBal = yrEndBal 'Setting up for next year
   Next rowNum1

   annualPmnt = annualPmnt + annualIncr ' New annual payment
   numOfIterations = numOfIterations + 1 ' Count iterations

Loop ' End of the iteration Do loop

' Write out the number of iterations used
Cells(outRow + loanLife + 4, 1).Value = "No. of iterations ="
Cells(outRow + loanLife + 4, 2).Value = numOfIterations

'*************************************************************
' Format data in table output
'*************************************************************
Range(Cells(outRow + 1, 4), Cells(outRow + loanLife, 8)). _
 Select
Selection.NumberFormat = "$#,##0"

End Sub
```

Analysis of the Code

To keep the code short and focus on the new features I want to illustrate, this code reads in the input data from the worksheet, omits data validation, and uses a preformatted worksheet. You already know how to change these if you want.

Since a lot of the code is the same as that in the last model, I discuss only the new material in it.

Lines 10–16: For demonstration purposes, I have included the data type for each variable here. As before, you can omit all of them and let VBA assume them to be `Variant` data type. Also, in some places you could use different data types (for example, `Double` for `Single`) if that were more appropriate. It is not required, but it is good practice to group related variables under separate `Dim` statements.

Line 29: Here I am specifying the constant annual increment amount (step size) to use. We will see later that depending on what we want to base it on, it may have to be specified somewhere else in the code.

Line 46: Here I am specifying the initial guess for the `annualPmnt`. This initial value has to be set outside the iteration `Do` loop. For the subsequent iteration this value will be modified inside the `Do` loop.

Line 47: I want to use `numOfIterations` to keep count of the number of iterations the program has to make to get to the answer. I am initializing it here as zero. After each iteration I will increase it by 1.

Line 50: This is the beginning of the `Do` loop and also includes the condition to end the iterations. The condition is based on the cell that will contain the final loan balance. The condition says that the iteration will continue only as long as the final balance is greater than or equal to zero because once the balance becomes negative we can stop.

Lines 53–69: These are essentially the same as in the previous model. The `For` loop here is nested inside the `Do` loop. Once control gets to line 56, the beginning of the `For` loop, the `For` loop is executed 10 times for a loan life of 10 years and so forth, creating a complete amortization table based on the annual payment being used for the current iteration of the `Do` loop.

Line 71: With the amortization table done, the annual payment is now increased by the specified step to get ready for the next iteration. Note that there may not be a next iteration because when control gets back to line 50 after the `Do` loop is completed, the check of the final balance may show that there is no need to do any more iteration.

Line 72: To keep track of the number of iterations, the iteration counter is incremented by 1.

Line 74: End of the `Do` loop. From here control goes back to line 50. If the test is `True`, VBA will do another iteration; if it is `False`, that is, the final balance is zero or negative, the iteration and Do loop will stop and control will jump to line 77 (because lines 75–76 have nothing executable in them).

Lines 77–78: Creates a label for the number of iterations and enters the value in the cell next to it. Just for illustration I decided to put it in a row below the last row of the table, and since the last row of the table depends on the loan life, I had to specify here a row number that depends on it. (As always, VBA will use the values of the variables to calculate the row number.) You could put these in a fixed row such as row 6.

Lines 82–85: Formats the amortization table as before.

Testing the Model

The final value used for iteration, shown in the column for Annual Payment is the answer that the model generates. If the final balance in the amortization table is zero, then this is the exact answer. Most of the time this will not be the case, and the final balance will be negative, meaning the model's answer is bigger than the actual answer—the more negative the final balance, the bigger the error.

Since we are stopping iteration when the final balance becomes negative, it is important in this case that we start with a guess that is too small. Otherwise, the final balance will become negative after the very first iteration and iteration will stop, most often with a fairly large error.

If the final balance when the iteration stops is too large, it means that the step size being used is too large. For example, since we are using a constant step size equal to the initial loan amount divided by 1,000, the step size used for a $100,000 loan will be $100. The final answer (not the final balance) may be off by as much as $100. For larger loans, the error may be even larger. One way to get around this problem is to use a smaller step size. For example, instead of tying the step size to the loan amount, you can make it $5, $10, or something else by specifying that number in line 29. Try this out and notice that as you use smaller step sizes, you need many more iterations and it takes much longer to get to the answer.

In the next model, we will try one of the methods we discussed before to get better answers even as we decrease the required number of iterations.

Conditions Used in Do Loops

The stopping conditions in a Do loop can be used either in the Do line or in the Loop line. We also have the choice of using a `While` condition or `Until` condition. Are they all interchangeable with the proper modification for `Until`? The answer is "Most of the time—but not always." Now that we have a model we can experiment with, we can study two important differences.

For the first experiment, make the condition in the Do line > 0 instead of >= 0. After all, we want to iterate only as long as the final balance is greater than zero.

Once it is zero we will have our answer and we should stop. Run the program with this change and you will have an empty output table and the program will stop without doing any iteration. (The iteration counter will show 0.) What happened?

When control gets to the `Do` the first time, we have an empty amortization table because the program clears it in the earlier step for a new run. So VBA evaluates the `While` condition to be `False` because the final balance is zero (empty cell) and not greater than zero, and the `Do` loop stops—control jumps to line 77 right away without doing any iteration.

Now cut and paste the same `While` condition with > 0 in the `Loop` line and run the program again. It will run correctly and produce the right answer because by the time the condition is tested in this version, the amortization table has been filled and the final balance cell is not empty anymore.

The conclusion is that the same conditions generally work the same way whether you put them in the `Do` line or the `Loop` line. But at times when the condition is satisfied before getting into the loop, if the condition is in the `Do` line the `Do` loop will not be executed at all. However, as is the case here, if the condition is in the `Loop` line, the `Do` loop will be executed at least once. Sometimes you may want one or the other to happen, and you should make sure you are putting the condition in the line where it will behave the way you want.

Another point to keep in mind is that sometimes you may get slightly different effects with `While` and `Until`. In this example, you could write the condition as `Until < 0` instead of `While >= 0`. If you use the = in the `While` condition to make it work in the `Do` line for the first iteration, as we did, then if by chance your iteration hits the perfect answer and the residual balance goes to 0, the iteration will not stop. It will go through one more iteration with a one-step higher annual payment, making a perfect answer into a less-than-perfect one! If instead you use `Until < 0`, then it will not stop before the first iteration and it will stop if you hit the perfect answer. Because in some situations there can be subtle differences, you should always carefully analyze the conditions you write.

Limitations of the Model

We can get this model to produce as accurate an answer (estimate of the periodic payment) as we want by specifying smaller and smaller steps. For example, if we specify a step size of $1, iteration will stop only when increasing the payment amount by $1 and will flip the remaining balance at the end of the period from positive to negative. It therefore will produce an answer that is accurate to within $1.

However, the larger the input values and the more accurate an answer we want, the more iterations and time this model will take to produce an answer. So this model is very inefficient.

This model also does not provide any way to directly specify the accuracy of the answer as measured by the residual final balance.

MODEL 3: LOAN AMORTIZATION TABLE, VERSION 3

The Problem

Create a model to produce an amortization table for a fixed rate loan. The loan is to be repaid in equal annual installments over its life and the first payment is to be made at the end of the first year. Determine the required annual payment amount by iteration instead of using VBA's `Pmt` function. To speed up the accuracy of the previous model, use a step size that is relatively large in the beginning and gets smaller as the guesses get closer to the actual annual payment. The iteration should stop when the final balance becomes smaller than a specified margin of error. The output sheet should look like Figure 26.3 and show the number of iterations used to arrive at the solution.

Modeling Strategy

Since the magnitude of the final balance is the measure of how close we are to the actual answer, make the step size smaller as this final balance gets smaller, that is, make the step size depend on the final balance. A simple

	1	2	3	4	5	6	7	8
1	Input Data							
2	Interest rate (% per year)	10%						
3	Loan life (years)	10						
4	Initial loan balance ($)	$100,000						
5								
6			Year	Year-beg	Annual	Interest	Principal	Year-end
7				Balance	Payment	Component	Repaid	Balance
8								
9			1	$100,000	$16,274	$10,000	$6,274	$93,726
10			2	$93,726	$16,274	$9,373	$6,902	$86,824
11			3	$86,824	$16,274	$8,682	$7,592	$79,232
12			4	$79,232	$16,274	$7,923	$8,351	$70,880
13			5	$70,880	$16,274	$7,088	$9,186	$61,694
14			6	$61,694	$16,274	$6,169	$10,105	$51,589
15			7	$51,589	$16,274	$5,159	$11,116	$40,473
16			8	$40,473	$16,274	$4,047	$12,227	$28,246
17			9	$28,246	$16,274	$2,825	$13,450	$14,796
18			10	$14,796	$16,274	$1,480	$14,795	$1
19								
20								
21								
22	No. of iterations =	8						
23								
24								

FIGURE 26.3 Model 3: Loan amortization table using decreasing step size.

approach would be to make the step size equal to the final balance divided by the loan life. This will overshoot the answer, however, because if we assume a 10-year loan life and have a final remaining balance of $100, we will have a step size of $10. Ten annual payments of $10 each will pay off more than the remaining $100 unpaid balance at the end of the tenth year. So try a step size half as big, that is, step size = final balance/loan life/2. (This is an illustration of the intuitive approach to finding an iterative solution we discussed earlier.)

As required in the problem, have the program check the final balance against the specified margin of error at the end of each iteration. Stop when the final balance becomes smaller than the margin of error.

The Code for the Model

```
Option Explicit
Sub Loan_Amort_Ver3()

' This model calculates the annual payment amount
' using an iterative procedure. It starts with a safe low
' estimate of annual payment and then increases it
' in steps that start large and get successively smaller.
' In this model the user can specify desired accuracy but
' for high interest rate and/or long loan life the step
' size used here may be too large to produce an answer of
' desired accuracy.

Dim intRate, initLoanAmnt, loanLife
Dim yrBegBal, yrEndBal, finalBal
Dim annualPmnt, intComp, princRepay
Dim outRow, rowNum1, numOfIterations, balTolerance
Dim outSheet

'**********************************************************
' User inputs
'**********************************************************
' Read in from entered by user on worksheet
intRate = Cells(2, 2).Value 'In decimals
loanLife = Cells(3, 2).Value 'in full years
initLoanAmnt = Cells(4, 2).Value 'initial loan balance

'**********************************************************
' Programmer inputs
'**********************************************************
outSheet = "Loan Amort"
balTolerance = 5 'Specifies desired accuracy
outRow = 8 'row below which repayment schedule would start
```

```

'*********************************************************
' Preliminaries
'*********************************************************
' Make the outSheet the active sheet
Worksheets(outSheet).Activate

' Clear previous data
Rows(outRow + 1 & ":" & outRow + 300).Select
Selection.Clear

'*********************************************************
' Computations and output
'*********************************************************
annualPmnt = initLoanAmnt / loanLife ' Initial guess
numOfIterations = 0 ' Counter for number of iterations

' This Do loop controls the iteration
Do
    ' Initialize balance at the beginning of year 1
    yrBegBal = initLoanAmnt

    ' Loop to calculate and output year-by-year data
    For rowNum1 = 1 To loanLife

        intComp = yrBegBal * intRate
        princRepay = annualPmnt - intComp
        yrEndBal = yrBegBal - princRepay

        Cells(outRow + rowNum1, 3).Value = rowNum1
        Cells(outRow + rowNum1, 4).Value = yrBegBal
        Cells(outRow + rowNum1, 5).Value = annualPmnt
        Cells(outRow + rowNum1, 6).Value = intComp
        Cells(outRow + rowNum1, 7).Value = princRepay
        Cells(outRow + rowNum1, 8).Value = yrEndBal

        yrBegBal = yrEndBal 'Setting up for next year

    Next rowNum1

    finalBal = Cells(outRow + loanLife, 8).Value

    ' Calculate the next annual payment to try
    annualPmnt = annualPmnt + finalBal / loanLife / 2

    numOfIterations = numOfIterations + 1 ' Count iterations

```

```
80:  Loop While finalBal >= balTolerance
81:
82:  ' Print out number of iterations used
83:  Cells(outRow + loanLife + 4, 1).Value = "No. of iterations="
84:  Cells(outRow + loanLife + 4, 2).Value = numOfIterations
85:
86:  '*********************************************************
87:  ' Format data in table
88:  '*********************************************************
89:  Range(Cells(outRow + 1, 4), Cells(outRow + loanLife, 8)). _
90:    Select
91:  Selection.NumberFormat = "$#,##0"
92:
93:  End Sub
```

Analysis of the Code

I discuss here only the parts of this code that are different from the code for the previous model.

Line 31: This new variable `balTolerance` is used to specify the desired margin of error.

Line 73: To make the subsequent code more readable, I am defining a new variable `finalBal` here to read in and store the residual final balance. It is generally better to keep your code lines short by defining such intermediate variables.

Line 76: After an amortization table is created using a guess for annual payment, I increase it here by the variable step size based on the remaining loan balance as discussed under the modeling strategy.

Line 80: Here the code checks if the final balance has become smaller than the required margin of error and either continues the loop or ends the loop and goes on to the next step depending on the result.

Testing the Model

Set the margin of error `balTolerance` equal to 5 and test the model for a $100,000 loan at 10% interest and 10-year loan life. The final balance will reach $1 after just 8 iterations. If you run the previous model for the same loan, it will stop after 64 iterations with a final balance of –$406. So, as expected, the new model is much faster and produces a much more accurate answer. In addition, this model lets you specify the margin of error, whereas in the previous model the only way you can control the error is by specifying a smaller step size, which increases the required number of iterations.

To be safe, you should always test a model with many different inputs. Run this model with an interest rate of 50%, leaving everything else the same. The model will stop after the second iteration with a large negative final balance. Obviously it does not work for large interest rates. It will have similar problems with long loan lives as well. Why?

There are two problems. First, the way we have set up the stopping condition, the program stops any time the final balance becomes negative. If we overshoot the answer by a small or large amount, iteration will stop no matter how poor the answer is. Second, as will become clearer in the next model, the formula we have used to specify the decreasing step size can overshoot the answer right away and by a large amount for high interest rates and long loan lives.

These are typical problems of using the intuitive approach to specifying initial guess and step size for an iteration. Unless you have a good understanding of the problem and are careful, you can have a situation like this where the model will work fine for certain input values but not for others. This is why you must always thoroughly test a model for a wide range of values.

One other thing you can do is use data validation to limit the values of the inputs that a user can specify. For example, you can limit interest rate to a maximum of 15% because higher values are not realistic, and then test to make sure that your model works for interest rates up to that limit.

MODEL 4: LOAN AMORTIZATION TABLE, VERSION 4

The Problem

Create a model to produce an amortization table for a fixed rate loan. The loan is to be repaid in equal annual installments over its life and the first payment is to be made at the end of the first year. Determine the required annual payment amount by iteration instead of using VBA's `Pmt` function. Improve on the previous model by incorporating a better initial estimate of annual payment and a decreasing step size that works for all values of inputs. The iteration should stop when the final balance becomes smaller than a specified margin of error. The output sheet should look like Figure 26.4 and show the number of iterations used to arrive at the solution.

Modeling Strategy

The annual payment on any fixed-rate amortizing loan must be greater than the interest due in the first year. Otherwise the remaining loan balance will start increasing instead of decreasing. So use the first year's interest, that is, the interest on the initial loan amount as a simple and safe initial guess for annual payment

	1	2	3	4	5	6	7	8
1	**Input Data**							
2	Interest rate (% per year)	10%						
3	Loan life (years)	10						
4	Initial loan balance ($)	$100,000						
5								
6			**Year**	**Year-beg**	**Annual**	**Interest**	**Principal**	**Year-end**
7				**Balance**	**Payment**	**Component**	**Repaid**	**Balance**
8								
9			1	$100,000	$16,275	$10,000	$6,275	$93,725
10			2	$93,725	$16,275	$9,373	$6,902	$86,824
11			3	$86,824	$16,275	$8,682	$7,592	$79,231
12			4	$79,231	$16,275	$7,923	$8,351	$70,880
13			5	$70,880	$16,275	$7,088	$9,187	$61,693
14			6	$61,693	$16,275	$6,169	$10,105	$51,588
15			7	$51,588	$16,275	$5,159	$11,116	$40,473
16			8	$40,473	$16,275	$4,047	$12,227	$28,245
17			9	$28,245	$16,275	$2,825	$13,450	$14,795
18			10	$14,795	$16,275	$1,480	$14,795	$0
19								
20								
21								
22	No. of iterations =	14						
23								
24								

FIGURE 26.4 Model 4: Loan amortization table using improved step size.

that will work for all input values. (As a challenge, try to come up with an even better guess.)

For the step size, use the present value of the residual final balance divided by the loan life. This is a safe amount because we could pay off the entire residual final balance by paying an incremental amount equal to its present value in the first year. Therefore, if we stretch out the same amount by paying it in equal installments over the loan life, we will be paying off a little less than the residual final balance.

For the above initial guess and step size, we are sure—based on our understanding of the problem—that our guess for annual payment will never exceed the actual answer. So, as required in the problem, have the program check the final balance against the specified margin of error at the end of each iteration and stop when the final balance becomes smaller than the margin of error.

The Code for the Model

```
Option Explicit
Sub Loan_Amort_Ver4()

' Here we start with a better initial guess and the step
' is chosen so that it will work for large inputs as well

Dim intRate, initLoanAmnt, loanLife
```

```
Dim yrBegBal, yrEndBal, finalBal
Dim annualPmnt, intComp, princRepay
Dim outRow, rowNum1, numOfIterations, balTolerance
Dim outSheet

'********************************************************
' User inputs
'********************************************************
' Read in from data entered by user on worksheet
intRate = Cells(2, 2).Value 'In decimals
loanLife = Cells(3, 2).Value 'in full years
initLoanAmnt = Cells(4, 2).Value 'initial loan balance

'********************************************************
' Programmer inputs
'********************************************************
outSheet = "Loan Amort"
balTolerance = 5 'Specifies desired accuracy
outRow = 8 'row below which repayment schedule would start

'********************************************************
' Preliminaries
'********************************************************
' Make the outSheet the active sheet
Worksheets(outSheet).Activate

' Clear previous data
Rows(outRow + 1 & ":" & outRow + 300).Select
Selection.Clear

'********************************************************
' Computations and output
'********************************************************
annualPmnt = initLoanAmnt * intRate
numOfIterations = 0 ' Counter for number of iterations

' This Do loop controls the iteration
Do While finalBal > balTolerance Or finalBal = 0

   ' Initialize balance at the beginning of year 1
   yrBegBal = initLoanAmnt

   ' Loop to calculate and output year-by-year data
   For rowNum1 = 1 To loanLife
      intComp = yrBegBal * intRate
      princRepay = annualPmnt - intComp
      yrEndBal = yrBegBal - princRepay
```

```
55:
56:         Cells(outRow + rowNum1, 3).Value = rowNum1
57:         Cells(outRow + rowNum1, 4).Value = yrBegBal
58:         Cells(outRow + rowNum1, 5).Value = annualPmnt
59:         Cells(outRow + rowNum1, 6).Value = intComp
60:         Cells(outRow + rowNum1, 7).Value = princRepay
61:         Cells(outRow + rowNum1, 8).Value = yrEndBal
62:
63:         yrBegBal = yrEndBal 'Setting up for next year
64:     Next rowNum1
65:
66:     finalBal = Cells(outRow + loanLife, 8).Value
67:
68:     ' Calculate the next annual payment to try
69:     annualPmnt = annualPmnt + (finalBal * (1 + intRate) ^ _
70:       (-loanLife)) / loanLife
71:     numOfIterations = numOfIterations + 1 ' Count iterations
72:
73: Loop
74:
75: ' Print out number of iterations used
76: Cells(outRow + loanLife + 4, 1).Value = "No. of iterations="
77: Cells(outRow + loanLife + 4, 2).Value = numOfIterations
78:
79: '**********************************************************
80: ' Format data in table
81: '**********************************************************
82: Range(Cells(outRow + 1, 4), Cells(outRow + loanLife, 8)). _
83:   Select
84: Selection.NumberFormat = "$#,##0"
85:
86: End Sub
```

Analysis of the Code

Here I discuss only the parts of this code that are different from the code for the previous model.

Line 41: I am setting the initial guess equal to the interest payment for the first year.

Line 45: This is the condition for stopping the iteration. As discussed before, since the final balance will be zero (empty cell) at the beginning of the first iteration, the second part of the condition (`Or finalBal = 0`) is necessary. If this condition is omitted, control will never enter the `Do` loop. To check this, comment out this last part and run the code.

Lines 69–70: Here I am calculating the present value of the residual final balance, dividing it by the loan life, and adding it to the current annual payment guess to come up with a new guess.

Testing the Model

Since our objective was to solve the problems that the previous model was having in handling large values for inputs, you should test this model with large input values to check that it works. Notice that we have paid a small price for this additional flexibility. For input values in the normal range, this model may take some extra iterations to get to the answer within the specified margin of error. The penalty in computation time is negligible, however, and we have gained reliability for that price.

MODEL 5: LOAN AMORTIZATION TABLE USING GOAL SEEK

The Problem

Create a model to produce an amortization table for a fixed rate loan. The loan is to be repaid in equal annual installments over its life and the first payment is to be made at the end of the first year. Use Excel's Goal Seek to determine the necessary annual payment. The output sheet should look like Figure 26.5.

	1	2	3	4	5	6	7	8
1	**Input Data**							
2	Interest rate (% per year)	10%						
3	Loan life (years)	10						
4	Initial loan balance ($)	$100,000						
5								
6			**Year**	**Year-beg**	**Annual**	**Interest**	**Principal**	**Year-end**
7				**Balance**	**Payment**	**Component**	**Repaid**	**Balance**
8								
9			1	$100,000	$16,275	$10,000	$6,275	$93,725
10			2	$93,725	$16,275	$9,373	$6,902	$86,823
11			3	$86,823	$16,275	$8,682	$7,592	$79,231
12			4	$79,231	$16,275	$7,923	$8,351	$70,880
13			5	$70,880	$16,275	$7,088	$9,187	$61,693
14			6	$61,693	$16,275	$6,169	$10,105	$51,588
15			7	$51,588	$16,275	$5,159	$11,116	$40,472
16			8	$40,472	$16,275	$4,047	$12,227	$28,245
17			9	$28,245	$16,275	$2,825	$13,450	$14,795
18			10	$14,795	$16,275	$1,480	$14,795	$0
19								
20								

FIGURE 26.5 Model 5: Loan amortization table using Goal Seek.

Modeling Strategy

Since Goal Seek solves problems by iteration, it can be used to solve a problem like this one where the answer has to be found by iteration. However, Goal Seek can only work with worksheet models, that is, models that are built using formulas in worksheets. Here, then, use VBA to enter all the necessary formulas in the amortization table and then use it to run Goal Seek with the appropriate cell addresses for the independent and dependent variables and the target value for the dependent variable. The formulas you need to enter in the amortization table are the same as the ones we used in the corresponding Excel model.

The Code for the Model

```
Option Explicit
Sub Loan_Amort_GoalSeek()

' This version creates an amortization table with formulas
' and then uses Goal Seek to find the answer

Dim intRate, initLoanAmnt, loanLife, outRow, outSheet

'**********************************************************
' User inputs
'**********************************************************
' Read in from data entered by user on worksheet
intRate = Cells(2, 2).Value 'In decimals
loanLife = Cells(3, 2).Value 'in full years
initLoanAmnt = Cells(4, 2).Value 'initial loan balance

'**********************************************************
' Programmer inputs
'**********************************************************
outSheet = "Loan Amort"
outRow = 8 'row below which repayment schedule would start

'**********************************************************
' Preliminaries
'**********************************************************
' Make the outSheet the active sheet
Worksheets(outSheet).Activate

' Clear previous data
Rows(outRow + 1 & ":" & outRow + 300).Select
Selection.Clear

```

```
33:  '***********************************************************
34:  ' Create table in spreadsheet with formulas
35:  '***********************************************************
36:  Cells(outRow + 1, 3).Value = 1
37:  Cells(outRow + 1, 4).Value = initLoanAmnt
38:  Cells(outRow + 1, 6).Formula = "=D9*$B$2"
39:  Cells(outRow + 1, 7).Formula = "=E9-F9"
40:  Cells(outRow + 1, 8).Formula = "=D9-G9"
41:
42:  Cells(outRow + 2, 3).Formula = "=C9+1"
43:  Cells(outRow + 2, 4).Formula = "=H9"
44:  Cells(outRow + 2, 5).Formula = "=E9"
45:  Cells(outRow + 2, 6).Formula = "=D10*$B$2"
46:  Cells(outRow + 2, 7).Formula = "=E10-F10"
47:  Cells(outRow + 2, 8).Formula = "=D10-G10"
48:
49:  Range("C" & outRow + 2 & ":H" & outRow + 2).Copy _
50:    Range("C" & outRow + 3 & ":H" & outRow + loanLife)
51:
52:  '***********************************************************
53:  ' Use Goal Seek to find answer
54:  '***********************************************************
55:  Range("H" & outRow + loanLife).GoalSeek Goal:=0, _
56:    ChangingCell:=Range("E9")
57:
58:  '***********************************************************
59:  ' Format data in table
60:  '***********************************************************
61:  Range(Cells(outRow + 1, 4), Cells(outRow + loanLife, 8)). _
62:    Select
63:  Selection.NumberFormat = "$#,##0"
64:
65:  End Sub
```

Analysis of the Code

Lines 1–32: This part of the code is very similar to the codes of the previous models except that we do not need many of the variables we were using before.

Lines 36–40: Here I am entering the formulas into the cells of the first row of the amortization table. To enter a formula instead of value into a cell, the cell reference has to be followed by `Formula` instead of `Value`, that is, we have to set the `Formula` property. The formula to be assigned has to be specified as a text within quotation marks and preceded by the equals sign.

Lines 42–47: Here I am entering the formulas for the second row of the table because some of them are different from the formulas in the first row. For example, the beginning of the year loan balance in the first row is the same as the initial loan amount, but in the second row it equals the end of the year balance from the first row. Although some of the formulas here are the same as those in the first row, I am entering all of the formulas in this row for convenience.

Lines 49–50: Here I am copying all the formulas in the second row and pasting them into all the remaining rows of the mortgage table. This is exactly what you would do to create this model in Excel. Since the necessary number of rows in the mortgage table depends on the loan life, the range of cells into which the formulas have to be pasted must reflect the loan life. The first part of the statement indicates the range to be copied. The structure of the statement is such that you do not have to add the word "paste" to the destination range. VBA automatically recognizes the second range referenced as the destination range. Study closely how I concatenate various texts and variables to create the appropriate arguments for the `Range` reference. Remember that whenever VBA sees a variable, it substitutes its value in its place and then works with that value.

Lines 55–56: Once I have my Excel model set up, I can use Goal Seek by specifying the addresses for the independent and dependent variables and the target vale. This is what I am doing here. The first reference is to the target cell, that is, the final balance cell. Then I specify the target value, which in this case is zero because I want the final balance to go to zero. The third reference is the independent variable cell. This is the statement syntax you have to use with Goal Seek. (I found it out by recording a macro while using Goal Seek.)

Testing the Model

Test the model by running it for various combinations of input values and checking that the numbers in the table make sense and the final balance is zero.

Advantages and Disadvantages

First notice that in this model there are formulas (instead of just numbers) in the various cells in the amortization table. The VBA code has created a working worksheet model that you can use without running the VBA model again.

The key advantage of this model is that you can use a very efficient iteration method without having to worry about all the details of iteration like specifying initial guess, step size, and so on. Another advantage relative to the parallel Excel model is that even a user who does not know how to use Goal Seek can use this model and use it for any loan life.

The major disadvantage is that before you can use Goal Seek this way you have to create the entire worksheet model first. This may be fine for small models like this one, but for large, complex models that involve hundreds of worksheet formulas, this is not a convenient approach. You are better off creating models in Excel or VBA depending on what will work better in a particular situation. If you have to use Goal Seek in an Excel model you have created and want to automate its use, you can write a small VBA program to run just the Goal Seek part. Then you will be able to run it without having to enter cell references, and so on, into Goal Seek every time you want to run it. Users who do not know how to run Goal Seek will be able to use the program as well.

Also, if you want to run Goal Seek several times on a worksheet model for different target values, then you can automate that process by embedding Goal Seek in a VBA program (inside a loop if necessary).

MODEL 6: LOAN AMORTIZATION TABLE USING ARRAYS

The Problem

Create a model to produce an amortization table for a fixed rate loan. The loan is to be repaid in equal annual installments over its life and the first payment is to be made at the end of the first year. Determine the required annual payment amount by iteration instead of using VBA's `Pmt` function. Use the same initial guess and step size formulas we used in Model 4, but use arrays for all intermediate calculations to speed up the model's operation. The output sheet should look like Figure 26.4 and show the number of iterations used to arrive at the solution.

Modeling Strategy

In VBA, reading in data from a worksheet and writing out data to a worksheet take a relatively long time. Since in the previous models we write out the full amortization table for each iteration, they take much longer to execute than is necessary. However, in small models like these this slower operation does not matter much. In large models that involve reading in and writing out lots of data, it is best to avoid most of the interactions with worksheets by storing all intermediate values in arrays and writing out to the worksheet only the final results. VBA can handle data much faster when they are stored in arrays. Also, you can store larger amounts of data more conveniently in arrays. For example, if for some reason you want to save the entire amortization table for each iteration, it will be much easier to do so if you are using arrays than if you try to write them out (that is, effectively store them) in worksheets.

For this version of the model, set up arrays for all the variables in the amortization table, store the results of all the intermediate iterations in them, and then write out the final results in the amortization table on the output worksheet. (You may want to review the basics of arrays in Chapter 22: VBA Essentials before going further.)

The Code for the Model

```
Option Explicit
Option Base 1
Sub Loan_Amort_Arrays()

' This version uses arrays. Otherwise similar to Ver 4.
' We start with a good initial guess and the step
' is chosen so that it will work for large inputs as well.

Dim intRate, initLoanAmnt, loanLife
Dim yrBegBal(100), yrEndBal(), finalBal
Dim ipPay(1 To 100, 1 To 2)
Dim annualPmnt, aPmtOld
Dim outRow, rNum, numOfIterations, balTolerance
Dim outSheet, iCol, pCol

'*********************************************************
' User inputs
'*********************************************************
' Read in from data entered by user on worksheet
intRate = Cells(2, 2).Value 'In decimals
loanLife = Cells(3, 2).Value 'in full years
initLoanAmnt = Cells(4, 2).Value 'initial loan balance

'*********************************************************
' Programmer inputs
'*********************************************************
outSheet = "Loan Amort"
balTolerance = 1 'Specifies desired accuracy
iCol = 1
pCol = 2
outRow = 8 'row below which repayment schedule would start

'*********************************************************
' Preliminaries
'*********************************************************
' Make the outSheet the active sheet
Worksheets(outSheet).Activate

' Clear previous data
Rows(outRow + 1 & ":" & outRow + 300).Select
Selection.Clear
```

```

ReDim yrEndBal(loanLife) 'Redimension the array

'**********************************************************
' Computations and output
'**********************************************************
annualPmnt = initLoanAmnt * intRate
numOfIterations = 0 ' Counter for number of iterations

' This Do loop controls the iteration
Do While finalBal > balTolerance Or finalBal = 0

   ' Initialize balance at the beginning of year 1
   yrBegBal(1) = initLoanAmnt

   ' Loop to calculate and store year-by-year data
   For rNum = 1 To loanLife
      ipPay(rNum, iCol) = yrBegBal(rNum) * intRate
      ipPay(rNum, pCol) = annualPmnt - ipPay(rNum, iCol)
      yrEndBal(rNum) = yrBegBal(rNum) - ipPay(rNum, pCol)

      yrBegBal(rNum + 1) = yrEndBal(rNum)
   Next rNum

   finalBal = yrEndBal(loanLife)
   aPmtOld = annualPmnt
   ' Calculate the next annual payment to try
   annualPmnt = annualPmnt + (finalBal * (1 + intRate) ^ _
     (-loanLife)) / loanLife
   numOfIterations = numOfIterations + 1 ' Count iterations

Loop

'**********************************************************
' Output data to worksheet
'**********************************************************
For rNum = 1 To loanLife
   Cells(outRow + rNum, 3).Value = rNum 'Year number
   Cells(outRow + rNum, 4).Value = yrBegBal(rNum)
   Cells(outRow + rNum, 5).Value = annualPmnt
   Cells(outRow + rNum, 6).Value = ipPay(rNum, iCol)
   Cells(outRow + rNum, 7).Value = ipPay(rNum, pCol)
   Cells(outRow + rNum, 8).Value = yrEndBal(rNum)
Next rNum

' Print out number of iterations used
Cells(outRow + loanLife + 4, 1).Value = "No. of iterations="
Cells(outRow + loanLife + 4, 2).Value = numOfIterations
```

```
90:
91:   '************************************************************
92:   ' Format data in table
93:   '************************************************************
94:  Range(Cells(outRow + 1, 4), Cells(outRow + loanLife, 8)). _
95:    Select
96:  Selection.NumberFormat = "$#,##0"
97:
98:  End Sub
```

Analysis of the Code

Line 2: This changes the default lower bound for array subscripts from 0 to 1. (See explanation later.)

Line 10: Here I declare (set up) two arrays. For each array, we have to specify the number of dimensions and the number of elements in each dimension. Declaring the first array as `yrBegBal(100)` means that it has only one dimension (think of it as rows). Normally the elements in each dimension are counted from 0 to the upper bound shown for it. An upper bound of 100 as specified here, then, would mean 101 elements or rows counted with the first element referred to as the 0th element or row and so on. However, because we specified Option Base 1 in line 2, the counting here will start from 1 and the number of elements in this array will be 100. In most cases this is more convenient than starting the count at 0.

I am also declaring `yrEndBal()` as an array by including the pair of parentheses after it, but I am not specifying the number of dimensions or number of elements here. I will have to do so before I use the array (see line 43). In this model I am using arrays to store all the values for each variable of the amortization table. Ideally, the number of rows in each array should equal the loan life. Loan life, however, is a user input that I do not know at the time of writing the code. So I can either specify a large enough number of elements that I believe will always be larger than the loan life—for example, 100—or I can wait to declare the size of the arrays until after the user has entered the loan life. I am using a mix of the two approaches here for illustration.

Note that in a situation like this, the number of elements you need in an array may depend on a user input. Therefore, if you want to declare the size of the array permanently then it may be safer to validate the related input to make sure that it does not exceed the array size you specified.

Line 11: Specifying 1 to 100 and 1 to 2 instead of just 100 and 2 are redundant because in line 2 I already declared that the numbering of elements should start with 1 and not 0. This is just an illustration to show that, if you wish, this is how you would override the default you have specified. For example, if you indicated

50 to 149, the array would still have 100 rows but they would be numbered 50 to 149.

Lines 29–30: I am defining these variables to use them for referring to specific elements of arrays. For example, I am planning to store the interest payment for a year in the first column and principal payment in the second column of the array `ipPay`. To refer to the interest payment in the third year, then, I will have to use `ipPay(3,1)`. Since I will have to make such references at many places in the program, I may at some point use (by mistake) the first column for principal and the second column for interest payments. But if I create—as I have done here—a variable `iCol` with a value 1 and `pCol` with a value 2 and (when I want to refer to the interest payment for the third year) write `ipPay(3, iCol)`, then I will be much less likely to use the wrong column numbers. Whenever possible, it is safer to create variables with appropriate names and values and use them to refer to different elements of an array.

Line 43: Here I am assigning dimension to the `yrEndBal` array because I wanted to base it on the loan life the user enters. Note that I have to use a `ReDim` statement and not the `Dim` statement. You can redimension an array within a program as many times as you want, but you have to be careful if you want to preserve the data that were in the array before you `ReDim` it.

Lines 52–73: This is the same `Do` loop we used before and it will do the iterations until it is stopped by the same conditions.

Lines 58–64: If you think of two-dimensional arrays in terms of rows and columns, then referring to an element of an array is similar to referring to a cell in R1C1 convention. The code in these lines is similar to the code we used to write out the different values to the amortization table on the worksheet. Here I store them instead in the different elements of the arrays.

Line 67: Here I am saving the annual payment I used in the latest amortization calculations before incrementing it for use in the next iteration. If I do not save this value, then when iteration ends I will not have available the annual payment amount to which the other values correspond.

Lines 78–85: Control gets to this loop when the iteration is completed. The final values for the amortization table are now stored in the different arrays and I am using this `For` loop to write them out to the amortization table on the worksheet. The counter of the `For` loop (`rNum` here) is always a very useful variable that can be used in many different ways. Here I am using it to track the year number I am using in each pass through the loop.

Note that in line 81 I am writing out the value stored in `aPmtOld` because it—not the value stored in `annualPmnt`—corresponds to the other values in the table.

Testing the Model

Because this model is exactly the same as Model 4, you only need to check that the final amortization table looks right. Things can go wrong if—because of some programming or typing error—you store the different values in wrong elements of the arrays.

The next thing you should notice is that for the same set of input variables, this model and the earlier model get the same answer and take the same number of iterations. This is not surprising because we are doing exactly the same calculations. The big difference, though, is that this model runs much faster, that is, gets to the answer much faster. To appreciate this, run both models with some large numbers (for example, a 100-year loan at 30% interest). You will not even have to look at your watch to notice the difference.

MODEL 7: MYPMT FUNCTION

The Problem

Create a user-defined worksheet function `MyPmt` to calculate the equal annual payment that is necessary to pay off a fixed-rate amortizing loan given the initial loan amount, the interest rate, and the loan life. The function should determine the required annual payment by iteration instead of using VBA's `Pmt` function.

Modeling Strategy

This function is going to be very similar to VBA's `Pmt` function. We have solved this problem several times before. The only difference here is that we want to cast it in the form of a worksheet function that a user can use in worksheet models the same way as he uses Excel's built-in function.

Here you have to write a Function procedure instead of the Sub procedures you have been writing so far. One of the limitations of a Function procedure that you want to use in worksheet formulas is that it cannot write out anything to a worksheet. So even though you can use amortization tables and iterations as before, you will have to store all your intermediate results in arrays. We already saw how to do this in Model 6. You can take most of the code for this model from the Model 6 and add the few things necessary to cast it in the form of a Function procedure.

The Code for the Model

```
Option Explicit
Option Base 1
Function MyPmt(intRate, loanLife As Integer, initLoanAmnt)
```

```

' This program creates a user-defined function from a
' loan amortization program we wrote before.
' It can be used as a worksheet function to calculate
' the periodic payment for an amortizing loan.

Dim yrBegBal(100), yrEndBal(), finalBal
Dim ipPay(1 To 100, 1 To 2)
Dim annualPmnt, aPmtOld
Dim rNum, balTolerance
Dim iCol, pCol

'**********************************************************
' Programmer inputs
'**********************************************************
balTolerance = 1 'Specifies desired accuracy
iCol = 1
pCol = 2

ReDim yrEndBal(loanLife) 'Redimension the array

'**********************************************************
' Computations and output
'**********************************************************
annualPmnt = initLoanAmnt * intRate

' This Do loop controls the iteration
Do While finalBal > balTolerance Or finalBal = 0

    ' Initialize balance at the beginning of year 1
    yrBegBal(1) = initLoanAmnt

    ' Loop to calculate and output year-by-year data
    For rNum = 1 To loanLife
        ipPay(rNum, iCol) = yrBegBal(rNum) * intRate
        ipPay(rNum, pCol) = annualPmnt - ipPay(rNum, iCol)
        yrEndBal(rNum) = yrBegBal(rNum) - ipPay(rNum, pCol)

        yrBegBal(rNum + 1) = yrEndBal(rNum)
    Next rNum

    finalBal = yrEndBal(loanLife)

    aPmtOld = annualPmnt

    ' Calculate the next annual payment to try
```

```
50:     annualPmnt = annualPmnt + (finalBal * (1 + intRate) ^ _
51:       (-loanLife)) / loanLife
52:
53: Loop
54:
55: MyPmt = aPmtOld
56:
57: End Function
```

Analysis of the Code

Almost all of the code for this model is copied from Model 6. The difference is that because we do not have to write out the final amortization table to the worksheet, we do not need the portion of the code used for doing that. Here I discuss only the new elements.

Line 3: The Function procedure is declared with the word Function followed by the name you want to give the function. As with Sub procedures, this has to be followed by a pair of parentheses, which can be empty or include one or more arguments. As with Excel's built-in functions, the user provides inputs to a function through these arguments.

If you want to specify any of the arguments as anything other than `Variant` data type, then you have to do it here. For example, you must indicate `loanLife As Integer` here; you cannot do it in subsequent `Dim` statements. As with Sub procedures, specifying data type is optional. The names you use for the arguments will show in the input box for the function. So you should make them short but self-explanatory.

Line 55: The output of a Function procedure always has to be assigned to (stored in) a variable with the same name as the function. (If there is more than one output then this variable can be an array.) In this line I am doing just that.

Testing the Model

To see where the function is stored, go to a worksheet in the same workbook and double-click the Function button on the tool bar. In the Function category in the Paste function dialog box, click the User function category and then look for the function `MyPmt` in the list of functions.

To use the function, double-click it; the dialog box where you enter the values for the arguments will open. As with built-in functions, you can enter values or cell references for these arguments.

You will notice that below the boxes for entering values for the arguments there is a short description of the function. You have to enter it for any function you create. (To learn how, see the section "Adding Description to a Custom Function" in Chapter 23: Sub and Function Procedures.)

You can use a custom function you create in both worksheets and in other VBA programs. You can use the `MyPmt` function in place of VBA's `Pmt` function in a VBA program, although the `Pmt` function is more versatile. The point is that you can now create functions to do things for which Excel or VBA does not provide built-in functions.

MODEL 8: LOAN AMORTIZATION TABLE USING THE BISECTION METHOD

The Problem

Create a model to produce an amortization table for a fixed rate loan. The loan is to be repaid in equal annual installments over its life and the first payment is to be made at the end of the first year. Use the bisection method to calculate the required annual payment amount by iteration. The output amortization table should look like Figure 26.6. The model should also create an output table similar to Figure 26.7 to show the steps of the iteration process.

	1	2	3	4	5	6	7	8
1	**Input Data**							
2	Interest rate (% per year)	10%						
3	Loan life (years)	20						
4	Initial loan balance ($)	$500,000						
5								
6			Year	Year-beg	Annual	Interest	Principal	Year-end
7				Balance	Payment	Component	Repaid	Balance
8								
9			1	$500,000	$58,730	$50,000	$8,730	$491,270
10			2	$491,270	$58,730	$49,127	$9,603	$481,667
11			3	$481,667	$58,730	$48,167	$10,563	$471,104
12			4	$471,104	$58,730	$47,110	$11,619	$459,485
13			5	$459,485	$58,730	$45,949	$12,781	$446,704
14			6	$446,704	$58,730	$44,670	$14,059	$432,644
15			7	$432,644	$58,730	$43,264	$15,465	$417,179
16			8	$417,179	$58,730	$41,718	$17,012	$400,167
17			9	$400,167	$58,730	$40,017	$18,713	$381,454
18			10	$381,454	$58,730	$38,145	$20,584	$360,870
19			11	$360,870	$58,730	$36,087	$22,643	$338,227
20			12	$338,227	$58,730	$33,823	$24,907	$313,320
21			13	$313,320	$58,730	$31,332	$27,398	$285,922
22			14	$285,922	$58,730	$28,592	$30,138	$255,784
23			15	$255,784	$58,730	$25,578	$33,151	$222,633
24			16	$222,633	$58,730	$22,263	$36,467	$186,166
25			17	$186,166	$58,730	$18,617	$40,113	$146,053
26			18	$146,053	$58,730	$14,605	$44,125	$101,928
27			19	$101,928	$58,730	$10,193	$48,537	$53,392
28			20	$53,392	$58,730	$5,339	$53,391	$1
29								
30								
31								

FIGURE 26.6 Model 8: Loan amortization table using the bisection method.

	1	2	3	4	5	6
1	**Progress of the Iteration Process for the Bisection Method**					
2						
3	No.	Lower guess	Step size	Upper guess	Final balance	Final balance
4					at lower guess	at upper guess
5						
6	1	$50,000.00	$1,000.00	$51,000.00	$500,000.00	$442,725.00
7	2	$51,000.00	$1,000.00	$52,000.00	$442,725.00	$385,450.00
8	3	$52,000.00	$1,000.00	$53,000.00	$385,450.00	$328,175.00
9	4	$53,000.00	$1,000.00	$54,000.00	$328,175.00	$270,900.00
10	5	$54,000.00	$1,000.00	$55,000.00	$270,900.00	$213,625.00
11	6	$55,000.00	$1,000.00	$56,000.00	$213,625.00	$156,350.00
12	7	$56,000.00	$1,000.00	$57,000.00	$156,350.00	$99,075.00
13	8	$57,000.00	$1,000.00	$58,000.00	$99,075.00	$41,800.00
14	9	$58,000.00	$1,000.00	$59,000.00	$41,800.00	($15,475.00)
15	10	$58,000.00	$500.00	$58,500.00	$41,800.00	$13,162.50
16	11	$58,500.00	$250.00	$58,750.00	$13,162.50	($1,156.25)
17	12	$58,500.00	$125.00	$58,625.00	$13,162.50	$6,003.13
18	13	$58,625.00	$62.50	$58,687.50	$6,003.13	$2,423.44
19	14	$58,687.50	$31.25	$58,718.75	$2,423.44	$633.60
20	15	$58,718.75	$15.63	$58,734.38	$633.60	($261.32)
21	16	$58,718.75	$7.81	$58,726.56	$633.60	$186.14
22	17	$58,726.56	$3.91	$58,730.47	$186.14	($37.59)
23	18	$58,726.56	$1.95	$58,728.52	$186.14	$74.27
24	19	$58,728.52	$0.98	$58,729.49	$74.27	$18.34
25	20	$58,729.49	$0.49	$58,729.98	$18.34	($9.63)
26	21	$58,729.49	$0.24	$58,729.74	$18.34	$4.36
27	22	$58,729.74	$0.12	$58,729.86	$4.36	($2.63)
28	23	$58,729.74	$0.06	$58,729.80	$4.36	$0.86
29						
30						
31						

FIGURE 26.7 Model 8: Progress of the iteration process for the bisection method.

Modeling Strategy

Start by reviewing the earlier discussion of the bisection method. Here, the amortization table is effectively the function whose root we want to calculate, and for each guess of annual payment the final balance is the value of the function. For each guess of annual payment, then, the program has to calculate the entire amortization table. For speed, it will be better to do this using arrays as we did in Model 6. Both for practice and to keep the main program uncluttered, write a Sub procedure to do the calculations for the amortization table so that the main procedure can call it with a guess of annual payment and the Sub procedure will return the value for the final balance.

The initial guess and step size are not very important when using the bisection method. However, the better they are, the faster the iteration process will reach an answer of desired accuracy. Use one of the methods we used before to come up with initial guesses.

The iteration process in the bisection method takes place in two stages. You can handle this in two separate loops so that the control will exit the first loop when stage 1 is over and go on to the second loop for stage 2. This approach may be a little easier than the one I have used where I use only one loop and a slightly complex `If` block to handle the differences in calculations for stage 1 and stage 2. The approach I have used requires fewer lines of code, but before or after you look at my approach you should try to write the code using two separate loops as well.

To decide when to stop iteration, your code should compare the absolute value of the final balance with the desired margin of error.

Store in an array the intermediate values from the iteration process that you will need to produce the table in Figure 26.7. Print out the table after the iteration is over.

The Code for the Model

```
Option Explicit
Option Base 1
Dim yrBegBal(100), yrEndBal(100)
Dim ipPay(1 To 100, 1 To 3), tCol, iCol, pCol
Sub Loan_Amort_Bisection()

' This version uses the bisection method for the
' iteration. We start with a good initial guess and a
' fairly large initial step and the bisection method
' takes over, halving the step size with each iteration.

Dim intRate, loanSize, loanLife
Dim annualPmnt, finalBal
Dim outRow1, outRow2, rNum, numOfIt, errMar
Dim outSheet1, outSheet2, aPmnt, aStep, fBalL, fBalH
Dim itStage, itTrack(100, 6) 'To track iteration results

'***********************************************************
' Programmer inputs
'***********************************************************
outSheet1 = "Loan Amort"
outSheet2 = "Iterations"
tCol = 1 'Column number for total payment
iCol = 2 'Column number for interest component
pCol = 3 'Column number for principal component
outRow1 = 8 'row below which repayment schedule would start
outRow2 = 5
numOfIt = 0 'Counter for number of iterations
itStage = 1 'Used to distinguish Stage 1 from Stage 2

errMar = 1 'Specifies desired accuracy
aStep = 1000 'Initial step size

```

```
'*************************************************************
' Preliminaries
'*************************************************************
Worksheets(outSheet2).Activate

' Clear previous data from Iterations sheet
Rows(outRow2 + 1 & ":" & outRow2 + 300).Select
Selection.Clear

Worksheets(outSheet1).Activate

' Clear previous data from Loan Amort sheet
Rows(outRow1 + 1 & ":" & outRow1 + 300).Select
Selection.Clear

'*************************************************************
' User inputs
'*************************************************************
' Read in from data entered by user on worksheet
intRate = Cells(2, 2).Value 'In decimals
loanLife = Cells(3, 2).Value 'in full years
loanSize = Cells(4, 2).Value 'initial loan balance

'*************************************************************
' Computations
'*************************************************************
aPmnt = loanSize * intRate 'Initial guess for annual payment

Call Calc_Table(loanSize, aPmnt, intRate, loanLife, finalBal)
fBalL = finalBal 'final balance for lower end of interval

Do
   numOfIt = numOfIt + 1
   Call Calc_Table(loanSize, aPmnt + aStep, intRate, _
     loanLife, finalBal)
   fBalH = finalBal 'final bal. for higher end of interval

   itTrack(numOfIt, 1) = numOfIt
   itTrack(numOfIt, 2) = aPmnt
   itTrack(numOfIt, 3) = aStep
   itTrack(numOfIt, 4) = aPmnt + aStep
   itTrack(numOfIt, 5) = fBalL
   itTrack(numOfIt, 6) = fBalH

   If (fBalL * fBalH) > 0 Then
      aPmnt = aPmnt + aStep
      fBalL = fBalH
      If itStage <> 1 Then aStep = aStep / 2
```

```
    Else
       itStage = 2
       aStep = aStep / 2
    End If

Loop While (Abs(fBalH) - errMar) > 0
'Loop While (2 * aStep - errMar) > 0 'Alternate criterion

'*************************************************************
' Output data to worksheet
'*************************************************************
For rNum = 1 To loanLife
    Cells(outRow1 + rNum, 3).Value = rNum 'Year number
    Cells(outRow1 + rNum, 4).Value = yrBegBal(rNum)
    Cells(outRow1 + rNum, 5).Value = ipPay(rNum, tCol)
    Cells(outRow1 + rNum, 6).Value = ipPay(rNum, iCol)
    Cells(outRow1 + rNum, 7).Value = ipPay(rNum, pCol)
    Cells(outRow1 + rNum, 8).Value = yrEndBal(rNum)
Next rNum

Range(Cells(outRow1 + 1, 4), Cells(outRow1 + loanLife, 8)). _
  Select
Selection.NumberFormat = "$#,##0"

Sheets(outSheet2).Activate

For rNum = 1 To numOfIt
    Cells(outRow2 + rNum, 1).Value = itTrack(rNum, 1)
    Cells(outRow2 + rNum, 2).Value = itTrack(rNum, 2)
    Cells(outRow2 + rNum, 3).Value = itTrack(rNum, 3)
    Cells(outRow2 + rNum, 4).Value = itTrack(rNum, 4)
    Cells(outRow2 + rNum, 5).Value = itTrack(rNum, 5)
    Cells(outRow2 + rNum, 6).Value = itTrack(rNum, 6)
Next rNum

Range(Cells(outRow2 + 1, 1), Cells(outRow2 + numOfIt, 1)). _
  Select
Selection.NumberFormat = "0"

Range(Cells(outRow2 + 1, 2), Cells(outRow2 + numOfIt, 6)). _
  Select
Selection.NumberFormat = "$#,##0.00_);($#,##0.00)"

End Sub

'---------------------------------------------
'---------------------------------------------
```

```
129:  Sub Calc_Table(loanSize, annualPmnt, intRate, loanLife, fBal)
130:  ' This program generates an amortization table and the
131:  ' remaining balance at the end of the final period
132:
133:  Dim rNum
134:
135:  yrBegBal(1) = loanSize
136:      For rNum = 1 To loanLife
137:          ipPay(rNum, tCol) = annualPmnt
138:          ipPay(rNum, iCol) = yrBegBal(rNum) * intRate
139:          ipPay(rNum, pCol) = annualPmnt - ipPay(rNum, iCol)
140:          yrEndBal(rNum) = yrBegBal(rNum) - ipPay(rNum, pCol)
141:
142:          yrBegBal(rNum + 1) = yrEndBal(rNum)
143:      Next rNum
144:
145:      fBal = yrEndBal(loanLife) 'final balance
146:
147:  End Sub
```

Analysis of the Code

In this model I have used two Sub procedures. This is partly to demonstrate how Sub procedures can be used to remove parts of the code that will be used repeatedly with various input values out of the way and then called from other procedures as needed. The first Sub procedure—named `Loan_Amort_Bisection`—is the main procedure, which calls the Sub procedure named `Calc_Table` to do certain calculations.

Line 2: This changes the default and makes all array indexes to be numbered starting at 1 instead of the default 0.

Lines 3–4: By declaring these variables (including arrays) before the first procedure in the module, I am making them module-level variables so that they will be available to both Sub procedures of the model. This is one way of reducing the number of variables that have to be passed back and forth between two procedures as arguments.

Line 21–32: Initializes several variables. Of special interest are: `itStage`, which I use to keep track of whether I am in stage 1 or 2 of iteration; `errMar`, which I use to specify the desired accuracy; and `aStep`, which is the step size. I am arbitrarily setting its initial value to 1000.

Lines 37–47: Clears out any old data from the two worksheets the model uses.

Lines 53–55: Reads in the user inputs from the worksheet.

Line 60: Sets the initial guess for `aPmt`, the annual payment amount, equal to the interest payment on the loan for the first year. (I could have made other choices.)

Line 62: Calls the Sub procedure `Calc_Table` to calculate the final loan balance (at the end of the loan life) for the initial values of the different variables specified. I will discuss this Sub procedure, including its arguments, in detail later.

Line 63: Sets the value of the lower final balance equal to the final balance for the initial values specified.

Line 65–87: The `Do` loop for iteration.

Line 66: The variable `numOfIt` keeps count of the number of iterations. This variable was initialized to 0. This statement adds 1 to it for each pass through the loop.

Lines 67–68: Calls Sub procedure `Calc_Table` to calculate the final loan balance for annual payment equal to the initial value plus one step.

Line 69: Sets the value of the upper final balance equal to the final balance for the higher guess for annual payment.

Lines 71–76: Stores the values for the iteration table.

Lines 78–85: This `If` block controls the iteration process for the bisection method. Analyze it thoroughly by referring to the discussion of the bisection method. In stage 1, the `True` branch is executed repeatedly and the step size is not changed because the `If` condition in line 81 is not satisfied. Once iteration gets into stage 2, the step size is halved in each step. If you have difficulty understanding the logic, study the details of the iteration process in Figure 26.7 in conjunction with the discussion in the next section, "Testing the Model."

Line 87: Continues looping as long as the absolute value of the final balance is greater than the specified accuracy.

Line 88: A possible alternate looping condition that is commented out. This condition will stop iteration when the last step size is smaller than the specified accuracy. This test is different from the previous one, and which one should be used depends on what definition of accuracy the user has in mind. Note that the step size is doubled for the test because the current value of the step size at this point is actually half of what was used for the last set of calculations. (It was halved in the pass through the `If` block in preparation for the next iteration.)

Lines 93–123: Outputs and formats the data for the two tables.

Line 129: Declaration statement for the Sub procedure `Calc_Table`. This Sub procedure generates an amortization table for the input values provided as arguments, calculates the final unpaid balance, and passes it back as `fBal`. Note that because certain variables were declared as module-level variables, their values generated and updated here are available in the main procedure as well.

Lines 133–143: Similar to code we used before to generate amortization tables.

Line 145: Assigns the value of the year-end balance for the last period to `fBal`, which is returned to the main procedure.

Testing the Model

If the final balance in the amortization table (in the Loan Amort worksheet) is less than or equal to the specified accuracy, then the model is likely to be working properly. However, examining the step-by-step details of the iteration process in the table on the worksheet iterations (Figure 26.7) is also informative and can confirm that the model is working correctly.

If you had difficulty visualizing how the bisection method works, look through the table in conjunction with the discussion of the bisection method. Through iteration 9, where the upper guess reached $59,000, the iteration was in stage 1 and in each iteration both guesses were moved up by the initial specified step of $1,000. In iteration 9, for the first time the final balances had opposite signs for the lower and upper guesses, thus marking the end of stage 1.

Starting with iteration 10, the iteration entered stage 2 and the step size was halved with each iteration. Then if the final values for the lower and upper guesses had opposite signs (for example, in iteration 11) the lower guess was kept unchanged in the next iteration and the upper guess was reduced by the new step size. Conversely, if the final values for the lower and upper guesses had the same sign (for example, in iteration 12), then the upper guess from the previous iteration was made the lower guess for the new iteration and a new higher upper guess was created using the new step size.

Run the model with a few different initial values and study the iteration table to fully understand the bisection method as well as the effects of the initial guesses for annual payment and step size. For example, if you change the loan life from 20 years to 10 years, you will see that the model takes many more iterations to arrive at the answer. Can you explain why?

MODEL 9: LOAN AMORTIZATION TABLE FOR CHANGING INTEREST RATE

The Problem

Create a model to produce an amortization table for a variable rate loan for which the interest rate can change in two steps over its life, that is, the loan life is broken down into three interest rate periods with different interest rates specified

	1	2	3	4	5	6	7	8	9
1	**Input Data**								
2	Initial loan balance ($)	$100,000							
3	Period 1 length (years)	5							
4	Period 2 length (years)	3							
5	Period 3 length (years)	7							
6	Interest rate, period 1 (%)	6%							
7	Interest rate, period 2 (%)	8%							
8	Interest rate, period 3 (%)	9%							
9									
10			Year	Year-beg	Annual	Interest	Principal	Year-end	Interest
11				Balance	Payment	Component	Repaid	Balance	Rate
12									
13			1	$100,000	$10,960	$6,000	$4,960	$95,040	6.0%
14			2	$95,040	$10,960	$5,702	$5,258	$89,781	6.0%
15			3	$89,781	$10,960	$5,387	$5,574	$84,208	6.0%
16			4	$84,208	$10,960	$5,052	$5,908	$78,300	6.0%
17			5	$78,300	$10,960	$4,698	$6,263	$72,037	6.0%
18			6	$72,037	$10,960	$5,763	$5,198	$66,840	8.0%
19			7	$66,840	$10,960	$5,347	$5,613	$61,226	8.0%
20			8	$61,226	$10,960	$4,898	$6,062	$55,164	8.0%
21			9	$55,164	$10,960	$4,965	$5,996	$49,168	9.0%
22			10	$49,168	$10,960	$4,425	$6,535	$42,633	9.0%
23			11	$42,633	$10,960	$3,837	$7,124	$35,509	9.0%
24			12	$35,509	$10,960	$3,196	$7,765	$27,745	9.0%
25			13	$27,745	$10,960	$2,497	$8,463	$19,281	9.0%
26			14	$19,281	$10,960	$1,735	$9,225	$10,056	9.0%
27			15	$10,056	$10,960	$905	$10,055	$1	9.0%
28									
29									
30									
31	No. of iterations =	18							
32									
33									

FIGURE 26.8 Model 9: Loan amortization table for changing interest rate.

for the three periods. The loan is to be repaid in equal annual installments over the life of the loan and the first payment is to be made at the end of the first year. The user will provide the lengths of the three interest rate periods (in years) and the interest rates for each of them. The model will have to calculate the appropriate equal annual payment. The output table should look like Figure 26.8.

Modeling Strategy

Because this model is similar to a number of previous models, it is easiest to build it by modifying one of them. Start with a copy of Model 6.

The primary change you have to make is to use different interest rates in different years. Create a new array for interest rates; before starting other computations, enter the right interest rate in it for each year. Then, in doing the calculations for the amortization table for each year, use the interest rate from this array.

Also be careful about specifying the initial guess for annual payment and the decreasing step size. To be safe, base the initial annual payment on the lowest interest rate. Remember that for the iteration approach used in Model 6 you must start with a value that is lower than the final answer. Using the lowest interest rate to generate the initial guess will ensure this. Similarly, to make sure that the step size will never make a new guess higher than the final answer, use the highest interest rate in the discounting used to specify the step size. If the reasons for these choices are not clear, review why we used the particular initial guess and step size in Model 6.

The Code for the Model

```
Option Explicit
Option Base 1
Sub Loan_Amort_IntChange()

' This version modifies Model 6 to accommodate 3 different
' interest rates specified by the user.

Dim initLoanAmnt, loanLife
Dim yrBegBal(100), yrEndBal(), finalBal
Dim ipPay(100, 2), intRate(1 To 100)
Dim prd1, prd2, prd3, int1, int2, int3
Dim annualPmnt, aPmtOld
Dim outRow, rNum, numOfIterations, balTolerance
Dim outSheet, iCol, pCol

'**********************************************************
' User inputs
'**********************************************************
' Read in from data entered by user on worksheet
initLoanAmnt = Cells(2, 2).Value 'initial loan balance
prd1 = Cells(3, 2).Value 'Length of period 1
prd2 = Cells(4, 2).Value
prd3 = Cells(5, 2).Value
int1 = Cells(6, 2).Value 'Interest rate for period 1
int2 = Cells(7, 2).Value
int3 = Cells(8, 2).Value

loanLife = prd1 + prd2 + prd3
'**********************************************************
' Programmer inputs
'**********************************************************
outSheet = "Loan Amort"
balTolerance = 1 'Specifies desired accuracy
iCol = 1
pCol = 2
outRow = 12 'row below which repayment schedule would start
```

```
'**********************************************************
' Preliminaries
'**********************************************************
' Make the outSheet the active sheet
Worksheets(outSheet).Activate

' Clear previous data
Rows(outRow + 1 & ":" & outRow + 300).Select
Selection.Clear

ReDim yrEndBal(loanLife) 'Redimension the array

'**********************************************************
' Computations and output
'**********************************************************
' Enter appropriate interest rates into the intRate array
For rNum = 1 To loanLife
   If rNum <= prd1 Then
      intRate(rNum) = int1
   ElseIf rNum <= prd1 + prd2 Then
      intRate(rNum) = int2
   Else
      intRate(rNum) = int3
   End If
Next

annualPmnt = initLoanAmnt * Application.Min(int1, int2, int3)
numOfIterations = 0 ' Counter for number of iterations

' This Do loop controls the iteration
Do While finalBal > balTolerance Or finalBal = 0

   ' Initialize balance at the beginning of year 1
   yrBegBal(1) = initLoanAmnt

   ' Loop to calculate and store year-by-year data
   For rNum = 1 To loanLife
      ipPay(rNum, iCol) = yrBegBal(rNum) * intRate(rNum)
      ipPay(rNum, pCol) = annualPmnt - ipPay(rNum, iCol)
      yrEndBal(rNum) = yrBegBal(rNum) - ipPay(rNum, pCol)

      yrBegBal(rNum + 1) = yrEndBal(rNum)
   Next rNum

   finalBal = yrEndBal(loanLife)
   aPmtOld = annualPmnt

```

```
85:      ' Calculate the next annual payment to try
86:      annualPmnt = annualPmnt + (finalBal * (1 + _
87:        Application.Max(int1, int2, int3)) ^ _
88:        (-loanLife)) / loanLife
89:      numOfIterations = numOfIterations + 1 ' Count iterations
90:
91:  Loop
92:
93:  '**********************************************************
94:  ' Output data to worksheet
95:  '**********************************************************
96:  For rNum = 1 To loanLife
97:      Cells(outRow + rNum, 3).Value = rNum 'Year number
98:      Cells(outRow + rNum, 4).Value = yrBegBal(rNum)
99:      Cells(outRow + rNum, 5).Value = aPmtOld
100:     Cells(outRow + rNum, 6).Value = ipPay(rNum, iCol)
101:     Cells(outRow + rNum, 7).Value = ipPay(rNum, pCol)
102:     Cells(outRow + rNum, 8).Value = yrEndBal(rNum)
103:     Cells(outRow + rNum, 9).Value = intRate(rNum)
104: Next rNum
105:
106: ' Print out number of iterations used
107: Cells(outRow + loanLife + 4, 1).Value = "No. of iterations ="
108: Cells(outRow + loanLife + 4, 2).Value = numOfIterations
109:
110: '**********************************************************
111: ' Format data in table
112: '**********************************************************
113: Range(Cells(outRow + 1, 4), Cells(outRow + loanLife, 8)). _
114:   Select
115: Selection.NumberFormat = "$#,##0"
116:
117: Range(Cells(outRow + 1, 9), Cells(outRow + loanLife, 9)). _
118:   Select
119: Selection.NumberFormat = "0.0#%"
120:
121: End Sub
```

Analysis of the Code

Most of this code is the same as the code in Model 6 (although the line numbers are different). Here I discuss only the changes.

Lines 8–14: Adds and delete variables as necessary.

Lines 20–26: Adds the three period lengths and corresponding interest rate.

Line 28: Calculates loan life from input data.

Line 36: Value of `outRow` is changed to move the table down on the spreadsheet.

Lines 54–62: Uses an `If` block to enter the right interest rates in the `intRate` array. Study the `If` block and for practice try to do the same with a different design.

Line 64: Calculates the initial guess for the annual payment. Uses Excel's built-in `Min` function to select and use the minimum interest rate. Because `Min` is an Excel function, it has to be preceded by `Application`.

Line 75: Instead of using one interest rate for all years, uses the interest rate for the specific year from the array.

Lines 86–88: Uses the maximum interest rate for discounting.

Line 103: Adds an interest rate column to the outputs for the table.

Lines 117–119: Adds formatting for the interest rate column of the table.

Testing the Model

Check that the interest rates in the output table are changing to the right values in the right years and that the interest component is being calculated using the right interest rate as well. Beyond that you can test this model the same way you tested Model 6.

MODEL 10: LOAN AMORTIZATION TABLE FOR CHANGING ANNUAL PAYMENT

The Problem

Create a model to produce a loan amortization table for a fixed rate loan for which the annual loan payment can change in two steps during the loan life. The first payment is to be made at the end of the first year. The user will provide the year numbers when the annual payments change and the percentages by which they change in each instance. The model will have to calculate the first annual payment. The output table should look like Figure 26.9.

Modeling Strategy

For this model it is easier to modify one of the earlier models than start from the beginning. Start with a copy of Model 6.

	1	2	3	4	5	6	7	8
1	**Input Data**							
2	Interest rate (% per year)	9%						
3	Loan life (years)	15						
4	Initial loan balance ($)	$100,000						
5	1st increase year	5						
6	2nd increase year	11						
7	1st increase percentage	10%						
8	2nd increase percentage	20%						
9								
10			**Year**	**Year-beg**	**Annual**	**Interest**	**Principal**	**Year-end**
11				**Balance**	**Payment**	**Component**	**Repaid**	**Balance**
12								
13			1	$100,000	$11,231	$9,000	$2,231	$97,769
14			2	$97,769	$11,231	$8,799	$2,431	$95,338
15			3	$95,338	$11,231	$8,580	$2,650	$92,688
16			4	$92,688	$11,231	$8,342	$2,889	$89,799
17			5	$89,799	$12,354	$8,082	$4,272	$85,528
18			6	$85,528	$12,354	$7,697	$4,656	$80,872
19			7	$80,872	$12,354	$7,278	$5,075	$75,796
20			8	$75,796	$12,354	$6,822	$5,532	$70,264
21			9	$70,264	$12,354	$6,324	$6,030	$64,235
22			10	$64,235	$12,354	$5,781	$6,573	$57,662
23			11	$57,662	$14,824	$5,190	$9,635	$48,027
24			12	$48,027	$14,824	$4,322	$10,502	$37,525
25			13	$37,525	$14,824	$3,377	$11,447	$26,078
26			14	$26,078	$14,824	$2,347	$12,477	$13,601
27			15	$13,601	$14,824	$1,224	$13,600	$1
28								
29	No. of iterations =	21						
30								
31								

FIGURE 26.9 Model 10: Loan amortization table for changing annual payment.

You can change the annual payment amount in many different ways. One possibility is to create a new array of multipliers with values by which you will multiply the initial annual payment to get the annual payment for each of the future years. The multiplier will be 1 for the years until there is a change. Starting with the year of the first change the multiplier will be 1 + the size (in decimals) of the first change, and so forth.

To be safe, you should also adjust the initial guess for the annual payment and the step size to reflect the changing annual payments.

The Code for the Model

```
Option Explicit
Option Base 1
Sub Loan_Amort_Arrays()

' In this version the annual payments change at
' specified times by specified amounts.

Dim intRate, initLoanAmnt, loanLife
Dim yrBegBal(100), yrEndBal(), finalBal
Dim ipPay(100, 2)
```

```
Dim annualPmnt, aPmtOld, pmntMult(100)
Dim outRow, rNum, numOfIterations, balTolerance
Dim outSheet, iCol, pCol
Dim chngYr1, chngYr2, chngSz1, chngSz2

'**********************************************************
' User inputs
'**********************************************************
' Read in from data entered by user on worksheet
intRate = Cells(2, 2).Value 'In decimals
loanLife = Cells(3, 2).Value 'in full years
initLoanAmnt = Cells(4, 2).Value 'initial loan balance
chngYr1 = Cells(5, 2).Value '1st increase year
chngYr2 = Cells(6, 2).Value
chngSz1 = Cells(7, 2).Value 'Size of 1st change, in decimal
chngSz2 = Cells(8, 2).Value

'**********************************************************
' Programmer inputs
'**********************************************************
outSheet = "Loan Amort"
balTolerance = 1 'Specifies desired accuracy
iCol = 1
pCol = 2
outRow = 12 'row below which repayment schedule would start

'**********************************************************
' Preliminaries
'**********************************************************
' Make the outSheet the active sheet
Worksheets(outSheet).Activate

' Clear previous data
Rows(outRow + 1 & ":" & outRow + 300).Select
Selection.Clear

ReDim yrEndBal(loanLife) 'Redimension the array

'**********************************************************
' Computations and output
'**********************************************************
'Set values for annual payment multiplier
For rNum = 1 To loanLife
   pmntMult(rNum) = 1
   If rNum >= chngYr1 Then pmntMult(rNum) = (1 + chngSz1)
   If rNum >= chngYr2 Then pmntMult(rNum) = _
     (1 + chngSz1) * (1 + chngSz2)
```

```
Next

annualPmnt = initLoanAmnt * intRate / (1 + chngSz1) / _
  (1 + chngSz2)
numOfIterations = 0 ' Counter for number of iterations

' This Do loop controls the iteration
Do While finalBal > balTolerance Or finalBal = 0

   ' Initialize balance at the beginning of year 1
   yrBegBal(1) = initLoanAmnt

   ' Loop to calculate and store year-by-year data
   For rNum = 1 To loanLife
      ipPay(rNum, iCol) = yrBegBal(rNum) * intRate
      ipPay(rNum, pCol) = annualPmnt * pmntMult(rNum) _
        - ipPay(rNum, iCol)
      yrEndBal(rNum) = yrBegBal(rNum) - ipPay(rNum, pCol)

      yrBegBal(rNum + 1) = yrEndBal(rNum)
   Next rNum

   finalBal = yrEndBal(loanLife)
   aPmtOld = annualPmnt
   ' Calculate the next annual payment to try
   annualPmnt = annualPmnt + (finalBal * (1 + intRate) ^ _
     (-loanLife)) / loanLife / pmntMult(loanLife)
   numOfIterations = numOfIterations + 1 ' Count iterations

Loop

'**********************************************************
' Output data to worksheet
'**********************************************************
For rNum = 1 To loanLife
   Cells(outRow + rNum, 3).Value = rNum 'Year number
   Cells(outRow + rNum, 4).Value = yrBegBal(rNum)
   Cells(outRow + rNum, 5).Value = aPmtOld * pmntMult(rNum)
   Cells(outRow + rNum, 6).Value = ipPay(rNum, iCol)
   Cells(outRow + rNum, 7).Value = ipPay(rNum, pCol)
   Cells(outRow + rNum, 8).Value = yrEndBal(rNum)
Next rNum

' Print out number of iterations used
Cells(outRow + loanLife + 2, 1).Value = "No. of iterations ="
Cells(outRow + loanLife + 2, 2).Value = numOfIterations
```

```
105:  '**********************************************************
106:  ' Format data in table
107:  '**********************************************************
108:  Range(Cells(outRow + 1, 4), Cells(outRow + loanLife, 8)). _
109:    Select
110:  Selection.NumberFormat = "$#,##0"
111:
112:  End Sub
```

Analysis of the Code

Most of this code is the same as the code in Model 6 (although the line numbers are different). Here I discuss only the changes.

Line 11: Adds a new array `pmntMult` for the annual payment multiplier discussed in the modeling strategy.

Lines 23–26: Reads in additional inputs.

Lines 53–58: Enters appropriate multiplier values in the annual payment multiplier array. After you understand the `If` structure used here, do the same with a different `If` structure for practice.

Line 60: Adjusts the initial guess for annual payment for the subsequent changes. This is a safety measure to make sure that the initial guess is not too high.

Line 73: For each year adjusts the annual payment for the first year using the multiplier for that year.

Lines 83–84: Adjusts the step size for safety.

Line 95: To output the correct annual payment, makes adjustments using the multiplier.

Testing the Model

Start by checking that the annual payments in the amortization table are changing by the right amounts in the right years. Beyond that you can test this model the same way you tested Model 6.

CHAPTER 27

Financial Planning and Investments

In this chapter, we will develop in VBA some of the same models we developed in the corresponding chapter in Part Two. As we have seen before, the VBA models are generally more flexible and will overcome some of the limitations of the Excel models. We do not need any additional theory or concepts for these models.

Modeling Examples

MODEL 1: SAVING FOR RETIREMENT, VERSION 1

The Problem

You are currently 40 years old. Starting today, you want to save in 25 growing annual installments enough money to accumulate $1 million (after all taxes) in today's dollars by the time you retire at age 65. You expect to be able to save every year an amount 2% more than the previous year. You currently have $100,000 saved, and you plan to invest this money and all new savings in a stock fund that is expected to return 8% per year, of which 2% will be dividends and 6% will be capital gains. All the money will be in taxable accounts; you will have to pay income taxes at a 15% rate on the dividend incomes as you earn them at the end of each year. In addition, assume that you will sell all holdings at the time you retire and pay the necessary capital gains taxes at the rate of 15%. Assume inflation rate will average 3% per year over the period.

How much money will you have to save in the first year?

Set this up as a model so that a user can input other values (for example, different tax rates) in order to do similar calculations for his own situation. The output for the model is shown in Figure 27.1.

	1	2	3	4	5	6	7
1	**Saving for Retirement**						
2							
3	**Inputs**						
4	Target balance (in today's dollars)	$1,000,000					
5	Current savings balance ($)	$100,000					
6	Expected annual inflation rate (%)	3.00%					
7	Planned savings increment rate (%)	2.00%					
8	Expected annual dividend income (%)	2.00%					
9	Expected annual capital appreciation (%)	6.00%					
10	Ordinary income tax rate on dividends (%)	15.00%					
11	Capital gains tax rate (%)	15.00%					
12	Current age	40					
13	Retirement age	65					
14							
15	Required first year annual saving	**$18,295**					
16	Number of installments of savings	25					
17	Target balance in future dollars	$2,093,778					
18	Final after-tax balance less target balance	**$0**					
19							
20							
21		Yr-beg bal	Annual	Dividend	Capital	Yr-end bal	Tax
22		(Pre saving)	Saving	Income	Appreciation	After div tax	Basis
23							
24	1	$100,000	$18,295	$2,366	$7,098	$127,404	$120,307
25	2	$127,404	$18,661	$2,921	$8,764	$157,313	$141,451
26	3	$157,313	$19,035	$3,527	$10,581	$189,926	$163,484
27	4	$189,926	$19,415	$4,187	$12,560	$225,461	$186,458
56	33	$4,134,107	$34,479	$83,372	$250,115	$4,489,567	$1,726,502
57	34	$4,489,567	$35,168	$90,495	$271,484	$4,873,140	$1,838,591
58	35	$4,873,140	$35,872	$98,180	$294,541	$5,287,005	$1,957,915
59							
60							

FIGURE 27.1 Model 1: Saving for retirement using the same table all the time.

Modeling Strategy

We developed the same model using Excel before. A limitation of the Excel model, however, is that to make it work for different numbers of years until retirement, the formula in B18 has to be changed every time. Also, whenever any input variable is changed, the user has to remember to run Goal Seek.

The Excel model is therefore not suitable for users who do not understand the model and know Excel. In VBA, we can take the same Excel model and have our code change the formula in B18 based on the difference between the retirement age and the current age. We can then run Goal Seek to generate the answer.

The Code for the Model

```
Option Explicit
Sub Saving_For_Retirement()

' Works with the worksheet that already has all formulas
' built in. It finds the initial annual savings
' requirement for different current and retirement ages by
' entering a new formula in B18 and then running Goal Seek.
```

```
8:
9:    Dim retAge, crntAge, numSav, fBal, tBase
10:
11:   Sheets("Model").Select
12:   Selection.Activate
13:
14:   retAge = Cells(13, 2).Value
15:   crntAge = Cells(12, 2).Value
16:   numSav = retAge - crntAge
17:
18:   fBal = "F" & 23 + numSav
19:   tBase = "G" & 23 + numSav
20:
21:   Cells(18, 2).Formula = "=" & fBal & "-(" & fBal & "-" & _
22:     tBase & ")*CapTax - B17"
23:
24:   Range("B18").GoalSeek Goal:=0, ChangingCell:=Range("B15")
25:
26:   End Sub
```

Analysis of the Code

Lines 14–16: Reads in the retirement and current ages and calculates the number of savings installments.

Lines 18–22: Defines some intermediate variables and uses them to create and insert a new formula in B18, using the cell from the table that should be used to reflect the number of savings installments. (Note that the table remains the same and still has the same number of rows as before, but the new formula inserted in B18 refers to a different cell in the table.)

Line 24: Runs Goal Seek.

Testing the Model

To test the model, clear the formula in B18. Run the model with the same inputs as before and make sure that you are getting the same answer. Also check the new formula in B18. If it works with the old input values then it should work with other values as well.

Limitation of the Model

One limitation of the model is that it does not create a table that neatly ends at the retirement age. You have to start with a table long enough to cover whatever number of years the user may enter and the table will remain the same. If you want a table that does not show extra years, you can either have VBA delete the extra lines or create a fresh table every time. The latter will require more code than the former, but it will give you some practice in creating worksheet formulas with VBA. We will develop the code in the next model.

MODEL 2: SAVING FOR RETIREMENT, VERSION 2

The Problem

Develop a model for the same problem as in Model 1. This time, though, have the code create a new table every time by recreating all the necessary formulas so that the output table will have only as many lines as necessary. The output will look like Figure 27.2.

Modeling Strategy

The objective of this model is to literally create an Excel model using VBA and find the answer using Goal Seek. The model is identical to the Excel model and so the formulas you have to create are the same.

	1	2	3	4	5	6	7
1	**Saving for Retirement**						
2							
3	**Inputs**						
4	Target balance (in today's dollars)	$1,000,000					
5	Current savings balance ($)	$100,000					
6	Expected annual inflation rate (%)	3.00%					
7	Planned savings increment rate (%)	2.00%					
8	Expected annual dividend income (%)	2.00%					
9	Expected annual capital appreciation (%)	6.00%					
10	Ordinary income tax rate on dividends (%)	15.00%					
11	Capital gains tax rate (%)	15.00%					
12	Current age	40					
13	Retirement age	65					
14							
15	Required first year annual saving	**$18,295**					
16	Number of installments of savings	25					
17	Target balance in future dollars	$2,093,778					
18	Final after-tax balance less target balance	**$0**					
19							
20							
21		Yr-beg bal	Annual	Dividend	Capital	Yr-end bal	Tax
22		(Pre saving)	Saving	Income	Appreciation	After div tax	Basis
23							
24	1	$100,000	$18,295	$2,366	$7,098	$127,404	$120,307
25	2	$127,404	$18,661	$2,921	$8,764	$157,313	$141,451
26	3	$157,313	$19,035	$3,527	$10,581	$189,926	$163,484
27	4	$189,926	$19,415	$4,187	$12,560	$225,461	$186,458
28	5	$225,461	$19,804	$4,905	$14,716	$264,150	$210,431
29	6	$264,150	$20,200	$5,687	$17,061	$306,244	$235,464
45	22	$1,592,273	$27,730	$32,400	$97,200	$1,744,743	$852,305
46	23	$1,744,743	$28,284	$35,461	$106,382	$1,909,551	$910,731
47	24	$1,909,551	$28,850	$38,768	$116,304	$2,087,658	$972,534
48	25	$2,087,658	$29,427	$42,342	$127,025	$2,280,100	$1,037,952
49							

FIGURE 27.2 Model 2: Saving for retirement using a new table each time.

The Code for the Model

```
Option Explicit
Sub Saving_For_Retirement2()

' Enters formulas only in as many lines as needed and
' also a new formula in B18 and then finds the initial
' savings requirement by running Goal Seek.

Dim retAge, crntAge, numSav, fBal, tBase

Sheets("Model").Select
Selection.Activate

retAge = Cells(13, 2).Value
crntAge = Cells(12, 2).Value
numSav = retAge - crntAge

' Clears the table from the previous run
Rows("24:124").Select
Selection.ClearContents

' Enter formulas in row 25
Cells(25, 1).Formula = "=A24+1"
Cells(25, 2).Formula = "=F24"
Cells(25, 3).Formula = "=C24*(1+SavIncr)"
Cells(25, 4).Formula = "=(B25+C25)*DivRet"
Cells(25, 5).Formula = "=(B25+C25)*CapRet"
Cells(25, 6).Formula = "=(B25+C25+E25)+D25*(1-OrdTax)"
Cells(25, 7).Formula = "= G24+C25+D25*(1-OrdTax)"

' Copy formulas into other rows
Range("A25:G25").Copy Range("A26:G" & 23 + numSav)
Range("A25:G25").Copy Range("A24:G24")

' Enter unique formulas in the first row (row 24)
Cells(24, 1).Formula = 1
Cells(24, 2).Formula = "=CurBal"
Cells(24, 3).Formula = "=AnlSav"
Cells(24, 7).Formula = "=B24+C24+D24*(1-OrdTax)"

' Create formula for B18
fBal = "F" & 23 + numSav
tBase = "G" & 23 + numSav
Cells(18, 2).Formula = "=" & fBal & "-(" & fBal & "-" & _
  tBase & ")*CapTax - B17"

```

```
46:     ' Run Goal Seek
47:     Range("B18").GoalSeek Goal:=0, ChangingCell:=Range("B15")
48:
49:     End Sub
```

Analysis of the Code

Lines 10–11: Makes the “Model” sheet the active sheet.

Lines 13–15: Reads in the current and retirement ages and calculates the number of savings installments.

Lines 18–19: Clears the previous table.

Lines 22–28: Inserts the formulas in the second row of the table. Note that the names used in the formulas are names of cells in the worksheet and not variable names in the VBA code. You will have to create the names in the worksheet.

Lines 31–32: Copies the formulas from the second row of the table into all other rows including the first row.

Lines 35–38: Inserts new formulas in the first row of the table where the formulas need to be different from those in the other rows.

Lines 41–46: Same as in Model 1.

Testing the Model

You can test this model using the results from Model 1 or the Excel version.

Uses of the Model

This model does not do much more than Model 1 or the Excel model, but it produces a more elegant output sheet, and unlike in the Excel model, the user does not have to remember to run Goal Seek every time. Note that the last row in the table here coincides with the retirement year. Also, as was the case with the other models, this is a versatile model with which to do calculations for savings requirements.

MODEL 3: RETIREMENT PLANNING IN NOMINAL DOLLARS, VERSION 1

The Problem

A friend of yours who is close to retirement has asked for your advice on how he should invest his assets and manage his withdrawals during retirement. He will need to withdraw a specific amount of money (growing at the rate of inflation) every year for living expenses. He wants you to develop a model for him. This model should estimate how much money your friend can expect to withdraw annually during retirement under various assumptions from a nest egg of certain size. It should also estimate what size nest egg he will have to accumulate by the time of retirement to be able to withdraw a certain inflation-adjusted amount annually. (All of the money is invested in taxable accounts.)

You explain to him the retirement planning approach we discussed earlier under "Nominal Dollar Retirement Planning" in Chapter 15: Financial Planning and Investments and he agrees to follow that approach. Build him a model that he can use to address his two concerns. The input variables for the model are: returns on fixed income and equity investments, ordinary income and capital gains tax rates, inflation rate, funds available for initial investment, initial annual withdrawal, and security horizon. The output worksheet for this model is shown in Figure 27.3.

Modeling Strategy

For this version I use exactly the same modeling strategy as in the Excel model. Effectively, what you have to do is give the value represented by each column in the Excel a variable name and write the equation to calculate it in terms of the other variables. The equations will be the same as the formulas in those cells. As we saw in the Excel model, most of the equations will be same for all years except for a few that are different in the first year. In VBA you will use a loop (I have used a `For` loop) to repeat the same calculations for all the years. Where necessary, use `If` statements to do a set of calculations differently for the first year than for the other years.

One thing to keep in mind about VBA is that if certain calculations use the results from other calculations, then you have to be careful to do them in the right order. This is not an issue in Excel because Excel figures out in what order it needs to do calculations. Also keep in mind that once you assign a value to a variable, the variable retains that value until you change it. When you do calculations for a new year, for example, most variables will still have their values from the previous year. Therefore, if you do not do the calculations in the right order, some of them may use outdated values. Once they creep into a code, such subtle errors are often difficult to trace.

Because in this version you will essentially imitate the Excel model, as happens with that model, the balance of the investment in stocks may become negative after a certain number of years and the model outputs will not be meaningful beyond that point. Unlike in the Excel model, though, here you can end the table once the stock balance becomes negative so that the table will not have meaningless numbers.

	1	2	3	4	5	6	7	8	9	10	11	12	13	14	15
1	**Retirement Planning in Nominal Dollars**														
2															
3	Return on fixed income		6%												
4	Return on stocks		12%												
5	Tax rate (ordinary)		25%												
6	Tax rate (cap. gains)		15%												
7	Inflation rate		3%												
8	Initial balance		$1,300,000												
9	Initial annual withdrawal		$65,000												
10	Security horizon (years)		15												
11															
12															
13	Year	Total Bal.	FI Holding	After-tax	Stock Hold.	Annual	Int Income	Return on	Stock Hold.	FI Holding	Total Bal.	Tax Basis	Basis	CG Tax	Check on
14		Year-beg.	Year-beg	Stock Sales	Year-beg	Withdrawal	After Tax	Stock	Year-end	Year-end	Year-end	of Stock	Used	Paid	Tax Paid
15															
16	1	$1,300,000	$817,873	$0	$417,127	$65,000	$36,804	$50,055	$467,182	$854,677	$1,321,860	$417,127			
17	2	$1,320,966	$842,409	($54,682)	$411,607	$66,950	$37,908	$49,393	$461,000	$880,317	$1,341,318	$367,507	$49,621	$893	$21,860
18	3	$1,339,551	$867,681	($56,322)	$402,911	$68,959	$39,046	$48,349	$451,260	$906,727	$1,357,987	$321,198	$46,309	$1,767	$20,351
19	4	$1,355,366	$893,712	($58,012)	$390,627	$71,027	$40,217	$46,875	$437,502	$933,929	$1,371,431	$278,040	$43,158	$2,621	$18,436
20	5	$1,367,975	$920,523	($59,752)	$374,294	$73,158	$41,424	$44,915	$419,209	$961,947	$1,381,156	$237,870	$40,170	$3,456	$16,065
21	6	$1,376,885	$948,139	($61,545)	$353,394	$75,353	$42,666	$42,407	$395,801	$990,805	$1,386,606	$200,525	$37,345	$4,271	$13,181
22	7	$1,381,539	$976,583	($63,391)	$327,343	$77,613	$43,946	$39,281	$366,624	$1,020,529	$1,387,154	$165,842	$34,683	$5,066	$9,721
23	8	$1,381,310	$1,005,880	($65,293)	$295,488	$79,942	$45,265	$35,459	$330,946	$1,051,145	$1,382,091	$133,664	$32,179	$5,844	$5,614
24	9	$1,375,487	$1,036,057	($67,252)	$257,090	$82,340	$46,623	$30,851	$287,941	$1,082,679	$1,370,620	$103,834	$29,829	$6,604	$781
25	10	$1,363,272	$1,067,138	($69,269)	$211,323	$84,810	$48,021	$25,359	$236,682	$1,115,160	$1,351,842	$76,205	$27,629	$7,348	($4,867)
26	11	$1,343,764	$1,099,153	($71,347)	$157,257	$87,355	$49,462	$18,871	$176,128	$1,148,615	$1,324,742	$50,633	$25,573	$8,078	($11,430)
27	12	$1,315,948	$1,132,127	($73,488)	$93,846	$89,975	$50,946	$11,261	$105,107	$1,183,073	$1,288,180	$26,978	$23,654	$8,794	($19,022)
28	13	$1,278,681	$1,166,091	($75,693)	$19,916	$92,674	$52,474	$2,390	$22,306	$1,218,565	$1,240,871	$5,112	$21,866	$9,499	($27,768)
29	14	$1,230,678	$1,201,074	($77,963)	($65,851)	$95,455	$54,048	($7,902)	($73,753)	$1,255,122	$1,181,369	($15,091)	$20,203	$10,193	($37,810)
30															

FIGURE 27.3 Model 3: Retirement planning in nominal dollars.

The Code for the Model

```
Sub Retirement_Planning_Ver1()

' In this version stock holdings can go negative
' Printing is stopped at that point

'*********************************************************
' Read in input data
'*********************************************************
Worksheets("Model").Activate

retFI = Cells(3, 3).Value 'Return on fixed income
retEq = Cells(4, 3).Value 'Return on equity
taxOI = Cells(5, 3).Value 'Ordinary income tax rate
taxCG = Cells(6, 3).Value 'Capital gains tax rate
inflRate = Cells(7, 3).Value
initInv = Cells(8, 3).Value
initAnnlDraw = Cells(9, 3).Value
secHrzn = Cells(10, 3).Value

outRow = 15

Rows(outRow & ":" & outRow + 200).Select
Selection.ClearContents

'*********************************************************
' Calculations
'*********************************************************
For yearNum = 1 To 30

annlDraw = initAnnlDraw * (1 + inflRate) ^ (yearNum - 1)
ybFIBal = PV((1 + retFI * (1 - taxOI)) / _
  (1 + inflRate) - 1, secHrzn - 1, -annlDraw,, 0)

If yearNum = 1 Then
    atEqSale = 0
    ybTotBal = initInv
    ybEqBal = ybTotBal - ybFIBal - annlDraw
    eqTaxBase = ybEqBal
Else
    atEqSale = yeFIBal - ybFIBal - annlDraw
    ybEqBal = yeEqBal + atEqSale / (1 - taxCG + taxCG _
    * eqTaxBase / yeEqBal)
  prevEqTaxBase = eqTaxBase
  eqTaxBase = eqTaxBase * ybEqBal / yeEqBal
End If
```

```
46:
47:     If yearNum <> 1 Then
48:         taxBaseUsed = prevEqTaxBase - eqTaxBase
49:         cgTaxPaid = (yeEqBal - ybEqBal - taxBaseUsed) * taxCG
50:         taxCheck = yeTotBal - ybTotBal
51:     End If
52:
53:     atIntInc = ybFIBal * retFI * (1 - taxOI)
54:     retOnEqBal = ybEqBal * retEq
55:     yeEqBal = ybEqBal + retOnEqBal
56:     yeFIBal = ybFIBal + atIntInc
57:     ybTotBal = ybFIBal + ybEqBal + annlDraw
58:     yeTotBal = yeEqBal + yeFIBal
59:
60:     'Data output section
61:     Cells(outRow + yearNum, 1).Value = yearNum
62:     Cells(outRow + yearNum, 2).Value = ybTotBal
63:     Cells(outRow + yearNum, 3).Value = ybFIBal
64:     Cells(outRow + yearNum, 4).Value = atEqSale
65:     Cells(outRow + yearNum, 5).Value = ybEqBal
66:     Cells(outRow + yearNum, 6).Value = annlDraw
67:     Cells(outRow + yearNum, 7).Value = atIntInc
68:     Cells(outRow + yearNum, 8).Value = retOnEqBal
69:     Cells(outRow + yearNum, 9).Value = yeEqBal
70:     Cells(outRow + yearNum, 10).Value = yeFIBal
71:     Cells(outRow + yearNum, 11).Value = yeTotBal
72:     Cells(outRow + yearNum, 12).Value = eqTaxBase
73:
74:     If yearNum <> 1 Then
75:         Cells(outRow + yearNum, 13).Value = taxBaseUsed
76:         Cells(outRow + yearNum, 14).Value = cgTaxPaid
77:         Cells(outRow + yearNum, 15).Value = taxCheck
78:     End If
79:
80:     If ybEqBal < 0 Then Exit For
81:
82:     Next yearNum
83:
84:     End Sub
```

Analysis of the Code

Lines 9–18: Activates the "Model" sheet and reads in the input data.

Lines 22–23: Clears the table from the last run.

Lines 28–82: The main `For` loop of the code, which is executed once for each row.

Lines 30–32: Calculates the annual withdrawal amount and required year-beginning balance of safe investment for the current year using the same equations as the Excel model.

Lines 34–45: This `If` structure is used to do separate calculations that are different between the first year and all other years. In both cases, the calculations are the same as in the Excel model.

Lines 47–51: Does the calculations related to tax basis, but the `If` structure bypasses them for the first year when these calculations are not needed.

Lines 53–58: Does the other calculations that are the same for all the years.

Lines 61–72: Outputs the data common to all the years.

Lines 74–78: Outputs the data related to tax basis. The `If` statement excludes the first year because these outputs are not meaningful for the first year.

Line 80: Exits the loop if the stock balance at the beginning of the year becomes negative. Note that because this condition is checked after the data for a particular year has been written out, the data for the first year when the balance becomes negative is included in the table (as it should be). If we had used a `Do` loop instead of a `For` loop, we could have included this condition in the `Loop` line as `Loop While` or `Loop Until`.

Testing the Model

You can check this model's output against the Excel model's output or you can use the method we discussed for the Excel model to test the model.

Uses of the Model

So far this model does not do anything more than the Excel model, although by ending the table when the stock balance becomes negative it avoids putting out meaningless numbers. As before, we can calculate from this output how long a certain amount of initial saving will last. We can also use a trial and error approach to calculate how much money one would need to start with to provide for a specific growing annual withdrawal for a specified number of years. It is easy to automate this process by putting an iteration loop around the code we already have.

Notice that although this model does the calculations the same way as the Excel model does, the equations are much easier to follow and audit in VBA: any changes that have to be made occur in only one place.

MODEL 4: RETIREMENT PLANNING IN NOMINAL DOLLARS, VERSION 2

The Problem

Modify the code in Model 3 so that it will create the correct draw-down table all the way until all money is completely drawn down. This means that the stock holdings will not go negative, and after all the stock holdings are used up, future withdrawals will be made from the fixed-income holdings until the retiree runs out of money. The output for this model is shown in Figure 27.4.

Modeling Strategy

This model should have three stages. The first stage is the same as Model 3. Once the stock holdings become negative, the code enters the second stage. In this stage you will effectively have to backtrack and sell in that year the remaining portion of the stock holdings and make up for the difference (that is, get the balance of the money to cover the withdrawal for the year) from the fixed-income holdings. Then, in the third stage, you will keep drawing down the fixed-income holdings and stop when you run out of money.

The Code for the Model

```
Sub Retirement_Withdrawals_Ver2()

' In this version stock holdings cannot go negative.
' After all stock is sold, fixed-income holdings is
' drawn down to zero and execution stops.

'**********************************************************
' Read in input data
'**********************************************************
Worksheets("Model").Activate

retFI = Cells(3, 3).Value 'Return on fixed income
retEq = Cells(4, 3).Value 'Return on equity
taxOI = Cells(5, 3).Value 'Ordinary income tax rate
taxCG = Cells(6, 3).Value 'Capital gains tax rate
inflRate = Cells(7, 3).Value
initInv = Cells(8, 3).Value
initAnnlDraw = Cells(9, 3).Value
secHrzn = Cells(10, 3).Value

outRow = 15

```

	1	2	3	4	5	6	7	8	9	10	11	12	13	14	15
1	**Retirement Planning in Nominal Dollars**														
2															
3	Return on fixed income		6%												
4	Return on stocks		12%												
5	Tax rate (ordinary)		25%												
6	Tax rate (cap. gains)		15%												
7	Inflation rate		3%												
8	Initial balance		$1,300,000												
9	Initial annual withdrawal		$65,000												
10	Security horizon (years)		15												
11															
12															
13	Year	Total Bal.	FI Holding	After-tax	Stock Hold.	Annual	Int Income	Return on	Stock Hold.	FI Holding	Total Bal.	Tax Basis	Basis	CG Tax	Check on
14		Year-beg.	Year-beg	Stock Sales	Year-beg	Withdrawal	After Tax	Stock	Year-end	Year-end	Year-end	of Stock	Used	Paid	Tax Paid
15															
16	1	$1,300,000	$817,873	$0	$417,127	$65,000	$36,804	$50,055	$467,182	$854,677	$1,321,860	$417,127			
17	2	$1,320,966	$842,409	($54,682)	$411,607	$66,950	$37,908	$49,393	$461,000	$880,317	$1,341,318	$367,507	$49,621	$893	$21,860
18	3	$1,339,551	$867,681	($56,322)	$402,911	$68,959	$39,046	$48,349	$451,260	$906,727	$1,357,987	$321,198	$46,309	$1,767	$20,351
19	4	$1,355,366	$893,712	($58,012)	$390,627	$71,027	$40,217	$46,875	$437,502	$933,929	$1,371,431	$278,040	$43,158	$2,621	$18,436
20	5	$1,367,975	$920,523	($59,752)	$374,294	$73,158	$41,424	$44,915	$419,209	$961,947	$1,381,156	$237,870	$40,170	$3,456	$16,065
21	6	$1,376,885	$948,139	($61,545)	$353,394	$75,353	$42,666	$42,407	$395,801	$990,805	$1,386,606	$200,525	$37,345	$4,271	$13,181
22	7	$1,381,539	$976,583	($63,391)	$327,343	$77,613	$43,946	$39,281	$366,624	$1,020,529	$1,387,154	$165,842	$34,683	$5,066	$9,721
23	8	$1,381,310	$1,005,880	($65,293)	$295,488	$79,942	$45,265	$35,459	$330,946	$1,051,145	$1,382,091	$133,664	$32,179	$5,844	$5,614
24	9	$1,375,487	$1,036,057	($67,252)	$257,090	$82,340	$46,623	$30,851	$287,941	$1,082,679	$1,370,620	$103,834	$29,829	$6,604	$781
25	10	$1,363,272	$1,067,138	($69,269)	$211,323	$84,810	$48,021	$25,359	$236,682	$1,115,160	$1,351,842	$76,205	$27,629	$7,348	($4,867)
26	11	$1,343,764	$1,099,153	($71,347)	$157,257	$87,355	$49,462	$18,871	$176,128	$1,148,615	$1,324,742	$50,633	$25,573	$8,078	($11,430)
27	12	$1,315,948	$1,132,127	($73,488)	$93,846	$89,975	$50,946	$11,261	$105,107	$1,183,073	$1,288,180	$26,978	$23,654	$8,794	($19,022)
28	13	$1,278,681	$1,166,091	($75,693)	$19,916	$92,674	$52,474	$2,390	$22,306	$1,218,565	$1,240,871	$5,112	$21,866	$9,499	($27,768)
29	14	$1,258,018	$1,142,837	($19,727)	$0	$95,455	$51,428	$2,390	$0	$1,194,265	$1,194,265				
30	15	$1,194,265	$1,095,946	$0	$0	$98,318	$49,318	$2,390	$0	$1,145,264	$1,145,264				
31	16	$1,145,264	$1,043,996	$0	$0	$101,268	$46,980	$2,390	$0	$1,090,976	$1,090,976				
32	17	$1,090,976	$986,670	$0	$0	$104,306	$44,400	$2,390	$0	$1,031,070	$1,031,070				
33	18	$1,031,070	$923,635	$0	$0	$107,435	$41,564	$2,390	$0	$965,199	$965,199				
34	19	$965,199	$854,540	$0	$0	$110,658	$38,454	$2,390	$0	$892,995	$892,995				
35	20	$892,995	$779,017	$0	$0	$113,978	$35,056	$2,390	$0	$814,073	$814,073				
36	21	$814,073	$696,675	$0	$0	$117,397	$31,350	$2,390	$0	$728,026	$728,026				
37	22	$728,026	$607,107	$0	$0	$120,919	$27,320	$2,390	$0	$634,426	$634,426				
38	23	$634,426	$509,880	$0	$0	$124,547	$22,945	$2,390	$0	$532,824	$532,824				
39	24	$532,824	$404,541	$0	$0	$128,283	$18,204	$2,390	$0	$422,746	$422,746				
40	25	$422,746	$290,614	$0	$0	$132,132	$13,078	$2,390	$0	$303,692	$303,692				
41	26	$303,692	$167,596	$0	$0	$136,096	$7,542	$2,390	$0	$175,138	$175,138				
42	27	$175,138	$34,959	$0	$0	$140,178	$1,573	$2,390	$0	$36,533	$36,533				
43															

FIGURE 27.4 Model 4: Retirement planning in nominal dollars.

```
Rows(outRow & ":" & outRow + 200).Select
Selection.ClearContents

'**************************************************************
' Calculations until equity lasts
'**************************************************************
For yearNum = 1 To 50

annlDraw = initAnnlDraw * (1 + inflRate) ^ (yearNum - 1)
ybFIBal = PV((1 + retFI * (1 - taxOI)) / _
  (1 + inflRate) - 1, secHrzn - 1, -annlDraw,, 0)

If yearNum = 1 Then
    atEqSale = 0
    ybTotBal = initInv
    ybEqBal = ybTotBal - ybFIBal - annlDraw
    eqTaxBase = ybEqBal
Else
    atEqSale = yeFIBal - ybFIBal - annlDraw
    ybEqBal = yeEqBal + atEqSale / (1 - taxCG + taxCG _
      * eqTaxBase / yeEqBal)

    If ybEqBal < 0 Then Exit For

    prevEqTaxBase = eqTaxBase
    eqTaxBase = eqTaxBase * ybEqBal / yeEqBal
End If

If yearNum <> 1 Then
    taxBaseUsed = prevEqTaxBase - eqTaxBase
    cgTaxPaid = (yeEqBal - ybEqBal - taxBaseUsed) * taxCG
    taxCheck = yeTotBal - ybTotBal
End If

atIntInc = ybFIBal * retFI * (1 - taxOI)
retOnEqBal = ybEqBal * retEq
yeEqBal = ybEqBal + retOnEqBal
yeFIBal = ybFIBal + atIntInc
ybTotBal = ybFIBal + ybEqBal + annlDraw
yeTotBal = yeEqBal + yeFIBal

'Data output section
Cells(outRow + yearNum, 1).Value = yearNum
Cells(outRow + yearNum, 2).Value = ybTotBal
Cells(outRow + yearNum, 3).Value = ybFIBal
Cells(outRow + yearNum, 4).Value = atEqSale
Cells(outRow + yearNum, 5).Value = ybEqBal
Cells(outRow + yearNum, 6).Value = annlDraw
```

```
Cells(outRow + yearNum, 7).Value = atIntInc
Cells(outRow + yearNum, 8).Value = retOnEqBal
Cells(outRow + yearNum, 9).Value = yeEqBal
Cells(outRow + yearNum, 10).Value = yeFIBal
Cells(outRow + yearNum, 11).Value = yeTotBal
Cells(outRow + yearNum, 12).Value = eqTaxBase

If yearNum <> 1 Then
    Cells(outRow + yearNum, 13).Value = taxBaseUsed
    Cells(outRow + yearNum, 14).Value = cgTaxPaid
    Cells(outRow + yearNum, 15).Value = taxCheck
End If

Next yearNum

'**********************************************************
' Calculations after equity is used up
'**********************************************************
'Starts with the year when all equity investment is used up
yrEqUsedUp = yearNum

For yearNum = yrEqUsedUp To 50

annlDraw = initAnnlDraw * (1 + inflRate) ^ (yearNum - 1)

If yearNum = yrEqUsedUp Then
    'Calculate assuming all remaining equity is sold
    atEqSale = -yeEqBal + (yeEqBal - eqTaxBase) * taxCG
    ybFIBal = yeFIBal - atEqSale - annlDraw
    ybEqBal = 0
    yeEqBal = 0
Else
    atEqSale = 0
    ybFIBal = yeFIBal - annlDraw
End If

atIntInc = ybFIBal * retFI * (1 - taxOI)
yeFIBal = ybFIBal + atIntInc
yeTotBal = yeFIBal

If yearNum = yrEqUsedUp Then
    ybTotBal = ybFIBal + annlDraw - atEqSale
Else
    ybTotBal = ybFIBal + annlDraw
End If

 'Data output section
 Cells(outRow + yearNum, 1).Value = yearNum
```

```
119:    Cells(outRow + yearNum, 2).Value = ybTotBal
120:    Cells(outRow + yearNum, 3).Value = ybFIBal
121:    Cells(outRow + yearNum, 4).Value = atEqSale
122:    Cells(outRow + yearNum, 5).Value = ybEqBal
123:    Cells(outRow + yearNum, 6).Value = annlDraw
124:    Cells(outRow + yearNum, 7).Value = atIntInc
125:    Cells(outRow + yearNum, 8).Value = retOnEqBal
126:    Cells(outRow + yearNum, 9).Value = yeEqBal
127:    Cells(outRow + yearNum, 10).Value = yeFIBal
128:    Cells(outRow + yearNum, 11).Value = yeTotBal
129:
130:    ' Goes out of For loop when year-beg FI holdings go negative
131:    If ybFIBal < 0 Then Exit For
132:
133:    Next yearNum
134:
135:    ' Deletes last line with negative year-beg FI balance
136:    Rows(outRow + yearNum).Select
137:    Selection.Delete Shift:=xlUp
138:
139:    End Sub
```

Analysis of the Code

Lines 1–84: This part of the code is same as that for Model 3 except for line 45.

Line 45: Exits the `For` loop when the year-beginning stock holdings become negative. In Model 3, this line was after the printout lines because we wanted to include in the table the numbers for the year in which the stock holdings go negative. In this model, however, we want to do the calculations for that year differently and so we want to get out of the loop without entering the numbers for the year in the table.

Line 90: Saves in a new variable the year number when the stock holdings run out.

Lines 92–133: Combines stages 2 and 3 in one `For` loop. The two stages are distinguished using an `If` structure inside the loop.

Lines 96–105: The `If` structure that does calculations differently for stages 2 and 3. In the first year of the loop in which the remaining portion of the stock holdings have to be sold, the `True` part of the `If` structure is executed. In the remaining years, the `Else` part of the structure is executed.

Lines 98–101: Sells all the remaining stocks and sets the values of the other variables appropriately.

Lines 103–104: For stage 3 years, makes after-tax stock sales zero and calculates year-beginning fixed-income balance differently.

Lines 107–109: Does a few more calculations that are common to both stages 2 and 3.

Lines 111–115: This `If` structure calculates the year-beginning total balance differently for stages 2 and 3.

Lines 118–128: Enters the results for the year in the table.

Line 131: Exits the `For` loop and ends the table when the year-beginning fixed income balance becomes negative.

Lines 136–137: In the last row of the table the year-beginning fixed-income holdings went negative, but we do not want it in the table. This code deletes the last row of the table.

Testing the Model

You can test the first stage of the model against the results of the previous versions. Then in the transition year (stage 2), check to make sure that the code is selling the right amount of stocks to get the stock holdings down to zero. The other numbers on the line should reflect that. In subsequent years, check that the right amount is being drawn down from the fixed-income holdings. The remaining balance in the last line should be less than the withdrawal requirement for the next year.

Uses of the Model

Here the output clearly shows that for this set of inputs, the money will last for a little more than 27 years. We were able to come to the same conclusion from the previous models as well. Here, though, the answer is clearer and the table shows correct numbers all the way to the last year.

As before, we can use a trial and error approach to calculate how much money one would need to start with to provide for a specific growing annual withdrawal for a specified number of years. We can also automate the process by putting an iteration loop around this code. Speed is not going to be much of an issue here. However, as I have discussed before, if we want to attempt an iteration solution, it will be better and faster to do everything using arrays and output only the final numbers to the table. In VBA, reading from and writing out to worksheets is a rather slow process (relative to many other operations) and therefore using this model—which will write out a table for each iteration—will somewhat slow down execution.

MODEL 5: PORTFOLIO STRUCTURING

The Problem

Create a model that an investor can use to structure a portfolio using the three-level approach discussed in Chapter 15: Financial Planning and Investments. The user will input the total portfolio size, the allocations at the levels of asset class, and the categories within each asset class in one worksheet ("Inputs"). The choice of funds within each category and the user's allocation to the funds he wants to invest in will be on a separate worksheet ("Funds"). The model's output should be in a third worksheet ("Portfolio") that shows a clear picture of the target portfolio and only the funds with investment in them.

Modeling Strategy

We have already developed the same model in Excel. The "Inputs" sheets, as shown in Figure 27.5, uses three asset classes: money market, stocks, and bonds. Within each asset class the worksheet provides for several asset categories. The user can quite easily add more categories as long as he uses the same format and provides a symbol for each category that ties to the same category in the "Funds" sheet. The user inputs his allocations to the asset classes and the categories within them here.

As before, instead of asking the user to show his allocation to each category as percentage of the entire portfolio, have him enter the allocation as percentage of the asset class to which it belongs. For example, if the user indicates that he wants 20% of his equity investments to go into large-cap value funds, then as he changes his allocation to stocks, the allocation to each category within it will change (as it should be). The allocations to all the categories within each asset class should add up to 100%.

The funds available for selection are included in the "Funds" worksheet under the appropriate categories as shown in Figure 27.6. New funds can be added easily and must include a symbol. Allocations to individual funds within each category should be as percentage of the category and not the asset class. The allocations to funds in each category should add up to 100%. This structure of the model has the advantage that any change in allocation at a higher level will cascade down to the lower levels.

Structure the output sheet ("Portfolio") as shown in Figure 27.7. This sheet should show only the categories and funds that are being used.

The calculations are straightforward. The dollar allocation to a fund is the dollar size of the portfolio multiplied by the percent allocations to the fund's asset class, its category (except in the case of a money market fund), and to the fund.

	1	2	3
1		**Portolio Targets**	
2			
3		**Total portfolio value**	$2,000,000
4			
5		**Asset allocation**	
6	MK	Money market percentage	10%
7		Stock percentage	60%
8			
9			
10		**Domestic Stocks**	
11	LC	Large cap	18%
12	LV	Large cap value	28%
13	SC	Small cap	8%
14	SV	Small cap value	16%
15	RE	REIT	10%
16	SO	Other special categories	0%
17		**Total domestic stocks**	80%
18			
19		**International Stocks**	
20	IT	International developed markets	20%
21	IE	Emerging markets	0%
22		**Total international stocks**	20%
23			
24		**Total stocks**	**100%**
25			
26		**Bonds**	
27	SB	Short-term bonds	70%
28	MB	Intermediate-term bonds	0%
29	LB	Long-term bonds	0%
30	TB	Total return bonds	30%
31	IB	Inflation-protected bonds	0%
32	JB	Junk bonds	0%
33	FB	Foreign bond	0%
34		**Total bonds**	**100%**
35			
36			

FIGURE 27.5 Model 5: User's allocation to asset classes and categories.

The Code for the Model

```
Option Explicit
Sub Portfolio_Structuring()

' Creates target portfolio given the total portfolio size,
' target asset allocation (among money market, stocks,
' and bonds), and allocation by fund within each category.
' To add new funds within any category, insert a line with
' fund symbol and fund name within the category in the "Funds"
' worksheet. To remove a fund delete its line in "Funds" sheets

Dim pValR, stkPR, mmktPR, stkR, bndR, dtC
Dim rOff, ppC, pdC
Dim portVal, sPrcnt, mPrcnt, bPrcnt
```

	1	2	3
1	**Selected Funds to Choose from in Each Category**		
2			
3	**MK**	**Money market funds**	
4	VMPXX	Vanguard Treasury Money Market	10%
5	VMMXX	Vanguard Prime Money Market	40%
6	VMSXX	Vanguard Tax-Exempt Money Market	50%
7			
8			
9		**Stocks**	
10		**Domestic stocks**	
11	**LC**	**Large cap**	
12	VFINX	Vanguard 500 Index, Investor shares	50%
13	VMCAX	Vanguard Tax-Managed Capital Appreciation	
14	VTSMX	Vanguard Total Stock Market Index	50%
15			
16	**LV**	**Large cap value**	
17	VIVAX	Vanguard Value Index	100%
18	CFIMX	Clipper	
19			
20	**SC**	**Small cap**	
21	VEXMX	Vanguard Extended Market Index	100%
22	NAESX	Vanguard Small-Cap Index	
23			
24	**SV**	**Small cap value**	
25	VISVX	Vanguard Small-Cap Value Index	100%
26			
27	**RE**	**REIT**	
28	VGSIX	Vanguard REIT Index	100%
29			
30	**SO**	**Other special categories**	
31			
32		**International stocks**	
33	**IT**	**International developed markets**	
34	VDMIX	Vanguard Developed Markets Index	100%
35	VEURX	Vanguard European Stock Index	
36			
37	**IE**	**Emerging markets**	
38	VEIEX	Vanguard Emerging Market Stock Index	100%
39			
40			
41		**Bonds**	
42	**SB**	**Short term bonds**	
43	VBISX	Vanguard Short-Term Bond Index , Investor shares	30%
44	VFSTX	Vanguard Short-Term Corporate, Investor shares	
45	VFSUX	Vanguard Short-Term Corporate, Admiral shares	70%
46			
47	**IB**	**Intermediate-term bonds**	
48	VFIIX	Vanguard GNMA, Investor shares	
49	VFIJX	Vanguard GNMA, Admiral shares	
50			
51	**LB**	**Long-term bonds**	
52			
53	**TB**	**Total return bonds**	
54	FBDFX	Fremont Bond	40%
55	HABDX	Harbor Bond	60%
56	DODIX	Dodge & Cox Income	
57			
58	**IB**	**Inflation-protected bonds**	
59	VIPSX	Vanguard Inflation-Protected Securities Fund	
60			
61	**JB**	**Junk bonds**	
62	**FB**	**Foreign bonds**	
63			

FIGURE 27.6 Model 5: Available fund choices and the user's allocations to them.

	1	2	3	4
1	**Target Portfolio**			
2				
3			**Percent**	**Dollar**
4			**Allocations**	**Allocations**
5		**Money market**	**10.0%**	
6	VMPXX	Vanguard Treasury Money Market		$20,000
7	VMMXX	Vanguard Prime Money Market		$80,000
8	VMSXX	Vanguard Tax-Exempt Money Market		$100,000
9				
10		**Stocks**	**60.0%**	
11		**Large cap**	10.8%	
12	VFINX	Vanguard 500 Index, Investor shares		$108,000
13	VTSMX	Vanguard Total Stock Market Index		$108,000
14		**Large cap value**	16.8%	
15	VIVAX	Vanguard Value Index		$336,000
16		**Small cap**	4.8%	
17	VEXMX	Vanguard Extended Market Index		$96,000
18		**Small cap value**	9.6%	
19	VISVX	Vanguard Small-Cap Value Index		$192,000
20		**REIT**	6.0%	
21	VGSIX	Vanguard REIT Index		$120,000
22		**International developed markets**	12.0%	
23	VDMIX	Vanguard Developed Markets Index		$240,000
24				
25		**Bonds**	**30.0%**	
26		**Short term bonds**	21.0%	
27	VBISX	Vanguard Short-Term Bond Index, Investor shares		$126,000
28	VFSUX	Vanguard Short-Term Corporate, Admiral shares		$294,000
29		**Total return bonds**	9.0%	
30	FBDFX	Fremont Bond		$72,000
31	HABDX	Harbor Bond		$108,000
32				
33		**Portfolio value**		**$2,000,000**
34				
35				
36				

FIGURE 27.7 Model 5: Portfolio structure based on allocations provided by user.

```
Dim mDollar, sDollar, bDollar
Dim typeR, rOut, r1, r2, fndAlloc, fDollar
Dim stkCat, bndCat, catAlloc

'**********************************************************
' Information on structure of worksheets used
'**********************************************************
' Layout of "Inputs" sheet
pValR = 3 'Portfolio value row
stkPR = 7 'Stock percentage row
mmktPR = 6 'Money market percentage row
stkR = 11 'Row where stock category allocations start
bndR = 26 'Row where bond category allocations start
dtC = 3 'Input data column
```

```
    'Layout of Portfolio sheet
    rOff = 5 'First row of output
    ppC = 3 'Column for percentage allocation
    pdC = 4 'Column for dollar allocation

    '**********************************************************
    ' Read input data and set up worksheets
    '**********************************************************
    Sheets("Inputs").Activate
    portVal = Cells(pValR, dtC).Value 'Portfolio value
    sPrcnt = Cells(stkPR, dtC).Value 'Stock percentage
    mPrcnt = Cells(mmktPR, dtC).Value 'Money market percentage

    bPrcnt = 1 - mPrcnt - sPrcnt 'Bond percentage
    mDollar = portVal * mPrcnt 'Money market investment in dollars
    sDollar = portVal * sPrcnt 'Stock investment in dollars
    bDollar = portVal * (1 - mPrcnt - sPrcnt) 'Bond in dollars

    ' Clear old data
    Sheets("Portfolio").Activate
    Cells.Select
    Selection.Clear

    Cells(1, 1).Value = "Target Portfolio"
    Cells(1, 1).Font.Bold = True
    Cells(1, 1).Font.Size = 12

    Columns(ppC).Select
    Selection.NumberFormat = "#0.0%"
    Columns(pdC).Select
    Selection.NumberFormat = "$#,##0"

    rOut = rOff ' Keeps track of row in output (Portfolio) sheet

    Sheets("Funds").Activate 'This sheet is kept active

    '**********************************************************
    ' Money market funds
    '**********************************************************
    Sheets("Portfolio").Cells(rOut, 2).Value = "Money market"
    Sheets("Portfolio").Range("B" & rOut).Font.Bold = True
    Sheets("Portfolio").Range("B" & rOut).Font.Size = 12
    Sheets("Portfolio").Cells(rOut, ppC).Font.Bold = True
    Sheets("Portfolio").Cells(rOut, ppC).Value = mPrcnt

```

```
rOut = rOut + 1
' Find location of money market category in "Funds" sheet
typeR = Application.Match("MK", Range("A1:A300"), 0)
For r1 = typeR + 1 To typeR + 50
If Cells(r1, 1).Value = "" Then Exit For
fndAlloc = Cells(r1, 3).Value
If fndAlloc <> 0 Then
   fDollar = mDollar * fndAlloc
   Sheets("Funds").Range("A" & r1 & ":B" & r1).Copy _
     Sheets("Portfolio").Range("A" & rOut)
   Sheets("Portfolio").Cells(rOut, pdC).Value = fDollar
   rOut = rOut + 1
End If
Next r1
rOut = rOut + 1
'***********************************************************
' Calculations for stock categories and funds
'***********************************************************
Sheets("Portfolio").Cells(rOut, 2).Value = "Stocks"
Sheets("Portfolio").Range("B" & rOut).Font.Bold = True
Sheets("Portfolio").Range("B" & rOut).Font.Size = 12
Sheets("Portfolio").Cells(rOut, ppC).Font.Bold = True
Sheets("Portfolio").Cells(rOut, ppC).Value = sPrcnt
rOut = rOut + 1
For r2 = stkR To bndR - 1
If Sheets("Inputs").Range("A" & r2).Value <> "" And _
  Sheets("Inputs").Range("C" & r2).Value <> 0 Then
   stkCat = Sheets("Inputs").Range("A" & r2).Value
   catAlloc = Sheets("Inputs").Range("C" & r2).Value
   typeR = Application.Match(stkCat, Range("A1:A300"), 0)
   Range("B" & typeR).Copy _
     Sheets("Portfolio").Range("B" & rOut)
   Sheets("Portfolio").Cells(rOut, ppC).Value = sPrcnt * catAlloc
   rOut = rOut + 1
```

```
    For r1 = typeR + 1 To typeR + 20
        If Cells(r1, 1).Value = "" Then Exit For
            fndAlloc = Cells(r1, 3).Value
            If fndAlloc <> 0 Then
                fDollar = sDollar * fndAlloc * catAlloc
                Range("A" & r1 & ":B" & r1).Copy _
                  Sheets("Portfolio").Range("A" & rOut)
                Sheets("Portfolio").Cells(rOut, pdC).Value _
                  = fDollar
                rOut = rOut + 1
            End If
    Next r1
End If
Next r2

rOut = rOut + 1

'**************************************************************
' Calculations for bond categories and funds
'**************************************************************
Sheets("Portfolio").Cells(rOut, 2).Value = "Bonds"
Sheets("Portfolio").Range("B" & rOut).Font.Bold = True
Sheets("Portfolio").Range("B" & rOut).Font.Size = 12
Sheets("Portfolio").Cells(rOut, ppC).Font.Bold = True
Sheets("Portfolio").Cells(rOut, ppC).Value = bPrcnt

rOut = rOut + 1

For r2 = bndR To bndR + 30
If Sheets("Inputs").Range("A" & r2).Value <> "" And _
  Sheets("Inputs").Range("C" & r2).Value <> 0 Then

    bndCat = Sheets("Inputs").Range("A" & r2).Value
    catAlloc = Sheets("Inputs").Range("C" & r2).Value
    typeR = Application.Match(bndCat, Range("A1:A300"), 0)
    Range("B" & typeR).Copy _
      Sheets("Portfolio").Range("B" & rOut)
    Sheets("Portfolio").Cells(rOut, ppC).Value = bPrcnt * catAlloc
    rOut = rOut + 1

    For r1 = typeR + 1 To typeR + 20
        If Cells(r1, 1).Value = "" Then Exit For
            fndAlloc = Cells(r1, 3).Value
            If fndAlloc <> 0 Then
                fDollar = bDollar * fndAlloc * catAlloc
                Range("A" & r1 & ":B" & r1).Copy _
                Sheets("Portfolio").Range("A" & rOut)
```

```
                  Sheets("Portfolio").Cells(rOut, pdC).Value _
                    = fDollar
                  rOut = rOut + 1
              End If
      Next r1
  End If
  Next r2

  rOut = rOut + 1

  '************************************************************
  ' Headings and portfolio value for double-checking
  '************************************************************
  Sheets("Portfolio").Activate

  Cells(3, ppC).Value = "Percent"
  Call FormatBoldRight(10, 3, ppC)

  Cells(4, ppC).Value = "Allocations"
  Call FormatBoldRight(10, 4, ppC)

  Cells(3, pdC).Value = "Dollar"
  Call FormatBoldRight(10, 3, pdC)

  Cells(4, pdC).Value = "Allocations"
  Call FormatBoldRight(10, 4, pdC)

  Cells(rOut, 2).Value = "Portfolio value"
  Call FormatBold(12, rOut, 2)

  Cells(rOut, pdC).Value = Application.Sum(Range _
    (Cells(rOff, pdC), Cells(rOut - 1, pdC)))
  Call FormatBold(12, rOut, pdC)

  End Sub

  '------------------------------------------------------------
  '------------------------------------------------------------
  Sub FormatBoldRight(fSize, rowN, colN)
  ' Bolds, font sizes, right aligns a cell in the active sheet

  Cells(rowN, colN).Font.Size = fSize
  Cells(rowN, colN).Font.Bold = True
  Cells(rowN, colN).HorizontalAlignment = xlRight

  End Sub
```

```
214:  '-----------------------------------------------------------
215:  '-----------------------------------------------------------
216:  Sub FormatBold(fSize, rowN, colN)
217:  ' Bolds and font sizes a cell in the active sheet
218:
219:  Cells(rowN, colN).Font.Size = fSize
220:  Cells(rowN, colN).Font.Bold = True
221:
222:  End Sub
```

Analysis of the Code

Lines 22–32: Defines as variables several row and column numbers in the "Inputs" and "Portfolio" sheets so that, if necessary, they can be changed easily later.

Lines 38–40: Reads in some data from the "Inputs" sheet.

Line 42: Calculates the percentage allocation to bonds.

Lines 43–45: Calculates the dollar allocations to money market, stocks, and bonds.

Lines 48–50: Clears the "Portfolio" sheet of all old data, formatting, and so on.

Lines 56–59: Formats the two columns.

Line 61: Initializes `rOut`. This variable keeps track of where the next line of output should go on the "Portfolio" sheet. It is incremented after each line of output to go on to the next line.

Line 63: Activates the "Funds" worksheet because the program does most of its work with this worksheet. As a result, whenever other sheets are used, specific references are made to them.

Lines 68–72: Creates and formats a heading and writes out the money market percent allocation.

Line 74: Increments `rOut` for next line of output. Similar statements are used throughout the program for the same purpose. I will not mention them again.

Line 77: Uses Excel's `Match` function to find the row number of the beginning of the money market funds in the "Funds" sheet.

Line 79–91: This loop goes row by row to check if there is a percentage allocation against any of the money market funds. If there is, then it calculates money to be invested in the fund and writes that out in the "Portfolio" sheet. It recognizes the end of the money market funds when it detects a blank in column 1.

Line 81: This If statement checks if the first column of a row is blank. When it is blank, it assumes that row to be the end of funds in this category and exits the For loop.

Line 83: Reads in the allocation for a fund.

Line 84–90: This If structure checks if the allocation for the fund is blank. If it is, then the rest of the For loop is skipped and the next iteration through the For loop is started to go on to the next row. Otherwise the dollar allocation to the fund is calculated.

Line 85: The dollar allocation to the fund is calculated by multiplying the percentage allocation to it by the dollar allocation to money market.

Lines 86–87: Copies the fund symbol and name to the "Portfolio" sheet.

Line 88: Writes the dollar allocation to the fund on the "Portfolio" sheet.

Lines 98–102: Creates heading for the start of stocks and enters the percentage allocation to stocks.

Lines 106–133: The outer For loop to work through the different categories of stocks. For each category, the code works essentially the same way as it does for money market. The starting and ending rows are based on specifications (earlier in the code) indicating where the stock categories and the bond categories begin.

Lines 108–109: Checks if a row is a stock category and has allocation. Otherwise the current iteration through the loop is ended and the next one starts.

Line 111: Reads in the symbol of the stock category.

Line 112: Reads in the percentage allocation for the stock category.

Line 113: Finds the row in "Funds" sheet where this category starts by matching the category's symbol using Excel's Match function.

Lines 114–115: Copies the fund category name into the "Portfolio" sheet.

Line 116: Calculates and writes out the percentage allocation to the category by multiplying its percentage allocation specified in the "Inputs" sheet by the percentage allocation to stocks. The multiplication is necessary because the category allocation for a stock category is specified as percentages of stock holdings and not portfolio holdings.

Lines 120–131: The inner loop to calculate and write out the dollar allocation to each fund in the current stock category. This loop works exactly the same way as the corresponding loop in the money market part of the code we saw earlier. Here, each stock category is comparable to the money market category.

Lines 140–175: Handles the bond part of the portfolio exactly the same way as the stock part.

Line 180: Activates the "Portfolio" sheet because the rest of the work will be done on it.

Lines 182–195: Creates several labels and formats them using two Sub procedures.

Lines 197–198: Uses Excel's `Sum` function to total the dollar allocations to the various funds (to make sure that the sum matches the portfolio value specified) and writes it out.

Lines 205–212: A Sub procedure to format a designated cell in the active sheet with the specified font size. It also bolds and right-aligns the contents of the cell.

Lines 216–222: A Sub procedure to format the designated cell in the active sheet with the specified font size. It also bolds the contents of the cell.

In this code we have used three `For` loops similar to the one in lines 79–91 that are quite similar. We could have created a Sub procedure to avoid repeating similar codes in three places. However, because each of these was only a few lines long, repeating them is also acceptable. The problem is that now if any change is made in one, the same change may have to be made in three places. This increases the chance of making mistakes when making changes.

Testing the Model

If the total portfolio value that the model calculates at the bottom of the "Portfolio" sheet matches the specified portfolio value, then you can be reasonably sure that the model is working properly. It is also easy to visually check the "Portfolio" sheet for proper organization, labels, and names of funds as well as the percentage and dollar allocations to the categories and funds.

Uses of the Model

This model is very useful for structuring different portfolios. One advantage of this design is that the user can easily add more funds in each category or even add more categories. Unlike the corresponding model in Excel, the output sheet here is clearer because it does not show any category or fund that is not being used in the portfolio. In the Excel model, unused funds and categories have to be manually hidden. Otherwise, if you are working with a lot of funds to have a wide selection but choose to invest only in a few of them, the output sheet can look cluttered. Here the list of funds is on a separate sheet and is out of the way.

CHAPTER 28

Analyzing Market History

In this chapter, we will use VBA to develop several models that we developed earlier using Excel to measure and show the performance of various asset classes both over time and relative to each other. The models will also plot the results in a few different types of charts commonly used to display them.

The key advantage of the models in this chapter over those we developed with Excel is that these models are more flexible. Even users who do not know Excel or VBA will be able to do a broader range of analysis with them.

This chapter does not introduce any new theory or concepts. Unless you are familiar with the material, you may want to first review the theory and concepts (as well as the models) in the chapter by the same name in Part Two.

Modeling Examples

MODEL 1: NOMINAL AND REAL GROWTH OF $1 INVESTMENT IN STOCKS

The Problem

Given the monthly price and dividend data for an index of large-cap stocks for the period from December 1945 to December 1999 and the corresponding CPI values, calculate in nominal and real terms the growth of an initial $1 investment over time. Make the starting and ending months input variables of the model so that the user can specify the period. Also calculate the nominal and real effective annual returns over the specified period.

Your model should provide a table showing the month-by-month growth of the investment and plot a chart to show the growth over time and compare nominal and real growths similar to Figures 28.1 and 28.2.

	1	2	3	4	5	6	7	8	9
1	**Nominal and Real Growth of $1 Investment with Dividend Reinvested**								
2									
3	Start year	1950		Nominal annualized return			12.23%		
4	Start month	1		Real annualized return			7.58%		
5	End year	1990							
6	End month	1							
7									
8									
9		Nominal	Real						
10	1950.01	1.00	1.00						
11	1950.02	1.03	1.03						
12	1950.03	1.04	1.03						
13	1950.04	1.07	1.07						
14	1950.05	1.12	1.11						
15	1950.06	1.14	1.13						
16	1950.07	1.06	1.04						
17	1950.08	1.13	1.10						
485	1989.08	101.53	19.15						
486	1989.09	101.99	19.17						
487	1989.10	102.28	19.14						
488	1989.11	100.43	18.75						
489	1989.12	103.18	19.23						
490	1990.01	100.89	18.61						
491									
492									

FIGURE 28.1 Model 1: Nominal and real growth of $1 investment in stocks.

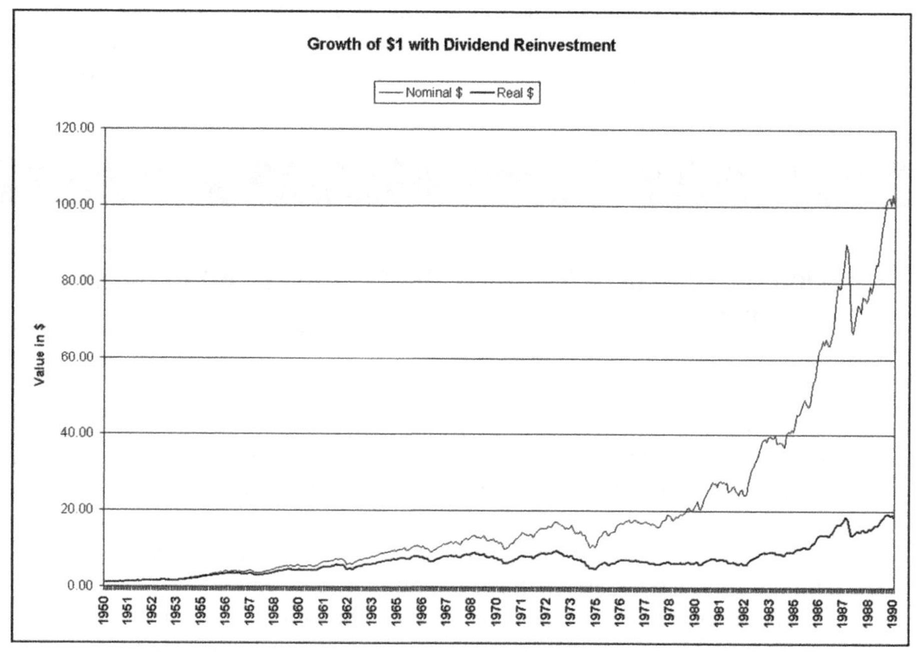

FIGURE 28.2 Model 1: Nominal and real growth of $1 investment in stocks.

Assume that the prices provided are per (notional) share at the beginning of the month, the dividends are paid monthly at the end of the month and are shown annualized (monthly values times 12), and the CPI values are for the beginning of the month. (Stocks generally pay quarterly dividends. However, since indexes comprise many stocks that pay dividends at different times, indexes are generally assumed to pay dividends on a monthly basis.)

Modeling Strategy

To calculate the total returns in nominal terms, use the definition of total return in the following steps: Start with an initial investment of $1 and calculate how many shares you will be able to buy with that money. At the end of the month, calculate the dividend you will receive on the shares you bought, and then calculate how many additional shares you will be able to buy at the stock price of the beginning of the next month using the dividend received. This gives you the number of shares you will own at the beginning of the next month, and then you can repeat the steps all the way to the end of the period.

At the beginning of each month, the nominal value of your portfolio (or initial investment) equals the number of shares owned times the price per share at that point. Calculate the real value or value in constant dollars of the beginning of the period by multiplying the nominal value by the ratio of the CPI at the beginning of the period and the current month.

Calculate the annualized returns using the cumulative values of the initial investment, that is, the final value of the $1 investment and the number of months in the period specified.

To write the procedure to plot the chart, turn on the Macro Recorder, create the chart using the Chart Wizard, and then convert it into a Sub procedure that your main procedure will call (execute) to plot the chart. You will need to modify the range of the data series that the procedure plots so that it always reflects the data period specified by the user. To accomplish this, you will have to pass on to the Sub procedure the row number of the last row of data to be plotted as an argument.

The Code for the Model

```
Option Explicit
Sub CalcCumReturn()

 ' Calculates how value of $1 invested at any point in time
 ' will grow in real and nominal terms to a terminal point.
 ' Uses monthly data and monthly reinvestment of dividend.
```

```

' Assume price in table is for beginning of month.
' Div shown on same line is collected at end of month and
' reinvested at next month's price.
' Inflation index assumed to be for the first day of the
' month shown in that row

Dim Stock(1 To 1000), Div(1 To 1000), Cpi(1 To 1000)
Dim YrMo(1 To 1000)
Dim inSheet, outSheet
Dim startYr, startMo, endYr, endMo, initInv
Dim firstDataRow, yrMoCol, stockCol, divCol, cpiCol
Dim numDataRows, printRow, outCol, roNum1, roNum3, rowOffset
Dim startRo, endRo, numShares, nomAccBal, realAccBal
Dim nomAnnlRet, realAnnlRet

'*********************************************************
' User inputs
'*********************************************************
' For use by others use InputBox for the follwoing
startYr = 1950 ' Year of initial investment
startMo = 1 'Month of initial investment
endYr = 1990 'Terminal year
endMo = 1 'Terminal month

'*********************************************************
' Programmer inputs
'*********************************************************
outSheet = "Cumulative Return"
inSheet = "Data"
rowOffset = 10
firstDataRow = 3
yrMoCol = 1
stockCol = 2
divCol = 3
cpiCol = 4

initInv = 1 'Initial investment
outCol = 2 'First column no on output sheet where output goes

'*********************************************************
' Computations and output
'*********************************************************
'Read in raw data
Sheets(inSheet).Activate

```

```
For roNum1 = 1 To 1000
    Stock(roNum1) = Cells(firstDataRow + roNum1 - 1, _
      stockCol).Value
    Div(roNum1) = Cells(firstDataRow + roNum1 - 1, divCol) _
      .Value
    Cpi(roNum1) = Cells(firstDataRow + roNum1 - 1, cpiCol) _
      .Value
    YrMo(roNum1) = Cells(firstDataRow + roNum1 - 1, _
      yrMoCol).Value

    If Stock(roNum1) = "" Then GoTo DataReadingDone
Next roNum1

DataReadingDone:
numDataRows = roNum1 - 1

' Determine row number in array for start month and year
startRo = MonthIndex(startYr, startMo)
endRo = MonthIndex(endYr, endMo)

Sheets(outSheet).Activate

' Clear data from previous run
Range(Cells(rowOffset, 1), Cells(2000, 3)).Select
Selection.Clear

' Output run parameters
Cells(3, outCol).Value = startYr
Cells(4, outCol).Value = startMo
Cells(5, outCol).Value = endYr
Cells(6, outCol).Value = endMo

printRow = 0
Cells(printRow + rowOffset, 1).Value = YrMo(startRo)
Cells(printRow + rowOffset, outCol).Value = initInv
Cells(printRow + rowOffset, outCol + 1).Value = initInv

numShares = initInv / Stock(startRo)

For roNum3 = startRo + 1 To endRo
    printRow = printRow + 1

    numShares = numShares + (numShares * Div(roNum3 - 1) _
      / 12) / Stock(roNum3)

    nomAccBal = numShares * Stock(roNum3)
    realAccBal = nomAccBal * Cpi(startRo) / Cpi(roNum3)

```

```
    Cells(printRow + rowOffset, 1).Value = YrMo(roNum3)
    Cells(printRow + rowOffset, outCol).Value = nomAccBal
    Cells(printRow + rowOffset, outCol + 1).Value = _
     realAccBal
Next roNum3

' Calculate and output annualized returns
nomAnnlRet = ((nomAccBal / initInv) ^ (12 / _
  (endRo - startRo))) - 1
realAnnlRet = ((realAccBal / initInv) ^ (12 / _
  (endRo - startRo))) - 1

' Output annualized retutrns
Cells(3, 4).Value = "Nominal annualized return"
Cells(3, 7).Value = nomAnnlRet
Cells(4, 4).Value = "Real annualized return"
Cells(4, 7).Value = realAnnlRet

'**************************************************************
' Format data and plot chart
'**************************************************************
' Format data
Range("A10:C1000").Select
Selection.NumberFormat = "0.00"
Range("G3:G4").Select
Selection.NumberFormat = "0.00%"

'Plot chart
Call PlotChart(rowOffset + printRow)

End Sub

Function MonthIndex(Year, Month)
' Calculates row number in the data arrays for the specified
' year and month

Dim startYear1, startMonth1

' The following start numbers show what data is in
' row 1 of array
startYear1 = 1945
startMonth1 = 12

MonthIndex = (Year - startYear1) * 12 + (Month - startMonth1) _
  + 1

End Function
```

Analysis of the Code

In this code, I first read the input data into some arrays and then do the calculations using the data from the arrays. You can use the data directly from the input worksheet. I am primarily using the arrays to provide some examples of how they are used. Generally speaking, repeatedly reading in the same data from worksheets slows down a program; in codes that use the same input data repeatedly, first reading the data into arrays speeds up execution. However, in small programs like this, reading the data into an array first is not essential.

Lines 1–21: As always, this part provides a description of what the code does and declares the variables and arrays used in the code. Note that I am explicitly declaring that the arrays should be dimensioned starting with 1 and not 0.

Lines 23–30: Here the user specifies the range of data to use for the analysis. If you are writing the code for your own use, you can change the input data here. If the code is to be used by someone else, you should use the `InputBox` function to get the input data from the user. You may also want to include some data validation to make sure that the user specifies a range that is within the range for which input data is available and does not enter invalid data, such as month names, numbers over 12 for months, and so on.

Lines 32–45: These are data that you (as the programmer) may want to change in the future. The use of some of these will become clear as we get further into the code. Instead of setting up some of these as variables, you can hard code them. For example, in the input data sheet the year and month are shown in column 1. When reading in this data, you can use 1 as the column number in the cell reference. Creating a variable like `yrMoCol` makes it easier to accommodate other sets of input data where the year and month may not be in the first column.

Lines 47–67: Here I am reading in the input data. I have to start by activating the proper worksheet. Then I am reading in the data using a `For` loop. In the "Programmer inputs" section I provided the row number for the first but not the last row of data. I am using the row number of the first row of data in the cell addresses from which each set of data is read in. But how do I know where the loop should end? For this, instead of providing the row number for the last row of data, I have the program stop reading in data when it reaches a blank cell. In line 63 I check if the stock price cell is blank. If it is, then control will exit the loop and go to the line with the label `DataReadingDone` (line 66). In the next line, I am capturing the number of rows of data the code has read in. It has to be 1 less than the last value of `roNum1` because the last row read in was blank.

Note that it would have been preferable to use `Exit For` in line 63. It would have avoided the use of the `GoTo`, which should be used as rarely as possible, and then there would not have been any need for the label in line 66. I used the `GoTo` only to show how it can be used, not because it is the best way to code this model.

Lines 69–71: Here I am using (calling) the function procedure `MonthIndex` to calculate the row numbers in the arrays for the first and last month the user specified. I will discuss this function procedure later. Note, however, that this is a nice way of keeping your main code uncluttered by removing from it certain side calculations or actions.

Lines 85–88: Here I am writing out the first year of output data in the output worksheet. Note how I am using two variables (`printRow` and `rowOffset`) to control where the data goes. The programmer specifies the value of `rowOffset`. The `printRow` moves the output one row at a time.

Lines 92–105: In this `For` loop, I am doing the calculations for each month of data. Note that `roNum3`, the counter of the loop, controls the row numbers in the arrays from which I am using the data and its values depend on the months of data that the user specifies. So I cannot use its value to control where the output data goes in the spreadsheet. I have to use a separate variable, `printRow`, to control this. Its value starts at 0 and goes up by one for each month. (Note that the calculations here are done the same way as we did them in Model 1 in Chapter 16: Analyzing Market History. If you have difficulty understanding these calculations, refer to that model.)

Lines 107–117: Here I am calculating the annualized return using the initial investment and its final value and then writing them out. To annualize the return, I express the length of the period in years by calculating the number of months and dividing it by 12, which can result in fractional years depending on the user's input. This calculates the effective annual return and not the APR return.

Lines 122–126: To generate these few lines of code to format the output sheet, I used the Macro Recorder as I formatted the worksheet and then cut and paste the code line from the recorded module.

Line 129: This calls the Sub procedure `PlotChart` to plot the data. (See the code for it at the bottom of Module1.) To create this Sub procedure, I turned on the Macro Recorder, created the chart using the Chart Wizard, and formatted it. After I was finished, I deleted some of the lines in the beginning the recorded macro that were superfluous, renamed the recorded macro, and cut and pasted it at the bottom of Module1.

I had to make one important modification. The recorded code referred to specific beginning and ending rows for the data to use from the output worksheet to plot the chart. The beginning row number will always remain the same (unless the `rowOffset` is changed), but the ending row number will depend on the data period that the user specifies. So I have to pass on to this Sub procedure the row number of the last row of data to plot, and I do this using the argument of the Sub procedure. In this Call line I provided this information as rowOffset + printRow. This value is assigned to lastRo, the argument of the Sub procedure whose declaration line reads:

```
Sub PlotChart(lastRo)
```

I then replaced the specific row numbers for the last row of data in the data series to plot with the variable lastRo. (See line numbers 157–158, etc., in Module1 where I use concatenation to create the variable range references using lastRo.) Another point to note is that because lastRo is an argument of the Sub procedure, it does not have be declared as a variable with a Dim statement.

Lines 133–135: This is the declaration line of the Function procedure MonthIndex and a description of what it does. Because Year and Month are arguments, they do not have to be declared with Dim statements.

Lines 141–142: Here I am specifying when the data begins. This will be the first row of data in the input data arrays such as Stock.

Lines 144–145: This statement calculates the row number for the specified year and month by calculating the number of months it is away from the first row of data. This value, which is the output of the Function procedure, has to be assigned to Monthindex, the name of the Function procedure.

Testing the Code

Because the model we created in Model 1 in Chapter 16: Analyzing Market History does the same calculations, you can test this model's results against the results from the previous model. In addition, you need to check that the code is doing the analysis for the range of data specified by the user and plotting this same range of data.

Uses of the Model

This is a more flexible model than the corresponding Excel model because here the user can specify the starting and ending points of data to see how the stock index performed, not just over the entire period but during any subperiod as well. The automatic plotting of a fully formatted chart is another timesaving feature of this model.

MODEL 2: GROWTH OF $1 INVESTMENT IN DIFFERENT ASSETS

The Problem

Given the annual total return data for four asset classes and the annual inflation rates, create a model to compare them by showing how an initial investment of $1 in each of them would have grown in nominal and real terms over a period of years specified by the user. The model should also calculate the corresponding nominal and real annualized returns and present the results in two separate charts for the nominal and real growths of the initial investments as shown in Figures 28.3, 28.4, and 28.5.

Modeling Strategy

Read the input data into an array and use two additional arrays to store the cumulative nominal and real values of the investments for the different asset classes. For convenience and practice, number the rows of the arrays by the year

	1	2	3	4	5	6	7	8	9	10	11
1	**Growth of $1 Investment in Different Assets**										
2											
3			**Nominal values**					**Real values**			
4		Small	Large	T-Bonds	T-Bills		Small	Large	T-Bonds	T-Bills	
5		Stocks	Stocks				Stocks	Stocks			
6											
7	Annualized ret.	9.0%	13.1%	10.6%	5.9%		5.7%	9.7%	7.2%	2.7%	
8											
9											
10	1982	$1.00	$1.00	$1.00	$1.00		$1.00	$1.00	$1.00	$1.00	
11	1983	$1.27	$1.22	$1.07	$1.11		$1.23	$1.18	$1.03	$1.07	
12	1984	$1.71	$1.49	$1.06	$1.21		$1.59	$1.39	$0.98	$1.12	
13	1985	$1.47	$1.59	$1.22	$1.33		$1.32	$1.42	$1.09	$1.18	
14	1986	$1.89	$2.10	$1.62	$1.43		$1.62	$1.81	$1.39	$1.23	
15	1987	$1.95	$2.49	$2.01	$1.52		$1.66	$2.11	$1.71	$1.29	
16	1988	$1.68	$2.62	$1.96	$1.60		$1.37	$2.13	$1.59	$1.30	
17	1989	$2.05	$3.06	$2.12	$1.70		$1.60	$2.39	$1.65	$1.33	
18	1990	$2.22	$4.02	$2.53	$1.85		$1.65	$3.00	$1.89	$1.38	
19	1991	$1.62	$3.89	$2.71	$1.99		$1.14	$2.73	$1.91	$1.40	
20	1992	$2.43	$5.08	$3.21	$2.10		$1.66	$3.46	$2.19	$1.43	
21	1993	$3.11	$5.48	$3.46	$2.18		$2.06	$3.63	$2.29	$1.44	
22	1994	$3.74	$6.02	$4.00	$2.24		$2.41	$3.88	$2.58	$1.45	
23	1995	$3.61	$6.09	$3.71	$2.33		$2.27	$3.83	$2.33	$1.46	
24	1996	$4.81	$8.39	$4.89	$2.46		$2.95	$5.14	$2.99	$1.51	
25	1997	$5.60	$10.33	$4.85	$2.60		$3.32	$6.12	$2.87	$1.54	
26	1998	$6.86	$13.75	$5.58	$2.73		$4.00	$8.01	$3.25	$1.59	
27	1999	$6.68	$17.68	$6.33	$2.87		$3.83	$10.14	$3.63	$1.65	
28	2000	$8.10	$21.40	$5.78	$3.01		$4.53	$11.96	$3.23	$1.68	
29	2001	$7.89	$19.46	$6.74	$3.19		$4.26	$10.51	$3.64	$1.72	
30	2002	$7.64	$17.14	$7.29	$3.31		$4.07	$9.12	$3.88	$1.76	
31	2003	$6.11	$13.35	$8.34	$3.36		$3.18	$6.94	$4.33	$1.75	
32											
33											

FIGURE 28.3 Model 2: Nominal and real growth of $1 investment in different assets.

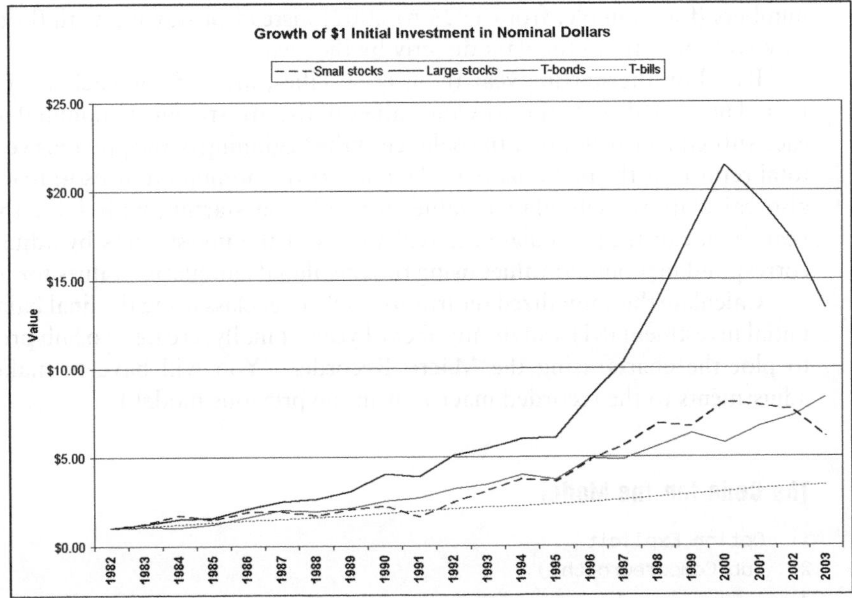

FIGURE 28.4 Model 2: Nominal growth of $1 investment in different assets.

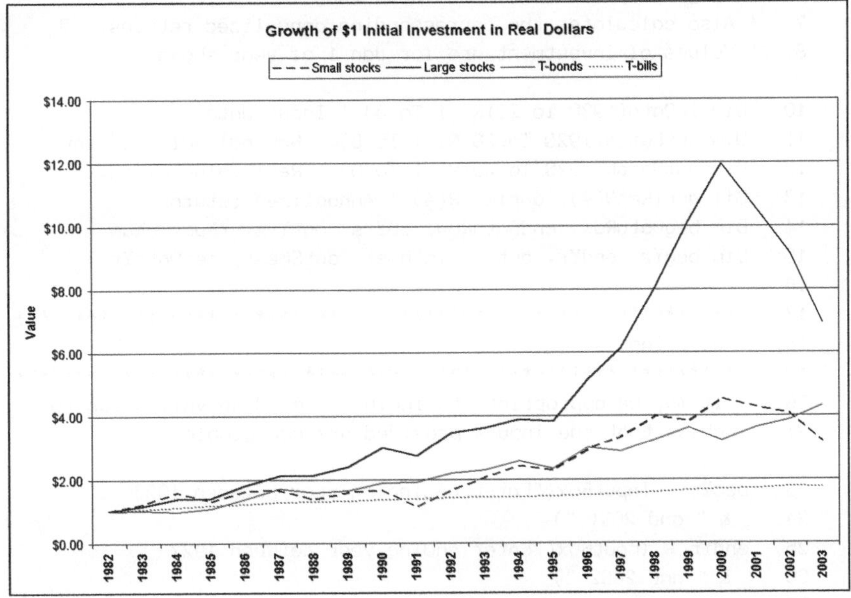

FIGURE 28.5 Model 2: Real growth of $1 investment in different assets.

numbers (for example, from 1926 to 2002) instead of starting with 0 or 1. This way you can refer to the data directly by the year.

Based on the starting year the user specifies, invest $1 in each asset for that year. Then to calculate the growing values of the investments in nominal terms for each subsequent year, grow the balance at the beginning of the previous year by the total return for the previous year. To convert the nominal returns to real returns, also calculate the cumulative values for inflation starting with 1 for the initial year. You can then calculate the real values of the investments by adjusting the corresponding nominal values using the calculated cumulative values for inflation.

Calculate the annualized returns for each asset class using the final balance, the initial investment ($1) and the number of years. Finally, create two Sub procedures to plot the charts using the Macro Recorder. (You will have to make minor adjustments to the recorded macros as in the previous model.)

The Code for the Model

```
Option Explicit
Sub CompareGrowth()

 ' Calculates the growth of initial $1 investment in 4 classes
 ' of assets in both nominal and real terms for specified
 ' range of years within the data range.
 ' Also calculates the corresponding annualized returns.
 ' Values of investment are for Jan 1 of year shown

  Dim inData(1920 To 2010, 1 To 5) ' Input data
  Dim outDataN(1920 To 2010, 1 To 5) ' Nominal value of inv
  Dim outDataR(1920 To 2010, 1 To 5) ' Real value of inv
  Dim annlRetN(4), annlRetR(4) ' Annualized returns
  Dim begDataRow, endDataRow, inYrs, outYrs, rNum, cNum
  Dim begYr, endYr, outRo, inSheet, outSheet, begDataYr

  '**************************************************************
  ' User inputs
  '**************************************************************
  ' It may be appropriate to include some data validation to
  ' check that the inputs provided are acceptable.

  begYr = InputBox("Enter beginning year between 1926" _
    & " and 2001.")
  endYr = InputBox("Enter ending year between 1927" _
    & " and 2002.")

```

```
'**********************************************************
' Programmer inputs
'**********************************************************
inSheet = "Input Data"
outSheet = "Cumulative Values"
outRo = 10 'Starting row for output table

begDataRow = 2
endDataRow = 78
begDataYr = 1926

'**********************************************************
' Analysis and computations
'**********************************************************
outYrs = endYr - begYr + 1 ' Number of years to compare

'Read in data
Worksheets(inSheet).Activate

inYrs = endDataRow - begDataRow + 1 'Years of input data

For rNum = 1 To inYrs
   For cNum = 1 To 5
      inData(begDataYr - 1 + rNum, cNum) = Cells(1 + rNum, _
       cNum + 1).Value
   Next
Next

' Set intial investments of $1
For cNum = 1 To 5
   outDataN(begYr, cNum) = 1
   outDataR(begYr, cNum) = 1
Next

' Calculate growing investment values in nominal dollars
' Includes cumulation inflation as well
For rNum = begYr + 1 To endYr + 1
   For cNum = 1 To 5
      outDataN(rNum, cNum) = outDataN(rNum - 1, cNum) * _
        (1 + inData(rNum - 1, cNum))
   Next
Next

' Calculate growing investment value in real dollars
' Use cumulated inflation data for adjustment
```

```
For rNum = begYr + 1 To endYr + 1
   For cNum = 1 To 4
      outDataR(rNum, cNum) = outDataN(rNum, cNum) / _
        outDataN(rNum, 5)
   Next
Next

Worksheets(outSheet).Activate

' Calculate and output annualized returns
For cNum = 1 To 4
   annlRetN(cNum) = outDataN(endYr + 1, cNum) _
     ^ (1 / outYrs) - 1
   annlRetR(cNum) = outDataR(endYr + 1, cNum) _
     ^ (1 / outYrs) - 1
   Cells(7, 1 + cNum).Value = annlRetN(cNum)
   Cells(7, 6 + cNum).Value = annlRetR(cNum)
Next

' Clear previous data
Range(Cells(outRo, 1), Cells(outRo + 100, 12)).Select
Selection.ClearContents

' Output calculated values of investment
For rNum = outRo To outRo + outYrs
   Cells(rNum, 1).Value = begYr + rNum - outRo

    For cNum = 1 To 4
       Cells(rNum, cNum + 1).Value = outDataN(begYr + rNum _
         - outRo, cNum)
       Cells(rNum, cNum + 6).Value = outDataR(begYr + rNum _
         - outRo, cNum)
    Next
 Next

 ' Plot charts
 Call PlotNominalChart(outRo, outYrs)
 Call PlotRealChart(outRo, outYrs)

 End Sub
```

Analysis of the Code

Here again I am using several arrays. It is not essential to do so, but it is instructive and makes the code run faster. To keep the code short, for the outputs I am using a worksheet that already has the appropriate headings, labels, and formatting. You could easily build them into the code as well by first generating the necessary codes using the Macro Recorder and then cutting and pasting the code into your code.

Lines 10–15: Notice two things about the arrays I am declaring. First, I am using two-dimensional arrays so that I can store similar data for all the assets in the same array. I am also using three different arrays, one for the input data and one each for the nominal and real value outputs. You could use one array for all of them, but it is better to keep different types of data separate using descriptive names for the arrays. Second, instead of assigning the arrays row numbers starting with 0 or 1, I am using the year for row numbers so that when I want to access the data for 1950 later on, I can use 1950 as the row number.

Lines 17–26: This section gets the user's input on the range of years to include in the analysis. The input dialog box that the user sees tells him the range of years he can use. Nonetheless, you may want to include a data validation to ensure that the user enters only acceptable data.

Lines 28–37: Various parameters that the programmer may want to change later. For example, `outRo` (line 33) specifies on what row of the output spreadsheet the output table starts and can be easily changed.

Lines 42–54: This section reads in the input data using nested `For` loops. You have to activate a worksheet to refer to cells in it without naming the worksheet repeatedly.

Lines 56–60: Here I am assigning $1 as the initial investment both for the nominal and real value arrays.

Lines 64–69: Using nested arrays, I calculate the value of the investment at the beginning of every year as the value at the beginning of the previous year times 1 plus the total return for the previous year. Although the CPI changes do not represent a growth, I am cumulating them the same way. If the analysis starts in 1950 then I have already set the value for that year in the CPI column in the array as 1. If by the beginning of 1955 that 1 grows to 1.3, then I can convert any dollar amount at the beginning of 1955 to constant dollars at the beginning of 1950 by multiplying the dollar amount by the ratio of 1 to 1.3.

Lines 73–78: I am again using nested loops to calculate the real values of the investment at the beginning of each year from the corresponding nominal values using the method described under lines 64–69.

Lines 83–90: In this section, I calculate the annualized returns. Since I already have the values to which $1 grows over the period for the various assets, calculating the annualized numbers is straightforward. I am also writing them out to the output worksheet.

Lines 93–106: Here I am writing out the table of the values of the investment in the different years. It is important to clear from the worksheet any old numbers that may be left from a previous run. To do this, I am selecting a range of the worksheet where previous numbers could have been and I am clearing the range (see line 93). The key here is to make sure that the range selected does not include any of the headings and labels because the program will not recreate them. At the same time, the selected area should be large enough to clear all possible previous outputs. This is why I am using a range that starts at the first line of the table (identified by `outRo`) and extends for 100 rows because I know there is less than 100 years of input data and so no previous analysis could have been done for more than 100 years.

Lines 109–110: In these statements, I am calling the Sub procedures I have created to plot one chart with the nominal values and one with the real values. As before, I recorded the codes for the charts and then modified them to accommodate the starting and ending years specified by the user. In the codes for these Sub procedures at the bottom of Module1, you can see which lines I have modified from the recorded versions and what modifications I have made. In the calls to these Sub procedures I pass on the necessary information about the first row of output data and the number of rows of output data that the charts should plot.

One interesting thing to note is that I am using the same variable names (`outRo` and `outYrs`) in both the main procedure and these Sub procedures. This does not confuse VBA because I am using them as local variables in each procedure. As such, VBA views them as different variables even though they have the same names in the different procedures.

Testing the Code

The calculations involved in this model are fairly simple and you can easily check them using a hand calculator. Also, Model 2 in Chapter 16: Analyzing Market History does the same calculations. So you can test this model's results against the results from the previous model. You should also carefully check the charts to make sure that they are starting at the right years.

Uses of the Model

This model, again, is more flexible than the Excel version because the user can easily choose different subperiods to examine. The automatic plotting of a fully formatted chart is another useful timesaving feature.

MODEL 3: COMPARING ROLLING PERIOD RETURNS

The Problem

Given the total annual returns for large-cap stocks and the year-end CPI values for the period 1946–2002, create a model to calculate the cumulative and annualized

	1	2	3	4	5	6	7
1	**Real and Nominal Rolling Period Returns**						
2							
3	Step size	1					
4	Start year	1946					
5	End year	2002					
6	Window length	10					
7		Nominal	Real				
8	Max cumulative return	517.2%	414.7%				
9	Min cumulative return	13.3%	-31.9%				
10	Average cumulative return	250.9%	147.7%				
11							
12	Maximum annualized return	20.0%	17.8%				
13	Minimum annualized return	1.3%	-3.8%				
14	Average annualized return	12.5%	8.2%				
15							
16							
17		**Window return**			**Window return**		
18		**Cumulative**			**Annualized**		
19		Nominal	Real		Nominal	Real	
20	1946	354.7%	208.8%		16.4%	11.9%	
21	1947	433.4%	315.5%		18.2%	15.3%	
22	1948	352.0%	272.4%		16.3%	14.1%	
23	1949	517.2%	414.7%		20.0%	17.8%	
24	1950	489.6%	373.3%		19.4%	16.8%	
25	1951	345.2%	273.5%		16.1%	14.1%	
26	1952	360.2%	306.5%		16.5%	15.1%	
62	1988	425.2%	275.7%		18.0%	14.2%	
63	1989	477.8%	324.8%		19.2%	15.6%	
64	1990	432.5%	299.0%		18.2%	14.8%	
65	1991	400.0%	284.5%		17.5%	14.4%	
66	1992	236.7%	162.8%		12.9%	10.1%	
67	1993	143.2%	90.8%		9.3%	6.7%	
68							

FIGURE 28.6 Model 3: Real and nominal rolling period returns.

nominal and real returns for all possible rolling periods (windows) of length specified by the user. The user should also be able to specify the data range to use, that is, the starting and ending years, as well as the forward step size. The model should plot two bar charts to compare the nominal and real values for cumulative returns and annualized returns.

Calculate the maximum, minimum, and average values for both nominal and real cumulative and annualized returns. The outputs of the model should look like Figures 28.6, 28.7, and 28.8.

Modeling Strategy

The code for this problem is more complex because you have to keep track of a number of things.

You can use essentially the same approach as we used in the last model to calculate the returns for each window. You have to start by picking the first window based on the beginning year and the window length the user specifies. For example, if the first year is 1950 and the window length is 10 years, then the first window will span the years 1950–1959. If the specified step size is 1 year, then the next window will be 1951–1960. If the step size is 3 years, it will be

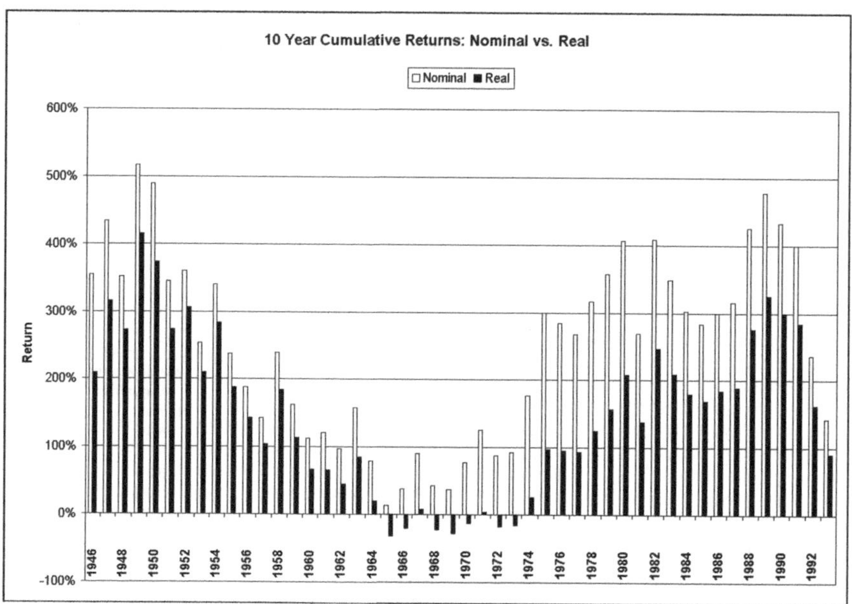

FIGURE 28.7 Model 3: Real and nominal cumulative returns.

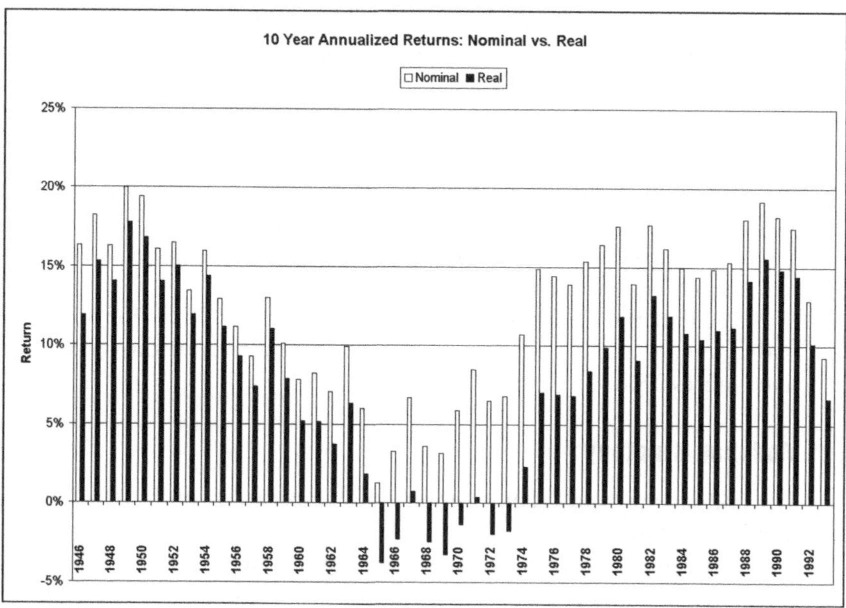

FIGURE 28.8 Model 3: Real and nominal annualized returns.

1953–1962. You have to repeat the same calculations for all possible windows, moving ahead in steps. When do you stop? For the last window, the final year will coincide with the last year specified by the user. If the user specifies 2000 as the last year and a step size of 1, then—in our example—the last window would be 1991–2000.

This strategy requires creating an inner loop to do the calculations for each window and an outer loop to choose windows in steps. Once the calculations for all the possible windows are done, you can output the data to the output worksheet and then use Excel's MAX, MIN and other functions on the columns of the output data on the worksheet to calculate the other statistics that the model has to generate. (I will show how you can also calculate these statistics using loops instead of any built-in function.)

To format the output worksheet, you can create a Sub procedure using the Macro Recorder and call it from the main procedure. Similarly, you can create the necessary Sub procedures to plot the data using the Macro Recorder, modify them as in the previous models, and call them from the main procedure.

The Code for the Model

```
Option Explicit
Sub CalcRollingReturns()
'
' Calculates real and nominal maximum, minimum and average
' cumulative and annualized returns for sliding windows.
' User specifies window length and years of data to use.
' Windows move forward based on specified step size in years.
' Uses annual total return data as input.
' Inflation index assumed to be for last day of year.
Dim outSheet, inSheet
Dim stkRet(1 To 100), Cpi(1 To 100), Yr(1 To 100)
Dim nomAccBal, realAccBal
Dim minCumNomRet, maxCumNomRet, minCumRealRet, maxCumRealRet
Dim minAnnlNomRet, maxAnnlNomRet
Dim minAnnlRealRet, maxAnnlRealRet
Dim realAnnlRet, nomAnnlRet
Dim avgNomRet, avgRealRet, avgCumRealRet, avgCumNomRet
Dim winLen, outCol
Dim startYr, endYr, startRo, endRo
Dim stepSize, initInv, rowOffset
Dim firstDataRow, firstDataYr, stkRetCol, cpiCol, yrCol
Dim roNum1, roNum2, roNum3, colNum
Dim numDataRows, stepCnt, winBeg
```

```

'**********************************************************
'User inputs
'**********************************************************
winLen = InputBox("Enter window length in years.")
startYr = InputBox("Enter first year of data to use as a" _
  & " 4 digit number. Earliest year available is 1946.")
endYr = InputBox("Enter last year of data to use as a" _
  & " 4 digit number. Last year available is 2002.")
stepSize = InputBox("Enter step size in years for moving" _
  & " forward.")

'**********************************************************
'Programmer inputs
'**********************************************************
outSheet = "Window Returns"
inSheet = "Input Data"
rowOffset = 19
firstDataRow = 4
firstDataYr = 1945
yrCol = 1
stkRetCol = 2
cpiCol = 3
outCol = 2 'Column no on Out Sheet where output goes
initInv = 1

'**********************************************************
'Read in raw data
'**********************************************************
Sheets(inSheet).Activate

startRo = startYr - firstDataYr + 1 ' row number of 1st year
endRo = endYr - firstDataYr + 1 'row number of last year

'Read data into arrays
For roNum1 = 1 To 100
   Yr(roNum1) = Cells(firstDataRow + roNum1 - 1, yrCol) _
     .Value
   stkRet(roNum1) = Cells(firstDataRow + roNum1 - 1, _
     stkRetCol).Value
   Cpi(roNum1) = Cells(firstDataRow + roNum1 - 1, _
     cpiCol).Value

   If stkRet(roNum1) = "" Then Exit For
Next roNum1

numDataRows = roNum1 - 1
```

```
'*********************************************************
' Computations and output
'*********************************************************
Sheets(outSheet).Activate

' Clear previous data
Range(Cells(rowOffset, 1), Cells(rowOffset + 100, 1)).Select
Selection.ClearContents

For colNum = 0 To 4
  Columns(outCol + colNum).Select
  Selection.ClearContents
Next

' Write out run parameters
Cells(3, outCol).Value = stepSize
Cells(4, outCol).Value = startYr
Cells(5, outCol).Value = endYr
Cells(6, outCol).Value = winLen

' Create headings for data colimns
Cells(7, outCol).Value = "Nominal"
Cells(7, outCol + 1).Value = "Real"
Cells(rowOffset, outCol).Value = "Nominal"
Cells(rowOffset, outCol + 1).Value = "Real"
Cells(rowOffset, outCol + 3).Value = "Nominal"
Cells(rowOffset, outCol + 4).Value = "Real"

' Initialize values
maxCumNomRet = -10000000
minCumNomRet = 10000000
maxCumRealRet = -10000000
minCumRealRet = 10000000
avgRealRet = 0
avgNomRet = 0
avgCumRealRet = 0
avgCumNomRet = 0

stepCnt = 0 ' Used to keep track of steps

For roNum3 = startRo To endRo - winLen + 1 Step stepSize
   stepCnt = stepCnt + 1
   nomAccBal = initInv
   winBeg = roNum3

   ' Calculate 1 + nominal cumulative return
```

```
        For roNum2 = winBeg To winBeg + winLen - 1
            nomAccBal = nomAccBal * (1 + stkRet(roNum2))
        Next roNum2

        realAccBal = nomAccBal * Cpi(roNum3 - 1) / _
          Cpi(roNum2 - 1)
        nomAnnlRet = (nomAccBal / initInv) ^ (1 / winLen) - 1
        realAnnlRet = (realAccBal / initInv) ^ (1 / winLen) - 1

        avgRealRet = avgRealRet + realAnnlRet 'Creating sum
        avgNomRet = avgNomRet + nomAnnlRet ' Creating sum
        avgCumRealRet = avgCumRealRet + (realAccBal - initInv) _
          / initInv
        avgCumNomRet = avgCumNomRet + (nomAccBal - initInv) _
          / initInv

        If nomAccBal > maxCumNomRet Then maxCumNomRet _
          = nomAccBal
        If nomAccBal < minCumNomRet Then minCumNomRet _
          = nomAccBal

        If realAccBal > maxCumRealRet Then maxCumRealRet _
          = realAccBal
        If realAccBal < minCumRealRet Then minCumRealRet _
          = realAccBal

        ' Output window returns
        Cells(stepCnt + rowOffset, 1).Value = Yr(roNum3)
        Cells(stepCnt + rowOffset, outCol).Value = (nomAccBal _
          - initInv) / initInv
        Cells(stepCnt + rowOffset, outCol + 1).Value = _
          (realAccBal - initInv) / initInv

        Cells(stepCnt + rowOffset, outCol + 3).Value _
          = nomAnnlRet
        Cells(stepCnt + rowOffset, outCol + 4).Value _
          = realAnnlRet
    Next roNum3

    '**********************************************************
    ' Calcualte and output averages
    '**********************************************************
    avgCumRealRet = avgCumRealRet / stepCnt
    avgCumNomRet = avgCumNomRet / stepCnt
    avgRealRet = avgRealRet / stepCnt
    avgNomRet = avgNomRet / stepCnt

```

```
168:  minCumNomRet = (minCumNomRet - initInv) / initInv
169:  maxCumNomRet = (maxCumNomRet - initInv) / initInv
170:
171:  minCumRealRet = (minCumRealRet - initInv) / initInv
172:  maxCumRealRet = (maxCumRealRet - initInv) / initInv
173:
174:  minAnnlNomRet = (1 + minCumNomRet) ^ (1 / winLen) - 1
175:  maxAnnlNomRet = (1 + maxCumNomRet) ^ (1 / winLen) - 1
176:
177:  minAnnlRealRet = (1 + minCumRealRet) ^ (1 / winLen) - 1
178:  maxAnnlRealRet = (1 + maxCumRealRet) ^ (1 / winLen) - 1
179:
180:  Cells(8, outCol).Value = maxCumNomRet
181:  Cells(9, outCol).Value = minCumNomRet
182:  Cells(8, outCol + 1).Value = maxCumRealRet
183:  Cells(9, outCol + 1).Value = minCumRealRet
184:  Cells(10, outCol).Value = avgCumNomRet
185:  Cells(10, outCol + 1).Value = avgCumRealRet
186:
187:  Cells(12, outCol).Value = maxAnnlNomRet
188:  Cells(13, outCol).Value = minAnnlNomRet
189:  Cells(14, outCol).Value = avgNomRet
190:
191:  Cells(12, outCol + 1).Value = maxAnnlRealRet
192:  Cells(13, outCol + 1).Value = minAnnlRealRet
193:  Cells(14, outCol + 1).Value = avgRealRet
194:
195:  ' Format worksheet
196:  Call FormatWorksheet
197:
198:  ' Create charts
199:  Call PlotCumRet(winLen, stepCnt + rowOffset)
200:  Call PlotAnnualRet(winLen, stepCnt + rowOffset)
201:
202:  End Sub
```

Analysis of the Code

Lines 2–26: Contains the description of the model and declaration of variables. Note that I use three separate arrays for the three input variables and number them by the year, starting with 1.

Lines 31–51: I am using these sections to get the user and programmer inputs.

Lines 58–59: Here I am calculating the row numbers in the data arrays that correspond to the beginning and ending years specified by the user.

Lines 62–73: Here I am reading in the input data using a loop. To decide where input data ends, I check the value in the stock price column in each loop and exit the loop when a blank cell is reached. In line 73, I store the number of rows of input data in the variable `numDataRows`.

Lines 78–87: This section of the code clears the worksheet of the data from the previous runs, making sure that I keep the permanent labels and column headings.

Lines 89–101: Here I am writing out the user inputs and creating some necessary data headings.

Lines 103–111: These are variables I will use later to calculate the maximum values, minimum values, and so on. I am assigning them initial values here. Why I am assigning them these initial values will become clear as we see how I use them.

Line 115: This is the beginning of the major outer loop that controls the stepping forward process. The counter of the loop `rowNum3` represents the lower end of a window. I start with `startRo`, which represents (in the arrays) the beginning year specified by the user. The counter is incremented by the `stepSize` specified by the user every time control goes through the loop. The lower end of the last window cannot be greater than `endRo - winLen + 1`. So this condition controls when the looping stops.

This loop ends in line 158.

Line 116: Keeps count of how many steps I am taking.

Line 117: Sets the initial balance, that is, the balance in the first year, for a window.

Lines 118–123: Here I am calculating the nominal final balance at the end of the window by going through it year by year. The value of the investment at the beginning of any year equals the balance at the beginning of the previous year multiplied by 1 plus the total return for the previous year.

Lines 125–126: Calculates the final balance in constant dollars of the beginning year of the window using the ratio of CPIs.

Lines 127–128: I am calculating here the annualized returns from the cumulative returns I have already calculated.

Lines 130–134: Here I am keeping a running total for each type of return. I will use them to calculate averages later. The totals are updated during each pass through the loop, that is, for each window. To keep a running total as here, the variable being used has to be initialized to zero as I did in lines 108–111. Also note that I am making the variables for the averages do "double duty" here. I am using them to keep the running totals and later I will divide them by the appropriate divisors to calculate the averages.

Lines 137–145: In this section, I keep track of the maximum and minimum returns in variables like `maxCumNomRet`. I initiated the variables for maximums to very small values and minimums to very large values. Then for each pass through the loop, that is, each window, if the new return is greater than the previous maximum, then the maximum is updated; otherwise it is left alone. The program captures the minimums by reversing the test.

In programming, this is a common technique used to calculate the maximum and minimum from any series of values and you should make sure you fully understand it.

Lines 148–157: In these statements I am writing out the various returns for the window.

Line 158: This is the end of the loop that controls the outer loop. From here, control goes back to the beginning of the loop to start calculation for the next window.

Lines 163–166: Here I am calculating the averages from all the running totals I kept before. Note that the divisor is the number of windows or steps I kept track of in line 116.

Line 168–178: These statements convert the final balances to cumulative returns.

Lines 180–193: Here I am writing out the various averages to the output worksheet.

Line 196: Calling the `FormatWorksheet` Sub procedure that I created using the Macro Recorder to format the finished worksheet.

Lines 199–200: Calling the Sub procedures to create the two charts. I created them using the Macro Recorder and then modified them to accommodate the different lengths of analysis period specified by the user.

Testing the Code

The calculations for this model can be easily checked with a hand calculator. For example, to check that the window returns are being calculated correctly, run the program with a window length of 3 and check the results. You can also use the previous model and Model 4 in Chapter 16: Analyzing Market History in the Excel part of the book to check the results of this model.

Uses of the Model

The output of this model, especially the charts, provides very useful information about the nature of the stock market. Using windows of different lengths (for example, 5, 10, or 15 years), you can see that the risk of investing in the stock market can be reduced considerably by using a buy-and-hold strategy.

CHAPTER 29

Simulating Stock Prices

In the parallel chapter in Part Two we saw that it is possible to build Excel models to simulate stock prices. However, a major use of simulations in finance is in Monte Carlo simulations used to value European options and other derivatives, especially in situations where the payoffs depend on several underlying market variables. For such simulations, we have to sample tens of thousands or even hundreds of thousands of paths, which cannot be done in Excel. Such simulations have to be done in VBA or other programming languages. Although we will not go into Monte Carlo simulations in this book, we will build a model in this chapter to simulate stock prices similar to the model we built in Excel. Unlike the Excel model, though, this model can be extended to do Monte Carlo simulations with appropriate modifications to speed up the computations and accommodate other requirements.

This chapter requires no additional theory or concept. However, it is important that you have a good grasp of the theory and concepts I discussed in Chapter 18: Simulating Stock Prices. It will also be easier to follow the models in this chapter if you have already worked through the models in Excel in the earlier chapter.

Modeling Examples

MODEL 1: ESTIMATING A STOCK'S VOLATILITY

The Problem

Create a worksheet function to calculate the annualized volatility for a stock based on daily closing price data. The user would enter the number of days of historical data to use for the estimate and the range in the worksheet containing the historical daily price data.

Modeling Strategy

We discussed the necessary formulas in the chapter by the same name in Part Two in the section on estimating volatility. To calculate the continuously compounded daily rate of return, first calculate the price relative of the stock (today's price divided by yesterday's price) for every day and then take its natural logarithm. Start the calculations with the most recent day in the data set and store the values in an array with 1 fewer elements than the number of days specified by the user. Use the array of daily return in Excel's STDEV function to calculate the daily standard deviation and then annualize it by multiplying it by the square root of 250.

The Code for the Model

```
1:   Option Explicit
2:   Option Base 1
3:   Function StkVol(N, PriceRange)
4:
5:    ' Calculates annualized volatility from daily price data.
6:    ' N = Number of days of data to use
7:    ' PriceRange is the range containing the daily prices
8:
9:   Dim i, DlyRet()
10:
11:  ReDim DlyRet(N - 1)
12:
13:   ' calculate daily returns
14:  For i = 1 To N - 1
15:      DlyRet(i) = Log(PriceRange(i) / PriceRange(i + 1))
16:  Next
17:
18:   ' Calculate and annualize standard deviation
19:  StkVol = Application.StDev(DlyRet) * Sqr(250)
20:
21:  End Function
```

Analysis of the Code

Line 3: Declares the Function procedure. `N` is the number of days of data the user wants used in estimating volatility. As the second argument, the user will enter the worksheet range containing the historical daily price data. `PriceRange` does not have to be specified as an array to accept an array (a worksheet range) input.

Line 9: The array `DlyRet` has to be declared as a dynamic range because its actual dimension will depend on the user input `N`.

Line 11: Redimensions `DlyRet` for N-1 elements.

Line 14–16: The `For` loop calculates the daily return as the natural logarithm of the daily price relatives.

Line 19: Calculates daily volatility using the daily return data in Excel's STDEV function and annualizes it assuming 250 trading days per year. Because STDEV is an Excel and not VBA function, it has to be preceded by `Application.` As always, the output value of the function has to be assigned to the function name.

Testing the Model

To test the model calculate the volatility of a stock using some historical data. For example, in a cell in the worksheet for this model with the historical data in the range B5:B258, you can enter the formula =StkVol(200,B5:B258). Then check the result using the results from the similar Excel model we developed earlier.

Uses of the Model

Although we developed the same model in Excel, this model is more versatile because anyone can use it as a worksheet function in other worksheet models. It can also be used in other VBA procedures.

MODEL 2: SIMULATING STOCK PRICES

The Problem

Develop a model to simulate the price of a stock given its current price, expected return, volatility, and the simulation step size. Make all of these input variables so that the user can change them. The user should also be able to generate new price paths easily. Create a chart like the one in Figure 29.1 to show the simulated price path for the stock and its certain and uncertain components.

Modeling Strategy

For this model we will use the same strategy we used in the Excel model. Use the equations we discussed to calculate the stock price at the end of a step based on the price at the beginning of the step and repeat the process for each step. To simulate the price for each step, you will need a random draw from a standard normal distribution. To do so, you can use VBA's Rnd function to draw a random sample between 0 and 1 from a uniform distribution and then use Excel's NORMSINV to convert it into a random draw from a standard normal distribution.

The Code for the Model

```
Option Explicit
Sub StkSimulation()
```

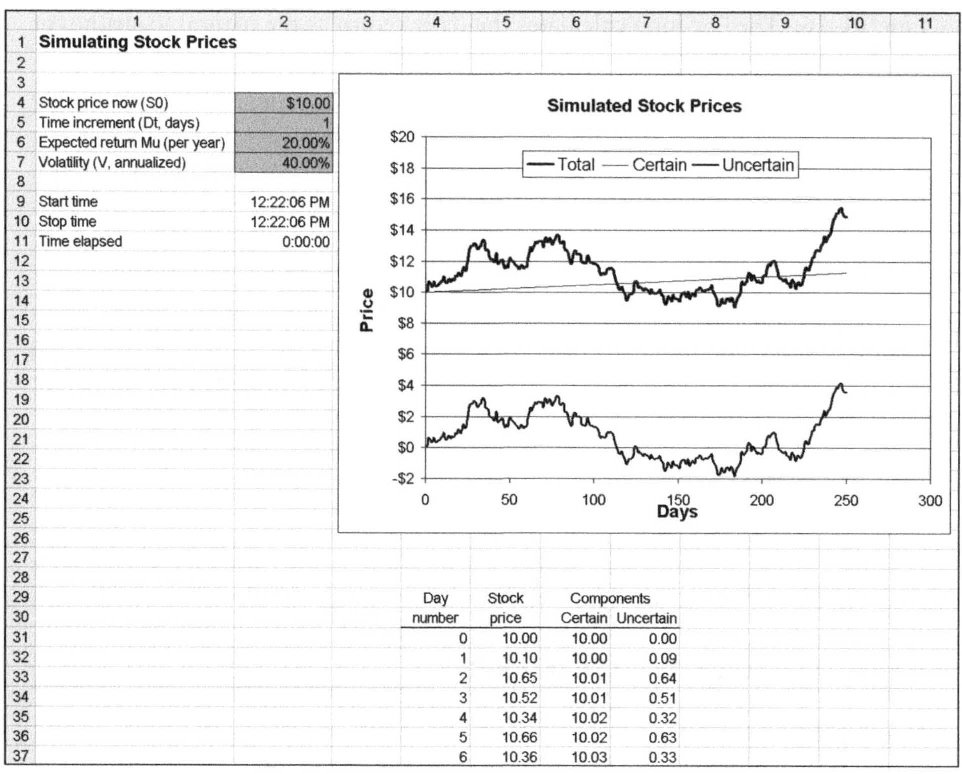

Day number	Stock price	Components Certain	Uncertain
0	10.00	10.00	0.00
1	10.10	10.00	0.09
2	10.65	10.01	0.64
3	10.52	10.01	0.51
4	10.34	10.02	0.32
5	10.66	10.02	0.63
6	10.36	10.03	0.33

FIGURE 29.1 Model 2: Simulation of a stock's price.

```

' Simulates daily stock prices assuming geometric
' Brownian motion.

Dim S0, dt, mu, vol, N, k
Dim sOld, sNew, cOld, cNew, uNew, rDraw
Dim rowOffset, i

Range("Starttime") = Time 'Records the starting time
Worksheets("Model InOut").Activate

'**********************************************************
' Read input data
'**********************************************************
S0 = Cells(4, 2).Value
dt = Cells(5, 2).Value
mu = Cells(6, 2).Value
vol = Cells(7, 2).Value
```

```
21:
22:  '**********************************************************
23:  ' Computations
24:  '**********************************************************
25: N = 250 'Number of days to simulate
26: rowOffset = 31 'used to control where data is written out
27:
28: k = mu - vol ^ 2 / 2
29:
30:  ' Initial values
31: sOld = S0 'Used to store stock price for previous day
32: cOld = S0 'Used to store certain component for previous day
33: Cells(rowOffset + i, 4).Value = 0
34: Cells(rowOffset + i, 5).Value = S0
35: Cells(rowOffset + i, 6).Value = S0
36: Cells(rowOffset + i, 7).Value = 0
37:
38: For i = 1 To N
39:     'Generates random draw from standard normal distributions
40:     rDraw = Application.NormSInv(Rnd)
41:
42:     sNew = sOld * Exp(k * dt / 250 + vol * rDraw * _
43:     Sqr(dt / 250))
44:     cNew = cOld * Exp(k * dt / 250) 'Certain component
45:     uNew = sNew - cNew 'Uncertain component
46:
47:     Cells(rowOffset + i, 4).Value = i
48:     Cells(rowOffset + i, 5).Value = sNew
49:     Cells(rowOffset + i, 6).Value = cNew
50:     Cells(rowOffset + i, 7).Value = uNew
51:
52:     sOld = sNew 'Saves old price before calculating next one
53:     cOld = cNew
54: Next
55:
56: Range("Stoptime") = Time 'Record ending time
57:
58: End Sub
```

Analysis of the Code

This code does the calculations exactly the same way as in the Excel model. It is therefore not necessary to discuss everything in detail.

Line 11: Records on the spreadsheet the time that the program starts running. This is not important for a code like this one because it takes less than a second to run. If you were doing 100,000 simulations using this same code, however, the time each run takes would be important. As you try out different techniques to speed up a code, it is useful to be able to measure if things are improving. You can calculate the time it takes to run a code by recording the time at the beginning and at the end (as we will do) and monitor the difference. In the worksheet, I used Starttime as a label for the cell where I want the time recorded (B9).

Line 25: Specifies the number of days for which simulation will be done. This could be made an input variable, but then one would have to include VBA code to recreate the chart for every run so that the different number of data points can be accommodated. (This is fairly easy to do using the Macro Recorder.)

Lines 38–54: Controls the daily simulation.

Line 40: Generates a random draw from a standard normal distribution using the method we have been using. Note that because VBA has its own Rnd function to draw a sample from a uniform distribution between 0 and 1, you cannot use the corresponding Excel function RAND here.

Lines 42–45: Calculates the stock price for the next day and its certain and uncertain components using the same equations we used before.

Lines 47–50: Writes out the calculated values for price and so on.

Lines 52–53: Saves the current stock price and certain component of it because they will be needed for next day's calculations.

Line 56: Records the ending time. The running time is calculated in B11 on the worksheet as the difference between the stopping and starting times.

Testing the Model

You can test the model's output against hand calculations, for which you will have to print out one or two random draws. Then you can calculate the simulated stock price starting with the previous day's price and using the value of the random draw. Also change the input variables and make sure that the changes taking place seem reasonable.

Uses of the Model

As with the Excel model, this model is useful for visualizing how stock prices develop under the geometric Brownian motion assumption and how changes in the different input variables change the simulated prices. For example, you can see the effect of volatility by changing it from 0 to high numbers. Because in this model μ is an input, if you hold it constant and increase volatility, κ, the expected continuously compounded rate of return will get smaller. The effect is that the line showing the certain component will become flatter but the variations around it will become more pronounced.

As I discussed at the beginning of the chapter, this model can be extended to do various Monte Carlo simulations, which you cannot do with the corresponding Excel model. For example, you can do a series of simulations by putting an outer loop around the appropriate portions of the code.

CHAPTER 30

Options and Option Portfolios

In this chapter, we will develop some of the same models in VBA that we developed in Excel for options and option portfolios. Doing so will allow us to see that even though we could develop these models in Excel, creating them in VBA offers several advantages. For example, we will develop a worksheet function for calculating option prices based on the Black-Scholes-Merton (BSM) model that can then be used in other worksheet or VBA models. We will also develop a function that automatically calculates implied volatility. In the Excel model, the user had to do so using the Goal Seek function. Most importantly, we will develop more useful option portfolio models for evaluating various option-trading strategies.

This chapter needs no theory or concepts beyond what I covered in Chapter 19: Options and Option Portfolios. If you have not studied that chapter yet, I recommend that you do so and work through the models there before working on the models here.

Modeling Examples

MODEL 1: PROFIT OF OPTIONS PORTFOLIO AT EXPIRATION

The Problem

Develop a model to calculate the projected profits of a portfolio of positions in stocks, calls, and puts at the time of expiration of the options for a range of terminal stock prices (that is, stock prices when the options expire). All the positions are on the same stock and all the options expire at the same time. For each position, the user should be able to enter the position type (stock, put, or call), exercise price or stock purchase price, position size, and premium paid

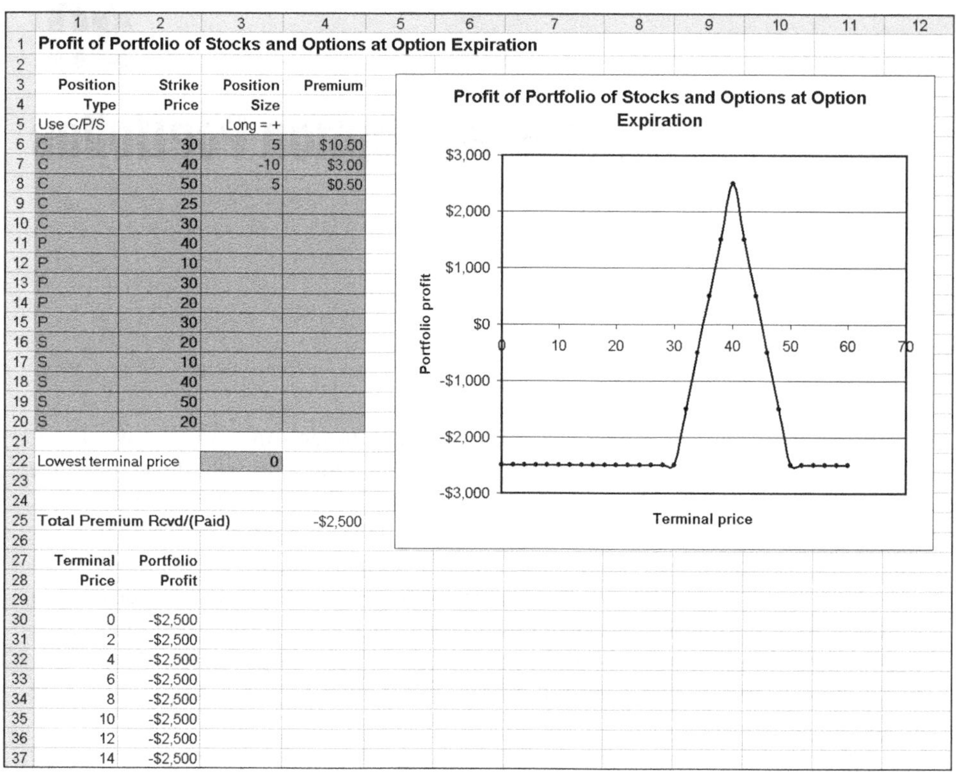

Profit of Portfolio of Stocks and Options at Option Expiration

Position Type	Strike Price	Position Size	Premium
Use C/P/S		Long = +	
C	30	5	$10.50
C	40	-10	$3.00
C	50	5	$0.50
C	25		
C	30		
P	40		
P	10		
P	30		
P	20		
P	30		
S	20		
S	10		
S	40		
S	50		
S	20		

Lowest terminal price: 0

Total Premium Rcvd/(Paid): -$2,500

Terminal Price	Portfolio Profit
0	-$2,500
2	-$2,500
4	-$2,500
6	-$2,500
8	-$2,500
10	-$2,500
12	-$2,500
14	-$2,500

FIGURE 30.1 Model 1: Profit of a portfolio of stocks and options at option expiration.

(if option). Create a chart to show the projected portfolio profits (values) for a range of terminal stock prices similar to the one shown in Figure 30.1.

Modeling Strategy

To provide flexibility, let the user provide the lowest terminal price to use for your calculations and use 30 more terminal prices at $2 steps. (You can make both the step size and the number of steps user inputs as well.)

Start by calculating the net total premium paid and received for all the positions. You can ignore the investment in the stock positions at this stage and calculate the profit on the stock positions at the terminal as the difference between the terminal price and the original price.

To calculate the profit on the portfolio for all the terminal prices, you will have to use nested loops. The outer loop will control moving through the terminal prices, one at a time, and the inner loop will accumulate the profit for all the positions for each terminal price. Because the calculation of the profit for a position is different for puts, calls, and stocks, you can use a `Select Case` structure or nested `If` structure to decide which type of calculation has to be done based on the position type.

You can have VBA create the chart fresh every time by including the appropriate code in your model. As I show in the models in Chapter 28: Analyzing Market History, you can use the Macro Recorder to generate the necessary code. Alternately, you can create the chart once manually, and it will get automatically updated every time the code is run and the data series for the chart changes.

The Code for the Model

```
Option Explicit
Sub Option_Port_Profit_Expiration()

' This program calculates the profit of a portfolio
' of puts, calls, and stocks at the time
' the options expire. All options expire at the same time.

Dim begPos, endPos, begTerm, totPremRow
Dim contSz, prcStep, numPrc, termPrcRow
Dim typeCol, strkCol, posCol, premCol, termCol, valCol
Dim premPaid, totPrem
Dim roCnt, roTerm, roPos
Dim numPos, optPrem, termPrc
Dim posStrk, posType, portVal

'**********************************************************
' Programmer inputs
'**********************************************************

begPos = 6          ' Row number where positions start
endPos = 20         ' Row number where positions end
termPrcRow = 22     ' Input row starting terminal price
begTerm = 30        ' Row number where terminal prices start

totPremRow = 25     ' Row for total premium

typeCol = 1         ' Column number for position type
strkCol = 2         ' Column number for strike prices
posCol = 3          ' Column number for positions
premCol = 4         ' Column number of premiums
termCol = 1         ' Column number for terminal prices
valCol = 2          ' Column number for terminal values
```

```
contSz = 100        ' Contract size, 150 shares/contract
prcStep = 2         ' Step for incrementing terminal prices
numPrc = 30         ' No of terminal prices to show

Worksheets("Options Portfolio").Activate

'*********************************************************
' Calculate total premium Received/(Paid)
'*********************************************************
totPrem = 0

For roCnt = begPos To endPos
    numPos = Cells(roCnt, posCol).Value
    optPrem = Cells(roCnt, premCol).Value
    premPaid = -numPos * optPrem * contSz
    totPrem = totPrem + premPaid
Next roCnt

Cells(totPremRow, premCol).Value = totPrem

'*********************************************************
' Calculate portfolio values at various terminal prices
'*********************************************************
'Create column of terminal prices
termPrc = Cells(termPrcRow, 3).Value

For roTerm = begTerm To begTerm + numPrc
    Cells(roTerm, termCol).Value = termPrc
    termPrc = termPrc + prcStep
Next

For roTerm = begTerm To begTerm + numPrc
    termPrc = Cells(roTerm, termCol).Value
    portVal = totPrem

    For roPos = begPos To endPos
        posStrk = Cells(roPos, strkCol).Value
        posType = Cells(roPos, typeCol).Value
        numPos = Cells(roPos, posCol).Value

        If posStrk <> "" Then

            Select Case posType

            Case "C"
```

```
79:                     If (termPrc > posStrk) Then
80:                         portVal = portVal + (termPrc - posStrk) _
81:                             * numPos * contSz
82:                     End If
83:
84:                 Case "P"
85:                     If (termPrc < posStrk) Then
86:                         portVal = portVal + (-termPrc + posStrk) _
87:                             * numPos * contSz
88:                     End If
89:
90:                 Case "S"
91:                     portVal = portVal + (termPrc - posStrk) _
92:                         * numPos * contSz
93:                 End Select
94:             End If
95:
96:         Next roPos
97:
98:         Cells(roTerm, valCol).Value = portVal
99:
100:    Next roTerm
101:
102:    End Sub
```

Analysis of the Code

Lines 1–38: Carries out various routine tasks such as declaring variables, assigning values to them, and so on.

Lines 43–50: The `For` loop calculates the premium paid or received for each position and accumulates them in the variable `totPrem`.

Line 52: Outputs the amount of net premium received.

Lines 58–63: Starts by reading in the lowest terminal stock price specified by the user and then creates the series of terminal prices using a `For` loop.

Lines 65–100: The outer `For` loop to move through one terminal price at a time.

Line 66: Reads in the terminal price for which net portfolio value is to be calculated.

Line 67: Sets the initial net value of the portfolio equal to the net premium received calculated earlier.

Lines 69–96: The inner `For` loop to calculate the values for all positions for the terminal value picked by the outer `For` loop.

Lines 70–72: During each pass, reads in necessary information for one position.

Line 74: Skips terminal value calculation if position strike price is not indicated (blank).

Lines 76–93: The `Select Case` structure that uses the position type to decide what type of calculation has to be done. Note that unless the position type is P, C, or S, the position is ignored.

Line 98: Once all the net values of all the positions have been calculated for one terminal price, the net value is written out and calculations start for the next terminal price.

Note that in Module2 there is an alternate version of the code that uses `If` statements instead of the `Select Case` structure. Otherwise the two codes are the same.

To complete, create the chart using the data from A30:B60 and label and format it.

Testing the Model

To test the model, run the program with just one call position of size 1. Check that the terminal prices properly reflect the lowest terminal price and the terminal price step size and that both the series of net terminal values and the chart are correct. Try the same test with a put position and a stock holding, and then use some simple combinations. (Use hand calculations for checking as needed.)

Uses of the Model

This model can be used the same way as the corresponding Excel model. Refer to the discussion there.

Limitations and Flexibility of the Model

This model has some of the same limitations as the corresponding Excel model. It is more flexible, however, because it can be extended more easily (for example, to include additional stocks and options). Also, its equations are easier to understand and check than the corresponding Excel model.

MODEL 2: OPTION PRICING USING THE BSM EQUATIONS

The Problem

Develop a function to calculate the price for European puts and calls on dividend-paying stocks based on the Black-Scholes-Merton (BSM) model.

Modeling Strategy

The advantage of creating this model as a function is that it can then be used in both worksheet models and other VBA models like built-in functions.

I discussed the BSM equations in Chapter 19: Options and Option Portfolios. The function should have as its arguments all the inputs that the user needs to provide for the BSM equations. An additional argument should be an indicator of option type. As we saw in the corresponding model in Excel, by incorporating an `optType` of 1 for calls and -1 for puts, we can use the same equations for both puts and calls.

Negative or zero values of stock price, strike price, and volatility do not make sense. As such, if the user enters any of these values then the function should produce an error value. You can use zero or any negative number to indicate an error value.

The BSM equations require calculating intermediate variables d_1 and d_2. For practice, you may want to create two separate functions to calculate them. An additional advantage of doing so is that you can then use these functions for other calculations as well.

The Code for the Model

```
Option Explicit
Function BSMOptPrice(optType, S0, K, r, q, T, sigma)

' Calculates Black-Scholes-Merton option price
' optType = 1 for call, -1 for put
' This function uses Functions BSD1 and BSD2

Dim exprT, expqT, ND1, ND2

If S0 > 0 And K > 0 And T > 0 And sigma > 0 Then
    exprT = Exp(-r * T)
    expqT = Exp(-q * T)
    ND1 = Application.NormSDist(optType * _
        BSD1(S0, K, r, q, T, sigma))
    ND2 = Application.NormSDist(optType * _
        BSD2(S0, K, r, q, T, sigma))
    BSMOptPrice = optType * (S0 * expqT * ND1 - _
        K * exprT * ND2)
ElseIf S0 > 0 And K > 0 And sigma > 0 And T = 0 Then
    BSMOptPrice = Application.Max(0, optType * (S0 - K))
Else
    'MsgBox "One of the inputs provided is invalid"
    BSMOptPrice = 0
End If
```

```
25:
26:  End Function
27:
28:  '-----------------------------------------------------------
29:  '-----------------------------------------------------------
30:  Private Function BSD1(S0, K, r, q, T, sigma)
31:
32:  ' Calculates D1 for Black-Scholes-Merton option pricing
33:
34:  BSD1 = (Log(S0 / K) + (r - q + 0.5 * sigma ^ 2) * T) / _
35:      (sigma * Sqr(T))
36:
37:  End Function
38:
39:  '-----------------------------------------------------------
40:  '-----------------------------------------------------------
41:  Private Function BSD2(S0, K, r, q, T, sigma)
42:
43:  ' Calculates D2 for Black-Scholes-Merton option pricing
44:
45:  BSD2 = BSD1(S0, K, r, q, T, sigma) - (sigma * Sqr(T))
46:
47:  End Function
```

Analysis of the Code

Line 2: Declaration statement for the Function procedure. The first argument `optType` is the call or put indicator. The user should use 1 for calls and -1 for puts.

Line 8: Declares (using `Dim`) all variables used in the function, but the ones included as arguments do not need to be separately declared here.

Lines 10–23: The `If` structured used to handle invalid arguments.

Line 10: Uses `If` statement with condition defined with the `And` operators. The condition evaluates to `True` only if all the conditions are satisfied, in which case the option price is calculated using the BSM model. If $T = 0$, that is, at expiration, the value of an option can be calculated directly. So the BSM equations are used only when $T > 0$; otherwise they are bypassed.

Lines 13–14: Calculates the necessary probabilities using Excel's built-in function `NormSDist` as we did in the Excel model. The function is preceded by `Application` because it is an Excel function being used in VBA. Invokes the Function procedure `BSD1` to calculate d_1.

Lines 17–18: Calculates the price of the option and assigns the value to the function as is required for Function procedures.

Line 19: If all inputs are valid but `T = 0`, then the option price is calculated in the line immediately following.

Line 20: For `T = 0`, that is, at expiration, this portion of code calculates option price as the greater of 0 or the difference between the terminal stock price and the strike price. The `optType` is used to provide the correct sign.

Line 23: If control gets to this line, then one of the inputs is invalid. In this case, the program assigns an option value of zero as an indicator of error. (You can also provide the error message and a negative value to the function, but these sometimes may cause problems when this function is used in other worksheet or VBA models.)

Line 30: Declares the Function procedure to calculate d_1. Declares it as a `Private` function so that it does not show up in the list of user-defined functions.

Line 34: Assigns the calculated value to the function name. Because the input data is already validated in the calling procedure, it is not necessary to check them here again.

Line 41: Declares the Function procedure to calculate d_2.

Line 45: Uses the function `BSD1` to calculate the value of d_2 and assigns it to the function name.

Function Description

To enter a brief description of the function that will show when the function is selected from the function list, press Alt+F8. In the Macro name box, type the function name `BSMOptPrice` and click Options. Enter a brief description in the Descriptions box. You cannot enter a separate description for the arguments.

Testing the Model

The only practical way to test this model is to compare its outputs with those from other option pricing models. You can compare the output of this model with those of the Excel model we developed earlier.

Uses of the Model

This is a useful function to have available. If you want to have it available at all times, you can copy it into a module in Personal.xls (it is always open in the background whenever Excel is open).

MODEL 3: IMPLIED VOLATILITY OF OPTIONS

The Problem

Create a function to calculate the implied volatility of an option using the BSM equations given its price and the other necessary inputs.

Modeling Strategy

As I discussed under the model for pricing options in Chapter 19: Options and Option Portfolios, the implied volatility has to be calculated from the BSM equations using iteration. While you can use a sophisticated iteration method such as bisection to minimize the necessary number of iterations, it is not critical to do so here for two reasons. First, volatility estimates are never very accurate, so we can do iterations in steps of 1%. Second, volatilities for stocks generally lie in the range of 20% to 60%. So for iteration you can safely start with an initial guess of 1%. Calculate the price of the option using the BSM option pricing function we developed earlier. If the calculated option price is less than the price specified, increase the volatility by 1% and keep trying until the calculated price exceeds the specified price. To guard against the possibility that the specified option price is wrong, stop the iteration at 200% volatility. If a more accurate estimate of volatility is desired, use one of the more sophisticated iteration schemes in which the step size decreases as the guess gets closer to the answer.

The Code for the Model

```
Option Explicit
Function ImpliedVol(optType, S0, K, r, q, T, optPrice)

' Calculates implied volatility for an option by iteration
' Uses the BSMOptPrice function.
' optType = 1 for call, -1 for put

Dim itCount, sigma, priceEst

sigma = 0.01
For itCount = 1 To 200
    priceEst = BSMOptPrice(optType, S0, K, r, q, T, sigma)
    If priceEst >= optPrice Then
        ImpliedVol = sigma
        Exit For
    End If
    sigma = sigma + 0.01
```

```
18:  Next
19:
20:  If itCount > 200 Then MsgBox "Volatility over 200%"
21:
22:  End Function
```

Analysis of the Code

Here I discuss only the `ImpliedVol` function because we have already discussed the other functions it uses.

Line 10: Initial guess for sigma.

Line 11–18: The iteration loop.

Line 12: Calculates the price of the option using the BSM model for the current guess for sigma.

Line 13–16: When the calculated price exceeds the specified price, this section of code assigns the current values of sigma to `ImpliedVol`, the function name, and exits the `For` loop.

Line 17: If control reaches this line bypassing the `If` structure, then the current sigma is incremented by 1% and the iteration continues.

Line 20: If control reaches this line because the limit of 200 iterations was exceeded (that is, iterations with volatilities of up to 200% did not find an answer), then it provides a message before ending the function.

Testing the Model

Test the model by calculating the option price using the implied volatility. The calculated price should be close to the option price you had originally specified.

Uses of the Model

This is another useful function to have available either for use in worksheet models or other VBA models.

Volatility Smiles

As I discussed in the Excel chapter on options, implied volatilities calculated from the observed prices of options with different strike prices maturing at the same time vary from one another for various reasons. It is customary to create plots of the implied volatilities of options with different strike prices. It is easy to calculate the volatilities for a series of observed option prices using this function and plot the results as a volatility smile. The same can be done in a worksheet as well.

MODEL 4: PROFIT OF OPTIONS PORTFOLIO AT ANY TIME

The Problem

Develop a model to calculate the projected profits of a portfolio of positions in stocks, calls, and puts at any time for a range of stock prices. All the positions are on the same stock and all the options expire at the same time. For each position, the user should be able to enter the position type (stock, put, or call), exercise price or stock purchase price, position size, and premium paid (if option). In addition, the user will also provide input values for time to expiration, volatility, interest rate, and the yield for the stock.

Create a chart to show the projected portfolio profits (value) for a range of stock prices. (The worksheet for this model is shown in Figure 30.2.)

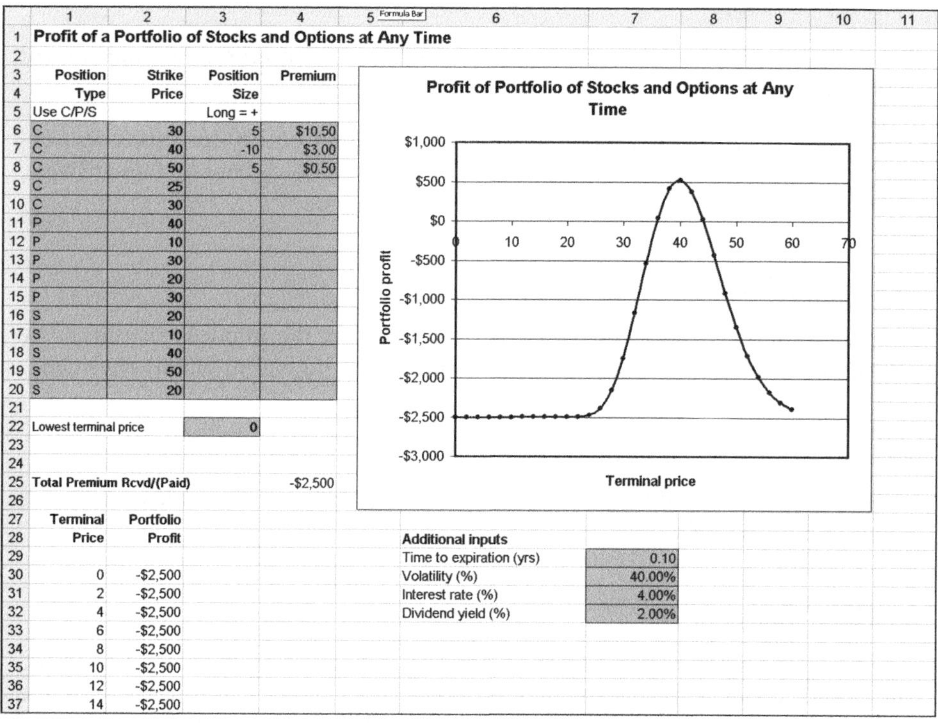

FIGURE 30.2 Model 4: Profit of a portfolio of stocks and options at any time.

Modeling Strategy

This model is similar to Model 1 except that you have to calculate the price of the options at the specified time using the BSM option pricing equations. The easiest way to do so is to use the `BSMOptPrice` function we developed in Model 2. At the time of option expiration, that is, if the user specifies time to expiration of zero, the calculations will be the same as those in Model 1. You can start with the code for Model 1, and where the price of the puts and calls are calculated, add `If` statements to calculate prices using the `BSMOptPrice` function as well.

The Code for the Model

```
Option Explicit
Sub Option_Portfolio_Val_AnyTime()

 ' This program calculates the value of a portfolio of
 ' puts, calls, stocks at any time using the
 ' BSM option pricing model. All positions are assumed to
 ' expire at the same time.

 Dim begPos, endPos, begTerm, totPremRow
 Dim contSz, prcStep, numPrc, termPrcRow
 Dim typeCol, strkCol, posCol, premCol, termCol, valCol
 Dim premPaid, totPrem
 Dim roCnt, roTerm, roPos
 Dim numPos, optPrem, termPrc
 Dim posStrk, posType, portVal
 Dim r, q, T, sigma, optPrice

 '*********************************************************
 ' Read in user inputs
 '*********************************************************
 r = Cells(31, 7).Value       ' Interest rate
 q = Cells(32, 7).Value       ' Dividend yield
 T = Cells(29, 7).Value       ' Remaining life in years
 sigma = Cells(30, 7).Value   ' Volatility

 '*********************************************************
 ' Programmer inputs
 '*********************************************************
 begPos = 6        ' Row number where positions start
 endPos = 20       ' Row number where positions end
 termPrcRow = 22    ' Input row starting terminal price
 begTerm = 30       ' Row number where terminal prices start

 totPremRow = 25 ' Row for total premium
```

```
typeCol = 1        ' Column number for position type
strkCol = 2        ' Column number for strike prices
posCol = 3         ' Column number for positions
premCol = 4        ' Column number of premiums
termCol = 1        ' Column number for terminal prices
valCol = 2         ' Column number for terminal values

contSz = 100       ' Contract size, 250 shares/contract
prcStep = 2        ' Step for incrementing terminal prices
numPrc = 30        ' No of prices for the stock to show

Sheets("Options Portfolio").Activate

'***********************************************************
' Calculate total premium received/(paid)
'***********************************************************
totPrem = 0

For roCnt = begPos To endPos
    numPos = Cells(roCnt, posCol).Value
    optPrem = Cells(roCnt, premCol).Value
    premPaid = -numPos * optPrem * contSz
    totPrem = totPrem + premPaid
Next roCnt

Cells(totPremRow, premCol).Value = totPrem

'***********************************************************
' Calculate portfolio values at various terminal prices
'***********************************************************
'Create column of stock prices
termPrc = Cells(termPrcRow, 3).Value

For roTerm = begTerm To begTerm + numPrc
    Cells(roTerm, termCol).Value = termPrc
    termPrc = termPrc + prcStep
Next

For roTerm = begTerm To begTerm + numPrc
    termPrc = Cells(roTerm, termCol).Value
    portVal = totPrem

    For roPos = begPos To endPos
        posStrk = Cells(roPos, strkCol).Value
        posType = Cells(roPos, typeCol).Value
        numPos = Cells(roPos, posCol).Value

```

```
        If posStrk <> "" Or numPos <> 0 Then
            Select Case posType

            Case "C"
                If T = 0 Then
                    If (termPrc > posStrk) Then
                        portVal = portVal + (termPrc _
                            - posStrk) * numPos * contSz
                    End If
                Else
                    optPrice = BSMOptPrice(1, termPrc, _
                        posStrk, r, q, T, sigma)
                    portVal = portVal + optPrice _
                        * numPos * contSz
                End If

            Case "P"
                If T = 0 Then
                    If (termPrc < posStrk) Then
                        portVal = portVal + (-termPrc _
                            + posStrk) * numPos * contSz
                    End If
                Else
                    optPrice = BSMOptPrice(-1, termPrc, _
                        posStrk, r, q, T, sigma)
                    portVal = portVal + optPrice _
                        * numPos * contSz
                End If

            Case "S"
                portVal = portVal + (termPrc - posStrk) _
                    * numPos * contSz
            End Select
        End If

    Next roPos

    Cells(roTerm, valCol).Value = portVal

Next roTerm

End Sub
```

Analysis of the Code

I developed this code by modifying the code for Model 1. So here I mostly discuss the changes I have made. (I have not included the codes for the functions that I have already discussed.)

Lines 21–24: Reads in additional inputs.

Lines 87–97: This `If` structure calculates the call price the same way as in Model 1 if `T = 0`; otherwise it uses the `BSMOptPrice` function.

Lines 100–110: Same modifications as in lines 87–97.

Testing the Code

Test the code by successively using 1 call, 1 put, and 1 stock position. Verify the values against calculations of the values of the put and call from any of the previous models. Then use one or two simple combinations to make sure that profits of all the positions are being added properly for each stock price.

Uses of the Model

This is a very useful model for trying out various option trading strategies. It is much more powerful than Model 1 because you can use it to see how the value of the portfolio will change with time as well as changes in the underlying variables such as volatility.

Compared to the corresponding Excel model, this model is easier to check and it can be extended more easily. For example, extending it for more than one stock or for options that expire at different times is relatively easy.

CHAPTER 31

Binomial Option Pricing

In this chapter, we will develop binomial option pricing models in VBA that will parallel the binomial models we developed in Excel in Part Two. It is generally easier to understand and learn to develop binomial trees with Excel. Therefore, if you have not covered the corresponding Excel chapter yet, I recommend that you work through at least the first model there before trying to develop binomial models in VBA. Also, this chapter does not use any additional theory or concepts, but you have to understand the theory and concepts that I discussed in the earlier chapter.

The models in this chapter will demonstrate that one of the key advantages of developing them in VBA is that it is easier to modify them and use them with any number of steps to get the kind of accuracy necessary for "real world" applications.

Modeling Examples

MODEL 1: EUROPEAN OPTIONS ON STOCKS WITH KNOWN DIVIDEND YIELD

The Problem

Develop a model to estimate the price of European options (both puts and calls) on stocks with known dividend yields using a 9-step Cox, Ross, and Rubinstein (CRR) binomial tree. (The worksheet for this model is shown in Figure 31.1.)

Modeling Strategy

You may find it easier to study the code of this first model of binomial trees before attempting to write it on your own. However, if you can proceed on your own using the following strategy, do so.

	1	2	3	4	5	6	7	8
1	**Binomial Pricing of European Options for Stocks with Known Dividend Yield**							
2								
3								
4	Option type (C=1, P=-1)	-1		Put price	$2.25			
5	Stock price (S)	$50.00						
6	Exercise price (K)	$50.00						
7	Interest rate (rr, annual)	8.00%						
8	Dividend yield (q, annual)	3.00%						
9	Volatility (V, annual)	20.00%						
10	Time to maturity (T, years)	0.5						
11	Number of steps (n)	9						
12								
13								
14								

FIGURE 31.1 Model 1: Binomial pricing of European options with known dividend yield.

In VBA, build the trees in arrays and visualize them as rectangles in the corresponding Excel spreadsheet. You may find it easier to do so if you use the columns for the steps and the rows for the different nodes at the same point in time. Also, to maintain the parallel, use the upper triangular half of an array for the tree. You may use separate two-dimensional arrays for each tree or you can use one three-dimensional array and use a different page of it for each tree. To conserve memory space, it may also be better to use dynamic arrays and `ReDim` them based on the number of steps specified. However, this is generally not necessary with modern PCs.

You may find it convenient to number the rows starting from 1 but the columns from 0 so that you can use column 0 for now. After you read in the inputs (as shown in Figure 31.1), follow essentially the same approach as we used for the Excel model. Start by calculating the parameters for the tree. Then generate the stock price tree using a two-level nested `Do` loop with the step (the column) as the outer loop. Make sure that you use a different equation for the first row (using an `If` statement) than you do for the remaining rows. To create the triangular shape of the tree, the index of the inner loop need only go to a maximum value that is dependent on the index of the outer loop.

You also have to use a pair of nested loops to generate the tree for option prices. The calculations are the same as those we used in the Excel model.

The Code for the Model

```
Option Explicit
Sub Euro_Div()

' Calculates European option prices for a stock with known
' dividend yield.
' In the arrays, the columns represent steps in time.
```

```

Dim Stk(), Euro()
Dim optType, S, K, sig, T, r, q, n
Dim dt, u, d, p, emrdt, i, j

'**********************************************************
' Read in user inputs
'**********************************************************
Worksheets("Inputs").Activate

optType = Cells(4, 2).Value
S = Cells(5, 2).Value
K = Cells(6, 2).Value
sig = Cells(9, 2).Value
T = Cells(10, 2).Value
r = Cells(7, 2).Value
q = Cells(8, 2).Value
n = Cells(11, 2).Value

'**********************************************************
' Computations
'**********************************************************
'Redimension the arrays based on number of steps specified
ReDim Stk(1 To n + 1, 0 To n)
ReDim Euro(1 To n + 1, 0 To n)

dt = T / n 'Step size in years
u = Exp(sig * Sqr(dt)) 'Up movement multiplier
d = 1 / u 'Down movement multiplier
emrdt = Exp(-r * dt) 'Discount factor per step

'p is risk neutral probability of up movement
p = (Exp((r - q) * dt) - d) / (u - d)

Stk(1, 0) = S 'Initial value, at time 0

'Generate stock price tree
For j = 1 To n ' Counts steps
    For i = 1 To j + 1
        If i = 1 Then
            Stk(i, j) = Stk(i, j - 1) * u
        Else
            Stk(i, j) = Stk(i - 1, j - 1) * d
        End If
    Next
Next

```

```
54:  ' Generate option value tree
55: For j = n To 0 Step -1
56:     For i = 1 To j + 1
57:         If j = n Then
58:             Euro(i, j) = Application.Max(optType * _
59:                 (Stk(i, j) - K), 0)
60:         Else
61:             Euro(i, j) = (p * Euro(i, j + 1) + (1 - p) _
62:                 * Euro(i + 1, j + 1)) * emrdt
63:         End If
64:     Next
65: Next
66:
67: 'Output calculated option value
68: Cells(4, 5).Value = Euro(1, 0)
69:
70: End Sub
```

Analysis of the Code

Lines 1–24: Performs preliminary tasks and reads in the input variables from the worksheet.

Lines 30–31: Redimensions the arrays based on the number of steps specified by the user.

Lines 33–39: Calculates the parameters of the tree.

Line 41: Specifies the initial stock price for the tree.

Lines 44–52: The nested `For` loops used to create the stock price tree. Note that I have made the upper bound for the counter of the inner `For` loop dependent on the step number to create a triangular-shaped tree.

Lines 55–65: The nested `For` loops used to generate the option value tree. As always, the option values are calculated starting at maturity, that is, the last step. The values at maturity (nodes where $j = n$) are calculated using Excel's `Max` function. The values at the earlier nodes are calculated as the present values of the expected values at the next forward step. As before, I have generated the triangular shape of the tree by appropriately specifying the range of the counter for the inner `For` loop.

Line 68: Writes out the option price as the value from the option value tree at time 0.

Testing the Model

Because here you can easily use a large number of steps, calculate the value of a few options using 100 or more steps. Then compare the calculated prices with those from the Black-Scholes-Merton (BSM) equations using one of the models we built earlier for them. The two should agree within a few cents.

Uses of the Model

The most important use of this model is for understanding how to build binomial trees. Because we can use the BSM equations to calculate the exact prices for European options for stocks with known dividend yields, we do not need binomial trees for them. Now it should be obvious how easy it is to change the number of steps for a binomial tree in VBA. Also note that you could easily create this model as a Function procedure and have it available for use as a user-defined function.

MODEL 2: AMERICAN OPTIONS ON STOCKS PAYING NO DIVIDEND

The Problem

Develop a model to estimate the price of American options (both puts and calls) on stocks that pay no dividend using a Cox, Ross, and Rubinstein (CRR) binomial tree. Simultaneously calculate the values of the equivalent European options. (The worksheet for this model is shown in Figure 31.2.)

Modeling Strategy

This model can be developed as a modification of Model 1. The key difference between calculating the price of American and European options is that American options can be exercised at any time; so we have to test at every node to see if

	1	2	3	4	5	6
1	**Binomial Pricing of American Options on Stocks Paying No Dividend**					
2						
3						
4	Option type (C=1, P=-1)	-1		**American put price**	**$3.28**	
5	Stock price (S)	$60.00		**European put price**	**$3.17**	
6	Exercise price (K)	$60.00				
7	Interest rate (rr, annual)	4.00%				
8	Volatility (sig, annual)	20.00%				
9	Time to maturity (T, years)	0.6				
10	Number of steps (n)	5				
11						
12						

FIGURE 31.2 Model 2: Binomial pricing of American options on stocks that pay no dividend.

exercising before expiration will have a higher payoff than the expected return from holding the option to maturity. Otherwise the two models are identical. (You can either drop the dividend yield q from both the input and the calculation of the risk-neutral probability of up movement or keep it and assign it a value of 0.)

The Code for the Model

```
Option Explicit
Sub Amer_NonDiv()

' Calculates American option prices for a stock that
' pays no dividend.
' In the arrays, the columns represent steps in time.

Dim Stk(), Amer(), Euro()
Dim optType, S, K, sig, T, r, n
Dim dt, u, d, p, emrdt, i, j, exVal

'************************************************************
' Read in user inputs
'************************************************************
Worksheets("Inputs").Activate

optType = Cells(4, 2).Value
S = Cells(5, 2).Value
K = Cells(6, 2).Value
sig = Cells(8, 2).Value
T = Cells(9, 2).Value
r = Cells(7, 2).Value
n = Cells(10, 2).Value

'************************************************************
' Computations
'************************************************************
'Redimension the arrays based on number of steps specified
ReDim Stk(1 To n + 1, 0 To n)
ReDim Amer(1 To n + 1, 0 To n)
ReDim Euro(1 To n + 1, 0 To n)

dt = T / n 'Step size in years
u = Exp(sig * Sqr(dt)) 'Up movement multiplier
d = 1 / u 'Down movement multiplier
emrdt = Exp(-r * dt) 'Discount factor per step

```

```
' p is risk neutral probability of up movement
p = (Exp(r * dt) - d) / (u - d)

Stk(1, 0) = S ' Initial value, at time 0

' Generate stock price tree
For j = 1 To n ' Counts steps
    For i = 1 To j + 1
        If i = 1 Then
            Stk(i, j) = Stk(i, j - 1) * u
        Else
            Stk(i, j) = Stk(i - 1, j - 1) * d
        End If
    Next
Next

' Generate option value tree
For j = n To 0 Step -1
    For i = 1 To j + 1
        If j = n Then
            Amer(i, j) = Application.Max(optType * _
                (Stk(i, j) - K), 0)
            Euro(i, j) = Application.Max(optType * _
                (Stk(i, j) - K), 0)
        Else
            Amer(i, j) = (p * Amer(i, j + 1) + (1 - p) _
                * Amer(i + 1, j + 1)) * emrdt
            Euro(i, j) = (p * Euro(i, j + 1) + (1 - p) _
                * Euro(i + 1, j + 1)) * emrdt
            exVal = Application.Max(0, optType * _
                (Stk(i, j) - K))
            Amer(i, j) = Application.Max(Amer(i, j), exVal)
        End If
    Next
Next

' Output calculated option value
Cells(4, 5).Value = Amer(1, 0)
Cells(5, 5).Value = Euro(1, 0)

End Sub
```

Analysis of the Code

Start with a copy of the workbook for Model 1. Note that I have dropped q as an input variable. Because most of the code is identical to the one for Model 1, I discuss only the differences here.

Lines 17–23: Changes the cell numbers as necessary to match the cell numbers for the input data on the input worksheet.

Line 39: Deletes q in this equation from the Model 1 version if you have decided not to use it as an input variable.

Lines 58–61: Calculates the (identical) values of the option at expiration for both the American and European option value trees.

Lines 63–66: As in Model 1, for both American and European options, calculates the (identical) values of the options at earlier nodes as the present values of the expected values.

Lines 67–68: Calculates the payoff from immediate exercise.

Line 69: For American options, chooses the higher of the two calculated values as the appropriate value.

Testing the Model

Check to see that the model produces identical values for American and European calls. The values of American puts maybe higher. But because we do not know how much higher, we cannot directly check this model. It is easier to check the calculations for the model in Excel because you can see the entire tree. (If you want to, you can print out a tree for the VBA model quite easily using two nested loops.) Because you already have the parallel Excel model, you can check the results of the VBA model against it.

Uses of the Model

This is a useful model for calculating the values of American options because you can easily increase the step size to 50 or 100 to get accurate estimates. You can also easily convert it into a user-defined function that can be used in both worksheet models and other VBA models.

MODEL 3: AMERICAN OPTIONS ON STOCKS WITH KNOWN DIVIDEND YIELDS

The Problem

Develop a model to estimate the price of American options (both puts and calls) on stocks with known dividend yields using a Cox, Ross, and Rubinstein (CRR) binomial tree. Simultaneously calculate the values of the equivalent European options. (The worksheet for this model is shown in Figure 31.3.)

	1	2	3	4	5	6	7
1	**Binomial Pricing of American Options on Stocks with Known Dividend Yield**						
2							
3							
4	Option type (C=1, P=-1)	-1		**American put price**	**$3.78**		
5	Stock price (S)	$50.00		**European put price**	**$3.66**		
6	Exercise price (K)	$50.00					
7	Interest rate (rr, annual)	7.00%					
8	Dividend yield (q, annual)	2.00%					
9	Volatility (sig, annual)	30.00%					
10	Time to maturity (T, years)	0.5					
11	Number of steps (n)	9					
12							
13							

FIGURE 31.3 Model 3: Binomial pricing of American options on stocks with known dividend yield.

Modeling Strategy

The only difference between this model and Model 2 is that here options are on stocks with know dividend yields. We can easily make this change to Model 2 to by adding q, the dividend yield, as an additional input and including it in the calculation of the risk-neutral probability of up movement (as we did in Model 1).

Start with a copy of the workbook for Model 2 and make the above changes. Because there is so little change in the codes of Model 2 and Model 3, I am not including the code for Model 3 here. It is, however, included in the workbook on the CD should you need it.

Testing the Model

For dividend-paying stocks, even the values of calls for otherwise identical American and European options can be different. You therefore have to check the model by doing hand calculations. It is easier to check the calculations for the model in Excel because you can see the entire tree. (If you want to, you can print a tree for the VBA model quite easily using two nested loops.) Because you already have the parallel Excel model, you can check the results of the VBA model against it.

Uses of the Model

This is a useful model for calculating the values of American options because you can easily increase the step size to 50 or 100 to get accurate estimates. You can also easily convert it into a user-defined function that can be used in both worksheet models and other VBA models.

MODEL 4: AMERICAN OPTIONS ON STOCKS WITH KNOWN DOLLAR DIVIDENDS

The Problem

Develop a model to estimate the price of American options (both puts and calls) on a stock that will pay a known dollar amount of dividend at a known time in the future. Simultaneously calculate the values of the equivalent European options. (The worksheet for this model is shown in Figure 31.4.)

Modeling Strategy

To build the binomial tree for this model, we have to calculate the present value of the dividend (using the risk-free rate of return as usual), subtract it from the initial price of the stock, and treat the remaining part of the stock price as its uncertain component. We can then build a tree for just the uncertain component of the stock price. Finally, we can create a tree for the total stock price by adding to the uncertain component at each node (from the previous tree) the present value of the dividend at that point in time. The present value will get larger as we step closer to the time of the dividend payment, and, of course, no adjustment for the dividend will have to be made at nodes beyond the time of the dividend payment.

Calculate the value of the options as before, using the tree for the total stock price.

It will be easiest to build this model starting with a copy of Model 2. Build two separate stock price trees, starting with the one for the uncertain component of the stock price. After you have the tree for total stock price, you can build the trees and calculate the prices for the American and European options as before.

	1	2	3	4	5	6	7
1	Binomial Pricing of American Options on Stocks with Known Dollar Dividend						
2							
3							
4	Option type (C=1, P=-1)	-1		American put price	$4.27		
5	Stock price (S)	$55.00		European put price	$4.07		
6	Exercise price (K)	$50.00					
7	Interest rate (rr, annual)	8.00%					
8	Volatility (sig, annual)	40.00%					
9	Time to maturity (T, years)	0.6					
10	Number of steps (n)	5					
11	Dividend amount	$2.00					
12	Time to ex-dividend date	0.25					
13							
14							

FIGURE 31.4 Model 4: Binomial pricing of American options on stocks with known dollar dividend.

The Code for the Model

```
Option Explicit
Sub Amer_DollarDiv()

' Calculates American option prices for a stock that
' will pay one known dollar dividend
' In the arrays, the columns represent steps in time.

Dim Stku() 'Uncertain component of stock price
Dim Stka() 'Total stock price
Dim Amer(), Euro(), stepTime()
Dim optType, S, K, sig, T, r, n, Su, div, exDiv
Dim dt, u, d, p, emrdt, i, j, exVal
Dim divPV

'**************************************************************
' Read in user inputs
'**************************************************************
Worksheets("Inputs").Activate

optType = Cells(4, 2).Value
S = Cells(5, 2).Value
K = Cells(6, 2).Value
sig = Cells(8, 2).Value
T = Cells(9, 2).Value
r = Cells(7, 2).Value
n = Cells(10, 2).Value
div = Cells(11, 2).Value ' Dollar amount of dividend
exDiv = Cells(12, 2).Value ' Time until exdividend date

'**************************************************************
' Computations
'**************************************************************
'Redimension the arrays based on number of steps specified
ReDim Stka(1 To n + 1, 0 To n)
ReDim Stku(1 To n + 1, 0 To n)
ReDim Amer(1 To n + 1, 0 To n)
ReDim Euro(1 To n + 1, 0 To n)
ReDim stepTime(0 To n)

dt = T / n ' Step size in years
u = Exp(sig * Sqr(dt)) ' Up movement multiplier
d = 1 / u ' Down movement multiplier
emrdt = Exp(-r * dt) ' Discount factor per step
Su = S - div * Exp(-r * exDiv) ' Initial uncertain component
```

```
' p is risk neutral probability of up movement
p = (Exp(r * dt) - d) / (u - d)
Stka(1, 0) = S
Stku(1, 0) = Su ' Uncertain component at time 0
stepTime(0) = 0

' Generate stock price tree
For j = 1 To n ' Counts steps
    stepTime(j) = j * dt ' Time distance for each step
    divPV = div * Exp(-(exDiv - stepTime(j)) * r)
    For i = 1 To j + 1
        If i = 1 Then
            Stku(i, j) = Stku(i, j - 1) * u
        Else
            Stku(i, j) = Stku(i - 1, j - 1) * d
        End If

        Stka(i, j) = Stku(i, j)
        If stepTime(j) < exDiv Then Stka(i, j) = Stka(i, j) _
            + divPV
    Next
Next

' Generate option value tree
For j = n To 0 Step -1
    For i = 1 To j + 1
        If j = n Then
            Amer(i, j) = Application.Max(optType * _
                (Stka(i, j) - K), 0)
            Euro(i, j) = Application.Max(optType * _
                (Stka(i, j) - K), 0)
        Else
            Amer(i, j) = (p * Amer(i, j + 1) + (1 - p) _
                * Amer(i + 1, j + 1)) * emrdt
            Euro(i, j) = (p * Euro(i, j + 1) + (1 - p) _
                * Euro(i + 1, j + 1)) * emrdt
            exVal = Application.Max(0, optType * _
                (Stka(i, j) - K))
            Amer(i, j) = Application.Max(Amer(i, j), exVal)
        End If
    Next
Next

' Output calculated option value
Cells(4, 5).Value = Amer(1, 0)
Cells(5, 5).Value = Euro(1, 0)

End Sub
```

Analysis of the Code

Since this code is based on the code for Model 2, I will only discuss the modifications.

Lines 8–10: Declares two separate arrays for stock prices and a one-dimensional array to store the time for each step.

Lines 27–28: Adds new input variables `div` and `exdiv`.

Line 44: Calculates the uncertain component of the initial stock price.

Lines 49–50: Initializes values at time 0.

Line 54: Calculates the time for each step.

Line 55: Calculates the present value of the dividend for each step using the difference between the ex-dividend time and time of the step.

Lines 57–61: Calculates the prices for the tree of the uncertain component of the stock price.

Lines 63–65: Calculates the total prices for the stock. The value is the same as the corresponding uncertain component except that the present value of the dividend is added at nodes prior to the ex-dividend time.

Lines 70–91: Essentially the same as in Model 2.

Testing the Model

The easiest way to check the model is against values from the corresponding Excel model. Otherwise it may be necessary to print out the trees so that you can check them with hand calculations.

Uses of the Model

The model can be easily extended to accommodate several known dollar amounts of dividends. It can produce accurate estimates of option values when used with large number of steps.

APPENDIX A

Keyboard Shortcuts for Excel

Press	To
	For moving and scrolling
Ctrl + arrow key	Move to the edge of the current data region
Home	Move to the beginning of the row
Ctrl + Home	Move to the beginning of the worksheet (A1)
Ctrl + End	Move to the bottom-right corner of the used area of the worksheet
PgDn	Move down one screen
PgUp	Move up one screen
Alt + PgDn	Move one screen to the right
Alt +PgUp	Move one screen to the left
F5	Display the Go To dialog box
	For entering data on a worksheet
Alt + Enter	Start a new line in the same cell
Shift + Enter	Complete a cell entry and move up one cell
Tab	Complete a cell entry and move to the right cell
Shift + Tab	Complete a cell entry and move to the left cell
Ctrl + Delete	Delete text to the end of the line
Shift + F2	Edit a cell comment
Ctrl + D	Fill down (a selected column of cells with the content of the first cell)
Ctrl + R	Fill to the right (a selected row of cells with the content of the first cell)
Ctrl + F3	Open the Define Name dialog box
	For working in cells or the formula bar
Ctrl + Shift + Enter	Enter a formula as an array formula
F2	Edit the active cell
F3	Open the Paste Name dialog box
Shift + F3	Paste a function into a formula
F9	Calculate all sheets in all open workbooks

Press	To
Ctrl + Alt + F9	Calculate all worksheets in the active workbook
Shift + F9	Calculate the active worksheet
Ctrl +; (semicolon)	Enter the current date
Ctrl + Shift + : (colon)	Enter the current time
Ctrl + ' (single left quote)	Alternate between displaying cell values nd formulas
•	**For inserting, deleting, and copying selection**
Ctrl + C	Copy the selection
Ctrl + X	Cut the selection
Ctrl + V	Paste the selection
Delete	Clear the contents of the selection
Ctrl + - (hyphen)	Delete the selection (and move other cells to fill the void)
Ctrl + Z	Undo the last action
Ctrl + Shift + Plus sign	Insert blank cells
	For selecting cells, columns, or rows
Shift + arrow key	Extend the selection by one cell
Ctrl + Shift + arrow key	Extend the selection to the last nonblank cell in the same column or row
Ctrl + space bar	Select the entire column
Shift + space bar	Select the entire row
Ctrl + A	Select the entire worksheet
	For working with worksheets and macros
Shift + F11	Insert a new worksheet
Alt + F8	Display the Macro dialog box
Alt + F11	Display the Visual Basic Editor (VBE)
Ctrl + PgDn	Move to the next sheet in the workbook
Ctrl + PgUp	Move to the previous sheet in the workbook
	Miscellaneous
Ctrl + S	Save active workbook
Ctrl + N	Open new workbook
Ctrl + O	Open an existing workbook
Shift + F5 or Ctrl + F	Display the Find dialog box
Ctrl + H	Display the Replace dialog box

Note: In most cases, the above shortcuts are not case sensitive (that is, both “s” and “S” will work the same)

APPENDIX B

VBA Quick Reference

Referring to Things in Excel

A workbook	Workbooks("MyBook.xls")
A worksheet	Worksheets("Sheet1") or Sheets("Sheet1")
A cell or range in A1 convention	Range("A1") or Range("A1:C5")
Several cells or ranges	Range("A1,C5,D11") or Range("A1:C5,F6,D2:E5")
A range in R1C1 convention	Range(Cells(1,1), Cells(5,10))
A cell in R1C1 convention	Cells(1, 5)
A range with a name	Range("RangeName")
An entire column or row in A1 convention	Columns("D:D") or Rows("6:6")
An entire column or row in R1C1 convention	Columns(1) or Rows(6)
A number of rows with fixed (that is, known) row numbers	Rows("6:100")
A number of rows with variable row numbers	Rows(startRow & ":" & endRow)
The 3rd row of a range (C5:G5 here)	Range("C3:G15").Rows(3)
All cells in a worksheet	Worksheets("Sheet1").Cells
A cell relative to a specified cell (C16 here)	Range("F15").Offset(1,-3)
A range relative to a specified range (D8:F13 here)	Range("B5:D10").Offset(3,2)
The currently selected object (cell, range, etc.)	Selection
The workbook containing the procedure being executed	ThisWorkbook
The currently active workbook	ActiveWorkbook
The currently active cell (may be part of selected range)	ActiveCell

Using Some Common Properties

To retrieve the value (contents) of a cell or range	cellVal = Cells(1,5).Value
To assign values to a cell or range	Range("A1:C3"). Value = 123
To assign values to a named cell or range	Range("RangeName"). Value = 123
To retrieve the text in a cell	cellText = Range("A1").Text
To get the column or row number of a cell	Range("C5").Column or Range ("C5").Row or Selection.Column
To get the number of the first column	Range("F5:H10").Column of a range or Selection .Column
To enter a formula into a cell or range in A1 convention	Range("A3").Formula = "=Sum(A1:A2)"
To enter a formula into a cell or range in R1C1 convention	Range("A3").FormulaR1C1 = "=SUM(R[-2]C:R[-1]C)"
To name a cell or range	Range("A1:C3"). Name = "RangeName"
To rename a worksheet	Worksheets("Sheet3").Name = "Stock Options"
Hide or unhide a worksheet	Worksheets("Sheet1").Visible = False or True

Using Some Common Methods

Activate a worksheet	Sheets("Sheet1").Activate
Select the entire active worksheet	Cells.Select
Select a range	Range("A1:C12").Select
Activate a cell within a selected range	Range("F6").Activate
Clear current selection (worksheet, range, etc.)	Selection.Clear
Clear both contents and format of a range	Range("D1:D7").Clear
Clear contents (but not format) of a range	Range("D1:D7").ClearContents
Clear format (but not contents) of a range	Range("D1:D7").ClearFormats
Delete several rows or columns	Rows("6:10").Delete or Columns("7:12").Delete
Copy a range and paste at a different location	Range("A1:C12").Copy Range("D1")
Insert a row before row 4	Rows(4).Insert
Insert a worksheet before the active sheet	Sheets.Add or Worksheets.Add
Delete a worksheet	Worksheets("Sheet1").Delete

APPENDIX C

Excel and VBA Built-In Functions

This appendix contains categorized selected lists of the built-in functions available for use in Excel (worksheets) and VBA along with a brief description for each. I have used the same categories as are used by Excel in the Insert Function (Paste Function in the earlier versions of Excel) dialog box to make it easy to find a function you are looking for. Each category includes both the available worksheet and VBA functions, and the scope of each function (discussed below) indicates where and how you can use it.

These are selected rather than exhaustive lists. To avoid clutter, in each category I have selectively included only the functions you are likely to find useful in financial modeling and analysis. I have completely omitted the Engineering, Database, and Trigonometric functions because you will rarely use them.

For brevity, the description of each function includes only the information needed to quickly decide if a particular function may be useful for a particular model or analysis. If you are not familiar with the function, you will have to look up its description in the relevant chapter in Part One or in Excel's Help.

Scope of a Function

For worksheet functions that have equivalent VBA forms, you must use the VBA form in VBA. These are identified with a # next to them. You can use the other worksheet functions in VBA, but you have to precede the worksheet function name by `Application` or `WorksheetFunction` followed by a period (.). For example, to use the worksheet function `Average` in VBA you will use `Application.Average` or `WorksheetFunction.Average`.

The VBA functions cannot be used in worksheets.

FINANCIAL FUNCTIONS

Function	What It Does
Worksheet Functions	
ACCRINT	Returns the accrued interest for a security that pays periodic interest
ACCRINTM	Returns the accrued interest for a security that pays interest at maturity
COUPDAYSBS	Returns the number of days from the (notional) coupon date preceding the issuance of a security to the settlement date
COUPDAYS	Returns the number of days in the coupon period that contains the settlement date (i.e., the first coupon period) for a security
COUPDAYSNC	Returns the number of days from the settlement date to the next coupon date
COUPONCD	Returns the next coupon date after the settlement date
COUPNUM	Returns the number of coupons payable between the settlement date and maturity
COUPPCD	Returns the coupon date preceding the settlement date
CUMIPMT	Returns the cumulative interest paid on an amortizing loan between two specified dates
CUMPRINC	Returns the cumulative principal repaid on an amortizing loan between two specified dates
DB	Returns the depreciation of an asset for a specified period using the fixed-declining balance method
DDB#	Returns the depreciation of an asset for a specified period using the double-declining balance method or a faster or slower depreciation rate specified
DISC	Returns the annualized discount yield (not compounded) on a security traded on a discount basis
DOLLARDE	Converts the dollar price expressed as a fraction into a dollar price expressed as a decimal number
DOLLARFR	Converts the dollar price expressed as a decimal number into a dollar price expressed as a fraction
DURATION	Returns the Macauley duration for a coupon-paying security
EFFECT	Returns the effective annual interest rate given the nominal annual interest rate and the number of compounding periods per year
FV#	Returns the future value of a constant annuity

FINANCIAL FUNCTIONS *(continued)*

Function	What It Does
FVSCHEDULE	Returns the future value of an initial principal after applying a series of specified periodic interest rates
INTRATE	Returns the interest rate (not compounded) on a security with no (remaining) coupon
IPMT#	Returns the interest payment for a specified period of an annuity
IRR#	Returns the internal rate of return for a series of cash flows that occur at equal intervals but are not necessarily equal
ISPMT	Returns the interest paid during a specific period of an investment
MDURATION	Returns the modified duration for a coupon-paying security
MIRR#	Returns the modified internal rate of return for a series of cash flows that occur at equal intervals but are not necessarily equal
NOMINAL	Returns the nominal annual interest rate given the effective annual interest rate and the number of compounding periods per year
NPER#	Returns the number of periods for an annuity
NPV#	Returns the present value of a series of unequal future cash flows that occur at equal intervals starting one period in the future
ODDFPRICE	Returns the price per $100 face value of a security having an odd (short or long) first period
ODDFYIELD	Returns the yield of a security that has an odd (short or long) first period
ODDLPRICE	Returns the price per $100 face value of a security having an odd (short or long) last coupon period
ODDLYIELD	Returns the yield of a security that has an odd (short or long) last period
PMT#	Returns the constant periodic payment for an annuity
PPMT#	Returns the total principal payment over a specific number of periods for a constant annuity
PRICE	Returns the price per $100 face value of a coupon paying security at a specified yield
PRICEDISC	Returns the price per $100 face value of a security traded on a discount basis at a specified discount rate
PRICEMAT	Returns the price per $100 face value of a security that pays interest at maturity given its annual yield

FINANCIAL FUNCTIONS *(continued)*

Function	What It Does
PV#	Returns the present value of a constant annuity
RATE#	Returns the interest rate per period for a constant annuity
RECEIVED	Returns the amount received at maturity for a security traded on a discount basis
SLN	Returns the straight-line depreciation per period of an asset
SYD#	Returns the sum-of-years' digits depreciation of an asset for a specified period
TBILLEQ	Returns the bond-equivalent yield for a Treasury bill
TBILLPRICE	Returns the price per $100 face value for a Treasury bill
TBILLYIELD	Returns the annualized (not compounded) discount yield for a Treasury bill
VDB	Returns the depreciation for any specified number of periods using the double-declining balance method or other specified faster or slower depreciation rate
XIRR	Returns the internal rate of return for a series of cash flows that are not necessarily equal or periodic
XNPV	Returns the present value of a series of cash flows that are not necessarily equal or periodic
YIELD	Returns the yield on a security that pays periodic interest
YIELDDISC	Returns the annual yield for a discounted security
YIELDMAT	Returns the annual yield of a security that pays interest at maturity

In VBA must use available equivalent function by the same name

STATISTICAL FUNCTIONS

Function	What It Does
Worksheet Functions	
AVEDEV	Returns the average of the absolute deviations of the data points from the mean
AVERAGE	Returns the arithmatic average of the arguments that are numbers
AVERAGEA	Returns the arithmatic average of the arguments including texts, logical values in special ways
CHIDIST	Returns the one-tailed probability of the chi-squared distribution
CHINV	Returns the inverse of the one-tailed probability of the chi-squared distribution
CHITEST	Returns the value from the chi-squared distribution for the test for independence
CONFIDENCE	Returns the confidence interval for a population mean
CORREL	Returns the correlation coefficient between two data sets
COUNT	Counts how many numbers are in the list of arguments
COUNTA	Counts how many values (including logical values, texts, and error values) are in the list of arguments
COUNTBLANK	Counts the number of blank cells in the argument range
COUNTIF	Counts the number of cells that meet the criteria specified in the argument
COVAR	Returns the covariance of a set of data point pairs
DEVSQ	Returns the sum of squares of deviations of data points from the sample mean
EXPONDIST	Returns the exponential distribution
FDIST	Returns the F probability distribution
FINV	Returns the inverse of the F probability distribution
FORECAST	Predicts a future value based on known pairs of values using linear regression
FREQUENCY	Returns the frequency distribution (by specified baskets) for a set of data
FTEST	Returns the result of an F-test
GEOMEAN	Returns the geometric mean
GROWTH	Returns predictions based on an exponential trend

STATISTICAL FUNCTIONS *(continued)*

Function	What It Does
INTERCEPT	Returns the intercept of a linear regression line
KURT	Returns the kurtosis of a data set
LARGE	Returns the k-th (specified) largest value in a data set
LINEST	Returns the parameters and detailed statistics for a linear regression
LOGINV	Returns the inverse of the lognormal distribution
LOGNORMDIST	Returns the cumulative lognormal distribution
MAX	Returns the maximum value in a list of arguments ignoring logical values and texts
MAXA	Returns the maximum value in a list of arguments including logical values (TRUE=1 and FALSE=0) and texts (=0)
MEDIAN	Returns the median of the given numbers
MIN	Returns the minimum value in a list of arguments ignoring logical values and texts
MINA	Returns the minimum value in a list of arguments including logical values (TRUE=1 and FALSE=0) and texts (=0)
MODE	Returns the mode (most frequently occurring value) in a given data set
NORMDIST	Returns the cumulative normal distribution for the specified mean and standard distribution
NORMINV	Returns the inverse of the cumulative normal distribution for the specified mean and standard distribution
NORMSDIST	Returns the cumulative standard normal distribution
NORMSINV	Returns the inverse of the cumulative standard normal distribution
PERCENTILE	Returns the k-th percentile of values in a range
PERCENTRANK	Returns the percentage rank of a value in a data set
PERMUT	Returns the number of permutations for a given number of objects that can be selected from the total objects
POISSON	Returns the poisson distribution
PROB	Returns the probability that values in a range are between two limits
QUARTILE	Returns the quartile of a data set
RANK	Returns the rank of a numbers in a list of numbers
SKEW	Returns the skewness of a distribution

STATISTICAL FUNCTIONS *(continued)*

Function	What It Does
SLOPE	Returns the slope of a linear regression line through a set of data points
SMALL	Returns the k-th smallest value in a data set
STANDARDIZE	Returns the normalized value from a distribution given its mean and standard deviation
STDEV	Returns the estimate of population standard deviation based on a sample, ignoring text and logical values
STDEVA	Returns the estimate of population standard deviation based on a sample, including text (=0) and logical values (TRUE=1, FALSE=0)
STDEVP	Returns the sample standard deviation of a set of data, ignoring text and logical values
STDEVPA	Returns the sample standard deviation of a data set, including text (=0) and logical values (TRUE=1, FALSE=0)
STEYX	Returns the standard error of the predicted y-values for each x in a regression
TDIST	Returns the probability for the Student's t-distribution
TINV	Returns the inverse of the Student's t-distribution
TREND	Returns the value along a linear trend line
TTEST	Returns the probability associated with a Student's t-test
VAR	Returns the estimate of population variance based on a sample, ignoring text and logical values
VARA	Returns the estimate of population variance based on a sample, including text (=0) and logical values (TRUE=1, FALSE=0)
VARP	Returns the sample variance of a set of data, ignoring text and logical values
VARPA	Returns the sample variance of a data set, including text (=0) and logical values (TRUE=1, FALSE=0)

MATHEMATICAL FUNCTIONS	
Function	**What It Does**
Worksheet Functions	
ABS #	Returns the absolute value of a number
CEILING	Returns a number rounded away from zero to the nearest multiple of a specified number
COMBIN	Returns the possible number of combinations for a given number of items
EVEN	Returns a number rounded to the nearest even integer away from zero
EXP #	Returns *e* raised to a power
FACT	Returns the factorial of a number
FLOOR	Returns a number rounded towards zero to the nearest multiple of a specified number
INT	Rounds a number down to the nearest integer
LN	Returns the natural logarithm of a number
LOG	Returns the logarithm of a number to the base specified
LOG10	Returns the base-10 logarithm of a number
MOD	Returns the remainder after a number is divided by a specified divisor
MROUND	Returns a number rounded up or down to the nearest multiple of a specified number
ODD	Returns a number rounded to the nearest odd integer away from zero
PI	Returns the value of pi
POWER	Returns the result of a number raised to a specified power
PRODUCT	Multiplies all the numbers given as arguments and returns the result
QUOTIENT	Returns the integer portion of the result of a division
RAND	Returns a random draw from a uniform distribution between 0 and 1 (both included)
RANDBETWEEN	Returns a random draw from a uniform distribution between two specified numbers
ROUND #	Rounds a number to a specified number of digits

MATHEMATICAL FUNCTIONS *(continued)*

Function	What It Does
Worksheet Functions	
ROUNDDOWN	Returns a number rounded toward zero to a specified number of digits
ROUNDUP	Returns a number rounded away from zero to a specified number of digits
SIGN	Returns the sign of a number: 1 for positive, 0 for 0, and −1 for negative
SQRT	Returns the positive square root of a number
SUM	Returns the sum of its arguments
SUMIF	Sums the values in cells (in a range) selected by applying a specified criteria to a parallel set of cells
SUMSQ	Returns the sum of the squares of its arguments
TRUNC	Truncates a number to a specified number of decimal points by removing the rest
VBA Functions	
Fix	Returns the integer portion of a number (differs from Int function for negative numbers)
Int	Returns the integer portion of a number (differs from Fix function for negative numbers)
Log	Returns the natural logarithm of a number
Rnd	Returns a random draw from a uniform distribution between 0 and 1 (both included)
Sgn	Returns the sign of a number: 1 for positive, 0 for 0, and −1 for negative
Sqr	Returns the square root of a number

In VBA must use available equivalent function by the same name

LOOKUP AND REFERENCE FUNCTIONS

Function	What It Does
Worksheet Functions	
ADDRESS	Creates a cell address as text given row and column numbers
CHOOSE #	Based on a specified index number (1st, 2nd, etc.) chooses a value from the list of its value arguments
COLUMN	Returns the column number of the specified reference
COLUMNS	Returns the number of columns in an array or reference
GETPIVOTDATA	Retrieves specified data from a PivotTable report
HLOOKUP	Searches for a value in the top row of a table or an array of values, and then returns the value from a specified row in the same column of the table or array
INDEX	Returns the value or reference to the value of the specified row and column of a table or range
INDIRECT	Returns the contents of a reference (after any necessary evaluation) specified by a text string
LOOKUP	Looks in a one-row or one-column range for a value and returns a value from the same position in a second one-row or one-column range
MATCH	Returns the relative position of an item in a range of contiguous cells in a row or a column that matches a specified value
OFFSET	Returns the reference to a single cell or a range of cells that is a specified number of rows and columns from a cell or range of cells
ROW	Returns the row number of the specified reference
ROWS	Returns the number of rows in an array or reference
TRANSPOSE	Transposes an array (as defined in matrix algebra) so that the first row becomes the first column, etc.
VLOOKUP	Searches for a value in the leftmost column of a table or an array of values, and then returns the value from a specified column in the same row of the table or array

In VBA must use available equivalent function by the same name

DATE AND TIME FUNCTIONS

Function	What It Does
Worksheet Functions	
DATE	Returns the serial number of a date specified by year, month, and date as separate arguments
DATEVALUE	Returns the serial number of a date specified as a text (that is, in quotations) in one of Excel's date formats
DAY#	Returns the day of month of a date given as a serial number or a text in one of Excel's date formats
DAYS360	Returns the number of days between two dates specified in Excel formats or as serial numbers, based on a 360 day year
EDATE	Returns the serial number of the date that is a specified number of months before or after the start date
EOMONTH	Returns the serial number of the last day of the month that is a specified number of months before or after a specified date
HOUR#	Returns the hour of a time value
MINUTE#	Returns the minutes of a time value
MONTH#	Returns the month of a date value
NETWORKDAYS	Returns the number of whole working days between two specified date values.
NOW#	Returns the serial number of the current date and time
SECOND#	Returns the seconds of a time value
TIME	Returns the decimal number for time entered as hour, minute, and seconds separated by commas
TIMEVALUE	Returns the decimal number of a time specified by a text string
TODAY	Returns the serial number of current date
WEEKDAY#	Returns an integer indicating the day of the week for a date
WEEKNUM	Returns a number that indicates where the week of a specified date falls numerically within a year
WORKDAY	Returns the serial number of the date that is a specified number of workdays before or after a date
YEAR#	Returns the year of a date
YEARFRAC	Returns the number of years and fraction of years between two specified dates

DATE AND TIME FUNCTIONS *(continued)*

Function	What It Does
VBA Functions	
Date	Returns the current system date
DateAdd	Adds a specified time interval to a date
DateDiff	Returns the time interval between two dates
DatePart	Returns a specified part of a date
DateSerial	Returns a Variant (Date) for a specified year, month, and day
DateValue	Converts a string expression to a date
MonthName	Returns the month name as a string given a month number
Time	Returns the current system time
TimeSerial	Returns a Variant (Date) containing the time for a specified hour, minute, and second
TimeValue	Returns a variant containing the time
WeekdayName	Returns the name of the day of the week for a date

In VBA must use available equivalent function by the same name

TEXT FUNCTIONS

Function	What It Does
Worksheet Functions	
CONCATENATE	Joins several text strings into one text string
EXACT	Checks whether two text strings are identical (case-sensitive) and returns TRUE or FALSE
FIND	Finds and returns the position of one text string within another (case-sensitive)
FIXED	Returns a number as a text string after formatting it with a specified number of decimals
LEFT#	Returns a specified number of characters from the beginning of a text string
LEN#	Returns the number of characters in a text string
LOWER	Converts all uppercase letters in a text string to lowercase
MID#	Returns a specified number of characters from a text string, starting at a specified position
PROPER	Capitalizes the first letter of each word in a text string and converts all other letters to lowercase letters
REPLACE#	Replaces a specific number of characters at a specific position in a text string with a new text string (of any length)
REPT	Creates a new text string by repeating a given text string a specified number of times
RIGHT#	Returns a specified number of characters from the end of a text string
SEARCH	Finds and returns the position of one text string within another (not case-sensitive)
SUBSTITUTE	Substitutes new text for specific old text in a text string
TEXT	Converts a value to text in a specified number format
TRIM#	Removes all extra spaces from a text string except for single spaces between words
UPPER	Converts text to uppercase
VALUE	Converts a text string that represents a number to a number

TEXT FUNCTIONS *(continued)*

Function	What It Does
VBA Functions	
InStr	Returns the position of a string within another string
InStrRev	Returns the position of a string within another string, from the end of the string
LCase	Returns a string converted to lowercase
LTrim	Returns a copy of a string with no leading spaces
RTrim	Returns a copy of a string with no trailing spaces
Space	Returns a string with a specified number of spaces
Str	Returns the string representation of a number
StrComp	Returns a value indicating the result of a string comparison
StrConv	Returns a string converted as specified
String	Returns a string containing repeating character strings of the length specified
StrReverse	Returns a string, reversed
UCase	Converts a string to uppercase

In VBA must use available equivalent function by the same name

LOGICAL FUNCTIONS

Function	What It Does
Worksheet Functions	
AND	Returns TRUE if all its arguments are TRUE; otherwise returns FALSE
FALSE	Returns the logical value FALSE
IF	Returns one value if a specified condition evaluates to TRUE and another value if it evaluates to FALSE
NOT	Reverses the logical value of its argument
OR	Returns TRUE if any one of its arguments is TRUE; otherwise returns FALSE
TRUE	Returns the logical value TRUE
VBA Functions	
IIF	Returns one of two parts, depending on the evaluation of an expression
Xor	Performs a logical exclusion on two expressions and returns True if one and only one of them is True

INFORMATION AND MISCELLANEOUS FUNCTIONS

Function	What It Does
Worksheet Functions	
CELL	Returns information about the formatting, location, or contents of a cell
ISBLANK	Returns TRUE if a cell referred to is empty
ISERR	Returns TRUE if the value is any error value except #N/A!
ISERROR	Returns TRUE if the value is any error value
ISEVEN	Returns TRUE if the number is even
ISLOGICAL	Returns TRUE if the value is a logical value
ISNA	Returns TRUE if the value is the error value #N/A!
ISNONTEXT	Returns TRUE if the value is not text
ISNUMBER	Returns TRUE if the value is a number
ISODD	Returns TRUE if the number is odd
ISREF	Returns TRUE if the value is a reference
ISTEXT	Returns TRUE if the value is text
N	Converts a value to a number based on a set of rules
TYPE	Returns a number indicating the type of a value
VBA Functions	
Array	Returns a variant containing an array
CCur	Converts an expression to a currency data type
CDate	Converts an expression to a date data type
CDbl	Converts an expression to a double data type
CDec	Converts an expression to a decimal data type
CInt	Converts an expression to an integer data type
CLng	Converts an expression to a long data type
CSng	Converts an expression to a single data type
CStr	Converts an expression to a string data type
CurDir	Returns the current path
CVar	Converts an expression to a variant data type
Format	Displays an expression in a particular format

INFORMATION AND MISCELLANEOUS FUNCTIONS *(continued)*

Function	What It Does
InputBox	Displays a dialog box to get user input
IsArray	Returns True or False depending on whether a variable is an array
IsDate	Returns True or False depending on whether a variable is a date or can be converted to a date
IsEmpty	Returns True or False depending on whether a variable has been initialized or explicitly set to empty
IsError	Returns True or False depending on whether an expression is an error value
IsMissing	Returns True or False indicating whether an optional variant argument has been passed to a procedure
IsNull	Returns True or False depending on whether an expression contains no valid data (null)
IsNumeric	Returns True or False depending on whether an expression can be evaluated as a number
LBound	Returns the smallest subscript for a dimension of an array
MsgBox	Displays a dialog box with a message
TypeName	Returns a string that describes the data type of a variable
UBound	Returns the largest available subscript for a dimension of an array
VarType	Returns an integer indicating the subtype of a variable

About the CD-ROM

This appendix includes information on the contents of the CD that accompanies this book. For the latest and greatest information, please refer to the ReadMe file located at the root of the CD.

What's on the CD

This CD contains full working versions of all the models discussed in the book, along with the data used in the models and a few other Excel and VBA examples. The workbooks are organized in folders by chapter, and the workbook for each model is labeled with chapter and model numbers and a brief model description, all of which tie to the book. (There are no folders for chapters that do not contain any models or examples.) Three additional workbooks contain the material presented in the appendices in the book.

There are instructions throughout the book that will guide you through the customization of each model to suit your specific investing needs.

System Requirements

- A computer with a processor running at 120 Mhz or faster.
- At least 32 MB of total RAM installed on your computer; for best performance, we recommend at least 64 MB.
- A CD-ROM drive.

NOTE: Many popular word processing programs are capable of reading Microsoft Word files. However, users should be aware that a slight amount of formatting might be lost when using a program other than Microsoft Word.

USING THE CD WITH WINDOWS

To install the items from the CD to your hard drive, follow these steps:

1. Insert the CD into your computer's CD-ROM drive.
2. The CD-ROM interface will appear. The interface provides a simple point-and-click way to explore the contents of the CD.

   If the opening screen of the CD-ROM does not appear automatically, follow these steps to access the CD:
3. Click the Start button on the left end of the taskbar and then choose Run from the menu that pops up.
4. In the dialog box that appears, type *d*:**start.exe**. (If your CD-ROM drive is not drive *d*, fill in the appropriate letter in place of *d*.) This brings up the CD Interface described in the preceding set of steps.

USING THE CD WITH MACINTOSH

To install the items from the CD to your hard drive, follow these steps:

1. Insert the CD into your computer's CD-ROM drive.
2. The CD icon will appear on your desktop; double-click to open.
3. Double-click the Start button.
4. Read the license agreement and click the Accept button to use the CD.
5. The CD interface will appear. Here you can install the programs and run the demos.

APPLICATIONS

The following application is on the CD:

OpenOffice.org. OpenOffice.org is a free, multiplatform, office productivity suite. It's similar to Microsoft Office or Lotus SmartSuite, but OpenOffice.org is absolutely free. It includes word-processing, spreadsheet, presentation, and drawing applications that enable you to create professional documents, newsletters, reports, and presentations. It supports most file formats of other office software, so you should be able to view and edit any files created with other office software. Certain features of Microsoft Excel documents may not work as expected from within OpenOffice.org.

Shareware programs are fully functional, trial versions of copyrighted programs. If you like particular programs, register with their authors for a nominal fee and receive licenses, enhanced versions, and technical support.

Freeware programs are copyrighted games, applications, and utilities that are free for personal use. Unlike shareware, these programs do not require a fee or provide technical support.

GNU software is governed by its own license, which is included inside the folder of the GNU product. See the GNU license for more details.

Trial, demo, or evaluation versions are usually limited either by time or functionality (such as being unable to save projects). Some trial versions are very sensitive to system date changes. If you alter your computer's date, the programs will "time out" and no longer be functional.

Customer Care

If you have trouble with the CD-ROM, please call the Wiley Product Technical Support phone number at (800) 762-2974. Outside the United States, call (317) 572-3994. You can also contact Wiley Product Technical Support at **http://support.wiley.com**. John Wiley & Sons will provide technical support only for installation and other general quality control items. For technical support on the applications themselves, consult the program's vendor or author.

To place additional orders or to request information about other Wiley products, please call (877) 762-2974.

Index

For more information about the CD-ROM, see the About the CD-ROM section on page 777.

CUSTOMER NOTE: IF THIS BOOK IS ACCOMPANIED BY SOFTWARE, PLEASE READ THE FOLLOWING BEFORE OPENING THE PACKAGE.

Printed and bound by CPI Group (UK) Ltd, Croydon, CR0 4YY

23/04/2025

14660934-0002